New England Dissent, 1630–1833

Volume II

A Publication of
The Center for the Study of
the History of Liberty in America / Harvard University

New England Dissent
1630-1883

*The Baptists and the Separation
of Church and State*

VOLUME

II

William G. McLoughlin

HARVARD UNIVERSITY PRESS, Cambridge, Massachusetts

1971

Contents

VOLUME II

IX

*The Baptists Confront Pluralism in the New Republic,
1780–1810*

37 The Baptists, the Shakers, and the Universalists, 1780–
1810   697

38 The Methodists, the Freewill Baptists, and the
Christ-ians, 1780–1810   723

39 The Baptists' Views on Government, Morality, and
Slavery, 1780–1810   751

40 The Baptists' Views on Education, Science, Politics,
and National Destiny, 1780–1810   770

X

*Disestablishment in Vermont and New Hampshire,
1768–1819*

41 Disestablishment in Vermont, 1768–1807   789

42 The Baptists and the Vermont Glebelands, 1790–1820   813

43 Dissent in New Hampshire, 1640–1792   833

44 The Dissenters and the Courts in New Hampshire,
1792–1807   855

45 The Dissenters and the Republican Party in New
Hampshire, 1800–1816   877

46 Disestablishment in New Hampshire, 1816–1819   894

Contents

XI

Disestablishment in Connecticut, 1776–1818

47 John Leland and the Era of "Modern Liberality" in Connecticut, 1776–1800   915

48 The Decline of the Parish System in Connecticut, 1784–1800   939

49 Expedients to Prop Up the Establishment in Connecticut, 1780–1800   962

50 The Baptist Petition Movement, 1800–1807   985

51 The Dissenters and the Republicans in Connecticut, 1800–1812   1006

52 The Rise of the Toleration Party, 1816–1817   1025

53 Disestablishment in Connecticut, 1817–1818   1043

XII

The Dissenters and the Jeffersonian Republicans in Massachusetts, 1800–1820

54 James Sullivan and the Republican Party, 1800–1808   1065

55 The Barnes Case and the Religious Liberty Act, 1810–1812   1084

56 The Baptists Seek Respectability, 1800–1830   1107

57 The Baptists and the Trinitarian-Congregationalists, 1812–1828   1128

58 Political and Sectarian Viewpoints on Disestablishment, 1820   1145

59 The Debate over Article Three in the Constitutional Convention of 1820   1160

XIII

The Final Downfall of the Massachusetts Establishment, 1820–1833

60 The Dedham Case and the Amendment of the Religious Liberty Act, 1821–1824   1189

Contents

61   The Trinitarian-Congregationalists Abandon the
Establishment, 1824–1830   1207

62   The Universalists and the Eleventh Amendment to the
Massachusetts Constitution, 1830–1833   1230

63   The Abolition of Compulsory Religious Taxes in
Massachusetts, 1832–1834   1245

64   The Baptists Enter the Mainstream   1263

Epilogue   1277

Bibliographical Essay   1285

Index   1295

PART IX

The Baptists Confront Pluralism in the New Republic,

1780–1810

"The Methodists have followed the Baptists thro' the country with much zeal, but they earnestly strike against the most essential doctrines of the gospel . . . To hold up light against their errors, as others, is of great importance in this time when many have an ear to hear."

Isaac Backus, 1789

Chapter 37

The Baptists, the Shakers, and
the Universalists,
1780–1810

As it is a time of the prevalence of errors of every kind and of the apostasy of many from the faith of the gospel, it is recommended to the churches that they express in their annual letters to the Association their particular adherence to the doctrines of grace.

Vote of the Warren Baptist Association, 1784

Between the years 1780 and 1810 the Baptists of Massachusetts (as well as those elsewhere in New England) were torn between hope and frustration, between increasing self-confidence and increasing self-consciousness. Although they shared the general American optimism over the successful founding of the new nation and were elated by their own increasing size, power, and prestige, they found their aspirations constantly thwarted by divisions from within and persistent social prejudice from without. In 1788 the question of religious taxation seemed so threatening to Isaac Backus that he urged on the Warren Association the necessity for another petition movement to the legislature: "This is our only possible way of union and happiness — No men can enjoy that happiness who force their neighbours to support any religious teacher whom they never chose." [1] But for the first time the Baptists were reluctant to follow their old champion. His call for action met opposition and only "after some debate" did the Association vote: "As many of our societies are still under oppression on account of ministerial taxes, a memorial and petition to the Legislature of the Commonwealth for its removal, and the establishment of equal religious liberty in this government was laid before the Association by Rev. Mr. Backus and was approved." [2] However the committee appointed to

1. Ms. letter from Isaac Backus to the Warren Association, October 3, 1788; this letter is among the BP(AN).
2. Warren Association Minutes, 1788, and Isaac Backus, ms. "Diary," XI, 101, in the BP(AN).

draw up and present the petition "in such time and manner as they shall think proper" could not agree and never presented a petition.

Some Baptists were obviously tired of the futile efforts to obtain political redress and wanted to devote their energy increasingly to evangelism and denominational organization. Others believed church-state relations were improving and safely could be left to the good will of the towns and parishes. By 1795 even Backus showed some optimism on this issue: "the power of one sect in our land to compel all others to bow to them in re-ligious affairs is daily consuming [i.e., being consumed] by the light and power of the gospel." [3] When a motion was made in the Shaftesbury As-sociation in 1801 to create a legal defense fund to aid those unjustly dis-trained or imprisoned for religious taxes, the Association voted: "The As-sociation esteem it duty to afford relief to Churches or Brethren who are suffering by oppression . . . as far as we have opportunity: but as there are but few of our Churches in a situation to suffer in this way, we do not think it necessary to raise a fund for that purpose." [4]

Behind this change in the hitherto militant and aggressive, even trucu-lent, attitude of the Baptists was the growth in the size, wealth, learning, and respectability of their membership so that it no longer seemed neces-sary or proper to resort to the sectarian outlook and behavior of the two generations which followed the Great Awakening. Sociologically, the Bap-tists were going through the important transition from a sect to a denomina-tion. A new generation of Baptists came of age after 1780; their needs, desires, and outlook differed greatly from those of the generation which had lived through the fervent zeal of the Awakening and its aftermath of "persecution." Turning from politics to internal development, these younger Baptists strove to achieve by institutional respectability what they lacked in social and political influence.

In one sense they were forced to do this by the increasing size and com-plexity of the Baptist movement in these years. The statistical evidence of their rapid growth is considerable. Starting with the formation of the Warren Association in 1767 all of the Baptist Associations kept and pub-lished annual records of the membership growth of each of their churches. In 1770 the Warren Association reported eleven churches in Massachusetts with 530 baptized members. Twenty-five years later Backus listed 136 churches in Massachusetts with 8,463 members.[5] Backus said that in 1734, the year the Great Awakening started in Northampton, there were six Bap-tist churches in all of New England (excluding Rhode Island) with a membership of perhaps 200, but by 1795 there were 198 churches with

3. Isaac Backus, *History of New England,* ed., David Weston (Newton, 1871), II, 379.

4. Shaftesbury Association Minutes, 1801, p. 7. This grew from a case of taxation and distraints on the Baptists in the town of Partridgefield (now Peru) Massachusetts in 1799.

5. Backus, *History,* II, 412.

15,052 members. Doubtless there were many Baptists and Baptist congregations of whom Backus did not know. It is reasonable to estimate that there were five times as many (including children) who attended the churches and were nominal Baptists — say 42,000 Baptists in Massachusetts by 1795 of a population of 395,000 or roughly twelve per cent. (Other dissenting groups, like the Episcopalians, Quakers, Methodists, Sandemanians, Shakers, and Universalists, probably added another 30,000 to those outside the Standing Order.) [6] Not only was this a significant numerical growth in two generations, but it was a twelvefold proportional growth from less than one per cent of the population in 1740. Between 1795 and 1820 the Second Great Awakening produced an equally rapid growth among the Baptists and other dissenters at the expense of the Congregationalists, but in this movement the Baptists had to share a larger number of the converts with the Methodists and Universalists.

Perhaps one of the most important indications that the New England Baptists had arrived at a position of consequence was the publication in 1794 of a tract by the Rev. Noah Worcester of the Congregational church in Worcester entitled, *Impartial Inquiries Concerning the Progress of the Baptist Denomination.* Worcester expressed surprise, alarm, and chagrin that the Baptists had grown so large and were continuing to expand so rapidly by proselyting persons who were nominally, and by all rights, members of the Congregational parishes into which they were born. His tract was primarily an attack on the lack of zeal and vitality among the Congregationalists and an attempt to arouse them to new evangelistic endeavors. It was an urgent prelude to the revival spirit of the Second Great Awakening.

Worcester found no reason to praise the Baptists, however. He did admit that they had "been treated with disrespect," and he candidly confessed that a certain amount of persecution by the established churches had given their cause some popular sympathy. He noted that their preachers showed "a greater degree of engagedness" than most Congregationalists and that they were willing to itinerate to everywhere, reaching directly into the most remote hamlets and homes of persons who seldom came to public worship. But generally he credited the Baptists only with the least attractive forms of demagogy and proselyting. He criticized their preaching for the "confident manner and affecting tone with which they address the passions of their hearers" rather than using reason. Baptist preachers spoke rapidly and interminably but not very intelligibly. They quoted much Scripture,

6. In 1786 Backus wrote that since 1744 "above forty thousand people in New England have withdrawn from [the Standing Order] and the most of them have turned to the baptist denomination." *Testimony of the Two Witnesses* (Providence, 1786), p. 30. For other statistical estimates on denominational sizes in this period see Edwin S. Gaustad, *Historical Atlas of Religion in America* (New York, 1962), pp. 10–13, and Ezra Stiles, *Extracts from the Itineraries of Ezra Stiles,* ed., F. B. Dexter (New Haven, 1916), pp. 92–96.

usually from memory, but they jumbled their texts and usually miscon-strued them. They were great showmen of the pulpit, arousing the emo-tions and titillating the affections of their hearers but, Worcester said, they reached only the most shallow, ignorant, and uneducated classes — those "who possess weak judgments, fickle minds and quick and tender pas-sions." Therefore their churches were hardly fit spiritual homes for serious, devout, or reasonable Christians.

Though Worcester did not think them any credit to religion, he in-directly praised the Baptist ministers for their earnest, dedicated, indefati-gable search for new converts. Yet he insisted that they took advantage of revivals in Congregational churches to wean away the more excitable and unstable of the newly awakened. They were quick to capitalize on any "disaffection to settled ministers," drawing members away from a parish minister who did not please them or "artfully" catering to one faction against another in order to fill their own meetinghouses. Worcester, like most Standing ministers, was convinced that "covetousness with regard to supporting the gospel" was a principal reason why many joined the Bap-tists and accused their ministers of furnishing eagerly such tax-dodgers "with certificates" to increase their church rolls. "The annual accounts published by the Baptists of their success in gaining proselytes" deceived the gullible into believing God favored their practices. Others joined them because they could not stand the higher-toned morality and stricter church discipline required of members in the established churches.

Nevertheless, it was a tribute to the Baptists that as eminent a cleric as Worcester found them a threat worth published concern and thought it necessary to arouse the Standing Order to action lest they soon find themselves without congregations. Baptists could withstand these outraged cries of fanaticism, bigotry, enthusiasm, ignorance, and "sheep stealing" far more easily from persons fearful of their victory than they could stand disdainful silence from persons too contemptuous to take notice of them. Worcester's tract, for all its abuse, was a symbol of which they could be proud. The establishment was wounded, perhaps fatally. Let the establish-ment rage. To the victor would belong the spoils; and the Baptists did not doubt that, as the century ended, victory would be theirs. They had less to fear from the Rev. Mr. Worcester's ill-natured attacks than from the prob-lems of coordinating and administering their rapidly growing denomination.

The Warren Association, which in its early years had tried to unite all the New England Baptists, obviously could not absorb all of these new churches. It reached a peak membership of forty-five churches in 1785. Since distant churches could not send delegates to the annual meetings they began to organize their own regional associations, some of which have al-ready been mentioned. The New Hampshire Association was formed in 1776 for the churches north of Boston. The Shaftesbury Association in 1781 gathered the churches of western Massachusetts and southern Vermont. The Woodstock Association split off from Shaftesbury in 1783 with churches from southeastern Vermont, western New Hampshire, and a few from the northern border of Massachusetts. After this, creation of new associations increased rapidly: Bowdoinham (1787), Vermont (1787), Meredith (1789), Danbury (1790), Leyden (1793), Richmond (1795). By 1804 there were thirteen Baptist Associations in New England with 312 churches and 23,638 baptized members.[7] And these were only the closed communion Calvinistic Baptists. There were also associations of the Six-Principle Baptists, the open-communion Separate-Baptists, the Seventh Day Baptists, and, after 1784, the Free Will Baptists. By the end of the Second Great Awakening in 1830 the Baptist churches were sufficiently numerous everywhere so that the associations existed on a county basis. Though they had no organizational structure to unite the associations, the use of fraternal delegates or "messengers" provided close links among them all, and all of them operated on principles similar to those the Warren Association adopted.

Each of these associations held annual meetings to which each church sent pastors and delegates. Here they discussed their current problems of theology, church discipline, polity, ordination, and religious liberty and tried to arrive at amicable solutions to internal disputes of all kinds. However, as Backus said, these associations refused "to hear and judge of any personal controversy in any church, or to intermeddle with the affairs of any church which has not joined with them." [8] The individual autonomy of each congregation was considered sacred.

However, it often happened that the associations did have to make certain judgments concerning the individual churches. The simple question of which churches should be admitted to membership and which should be excluded required a judgment; if a church had a schism and sent two sets of delegates some choice had to be made.[9] In 1782, when Universalism began to infect some of the churches, the Warren Association voted that if any church should deviate from the faith and order of the Baptists "the neighbouring Churches ought to inform the deviating Church of their uneasiness and desire a candid hearing"; if this were denied or "satisfaction is not obtained, they should withdraw fellowship from said Church . . . and give information to the next Association who have a right to drop such

7. Isaac Backus, *An Abridgement of the Church History of New England* (Boston, 1804), p. 237.
8. Backus, *History,* II, 412.
9. For example, in 1788, the Warren Association voted, "Having received information that the majority of the church at Ashfield have withdrawn themselves from the pastor, the Rev. Mr. Smith, in a disorderly manner, we think it our duty to drop them from this association . . . But as it appears to us that he hath in all respects held to the doctrines of faith, to which said church first agreed, and hath conducted himself as becometh a minister of Christ, we are in full fellowship with him as such." And in 1794 the Association voted not to readmit the Ashfield Baptists who had split off from Smith.

Church from this body; though we disclaim all power and jurisdiction over the churches." [10] But generally speaking the associations did show remarkable consistency in refusing to sit in judgment on individual cases brought before them. Two or three times during these years member churches complained that the Warren Association was intermeddling too much, and two or three churches withdrew on these grounds. But most of the churches agreed that they gained far more than they lost by belonging to these associations.[11]

What they gained was a sense of unity and solidarity *against* their opponents and *for* the promotion of gospel truth. They learned the value of cooperative effort in common tasks too involved for one or two churches. They gained a sense of fellowship from interchanging ideas, problems, and faith. As they watched the associations grow and found that they were able to achieve many of their aims more rapidly than they had ever hoped, they became convinced that God was aiding their cause, for surely they could not have accomplished these things unaided. It is fair to say that by 1795 the promotion of denominational harmony and growth was of more importance to the associations than was the fight for full religious liberty. The principal functions of the associations were now to provide supplies for vacant churches, to ordain evangelists, and to encourage missionary tours to destitute or frontier areas where the gospel according to the Baptists might be spread.

One of the prime missionary tasks which the Warren Association set for itself almost from its outset was to win over the Separate-Baptists of eastern Connecticut who had formed themselves into the Stonington Association in 1772 and those open-communion churches which later formed the Groton Union Conference in 1785. The Stonington Association began on an informal basis in 1772 among the Baptists at Stonington, Groton, Montville, and New London. By 1795 it included three churches in Stonington, Groton First, New London, Saybrook, Colchester, Montville, Chatham, East Haddam, Ashford Second and Third, Woodstock Second, Hampton, Plainfield, Exeter, West Greenwich, and Richmond First and Second. Why this group of churches was hostile to the Warren Association in its early years is unclear. Partly they resented the leadership of the educated ministers from the Middle Colonies like Manning, Hezekiah Smith, and Stillman; partly they were provincial in their distrust of the implications in the founding of Rhode Island College; and partly they seem to have harbored some old grudges from the early days of the Separate-Baptist movement when Connecticut and not Massachusetts was the center of the radical pie-

10. Warren Association Minutes, 1782, p. 4.
11. See however the letter from John Rathbun, clerk of the Second Baptist Church of Ashford to the Warren Association in 1788 stating the withdrawal of that church from the Warren Association "fearing an Interference with the Independency of Churches." This letter is among the BP(AN).

tism of the Awakening. But in their actual tenets and practices there was no significant difference between the churches of this association and those of the Warren Association.

Isaac Backus, who by birth had close personal ties with eastern Connecticut, began attending the annual meetings of the Stonington Association in 1783 to promote closer relations between the two groups. He wrote in his diary, October 20, 1783, that he was happy to find that the "prejudices against our order and against our college appeared to be much removed" by what he told their elders and delegates. He continued to attend their meetings regularly and in 1788 delivered a lecture to the association on "the cause and nature of the meeting of forty separate and baptist churches" in Stonington in 1754 which led to the schism between open- and closed-communion Separates and Baptists. In 1788 he noted that Elder Zadock Darrow's church in New London that year gave up open-communion and left the Groton Union Conference to join the Stonington Association. In 1791 Backus was chosen as moderator of the Stonington Association. And four years later he noted that it caused quite a stir in Connecticut when Elder Stephen Parsons of Middletown, the successor of the old Separate stalwart Ebenezer Frothingham, gave up pedobaptism and brought his church into the Stonington Association. By this time all friction had ceased between the Stonington and Warren Association and thanks to Backus the groups were on as happy fraternal relations as any other Calvinistic Baptist associations.

The Groton Union Conference, formed in 1785, included the Baptist churches of Dartmouth, New Bedford, two in Rehoboth, two in North Kingstown, two in Westerly, and one each in Groton, South Kingstown, New Shoreham, Dighton, Attleborough, Stonington, Lyme, Saybrook, Sutton, Preston, and Canterbury. All of the churches practiced open, mixed, or occasional communion with pedobaptists and hence were not in fellowship with the closed-communion Baptists. Backus and others in the Warren Association made considerable efforts to persuade these churches to give up mixed communion and noted it as a signal victory for their cause whenever one of them did so. In December 1772, Backus, Noah Alden and Ebenezer Hinds were called to be a council to settle a dispute about open-communion in the Rehoboth Baptist Church over which Elhanan Winchester was pastor. This church belonged to the Groton Union Conference and, said Backus, "Winchester when he was settled here promised in strong terms to give fellowship and administer the ordenance of the Supper to pedobaptist as well as baptist bretheren." In the summer of 1772 Winchester changed his mind and refused to countenance pedobaptism. The majority of his church members censured him for breaking his covenant. Winchester and the minority called the council and naturally invited three closed-communion elders to hear the case. The council asked Winchester to retract his "unbecoming" covenant accepting the practice of open- or mixed communion, and when he had done so the council then proceeded to admonish the majority of his church because they "had censured men's consciences and that for retracting error and embracing the truth." When the majority would not accept Winchester as elder on closed-communion terms, the council instructed him to form a new church with his minority or to join some nearby closed-communion church.[12] In 1795 Backus noted optimistically that several open-communion churches in Massachusetts, notably those in Dighton and Attleborough, had recently adopted closed-communion "and the rest of those churches appear inclined to do the same and to come into fellowship with our associated churches." [13] And in 1805 he wrote that more of the Groton Union churches "have given up mixed communion . . . and are come into connexion with the rest of our associations." [14] But in 1805 the Groton Union Conference still had twenty churches in its membership and it was not until 1815 that conferences were held with serious intentions of merging it with the Stonington Association. This was finally accomplished in 1817 when the practice of closed-communion was accepted by all those still in the Groton Union.[15]

The attempt to amalgamate the Six-Principle Baptists with the Separate-Baptist denomination also received considerable attention. As noted above, two groups of Six-Principle churches existed in the mid-eighteenth century: the old Arminian Six-Principle Baptists who were principally in Rhode Island and who had formed their own association or annual conference in 1692; and a new group of Calvinistic Six-Principle Baptists who grew out of the Awakening in the 1750's. Little is known of this latter group. Backus attended a conference of the Six-Principle Calvinistic Baptists in Gloucester, Rhode Island in 1763 and noted in his diary that elders and messengers from six churches were there: Elder Noah Alden of Stafford; Whitman Jacobs of Thompson; James Smith of South Hadley; Nathaniel Green of Spencer; David Morse of Sturbridge; and Joseph Winsor of Gloucester.[16] He asked those present

> whether they would hold communion with our Churches [i.e., the Separate-Baptist churches in eastern Massachusetts] who were agreed in general with 'em in principle and practice except in holding the laying on of hands on all after baptism. And they said yt they held that [rite] as a standing ordinance in ye Church and also a term of communion but were willing to give or receive light in ye case.

12. Backus ms. "Diary," VIII, 56 (December 23, 1772). Also *ibid.,* VIII, 63. Winchester and his minority did form a new church in Rehoboth, February 3, 1773.
13. Backus, *History,* II, 415, 510. Also his ms. "Diary," VI, 79, and XII, 52.
14. Backus, *Abridgement,* p. 235.
15. *Historical Sketch of the New London Baptist Association* (Boston, 1851), p. 3; David Benedict, *A General History of the Baptist Denomination* (Boston, 1813), I, 526.
16. Backus, ms. "Diary," VI, 11–12. W. G. McLoughlin, "The First Calvinistic Baptist Association in New England." *Church History,* XXXVI (1967), 410–418.

The conference then appointed a committee consisting of Alden and Jacobs "on their side," and Backus gathered some of his friends to meet with them in Cumberland in April 1764. At this conference they discussed at great length "concerning laying on of hands wth prayer after baptism upon all y^t are rec^d into ye church." Backus reported that "they tho't yt they ought to retain yt practice yet they sc[r]upled whether ye rule would warrant there holding of it as a term of communion." [17] Thus, there seemed some willingness to consider the laying on of hands an indifferent or non-essential point and to hold open-communion with churches which did not make this rite a point of communion. But when the matter was brought before the general conference on September 27, 1765, "they were much divided" on it. And "more than half ye elders are bro^t to think yt it wont do to hold yt as a bar of com^n as they have done." [18] No further record of this association exists and it is probable that with the founding of the Warren Association in 1767 it ceased to meet and those who were willing to consider the laying on of hands upon all candidates for church membership non-essential, as was the practice among the churches of the Warren Association, joined the new organization. The few which insisted on maintaining the rite continued without any known association or regular conferences.

The association of the Arminian or General Six-Principle churches, "the Old Baptists," sometimes referred to as the Rhode Island Association or Conference, continued to meet annually during the Awakening and Backus reports that in 1774 its membership consisted of the Cumberland First Baptist Church, Newport Second, Swansea Second, two churches in Rehoboth, two in Scituate, two in Gloucester, two in Warwick, Foster First, Coventry First, North Kingstown First, Richmond First, Cheshire Second, Shaftesbury Third, and one church each in Johnston, Smithfield, and East Greenwich.[19] (The distant churches in Cheshire and Shaftesbury had been formed by migrants from Rhode Island.) The Separate-Baptists did their best to persuade these churches to abandon their Arminianism as well as to abandon their rigid stand on the laying on of hands, but they had only limited success. Backus reported several times in his diary that he was happy "to see ye doctrines of grace [Calvinism] bear such sway among these old Baptist Societyes where Arminianism has almost universally prevail^d for many years." [20] He noted many quarrels and church councils over the years, particularly among the Arminian Baptists in Swansea, Newport, and Rehoboth because "the clear doctrines of grace have lately gained ground among them, and some who disliked them had raised a clam-

17. Backus ms. "Diary," VI, 35 (April 11, 1764).
18. *Ibid.,* VI, 94. Backus mentioned as present at this meeting elders Alden, Jacobs, Nathaniel Green, Bennet, Young, Winsor, Worden, Angel, and Miller.
19. Backus, *History,* II, 415.
20. Backus, ms. "Diary," IV, 121–122 (February 2, 1758), VI, 44–47, 66; VIII, 56, 58, 114.

our." [21] But the Arminians generally held their own and remained outside the Calvinistic mainstream of the denomination. In 1795 Backus could name only three of these "old Baptist" churches which had come over to Calvinism: Newport Second, Swansea Second, and Cumberland First.[22] Nor were the Separate-Baptists ever successful in persuading the Seventh Day Baptists to return to First Day Worship.[23]

Another sign of the Baptist's concern for denominational unity, order, and respectability after 1780 was their effort to insure the regular and generous support of their ministers. As pietistic sectarians they had previously shown a typical disdain for this mundane problem, trusting in the charity of the brethren, the dedication of the ministry, and the providence of God to sustain the temporal needs of the church. But in 1771, 1780, and 1789 the Warren Association in its pastoral letters used particularly strong words in warning against "the sin of covetousness" which leads church members to fail to give adequate support to their pastors. By 1789 the association was ready to point out that voluntary subscriptions had proved totally inadequate as a means of supporting the ministry. Instead it urged either the raising of a ministerial endowment fund, which could be invested to provide a steady income, or the annual assessment of the estates of each member in proportion to his wealth. The latter practice led a number of Baptist churches at this time to seek incorporation, though the association meant only that such an assessment should have just the spiritual power of church censure behind it. Backus, the wheelhorse of the denomination, in 1790 published his tract on *The Liberal Support of Gospel*

---

21. *Ibid.*, VIII, 114 (June 4, 1774).

22. Backus, *History*, II, 415. For the influence of Manning, Gano, Morgan Edwards, and other "ministers who have lately travel'd from the Jerseys" in persuading the Newport Arminians to change their views see Backus, ms. "Diary," VI, 66 (January 19, 1765). In 1781, Backus wrote an optimistic letter to the prominent London Baptist, Dr. John Gill, concerning the progress of Calvinism among the old Baptists in which he said, "among sever[l] old Bap[ts] Cong[ns] Particularly in and near Swanzy where Armin[sm] has been too much entertained, the doct[ns] of grace both in their theory and divine efficacy have gan[d] considerab[l] ground within a few years." This letter, dated March 10, 1781, is among the BP(AN). In 1788, Backus wrote, but never published, a sixteen-page tract entitled "Remarks upon David Jones's vindication of Laying on of Hands." Jones's tract appeared in Philadelphia in 1786 and was an attempt to reassert the Six-Principle view that this was an essential ordinance or rite for all Baptist churches. Backus in his answer noted that this doctrine could only lead to further strife and division and said he deplored anything "which threatenes a . . . division in our Baptist Churches." Laying on of hands, he went on, was a matter "of doubtful disputation" and it should not be made an issue. This ms. tract is among the Backus Papers at the American Baptist Historical Society, Rochester, New York. Apparently Backus realized that the best way to keep this matter from becoming an issue was not to publish his tract. The rite of laying on of hands eventually disappeared from most Baptist churches.

23. The Seventh-Day Baptist Churches were, however, Calvinist. Backus reported in 1795 that their association, which always remained small, contained only four churches, in Newport, Hopkinton, New London, and Bristol (Connecticut). *History*, II, 415.

Ministers to arouse the laity to their duty. No longer were Baptists to be allowed to plead poverty as an excuse for failing to pay adequate ministerial salaries.

The efforts to collect funds to endow certain charitable and educational activities were additional signs of growing denominational maturity and a willingness to think in longer-range terms rather than trusting wholly in the Lord to provide. In 1783 the Warren Association voted to urge a system of annual subscriptions on all member churches for the support of Rhode Island College. In 1791 it established a permanent Education Fund with a board of trustees incorporated by the state; the purpose was to build up an endowment fund to send needy students to the college. After 1794 the association minutes record annual collections taken for the aid of minister's widows, and in 1798 it established a permanent Missionary Fund.[24]

Although the transition to denominational status is clear, so is the fact that a great many aspects of pietistic sectarianism still remained, providing at times a useful and at others a baneful tension within the denomination. One indication of these tensions is the requests for advice on their problems sent into the associations each year by member churches. The more pietistic inquiries usually came, as one might expect, from recently formed churches on the frontier or in isolated rural areas. In 1783 a church asked whether it was really proper for the Warren Association to try to collect membership statistics: "Some have scrupled whether it is lawful to collect and publish the members of our Churches because of the divine judgment which fell upon Israel for David's numbering of the people." To this the Warren Association answered that David took his census without cause while the list which the Association was making would demonstrate specifically the advance of Baptist truth and might serve to "restrain others from oppressing them as they have often done."[25] Another church asked in 1785, is it "a transgression for a brother to appear in a court of judicature and plead as an attorney against another brother?" The Association answered "If an attorney in all other respects conducts himself in character as a church member, he is not censurable for acting as an attorney."[26] In 1786 it was queried whether an elder who was properly dismissed from one church to become an elder in another church needed to be ordained again. This was the practice of the Congregational churches, but the Association answered that he did not.[27] When the church at New Salem inquired in 1781 whether they should dismiss an aged or incapable pastor, the Association answered no, that instead they should assist him in his in-

24. Backus, *Abridgement*, p. 260.
25. Warren Association Minutes, 1783, p. 3. See also the letter from Matturean Ballou of the Richmond Church to the Warren Association in 1785 protesting the numbering of members and citing II Samuel, 24:10 and Exodus, 30:12.
26. Warren Association Minutes, 1785, p. 2.
27. Warren Association Minutes, 1786, p. 4. However, the Baptists adopted a ritual called "the installation" which was used to settle new pastors.

firmity.[28] That same year the church at Royalston asked "Whether the advice of a Mutual Council to an individual Church be so binding that if ye sd. Chh. does not Comply with ye advice of ye sd Council whether it is a just cause to break fellowship with sd Chh.?" And the Association "answered in ye Negative." [29] In 1792 the Hollis church wrote, "We wish your advice on the account of persons that is Contious [conscience] bound against bareing arms in the Millitary Cervice." [30] The answer to this is not recorded but it was certainly negative; pacifism was never a New England Baptists' doctrine, though some converts from Quakerism doubtless carried this conviction with them into the denomination.

Of all the queries with pietistic overtones which came to the associations, by far the most numerous concerned church discipline; i.e., questions asking on what grounds persons could be censured, excommunicated, restored to good standing. The congregational polity of the Baptists, like that of the Congregationalists from whom they sprang, had no clearly established judicial system beyond the majority vote of the members in good standing of each particular church, and no fixed set of rules by which to judge infractions of faith or morals other than the Bible and those principles accepted by each church in its own articles of faith and covenant. Except for the system of *ad hoc* advisory councils of neighboring ministers, there was no ultimate source of authority to whom persons who felt aggrieved by a particular majority vote could appeal. The pietistic concern for keeping the church pure and at the same time for rendering adequate charity, mercy, and justice to offenders produced endless quarrels and schisms not only within churches but between neighboring churches and between pastors as well. Queries to the associations on these points reveal that the pietistic element was still strong in the denomination. For example, in 1787, the Templeton Church asked whether a church could properly admit a member who had been excommunicated by another church if that member had been denied a council or conference or if, at the council, he had been unable to produce evidence of his innocence of the sin he was accused of? [31] In 1788 the South Brimfield church asked whether admonition barred a member from communion or whether only excommunication did so? In 1790 the Cambridge church submitted four queries: (1) Can a candidate for the ministry baptize before he is ordained? (2) Can a person be admitted to membership who has been baptized by someone who is not ordained? (3) Should such a person be re-baptized? (4) Should evidence

28. Ms. letter from the New Salem Church to the Warren Association, 1781, among the BP(AN).

29. Ms. letter from the Royalston-Athol Church to the Warren Association, 1781, among the BP(AN).

30. Ms. letter from Hollis Church to the Warren Association, September 1, 1792, among the BP(AN).

31. Ms. letter from the Templeton Church to the Warren Association, 1787, among the BP(AN).

from non-church members be accepted in a trial of a member before the church? That same year the Royalston church asked what should be done when a person under admonition at another church applied for admission? The Charlton Church asked in 1792 what it should do with a brother who was aggrieved at the way he had been disciplined and asked for dismission to another church on grounds of liberty of conscience? [32]

Some of these questions the associations were ready to answer, some they would not or could not. Among the more difficult questions were, "What are matters of public offense to a church?" What is to be done when a church refuses to take the advice of a council or to call another one? What is to be done when two succeeding councils give conflicting advice, one siding with the majority and the other with the minority? [33] Despite the Baptists' growing denominational maturity, these questions, imbedded in the congregational polity and the pietistic character of their principles, never ceased to plague them. But within these limits, by 1790 the Baptists in New England had achieved remarkable stability and order.

However, just as they began to congratulate themselves on the consolidation of their position as the most dynamic dissenting group in New England, just as they became convinced that their success was inescapable proof that their doctrines and practice were indeed the true interpretation of Scripture, a rash of new dissenting movements which cut deeply into their ranks arose and threatened their security and their self-confidence. Calvinism in these years was in the throes of a life and death struggle with the rising tide of rationalism in philosophy and Arminianism in theology. The Baptists, like every other Calvinist denomination, could not escape the ravages of this intellectual reorientation.

Their four most important competitors after 1780 were the Universalists, the Shakers, the Methodists and the Free Will Baptists. The Baptists never feared the inroads of deism or Unitarianism into their ranks. These were blatant anti-Christian heresies which found their foremost adherents among the upperclasses and which provided such perfect Satanic foils for orthodox Baptist preachers that they would have had to be invented had they not actually existed. Nor did the Baptists feel threatened by the neo-Edwardseans or Hopkinsians in the established church, though it was these dedicated New Lights who saved the Congregational churches from Unitarianism in the latter half of the eighteenth century. Congregationalists in any form were familiar enemies and so tainted with the onus of religious taxation that theological divergencies were of secondary importance. But the Universalists, Shakers, Methodists, and Free Will Baptists were all direct and immediate competitors for the allegiance of lower and middle

32. Ms. letters from these churches to the Warren Association, among the BP(AN).

33. Ms. letters from the Royalston and Cambridge churches to the Warren Association, 1790, among the BP(AN).

class pietists and each of them presented such striking and dynamic characteristics that the former sensationalism of antipedobaptism and dipping paled into insignificance by comparison. What was more, all of these were anti-Calvinist in their central doctrines and thereby more attuned to the temper of the times than were the Calvinistic Separate-Baptists. To be both anti-Calvinist and pietistically and evangelistically Christian, as these sects claimed to be, posed threats of such proportions to Baptists that it may well account for their dramatic shift in attention from the politics of church and state to the ecclesiastical warfare of soul-winning revivalism. They fought as much to preserve their churches as to expand them.

Thus, the letters from member churches to the Warren Association and other associations were from 1780 onward filled with constant lamentations about the inroads of these new heresies, errors, fanaticisms, false prophets, and schismatics who threatened both the new and the old churches of the denomination. Quite logically the pastoral letters of all the associations in these years rang with constant warnings to their congregations that heretics were among them and that they must hold fast to the old faith. By 1784 the Warren Association felt it necessary to protect itself from possible heretical inroads among its membership by establishing what was tantamount to a creedal test of orthodoxy — a loyalty oath — for all member churches and their delegates: "As it is a time of the prevalence of errors of every kind and of the apostacy of many from the faith of the gospel, it is recommended to the churches that they express in their annual letters to the Association their particular adherence to the doctrines of grace." [34] And by "the doctrines of grace" it was clearly understood that the Association meant the doctrines of Calvinism imbedded in the Baptist Confession of Faith of 1689 and asserted to be "The faith and order of this Association" in its original constitution. From that time, though no special formula was prescribed or followed, all the annual letters to the Association accrediting the delegates or messengers from the member churches began with an affirmation of the fundamental points of Calvinism. Three samples from letters sent in 1786 will illustrate the responses:

> The third church of Christ in Middleborough, Holding to the doctrine of Original Sin and total depravity of all the human race; Particular, absolute, personal and Eternal Election of Some to Everlasting life, the final perseverance of Saints, immersion for Baptism, resurrection of the dead, and future Eternal rewards and punishments . . .

> The first Baptist Church of Christ in Attleborough, still holding the Doctrine of original Sin, universal moral depravity, Perticular Election, Free justification by the imputed Righteousness of Christ, Regeneration, Perseverance of the Saints, from Grace to glory, And that the rewards of the Righteous and the punishments of the Wicked will be endless . . .

> [First Baptist Church of Newport] The Doctrines upon which this church

34. Warren Association Minutes, 1784, p. 4.

was at first founded and which we still maintain are the totally ruined state of man by the fall, his recovery only by Divine unmeritted grace, the necessity of the special and sovereign influences of the Holy Spirit, the unchangeable love of God to his people, justification only by the imputed righteousness of Christ, the importance of maintaining good works, the resurrection of the dead, the everlasting happiness of the righteous, and the everlasting punishment of the wicked.[35]

This new emphasis on doctrinal orthodoxy was reinforced by apostrophes in the annual pastoral letters of the associations to their members defending Calvinism from the various theological errors of the day, especially concerning the doctrine of everlasting hellfire (repudiated by the Universalists), the doctrine of perseverance of the saints (rejected by the Methodists), the doctrine of sovereign grace (rejected by Arminians in general), the divinity of Christ (rejected by the Unitarians), and the truth of the atonement (repudiated by deists, atheists, and infidels generally). In 1790 the Warren Association admonished over-fervent pietists "who place the whole of religion in certain feelings," — an obvious reference to the impact the Shakers were having on some Baptist adherents.

Their fears of growing religious confusion even led the Baptists on one occasion to cooperate with the Congregationalists. This was in a petition sent to Congress in 1790 asking the Congress to regulate and certify the accuracy of all Bible publication. No publisher should be permitted to publish or sell a Bible, said this petition, "without its being carefully inspected and certified to be free from error" by some committee appointed by Congress.[36] Presumably the Baptists and Congregationalists expected merely a supervision of the authenticity and typographical accuracy of reprints of the King James version of the Bible, but the assumption that the duty and the right to maintain and license this essential item of religion (and therefore the duty and power to ban any translation of the Bible which did not conform to its standards) rested with the state once again indicates the difference between the theories of separation and of religious freedom held by the Baptists at this time and those held by the Jeffersonian liberals. It also reflects the high value the orthodox Protestants of the period placed on Biblical literalism. What would Backus, Manning, and Stillman have done, one wonders, had they been appointed to a Congressional committee to license the various revised versions of the Bible which have appeared since 1790?

In some respects it seems unlikely that the Separate-Baptist's first serious

35. These letters are among the BP(AN). It may be significant that in 1785 the Warren Association had refused to approve the Newport church's application for membership, probably suspecting that it was still tinctured with Arminianism from the Six-Principle Churches of Rhode Island.

36. Warren Association Minutes, 1790, p. 7. The Congregationalists originated the petition and the Baptists accepted an invitation from them to join in recommending the action to Congress.

competition came from the Shakers. The two groups appeared to have little in common. The explanation lies in part in the fact that the Baptists had, because of the absence of any other significant pietistic group, brought into their ranks many who merely found there a temporary home until a more radical pietism presented itself. On the other hand, the growth of Shakerism may be seen as simply a consequence of the perennial search among the extreme pietists to find an ultimate and clearcut authority which could settle all of the doubts that made them feel uncomfortable in the corruptions of a Standing church or in the unstable, majority-ruled congregations of the Baptists.

Shakerism, or the United Society of Believers, came to America from Manchester, England, in 1774 with Ann Lee who had separated from her husband (a blacksmith named Stanley) after four of her children died in infancy. She had joined a sect called the Shaking Quakers in England in 1758. Their worship was distinguished from the Quakers by their practices of dancing, singing, and prophesying in tongues — a typical holiness formula. "Mother" Ann rose to prominence through her strong character and remarkable eloquence, despite her lack of formal education. When she came to America in 1774 she was joined by eleven followers in Watervliet (then Niskeyuna), New York, nine miles northwest of Albany. They bought land here and began farming on a communal basis. In addition to their communism, pacifism, faith healing, and celibacy, a most remarkable feature of Shakerism was Ann Lee's claim that in her dwelt the spiritual aspects of Christ and that as the female embodiment of the divinity her work was fulfilling the prophecy of the Second Coming. According to Backus,

> On April 17, 1780, Talmage Bishop brought news into New Lebanon of a number of Strange and wonderful Christians at Nisqueunia, 9 miles above Albany, which had a great effect upon the people; and by degrees mr. Samuel Jones [Yale, 1769], a presbyterian minister at New Lebanon, and the main of its inhabitants, baptists and others, fell in with them; as also did elder Rathbun, and the main of his [Baptist] church of Pittsfield, with many others.[37]

The authorities in Albany began to persecute the Shakers for sowing disunity and for suspected Tory activities; as recent immigrants they were

---

37. Backus, ms. "Diary," X, 41 (June 14, 1781). John Farrington, a Baptist elder in New Lebanon, soon after became a convert to Shakerism. The standard histories of the Shakers are Edward Andrews, *The People Called Shakers* (New York, 1953); Arthur Joy, *The Queen of the Shakers* (Minneapolis, 1960); Marguerite Melcher, *The Shaker Adventure* (Princeton, 1941); and Julia Neal, *By Their Fruits* (Chapel Hill, 1947). The Shakers always paid any religious taxes levied on them either as individuals or later as communities; they justified this on their principles of withdrawal from the world and their pacifism which forbade them to engage in quarrels with the state.

considered an alien and untrustworthy element in wartime.[38] Their religious peculiarities contributed to the local desire to be rid of them. Consequently Mother Ann and her followers moved on to other towns to proselyte and to find a place to settle. Traveling through the Berkshire region of western Massachusetts in 1781–1783 they made converts in Pittsfield, Ashfield, Cheshire, and Harvard; by 1786 their preachers were itinerating throughout New England. After twice being driven out of the town of Harvard in 1781–82, they returned in 1783 and in 1784 Mother Ann died there.

From the various accounts of those among the Baptists who were attracted to her teaching or who talked to those who were, there were apparently many aspects of it which were appealing to the pietistic mind. First and foremost was the strong, charismatic, and authoritarian figure of Ann Lee herself and her followers' complete dedication to her. Mother Ann, who claimed to have the power of the Godhead dwelling in her, could settle immediately and infallibly all the many disputed points of doctrine and practice which so troubled the perfectionist desires of the radical pietist. Furthermore her teaching was extremely literalistic in its reliance on the Bible; thus, it did not seem to the believer to constitute a flagrant departure from revealed truth. In addition, the fervor in Shaker worship, the stories of Ann Lee's prophecies fulfilled, and the miracles of faith healing seemed to the credulous to be divine attestations to her authentic apostleship if not of her incarnation. Many were also attracted by the ascetic and communal aspects of Shaker communities, the celibacy of which could be justified by the practice of the apostles. Its monastic aspects certainly offered a stark contrast to the growing materialism and atomism of American life. The practice of oral confession of sins combined with the belief that eternal salvation was available to all who joined the sect but to none outside provided the attraction of assurance and exclusiveness which radical pietists always seek in a church of truly gathered saints. Finally, their strong millennialism was a vital element to many pietists who had always expected that this event was imminent and was bound to happen in America. Although the fact that God had chosen to be reincarnated in a woman was the most serious stumbling block for the uninitiated, there is no doubt that many pietists have felt the lack in Protestantism of that function the Virgin Mary performs in Catholicism. And the practice of celibacy guarded against the free love or spiritual wifery which had detracted from the perfectionists of the Great Awakening.

Had the Baptists been more sophisticated (or more cynical) they might have comforted themselves with the thought that they were probably well rid of persons whose religious needs were better fulfilled by the radical pietism of Mother Ann's sect. But they could not be sure how many of

38. Ezra Stiles, *The Literary Diary of Ezra Stiles*, 3 vols., ed., F. B. Dexter (New York, 1901), II, 510–511.

their followers might yield to these temptations of the Devil.[39] Like all heresies, this appeared to them an obvious work of Satan designed to impede the progress and ultimate glory of the true faith.

Backus obtained some firsthand experience with the Shakers in 1782 when he went to Shaftesbury, Vermont as a fraternal delegate from the Warren Association to the Shaftesbury Association. The Shaftesbury Association, which then included most of the Baptist churches in the Berkshire area, wanted Backus's help to reclaim some of their members from the new sect. Elder Valentine Rathbun of Pittsfield, one of the leading Baptists in the western part of the state, had become a follower of Mother Ann in the fall of 1780, though after three months in the sect he recanted. After his recantation he wrote in December 1780 a vehement attack on and exposé of all their views and practices; this was widely read and often reprinted.[40]

Rathbun became so bitter against the Shakers that he entirely forgot the Baptist principle of religious liberty. In March 1781, he made a motion in the Pittsfield town meeting to devise "some measures to take with those people known as Shakers." The town appointed a committee of five, including Rathbun and the Rev. Thomas Allen, to discover whether the Shakers were such a threat to civil order that they should be banished. On April 2, 1781 the committee reported to the town:

> That they have attended to the object of their commission so far as they imagined in duty and prudence they ought and that they have reason to apprehend that those people called Shakers are in many instances, irregular and disorderly in their conduct and conversation, if not guilty of some high crimes and misdemeanors. The committee therefore recommend it to the town to direct their selectmen to take such cognizance of all disorderly and idle persons in the town, and of their families, as in prudence and by law they may and ought; and further, that the town give particular instructions to their respective grand jurors to be chosen for the next courts to inquire into all the conduct and practices of said people which are contrary to law, and make due presentment thereof, particularly all blasphemies, adulteries, fornications, breaches of sabbath, and all other breaches of law which they may have been guilty of; and that all tithingmen and other persons use their best endeavors, according to law to suppress all disorders and breaches of the peace of every kind; and also that the town direct their town-clerk to inform the commissioners, or other proper authority in the country of Albany, that great and manifest inconveniences and dangers arise from the correspondence and intercourse

39. Stiles heard that they had made 400 converts by February 1781, *ibid.*, II, 510–511.

40. Valentine Rathbun, *An Account of the Matter, Form and Manner of a New and Strange Religion* (Providence, 1781), and *Some Brief Hints of a Religious Scheme Taught and Propagated by a Number of Europeans Living in a Place Called Nisqueunia* (Hartford, 1781). Rathbun concluded, "I am very sensible that the spirit which leads on this new scheme is the spirit of witchcraft." *Ibid.*, p. 20.

subsisting between the people of Niskeuna called Shakers and some people of this town and county disposed to embrace their erroneous opinions, and that they be requested to co-operate with us in endeavoring to prevent such intercourse and correspondence by all possible ways and means.[41]

In short, if new and dangerous "erroneous opinions" concerning religion were vented in a town, Rathbun believed that the civil authorities were justified in defining these opinions as religious blasphemy and prosecuting or banishing those persons who held them. That Baptists had protested vigorously when their itinerant ministers were arrested as vagrants and disturbers of the peace by town officers did not seem to them inconsistent with this action toward the Shaker itinerants.

When Backus came to Shaftesbury in June 1782, two of Rathbun's brothers, one of his brothers-in-law, and four of his children were still Shakers — which may account for the elder's vehemence on the subject. Backus went to the nearby town of Richmond and spent four hours talking with one of the brothers, Daniel Rathbun, "a man of considerable capacity." But he could not dissuade him from his errors.[42] Backus was also told about the wife of Elias Sawyer, a Baptist who "danced with the Shakers till late in the evening" and then "catcht a bad cold and was seized with billious colic but next day danced again and died before night." He heard tales about miraculous faith healings which proved to be fraudulent. And he left Shaftesbury convinced that Ann Lee was nothing but "a common prostitute."

A year later a Shaker itinerant named Stephen Williams brought the heresy into Backus's own region of New England and Backus went to the town of Raynham to meet Williams and refute him.[43] Backus summarized the Shakers's views in this way: "Those Shakers evidently are like the papists in the following points: 1. In holding an earthly head to their church. 2. That out of it is no salvation. 3. That none can enter into it but by confessing their sins to a creature. 4. That they must implicitly believe and do as their leaders say. 5. That the way of salvation is, do and live."[44] In writing his *History of New England,* the second volume of which he published in 1784, Backus added to these errors of the Shakers that "Their doings are unnatural and violent" and that "They endeavor to enforce and

41. J. E. A. Smith, *The History of Pittsfield, Massachusetts,* 2 vols. (Springfield, 1869), I, 454. Backus made no mention in his history of this instance of Baptist intolerance toward religious non-conformity.

42. Isaac Backus's ms. "Journal of a trip to Shaftesbury, 1782," among the BP(BU). Daniel Rathbun eventually did leave the Shakers and published a long account of their practices, *A Letter from Daniel Rathbun to James Whittacor* (Springfield, 1785), with a preface by Valentine Rathbun. Rathbun became disillusioned when he discovered that Mother Ann seemed often to be under the influence of alcohol. See also Ezra Stiles, *Diary,* II, 509.

43. Backus ms. "Diary," X, 60 (March 30, 1783).

44. *Ibid.,* X, 60.

propagate their scheme with a strange power, signs, and lying wonders."
He even added gratuitously,

> their chief leaders delight themselves much in feasting and drinking spiritu-
> ous liquor . . . Some of them at Norton and elsewhere have carried mat-
> ters so far this year [1784] as for men and women to dance together entirely
> naked, to imitate the primitive state of perfection. And their forcibly strip-
> ping a woman of one of their families, who testified against their wicked-
> ness, has moved the authority of Bristol county lately to take them in
> hand therefor.[45]

Backus is also the source for the report that "a motion was made in our
legislature to have them punished by authority, which motion was negatived
by the majority of a single vote." [46]

President James Manning of Rhode Island College showed the same
desire to put the Shakers in the worst light. He wrote to Samuel Stennett,
the prominent London Baptist, on November 8, 1783:

> They pretend to absolve the sins of their disciples, and of course require
> particular confession to be made to them. Their particular worship consists
> in dancing, turning round on the heel, jumping, singing, and embracing
> each other, while they pretend to talk in unknown tongues, work miracles,
> etc. etc. They interdict all intercourse between the sexes, declaring the
> marriage contract void, and pretending to a state of absolute perfection.
> Some carnal fruits, however, have inadvertently resulted from their chaste
> embraces. And — would you believe it? — vast numbers of those who
> once appeared serious, well-disposed persons, have followed their pernicious
> ways. They are not to be reasoned with; alleging that they know they are
> right, and they will rave like madmen when opposed, calling this the
> effect of the Spirit of God.[47]

These reports are more indicative of the Baptists' hostility than of the
Shakers' true nature. This vindictiveness may be accounted for partly because Baptists provided the chief source of Shaker converts. Ezra Stiles
reported of the New Lebanon Shaker colony in 1786, "I find these Shakers
are almost to a man Converts fr. the Rh. Isld. & Narraganset Baptists
called there New Lights & Separates — accustomed in their Narrag. Meet-

45. Backus, *History*, II, 297–298.
46. *Ibid.*, II, 462–463. In 1782, according to Backus, the Shakers moved into the
towns of Norton and Rehoboth, making heavy inroads among the Baptists and

> they prevailed with many of their society to sell their estates in order to build
> a ship to carry the church to the New Jerusalem, as they said. And a large
> vessel was built in Rehoboth; but it was sent a voyage to the West Indies, from
> whence a rich cargo was brought, and the vessel and cargo were sold, and a
> few men cheated the rest out of their estates . . .

47. Reuben Aldridge Guild, *Early History of Brown University Including the Life,
Times and Correspondence of President Manning* (Providence, 1897), p. 364.

ings to work themselves up to high Enthusiasm, so as in Worship all the Congregation to get to speek^g, pray^g, & singing all at the same time." [48]

Evidence supports Stiles that it was among Separate-Baptists, who, after 1770 moved in great numbers to the frontier areas from Rhode Island, eastern Connecticut, and the Old Plymouth Colony region, that the Shakers found their most fertile source of converts. However, rarely did entire congregations go over to the Shakers, as in Pittsfield. Most Baptist church records report that only a handful of members "went off to the Shakers" in the years 1780–1785, though among these, unfortunately, were a number of Baptist elders.[49] Since the Shakers never had more than two thousand members in these years it seems that the Baptists were far more worried over potential Shaker inroads than they need to have been. In the third volume of his history, published in 1795, Backus reported that although in 1783 "the Shakers were a large body . . . yet we seldom hear of them now, unless it is by way of observing that the power which then actuated them is gone; and their attention is much fixed upon worldly schemes of gain." [50] The Shakers were to get renewed impetus from the camp meeting revivals on the southern and western frontiers after 1800, but after 1790 they ceased to be a force in New England.

The Universalist "delusion," however, was a far more serious affair for the Baptists. Insofar as John Murray can be considered the founder of Universalism in America, this sect too owed its origins to an English import in the 1770's. Murray was one of George Whitefield's converts in England, imbibed Universalist doctrines from James Relly in London, and came to America in 1770. Ezra Stiles says that when Murray began preaching in New England after 1772 he preached often in Separate and Separate-Baptist churches. In 1779 he organized the first Universalist Church in the United States in Gloucester, Massachusetts, and, to promote his views, he published an edition of James Relly's *Union, or a Treatise on the Consanguinity between Christ and his Church.*[51] Universalism was often called "Rellyism" in its early years.

But Murray was not the sole, nor perhaps even the most important, originator of this sect. At least of equal importance was Elhanan Winchester (1751–1797), a Separate-Baptist minister who, from 1771 to 1780, had been one of the most successful itinerant evangelists and pastors in the denomination. After he had preached widely in Massachusetts,

---

48. Stiles, *Diary,* III, 243.
49. Baptist church records in Ashfield (1781); Boston First (1782–1783); Cheshire (1781); Chelmsford (1782); and Harvard (1781–1782). The most important ministerial defection to the Shakers was Elder Joseph Meacham of Enfield, Connecticut. His departure ruined his church. He never recanted. Backus, *History,* II, 526.
50. Backus, *History,* II, 404.
51. *Ibid.,* II, 248, and Stiles, *Diary,* I, 289–290, 296, 417.

South Carolina, and Delaware, Winchester in 1780 went to Philadelphia to become pastor of the First Baptist Church, the most prestigious church of the denomination in the Middle Colonies if not in the country. Then, in the spring of 1781, to the consternation of Baptists everywhere and to the particular embarrassment of the Separate-Baptists in New England who had been so high in his praise, Winchester openly avowed his Universalist views.

In the 1790's another group of Universalists arose in the back country of New England under the leadership of Hosea and Matturean Ballou and Caleb Rich, all three of whom had been Separate-Baptists. However, it seems evident now that Universalism would have arisen even without these leaders. The movement represents one aspect of the many-sided revolt against Calvinism and the rise of optimistic, self-confident, humanitarianism which occurred in the latter half of the eighteenth century. It belongs with Unitarianism, deism, and Methodism as a version of that Arminian movement within Christendom which climaxed the Age of Reason and ushered in the Age of Romanticism and Evangelicalism.[52] Just as deism had its sophisticated exponents, like Jefferson and Franklin, and its provincial exponents, like Ethan Allen and Elihu Palmer, so Universalism was given its first sophisticated American exposition in 1782 in Charles Chauncy's *Salvation for All Men,* a volume which caused as much consternation among the Congregationalists of the Standing Order as had Winchester's defection among the Separate-Baptists a year earlier. And for the same reason: it was proof that Arminianism was making serious inroads into the heart of American Calvinism. For the Baptists the Arminian inroads into their denomination were particularly exasperating because they negated the claim that the Baptist separation from the Standing Order had been necessary to preserve Christianity from this heresy in the 1740's and later. Now it turned out that the Separation itself was polluted and that even the Baptist faith was not invulnerable to it.[53]

The rising threat of Universalism in New England can be traced in Backus's diary and papers. On October 25, 1778, Backus recorded in his diary, "John Murry has again been here of late preaching up universal

---

52. The standard history of Universalism is Richard Eddy, *Universalism in America* (Boston, 1886), 2 vols. For the concomitant rise of Arminianism and Unitarianism see Conrad Wright, *The Beginnings of Unitarianism in America* (Boston, 1955).

53. The case of Elder Jeremiah Barstow (or Bestow) of the Second Baptist Church in Sutton was one of the early outcroppings of this Arminianism among the Baptists. Backus was on a council, called by some aggrieved members of this church on September 30, 1772, who complained "about the doctrines of grace" Barstow preached. Barstow held that all men are "in a state of salvability" and that "the non-elect had such an interest in Christ's death as to be considered in a pardonable state till they sinned it away." Barstow's church voted 11 to 5 that this was heretical and the council agreed. *Ibid.,* II, 460–461; Backus ms. "Diary," VIII, 46; and the ms. decision of the council among the BP(AN).

salvation with much art and eloquence and had many followers, but as to true religion, people are exceedingly stupid about it." A year later in Norwich, Connecticut on October 10, 1779, he recorded, "John Murray who preaches up universal salvation pr^t at the separate meetinghouse . . . Mr. Tyler the episcopal minister and elder Rennels [Reynolds] both fall in with him and multitudes flock after him tho' his doctrine is really the same with that of the devil, 'Ye shall not surely die.' " Elder Gamaliel Reynolds later led the Separate-Baptist church of Norwich into the Universalist denomination. On September 5, 1780, Elder Nathaniel Green of the Charlton church wrote to the Warren Association that the town had been invaded by advocates of universal salvation but that fortunately brother Elhanan Winchester had arrived and was stirring up a revival among the Baptists which took people's minds off this heresy.[54] On September 11, 1781 Richard Montague, the lay leader of the Baptist church in Montague, wrote to the Warren Association that his church had lost three male and four female members who "Renounced their former profession and fully embraced that that is general called ye new Religion." [55] Three weeks later Backus recorded in his diary, "John Murry came to Taunton last Thursday and pr^t up the universal salvation of all men which is the first time of preaching that heresy so near us." And soon after Backus declared "The doctrine of salvation of all men had spread so far in our country that I thought it duty to write against it." [56] His tract was entitled, *The Doctrines of Universal Salvation Examined and Refuted* (Providence, 1782). It was not only an answer to Murray, but to Winchester's recent infidelity, to Chauncy's *Salvation to All Men,* and to a new edition of Relly's *Union or Treatise of the Consanguinity between Christ and his Church* which had appeared in Providence earlier that year.

In this polemic Backus acknowledged that there were certain variations in the doctrines put forth by Relly, Murray, Winchester, and Chauncy, but nevertheless they were all attacking the fundamental doctrines of true religion — Calvinism. They did this, said Backus, because they claimed that these hard doctrines were leading men of common sense to repudiate Christianity for deism. Relly argued, said Backus, that Calvinism was a system of "self-righteousness" and "bigotry" which taught "the obedience of fear." Relly opposed it because "where fear of punishment is judged necessary to obedience, unbelief is established. But the obedience of faith

---

54. Letter from Nathaniel Green to the Warren Association, September 5, 1780, among the BP(AN). A year earlier the Warren Association Minutes contain this acknowledgment of the spread of universalism: "Advice being asked by the church in Charlton about the opinion of some who hold to universal salvation or that all the human race will finally be saved by Jesus Christ: We look upon it to be a *damnable heresy.*"

55. Letter from Richard Montague to the Warren Association, September 11, 1781, among the BP(AN).

56. Backus ms. "Diary," December 31, 1782.

is genuine, free from artifice, without fear." Backus was astonished at such claims. "Can Relly's system be any other than a filthy dream?" For if Relly was opposed to the doctrine of divine punishment for sin, he was clearly opposed to all government; "No government can be maintained in civil states without appeals to God to avenge injustice, perjury, and unfaithfulness." It would appear from this that Backus agreed with the arguments which Theophilus Parsons used shortly thereafter to defend the right of the First Parish of Gloucester to levy religious taxes on Murray's church members for the support of the Congregational church.

The difference between Relly and Murray, Backus continued, was that "Relly builds upon an imaginery union with Jesus, but Winchester upon the benevolent nature of the Deity . . . Relly holds that salvation is already compleat in Christ so as to exempt men from all future punishment; but Winchester denies the need of Christ's blood to appease any wrath in the Deity." Winchester treats sin "as a natural and not a moral evil; as a calamity rather than a crime." On the other hand, "Relly declares sin to be an infinite evil, deserving of infinite punishment" but says that this penalty has already been settled and remitted by Christ's atonement. As for Chauncy, his great argument seemed to be, said Backus, that men would not turn deist if they realized that God was good and would damn no one eternally.[57] This, said Backus, was nothing but Romish superstition; it was the doctrine of purgatory, stated long ago by "St. Origen." Backus summed up his own Calvinistic arguments against universalism this way:

> Because it is a most important truth that God is no respector of persons, many deny his right to do what he will with his own grace, though in a way of perfect justice. He is perfectly just in all his dispensations, while he shews mercy to whom he will shew mercy. To deny this is to deny him the right which every freeman has with his own property. Oh, madness! It is also an essential truth, that God is love in the abstract; but it is a fatal delusion to imagine that he loves every individual sinner, so as not to inflict endless punishment upon such as die in impenitency. The devils are his creatures, and were a higher order of them then men; yet their endless punishment is declared as one evidence against those who turn grace into lasciviousness.[58]

One of the particularly distressing aspects of Winchester's apostasy in the spring of 1781 was that he confessed he had held Universalist views for two years before he announced them.[59] Not only did this indicate

57. For other arguments against Chauncy see Backus's *The Testimony of the Two Witnesses* (Boston, 1786), pp. 20–21.

58. Backus, *History*, II, 295. Backus's justification of God's arbitrary dispensation of grace in terms of the inalienable right of a freeman to dispose of his private property as he chooses must rank as a signal proof of the Lockean influence on American Calvinism.

59. Gardner Thurston to Isaac Backus, March 15, 1781, in BP(AN).

that he might have been insinuating these heresies to Baptists who heard him everywhere during that period, but even worse it indicated how difficult it was to spot heresy. President Manning, writing to John Rippon in London in 1784, expressed the Baptists's general dismay at the event: "The apostasy of Mr. Winchester has been for a lamentation amongst us. Self-exaltation was the rock on which he split. Though he had from the first been remarkable for instability of character, he inflicted a grievous wound on the cause, especially in Philadelphia." [60] Another thing which distressed Winchester's former brethren was that after his church split on the issue of dismissing him, he, with a slight majority, claimed the right to the church building and property. He lost his suit in court, but that he had tried to wrench this property away from the denomination made Backus lament, "he grasped at the temporal property of said church as long as he could hope for it" and then he (Winchester) hypocritically wrote in 1787 that he had martyred himself for the cause of truth.[61] The Philadelphia Baptists printed a long attack on Winchester in 1781 and it was not until 1794 that the apostate Baptist dared to return to New England to preach.[62]

The records of the Baptist churches of New England in this period indicate clearly the great inroads which the Universalists made into their membership ranks.[63] Almost every Baptist church lost some members and many lost ten or twenty. Moreover, at least six other Baptist elders besides Winchester apostatized to Universalism: Elder Reynolds of Norwich in 1783; Elder John Millington of Shaftesbury in 1787; Elder Elkanah Ingalls of Upton in 1788; Elder Ebenezer Lamson of Sutton in 1794; Elder Isaac Root of Danville, Vermont in 1799 and Elder Isaiah Parker of Harvard, Massachusetts in 1804.[64] Lamson could not persuade any of his church to join him, but Reynolds and Ingalls carried the majority of their congregations with them and wrecked their churches; Root was dismissed from his church and Parker had retired from preaching in 1798. Two other notable Baptists nearly joined the new denomination or were suspected of it. Morgan Edwards of Philadelphia, according to James Manning, wrote a book defending Winchester's view in 1783 but was persuaded not to publish it.[65] President Jonathan Maxcy of Rhode Island College, who succeeded Manning, was considered by several persons,

---

60. Guild, *Brown University,* p. 378.
61. Backus, *History,* II, 440, and 441–442 n.
62. Guild, *Brown University,* p. 383.
63. For a graphic account by a Baptist who was almost "ensnared" by "One of the Univeselers" see letter from Abigail Macomber to the Bowdoinham Association, August 16, 1790, in BP(AN). Other correspondence in BP(AN) mentions Universalist converts from the Baptist churches in Chelmsford, Newton, Upton, Charlton, Carver, Montague, Grafton, and Douglas.
64. Letter from the Upton Baptist Church to the Warren Association in 1788 about Ingalls; Backus, ms. "Diary," XII, 118.
65. Guild, *Brown University,* pp. 375, 378.

including Backus, to be heretical in his views on this question in the 1790's, but he managed to defend his position.[66]

Backus tried to be optimistic about a bad situation by insisting that Universalism had weakened the Standing Order more than it had the Baptists. In a letter to Thomas Ustick, on June 3, 1796, he discussed the posthumous book written by Dr. Joseph Huntington in favor of Universalism: "How popular has this doctrine grown? Though it strikes at the root of all true religion, as much as infidelity itself. But it has had an influence towards pulling down what men have called their established religion in New England. Dr. Huntington has been a great leader therein. Thus God makes all things work for the good of his children." [67]

If one pairs Universalism with Unitarianism, as Backus did, then perhaps he was right in pointing out that it irrevocably split the Congregationalists and eventually was a prime force in the fall of the establishment. He was correct as well in that the Baptists continued strong despite Universalism's inroads. But he probably would not have approved the way in which the Baptists coped with the rising anti-Calvinism in the Second Great Awakening gradually shifting their doctrinal emphasis away from the harsher aspects of Calvinism and toward a clearly Arminian or evangelical interpretation of "the doctrines of grace." Fortunately for the Baptists, the Universalists also had growing pains from 1790 to 1830; they became badly divided over the specifics of their doctrines. But had Backus lived until the 1830's he would have had to admit that this sect, of which he so thoroughly disapproved, was at that time more active than were the Baptists in bringing about the final overthrow of compulsory religious taxes in Massachusetts.

66. For an accusation of Maxcy's heresy see William Rogers's letter to Isaac Backus, November 2, 1791, and the correspondence between Backus and Maxcy on this subject in 1797 among the BP(AN). Maxcy claimed he had been misrepresented and Backus appeared to be reassured by this. Also Alvah Hovey, *A Memoir of the Life and Times of the Rev. Isaac Backus* (Boston, 1858), pp. 352–360.

67. This letter is in the American Baptist Historical Society in Rochester.

Chapter 38

The Methodists, the Freewill Baptists and the Christ-ians, 1780–1810

One thing which much discourages us is the Weslien methodist[s] are all around us and appear determined to spread their tenets which appear to us contrary to truth and our articles of faith.

Weston Baptist Church to the Warren Association, 1792

At the turn of the century, Methodism was the third, and ultimately the most serious rival of the Baptist persuasion in New England (and throughout the United States). It did not begin to appear in New England until the 1790's, and it grew very slowly. Its frank Arminianism, its perfectionism, its episcopal form of government, and undoubtedly its old associations with Toryism worked against it in its early years. But with the rise of the Second Great Awakening and the ultimate revision of Calvinism into evangelicalism after 1800, Methodism came to rival the Baptist denomination throughout the new nation. Like Universalism and Shakerism, Methodism came to America from England in the Revolutionary years. It formally arrived in 1769 when John Wesley commissioned Richard Boardman and Joseph Pilmoor to look after the Methodists who had already immigrated to America. In 1771 Francis Asbury, its greatest early leader, arrived. Because Wesley was a Tory and because his movement remained technically a part of the Church of England in the colonies until 1784, the denomination suffered a serious setback between 1775 and 1783. But after that it began to flourish. In 1789, Jesse Lee brought his circuit riding evangelism to New England and the Baptists soon became aware of this threat to their unity.

However, Wesley's movement was well-known to the Baptists long before it actually arrived in New England. John Allen, the Revolutionary pamphleteer who for a time occupied the pulpit of the Second Baptist Church in Boston, denounced Wesley in his widely read tract, *The Spirit of Liberty,* published in London in 1770:

723

My thoughts of Mr. Wesley as a Gentleman and as a Scholar are very respectable, and what he is worthy of, — that he is a Man of surprising parts, a great Historian, and is as enterprizing as he is great . . . — but as to Mr. Wesley being a Christian, I dare not . . . attempt to deceive him or you in thinking so . . ." [1]

One of the first mentions of Wesley by a New England Baptist appeared in Backus's *History of New England,* second volume, in 1784. He called it "a new sect which is now formed in America" and commented that there were now three different forms of episcopacy in the United States (that of Coke and Asbury, through Wesley; that of Samuel Seabury through the Scottish Church, and that of Samuel Provost and William White, ordained by the Church of England through a special act of Parliament). [2] Backus also deplored the Arminian and perfectionist aspects of the new sect whose "teachers have taken great pains to draw off people from all other religious communities in our land by confounding works and grace together." He quoted Wesley's attack on "unconditional election" and "unlimited reprobation" and claimed that Wesley was perverting Scripture in linking the two doctrines. He also rebutted Wesley's refutation of the doctrine of perseverance of the saints by quoting the text from John 6:37, "Him that cometh to me, I will in no wise cast out." [3] Backus later summed up his conception of Wesleyanism in two sentences: "Mr. Wesley held that Christ died equally for all mankind, but that men are saved by their own faith and obedience, which yet they may fall from, and perish forever . . . How stupid is this!" [4]

During the first five months of 1789 Backus made an extended preaching tour in Virginia and North Carolina; he noted that while the Baptists were rapidly growing in the South, "The Methodists are the next most numerous." [5] "The Methodists have followed the Baptists thro' the country with much zeal, but they earnestly strike against the most essential doctrines of the gospel . . . To hold up light against their errors, and others, is of great importance in this time when many have an ear to hear." [6]

For this reason, and because he was urgently requested to do so by his

1. This was quoted by Ezra Stiles in his *The Literary Diary of Ezra Stiles,* ed. F. B. Dexter 3 vols. (New York, 1901), I, 244.

2. Isaac Backus, *History of New England,* ed. David Weston (Newton, 1871), II, 323–326; Isaac Backus, *An Abridgement of the Church History of New England* (Boston, 1804), p. 281; Isaac Backus, ms. "Diary," X, 115.

3. He also accused Wesley of apostasy for renouncing the high church views he had held prior to 1739. *History,* II, 323–326.

4. *Ibid.,* II, 325; and Backus ms. "Diary," XIV, 6. In 1795 Backus declared that John Callendar was wrong when he called Whitefield "a second George Fox" in 1743; it was really "Mr. Wesley and his followers" who "have been exceedingly zealous for the doctrines which Fox held" presumably about perfectionism. *History,* II, 505–506.

5. See his letter to his brother Elijah, May 25, 1790, in the BP(AN).

6. Backus to his wife, March 29, 1789, among the BP(AN).

Southern brethren, Backus spent the latter part of 1789 writing a tract designed to refute Wesley's doctrines. The tract, *The Doctrine of Particular Election and Final Perseverance,* specifically attacked Wesley for denying these Calvinistic articles of faith and as well attacked his Toryism and his veracity. Here, as elsewhere, the Calvinists defensively denied that their doctrines were based on preaching fear of hellfire and damnation: "All the world have now seen," he concluded, "that love is a vastly more powerful principle of action than fear;" why else would God have deigned to save any of the depraved race of men except for his great mercy and love? Backus thought in 1789 that "their influence is now on the decline." [7] But he had to revise his opinion in the 1790's as Methodist itinerants poured into New England and began to cut into the Baptist ranks at a faster rate than the Universalists or Shakers had ever done.

This letter from Weston in 1792 is typical of the letters which the Warren Association began to receive in this period from member churches: "One thing which much discourages us is the Weslien methodist[s] are all around us and appear determined to spread their tenets which appear to us contrary to truth and our articles of faith." [8] A letter in 1798 from Elder Abner Lewis of the Harwich church voiced the same fear: "Their is at present a number of this Church that Neglect to assemble with us and assemble with the meathedis [Methodists]." [9] Apparently there were no Baptist elders in New England who became Methodists, but the church records show that many of their members did. This "new sect" had just the right combination of pietistic fervor, optimism, and Christian truth to provide what many in the Baptist ranks wanted: a religion which abandoned the pessimism and implicit determinism of "high-toned" Calvinism; which gave the individual a larger measure of free will in controlling the destiny of his soul here and hereafter; which was just as ascetic as the Baptist religion in its demands on personal morality; which in no sense abandoned the preaching of hellfire and damnation (as the Universalists did) or belief in the Trinity (as the deists and Unitarians did). Moreover, the Wesleyan doctrine of perfectionism, or "growing in grace," fitted admirably with the faith in progress and in the imminent millennium which dominated pietistic thought in the young republic.

It is true that the doctrine of episcopal church government was a drawback to many, but the Methodists lessened this by democratizing it; besides, in the early period the role of bishops was small compared to that of the class leaders and the itinerant circuit riders. The Methodists sought to remove the stigma of Toryism by emphasizing after 1784 their break with

7. *Ibid.,* March 29, 1789, BP(AN). Also George C. Baker, *An Introduction to the History of Early New England Methodism* (Durham, 1941).

8. Letter from Samuel Pratt, clerk of the Weston Church to the Warren Association, September 7, 1792, in the BP(AN).

9. Abner Lewis to the Warren Association, 1789, in the BP(AN).

the Church of England and by denouncing establishments of religion as vigorously as any Baptist:

> We are not ignorant of the spirit and designs it [the Church of England] has ever discovered in Europe of rising to preeminence and worldly dignities by virtue of a national establishment . . . and we fear the same spirit will lead the same church in these United States (although altered in name) to similar designs and attempts . . . For these reasons we have thought it our duty to form ourselves into an independent state.[10]

The Baptists, especially those better educated, displayed their own hard-won respectability by ridiculing the ignorant fanaticism of the Methodists in terms similar to those the Congregationalists had used against Separate-Baptists in the 1740's. Edmund Botsford, a graduate of Rhode Island College and elder in Georgetown, Virginia, wrote to Backus in 1804 describing the Methodist meetings in his community: "They sing, pray, clap hands, fall down. laugh, holloo, etc. some times all together, that you would think they were deranged;" they court persecution; they are extremely censorious of all other churches, and "their conversions are of short duration." [11] Backus wrote disapprovingly in 1805, "Many have doubtless been reformed by their [the Methodist's] means, and some converted; but they readily receive awakened persons to communion without a profession of regeneration." He particularly resented that "if any one who was sprinkled in infancy is not satisfied with it and will join with them, they [Methodist ministers] will go into the water and baptize them." [12]

The Methodists would have gained more converts from the Baptists in New England if the Baptists had not produced a schism of their own over the question of Calvinism and free will. It was ironic that the schism which produced the Free Will Baptist sect under the leadership of Benjamin Randall in 1780 in Maine and New Hampshire came just when the Baptists were congratulating themselves at winning over so many of the Arminian Six-Principle Baptists in Bristol and Plymouth counties. The story of the Free Will Baptists in this period belongs to the history of the denomination in New Hampshire and Vermont. Before 1810 there were no Free Will Baptist Churches founded south of these states.[13] Benjamin Randall (1749–1808) lived in New Castle, New Hampshire where he was a sailmaker and tailor. Randall was brought up in the Congregational church; after he heard Whitefield preach in 1770, he was converted and joined the Standing church in New Castle in 1772. He was dissatisfied with

10. Backus quoted the statement from the Methodist Discipline of 1787; *History,* II, 325.

11. Edmund Botsford to Backus, January 3, 1804, among the BP(AN).

12. Backus, *Abridgment,* p. 219.

13. Norman A. Baxter in his *History of the Freewill Baptists* (Rochester, 1957) writes that one hundred Freewill churches were founded between 1780 and 1810, two of these in Vermont and the other ninety-eight in New Hampshire; p. 31,

its formality and coldness, separated from it in 1775 and began meeting with some other pietists in his home. In 1776 he followed the usual Separate path and renounced infant baptism. He was immersed by William Hooper, pastor of the Baptist church in Madbury,[14] and became a member of this church. The following year he felt a call to preach and after itinerating for a time he was asked to form a church among some of his converts in New Durham. He did this, but after he preached to this congregation for some time, his members noted he was not preaching Calvinism. When he was asked why he did not, he replied, "Because I do not believe it." [15] Several conferences and councils on the issue of his orthodoxy resulted, and in July 1779, after one such council, Elder Walter Powers of the Gilmanton Baptist church said he could no longer have fellowship with Randall because he was not a Calvinist.

At the same time that Randall was making this transition to Arminianism, two other Baptists in that region were doing the same thing. Elder Edward Lock, pastor of the church in Loudon-Canterbury, was declared heretical by a council in December 1779. Several of Lock's congregation formed a new church in Gilmanton and called Lock as their pastor; the other Baptist ministers in the vicinity refused to ordain Lock at a council called for this purpose in February 1780. At this council, however, Elder Tozier Lord of the Lebanon church declared that he agreed with Lock's doctrines and he agreed to ordain Lock by himself since the rest of the council would not. In April 1780, Lord and Lock ordained Randall as elder of a Free Will Baptist church in New Durham. Because both Lock's and Tozier's churches broke up in 1782, while Randall remained at New Durham and expanded his following, he is generally given credit for founding the new denomination. But it was obviously a spontaneous, joint venture.

Under the ardent evangelism of Lock and Randall, the new denomination grew rapidly. Between 1780 and 1792 eighteen new churches were formed; between 1792 and 1800, thirty-three more were formed; from 1800 to 1810, forty-nine more.[16] Free will was a popular doctrine on the frontier and this growth might have been even more rapid except for the advent of Shakerism in New Hampshire in 1782. A great many "Freewillers" and potential freewillers, including some of the elders of the new

---

14. Hooper lived in Madbury but he really was pastor of two congregations, one in Madbury and one in Berwick; Backus, *History*, II, 480.

15. Baxter, *Freewill Baptists*, p. 21.

16. *Ibid.*, pp. 28–29. Elder Nathaniel Lord wrote to Backus from Berwick, October 26, 1778: "There seems to be Great Division at hand. Ranglings and Disputings through the Churches . . . the things most in Disput at present are as follows — how the Universal Call or the free proclamation of the Gospel to Every Creature Can be Reconcile with the Doctrine of perticular Election. See also the letter from William Hooper to Backus, May 3, 1780, which said that "the Free will Plan" was causing divisions in Madbury.

Free Will churches, chose the Shakers.[17] In addition, the Calvinist Baptists' formation of the New Hampshire Association led to a vigorous counter-attack against the Arminian heresy. In 1784 the New Hampshire Association wrote to the Warren Association, "Some Brethren who seemed to be Tip[p]ed To and Fro by the Freewillers (so called) have Returned and given Satisfaction. And the Free will Doctrine so Diligently Promulgated by One Lock and his Brethren for a Time has visiably Decreased Since the Frenzical, if not Magical Religion of the Shakers hath been Embraced by some of Lock's People." [18] The only mention of Randall in all of Backus's personal papers is a brief note in his diary for July 15, 1799, where he stated that a revival began in Marshfield, Massachusetts the previous fall and "went on gloriously until one Benjamin Randel, an arminian baptist of Newhampshire, came there in March and laboured for above a fortnight" until he produced a schism in Elder Timothy Williamson's Marshfield church.[19]

When Randall and his brethren finally got around to moving southward after 1799, they found their best harvests in the towns of the old Plymouth colony, on the Cape, and among the Six-Principle Baptists of Rhode Island. The doctrine of free will had always been popular in this area and several debates had arisen between the Calvinists and the old Arminian Baptists prior to 1799. In 1767 Backus wrote a tract entitled *True Faith Will Produce Good Works* which he intended as an attack upon the Standing Order and the Arminian tendencies of Stoddardeanism (though he also added "some remarks" against the new teachings of Robert Sandeman whose doctrines were then becoming popular in New England).[20] To his great surprise, his book was taken as an attack upon the Six-Principle Arminian Baptists as well, and Elder Daniel Martin of the "old Baptist" church in Rehoboth wrote an answer to it in 1770 entitled *Some Meditations* in defense of Arminianism. Backus was urged not to engage in an intramural pamphlet war with other Baptists, but as the champion of the Baptist cause he felt that it was his duty to protect the name of the denomination from aspersions on its Calvinistic orthodoxy. He therefore answered Martin in 1771 with a tract entitled *The Doctrine of Sovereign Grace Opened and Vindicated*. Martin had argued, "Since it is the good will of God that all men should be saved and come to the knowledge of the truth, what doth hinder, or indeed what can hinder or prevent, but the want of man's good will?" To which Backus replied, "His plan [Martin's] would make the will of the Creator dependent on the will of the

17. *Ibid.*, pp. 61–64.
18. Letter from New Hampshire Association to the Warren Association, 1784, among the BP(AN).
19. Backus, ms. "Diary," XIII, 43.
20. Sandeman and his views are discussed below. Backus often included two tracts for the price of one.

creature . . ." It was not true, said Backus, following Jonathan Edwards, that men can "act with motive or against motive." They have no free will in this sense. He then offered historical evidence that Roger Williams, in founding the first Baptist church in America, had taken strong Calvinistic grounds and concluded that Martin and the Arminians had "warped off" from Baptist orthodoxy when they took up Arminianism. He also added an attack upon the practice of laying on of hands as an essential rite for church membership. Quoting the noted English Baptist historian, Thomas Crosby, Backus pointed out that the General Baptists in England had adopted this rite from the Anglican practice of confirmation, and that it could not be justified by Scripture.

The debate was unproductive, but Backus was convinced that God was clearly demonstrating the truth of the Calvinistic interpretation of the gospel by the continued success of the Separate-Baptists and the steady decline of the Arminian, Six-Principle Baptists. He noted in the third volume of his history, published in 1795, that "The doctrines of grace and the power of godliness, have lately gained ground among" those Six-Principle churches in Rehoboth where Daniel Martin and his colleague, Elder Nathan Pierce, had formerly preached. Following Martin's death in 1781 his church had entered a sharp decline.[21] Backus simply could not entertain the possibility that Calvinism might be declining.

Another aspect of this controversy appeared in the private correspondence which Backus had with an Arminian layman named Josiah Briggs in November 1772. Briggs argued in opposition to the doctrine of a predestined elect, "It is as much a denial of Gods mercy to say he is merciful to some objects of it and not to others as it wo'd be of the perfection of his truth to say he is true to some and not to others." Moreover, he asked, "whether such a nature in man as to pity some and not others yt are no less objects of pity, be the image of God?" To which Backus answered that only God had universal knowledge of man's moral perfection; it was not inconsistent of God to save some and damn others, for it was infinite mercy on His part that any were saved at all: "Every soul that is punished either here or hereafter, it will be but what they deserve for their crimes, and it is all of mercy that any are saved." [22]

The argument represented the changing intellectual climate of New England, and of America, in the Revolutionary era. As Backus said testily, the Americans had come to the conclusion "That they will receive nothing for truth but what they can comprehend with their reason." [23] They were certain that God was benevolent and that he had given men the power of reason to comprehend his laws. Josiah Briggs was the archetype of the common man using his common sense to prove that the God of John

21. Backus, *History*, II, 434.
22. Josiah Briggs to Backus, September 5, 1772, in the BP(AN).
23. Isaac Backus, *True Faith Will Produce Good Works* (Boston, 1767), p. 63.

Calvin could not be benevolent and merciful because otherwise he would not be so arbitrary and tyrannical as to show favoritism to some while sending others, who were no worse, to eternal hellfire. But Backus saw in this view only the old sin of human pride and self-righteousness. "Nothing is more certain than this," he said in words worthy of John Cotton, or of Edwards himself, "that a God which a creature can comprehend is an idol." [24] The ways of God were a mystery too profound for mere mortals to probe with their puny reason.

Ultimately, of course, the anthropocentric view won and the Baptists themselves modified their Calvinism to accommodate it. It was one of the tragedies of Backus's life that he lived to see the man who succeeded him in the pulpit of the First Baptist Church in Middleborough preach views closer to Martin's and Briggs's than to Edwards' and his. [25]

Inasmuch as the New Light wing of the Standing Order was traveling much the same path in this period — from Calvinism to evangelicalism, from Edwardseanism to Taylorism — it might have been expected that some general rapprochement might have taken place between them. Certainly they faced the same common enemies in deism, Unitarianism, Universalism, Methodism, and the other departures from the old Calvinism of New England. Such a rapprochement finally did come about in the third decade of the nineteenth century — at least to the point where the Trinitarian Congregationalists agreed with the Baptists that the spread of Unitarianism made the establishment in Massachusetts no longer worth defending. But from 1780–1810 nothing of the sort took place. If anything, the theological antagonism between them increased. As Backus saw it, the Congregationalists were, by 1784, divided into two equally pernicious camps, both equally willing to persecute the Baptists and both equally apostate from the true Calvinism of Jonathan Edwards. The first group were the Unitarians, led by Jonathan Mayhew and Charles Chauncy, who had repudiated Edwards's view on the freedom (or lack of freedom) of the will and thus came to "the turning point of Arminianism, to which the opinion of universal salvation naturally succeeds." The second group — "the Hopkintonians," Backus called them (Samuel Hopkins, Nathanial Emmons, Joseph Bellamy, Jonathan Edwards, Jr.) — claimed to be the true heirs of Edwards but they had pushed his doctrine of the will to the opposite extreme and produced a system of determinism or "antinomianism" which made God the author of sin. [26] When a British theologian tried to argue in 1783 that Edwards's statement "The will is always determined

24. *Ibid.*, p. 63.

25. Backus to Ezra Kendall, February 5 and 21, 1805, among the BP(AN) and letter of January 27, 1805, in the American Baptist Historical Society. See also Backus's attacks on Elder Nickerson of Harwich, ms. "Diary," X, 46 and 54.

26. Backus, *History*, II, 248–252.

by the strongest motive," destroyed human responsibility for man's actions, Backus answered:

> I must tell him and all his friends, that I am much better acquainted with Edwards's writings than they are, and I absolutely know that the ideas naturally arising from the words 'Forcibly' and 'Inevitable' [which some ascribe to Edwards's doctrine of the will] as here used, when charged upon Edwards, are entirely unjust and abusive. And it tends to raise an evil temper in those who read the same against all the friends of Edwards's writings, of whom I am heartily one.[27]

Backus's earliest attack on the Hopkinsian or neo-Edwardsian viewpoint was in 1773 in his tract *The Sovereign Decrees of God, Set in a Scriptural Light and Vindicated*. He summed up his argument this way: "It is a most wicked device . . . to use the word 'inevitable' concerning the reprobate and 'irresistible' concerning the elect in such a manner as to exclude the idea of their own choice," and thus to lay the blame for sin on God. Hopkins and his school did not, as they understood it, make God the author of sin in the pejorative or deterministic manner in which Backus thought they did. The title of Hopkins's tract on this subject refuted this: *Sin, through Divine Interposition, An Advantage to the Universe, and yet This no Excuse for Sin or Encouragement to it*. All that Hopkins meant was that God, as Creator of the Universe, must have created or willed that sin should exist — for what specific purpose we cannot know, though we can of course assume that God has some good reason for this and that, in the long run, sin is part of God's will and is being used to work out his purposes.

Backus, however, took a simpler way out of the dilemma. He said that while God created the fundamental laws of the universe, he is not responsible for all the consequences of those laws, especially since he has revealed to us in Scripture that he considers man a morally responsible agent. Hence, said Backus, illegitimate children are in a broad sense created by God according to the laws of life, but it is clear that the children's illegitimacy is caused by the parents's immorality and not by God.[28] For Backus, man's relationship to God's moral laws is similar to that of a rebellious child to his parents: the parents lay down the law, the child is aware of it and capable of obeying it to a certain extent (such as when a parent insists that the child remain quiet for a period of time or sit straight in his chair) but the child is by nature both rebellious and

---

27. *Ibid.*, II, 252.
28. Isaac Backus, *The Sovereign Decrees of God* (Boston, 1773), pp. 8–9. Backus also pointed out that the heat of the sun, working in accordance with the laws of God, draws out the secret virtues of the earth, but the sun is not the cause of the stink of the dunghill. Backus, *History*, II, 300.

forgetful and lacks the strength to control his own instincts to the point of complete obedience to the parents's wishes, even though he realizes his obligation to the parent and is aware that the parents's commands are in his own best interest. Hence rebellious humans, like rebellious children, deserve punishment. To Backus, as to most of the Separate-Baptists, the Bible contained the revealed will of God which was the external motive obliging all men to act rightly:

> The means of grace are calculated in infinite wisdom to open the eyes of men, and to turn them from darkness to light, and from the power of Satan unto God. Precepts and promises, rewards and punishments, calls and warnings, are all motives to influence the choice of man. And the strongest hold that the devil has in this world is to persuade man, that a being governed in his choice by motives without himself, is inconsistent with the liberty of moral agents; and to persuade him at the same time that necessity obliges God to pardon and save them, whenever they shall become sincere penitents. Thus they assume a sovereignty to themselves, which they deny to their Maker.[29]

The Hopkinsians and the Unitarian-Universalists, were two sides of the same coin of infidelity. The Hopkinsians were tools of the devil to say that man can do nothing to save himself and that he is not even responsible for his sins but must wait for irresistible grace to convert him in God's own time — or perhaps never. The Universalist-Unitarians were tools of the devil to say that God could not possibly be so sovereign as Calvinism maintains and that man really can and should take on himself the duty of converting himself. In either case, men were being taught to reject an absolute moral law outside themselves as the highest motive for their good conduct:

> If motives without us do not determine choice, it would be impossible for God to govern us; and as the excellent Edwards observes, Arminian principles truly involve in their nature the horrid blasphemy which they falsely cast upon the Calvinists, of charging God with acting a deceitful part towards men in appointing the means of grace; for these are motives to determine their choice on the side of virtue, which he could not be sincere in appointing if their choice is not determined by motives without themselves.[30]

For men to say, fatalistically, "if we are entirely dependent upon the sovereign will of God, for renewing and saving grace, then all our use of means to attain salvation is vain," is as foolish as to say if God wants us to live he will send us manna and clothes from heaven and we need not work. God has appointed means in the natural world for us to work for

29. *Ibid.*, II, 301.
30. *Ibid.*, II, 301; Backus cites Edwards to confirm these views.

and attain food, clothing, and shelter; "and he has appointed the means and the end, and the means in order to the end, in the moral as well as natural world." The means of grace are the motivations to right conduct and to penitence for wrong conduct which Providence and the Bible hold up to us. But just as crops will only grow if God sends rain, so salvation will only come if God sends showers of blessing via the Holy Spirit.[31] But as God is sovereign, and men are all sinners, whether he chooses to send us natural or spiritual showers depends on his will and not on ours. We fully deserve that he send neither and should humbly praise him in either case.

Those who were the chief spokesmen for Hopkinsianism received short shrift from Backus and his colleagues. Nathaniel Emmons, he wrote in 1785, "has carried the doctrine of predestination so far as to assert that God positively produces or creates sin; a shocking error!"[32] Samuel Hopkins, he wrote to President Maxcy in 1797, had given the enemies of truth a handle with which to attack Calvinism: "Dr. Hopkins published a book, the year after Edwards died, and many others since, which have filled our land with controversy and given the enemy an occasion to reproach the truth, especially about the sovereignty of grace and the earnest and free calls of the gospel to all sinners, without any good in them."[33] President Maxcy of Rhode Island College so disliked Hopkins that he compared him to Joseph Priestley for the harm which he had done to Calvinism, but Backus thought this a bit unfair. In 1792, Elder William Rogers, a Rhode Island College graduate and pastor of the First Baptist Church of Philadelphia, wrote to Backus: "A kind of Poet in N. Jersey has given his Opinion of the New Divinity System in the following 4 lines —

You can and you can't
You shall and you shan't
You will and you won't
You'll be damn'd if you don't."[34]

The couplets referred to the various refinements on the doctrine of means which the New Divinity theologians had worked out — views which said that men could use means but could not attain salvation through them; that men should pray for assistance in salvation if they were pure in heart, but should not if they were not; that men would be saved if they used means but would not be saved just because they used means; that men might be damned whether they tried their utmost or whether they did not; and that the true test of a man's holiness was his willingness to be damned

31. *Ibid.,* II, 301.
32. Backus, ms. "Diary," XI, 12.
33. Backus to Maxcy, March 17, 1797, in BP(AN).
34. Letter to Backus, December 10, 1792, among the BP(AN).

for the glory of God (anyone truly having such willingness would of course *not* be damned). This was a gross over-simplification and mis-representation of the New Divinity made by men too unsophisticated really to comprehend the sincere efforts which Edwards' successors were making to save Calvinism from the attacks of the Age of Reason by making it seem more consistent and logical. Yet in a pragmatic sense the accusations were correct. The abstruse logic of the neo-Edwardsians was too involved for the comman man; Hopkinsianism's incomprehensibility was a primary reason for the rapid growth of deism as well as for other forms of Arminianism, and even for the increase of the Baptists themselves, who were less logical but more believable.[35]

The Baptists, however, were not immune to this new teaching. Elder Noah Alden was dismissed in 1765 from his church in Stafford, Connecticut for preaching such "antinomian principles." And after he had become pastor of the Bellingham church a letter to the Warren Association from some of his members complained that he had been preaching the false doctrine that no minister can "caul or invite aney Sinner in the Carrecter [character] of a Sinner to Come to Christ." [36] Alden was not dismissed for this because it was too fine a point of theology. But he was verging close to the Hopkinsian logic that preachers could do nothing for sinners until they were first taken in hand by God. (This rigid pre-destinarianism was the basis of "the hardshell" Baptist movement, a reaction to the growing Arminianism of the denomination in the nineteenth century.)

On the other hand, the Baptist church in Chelmsford rejected Elder Samuel Hovey as their preacher in 1770 "for certain things he advanced in publick one of which among others was for encouraging Sinners as such, vizt. Swearers, drunkards, Blasphemers, etc. to hope in God in the circumstances they stood in." [37] Hovey was considered unorthodox for preaching the opposite of that for which Alden had been criticized. This illustrates the difficulties among all Calvinists in this period in their attempts to reach a consistent and logical solution to the inherent paradoxes of Calvinism. In claiming that they followed Edwards, the Separate-Baptists meant only that they avoided trying to resolve the problems which he had left unresolved.

One aspect of the New Divinity which the Baptists did admire, however, was its strong opposition to the halfway covenant. When Joseph

---

35. E. S. Morgan, *The Gentle Puritan* (New Haven, 1962), pp. 410–411, confirms this view.

36. Backus, ms. "Diary," VI, 91, and letter of Elder Job Seaman to the Warren Association, September 9, 1775, in BP(AN).

37. Chelmsford Church to the Warren Association, September 17, 1781, in BP(AN).

Bellamy began writing his tracts against the practice in 1768, Backus felt that the separations of the Awakening were at last being justified by those who had opposed them.[38] The logic of Bellamy's position the Baptists said, should have led him to become a Baptist, for how could he defend the concept of a church of visible saints and at the same time sanction infant baptism? When Bellamy agreed that the old argument for infant baptism based on the typology of circumcision was invalid, the Baptists were convinced they had won their case. But the other Hopkinsians did not agree with Bellamy about this and Hopkins himself, in his *Systematic Theology* (1793) ridiculed Bellamy (and the Baptists) concerning this point in much the same terms that the Mathers had done in the seventeenth century.[39]

In addition to free will and predestination there was a third theological issue much debated during this period. Neither the Baptists nor the Hopkinsians were able to provide an answer satisfactory to the average man on the question of infant damnation. All varieties of anti-Calvinists derived great pleasure from baiting the Calvinists about this, and in the popular mind nothing was better proof of the tyranny and cruelty of the Calvinist's God than his willingness to send innocent infants to eternal hell-fire. Backus was frank to admit that

> As the wages of sin is death, God cannot be just in paying the same to infants but upon his right to constitute Adam as their head to act for them and dealing with them as sinners in him; for justice cannot pay wages where they are not due. And as Christ came into the world purely to save sinners, infants could have no part in his salvation, if they were not sinners.[40]

For some parents the fact that the Hopkinsians would at least baptize infants was a point in their favor, though the Hopkinsians had to admit that this had no direct effect on infants' salvation. Backus was annoyed that the question had been raised at all, since it was one of the many mysteries that God did not deign to reveal to his creatures: "What God does with all who die in infancy he has not informed us; and the horrid

38. Backus. *Abridgement*, p. 200.

39. For Backus's reaction to this see his *History*, II, 364. Bellamy did not give up infant baptism; he simply found other arguments for it.

40. *Ibid.*, II, 255–256. Backus adds here "That infants may partake of that salvation even in their mother's womb is certain. Luke i.44." Backus did not note the extent of this concession to the opponents of believers's baptism, but when his history was reprinted in 1871 the Baptist editor added the following note at this point: "Probably most of his readers will question the author's inference from this passage. The author himself might have considered it more carefully if the inference had been used in his day, as it has in later times, as an argument for infant baptism." *History*, II, 256 note.

idea of damnation to them which has been held up by some serves only to inflame the passions against the plain words of revelation." [41] It was a biased question raised by enemies of Calvinism just to embarrass the defenders of the faith. And it did embarrass them, for they had no answer to "the horrid idea." The Baptists were much better able to point out the heresies of others than they were to defend their own position in the changing theological milieu.

Apart from their opposition to the various pietistic sects which arose to threaten and compete with them for converts (Shakers, Universalists, Methodists, Free Will Baptists, and Hopkinsians), the Baptists also denounced such other errors and delusions as Unitarianism, deism, Quakerism, Episcopalianism, Roman Catholicism, and such eccentrics as the followers of Jemima Wilkinson, Robert Sandeman, and Shadrach Ireland.

Like most of their contemporaries, the Baptists considered Roman Catholicism not only the worst of heresies ("the Antichrist," "the Whore of Babylon") but also a deadly threat to the political safety of the nation. Almost every state in the Union had some restrictions on Catholicism, usually in the form of restrictions from holding public office. Backus thought it a good argument for propagandizing against Article Three of the Massachusetts constitution that the constitution did not limit office-holding to Protestants: "The framers of the Massachusetts Constitution in 1780 opened a door for Roman catholicks to become lawgivers and judges for us about soul guides." [42] Had there been more danger of numerous Roman Catholics being elected to office and influencing the ecclesiastical laws of the Standing Order, this argument might have had more weight.

The Unitarians Backus and the Baptists generally lumped with Arminians (the term Unitarian did not come into general use in New England until the nineteenth century). In 1795, Backus wrote "it is questionable whether there are not more Arminians in the churches who are supported by law in this country [i.e., Massachusetts] than there are of Calvinists." [43] The general terms for Unitarians in the eighteenth century were Arians and Socinians, and of these Backus said "both deny that Jesus Christ is God by nature, and the latter hold him to be no more than a man. But there is no such faith as theirs in heaven, nor in hell, nor in heathen darkness;" for even the devils said, "What have we to do with thee, Jesus, thou Son of

41. Backus to Ezra Kendall, January 27, 1805, in the American Baptist Historical Society.

42. Isaac Backus, *The Liberal Support of Gospel Ministers* (Boston, 1790), p. 33. Also his *Testimony of the Two Witnesses* (Providence, 1786), pp. 20–21, and 2nd ed. (Boston, 1793), p. 46. Some of the towns with strong Baptist elements were among those which urged in their ratifying reports that the term "Protestant" be substituted for "Christian" as a test for office-holding. On Backus's dislike of Catholicism see his remarks on the fall of the Papacy quoted in chapter 39.

43. Backus, *History*, II, 386.

God?" [44] The Warren Association issued several warnings against those who would "strip Christ of his eternal Deity," particularly in the circular letters of 1792 and 1795. But before 1800 so few persons in New England openly avowed this view that the Baptists had almost as little occasion to denounce it as they did Roman Catholicism.

Deism was, in its technical sense, a religious outlook which had even less impact on the Baptists than had Unitarianism. It was never an organized cult nor did it have any evangelists seeking converts (Elihu Palmer's short career was an exception). It flourished chiefly among the well-educated, the cosmopolitan, and the urban dwellers; most of those who might be properly called Deists never gave up whatever nominal denominational adherence they may have had. In rural and frontier regions a man who had read Tom Paine or Ethan Allen might set himself up locally as the chief exponent of these radical views, if he did not mind being an eccentric, but most of those whom the Baptists called deists were really anti-Calvinists and Nothingarians, members of no church. These cracker-barrel anticlericals attained a certain celebrity in this period and were pointed to by local and itinerant ministers as horrible examples. Their illnesses, accidents, and misfortunes were carefully noted as indications that God was not to be mocked. Very often they turned out to be among the most notable converts at the first revival meeting to be held in their vicinity (for which there is good psychological explanation). When a Baptist denounced them, as Elder Hezekiah Smith did in one of his sermons as an Army chaplain, he would refer to the type as "the deist or atheist." [45] Such men were held up as horrible examples, but they posed no serious threats to denominational growth — quite the contrary. They were perfect examples of the kind of social deviants who (like the Anabaptist-Munsterites of the Bay Colony) served primarily to give greater solidarity and identity to the values of the majority.

As for the Quakers, despite their close association with Rhode Island College, Backus probably reflected the general view of the Separate-Baptists toward them when he said of a Quaker he had met in 1752: "I am in hopes he is a Christian tho' I scarce ever saw a Quaker yt I thot was; he appears to have real Religion tho' he is out of ye way in some externals." [46] The Quakers were no doubt pious and pietists, but to a Calvinist they scarcely qualified as Christians.

In this respect the Baptists simply repeated the view of Roger Williams, who had made no bones about his contempt for the sect. It was out of his great regard for Williams that Backus became involved in a sharp contro-

---

44. *Ibid.*, II, 387–388.
45. Reuben A. Guild, *Chaplain Smith and the Baptists* (Philadelphia, 1885), p. 274.
46. Isaac Backus, "Travel Journals," February 4, 1752, among the BP(AN).

versy with the Quakers in the years 1779–1780. In the first volume of his *History of New England* (1777) Backus wrote at some length about Williams' controversy with the Quakers and made some harsh comments upon the fanaticism and unseemly behavior of the early Quakers — taking particular delight in relating the incidents in which Quaker women took off their clothes and paraded naked into the Puritan meetinghouses to testify against Puritan ungodliness. The leaders of the Quakers in Rhode Island (where Quakerism was the denomination of the most respectable people), particularly Moses Brown, Thomas Arnold, and Job Scott, were so angry at what they considered Backus' misrepresentations and errors that they nearly published a rebuttal by Scott. But some Baptists who were friends of both parties arranged a series of conferences to smooth out their differences. The Quakers demanded that Backus acknowledge his errors and publish a statement retracting them. In one of the letters he wrote to Moses Brown about the matter, Backus indicated that he would not be bullied into this:

> The greatest thing that moved me to insert any particular acc[t] of your predecessors in my history was their publicity representing Roger Williams as a bloody persecutor which was most glaringly unjust . . . And your not persuing the method we agreed upon [for settling the dispute] but pressing for my publishing such a memorandum [of retraction] before you will exert yourselves against the chains of tyranny now prepared for this State [Massachusetts — by the new constitution] causes a doubt of any happy issue of our conferences.[47]

The Quakers denied any such threat and eventually the matter was settled amicably. Backus printed an acknowledgment of some errors in his discussion of the Quakers as an appendix to the second volume of his history. But he by no means retracted all of his criticisms and there is no doubt that he still retained his distaste for their religious views.

The small sects formed by Robert Sandeman, Jemima Wilkinson, and Shadrach Ireland in New England in the latter half of the eighteenth century caused the Baptists some anxious moments, but did no serious damage to their growth. Shadrach Ireland was the first of these charismatic leaders to arrive on the scene. His sect, a direct outgrowth of the perfectionist tendencies among the Separates of the Great Awakening, attracted a num-

47. This and other letters and reports are among the BP(AN) and among the Moses Brown Papers at the Rhode Island Historical Society. The RIHS also has the original ms. written by Job Scott entitled "The Cause of Truth Maintained." See also the unpublished seminar paper by Jerome H. Wood, Jr., "A Society-Touching Matter: The Friends' Dispute with Isaac Backus" (1963) at the Brown University Library. A central point in the dispute was the extent to which the early Quakers repudiated civil government and advocated a theocracy. Though the eighteenth-century Quakers vigorously denied this, some recent historians have confirmed Backus's view. Thomas G. Sanders, *Protestant Concepts of Church and State* (New York, 1964), pp. 113–160

ber of Separates and Baptists in the years 1753 to 1778. Ireland was a pipe-maker and joiner in Charlestown, Massachusetts, when he was converted to New Light views by George Whitefield. He became an itinerant exhorter and gradually adopted the view of the Immortalists that those who were born again would never die. Whether because of his preaching "blasphemy" or his desertion of his wife and six children for a younger "spiritual wife," he was threatened with prosecution in Charlestown about 1760 and fled to the town of Harvard. Here a group of perfectionists who had separated from the Harvard Standing church in 1751 welcomed and hid him. He preached secretly, making a number of converts in the vicinity who in 1770 built a large "Square House" for him and his spiritual wife. He never appeared openly, and the authorities evidently did not try to prosecute him. His sect practiced pacifism and communal ownership of goods in addition to believing Ireland immortal. Stories about what happened after his death in 1778 (some say 1780) vary, but they all agree that his followers were loathe to bury him because he had warned them that while he might appear to be dead he would rise again. Eventually, said Backus, "the body scented so much that it was carried out in the night and buried in a corn-field." [48] The sect was temporarily shattered by this, but it remained together until 1781 when the Shakers came to Harvard and Ireland's followers joined them.

Elder John Davis reported in 1771 that the Baptist church in Grafton, Massachusetts, had been broken up by the departure of many of its members for Ireland's group and the Baptist church in Harvard wrote to the Warren Association in 1781 "we are surrouned on Every side with almost all sorts of Perswasions." But there is no record that many Baptists joined the sect. Ireland's sect was simply the most prominent of many such perfectionist groups in the post-Awakening years.[49]

Jemima Wilkinson's sect flourished from 1776 to 1785 in Rhode Island and eastern Connecticut and then moved to a community in New York State, where by 1800 it had about 250 members.[50] She was born in 1752, in Cumberland, Rhode Island, daughter of a well-to-do Quaker farmer, in whose faith she was raised. But the Quakers disowned her in August 1776 for attending New Light (Separate) meetings. In the fall of that year she

48. Henry S. Nourse, *History of the Town of Harvard* (Harvard, 1894), pp. 253–257; Backus, *History*, II, 297, 462–463; and Ezra Stiles, *The Literary Diary of Ezra Stiles*, 3 vols., ed. F. B. Dexter (New York, 1901), II, 558. Ireland is also mentioned in most accounts of the Shakers.

49. See John Davis's notes on a journey to the Baptist churches, 1771, and the Harvard Baptist church's letter to the Warren Association in the BP(AN). For other "Immortalist" groups see Backus, *History*, II, 88, and Ezra Stiles, *Extracts from the Itineraries of Ezra Stiles*, ed. F. B. Dexter (New Haven, 1916), p. 418.

50. There is an admirably balanced biography of Wilkinson by Herbert A. Wisbey, Jr., *Pioneer Prophetess* (Ithaca, 1964); for contemporary attacks see Abner Brownell, *Enthusiastical Errors, Transpired and Detected* (New London, 1783); Stiles, *Diary*, II, 380–382; Backus, *History*, II, 298–299.

became severely ill and suffered a mental breakdown. When she recovered she claimed that two archangels had appeared to her and that her original soul had departed and her body was now inhabited by "The Spirit of Life from God." "The Spirit took full possession of the Body it now animates" and God commanded her to preach repentance and "to warn a lost and guilty" world of coming Judgment. She began at once to exhort in public, claiming miraculous spiritual powers of prophecy, faith healing, and dream interpretation. Some who became her followers considered her the Messiah come "a second time" to save mankind. Henceforth she called herself "the Publick Universal Friend" and preached a moralistic version of millennial pietism with many similarities to Quakerism, including pacifism. But she also advocated (though did not require) celibacy and community of goods. She began itinerant preaching in 1777, often in the open air, and succeeded in founding small groups of adherents in many towns in southern New England; meetinghouses for her sect were built in New Milford, East Greenwich and South Kingstown. However, she met increasing hostility in New England and after trying for a time (1783–1785) to live in Philadelphia, she finally bought land in the Genessee area of New York and founded a community called "Jerusalem" where she lived with her followers until her death in 1819. The sect died out shortly thereafter.

Valentine Rathbun identified her with Ann Lee as one of the dangerous religious hoaxes of their era; James Manning said she "pretended to be Jesus Christ in the form of a Woman," and Backus ridiculed her in his history in 1784. But since her converts were few — and generally from among the upper class — she does not appear to have been a great threat to the Baptists outside of Rhode Island. Quakers warned their congregations against her but probably most of her followers had Quaker upbringing or were sympathetic to it.

The Sandemanians seemed a much greater threat to the Baptists; Robert Sandeman was the only one of the three whom Backus thought it necessary to refute in a polemical tract. Sandeman was born in Scotland in 1718 and in 1744 became an elder in the sect known as Glassites. This sect had been formed by the Rev. John Glas in 1730 after he had withdrawn from the Church of Scotland because of dislike for its Calvinism and its position as the established church. The Glassites also practiced certain primitive Christian rites like footwashing and the Christian kiss of charity (some derisively called them the Kissites). Sandeman came to New England in 1764 where the fame of his book, *Letters on Theron and Aspasia* (Edinburgh, 1757) had preceded him. He itinerated throughout New England for the next seven years but made his headquarters in Danbury, Connecticut. Churches of his sect were formed in Taunton, Massachusetts; Portsmouth, New Hampshire; and Newtown, Connecticut and groups of his followers worshipped regularly in New Haven, Providence, and Boston in the 1770's. The Sandemanians declined rapidly after Sandeman's death in 1771, but scattered remnants existed until late in the nineteenth century.

At least two Baptist churches were "infected" with Sandemanian notions in the controversies over Calvinism which raged in these years: the church at Stratfield, Connecticut and that at Chelmsford, Massachusetts. The Stratfield church lost five or six members who adopted Sandeman's views; in Chelmsford, according to Backus, the elder had his mind "somewhat entangled with Sandeman's notion of exalting the atonement in such a manner as to pay little or no regard to a divine work *within* us, of conviction by the law, and relief by the Gospel." [51] Backus's polemical *Remarks on the Writings of Mr. Sandeman* (Boston, 1767) defended evangelical Calvinism from Sandeman's more rationalistic concept of conversion, grace, atonement and perseverance. He also attacked the primitive rites of Sandemanianism and the fact that Sandeman opposed the practice of family prayer. Because Sandeman did preach a more "legalistic" form of Calvinism as opposed to the "heart religion" or experimental religion of the Separate-Baptists, his doctrines did not have as wide an appeal to the Baptists as did his pietistic practices.

Despite their fears of growing infidelity and the continual threats of sectarian competition from 1780 to 1810, the Baptists remained essentially optimistic. There were some Baptists who, under the stress of persecution or because of some particular upheaval (like Shays Rebellion at home or the French Revolution abroad) chose to emphasize the gloomier millennial interpretation of a Day of Judgment to precede the Second Coming. "We are threatened (as a nation)" wrote the Sturbridge Baptist Church to the Warren Association in 1798 when war with France or England seemed imminent, "with dire calamities, infidelity prevails on every hand and vice has become triumphant;" the time had come to prepare for Christ's return.[52] But this pessimistic exegesis was much less common than the optimistic one which foresaw increasing prosperity, peace, and evangelism ushering in the thousand years of millennial glory "on earth even as it is in heaven." The circular letter of the Warren Association in 1784 affirmed that the American Revolution was an act of God which foretold "the advancement and com-

51. For Sandeman, see Williston Walker, "The Sandemanians of New England," *Annual Report,* American Historical Association, 1901 (Washington, 1902), I, 131–162. For the schism in the Stratfield Church, see Backus's notes on the history of the Stratfield church in BP(AN). For the elder at Chelmsford see Isaac Backus, *Truth Is Great And Will Prevail* (Boston, 1781), p. 16. Also Backus, *History,* II, 127, 130–131, 296, 528. Stiles, *Itineraries,* 331, 453, 551, and Stiles, *Diary,* I, 184, 284, 502; II, 171, 228. Stiles says that while Sandeman's doctrines were "frigid," the practices of his adherents were "high Enthusiasm very much like that of the hottest New Lights." Most Sandemanians appear to have been Loyalists in the Revolution; this did not add to their popularity.

52. Letter from the Sturbridge Church to the Warren Association, August 29, 1789, in BP(AN).

pletion of the Redeemer's kingdom." "With what a surprising progress have we stepped up to our present importance and rank amongst the nations." The worldly man would of course think of the Revolution simply in terms of political freedom, but the Christian recognized it "as one important step towards bringing in the glory of the latter day." "Nor is it at all improbable that America is reserved in the mind of Jehovah to be the grand theatre on which the divine Redeemer will accomplish glorious things . . . If we observe the signs of the times we shall find reason to think he is on his way . . . Even so, come, Lord Jesus, come quickly." [53]

By identifying their future with that of the entire United States, the Baptists, like other Americans, lifted their horizons above the narrow borders of their own denomination or state. America became for the evangelicals of the nineteenth century what Massachusetts Bay had been for the Puritans of the seventeenth century — a city set upon a hill — the vanguard of the reformation of the world. Richard Montague, in a revealing letter to the Warren Association from the Baptist church in Montague in 1790, gave credit to Isaac Backus's *History of New England* for pointing out so clearly the role which God had ordained for the Baptists in America. It was now obvious, wrote Montague after reading the history, that in America God intended "to pave ye way effectually to ye Ushering in of ye glorious purposes of his grace" where no tyrant can "Lord it over God's heritage." In New England of the past, said Montague, this purpose was not so evident because the Baptists lived in bondage to the Standing Order: "But now liberty is gained for all of the Sects and denominations of Christians by ye constitution we live under," and the future was secure for "The Truth is great and will prevail." [54] Unlike the severely persecuted pietists of Europe (Mennonites, Moravians, Hutterites, Schwenkfelders), whose withdrawal from the world had expressed their belief that they had no stake in the social order around them, the pietistic New England Baptists had always believed, and now knew, that their destiny was America's destiny.

This sense of belonging was a fundamental factor in the Baptists's conservatism as a denomination. They had everything to gain by identifying their future with that of the United States. By the same token they wished to demonstrate that their own earlier rebelliousness was over. They considered that they had proven good and responsible citizens of the new nation and they wished to be treated with respect.

After 1770 most Baptist ministers began to drop the pietistic term "Elder" and to use the title of "Reverend," which before had been reserved for the learned clergy of the established churchs.[55] The graduates of Rhode

53. Warren Association Minutes, 1784.
54. Richard Montague to the Warren Association, September 3, 1790, in the BP(AN).
55. Backus in a letter to Ebenezer Hinds, May 31, 1784, said that he personally

Island College wrote A.B. and A.M. after their names. Honorary degrees of M.A. and D.D. were awarded by the college both as rewards to its friends and to enhance its own prestige. Everyone in the denomination was happy to hear its leaders referred to as the Rev. Dr. Samuel Stillman D.D. or the Rev. Dr. Hezekiah Smith, A.M. Smith wrote to a Congregational minister who attacked his views in a sermon in 1773 to call his attention to this matter: "In your sermon you did not even call me Revd or Mr. tho' I have a master's degree." [56] Backus took to wearing a large wig in the 1770's and after he received an honorary A.M. from the college in 1797 he regularly placed these letters after his name on the title pages of his publications.

When James Manning died in 1791, Backus wrote an obituary in which he exhibited the typical combination of pride and self-consciousness of the Baptists regarding their college: "He lived to see our college arise in esteem for learning, especially for the gift of public speaking, above the University at Cambridge [Harvard] so that many young men were sent to it from all parts of the country and from all denominations." Yet Backus explained Manning's failure to publish any significant work by saying "his *humility* was so great and his concern for the honor of our University, that he never could be prevailed with to publish any one discourse to the world. He knew how envious many were, and how ready they would be to make the use of the least mistake they could discover, against the honor of the Institution for learning which he served." This may explain why Backus, who had no college training, and hence no status to lose, was left to be the major polemicist for his denomination.[57]

But these indications of increasing respectability and upward mobility were not universally acclaimed within the denomination. The pietistic impulse was still strong; Baptists in the rural and frontier areas of New England still retained their primitive zeal for the old and simple ways. In 1790, for example, the Danbury Baptist Association in Connecticut voted not to replace the term Elder by the term Reverend. Throughout this period, and throughout the nineteenth century, the rural Baptists looked askance at the increasing institutionalism, sophistication, and status-con-

---

did not like to be called "Reverend," but Stiles said that the Baptists began to use the title in 1764, *Diary,* I, 122.

56. See Hezekiah Smith's 38-page letter to a Mr. Walker, March 3, 1773, among the BP(AN). Smith did not receive a D.D. till 1797 — from Rhode Island College. The college even awarded an honorary degree to John Adams in 1797. And in 1804 it changed its name to Brown University to honor Nicholas Brown of Providence for donating $5000 to endow a chair in Oratory and Belle Lettres. Though he was a Baptist in principle, Brown was not a member of any Baptist church. W. C. Bronson, *The History of Brown* (Providence, 1914), pp. 156–157.

57. This obituary was sent to John Rippon in London for publication in *The Baptist Annual Register,* but it was never printed. It is among the Rippon Papers at the Angus Library, Regents Park College, London, England. It has been published in *Books at Brown,* XXII (1968), 155–160.

sciousness of their brethren in the eastern, urban, and older settled regions. Even those urban Baptists most involved in the denomination's rising status continued to feel awkward at times. There was in the essence of the denomination (as in Christianity itself) a tension or conflict between the absolute and ultimate ideals of the faith and the relative, temporal demands of the denomination. The official letters of the association included many warnings and exhortations concerning the dangers of success and of increasing worldliness. One of the most searching of these appeared in a letter in 1794 which the Shaftesbury Association sent with its fraternal delegates to the Warren Association. It epitomized the denomination's ambivalence toward its own success. It began by noting that the Baptists had prospered greatly in America and that they could praise God for "Few enemies, the field maintained, and victory [over persecution] almost won." But it warned, "We are not out of danger" from Satan's wiles. It listed three major areas of concern on this score. First of these was "divisions and schisms" arising from "a turbulent spirit" and excessive "gospel freedom;" too many churches lacked "a system of gospel discipline" sufficient to restrain their members from excesses in feelings and practice. Speaking here with the accents of denominational conservatism, the Shaftesbury Baptists feared that in many churches "the idea of immediate impulse from ye Spirit of God" led many into the perennial pietistic excesses of perfectionism and emotionalism. The second concern was also voiced conservatively: there was, said the letter, a "popular clamour in this country [i.e., western Massachusetts and southern Vermont] against our ministers" because they "set everybody and every thing to preaching;" this indicated that the churches had opened "the doors of liberty" so wide that they were "thrown off from their hinges" and could not be shut. Too many persons who claimed to have the gift of preaching had been encouraged to do so and there had been "Unskillful inductions into the ministry" which did injury to the cause: "An improper person introduced [into the ministry] will endeavour to introduce men of his own Stamp" and soon the denomination would be flooded with eccentric, fanatical exhorters.

But the third danger, "our greatest danger," was the opposite of the first two. "As we grow numerous, wealthy, learned, and respectable," the denomination may decline in piety. This, said the letter, was what had happened to the Roman Church. "It will be rare" if the Baptists did not succumb to the same worldliness. The result would be to "diminish in holy zeal, grow formal, and lose the power of religion." If this occurred, then "another Separation must ensue" like that of the Reformation or of the First Great Awakening, as "holy souls . . . dissent from our establishment." When that day came, the Baptists, as had the Standing Order in 1740, would call these new separatists "enthusiasts." The letter concluded that the Baptists must be on their guard to prevent this.[58]

58. Peter Werden and Samuel Whelpley to the Warren Association, June 4, 1794.

A small pietistic schism which occurred in the Baptist denomination in 1804 demonstrated that this was not an idle warning. The result was a new sect called the Christ-ians. While this separation from the Baptist "establishment" was similar to that of the Free Will Baptists twenty years earlier in that it represented a rejection of Calvinist theology for that of Arminianism, it differed by being a more explicit reaction against the increasing formalism and worldliness of the denomination. The Free Will Baptists had started in the newly settled areas of New Hampshire and Vermont, but the Christ-ians began in the city of Boston and later spread to Portsmouth. The founder of the movement, Elias Smith, had been for a time one of the most prominent Baptist clergymen in the Boston area and a close friend and protégé of Samuel Stillman and Thomas Baldwin, the acknowledged leaders of the denomination. But as a country bred Baptist, he never became accustomed to big city ways.

In his colorful autobiography and biting tracts Smith provided copious documentation of the tension between the pietists and the denominationalists among the Baptists at this stage in their history. Smith bitterly criticized the extent to which the Baptists in the vicinity of Boston had departed from the primitive simplicity and fervor of Obadiah Holmes and Thomas Goold to mimic the clergy of the Standing Order.

Elias Smith was born in Lyme, Connecticut in 1769. His father was a Separate-Baptist farmer.[59] His mother was a pedobaptist Separate and insisted he be sprinkled as an infant by Daniel Miner, pastor of the Separate Church in Lyme. The family attended the Separate-Baptist Church of Elder Jason Lee in Lyme until they moved to Woodstock, Vermont in 1782. Because there was no Baptist church nearby the family attended the Congregational church. Smith had a conversion experience in 1785; in 1789 he became a Baptist and was immersed by Elder William Grow. He had been a school teacher since 1785 but in 1790 he felt called to become an itinerant exhorter. In 1791 he was invited to become the settled minister of the town of Danville, Vermont. Because the Baptists were a majority of the voters and the law in Vermont permitted a minister of any sect to become the town minister with a majority vote, Smith would have received the 200 acres of land set off in the town grant for the use of the first settled minister in Danville. But he preferred to continue itinerating. The next year he agreed to preach two-thirds of the time for the

---

See also the exchange of letters between Timothy Morse of Ipswich and Hezekiah Smith December 1781–March 1782, in which Morse accuses Smith of becoming too worldly. There is also the letter from the New Salem Church to the Warren Association in 1786 complaining that in the published minutes of the Association there was "much said and done about the burdens of civil taxes and how to get rid of them, and but little said about the burden of sin" which grips the world and the church. All of these are in the BP(AN).

59. Elias Smith, *The Life, Conversion, Preaching, Travels, and Sufferings of Elias Smith* (Portsmouth, New Hampshire, 1816).

town of Lee and one-third for the neighboring town of Stratham, Vermont. When the town of Lee asked him to accept the position as its established minister, he refused.

One of his parishioners gave him the money to buy the traditional black cloth for a minister's suit and when he first put it on, he noted, "My parents were not a little troubled to see me so richly dressed . . . Their fear was that such things might serve to lift me up and lead me to forget my dependence" on God. In 1792 he was ordained an evangelist by the New Hampshire Baptist Association. Shortly thereafter he visited Haverhill and preached at Hezekiah Smith's meetinghouse. Here, he noted, the church had grown respectable and "had more form than spirit." This same year he met Samuel Stillman who was traveling in Vermont: "He was dressed in black, wore a large white wig and three cornered hat. He looked as neat as is easy to be in a dirty world." Stillman told Smith with amazement how a man had once, during a sermon in his church in Boston, risen out of his seat in a burst of enthusiasm and shouted, "Free grace! Free grace!" "The Doctor thought it a very extraordinary circumstance that a common christian should feel so much as to be led to speak in a meeting-house" and disturb the meeting. But it surprised Smith even more that Stillman should frown on such behavior which was quite common in Vermont Baptist churches.

In 1793 Smith became the pastor of the Baptist Church in Salisbury, New Hampshire, and that same year made his first trip to Boston where Thomas Baldwin asked him to preach one Sunday in his meetinghouse, the Second Baptist Church. Baldwin was one of the rising leaders of the denomination who received an honorary A.M. from Rhode Island College in 1749, an honorary D.D. from Union College in 1803, and was chosen to give the Election Sermon in 1802 before the Massachusetts legislature.[60] Smith said that he felt very ill at ease speaking to the educated people of Boston. He was awed by the rich furnishings of Baldwin's church; he had never seen a church with a chandelier, "damask curtains," "cushing [for the pews] and silver candlesticks." Baldwin informed him that "some country preachers were apt to speak too long," so Smith took the hint and gave a short sermon. It was very well received. After other visits to Boston, he received a call in 1797 to settle over the church in the fashionable suburb of Woburn. He was rising in the world.

The Woburn church gave Smith a salary of one hundred pounds ($333) and expected him to conform to the style of dress and behavior set by his Boston colleagues, Stillman and Baldwin. Looking back on this episode after his break with the denomination, Smith wrote,

I became quite too respectable for a minister of Christ. They dressed me

60. William B. Sprague, *Annals of the American Pulpit* (New York, 1860), VI, 208, on Thomas Baldwin.

in black from head to foot; and on some occasions a part of my dress was silk with a large three-cornered hat and cloak of the best. I built a house there; kept a horse and carriage and lived in ease as other salary men do. Being so respectable I began to write my sermons [instead of delivering them ex tempore].[61]

Because Smith had already been ordained the Woburn church did not think it necessary to ordain him again. Instead, he went through what was called "an installation" ceremony, a new kind of ceremony to him.[62] Stillman, Hezekiah Smith, Baldwin, and Elder Joseph Grafton performed it for him in 1798. Smith wrote that this was "an high day with us. We made something of a splendid appearance as it respected the ignorant. We had two Doctores of Divinity; one or two A.M.'s and we all wore [Geneva] bands. When we came out of the counsel chamber and formed a procession to walk in baptist clerical order to the meeting house we looked as much like the cardinals coming out of the conclave after electing the pope as our practice was like theirs . . ." Up to this time he had never worn Geneva bands, but Hezekiah Smith advised him to do so whenever he preached. "Doctor Stillman, who was as fond of such foppery as a little girl is of fine baby rags, brought me one and put it on me." Smith asked Stillman why the wearing of bands was so important and he replied "That as I lived near the metropolis, it would make me appear respectable; and besides, said he, it will shew that you are an ordained minister." Once, while talking to Baldwin, who was as fond of appearances as Stillman, Smith remarked of the Baptist denomination, "We are going back to the place from whence we came out" — referring to the Separate movement of the 1740's. To which Baldwin replied, "We wish to make our denomination respectable." [63]

In 1799 Smith's church in Woburn decided to hold a memorial service in honor of George Washington. Jedidiah Morse was invited to come to deliver his famous funeral sermon on the great man. For this he was paid ten dollars. Smith was shocked to find that Morse not only delivered a written sermon but even wrote out his prayers. That same year Smith first began to think about politics. The famous newspaper letters of "Old South" (David Austin) convinced him that he should become a Jeffersonian

61. Smith, *Autobiography*, p. 292.

62. Smith's explanation of why his parishioners wanted him installed provides an interesting insight into the laws regarding religious marriages even at that late date and into John Murray's prosecution for performing marriages: "The laws of Massachusetts were such that no minister could marry people out of the town where he lived unless a town was destitute of a settled minister, and no minister was allowed to marry where he lived unless he was settled as the pastor of the church where he preached. This made some of my friends uneasy, as I could not marry them, nor get the money which the law gave the minister for every couple he married . . . I consented to be *installed* to have the benefit of the laws as a 'state minister.' " *Ibid.*, p. 277.

63. *Ibid.*, p. 279; p. 283.

Republican, and he always remained one. (Samuel Stillman was a Federalist.)

Smith's congregation had agreed to pay him by subscription but some of those who had promised to pay fell behind in their payments. This "caused a difficulty in my living," so Smith borrowed $1000 from his church, agreeing to pay them interest, and he invested the money in a general store in Woodstock, Vermont, with a partner to take care of the business. Then he began to be troubled by various theological questions which he had hitherto accepted without question. One of these was the Trinity; another was the imputation of Christ's righteousness, and the third was the doctrine of election. His doubts about Calvinism grew because he found the Baptists themselves were divided over it:

> Dr. Stillman held that Christ died for the elect only; Dr. Baldwin held that there was a propriety in preaching the gospel to all though but a small part would finally be benefited by it and these were given to Christ in the covenant of redemption before the world was. These two men differed so much on that point of doctrine that in a meeting each said to the other, if I held as you do I would preach no more.[64]

Smith generally had preached Baldwin's view, i.e., a general atonement rather than limited atonement. But he found that the articles of faith which his church had adopted at its founding subscribed to the older view of Stillman. On examining the doctrine of predestination and election for himself, he concluded that it was fatalistic; the doctrine of the Trinity seemed to him to be tri-theism. Faced with this and other doctrinal quandaries which he could not solve, he told some of his friends that he had reduced his theology "to two things, believe right and do right." One Baptist minister to whom he told this, Elder John Peak, "took occasion to say, I was either a Deist or a Universalist."

At last his uneasiness became so great that he asked for and received a dismission from his church. But his members, who had contributed much to building his house, were angry with him for deserting them. He left Woburn in 1801 after some bitter recriminations, and moved to Portsmouth, New Hampshire, where his brother lived. His brother persuaded him for a time to adopt Universalist principles. But he soon retracted these. He then began to write letters to the *New Hampshire Gazette* attacking the established church in that state. By 1803 he had clearly given up Calvinism and in that year he wrote a series of letters which he published in 1804 in which he denounced the Baptists of Boston and vicinity for "conforming to the world." This tract angered his former friends Stillman, Baldwin, and Hezekiah Smith; he attacked them personally. He even denounced Isaac Backus for accepting an honorary A.M. from Rhode Island College and for serving

64. *Ibid.*, p. 285.

as a trustee of the Warren Association's Education Fund which was incorporated by law.

In these letters Smith attacked the Boston ministers for "foppery," for praying for magistrates from the pulpit, for delivering election sermons at the request of the legislature, for refusing to call the brethren "brother" and "sister." He attacked the Haverhill Church for asking the legislature to incorporate it. He denounced Baldwin for refusing to let the Black Baptist minister, Thomas Paul, speak in his pulpit. He called the Warren Association a hierarchical body. He said the "installation" ceremony was popish. He said the desire to organize a missionary society was motivated by pride, love of power, and a desire for prestige. And he ended by renouncing the whole creed of Calvinism and adopting the doctrines of Arminianism.[65]

After he broke with the corrupt Baptist denomination, he formed a church in Portsmouth in 1803 based on his new principles; he called it "the Christ-ian church." Here he preached free will and what many considered little more than Unitarianism or Universalism. He opposed all creeds and articles of faith. In 1803 he met Abner Jones whom many consider the founder of the Christ-ian movement because in 1801 he had organized a church on similar principles in Lyndon, Vermont. Thereafter the two men worked together, and in 1804 they formed a Christ-ian church in Boston. In 1806 Elder Daniel Hix's Baptist Church in Dartmouth turned Christ-ian en masse.[66] Smith returned to Portsmouth where in 1808 he founded *The Herald of Gospel Liberty* devoted to promoting his system of religion and his Republican politics. He was a prolific pamphleteer and a popular speaker, but the vagueness of his tenets and his opposition to any form of denominational organization prevented him from attracting a large body of adherents.[67] Many confused his views with those of the Free Will Baptists or of the Universalists. He maintained a policy of open communion with all men of good will. But by 1819 his church in Boston had almost disappeared. His movement was not a serious threat to the denominational unity of the Baptists, but it was a significant demonstration of the contrast between the pietistic rural elements in the denomination and the more sophisticated urban element around Boston. The denomination obviously had become too large to be consistent if at one extreme it led to Shakerism and at the other to the Christ-ians. That in itself was proof that by 1800 the Baptists were no longer a sect, but a denomination.

65. Elias Smith, *Five Letters with Remarks* (Boston, 1804).
66. The papers of Daniel Hix at the New Bedford Public Library.
67. Elias Smith, *The Clergyman's Looking Glass* (1803); *A Short Sermon to the Calvinistic Baptists in Massachusetts* (1805); *The World Governed by a Jew* (1804); *Loving Kindness of God Displayed* (1809); and his magazine *The Christian Magazine* (Portland), 1805–1807. William Bentley, the Jeffersonian Unitarian of Salem, considered Elias Smith a more intelligent man than Stillman, Baldwin, or Hezekiah Smith and welcomed his attacks on the Calvinism and dogmatism of the Baptists.

But if the rural pietists distrusted the growth of educational snobbery, religious formality, institutional machinery, and social foppery, they did not need to fear that the denomination was coming under the control of a few sophisticated eastern Doctors of Divinity who might manipulate it to serve their own ends. The rural Baptists provided the guiding spirit of the denomination throughout the nineteenth century and the tone they gave it was essentially pietistic. But it was a divided pietism, torn between the evangelical Calvinism of Whitefield and Edwards and a new Arminian-ized Calvinism which was to evolve in the Second Great Awakening. In addition, the denomination was torn between the social conservatism of its New England Puritan heritage and a new Jeffersonian and individualistic ethic. The social and political views of the Baptists between 1780 and 1810 reveal even more strikingly than do their theological controversies the transitional stage of New England dissent as the Age of Jefferson emerged.

Chapter 39

The Baptists' Views on Government,
Morality, and Slavery,
1780–1810

Slavery grows more and more odious throughout the world; and as an honorable gentleman said some days ago, 'Though we cannot say that slavery is struck with apoplexy, yet we may hope it will die with a consumption.

Isaac Backus to the Massachusetts Ratifying Convention, 1788

The Baptists were *in* New England but not entirely *of* New England, just as they were in the world but not of the world. Their ambivalent position as pietists and New Englanders is evident in their schizophrenic reaction to social and political thought as well as in their theological and ecclesiastical thought. In religion they claimed to be Edwardsian Calvinists and in ecclesiology, Pilgrim Separatists. Hence "our forefathers" were New England's forefathers and "our Edwards" was the Standing churches' Edwards. Yet in reforming New England's church and state the Baptists consistently attacked the fundamentals on which it was based — the covenant theology, the coordinate system of government, the halfway covenant, the Saybrook Platform, the use of religious taxes, the territorial parish, and the corporate nature of Christian social order. Still they did not recognize (and perhaps would have deplored) the tendency of their revolution. To them it was a return to primitive Christian principles or Gospel Truth, not the advance of American democracy.

It is therefore not surprising that the social and political views of the maturing denomination differed very little from those of their Congregational neighbors. After 1800 the Baptists found themselves politically aligned with the Jeffersonian party, but it is clear that they did not see it as a Revolutionary party so much as the fulfillment of certain premises of Christian liberty inherent in their new reformation. Their social and political thought are perfect demonstrations of the inherent conservatism of the American Revolution. The fervor they evinced over natural rights and re-

751

ligious liberty had a very limited perspective. Rigid adherence to the virtues of the Protestant ethic guided their moral code; a steady devotion to good order and a Christian nation pervaded their political outlook. On no single issue, outside the realm of disestablishment, did the Baptists take a radical position, except perhaps on the French Revolution, which to them — as to Jefferson — was the mirror of their own fight against religious and political tyranny. What was radical in the Baptist, revolutionary, and Jeffersonian movements was implicit not explicit.

As pietists the Baptists were never greatly interested in political activity as such. Elder Elias Smith was a school teacher and minister for fifteen years before (at the age of thirty) he made a conscious effort to think about politics in 1799 and then discovered that he was a Jeffersonian. Isaac Backus, who was certainly the most active Baptist in this sphere, never considered political matters at all until he was fifty-one, during the Stamp Act crisis; he never attended a general election in Boston until 1774 and never spoke or voted in a town meeting until 1775.[1] Smith and Backus were ministers and ministers in New England had generally abstained from direct political action. Congregational ministers, who had a vital stake in the social order always had definite views about society and government which are easy to find. But one can read all of the New England Baptists' published literature in the colonial period without discovering more than passing references to these subjects.

From what little the Baptists did say on politics and government, the general outline of their position was essentially the same as that of John Locke, but with a definite Calvinist and pietist gloss. They believed that government was both a compact agreed on by men and an ordinance of God. They held firmly to the Lockean conception of natural rights and government by the consent of the governed, but believed also that men were innately too sinful to be trusted entirely with freedom. Although they thought men were fundamentally rational creatures — as opposed to animals — they also believed that reason was God-given and that man in his fallen state had lost so much of his rational wisdom that only through the grace of God could he hope to govern himself wisely. They disagreed with that rationalistic aspect of Locke which defined religion simply as saving souls and which therefore defined government in secular terms. The Baptists, like most New Englanders, thought of the good society as a Christian Commonwealth in which a "sweet harmony" existed between church and state. Despite the intrinsically individualistic aspect of experimental religion, the Baptists had not yet adopted an atomistic view of society. Like the Puritans, the Baptists were far more willing than Locke and Adam Smith to accept positive action by the state on behalf of the general welfare and were thus not satisfied with the conception of Locke and Smith that the gov-

1. Isaac Backus, ms. "Diary," VIII, 111 (May 26, 1774).

ernment should act only in the capacity of umpire among competing individuals. This complicated balance between individual freedom and the corporate welfare made the Baptists ambivalent toward the New England political system. Although the logic of their theological doctrines regarding experimental religion, believers' baptism, lay ordination, and the priesthood of all believers led them into the Jeffersonian anti-Federalist camp (and later into laissez-faire Jacksonianism), at the same time their beliefs in the sovereignty of God, original sin, and the depravity of man kept them wedded to many aspects of the Puritan (and later the Whig) conceptions of an organic Bible Commonwealth.

Thus there was always a fundamental belief in submission to the powers that be which governed the Baptists's social ethic, for these powers (whether inalienable moral laws or duly constituted civil authority) were ordained of God. Isaac Backus stated this conservative core of his faith succinctly when he maintained in 1788, that "every soul ought to feel a necessity always to obey the revealed will of God in the several relations which we sustain in life; and that in each community, necessity ought to be laid upon every member, to submit to the government of it, or to be excluded therefrom." [2] This explains why the Baptists were unwilling to abandon the Puritan "blue laws" or the laws restricting blasphemy, profanity, gambling, dancing, theater-going, and intemperance. On the more difficult social questions of the day — women's rights, slavery, test oaths, universal manhood suffrage, debtor and bankruptcy laws — they were divided. They were divided also on the central political question of the post-Revolutionary period — the extent to which government should be decentralized. The Massachusetts constitution of 1780, the rebellion of Shays, the ratification of the federal constitution, and the emergence of a Jeffersonian program for domestic and foreign affairs provided the testing ground for the formulation of the Baptist theory of social and political order. In the process the Baptist clergy, especially the more learned and urban of them, tended to exert a conservative influence upon the Baptist laity.

Since the Baptists followed the Puritans in requiring the signing of a covenant by all church members, the question of enforcing the moral laws of God began in the church. Regardless of what action the state might take against the sinner, his brethren felt it their duty to call him to task for any infractions of his compact to walk with them in all the ways of God. It is thus possible, by reading the church covenants and the cases of church discipline, to see what behavior the Baptists expected of an individual Christian. At the outset it may be noted that many Baptist churches forbade members to take disputes among themselves into a court of law without first trying to settle it through the church. Typical of this is article

2. *Ibid.*, XI, 85 (March 24, 1788).

number thirty-one in the Articles of Faith adopted by the South Brimfield Baptist church in 1747: "Christian brethren in church fellowship and communion ought not in case of any difference [to] proceed against each other in a course of civil law until such difference have had a hearing before the church." [3] Most Baptist church covenants also required the members to keep watch over each other not only for infringements of "gross sins" — such as breaches of the ten commandments — but also for "foolish talking and jesting," "Vain disputing about Words," "frolicking in promiscuous gatherings," "Disregarding Promises and not fulfilling of engagements," "Tatling and backbiting," "Spending time idly at Taverns or elsewhere," and "vain and unnecessary worldly conversation on Lords' days." [4]

Without attempting an all-inclusive statistical breakdown, it is safe to say from the examination of a large number of church records in this period that the major items of discipline (apart from theological heresies) were cases of intemperance (drunkenness), frolicking (attending mixed parties or dances), fornication (pre-marital intercourse), adultery, lying, backbiting (slander), cheating (failure to complete contracts), covetousness (usually failure to contribute to the support of the church), and profanity. While there were many other sins inveighed against in Baptist sermons — card-playing, theater-going, luxurious worldliness, dueling, price-gouging, and gambling — these were obviously sins of the rich and the urban dwellers in which the Baptists seldom found the opportunity or the inclination to indulge.

In every case of discipline which came before a church, if the sinner demonstrated sincere penitence and was willing to confess his crime and to make amends for it, he was forgiven and continued in good standing. Only the recalcitrant or stubborn sinner was "dealt with" — usually by pronouncing a censure which prohibited him from taking communion. If he still refused to confess and repent after two or three such censures or admonitions, the church proceeded to excommunicate him, pronouncing him a heathen and a publican and delivering him over to Satan and out of their care. Because communion and church membership meant so much to these pietists, the churches (not only the Baptist, but all the churches)

3. Records of the South Brimfield Baptist church in the church at Wales, Massachusetts. For an even stronger statement by a Separate church (which was adopted by many Baptist churches) compare this article in the Mansfield Articles of Faith: "That if any Civil Differences should happen between Brethren . . . we believe that we ought not to go to Law . . . but that all such Difficulties or Differences are to be decided by the Church." *The Result of a Council of the Consociated Churches of the County of Windham* (Boston, 1747), p. 8.

4. See the covenant written by Isaac Backus and signed by all members of his First Baptist Church in Middleborough after January 16, 1756. A copy of it is among the BP(AN). Many of the instances of church discipline are taken from the records of this church as kept by Backus and as reported in his diary, letters, and other papers, but other Baptist church records have been drawn upon as noted.

were a powerful moral force on the frontier and in the rural areas. But one thing which differentiated the pietistic Baptist (and Methodist) churches from those of the older denominations (Congregationalist, Presbyterian, Episcopal) was that they were usually just as rigid in their morality in urban areas as they were in rural areas. The decline in Baptist pietism and the transformation of their sect into a denomination can be measured by the gradual decline of church discipline, first in the urban areas, and then everywhere. For the Baptists this did not occur until well into the nineteenth century, even in the urban areas.

In addition to the evidence provided in church records, there is abundant evidence concerning the Baptist attitude toward personal and social morality in their sermons. Baptist ministers were always ready to call a spade a spade: "We delight not in hard names," Backus wrote in one of his tracts, "but every vice ought to be called by its proper name; and the custom in this adulterous age of calling those 'natural children' which God calls 'children of whoredom' has doubtless had a pernicious effect upon many to embolden them to go on in their filthy ways." [5] One of the sins of the times against which they often thundered was the growth of theaters in the large cities in this period. Despite the vigorous opposition of the clergy of all kinds, theaters were set up and did regular business in the 1790's in Boston, Providence, and Philadelphia. In 1792 Backus noted in his diary, "stage-plays were set up in Boston in open defiance of the law of the government;" and six years later he noted almost gleefully, that the Grand Theater in Boston had burned down "as they were preparing to mimock the burning of Sodom in a play; the fire catched in the house near night and consumed it . . . A plain testimony against mocking God!" [6] A member of the First Baptist Church of Boston, who was a tailor, found himself brought before his brethren in 1796 because "The church were informed that our brother, John Dyar, taylor, had an apartment in ye theatre, made ye clothes for ye players and attended every play night to dress and fit them for appearance on ye stage; by which conduct he had offended a number of ye church." The church sent a committee to investigate the matter which "reported that he [Dyar] had no connection at all with ye Theatre — yt he had a private room and was seldom interrupted by any

5. Isaac Backus, *An Appeal to the Public for Religious Liberty* (Boston, 1773), p. 45. The twentieth century pietistic evangelist, William A. (Billy) Sunday also resisted popular shifts in social attitudes in a similar fashion when he noted with disdain the attempts by psychologists to mislabel stealing as "kleptomania," adultery as "alienation," and murder as "temporary insanity" or "compulsion." W. G. McLoughlin, *Billy Sunday Was His Real Name* (Chicago, 1955).

6. Backus, ms. "Diary," XII, 76 (December 31, 1792), XIII, 22 (February 11, 1798). The letter from William Rogers to Backus, December 20, 1799, makes a similar comment about the burning of Ricket's Circus in Philadelphia when it was too vividly portraying a scene in Hell; in the BP(AN).

of ye players — that his time of engagement was nearly out — that he was very sorry he had hurt ye feelings of any of ye church. The church agreed to let ye matter rest as it had been misrepresented." [7]

As in the case of the burned theater, Baptist annals are filled with treasured tales of sinners who were punished by God for their actions. Backus told of a thoughtless girl in Hartford who "was going with her companions to a frolick." As she rode along in a sleigh she was cracking nuts and eating them; "she Put a Shell in her mouth and as they were going along very merry She happen^d as She was laughing to Suck ye Shell down her throat" where it became stuck and "She died in 2 or 3 hours — how terrable is Gods hand." [8]

There were continual warnings against "growing intemperance" in Baptist sermons.[9] Several Baptist elders passed the socially permissive boundary of spirituous consumption and were dismissed for chronic alcoholism. The most serious case was that of Elder Richard Chase of Harwich, who was finally censured and dismissed by his church in 1776 for "drinking" and "loose company." [10] Loose company or evil companionship and intemperance usually went together. A typical case of church discipline on this issue in 1784 reads, "Declared the sentence of excommunication passed last Friday against John Drake for going frequently into evil company, drinking to excess, and talking profanely. A solemn time." [11] Itinerant Baptist evangelists thanked God when they were fortuitously saved from sharing a table or room at an inn with hard drinking and "sporting" types.[12] They often complained that the worst part of going to jail for refusing to pay their religious taxes was the ungodly company they had to associate with there.

It is wrong, however, to associate this dislike of intemperance either with a belief in teetotalism or an advocacy of laws prohibiting the sale or manufacture of alcohol. The Baptists, like the Puritans, objected only to excessive use of alcohol. Isaac Backus always carried a small jug of rum in his saddle bags when he traveled. Elder Esek Carr of Attleborough was known to provide a jug of hard cider for internal warmth at his church meetings.[13] While the Baptists often deplored the fact that ordination cele-

---

7. Records of the First Baptist Church of Boston, February 29 and March 28, 1796, BP(AN). Dyar, once he was vindicated, could have brought charges against his brethren for slander or false witness but he did not.
8. Isaac Backus, "Travel Journals," November 29, 1750, in BP(AN).
9. Backus, ms. "Diary," VI, 134 (November 30, 1766).
10. *Ibid.,* IX, 17 (August 7, 1776).
11. *Ibid.,* X, 91 (May 23, 1784).
12. Isaac Backus, "Travel Journals," February 21, 1748/9, in the BP(AN).
13. William L. Chaffin, *History of the Town of Easton, Massachusetts* (Cambridge, 1886), pp. 184–185. It may be from this or a similar custom that the story became current that Baptists always concluded a communion service by "guzzling down" any wine which was left over. See Isaac Backus, *A Fish Caught in His Own Net* (Boston, 1768), p. 109, for a denial of this canard.

brations among the Standing Order were scenes of general intoxication,[14] the records show that when the Baptists of Middleborough built their first meetinghouse in 1756, they provided four pounds worth of rum (several Kegs) for those who helped to "raise the roof." [15]

The most notable instance of Baptist opposition to dancing was the story told of Elder Hezekiah Smith of Haverhill. It is virtually a classic of pietistic folklore and was often told of other ministers. Elder Smith, on one of his travels, was staying at an inn one night where the local citizens decided to hold a ball. Not realizing he was a Baptist elder, but recognizing him as a man of education and respectability, they asked him to "join in the mirth of the evening." He declined at first, but after they urged insistently he finally agreed. "After having acknowledged in his own easy and pleasant manner the attention which had been shown him, he remarked that he had always made it a principle through life never to engage in any employment without having first asked the blessing of God . . . Upon this he immediately commenced a prayer." And of course, this so altered the mood of the occasion that when he had finished the prayer he then launched into a "pathetic address to the consciences of his audience." By the time this ended, they were in no mood for dancing, the ball was canceled, and in the following days a great revival broke out and many of the thoughtless dancers were converted.[16]

While he was a chaplain in the army, Hezekiah Smith also delivered the most famous sermon against swearing in his day. General Washington had become so shocked by the amount of cursing among the troops that in July 1779, he issued an order to his officers to put a stop to this "vice, which is as unprofitable as wicked and shameful." Smith delivered a sermon to General Nixon's brigade on the subject, saying that the General's order was "sensible, pious, and polite" because it discountenanced "a vice pregnant with all the horrors of profaneness which violates the rules of decency and good order, and is repugnant to our blessed religion." Swearing, he said, "is a crime for which the great Jehovah positively declares he will not hold you guiltless and that for which you must severely suffer unless repented of." [17]

The Baptists were not entirely consistent regarding the enforcement of Sabbatarian laws. In 1774 Backus quoted favorably a sermon by the noted English Baptist minister, Benjamin Wallin, which had urged Parliament to enforce the Sabbath laws in England.[18] But when the Massachusetts

---

14. Backus, "Travel Journals," August 27, 1752, in BP(AN).

15. The bill for this is among the BP(AN).

16. Reuben A. Guild, *Chaplain Smith and the Baptists* (Philadelphia, 1885), pp. 138–139.

17. *Ibid.*, p. 257.

18. Isaac Backus, ms. "The Man of Sin Revealed," among the BP(AN). The sermon Backus referred to here was probably Benjamin Wallin's *Sonship of Christ* (London, 1771).

constitution required all persons to attend church on Sundays, Backus opposed it.[19] In Rhode Island, the Seventh Day Baptists petitioned the legislature in 1784 for the repeal of a law requiring all persons to attend church on Sunday; the petition was granted, but the existence of the law in that state dominated by Baptists and Quakers indicated the pervasiveness of the belief that the Sabbath must be kept holy.[20] Whatever the Baptists may have felt about compulsory church attendance, on which they were undoubtedly divided, they clearly believed the state had the right to prohibit all work, amusement, travel and other nonessential labor on that day.

Dueling was not a problem in New England, few examples of it have ever been found. But like all New Englanders, the Baptists disliked the practice. They were horrified when in 1803 Aaron Burr shot Alexander Hamilton in a duel. Backus recorded in his diary: "Vice President Burr shot Genl Hambleton in a duel at New York, July 11, and he died the 14th. Such is the madness of man!" [21]

Lotteries proved to be a thornier problem. In New England, as elsewhere in America and Europe, after 1760, lotteries became a very popular device for raising funds for all kinds of charitable purposes.[22] Churches, parsonages, hospitals, schools, and asylums were strengthened by this appeal to the human penchant (or vice) for gambling. The records of the legislature in Rhode Island are filled with petitions from Baptists asking permission to raise money for their churches this way. Rhode Island College, like Harvard and Yale, made use of lotteries to build college buildings as early as 1767.[23] When the college needed more funds in 1772, Manning wrote a letter to a leading Baptist in London, John Ryland, asking "Wd. a well concerted scheme of a Lottery to raise 1000 or 2[000] Sterl. meet wt. Encouragmt. by ye Sale of Tickets in England?" Ryland replied, "We have our fill of these cursed gambling Lotteries in London every Year; they are big with ten thousand Evils. Let the Devils Children have

19. He and other Baptists may have opposed it not so much from principle but because of the possibility that it was so worded that a dissenter who had no church of his own denomination nearby could be forced to attend the established church in his parish.

20. Ms. petitions, Rhode Island State Archives, XXI, 50 (June, 1784). The problem of Sabbath attendance in Rhode Island went back to the seventeenth century when the first Seventh Day Baptist churches were formed. In May 1725, a complaint was brought against the Seventh Day Baptists in the town of Westerly and the General Assembly cautioned them "that although the ordinances of men may not square with their private principles, yet they must be subject to them for the Lord's sake." Roger Williams had also maintained this view. Samuel G. Arnold, *History of Rhode Island* (Providence, 1899), II, 80.

21. Backus, ms. "Diary," XIV, 23 (July 22, 1803).

22. See John S. Ezell, *Fortune's Merry Wheel* (Cambridge, 1960), for a general history of lotteries in America.

23. W. C. Bronson, *The History of Brown University* (Providence, 1914), pp. 37, 59, 143.

them all to themselves. Let us not touch or taste." To which Manning replied:

> Your opinion of lotteries coincides with mine; but some of our friends urged me to mention the subject, as they could not see a prospect of supplies in any other way. Besides, I believe there have not been such iniquitous methods used in this matter with us, as in the State lotteries at home. They have been used to promote good designs.[24]

Manning seems to have dropped this method of raising money, but his successor, President Maxcy, led the appeal for another one in 1795.[25] Since all lotteries were subject to license by the state legislature, one might think some Baptist would consider this as much a form of state aid to religion as was incorporation, but none appear to have raised the issue.

Concerning the sin of fornication or pre-marital sexual relations, the Baptists followed the common custom of New England and considered the birth of a child within six months following marriage as *prima facie* evidence. Almost all cases of church discipline against members for this sin were based on this evidence. The Baptists were as subject to this sin as were the Puritans, even in the best of families; this was obvious from their church records. It was not, however, considered a heinous crime in the eighteenth century as long as the couple involved (having been married in time) confessed their sin and repented of it.[26] When Isaac Backus discovered that his own daughter had committed it, he commented, "Lois was married to Parker Allen, Dec. 17, 1786, and had a son born April 3, 1787. Their fall is lamented by them and others . . . and may he grant them repentance unto eternal salvation." [27]

Membership in the Masonic societies was another form of sin against which the Baptists pronounced in the eighteenth century. This was to have profound political consequences among pietists of the 1820's and 1830's. As early as 1768 Isaac Backus recorded his opposition to the Masons: "Saw a grand procession of free masons pass thro' ye strets [of Boston]

---

24. Reuben Aldridge Guild, *Early History of Brown University Including the Life, Times and Correspondence of President Manning* (Providence, 1897), p. 242.

25. Bronson, *Brown University*, pp. 143–144. Another form of indirect aid from the state which the Baptists utilized was in the form of interest on loans. In 1776 Rhode Island College had $4,000 of its endowment fund on loan to the state. The state, for reasons of its own, decided to return this money to the college. Isaac Backus and other leading Baptists and Quakers interested in the college at once presented a petition to the state, asking the state please to reconsider its decision, for the college did not know where else it could loan its money at such a good and safe rate of interest. Vol. 16, Rhode Island Archives, petition dated September 5, 1776.

26. In seventeenth-century Massachusetts the crime was usually punished by fines or whippings of one or both parties.

27. Backus, ms. "Diary," XI, 57 (April 24, 1787).

with a band of music" on their way to hear a sermon at Trinity Church; "they lookt to me more like worshippers of Diana than ye lowly Jesus." [28] Backus' objection seems to have been partly a dislike for their costumes and music and partly for their association with the upper classes and the Anglicans. But not until the 1790's did the Baptist churches begin to discipline members who joined the organization; probably few Baptists belonged to one before that date. On August 31, 1794 the matter came before the Second Baptist Church in Cheshire when some member asked the church's advice on joining the order. The Church voted

> Altho' the Church is ignorant of the Secrecy of Masonry and know not the advantages of that Ordor yet for members of this Church to Join them in their Lodges, looks so much like being yoked together with Unbelievers, and fellowshipping the Works of Darkness; and being unnecessarily Conformed to the World, that the Church agrees to Withdraw the right of Fellowship from any of the Members that frequent the Lodges.[29]

Four years later the Shaftesbury Association voted that if the members of any church were offended at a brother's joining the Masons he [the Mason] must either resign from the Masons or be excommunicated.[30] In these latter cases there seemed to be a suspicion that freemasonry was antireligious. Doubtless in some areas the lodges were centers for those with deistic leanings. But the more obvious reason for opposition to these new social organizations was the threat of divided loyalty and divided financial support which they presented to the churches. Under the mask of considering them irreligious or frivolous, the churches actually expressed a hostility for any activity which took a Christian's mind and energy away from his church.

The churches became involved in more complicated cases when they considered charges against a member for breach of a covenant or contract, mistreatment of an apprentice, embezzling an estate or failure to pay debts. Many pages in the church records are taken up with accounts of complex problems which in civil law would come under the headings of torts and contracts. Oral testimony, written statements, contractual evidence, witnesses for both sides, testimony and rebuttals for both sides often became so overwhelming that the church members who, like a jury without a judge, were required to render a decision, often became hopelessly confused in trying to pin down the specific moral sin of the accused. At the

28. *Ibid.*, VII, 44 (November 23, 1768). Samuel Stillman, however delivered an address to a Masonic society in Charlestown in 1785 in which he praised them for their devotion to God and public worship. For Backus's opposition to the Society of the Cincinnati see his *History of New England,* ed. David Weston (Newton, 1871), II, 260.

29. A typescript of the records of this church is in the Berkshire Athenaeum, Pittsfield, Massachusetts.

30. *Minutes* of the Shaftesbury Baptist Association, 1798, 1803.

other extreme, an extremely simple matter could produce the same endless wrangling. The members of Isaac Backus's church spent many weeks trying to settle the case of a woman who was accused of having borrowed two pins or needles from a neighbor and having failed to return them.[31] During the 1780's the enormous depreciation of paper money produced numerous cases of church discipline against shrewd church members who tried to pay off old debts in the depreciated bills. The Second Baptist Church of Newport contains a typical entry in a case of this kind:

> At our Church Meeting on August 2d A.D. 1787, the conduct of Bro^r Benoni Peckham was taken into Serious consideration respecting his tendering a Sum of paper Money in order to discharge a Mortgage of Lydda Sanford when the Discount was Six and Seven for One; the Brethren unanimously concluded it to be unjust on his part and quite unbecoming the christian . . . [and] did withdraw all fellowship from him until the fruits of repentance doth appear in him.[32]

Baptist church discipline was not limited to the delinquencies of members; it included pastors' delinquencies as well. Moses Thomas's complaint to the Warren Baptist Association in 1782 is an example. Thomas had been admonished and then excommunicated from the Third Baptist Church of Middleborough led by Elder Asa Hunt because he had brought what the church considered false accusations against his pastor. Thomas, in his letter to the Association, demanded a fair hearing on the case and said that he was willing to prove that Hunt had been guilty of sharp dealing in business affairs and had condoned such practices by other church members. For example, Hunt had justified a brother who overcharged Thomas for some corn by saying "that a man had a right to ask as many prices as he pleased and that a Bushel of Corn was worth what it would fetch"; it had no fixed or just price. Elder Hunt, who was a cobbler by profession, also "asked a bushel of rye or four shilings in money for making a pair of shoes" which was price-gouging. Further, he "Bought a yoke of oxen and sold them again for five Dollers more than he gave and never Moved them from the place where he Bought them." And finally

> it apered to me Extravagant that Crispus Shaw Being in want of a sum of money Elder hunt [said he] would procure the money which was 250 pounds old tenner [;] the said Shaw was to Bind over the Land for security and pay the interest and pay to Elder hunt 50 pounds old tenner in Labour

31. Records of the First Baptist Church of Middleborough.
32. Records of the Second Baptist Church of Newport, p. 88 (August 2, 1787), in the Newport Historical Society. The churches usually became involved in such cases only when both parties were members since the church had no control over non-members and the witness of non-members against members could not be properly accepted because they were not in the covenant. However, a member who was offended at the treatment of a non-member by one of his brethren could bring the matter before the church.

at twenty two shillings and six-pence a Day for Elder Hunts procuring the money and being his Bonds man.

The church members had declared these accusations false or unsubstantiated but Thomas was not satisfied with their decision because they were partisans in the case.[33]

On such problems of personal behavior and morality there was little to distinguish the Baptists from the Congregationalists, Methodists, or other pietistic denominations, except that the Baptists were apt to be more picayune and perfectionist than was the average Congregational church. Nor does there seem to be anything distinctive about the Baptist position on larger social issues — the role of women, of the Indian, or of the Negro in American society. The Separates did have some radical ideas about the role of women in the churches and were inclined to give them more freedom to pray and exhort in mixed meetings and even to vote in church meetings. And Ezra Stiles, after a careful investigation of the role of women in the Rhode Island Six-Principle Baptist churches concluded, "it appears plain to me that it is a Usage & practical Principle among the Baptists of this colony . . . to admit the Sisters to equal Votes in the Chh. meetings." [34] But the regular Baptists disagreed. Some Baptist articles of faith specifically stated "a woman hath no right to act either in teaching or governing the Church." [35] Most followed the traditional Congregational practices, giving women little more than a silent participation in church affairs. Nor did the Baptists have any radical notions about the role of women in secular affairs. The most they argued for was the right of a woman to obey her conscience rather than her husband if he forbade her to attend a Baptist meeting.[36] Women members were censured if they used this excuse for failure to attend church regularly. Whether a wife could disobey her husband if he were a Baptist and she a Shaker or Universalist does not appear to have come up. Isaac Backus, who published tributes to the two most important women in his life, his mother and his wife, praised them for their piety and their submissiveness, for their faithfulness as mothers and wives — for fulfilling the traditional New England concept of the woman's role as loyal helpmeet, devoted mother, and dedicated handmaiden of the church.[37]

33. Moses Thomas's letter to the Warren Baptist Association, June 11, 1782, is among the BP(AN). There is no record of the association's action, but it seems unlikely that they would interfere in such a matter. At most they might have recommended calling a council to settle the dispute. Also records of the Third Baptist Church of Middleborough at Andover Newton Theological School.

34. Ezra Stiles, *The Literary Diary of Ezra Stiles,* 3 vols., ed. F. B. Dexter (New York, 1901), I, 145–147.

35. Francis Jackson, *A History of the Early Settlements of Newton* (Boston, 1854), p. 149.

36. Isaac Backus's letter to "Sister" Hooper, June 30, 1774, in BP(AN).

37. For Backus on his mother see *Gospel Comfort under Heavy Tidings* (Provi-

With respect to the Indians and Blacks, the Baptists welcomed them somewhat more warmly as converts than did the Congregationalists — or at least the Indians and Blacks in New England felt more at home in Baptist churches — perhaps because they found the Baptist meetings more lively and the Baptists more sincerely dedicated to Christian brotherhood, or perhaps because they felt less of a gap between their own out-group position and that of the Baptists. Ezra Stiles noted in his diary in 1792, however, that of thirty Black church members in Newport (where there were more Blacks than anywhere else in New England) only seven belonged to the three Baptist churches in that city.[38] This matter is confused, however, by the general custom of requiring slaves to attend where their masters attended. Outside of Newport, and especially among the free Blacks, the Blacks preferred the Baptist churches, though there is no evidence that Congregational churches ever showed any reluctance to admit them to membership. But the Congregationalists, as the Separates had said, disliked permitting lay brethren to exhort and in at least one case an Indian who was censured for doing this in a Congregational church left it and formed his own Indian church where he practised open communion with antipedobaptists. The Separates and Separate-Baptists shared the common racial prejudices of the time against Indians and Blacks and when this particular Indian exhorter, Samuel Niles, sought ordination from the Separate elders near Westerly, they refused to perform it. However, another Indian exhorter in the same area, James Simon, was ordained by Elder Stephen Babcock of the open-communion Separate-Baptist church in Westerly.[39] Isaac Backus invited Simon to preach in his church when he visited Middleborough to baptize an Indian woman.[40] Both the Baptists and the Congregationalists usually noted in their records whenever a newly admitted member was an Indian or a "Negro." There was clearly a distinction between Christian fellowship and social equality.

Backus did have one radical notion about the Indians, however, which he shared with Roger Williams and the Quakers. Europeans, said Backus, had no right to take land from the Indians without making regular agreements and paying them for it. The falsely assumed right of Christian Europeans "to claim the property of infidels in America," he wrote in 1779, had brought about all the misery of the Indian wars, "from the poison whereof we are not yet thoroughly purged" — presumably reference to the Revolution when most Indians in the West sided with the British.[41] How many Baptists agreed with Backus and what, if anything they did about

dence, 1769); the second edition of this in 1803 contained "A Short Account of His Wife."

38. Stiles, *Diary,* I, 214.

39. *Ibid.,* I, 232–233. Perhaps one reason Niles was not ordained by the Separates was because he could neither read nor write.

40. Backus, ms. "Diary," III, 142.

41. Isaac Backus, *Policy as Well as Honesty* . . . (Boston, 177), p. 4.

it, is not evident. Backus had particular reasons for being friendly toward the Indians, however, for a church of Christian Indians had existed in Titicut parish when he first came there as a Separate minister in 1748 and these Indians gave to the members of Backus's church the land on which they built their first meetinghouse.[42] The Indian church in Titicut died out about 1760 and Backus's few references to his Indian neighbors indicate that from his standpoint they were a dissolute and bad-tempered lot. They played no significant part in Backus's church.

The Baptists of New England took conservative stands on the three principle issues concerning Blacks: social discrimination, the slave trade, and the abolition of slavery.[43] The issue of social discrimination arose most clearly regarding intermarriage. In 1774 Elder Asa Hunt of the Third Baptist Church in Middleborough wrote to the Warren Association:

> An English woman that has lived as a wife with a Negro desires to joine to the chh. We are well satisfied that she is a meet subject [for membership] only as we suppose it is not lawfull for such to be married together and the above persons upon a justice of the Peace Refusing to marry them Took Each other as husband and wife and have dwelt together Ever since. We Request your advice and counsel in the Case.[44]

The answer of the Warren Association is unknown and so is the resolution of the question. However, until 1786 no law was passed in Massachusetts prohibiting marriage between whites and Blacks; belief that such a law existed was simply a reflection of the common prejudice in the matter. Yet that the Baptists were willing to consider this woman for membership indicates a certain tolerance.

A similar, though more serious case, took place in Rhode Island in 1781, in the Second Baptist Church of Newport. "At our Church Meeting, February 1st 1781 . . . Agreed that Brother Jethro Brigs Cite Kingston Pees a Black Brother to appear at our next Church Meeting to account for his Conduct on Account of his keeping Company with a White Girl and Wanting to Marry her contrary to the Distinctions God had Made . . ."[45] Here the racial ban is given divine rather than legal sanction. On March 1, the church reported, "our Black Brother Kingston Pees appeared in Church Meeting and did not appear in any shape to be convinced of any Error in keeping Company with a White Girl, and Wanting to Marry her; Moreover he seemed rather to blame his Brethren than himself." However, the

42. Thomas Weston, *History of Middleboro* (Boston, 1906), pp. 18, 401.
43. For an early Baptist sermon urging slaves to be content with the lot which God had ordained for them see John Callendar, *A Discourse on the Death of the Rev. Nathaniel Clap* (Newport, 1746), pp. 31–33.
44. Letter from Elder Asa Hunt to the Warren Association September 2, 1774, in BP(AN).
45. This and the entries quoted below are from the Records of the Second Baptist Church of Newport in the Newport Historical Society.

church decided to reason with him a little longer. Finally, on March 28, "our Black Brother Kingston Pees appeared and confessed his Error in Sinning against God and Wounding his Brethren as touching the things accused of . . ." and he was forgiven. But the matter did not end here. On October 3, 1782 "Our Black Brother Kingston Pees Appeared and did not Deny the Accusation brought against him respecting Ann Mackumber a White Woman being with Child by him." The church therefore excommunicated him "as an Unclean Person . . . an Heathen Man and an Adulterer or Fornicator." On May 29, 1783, another Black brother, Case Mumford, was also excommunicated because he "did not in any degree appear to be convince[d] of his Error . . . for his Associating himself with Kingston Pees an Excommunicated Person." Kingston Pees was a free Black, not a slave; he later moved to New York City. Other than indications of racial prejudice implicit in the constant reference to "our Black Brother," this Baptist church habitually used its Black members whenever it had to send a message or a committee to visit another Black member on church business. Discrimination, or social propriety, required that Black Christians deal with Blacks and white Christians with whites.

Elder Elias Smith, as a Baptist minister in Woburn in the 1790's, noted that neither Samuel Stillman nor Thomas Baldwin would let the Black Baptist preacher, Thomas Paul, preach in their churches:

> When Thomas Paul came to Boston the Dr. [Stillman] told him it was *Boston*, and that they did not mix colours; or words of that import. He was not even willing he should preach in the vestry. Mr. Baldwin told me about these words [and added] . . . 'There are some of my congregation who would leave the meeting if Paul should preach here . . . and as long as there are other white men to preach, I do not think it best for him to preach here.' [46]

Stillman's church had many Black members, however, and in 1805 they asked to be dismissed to form a church in West Boston. They chose Thomas Paul as their pastor and asked the two Baptist churches in Boston to help ordain him. Stillman's church voted to send its pastor and deacons "to attend on that occasion, and that the delegates plainly dissuade them from ye admission of white members among them: as they may ultimately become the majority & defeat ye intention of their being an *African* church." [47] It is not clear how much of this was concern for the Blacks' benefit and how much was a dislike for social "amalgamation" which might have placed white church members in the position of being disciplined by a

46. Elias Smith, *Five Letters* (Boston, 1804), p. 18. For a case involving a Baptist church in Londonderry, New Hampshire which was reluctant to ordain a Black in 1806 see chapter 45, note 2.
47. Nathan E. Wood, *The History of the First Baptist Church of Boston* (Philadelphia, 1889), p. 297.

Black majority. In any case, Stillman did deliver the installation sermon in December 1806 (with the whites seated in the pews and the "people of color" in the galleries) and the African Baptist church in Boston was admitted to the Warren Baptist Association. Paul remained the official pastor here until his death in 1831, though he was often away on evangelistic or missionary trips. The church had about seventy members and remained on friendly terms — separate but equal — with the white Baptists of New England.[48]

Not many Baptists were wealthy enough to own slaves, but some did. Jeremiah Condy owned two; Hezekiah Smith owned one which he sold to his brother for $125 in 1776; Samuel Stillman owned one; Ephraim Bound in Boston and James Manning in Providence owned one; and several of the wealthy Baptist laymen in Rhode Island owned slaves.[49] There are few public statements by New England Baptists on the subject of slavery. An exception is the anonymous pamphlet, *An Oration on Liberty,* published in 1773. Its author, John Allen, was a Baptist preacher only recently come from England. Allen never found a welcome among the Baptists in New

48. Surprisingly little has been written about Thomas Paul although his was the first independent Black church in the North, and he was the first Black pastor in the Baptist churches of New England. He was born in Exeter, New Hampshire on September 3, 1773, was converted to Baptist views in 1789 and (according to one source) baptised by Edward Lock, a leader of the Freewill Baptists (though Paul himself was always a Calvinist). He began preaching in 1801 and for a time preached to the Baptists in Weare, New Hampshire. He was ordained in West Nottingham, some sources say in 1804 and others in 1805. He preached to the Blacks of Boston in Franklin Hall on Nassau Street in 1805–1806 until the meetinghouse was built in 1806 on Joy Street (the same building in which William Lloyd Garrison organized the Boston Anti-Slavery Society in 1832). The funds for this church were raised largely by a committee of whites who advertised the enterprise as a charity project chiefly because the building included a schoolroom for Black children. However a Black church member, Cato Gardiner, was also prominent in the fund-raising. The minutes of the Warren Association indicate that the church grew rapidly until 1812 but Paul's frequent absences often left the congregation confused. Paul preached in New York City in 1808–1809; he was responsible for the formation of the Abyssinian Baptist Church there in 1809. In 1823 he volunteered to serve as a missionary to Haiti and the Baptist Missionary Society of Boston supported him there for five years. "Ignorance of the French language hindering his reaching the class desired, he returned home to labor" in the Boston church until his death. Described in his obituary as "a gifted eloquent preacher," "an extraordinary man," Thomas Paul deserves more notice than he has yet received. Carter G. Woodson, *History of the Negro Church* (Washington, 1921), pp. 88–91; Walter H. Brooks, "The Evolution of the Negro Baptist Church," *Journal of Negro History* VII (January, 1922), 17; Ruby F. Johnston, *The Development of Negro Religion* (New York, 1954), p. 34; Caleb H. Snow, *History of Boston* (Boston, 1828), p. 342; Lee M. Freedman, "A Beacon Hill Synagogue," *Old Time New England,* XXXIII (July, 1942), 2–4; N. F. Carter, *The Native Ministry of New Hampshire* (Concord, N.H., 1906), p. 239; William Little, *History of Weare, N.H.* (Lowell, 1888), pp. 283, 335.

49. Guild, *Smith,* p. 176; also Thomas B. Maston, "The Ethical and Social Attitudes of Isaac Backus," Yale dissertation, 1939, chap. 6, "Slavery and War," pp. 137–157.

England and disappeared soon after 1773.[50] That same year, Elder Ebenezer Smith of Ashfield wrote a letter to Isaac Backus in which he denounced slavery. He had evidently been reading Allen's pamphlet and he took as his Scriptural text for this stand, Acts 17: 26, God "hath made of one blood all nations of men." [51] Backus noted on the back of this letter that he had read it to his church. In a petition to the Massachusetts Legislature for religious liberty in 1774, Backus made a passing reference to the Continental Congress "who have wisely extended their regards to the rights and freedom of the poor Africans;" but he did not pursue the point.[52] Later, in his tract, *The Testimony of the Two Witnesses* (1786), Backus referred in passing to "the cruel slave trade." [53] In 1787 Elder Caleb Blood's church in Newton wrote to the Warren Association, "Whereas we are informed that the Horred practice of the slave trade is reviveing again in New England it is our desire that the Association would strongly recommend it in their minutes to our Churches and friend[s] to manifest by word and deed their total avertion to such a wicked practice." [54] The Warren Association responded by including in its circular letter that year the following statement:

> Notwithstanding the great expense of blood and treasure during the late war to ward off slavery from ourselves, we are informed that in various parts of this country many have recurred to the horrid practice of sending our shipping to Africa to bring from thence the natives and to sell them as slaves in the West Indies: And as man-stealing is a capital crime by the laws of God — see Deut. xxiv. 7 — I Tim. i.10 — we therefore earnestly desire all our brethren to guard against giving the least countenance to that heaven-daring wickedness.[55]

The following year, Isaac Backus made a speech in the convention which ratified the federal constitution in Massachusetts in which he commended the Constitution for its requirement that the slave trade be ended by act of Congress in twenty years:

> I believe that according to my capacity no man abhors that wicked practice

50. John M. Bumsted and Charles E. Clark, "New England's Tom Paine: John Allen and the Spirit of Liberty," *William and Mary Quarterly,* 3rd. ser. XXI (October, 1964), 561–570.

51. Letter from Ebenezer Smith to Isaac Backus, October 16, 1773, in the BP(AN).

52. Alvah Hovey, *A Memoir of the Life and Times of the Rev. Isaac Backus* (Boston, 1858), p. 216.

53. Isaac Backus, *The Testimony of the Two Witnesses* (Providence, 1786), p. 45. Although Backus made an extended evangitistic trip to Virginia and North Carolina in 1789 and was confronted with the religious and moral problems of slavery he never, as John Leland did, denounced his Southern brethren for not abolishing slavery. W. G. McLoughlin, *Isaac Backus* (Boston, 1967), pp. 205–206.

54. Caleb Blood to the Warren Association, September 9, 1787, in the BP(AN).

55. Warren Association Minutes, 1787, p. 5.

["the importation of slaves into this country"] more than I do; I would gladly make use of all lawful means towards the abolishing of slavery in all parts of the land. But let us consider where we are, and what we are doing. In the Articles of Confederation no provision was made to hinder the importation of slaves into any of these states; but a door is now open hereafter to do it, and each state is at liberty now to abolish slavery as soon as they please . . . slavery grows more and more odious throughout the world; and as an honorable gentleman said some days ago, 'Though we cannot say that slavery is struck with apoplexy, yet we may hope it will die with a consumption.[56]

Backus never expressed more than that pious hope. His strongest statement on the subject was in this same speech when he said, quoting the Bible, " 'Ye are bought with a price; be not ye servants of men.' Thus the gospel sets all men upon a level, very contrary to the declaration of an honorable gentleman in this house, that 'the Bible was contrived for the advantage of a particular order of men.' " But this ambiguous statement of equality under the gospel said nothing about equality under the law. Backus grew up in a family which owned slaves and he seems to have felt the problem was outside the scope of religious or social action, and instead in the Providence of God. He personally abhorred slavery and he believed the Bible spoke against it, but it was not a matter about which he felt any strong urge for action. One may assume from the Baptists' lack of action in New England that this was the general feeling of the denomination.

However, in Rhode Island, where Quaker influence was strong, the Baptists were participants in the movement to end slavery. James Manning joined with the Quaker reformer, Moses Brown, and the Congregationalist theologian, Samuel Hopkins, to get a law passed declaring all slaves born in the state after March 1, 1784 were free; their educational expenses were to be borne by their mother's masters.

In 1789 a society for the abolition of slavery began in Providence under the leadership of Moses Brown and the Quakers. Its primary purpose was to prevent Rhode Islanders from engaging in the slave trade. James Manning (who had sold his slave boy, Cato, twenty years earlier) was a member, as was Samuel Stillman. There were 118 members in all; sixty-seven of them lived in Massachusetts. But Backus did not join them nor did any other Baptist minister in Massachusetts except Stillman.[57] Manning noted in a letter to Backus on December 8, 1790, that his leading parishioner, John Brown, quarreled with those members of the First Baptist Church who joined the abolition society. Brown was heavily engaged in the slave trade, and he did not think the church should meddle with business.

56. Jonathan Elliot, *The Debates in the Several State Conventions* . . . (Philadelphia, 1876), p. 149.
57. Letter from Manning to Backus, December 8, 1790, in the BP(AN); Mack Thompson, *Moses Brown* (Chapel Hill, 1962), pp. 195 ff., and Irving F. Bartlett, *From Slave to Citizen* (Providence, 1954), p. 21.

In 1792 the Shaftesbury Association took a stand on slavery and the slave trade which was the strongest public statement by any of the New England Baptists in the eighteenth century:

> The association being impressed with a sense of that freedom which every child of Adam is entitled to by nature; and of which they cannot be deprived but by hostile usurpation; take this method of manifesting their hearty detestation of the SLAVE TRADE: and recommend it to all our brethren to pray Almighty God to hasten the auspicious day when the Ethiopians, with all the human race, shall enjoy that liberty due to every citizen of the commonwealth and the name of SLAVE be extirpated from the earth.[58]

But apart from this statement, the Baptists were far less outspoken on slavery than were the Quakers. There is no record of any Baptist being censured or excommunicated for owning a slave or for engaging in the slave trade, comparable to the way Quakers "disowned" members of their congregations for these sins.

58. Shaftesbury Association Minutes, 1792, p. 11.

Chapter 40

The Baptists' Views on Education, Science, Politics, and National Destiny, 1780–1810

I have said little about the family quarrel [Shays's Rebellion] that has been the past year in this common wealth, but what I have said has been to condemn both sides.

Elder Samuel Bigelow to Isaac Backus, August 31, 1787

The Baptists' position on social order, morality, and the Negro were no more advanced than were those of their Congregational neighbors. Their stands on education, science, and politics were equally unexceptional. In James Manning they did have a leader especially dedicated to the promotion of education, but he did not have an easy time either in keeping the Baptist College going or in promoting public education in Rhode Island. Manning tried, in 1786, to persuade the national government to pay $4000 for rent and repairs to the college building (which had been used as a hospital for the French Army during the Revolution) but he was unsuccessful. However, after his death, in 1800 Congress did give the college $2800. By contributing to the Baptist education fund after 1792, Baptists demonstrated their determination to produce an educated ministry as well as to provide a useful liberal education for their children. The number of graduates from the college continued to be small (the largest graduating class was twenty students in 1790); most Baptists still believed that the gifts of the Holy Spirit were more important to ministers and laymen than education. Nonetheless, a general growth in sympathy toward the values of education among the Baptists marked a change from the earlier anti-intellectual quality of their pietism. Many Baptist elders were elected to and served on school committees in their towns in these years: among them, Hezekiah Smith in Haverhill; Noah Alden and Valentine Rathbun in Bellingham; Caleb Blood in Newton; and James Manning in Providence. Baptist laymen served on school committees even more frequently. Surprisingly, one of the functions these elders performed as school committeemen was to see that the children in the public schools were being taught the Westminster catechism by their teachers.[1]

In 1782, however, the Warren Association "Voted that a spelling book containing a good English grammar and the Baptist catechism be published" to serve as an alternative to the primers of the time which included the Westminster Catechism with its justification for infant baptism. The Association appointed a committee — Manning, Backus, Foster, Stillman, and Skillman — to do this. In 1784 the Association noted that a Mr. Howe had drawn up "a Spelling Book and Grammar" which the Association was willing to publish. But Stillman and Skillman did not think it proper to do so. Apparently nothing came of this, perhaps because the conservative faction in the Association, led by Stillman and Skillman, feared that publication of this primer as a competitor to those already in use would lead to unnecessary religious friction in the public schools. The issue raised important questions concerning the role of the public schools in inculcating religious doctrines which the Baptists apparently did not want to face.

Although there was undoubtedly a strong element of anti-intellectualism inherent in the Separate-Baptist movement, as there was in all pietistic movements, the Baptists demonstrated again their Puritan heritage by their general desire for and support of education. Most of them were products of the public school system in New England and most of them agreed with the efforts of James Manning, as chairman of the school committee in Providence, when he tried to persuade the people of Rhode Island to imitate their neighbors in Connecticut and Massachusetts in support of public schools. Manning's report to the town of Providence in 1791 led to the beginnings of such a system in Rhode Island, though the system did not get under way until 1800. Manning's Report indicates the feelings of a leading New England Baptist about education:

1. Useful knowledge, generally diffused among the people, is the surest means of securing the rights of man, of promoting the public prosperity, and perpetuating the liberties of a country.
2. As civil community is a kind of joint tenancy in repect to the gifts and abilities of individual members thereof, it seems not improper that the disbursements necessary to qualify those individuals for usefulness should be made from common funds.
3. Our lives and properties, in a free state, are so much in the power of our fellow-citizens, and the reciprocal advantages of daily intercourse are so much dependent on the information and integrity of our neighbors, that no wise man can feel himself indifferent to the progress of useful learning, civilization and the preservation of morals in the community where he resides.

1. For an example of a Baptist school teacher in East Hartford who taught the Westminster Catechism to his pupils in the 1780's even over the objections of Episcopal parents see Elias Smith, *Life* (Portsmouth, 1816), pp. 119–123.

4. The most reasonable object of getting wealth, after our own wants are supplied, is to benefit those who need it; and it may with great propriety be demanded, in what way can those whose wealth is redundant benefit their neighbors more certainly and permanently than by furnishing to their children the means of qualifying them to become good and useful citizens?

5. In schools established by public authority, and whose teachers are paid by the public, there will be reason to hope for a more faithful and impartial discharge of the duties of instruction, as well as of discipline among the scholars than can be expected when the masters are dependent on individuals for their support.[2]

The reasons offered here were not much different from those Thomas Jefferson offered in his "Bill for the Diffusion of Knowledge" in Virginia in 1779 or from those the New York Public School Society under DeWitt Clinton offered in 1805. They represented the general attitude of the period and the belief that a republican society needed an educated citizenry. The concept of the civil community as "a kind of joint tenancy" was a holdover from the organic view of society held by the Puritans, but significantly the report assumes that such schools will inculcate morality rather than religion. The doctrine of stewardship in paragraph four told the rich their obligations toward the poor (it was assumed public education would be supported by proportional taxation which would fall most heavily on the rich).

Baptists shared the Calvinists' view generally that education — that all research and scholarship — would necessarily lead only to a greater knowledge of and faith in God. Thought of a conflict between religion and science did not arise. Thus, even a pietist could accept the goal of more education for all. But this did not mean that the Baptists shared the more liberal views of the Enlightenment or were free from superstition and folklore about the supernatural forces of good and evil. Even an intelligent and widely read Baptist like Backus, filled his diary with credulous stories about the mysterious occurrences reported to him as fact — stories about stewpies, puddings, and dumplings which when baked "appeared like as if they were mingled with blood;"[3] stories of young men who saw visions and heard voices which seemed to prove that they were "bewitched;"[4] and, above all, stories in which the hand of God was clearly seen taking some action designed to awaken men to the necessity of their salvation. Backus told of scoffers at religion who were struck dead by God and of earthquakes sent to warn men that the day of judgment might come at any time.[5] To him all sudden

2. Printed in Reuben Aldridge Guild, *Early History of Brown University Including the Life, Times and Correspondence of President Manning* (Providence, 1897), p. 463.

3. Isaac Backus, "Journey to Cape Cod," November 29, 1755, in the BP(AN).

4. Isaac Backus, ms. "Diary," XII, 3 (August 3, 1789).

5. Isaac Backus, "Travel Journals," November 29, 1750, in the BP(AN).

deaths or accidents were solemn warnings from God which he, as a minister, should "improve" for the spiritual benefit of his congregation.

An incident which provides insight into the mixture of superstition, and millennialism even on the part of the most learned Baptists occurred on May 19, 1780 — the famous "Dark Day" of eastern New England. That morning the sky became so filled with dense black clouds that the sun was blotted out after eleven along the whole southeastern quarter of New England. People had to light candles to eat their noon meal and as the strange darkness persisted the streets became filled with fearful people milling about seeking an explanation. "In the evening, the blackest darkness was so palpable that a candle at the window gave no light outside." In Providence, a resident

> went into the street, where many persons were assembled, apparently in astonishment at the darkness, among others, Dr. [James] Manning. A powerful man, but profligate, advanced up to the president, and said, "How do you account for this darkness, sir? What does it mean?" The president, with great solemnity of manner, replied, "I consider it sir, as a prelude to that great and important day when the final consummation of all things is to take place." [6]

The Baptists were not averse to newer modes of thought, even if they still harbored many of the older superstitions. Backus admired Locke's *Essay on Human Understanding* and had read Cesare Beccaria's *Essay on Crime and Punishment*. Like Ezra Stiles and Thomas Jefferson, he was an inveterate and meticulous keeper of statistics and tables of mortality. He wrote a scholarly geographical account of the region around Middleborough with a note about its mineral deposits and iron ore which the Massachusetts Historical Society published, and he sent a series of detailed corrections and critical comments to Jedidiah Morse after he read the first edition of Morse's famous *Geography*.[7] In his descriptions of some of the natural wonders which came to his attention he displayed more of the scientific than the pietistic temper:

6. The darkness disappeared the next day and was subsequently explained by Professor Samuel Williams of Harvard as what we now call smog — a combination of heavy fog mixed with the soot and ashes from extensive forest fires in Vermont where "the people in the new towns had been employed in clearing their lands" for "two or three weeks before." W. G. McLoughlin, "Olney Windsor's Memorandum of the Phenomenal Dark Day," *Rhode Island History,* XXVI (July, 1967), 88–90. Though Manning, as Ezra Stiles said, was no scientist, his college probably did as much in this respect as other colleges its size in the eighteenth century. Donald Fleming, *Science and Technology in Providence, 1760–1914* (Providence, 1952).

7. MHS *Collections,* III (1794), 148–152, 162–166, 175–176; and Isaac Backus "Remarks on Morse's Geography, March 9, 1791," in the BP(AN). This 32-page ms. has been edited and annotated and given an historical introduction by Cynthia Kersten as a Master's thesis at Brown University.

Mr. Nicholas Wade of Bridgr. near the border of Halifax had a sheep which seem'd to swell till she could not go nor stand, and at last died on the 17th instant and next morning he cut her open, when to his great surprise there came out a thing that had some features of a lamb, but much more of a negro female child. It was larger than a middling child is at its birth, was ten inches broad across the breast and shoulders, its back and thighs shaped like a child and smooth all over except a woolly hair upon its head. Great numbers of people flockt to see it and dr. Isaac Otis dissected it and found that inwardly as well as outwardly it had more resemblance of a child than a beast, and tis suspect to be the effect of the beastiality of a Negro in the neighbourhood. Such an awful instance I have not heard of in my day before.[8]

He felt no call to make any religious comment about this incident, though his willingness to believe the worst about Negroes is evident.

Backus also appears up to date in his willingness to accept the value of inoculation for smallpox. He refused to heed the argument of a rural Baptist elder named Peleg Burroughs that inoculation was contrary to the word of God. Burroughs cited as proof for his contention Matthew 9:12, "They that be whole need not a physician, but they that are sick." [9] But in 1778 Backus had himself and his entire family inoculated. He made this clinical report of the virus which was injected into his arm:

I began to feel the symptoms of the distemper the 23d and began to break out the 28th my arm was prety sore, and the pocks were thick around the incision; besides which I had perhaps 100 all over me whereof about 30 were on my face, and they generally filled: my wife had not quite so many; Eunice had more; but we were all carried well through it.[10]

Despite this scientific objectivity, Backus always felt that the smallpox plagues which regularly hit Boston and other major cities in this period were visitations of God for the wickedness of these dens of iniquity.

Probably the outstanding example of the Baptists' intellectual stance in this period was Backus's three-volume *History of New England,* a work which mingled the best historical methods of the Enlightenment with the worst polemical qualities of Cotton Mather's *Magnalia.* Its full title was *A History of New England with Particular Reference to the Denomination of Christians Called Baptists.* The first volume appeared in 1777, the second in 1784, and the third in 1795; and in 1804 Backus published an abridged version of the history in one volume which brought the material up-to-date and included a section on the Baptists in the middle and southern states. This remarkable work compares with the best historical productions to appear in America in the eighteenth century.[11] Backus took great care to

8. Backus, ms. "Diary," VII, 149 (January 23, 1771).
9. Diary of Peleg Burroughs at the Newport Historical Society.
10. Backus, ms. "Diary," IX, 35 (March 15–23, 1778).
11. Backus has been described by Samuel Eliot Morison as "one of the most re-

base his account on the original records; he devoted many hours to scouring the old court papers and legislative archives in Plymouth, Boston, Providence, and Newport. He also consulted all the available manuscript materials (including John Winthrop's yet unpublished journal), old church records, family letters and diaries, and all the available printed materials he could find, including the forgotten works of Roger Williams. Since he had lived through much of the period he wrote about, he consulted with persons still living and asked them for written accounts of their own experiences. He collected a large number of valuable historical documents which were given to him for this work, and the extracts which he took from other manuscripts (since lost) form the only record now extant of these important materials.[12] Because of his careful attention to the written record Backus's history of the Baptists has stood for almost two centuries. Only minor errors have been found in the historical portions of his work. He felt this scrupulous regard for accuracy was forced on him. As a member of a minority group writing of persecutions which the majority had long since forgotten or wished to have forgotten, he recognized that every effort would be made to discount or discredit his claims. Moreover, he was so convinced of the obvious injustices done to the Baptists that he felt the record would speak for itself. His history revealed in authentic detail a segment of New England history which other historians of his day had neglected.

However, the work is not without serious faults in style and presentation. Backus was convinced that the Puritans acted both from spiritual ignorance and tyrannical spite in their dealings with the Baptists. Like most spokesmen for minority groups, he wrote from an exaggerated sense of persecution and often saw slights and intentional injuries where none were intended. In addition, the volumes were marred by the pietistic tone of righteous indignation and polemical pleading for the spiritual correctness of the Baptist persuasion over all others. He was almost as derisive of the other dissenting sects as were Puritan historians of the Baptists. Moreover his long digressions in which he incorporated large sections of his tracts defending sovereign grace or particular election or baptism by immersion with extensive proof texts detract seriously from the more straightforward side of his history — at least for the modern reader.

Not the least valuable of his contributions in this history were his detailed lists of Baptist churches with their dates of founding, ministers, and membership, county by county throughout New England. He also included at the

---

markable New Englanders of the Revolutionary period," a man "at once a worthy successor of Roger Williams and a historian who ranks with Belknap and Minot." MHS, *Proceedings*, L (1916–1917), 372–373. Ezra Stiles said of Backus's works (and of Israel Holly's) that they "would be considerable even for University Men." Ezra Stiles, *The Literary Diary of Ezra Stiles*, 3 vols., ed. F. B. Dexter (New York, 1901), I, 68.

12. For example, the only known copy of Samuel Hubbard's diary and letters now extant is the copy and extracts made by Backus.

end of the work short historical sketches of every Baptist church in New England about which he could obtain information. He obtained this through requests by the Warren Association to member churches to provide him with accounts and through his own voluminous correspondence and itinerant travels. Only supreme self-confidence that even the smallest beginnings of this denomination would ultimately be important as God worked out the destiny of the Baptist movement could have produced such a work. What the modern historian therefore sees as a heroic assemblage of facts was the creative effort of supreme faith, a conscious effort to promote pride and identity in a hitherto despised and neglected minority. In this mingling of fact and faith, of statistics and exegesis, of self-conscious denominationalism and inspired prophesy Backus captured the spirit of his age. In 1795, at the conclusion of his volumes, he wrote

> How great has been the increase of the Baptist churches . . . And though vast pains have been taken by men who have supported their worship by force, to make the people believe that the Baptists were enemies to good government, yet how are they now confounded in those attempts! For it now appears that government and liberty are united in their plan of conduct, which tends to bring all wars to an end.[13]

Here, if anywhere, an historian may trace the ways the spiritual force of the Great Awakening merged with the patriotic fervor of the American Revolution to create that unique mixture of pietistic humility and patriotic pride which has constituted the essence of the American character ever since.

Backus saw the freedom of the individual soul from Satan's spiritual bondage, which the evangelical conversion experience represented (and which influenced the large majority of Americans directly or indirectly during the Awakening), as an essential precondition and counterpart of the later freedom of the nation from the equally Satanic bondage of political tyranny. The merging of the two forces, or the evolution of the latter from the former, and their continuing together, could only be interpreted by those who lived through those exciting events as the clearest indication that God had predestined the United States for a preeminent role in the ultimate defeat of Satan and the triumph of the divine will over this world of sin. The Revolution itself was guided to a successful conclusion by the hand of Providence not only on the battlefield but through a great outpouring of divine grace — a second great awakening — in the years 1779–1780. "This revival," wrote Backus in 1784, "was undoubtedly a great means of saving this land from foreign invasion and from ruin by internal corruption." This was the message of Backus' history and it represented the basic philosophical outlook of the Baptists and of evangelical Protestantism in America for more than a century.

13. Isaac Backus, *History of New England,* ed. David Weston (Newton, 1871), II, 558.

If the Baptists showed a consistent ambivalence toward the moral problems of the post-Revolutionary generation, their approach to specific economic and political problems was equally confused. However certain the ultimate glory of the United States seemed, the Baptists floundered trying to discern God's immediate purposes. For example, they could find no explanation for the serious economic crisis in the 1780's, climaxed by Shays's Rebellion, except as the selfish materialism of immoral men. Backus said in 1786, the Revolution

> was no sooner over than the merchants of Babylon [London] even the great men of the earth, filled this country with her splendid and costly wares; by means of which public credit . . . has been bought and sold for a trifle. And the spirit of pride and luxury, like Sodom . . . has prevailed amazingly. No effectual care was taken to secure a medium of trade among us, and yet public and private debts are demanded with a great rigour as if brick could be made without straw.[14]

Like most pietistic people, Backus was looking for someone to blame and he could not decide which of three possible groups was the most guilty — the great British and American merchants who forced their goods on the public; the feckless average citizens who bought gaudy baubles which they could not afford; or the legislators who failed to secure a proper medium of trade. In 1781 he had publicly denounced the Massachusetts legislature for lowering the value of paper money to "but a 75th part of what they were three years and an half ago" and for giving as their reason "that thereby our public debts will be more easily paid! Whereas money was never harder to get." [15]

When the crisis of Shays's Rebellion came on "the poor of the world," the Baptists were sorely divided. Generally, the Baptist ministers sided with the forces of law and order; but the Baptist rank and file sided with the rebels — and were a large proportion of the rebel ranks according to some reports. To a Yale graduate and tutor like Barnabas Bidwell, it was only to be expected that the Baptists would be on the side of disorder and rebellion:

> The Gentlemen of learning & liberal professions, especially the Clergy [Congregational] are universally for Goverment. Debtors are generally on the other side; and this class comprehends more than half of the people. Persons guilty of crimes, or who wish to commit crimes; Rhode Island Emigrants and almost all of the denomination of Baptists; men of warm passions & little reason; men of fickle minds, fond of every new scheme and proud of an enterprising spirit — such have pretty generally engaged in the Insurrection.[16]

14. Isaac Backus, *Testimony of the Two Witnesses* (Providence, 1786), p. 14.
15. Isaac Backus, 22-page ms. proposal for the second volume of his history, written April 9, 1781, in BP(AN).
16. American Antiquarian Society *Proceedings,* n.s. IV (1887), 368.

Although the available evidence confirms Bidwell's claim that the Baptists provided more than their share of men to Shays's rebels, no Baptist minister is known to have supported the movement and several of them either condemned both sides or sided firmly with the government. A letter from Elder Samuel Bigelow of New Salem on August 31, 1787 probably reflected the ministers' general ambivalence:

> Spiritual things are at a very low ebb here . . . Church travel and ordinances have ceased ever since the people riss [arose] in arms against the government, and disunion took place, tho' at present we are better united as to publick worship but not as to chh privildges. I have got a full and final dismission from this Chh and people as their Pastor, tho' at present I continue labouring with them as a teacher and know not but I shall continue [to do so].
>
> I have said little about the family quarrel that has been the past year in this common wealth, but what I have said has been to condemn both sides. I think the political fathers have provoked their children to wrath, and by oppression wise men have been [made] mad, the children have been unruly and rebellious, turbulent and riotous. I think that all who have had any hand in either beginning or carrying on, aiding or assisting in the quarrel have acted out of character, and especially such as make the profession that our denomination does, and I think that such of our denomination as have had a hand in it are deepest in guilt and have fallen most out of character, and I think that the blood that has been shed in the quarrel will be required of all on both sides who have had any hand in beginning, carrying on, aiding or assisting in the matter, therefore I chuse to be deprived of special ordinances while I live rather than take them with any on either side, till they repent, turn from, and confess their sin of shedding blood wrongfully.[17]

In 1787 the Warren Association received a similar letter from Elder Isaac Bealls of the church in Leicester: "We have not only felt the Shock of our Publick calamities the Season past in common with our fellow-citizens, but have felt the dire effects thereof in our church and congregation: by which the Hearts of many Seemed to be converted into a petrifying quality; Members withdrew from us, the congregation decreased, falsehood greatly abounded, our Enemies grew confident, bold and daring."[18] But, he added, "the threatening Storm was a means of causing some that had been long wandering to return and Seek Shelter in the fold of Jesus."

As evidence of Baptist sympathy with the rebels, Elder Abishai Crossman of Chelmsford and most of his members signed a petition in 1787 urging

17. Samuel Bigelow to Isaac Backus, August 31, 1787, in BP(AN). In 1788 Bigelow reported to the Warren Association that peace and union had returned as a result of a religious revival. But Backus stated in his history that Bigelow was forced to leave the church in 1789. *History,* II, 470.

18. Isaac Bealls to the Warren Association, September 4, 1787, in the BP(AN). By "our Enemies" Bealls meant the spiritual enemies of the Baptist cause.

the legislature to pardon the rebel leader Job Shattuck.[19] And in Ashburn-ham, a Baptist, Jacob Willard, was elected to the legislature in May 1787; he was instructed by the town to work for the enactment of three measures which the Shaysites supported: 1. to continue the tender law; 2. to support an amnesty for the rebels; 3. to move the capitol from Boston to some place farther west.[20]

The Warren Association took no formal stand on the rebellion other than to proclaim in 1786 the need for "a more general and extensive ref-ormation [i.e., religious revival] which alone can save our country from ruin." [21] Isaac Backus seems to have shared the general antagonism toward the rebels which Bigelow and Bealls expressed. On March 28, 1787 he published *An Address to the Inhabitants of New-England Concerning the present Bloody Controversy Therein.* Here, although he began by berating the lawyers for fomenting trouble in suing debtors, the main issue of his six-page tract was to side with the statement made by the General Assembly in November 1786:

> We feel in common with our neighbours the scarcity of money; but is not this scarcity owing to our own folly? At the close of the war . . . immense sums have been expended for what is of no value, for the gewgaws im-ported from Europe, and the more pernicious produce of the West Indies [rum] . . . Without a reformation of manners we can have little hope to prosper in our publick or private concerns.

Backus added that no one could deny "this view of the cause of our distress. . . . I fully agree with our General Court that a paper currency would produce calamities without end." And he concluded, "The Command of God is 'Submit yourselves to every ordinance of man for the Lord's sake.' " Which was rather a strange argument from the man who had preached pas-sive resistance and civil disobedience fourteen years before.

The Baptist ministers' conservative approach was not inconsistent with their Calvinist attitude toward government nor with their individualistic approach to social ethics. The same impulse which led the Baptists to fight so hard for the personal right to complete liberty of conscience also led them to place the full blame for social problems upon the sins of in-dividuals who made up society. But there may also have been another factor at work in this. The Baptist in the 1780's may have been suffering from the same kind of "over-compensation" which the college-educated Arminian Baptists in 1740 displayed in opposing the Great Awakening. As an out-group seeking desperately to associate itself with the ruling elite,

---

19. Wilson Waters, *History of Chelmsford, Massachusetts* (Lowell, 1913), pp. 356–361.

20. Ashbursham Town Meeting Records, I, May 16, 1787.

21. Backus, ms. "Diary," XI, 43 (September 12, 1786). Warren Association Minutes, 1786.

feeling embarrassed for the more *outré* or socially deviant elements among their members, and believing that they were at last on the verge of attaining acceptance and participation in the power structure, the Baptist ministers in 1785 chose to identify themselves strongly with the forces of law, order, and propriety and to repudiate, or at least to deplore, the unruly and disruptive forces.

This may also help to explain the stand which Backus, Stillman and Manning took in 1788 on the ratification of the federal constitution. Since the delegates to the convention which was to ratify this constitution were chosen in the fall of 1787, when feelings over Shays's Rebellion still were strong, it was not surprising that those towns which had fought against the dominance of the state by eastern merchants, bankers, and lawyers expressed antifederalist views. Most of those towns where large number of the inhabitants supported the rebellion sent delegates who were instructed to vote against ratification. Of the four hundred delegates, about twenty or twenty-five were Baptists; the majority of these were instructed to vote against it. The town of Ashburnham sent Jacob Willard with this instruction. Five Baptist elders were elected; the majority of them were told to vote against it.[22] But Isaac Backus and Samuel Stillman were in favor of ratification, and James Manning, who was unable to persuade his own state to ratify it at this time, went to Boston to make what efforts for it he could. Governor John Hancock, who presided at the convention, asked Manning to deliver the closing prayer of the session[23] — an indication of the Baptists' rising status.

Stillman stated his reasons for supporting the constitution in a long speech at the convention. He believed that the Articles of Confederation were inadequate. While the proposed constitution might not be perfect, if it were rejected now the country might never have another chance to make a second constitution before it collapsed into anarchy. The frequent election of representatives would keep the government closely in the hands of the people. "Every two years there will be a revolution in the general government in favor of the people," he said. The Constitution would guarantee a republican form of government to each state but would leave each state free to adopt its own particular form of republic, thereby uniting the principle of federal control and local home rule. The constitution would provide for the impeachment of all officers of government found guilty of misconduct. There would be sufficient checks on the powers of Congress written into the constitution, the ultimate one the right to amend the constitution.

Stillman designed all of these arguments to quiet the apprehensions of

22. Noah Alden of Bellingham; Valentine Rathbun of Pittsfield; Peletiah Tingley of Waterbury, Maine; Isaac Backus and Samuel Stillman. Stiles, *Diary*, II, 302; Backus, ms. "Diary," XI, 79.

23. Guild, *Brown University*, pp. 448–450.

the antifederalists and presumably to persuade some of the Baptist delegates to defy their constituents and vote for ratification. Stillman was so convinced that the constitution was necessary and viable, he said, that he was willing to vote for it "without any amendments at all." With the millennial confidence of his persuasion, he concluded, "While Americans remain in their enlightened condition, and warmly attached to the cause of liberty they cannot be enslaved." Significantly, Stillman made no direct references to the Bible or to God in his address.[24]

Isaac Backus was the only other Baptist whose views at the convention have been recorded. His speech on behalf of ratification was so complicated by the Biblical exegeses which he used to support his points that it is often difficult to follow. He stressed three elements in the constitution which led him to favor it. First, he was pleased "with the exclusion of any religious test" for office holding in the national government. "Some serious minds discover a concern lest, if all religious tests should be excluded, the Congress would hereafter establish Popery, or some other tyrannical way of worship." These men had the matter backward. "It is most certain that no such way of worship can be established without any religious test."

Second, he was pleased that the constitution opened the way for the eventual abolition of the slave trade. His complex Biblical discussion of this item (based upon God's injunctions to Israel not to enter the lands of the Amorites, Edomites, Moabites, and Ammonites) led to a rather strained comparison between those who made "merchandise of slaves" and those who asserted control over the "souls of men" — a covert attack on the Congregational establishment.

Third, he was pleased that the constitution excluded "all titles of nobility or hereditary succession of power." The power of the people to return all officers of government "to a private station" was the most certain check "against their invasion of others' rights or abusing of their power." Like Stillman, he concluded with a millennial hope: "Such a door is now opened for the establishment of rightious government and for securing equal liberty as never was before opened to any people upon earth." [25] If any Baptist feared that the constitution, lacking a bill of rights to guarantee religious liberty, might permit Congress to make some laws on establishment of a state religion, he should have been reassured that the foremost Baptist champion against religious persecution supported it.

Backus said in his diary that when he was first informed that he had been chosen as one of the four delegates from Middleborough, "I thought I

24. Jonathan Elliot, *The Debates in the Several State Conventions* . . . (Philadelphia, 1876), pp. 162 ff.
25. *Ibid.,* pp. 148–151. Backus seems to have been convinced that the Constitution as written, even without the First Amendment, clearly prohibited Congress from ever making any laws respecting an establishment of religion. Backus, "Diary," XI, 77–81.

should not go, but as religious liberty is concerned in the affair, and many were earnest for my going, I consented." After he had arrived in Boston and had attended the convention for two weeks, he wrote to his wife,

> It is very disagreeable to be detained here for so long . . . but I can't think it advisable to leave the convention until the great point is turned, which is of vast importance.[26]

Five days after he wrote, the convention voted by a vote of 187 to 169 to ratify the constitution. Backus noted in his diary that "elder Alden of Bellingham, elder Rathbun of Pittsfield, elder Tingley of Waterborough (county of York) all voted against it, and so did two thirds of the lay Baptist members of the Convention, of which there were above twenty. Elder Stillman and I, with twelve congregational ministers, voted for it; though doubtless with very different views." [27] Backus, Stillman, and Manning may have deserved credit for persuading at least one third of the lay Baptist delegates to support the constitution.

But when Backus returned to Middleborough he found that his fellow townsmen, particularly the Baptists among them, wanted some explanation for his federalism. "Pr't [preached] twice to our people," he wrote in his diary on February 10, 1788, "tho' some are very uneasy at my voting for the new Constitution." How he satisfied these antifederalists he did not say.

Samuel Stillman probably did not have to justify his stand to the members of his church in Boston, for the Baptists there seem to have shared the feelings of the city in favor of federalism. The Second Baptist Church of Boston, through its elder, Thomas Gair, sent the following letter to the Warren Association in 1788:

> It is a matter of praise that we live in a period of such improvements, such liberty, peace, and good government, as the present is. The prospects of the still greater enlargement of these favours under a Federal Government animate our hope. We congratulate you on the pleasing expectation of its many advantages to this great and enlightened country. A country in which learning, candor, and freedom has made the most rapid and astonishing progress, and in which they must and will prevail amidst all opposition.[28]

26. Isaac Backus to his wife, February 1, 1788, in the BP(AN). The convention began January 9, 1788, but Backus did not arrive until January 15.

27. Backus, ms. "Diary," XI, 79 (January 15, 1788). By the different views of the Congregationalist clergy Backus probably meant that they did not, as he, see in the constitution a strong force working against any establishment of religion, but only a political victory for a more effective federal government.

28. Thomas Gair to the Warren Association, September 9, 1788. The occurrence of the term "candor" in this context raises echoes of the pre-Awakening "liberalism" of the Harvard-educated Boston Baptists like Callendar and Condy. Gair was a graduate of Rhode Island College, class of 1777.

This was another indication of the gap between the rural and the urban Baptists.

One of the most inexplicable aspects of the ratifying convention in Massachusetts is that none of the over twenty Baptist delegates appears to have suggested an amendment to the constitution to guarantee that Congress would not interfere with religious liberty. Although the Congregationalists would have opposed any amendment threatening their state establishment, it should have been possible to word an amendment which would have applied only to Congress. Nor could the Congregationalists have opposed such an amendment simply guaranteeing the inalienable right of freedom of conscience. Though nine amendments were presented to the convention and were recommended by the convention to Congress, none of them concerned religion. Nor was there any discussion in Massachusetts, public or private, concerning such an amendment.

There seem only two possible explanations for this. First, that the Baptists assumed, like Backus, that the Constitution as it stood prohibited Congress from taking any action which might abridge religious liberty.

Second, that the Baptists believed that even if Congress wanted to take some action in the sphere of religion (either to prohibit such establishments as already existed or to encourage them) the laws in each state should and would take precedence. For the antifederalist dissenters, as for the Congregationalists, religion, like education and voter qualifications, was considered a matter of states' rights. When the First Amendment was passed by Congress and ratified by the states, it guaranteed this — it left the question of religious establishment to each state and merely prohibited Congress from making any law "respecting an establishment of religion or prohibiting the free exercise thereof." In any case, it aroused no public comment in New England, even though the legislatures of Massachusetts and Connecticut refused to ratify it (it had sufficient support without their votes to become law). Backus mentioned the amendment briefly in the third volume of his history in 1795 and in his abridged history in 1804, but for some reason in both cases he quoted an early version of the amendment dated September 23, 1789, and not the version which was finally adopted. The version which he quoted, and which he assumed had become part of the Constitution read:

> Congress shall make no law, establishing articles of faith, or a mode of worship, or prohibiting the free exercise of religion, or abridging the freedom of speech, or of the press, or the right of the people peaceably to assemble, and to petition to the government for a redress of grievances.[29]

Backus's only comment was that "it is part of the constitution of our general government and yet the Massachusetts and Connecticut act contrary to it to

29. Backus, *History,* II, 341; Isaac Backus, *An Abridgement of the Church History of New England* (Boston, 1804), p. 225.

this day." Thus, the Baptists recognized that the battle would have to be fought at the state level with no help from outside.

The Baptists were no more united on political and economic issues in the 1790's than they had been before; their general viewpoint was probably accurately reflected in the diary and letters of Isaac Backus in these years. The five issues about which he offered comment were the French Revolution, the Whiskey Rebellion, the public debt, the possibility of war with France, and the downfall of the Papacy. Generally he took the side which was associated with Thomas Jefferson and the party which evolved under Jefferson's leadership at this time. But he did so from personal conviction and not from allegiance to any party. The Democratic-Republican Party did not manufacture the platform which drew the support of the Baptists in New England for the succeeding generation. It simply built its platform of the planks which it found already hewn, stacked, and waiting to be assembled. Backus wrote of the British declaration of war against France in 1793, "protestants are now joining with papists [Royalists] in bloody attempts against liberty and religion in France" — to him this was another indication of the deviltry of the Church of England.[30]

In December 1794 Backus commented about France and the Whiskey Rebellion in a noncommittal fashion:

> By an order of the British court a large number of our vessels were seized in the West Indies, and many were in earnest for an open declaration of war with that nation, which our Congress had hard work to avoid. At the same time an open insurrection appeared against our government in the west part of Pennsylvania against whom President Washington marched up with 15,000 men which cost the government not less than a million dollars.[31]

The Baptists, like all Yankees, and especially the antifederalist Yankees, were always concerned with the expense of government. Two years later in 1795 Backus took a more pietistic view of the world situation:

> Europe is full of confusion and blood; and America is become so wanton and extravagant, that it cost above a million of dollars, and required an army of 15,000 men last year, to compel a few countries in Pennsylvania to submit to the taxing power of our government . . . the whole country has been full of controversy ever since. And are not these the shakings among the nations which God will pursue until the Desire of all Nations shall come? Hag. ii.7.[32]

However, his friend Elder William Rogers of Philadephia wrote to Hezekiah

30. Isaac Backus, *Testimony of the Two Witnesses,* 2nd ed. (Boston, 1793), p. 22.
31. Backus, ms. "Diary," XII, 124, December 28, 1793.
32. Backus, *History,* II, 385 and 569 — "the debt is clearly increasing and many have tried all their arts to draw America into another war with foreign nations."

Smith more optimistically that same year, "The French go on gloriously, surely the Lord will in his own appointed time Smile upon his People universally and build up the walls of his Jerusalem."[33] On June 3, 1798, Backus was himself more optimistic: "Wonderful are the events in Europe! The French have conquered Rome, and the Pope fled to the island of Malta."[34]

In December, 1798, Backus made his first comment against the foreign policies of the Federalist Party:

> The changeableness of man is wonderfull. The French nation was greatly applauded for a number of years as the good allies of America who helped us to independence from the tyranny of Britain; but the last spring and summer every art was made use of by our highest rulers as well as others to render them as odious as possible; and the Congress broke off all trade with them and exerted all their powers to raise a fleet and army against them while they continued a strong connection with Britain tho' they took more of our vessels in the year than the French had. Dr. [Jedidiah] Morse of Charlestown prt. a sermon upon this subject on the thanksgiving.[35]

A year later he noted hopefully that "The tide of opinion is again turned in favour of the French nation."[36]

Backus, and the Baptists, were evidently almost all Jeffersonians by 1800. Once again, Backus may be accepted as a typical spokesman. After Jefferson's election he commented: "The man who was the Chief Magistrate of these United States for four years, was very fond of partiality. But a man was elected into that office in 1801 who is for equal liberty to all the nation."[37] Backus had read Jefferson's *Notes on Virginia* and quoted in the third volume of his history Jefferson's bill for religious freedom as a model for New England. Second only to his admiration for Jefferson's support of religious liberty (and to his friendship for France) Backus admired Jefferson's frugality in government. "Though our government was so managed, that our national debt had been increasing ever since the war, and very vast under the administration of Mr. Adams, yet in two years since Mr. Jefferson was president the debt has been lessened about ten million dollars & they are going to extinguish it wholly."[38] And when Jefferson was reelected he noted:

> Since Mr. Jefferson became President in 1801 our national debt has been much diminished and last March he was elected again into that office

33. William Rogers to Hezekiah Smith, April 14, 1795, in the BP(AN).
34. Backus, ms. "Diary," XIII, 25, June 3, 1798. He later corrected this entry to say that the Pope was confined in Italy.
35. *Ibid.*, XIII, 35, December 30, 1798.
36. *Ibid.*, XIII, 55, December 29, 1799.
37. Backus, *Abridgement*, p. 264.
38. Backus, ms. "Diary," XIII, 103, December 31, 1802.

by 162 votes when there was but 14 for any other man. And he has been gaining in esteem in the minds of people, tho' I suppose there never was any chief Magistrate in any government so much belied in print without punishment as he has been, till the lying party is become very comtemptible.[39]

The emergence of a two-party system in New England after 1796 at last provided the Baptists with the means for winning their long struggle against the establishment. At first the Democratic-Republicans made no particular attempt to win the allegiance of the dissenters as a bloc or to appeal directly to them for votes. In their effort to split the Federalist Party the Jeffersonians tried to argue that religion, and particularly the clergy, should keep out of politics, for there was no doubt that the Congregational ministry were solidly in back of the Federalists. When the Jeffersonians found that the Congregational ministers would not keep out of politics, then the way was opened, of necessity, for rallying whatever ministerial support could be found among the dissenters against the Standing Order. But the alliance between the anticlerical Jeffersonian politicians and the pietistic dissenters was never so secure and forthright as one might have expected.

Before proceeding to the final episode in the Baptists' long struggle in Massachusetts, it will be helpful to look first at how the denomination fared in the frontier states of Vermont and New Hampshire. For it was these states which set the pattern of disestablishment which Connecticut and Massachusetts belatedly had to follow.

39. Backus to William Richards in London, April 20, 1805, in the BP(AN).

PART X

Disestablishment in Vermont and New Hampshire,

1768–1819

"The Methodist Church being released from this yoke, now shot ahead . . ."

The Reverend Dan Young, Methodist minister, describing the results of the law for disestablishment in New Hampshire which he introduced.

Chapter 41

Disestablishment in Vermont,
1768–1807

And there is such a mixture [of religious views] in Vermont that I have no account of great sufferings there.

Isaac Backus in his *Abridgment of the Church History of New England* (1804)

The Baptists in Vermont were rarely persecuted for nonpayment of religious taxes. Moreover, there was much less of that social and political animosity between them and the Congregationalists which characterized their relationship in Massachusetts and Connecticut. However, complete religious liberty and equality did not exist in Vermont. "Although many of our brethren were amongst the first settlers in most parts of this State," said Baptist historian David Benedict in 1812,

> yet the greater part of the settlers were of the Congregational order, from the States of Massachusetts and Connecticut. These people carried with them the religious maxims of their native States, and by their influence the country was divided into parishes, in most of which Congregational churches were established, and a law was passed similar to those in the other New-England States, empowering these parishes to levy a general tax for building meeting-houses and supporting their ministers.[1]

Not until 1807, after some hard fights, were the Baptists and other dissenters in Vermont able to persuade the legislature to pass a law abolishing the system of compulsory religious taxation which generally favored the predominant denomination.

1. David Benedict, *A General History of the Baptist Denomination in America,* 2 vols. (Boston, 1813), I, 351. In the earliest period of settlement, 1725–1741, the area settled in southern Vermont was claimed by Massachusetts. From 1741 to 1764 that area of Vermont was annexed to New Hampshire. In 1764 the King transferred this territory to the colony of New York. Between 1777 and 1791 the Yankees and Yorkers wrangled bitterly for control of the area but the state's autonomy was generally securely in its own hands long before it achieved statehood in 1791. Before 1770 the number of settlers was very small.

Several factors account for the different, and easier, position of the Baptists in Vermont. Because Vermont was settled so late in the eighteenth century the major issues of church and state had already been thrashed out in Massachusetts and Connecticut and the Baptists took these gains with them to the frontier. Although in theory, and to some extent in law, the ecclesiastical system in Vermont followed that of Massachusetts, in practice the complex and carefully regulated social and religious structure of the old Puritan township seldom appeared on this new frontier. Vermont was not settled by carefully directed and well-financed mass migrations, one town at a time, but by the slow, haphazard and piecemeal clearing away of the forest by one or two families at a time over widely scattered areas.[2] Furthermore, while the racial and national stock of the emigrants was fairly homogeneous, their religious outlooks reflected the growing variety of sectarian persuasions in New England after 1770. The frontier emigrants, by a process of self-selection, consisted of a more individualistic, radical, uneducated, and generally poorer group of people than those who remained behind. Without accepting all of F. J. Turner's characterization of the frontier, it is easy to see in the configurations of Vermont life much of what Turner called "frontier democracy" in its more individualistic form. Among these poor but stubborn and self-willed emigrants evidence sustains the view of a high percentage of religious dissenters and radicals — persons who, if asked, would have said that one reason for their emigration was to escape the ecclesiastical confinements of the Massachusetts and Connecticut systems. Disliking intolerance toward themselves, these Vermont settlers recognized the virtue of tolerating their neighbors. Moreover, the unstable and unresolved political administration of Vermont in the years before 1791 encouraged a very flexible, almost anarchic, system of local rule in which over long periods of time towns were virtually sovereign political units, able and willing to settle their own problems in their own ways.

The result of these circumstances was a climate of freedom and equality that the dissenters of New England had not known before outside the traditionally "unwholesome" atmosphere of Rhode Island. Although Vermont towns relished the practice of majority rule, the majority always tempered its actions by respect for minority rights.[3] Most important, because the frontier climate fostered equality, it also fostered that social mobility and social mixing which had been lacking in the older Puritan

2. Walter T. Bogart, *The Vermont Lease Lands* (Montpelier, 1950), pp. 66–67, 307.

3. This does not mean that there were no instances of prejudices against dissenters. Henry Crocker, historian of the Baptists in Vermont, reports that Elder Elisha Rich, a Baptist itinerant preacher born in Sutton, Massachusetts, "experienced no little rough opposition in Clarendon" where he preached for five years in the 1780's. "Persons in disguise would surround his house and cruelly beat his cattle that they might have opportunity to abuse him also." They even tore up the pulpit in his church. Crocker, *History of the Baptists in Vermont* (Bellows Falls, 1913), p. 114.

colonies. On the frontier, Baptists and Congregationalists shared their hardships and resources, attended the same limited social and religious functions, permitted their children to intermarry, accepted each other as business equals, and ignored denominational distinctions in choosing the best available men for political leadership. From 1779 to 1781 a Baptist was the lieutenant governor of the state; in 1813–1814 a Baptist was sent to Congress as state representative, and finally, in 1826, a Baptist was elected to the governorship. And from its founding in 1791, Baptists were also given a share of the appointments to the board of trustees of Vermont University. That at last such possibilities were open to them in New England was a climactic turning point in Baptist history and a symbol of the final disintegration of the Puritan closed society. This openness at the top was proof of equal openness below.

Although the Baptists were never a majority of the population or even of the church members or churchgoers in Vermont, their denomination grew proportionately more rapidly than did any other, including the Congregational, from 1768 to 1807. As long as the Congregationalists adhered to their old system of religious taxation and a learned ministry they were at a serious disadvantage on the frontier. From an economic viewpoint the old Puritan system of town and parish organization would have produced a more effective religious structure. Few Vermont towns could afford to support even one church and minister adequately; two or three were that much more difficult. But pietistic settlers were strongly averse to community churches (except in the earliest days as an alternative to no religious services at all); they were even more divided about compulsory religious taxes. The poverty of their own adherents, not the tyranny of Congregational ecclesiasticism, was the real enemy of Baptist growth in Vermont. Before 1807, however, this problem was met by the system of itinerant evangelism in that state as elsewhere on the American frontier.

There is no accurate statistical index for the proportion of Baptists to other denominations in Vermont in this period. But there is ample evidence that a considerable number of the immigrants to that region came from areas in southern New England where Baptists (and Separates) were numerous: from Rhode Island; from the eastern part of Connecticut; southeastern Massachusetts; the southern part of Worcester County; and from the more newly settled regions in the Berkshires. Local histories and genealogies for the Vermont towns attest to this. Lois K. Mathews in *The Expansion of New England* and Abby M. Hemenway in her multi-volumed *Vermont Historical Gazetteer* describe numerous parts of Vermont where the early immigrants came from these dissenting sections of New England. Discussing the seventy-four new towns begun in Vermont before 1776, Mathews wrote, "Rhode Island was represented in Marlborough, Bennington, Shaftesbury, Danby, Londonderry, and probably others; Smithfield [R.I.] was the town which sent the most families . . . Norwich [Vermont] was a town which attracted Preston and Mansfield settlers" where New Light Separatism had been strong.

> Bennington will serve as a type of the old methods of planting towns, combined with new features. There was an organized emigration to Bennington from Hardwick, Massachusetts, in 1761 . . . The Hardwick emigration was distinctly a religious movement; the people had gone 'to gain greater freedom in ecclesiastical affairs.' [4]

David Ludlum, in *Social Ferment in Vermont 1791–1850,* states that although ultimately conservative Congregationalists probably constituted the majority of the immigrants, "for the first four decades of Vermont's existence, until 1800, radicals in politics and religion were in the ascendancy." He found that "among the early residents of Guilford were numbered Baptists who had passed over the border from Massachusetts to escape burdensome religious taxes." Although conservative Congregationalists dominated the southeastern Vermont area, west of the Green Mountains "those religious revolutionaries, the Separates, settled to escape the persecution of the Standing Order of southern New England. Here, too, were found 'Rhode Island haters of religion' as well as recruits to the Methodist faith. To the western settlements rebellious Daniel Shays and his associates fled . . ." Until "By the election of 1800 . . . Thomas Jefferson carried every county west of the mountains . . ." [5]

In Bennington, where in 1762 the first church of any denomination in Vermont was founded, the settlers included a large majority of Separates from Amherst, Hardwick, and Sunderland, Massachusetts and from Newent, Connecticut. They formed a Separate or Strict Congregational church in 1762 and in 1763 were joined by members of a Separate church in Westfield, Massachusetts. This Separate church was the only church in Bennington for some years. When a quarrel arose in 1780 some of the members moved to Poultney and founded another Separate church.[6] Mean-

---

4. Lois K. Mathews, *The Expansion of New England* (Boston, 1909), pp. 115–117, 143–145; also T. D. Seymour Bassett, University of Vermont Library, "Migration to Vermont, 1761" (mimeograph). I should like to thank Professor Bassett for sending me this paper and for his helpful comments on this chapter which he read in manuscript.

5. David Ludlum, *Vermont in Ferment: 1791–1850* (New York, 1939), pp. 5–6, 11, 13–15. Ludlum stresses that this radicalism became embedded in the Vermont constitution of 1777 by universal manhood suffrage and the creation of a Council of Censors whose actions produced three constitutional revisions within thirty years, all of which were in the direction of Jeffersonian democracy. He probably exaggerates the clearcut geographical division of eastern and western Vermont. Isaac Backus, historian of the Baptists, surprisingly (but not altogether inaccurately) attributes the settlement of Vermont to "The folly of many in Connecticut and the Massachusetts, who ran into debt at the close of the wars in 1763 and 1783." Isaac Backus, *History of New England,* ed. David Weston (Newton, 1871), II, 545.

6. C. C. Goen, *Revivalism and Separatism in New England, 1740–1800* (New Haven, 1962), p. 108.

while some of the Separates in Bennington became Baptists; these moved out to the southwest part of Shaftesbury and to southern Pownal. The first three elders of the Pownal Baptist church (formed in 1773) were from Rhode Island.[7]

The first Baptist church in Vermont was formed in Shaftesbury in 1768. It was led by Bliss Willoughby, who had been pastor of the Separate church in Newent, Connecticut and had taken the Separate petition to England in 1756. He became a Baptist in 1764. A second Baptist church was formed in Shaftesbury in 1780 and was known as "The Rhode Island Church" because of its members' origin. In 1781 a third church was formed by some of the "Old Baptists" of Rhode Island, Six Principle Baptists, who believed that the laying on of hands was required for full church membership. In 1783 a fourth Baptist church was formed in Shaftesbury and its second pastor, Elder Caleb Blood, achieved a reputation such that in 1792 he was invited to give the election sermon before the Vermont legislature.[8] By 1780 the Baptist churches in Vermont and on its borders in New York and Massachusetts were sufficiently strong and numerous to break away from the Warren Association and to form their own association. The Shaftesbury Association, formed in 1781, had forty-seven member churches by 1797, though most of them were across the border in the neighboring states.

Settlement of Woodstock was equally typical of the early and rapid influx of dissenters into Vermont. A Baptist church was organized here in the northern part of the town in 1780. It joined the Warren Association in 1781 but in 1783 it joined three Baptist churches in the vicinity to form the Woodstock Association. A second Baptist church was formed in the southern part of Woodstock in 1785. South Woodstock was known locally as Cottletown because it was dominated by the numerous members of the Cottle family. The Cottles had originally settled in Tisbury, Martha's Vineyard, in the seventeenth century. Sylvanus Cottle had been a deacon of the Congregational church there in the 1740's. He became a New Light in the 1750's and after he moved to Rochester, Massachusetts, he became a Separate-Baptist in 1772. His sons, Jabez and Warren, moved from Rochester to Woodstock in 1768, fought in the Revolution, then became farmers and clothiers. Other members of the family moved to Woodstock; finally, by 1790 there were forty-seven Cottles living in Cottletown. They became leaders of the community; Jabez was elected to the legislature and appointed a Justice of the Peace. Some members of the family moved west to Missouri in the late 1790's but many, including Jabez, remained. Jabez became a Baptist preacher in 1802 and was later pastor of the Woodstock church and

---

7. Crocker, *Baptists in Vermont*, pp. 14–15. See also Backus, *History*, II, 546, and Benedict, *History*, I, 337.

8. Backus, *History*, II, 546; Crocker, *History*, pp. 15–22; Benedict, *History*, I, 335–336.

the Windsor church. After 1808 he made frequent missionary trips to northern Vermont, New York, and lower Canada.[9]

Although early statistics on Baptist churches in Vermont, as for other denominations, are questionable, one can gain an idea of the proportional growth of Baptists and Congregationalists from the generally accepted totals: in 1776 there were eleven Congregational churches and two Baptist churches in the state; by 1790 there were fifty-eight Congregational churches and thirty-four Baptist; and by 1807, one hundred Congregational and seventy-six Baptist.[10] If these figures are even roughly accurate, they indicate that the proportion of Baptists to Congregationalists increased from about 15 percent to over 42 percent. And if one adds the numbers of other dissenting churches (Methodist, Freewill Baptists, Universalists, Christians), the dissenters would have had a majority by 1807. Ludlum pointed out, however, that Puritan Counter-Reformation began in Vermont after 1800 with the aid of the Connecticut and Massachusetts home missionary agencies. By 1820 they helped the Congregationalists to regain their predominant position, though the Congregationalists were able to compete with the dissenters only by dropping their strict Hopkinsian Calvinism and adopting the popular evangelical or Arminianized Calvinism of their competitors.[11]

It is characteristic of the frontier that the Baptists in Vermont in their early years were led by men who had been Baptists before they came to Vermont or who had been born in Baptist families before they came there. They were not native Vermonters. As one might also expect, these leaders, like the laymen to whom they preached, came predominantly from Rhode Island, eastern Connecticut and southeastern Massachusetts. Of the twenty-one prominent elders of the Shaftsbury Association during its first forty years, 1781–1820 (for whom Stephen Wright provided biographical data in his history of that Association), all of them were apparently born to Baptist parents. Seven came from southeastern Massachusetts, three from Rhode Island, two from eastern Connecticut, two from the Berkshire area, one from Hanover, New Hampshire. Only one was born in Vermont, and the others were from scattered towns in Massachusetts and Connecticut where there were Separate or Baptist churches. Most of them emigrated to Vermont either with their parents or soon after they became adults. Only two were ordained elders before they emigrated. Though the majority did not settle permanently in Vermont, almost all of them preached there at one

---

9. Henry Swan Dana, *History of Woodstock, Vermont* (Boston, 1889), pp. 373–386 and W. G. McLoughlin, "The Life of Elder Jabez Cottle," *New England Quarterly*, XXXVIII (1965), 375–386.

10. For these and other statistics see Ludlum, *Vermont*, p. 23; Benedict, *History*, I, 333–334, 353; A. H. Newman, *A History of the Baptist Churches in the United States* (New York, 1894), p. 271; Williston Walker, *A History of the Congregational Churches in the United States* (New York, 1894), pp. 309–310; and the minutes of the various Baptist associations.

11. Ludlum, *Vermont*, p. 40.

time or another (the Shaftsbury Association was not restricted to Vermont churches).[12] Also significant of the frontier is that the highest political offices in Vermont were not held by Vermont-born citizens until well into the nineteenth century.

Before the state constitution was formed in 1777, each Vermont town had a high degree of autonomy. But the settlers brought with them the principles and practices of a system with which they had been familiar in Massachusetts, Connecticut, and Rhode Island. The town meeting was the political forum and the selectmen the executors of the majority will. Where churches were organized, the towns played the customary role of concurring in the choice of the minister and in most towns, despite protests, the towns levied taxes for the building of the meetinghouse and the salary of the minister. In Bennington in the early years the strong Separate majority prevented any religious taxes from being levied, but after 1780, with the influx of other Congregationalists who did not share this view, a sufficient number of Separates apostasized from the Separate position to agree to levying taxes so long as the minister appointed shared their radical New Light views. The minority who opposed this left Bennington rather than submit. Even after the adoption of the state constitution, which incorporated the Massachusetts ecclesiastical system in principle, the General Assembly was slow to pass legislation to institute a uniform system of support for religion. The first such law was passed in 1783, and from that time until 1807, Vermont, like Massachusetts, was in the anomalous position of guaranteeing full liberty of conscience in its bill of rights while simultaneously requiring a general establishment of religion from which dissenters could be exempted only after they filed certificates. Unlike the people of Massachusetts and Connecticut, however, the people of Vermont were far more lenient in their execution of the certificate system. There are few instances of dissenters who were distrained or imprisoned for refusing to turn in certificates or because their certificates were declared invalid. "There is such a mixture [of religious views] in Vermont," wrote Isaac Backus in 1804, "that I have no account of great sufferings there." [13] And David Benedict, Backus's successor as Baptist historian, wrote of Vermont in 1812, "The Baptists in a few instances, and but a few, have been oppressed with these taxes." [14]

There was another reason for the low incidence of persecution for religious taxes in Vermont besides the general religious tolerance of the frontier milieu. This tolerance, or mutual respect, took the stigma off the certifi-

12. Stephen Wright, *History of the Shaftsbury Association* (Troy, 1835).

13. Isaac Backus, *An Abridgement of the Church History of New England* (Boston, 1804), p. 218. In discussing Vermont in the third volume of his history, published in 1795, Backus spoke less charitably of "the ministerial tyranny which has been carved into that wilderness from the states of Connecticut and the Massachusetts." *History,* II, 548.

14. Benedict, *History,* I, 351.

cate system itself. In Vermont the Baptists appear to have accepted the certificates not as a badge of inferiority or second-class citizenship but simply as a legal technicality designed to protect and guarantee their rights. This was the way in which the Congregationalists of Massachusetts and Connecticut had thought of the system. But where social and religious prejudice against the Baptists was strong, the certificates inevitably became symbols of this prejudice both to those "forced" to give them and those "forced" to accept them.

Nevertheless, the Baptists had, by 1777, developed scruples about church-state relations which transcended state boundaries. The principle of separation had come to include the refusal to acknowledge the right of the state to demand even this token of its authority of "the things which are God's." Although in Vermont it was more difficult to arouse the Baptists to a sense of righteous indignation against the certificate system than it was in Massachusetts or Connecticut, there were always enough Baptists and other dissenters who felt strongly about it to maintain a steady pressure for its abolition. It took them thirty years to obtain it.

Article Three of the Vermont constitution's Declaration of Rights indicated that even on the frontier in 1777 New Englanders had not yet thrown off their Puritan heritage. Though it was copied from a similar article in the Pennsylvania Bill of Rights, it added certain restrictive phrases (here italicized) which seriously altered the more liberal view of the Quaker State:

> That all men have a natural and unalienable right to worship Almighty God according to the dictates of their own consciences and understanding, regulated by the word of God; and that no man ought, or of right can be compelled to attend any religious worship, or erect or support any place of worship or maintain any minister contrary to the dictates of conscience; nor *can any man who professes the protestant religion,* be justly deprived or abridged of any civil rights, as a citizen, on account of his religious sentiment, or peculiar mode of religious worship, and that no authority can, or ought to be vested in, or assumed by, any power whatsoever, that shall in any case interfere with, or in any manner controul, the rights of conscience, in the free exercise of religious worship; *nevertheless, every sect or denomination of christians ought to observe the Sabbath, or the lord's day, and keep up, and support some sort of religious worship, which to them shall seem most agreeable to the revealed will of God.*

These additions to the Pennsylvania article deprived Vermont non-Protestants of civil rights (notably the right to hold office), in effect required every citizen to attend worship regularly,[15] and to contribute to the support of some form of revealed religion (presumably that of the King James

15. There is no evidence of any serious attempt in Vermont to enforce this requirement of church attendance.

Bible). This was clearly an establishment of Protestantism, though the constitution did not include any articles similar to Article Three of the Massachusetts Constitution describing the manner in which such an established religion should be supported.

This constitution also prescribed a religious test for officeholders requiring them to swear belief "in one God" who was "rewarder of the good and punisher of the wicked"; it also required acknowledgment that "the scriptures of the old and new testament" were "given by divine inspiration" and profession of "the protestant religion." By this means Jews, Roman Catholics, and probably deists and Universalists were presumably to be excluded from office.

Other clauses in the Vermont constitution gave the right of incorporation to all religious societies who applied to the legislature for it and stated that "Laws for the encouragement of virtue and prevention of vice and immorality shall be made and constantly kept in force." This constitution did not prescribe the kind of separation of church and state which Jefferson and Madison (or, in Pennsylvania, Benjamin Franklin) advocated. But it was probably not, on the face of it, opposed to the general principles of Backus and the Baptists, for it made no mention of compulsory religious taxes. Several Baptists were in the constitutional convention which drafted this constitution for Vermont and there is no evidence that they, or any other Baptist in the state, opposed any of the clauses in the constitution at that time. Nor did Backus ever write anything specifically about it. The vagueness of this constitution on religion has led some historians to assume erroneously that Vermont abolished religious taxes in 1777.

In 1781 the legislature passed the first specific law dealing with religious taxation. This law dealt only with levying religious taxes on the land of non-resident proprietors, but it was based on the clear assumption that a system of tax supported religion was already in effect in most towns. The act was specifically designed to strengthen this system of support for religion. Since "the value of the landed interest of the non-resident proprietors is greatly advanced by settlements being formed in the towns where such lands lie, and especially by public buildings being erected therein," the towns shall be permitted to levy taxes upon all except public land "not exceeding in the whole two pence per acre, for the purpose of building houses of public worship, school houses, and bridges." [16]

However, not until 1783 did the legislature pass a bill which clarified precisely how religious taxes were to be levied throughout the state and how

16. R. A. Perkins in "Early Relations of Church and State in Vermont" in *The Republican Observer* (White River Junction) January 31, 1879. In newly settled areas where much land, especially timberland, was held by non-resident for speculative purposes, the towns felt entitled to such a law. There were many precedents for it in Massachusetts, though usually such rights were granted to towns on an ad hoc basis after petition.

dissenters were to obtain exemption from them. The law was obviously a response to general confusion in the towns about the matter. It was a unique bill in the history of separationism, an elaborate attempt to create a general establishment of religion without giving preference to any particular group of believers and without obliging anyone who conscientiously objected to it to support the establishment. Far better than Article Three of the Massachusetts Constitution, it embodied the principle that the majority of voters in each town was to decide which religious denomination should constitute the established church in that town while simultaneously guaranteeing that all who belonged to any other sect should be exempt from paying taxes for the support of that establishment after presentation of certificates. Unlike the systems in Massachusetts and Connecticut — which, without specifically saying so, clearly favored the Congregationalists — the Vermont ecclesiastical system set forth in this law was an honest attempt to accommodate the religious diversity of the new state while retaining the principle of a general assessment for the support of the Protestant religion. One of the most significant aspects of the act was its requirement that two-thirds of a town's voters must agree on the choice of the minister; considering the diversity within each town, this meant that the major elements would have to be satisfied before any action could be taken.[17]

"An Act to enable Towns and Parishes to erect proper Houses for Public Worship and Support of Ministers of the Gospel" began by stating that it was "of the greatest Importance to the Community at large as well as to Individuals that the Precepts of Christianity and rules of Morality be publickly and statedly inculcated." Consequently whenever "any Town or Parish shall think themselves sufficiently able to build a Meetinghouse or settle a Minister" it was their duty to call a town meeting at which "two thirds of the Inhabitants of such Town or Parish" who were legal voters should "appoint a Place" for public worship and "vote a tax or taxes sufficient to defray the expence of such Building or Buildings, and also to hire or otherwise agree with a Minister or Ministers to preach in such Town or Parish." [18] The act specifically required that the two-thirds majority must be "of similar Sentiments with respect to the mode of Worship," but how this was to be determined the act did not say. Obviously it counted upon a large amount of tolerant good will and probably, in many towns, a willingness to

17. As in Massachusetts, the law gave no role to the church members in the choice of the ministers though tradition had always given the church a concurring voice, if not a veto. In many Vermont towns the action was taken jointly with the church. How strictly the clause requiring a "two-third" vote was adhered to is unknown, but it clearly gave minorities an important role in the decision of choosing a minister or laying religious taxes.

18. This provision was to prevent a minority from appearing at a meeting and passing a vote which bound all the other inhabitants. We have noted that this often happened in Massachusetts. The County Court was given the right to decide on the site of the meetinghouse in case of a disagreement in the town.

compromise somewhat in the direction of latitudinarianism or open communion. Otherwise it would be impossible for such a large majority to agree on a particular minister. As we shall see, this requirement also resulted in various efforts to divide up the use of the meetinghouse and tax support among irreconcilable denominationalists. Had not Americans been so pietistically sectarian, the kind of tolerant establishmentarianism which Vermont struggled with for thirty years might have worked. The Baptists in Vermont appear, like the other sects, to have been willing for a time to try it.

The act of course took pains to assert that "no Person shall be obliged to pay" religious taxes "who shall be hereafter described and exempted by this Act." But it also noted that there were "some perhaps who pretend to differ from the Majority with a Design only to escape Taxation." Therefore, tax exemption for conscientious dissenters required, as it did in Massachusetts and Connecticut, some form of certificate system. By the terms of the law

> every person or persons being of adult age shall be considered as being of Opinion with the major part [i.e., the two-thirds majority] of the Inhabitants within such Town or Parish where he, she or they shall dwell until, he, she, or they shall bring a certificate signed by some Minister of the Gospel, Deacon, or Elder or the Moderator in the church or Congregation to which he, she, or they pretend to belong.

Until a person produced such a certificate, he was "subject to pay all such Charges with the major part as by Law shall be assessed" for the support of the minister and meetinghouse in his town or parish.[19]

While the Baptists and other dissenters who were opposed in principle to a certificate system of any kind found this law of 1783 obnoxious, they had to admit that it was the most liberal certificate system yet devised in New England. The certificate had only to be signed by a deacon or elder and did not require him to attest to the conscientiousness of the adherent whom he certified. Nor did the law require that such a certificate must be submitted annually. Presumably once a dissenter's certificate was recorded by the town or parish clerk he was forever exempted from religious taxes. Most important, the dissenters did not have to pay the tax and then ask that it be paid to his own minister; once certified as "being of a different Persuasion" he was exempted from paying entirely — or at least until he changed

19. Ms. Laws of Vermont, I, 389–391, Vermont State Archives; and *Vermont State Papers,* ed. William Slade (Middlebury, 1823), I, 472–473. This act also contained a final clause stating that it did not apply to any church currently in existence until it applied for incorporation; it gave such churches one year to do this. This seems to indicate that certificates were to be accepted only from incorporated dissenting bodies, though in practice this was not done. There were at this time only six or seven Baptist churches in Vermont and only twelve to fifteen Congregational churches.

his persuasion. The act was also unique in its failure to specify by name which of the dissenting persuasions the state found acceptable. Whereas in Connecticut and Massachusetts the tax exemptions laws had specifically exempted only Quakers, Baptists, and Anglicans (so that even after 1780 the burden of proof fell upon the dissenters of all other sects before their Protestantism was considered legitimate), exemption in Vermont was hereby granted to any man certified as an adherent by "*some* Minister of the Gospel." Presumably a tax assessor could have denied that any Universalist, Shaker, or Methodist circuit rider was a legitimate minister of the gospel, but there is no record of any such challenge brought before the courts.

So far as available evidence is concerned, this act aroused no opposition from the Baptists or from any other dissenters. No petitions were presented; no Associations passed resolutions against it; no newspaper letters, tracts, or published sermons appeared. Town records indicate that the Baptists and other dissenters did file certificates under this law; probably in most places the act merely ratified a system already in operation. It posed no new threat to religious liberty and may have been taken by the Baptists as a helpful clarification and definition of their position. Apparently they were content, for they made no protest.

Two years later, however, in 1785 the legislature considered passing a bill which would have altered the system so as to pose a threat. Then the Baptists did protest. According to Elder John Peck, the bill proposed was one modeled on the Massachusetts system or perhaps it derived from the general assessment bill Patrick Henry and George Washington were then supporting in Virginia. It would have required every rateable taxpayer in each town to pay a tax for the support of religion. These funds would then have been distributed to the various churches in each town in proportion to the adherents of each denomination in that town. A Baptist layman named Asaph Fletcher, who lived in Cavendish, engaged in a spirited newspaper debate with a Congregational minister on the merits of the bill. According to Elder Peck, Fletcher's arguments were so convincing that the legislature decided against the bill.[20]

In 1786 the constitution of Vermont was revised and Article Three of the Declaration of Rights was rewritten. The phrase "who professes the protestant Religion" was omitted thereby granting religious liberty to deists, Jews, and Roman Catholics. And by the same token the word "Christians" was changed to "People" to extend the obligation to attend religious worship to all inhabitants. But the most important change was the omission of the words "and support" from the obligation of every sect or denomination toward religious worship.[21] However, the liberalization was more apparent

20. Crocker, *History,* p. 262. I have found no record of this bill or of the debate concerning it.
21. Ms. Laws of Vermont, II, 5, in the Vermont State Archives.

than real. Since the test oath for officeholders remained unchanged a requirement of belief in the old and new testaments still kept deists and Jews out of office and the requirement of belief in hell's punishments placed Universalists in an awkward position.[22] As for the omission of "and support" from the Declaration of Rights, this did not lead to invalidation or repeal of the law of 1783. Nor was there any attempt to repeal the state law requiring Sabbath attendance or the law prohibiting travel and business on the Sabbath.

When Vermont revised all of its laws in 1787 it added a clause to the act of 1783 for supporting ministers of the gospel which resolved the confusion regarding the incorporation of churches or congregations. The law of 1783 had implied that only incorporated religious bodies could legally obtain tax exemption through certificates. By the law of 1787 all religious bodies became automatically incorporated as soon as they formed an association to hire a minister or to build a meetinghouse.

> Be it enacted by the General Assembly of the State of Vermont that whenever any number or description of persons now included in any corporated Towns shall voluntarily associate and agree to hire or Settle a Minister of the Gospel or to build a house for public worship all contracts made by Such persons with Such Minister or with each other for the purposes aforesaid shall be valid and binding to all intent and purposes. And whenever such number of persons Shall agree to raise money by Subscription or upon the List of Polls or rateable estates of the persons associating it shall be lawful for the association to elect from time to time one or more meet persons to collect the same who shall be invested with the like powers and be liable to be proceeded against in like manner as Collectors of town rates by law are.

For the Baptists, the right by force of law to levy on and collect taxes from their own members was seldom thought desirable and few, if any, took advantage of it. But the new clause did clear up any doubts about their rights to give certificates to their members or adherents. Vermont was not going to adopt the precedents of the Massachusetts courts. Except for this, however, the law of 1783 was reenacted in 1787 virtually without change. Once again there was apparently no public protest by the Baptists or other dissenters.

Part of the constitution drawn up January 21, 1793, by the Baptist congregation, or society of Woodstock, provides a clear idea of the kinds of voluntary associations which the Baptists designed under this law and indicates that they opposed on the whole any system but a voluntary and free subscription for the support of the ministry:

> The light of Divine truth being in these latter days so far diffused abroad that it is found that in all religious establishments (so-called) which bind

22. In 1793 the test oath was revised to open this privilege to men of all faiths.

men in acts of building meetinghouses, settling ministers &c. which in their judgments they esteem themselves not benefited by, to be incompatible with, and repugnant to the nature of the gospel of peace which enjoins those who have received the truth in the love of it, that *as they have freely received, so freely give.* And it is well known that they are and ever have been not only very prejudicial to the cause of truth, piety and harmony, but have stirred up dissentions and animosities in towns and societies and been productive of cruel and bloody persecutions in states and kingdoms as all Europe can testify. And altho' we mean to pay all due respect to the memory of our pious ancesters who first emigrated from Europe to enjoy the benefits of gospel freedom; yet it must be confessed that they brought from that land of tyranny a tincture of religious oppression which quickly spread thro' church and state to the great detriment of religion itself as well as very injurious to those who suffered thereby both in their persons and estates. But we aim not at persons but facts, believing harsh judging and censuring to be condemned by the peaceable, passive spirit of the gospel; yet may we say without wrong to particular persons that we believe the confining the ministry of the gospel to a class of men who must of necessity be educated in some seminary of learning, and consequently crampt down by certain rules, notes, forms, &c. and their receiving approbation, license and ordination from none but their own brethren has a direct tendency to corrupt the simplicity of the gospel, and deprive the people of their inherent right of judging of the qualifications of their teachers and to impose such teachers on towns and parishes is a flagrant breach of justice and equality . . .

Therefore, We, the *United Baptist Society,* being guaranteed by the Constitution of the United States and the State of Vermont, and being fully convinced that religious and social worship ought to be kept up and maintained in towns and societies for the mutual edification of christians, and to propagate and increase the knowledge of the gospel among men in general, and also in special manner to inculcate and diffuse among our children and youth the wholesome precepts of christianity which are so essential to the forming their morals for civil life, as well as their future well-being in the coming world . . .

The Society pledge themselves to each other to support a public Teacher in a comfortable and decent manner by free contributions only . . .

Finally, as we wish to have this Society formed on the broad and firm basis of Christian liberty, no member thereof shall be subjected to any civil prosecution for the support of the gospel, nor shall this Society have power to vote any settled stipend for their minister, nor to collect by civil law any subscription for the above purpose. Yet the Society may expel any member whom they shall judge to be under the influence of a contracted, niggardly disposition in supporting the gospel or for any other behavior below the christian character.[23]

23. Dana, *Woodstock,* pp. 373–377. The Society had this statement printed in Spooner's *Vermont Journal,* February 11, 1793, which seems to indicate that it constituted a kind of Baptist Manifesto. While the members of the church were members of the society, not all the members of the society by any means were members of the church. For other details of this society and its constitution see below.

Probably the bulk of the self-incorporated Baptist societies or congregations in Vermont in these years adopted similar constitutions and acted on similar principles.

The only piece a Vermont Baptist wrote in these years on the problems of church and state was the election sermon Elder Caleb Blood preached to the Vermont legislature in 1792. Blood, the Elder of the Baptist Church in Shaftesbury, devoted three pages to the issue, quoting the election sermon of Elder Samuel Stillman to the Massachusetts legislature (in 1778) and paraphrasing Backus to the effect that "religion at all times is a matter between God and individuals." He was not vehement about the matter, but neither did he hide the fact that he thoroughly opposed "religious establishments by law" because "forcing men to support ministers is a damage both to church and state." It damaged the state and the church because it injured the consciences of good men and made conscienceless men even more hard-hearted and irreligious. Good men would contribute "freely" toward religion, and the irreligious would have to be won over by spiritual means.

Blood wished the legislators to understand, however, that true religious liberty "by no means prohibits the civil magistrate from enacting those laws that shall enforce observance of those precepts in the christian religion the violation of which is a breach of the civil peace . . . among others, that of observing the Sabbath should be enforced by the civil power." He left no doubt that he meant compulsory religious attendance as well as prohibition of all travel, work, and recreation on the Sabbath; "otherwise those irreligious persons who are so lost to virtue as neither to regard divine worship nor the appointed time for it" would disturb those who were worshipping, would "draw off our children" from worship, and would encourage wicked masters to force seven days of labor from their servants and apprentices. Consequently Blood, speaking no doubt for most of his denomination, firmly endorsed "those friendly aids to the cause of our holy religion which may justly be expected from our political fathers."

The dissenters' general mood of compliance with the existing system in Vermont was finally broken in the fall of 1794 when the Baptists made a concerted effort to obtain the repeal of the act of 1787 regarding the support of ministers. The leaders of this movement appear to have been Elisha Ransom, Ezra Butler, Roswell Mears, Elisha Andrews, John Spenser, Joseph Randall, and Richard Southgate. These men, some of them elders, some deacons and laymen, were among two hundred persons who signed various petitions presented to the General Assembly on October 11 and 13, 1794, for the repeal. The Baptist congregations in Clarendon, Woodstock and Wallingford seem to have originated the action; their petitions were identically worded. They claimed that the act of 1787 was "unconstitutional" because the third article of the Declaration of Rights stated "that all men have an unalianable right to worship God according to their own Consciences,

& that no man can of Right be compelled to maintain any Minister or place of Worship contrary thereto." [24] The petition signed by Butler, Mears, Andrews and others was more vehement in its claim: the act of 1787

> we conceive to be subversive of the Rights of conscience and Derogatory to the Spirit of the Constitution of the State of Vermont and of an exceeding dangerous Tendency depriving us of the sacred Rights of free citicens of the State of Vermont for it is our conscientious & avowed Sentiments that civil Authority have no Right to intermeddle with ecclesiastical affairs, and that we ought not either directly or indirectly to acknowledge their Power in those Matters — That the Church is in no sence dependent on the civil Power for its support — that there is no worrant in the word of God for coersive and forcible Means to be used in the support of Religion . . .

The petition signed by Richard Southgate and others called the act "both unconstitutional and oppressive to the peaceable subjects of the State" as well as "detrimental to the interest of true Religion" since it "has a tendency to increase the number of hypocrites and infidels, and to conceal their character as such; creating prejudices *among* different sects, and *against* divine Revelations; causing animosity and ill-will in society and disturbing the peace of neighbours." The petition signed by Elisha Ransom, Joseph Cottle and others of Woodstock, was the only one which implied that actual oppression of dissenters had taken place under the act by placing

> power in the hand of some against others & thereby drove them into the Courts of Common pleas to contend (at least some times) in vain for their Constitutional Rights which makes scarce their Portion & inheritance in the Constitution. We Pray, where is the God of [John] Lock, [Isaac] Watts, [Richard] Price, and [Thomas?] Pain for we fear our Constitution begining by degrees at length may be set at naught.

The inclusion of Thomas Paine in the petition, especially at a time when his *Age of Reason* had blackened his name throughout most of America, must be one of the few Baptist testimonies in his favor though it springs more from admiration for his love of freedom than for his anticlericalism. Yet there is a strongly anticlerical note in this petition which helps to account for the Baptists' admiration of Jefferson.

> Whatever good was intended by this Power put into the hands of Ecclesiasticks or Town & Parish we look upon it bad in its effects being the bane of Peace, the hinge of Contention: for as on the one hand all depraved nature is thirsting for Power the most ambicious that can gain a soficient majour [vote] in Town or Parish will improve it to set up his own Re-

24. *State Papers of Vermont: General Petitions,* ed. Allen Soule (Montpelier, 1958), X, 90–96.

ligion & then will not fail to domineer with an Iron Rod over the Consciences of others. The consequences are confiscation of goods & imprisonment attended with the loss of much time & money . . .

The most notable aspect in all five of these petitions was the predominance of political arguments in terms of Locke and the rights of man rather than of the old pietistic arguments in terms of Scripture and the rights of Christ. For the Baptists, as for the rest of America, Christ and culture were slowly becoming merged into one faith.

None of the petitions mentioned any concrete or specific cause for the origin of these petitions. One can only speculate that about this time the influx of additional Congregationalists and their missionaries began to produce more local conflicts over these matters than had prevailed during the earlier period when the dissenters were a larger proportion of the population. It may also be that at this time many towns, having passed through the most difficult period of conquering the wilderness, were now preparing to establish the more permanent and closely knit institutions of settled communities and it therefore became necessary to decide conclusively whether the old ecclesiastical system would or could be maintained, or whether it should be dropped entirely. Evidence for the former cause is available in the records of the General Association in Connecticut which, at its meeting in June 1793, designated eight missionaries "to the new settlements" and appointed a committee consisting of Ezra Stiles, Benjamin Trumbull, Jonathan Edwards, Jr., Nathan Williams, and Thomas Wells "to draw up a plan of missions and an address to the new Settlements" informing them of the benefits they would soon receive from these itinerants and soliciting donations both in Connecticut and in the new settlements themselves for their support.[25] These efforts were greeted by many in Vermont with the same animosity that the Puritans had shown earlier in the century toward the missionaries of the Society for the Propagation of the Gospel in Foreign Parts. Some of the letters the Connecticut newspapers received from Vermonters commenting upon these efforts indicate this.

One of these, addressed to Stiles and his committee and signed "Vermonters," appeared in the Connecticut *Courant* on December 23, 1793. It denounced the missionaries, all of whom were college graduates, as men who came to Vermont principally to speculate in land, to hobnob with the rich, and to stir up religious controversies among the people. Another letter signed "Freemen" of Vermont, appeared in the same journal on July 28, 1794, and was more detailed: "Will you print this," said the writers, "and thus inform the good people of Connecticut that their mission of Clergy is offensive to the inhabitants in general of Vermont . . . The 'crude divinity' sent from Connecticut has for many years impeded the progress of chris-

25. *The Records of the General Association of the Colony of Connecticut* (Hartford, 1888), p. 148, and Walker, *Congregationalists*, p. 312.

tianity. Vermonters are too well informed and too wise to adopt it." The people of Vermont, continued this letter

> are happy to treat clergymen with attention; but they enjoy too great felicity from having escaped the disagreeable effects of party colleges and the hierarchy of Massachusetts and Connecticut to introduce either here . . . We are not willing that any under the pretext of spreading the divine gospel system of piety and morality should undermine our religious liberty or perpetuate that domination by the union of clerical and civil power which prevails in Connecticut . . . Your ministers meetings are chiefly political clubs, self created, unconstitutional, secret, uncontrouled, unexamined and unprecedented in the oracles of heaven.[26]

Whether these letters were written by Baptists or by deists, they showed a common hostility to Connecticut's Congregational imperialism.

Whatever their origin, the petitions to end the certificate system and with it the general establishment of religion in Vermont met with stiff opposition. After they were read before the General Assembly the petitions were referred to a committee. On a motion by Ezra Butler, himself a member of the Assembly (and later a Baptist elder and the first Baptist Governor of the state), Elder Elisha Ransom was given liberty to appear before the Assembly and speak on behalf of the petitioners. The matter was then referred to a committee of one member from each county which drew up an amendment to the act of 1787. This proposed amendment granting dissenters the power to certify themselves would have considerably liberalized the certificate system along the lines taken three years earlier in Connecticut, but it was not a repeal of the system:

> It is hereby Enacted by the General Assembly of the State of Vermont that every person being of Adult Age shall be considered as being of Opinion with the Major part of the inhabitants of the Town or parish to which he, or she, or they belong unless he, she, or they shall make known to the town or parish Clerk by a certificate under his, her, or their own hand that he she or they are of a Different Denomination of Religious Worshippers and shall also in sd Certificate declare to what Sect or Denomination they actually do belong — and untill such Certificate shall be produced and shown to the town or parish Clerk (whose duty it shall be to record the same) Such person shall be subject to be rated . . . [27]

When Ezra Butler and Elisha Ransom stated that this amendment was an

26. Connecticut *Courant*, July 28, 1794, p. 3. The references to "self-created, unconstitutional, secret" organizations is obviously intended to turn George Washington's condemnation of the Democratic Clubs against the Federalists. Considering that the Baptists of Vermont were strongly Jeffersonian, there is a clear indication of political rivalry involved in this whole religious dispute.

27. Vermont State Papers (1793–1794), mss. "Laws," IV (no pagination), Vermont State Archives; *Vermont State Papers*, ed. Soule, X, 91, n. 21.

unsatisfactory answer to their petitions, the Assembly voted not to accept it, and there the matter ended. Elder Ransom wrote his comment on the affair to Isaac Backus a few months later:

> Five petitions were carried into the Vermont Assembly last fall, with more than two hundred signers, against the certificate law, and I went to speak for them; and after my averment that the certificate law was contrary to the rights of man, of conscience, the first, third, fourth and seventh articles of our constitution, and to itself, for it took away our rights and then offered to sell them back to us for a certificate, some stretched their mouths. And though no man contradicted me in one argument, yet they would shut their eyes, and say they could not see it so. I had many great friends in the house, but not a majority. They sent out a committee who altered the law much for the better, if any law could be good of that kind, which was that every man might assert his own sentiments to the town clerk, and that should answer; but because it would still be a bad law, and I would not thank them for it, and none of our friends would acknowledge it as a favor, it fell back to where it was before.[28]

Ransom concluded his account with a typical pietistic interpretation of his failure: "Only we have this to comfort us, The Lord reigneth, and their power is limited, and we shall have no more affliction than is needful for us. Duty is ours, the event is the Lord's."

In 1797 the state again repealed all of its laws and reenacted those it wished to keep. The act for the support of the gospel was reenacted with only minor changes, except that it this time specified the wording of the certificates:

> To all people to whom these present shall come — Greeting — Know ye that I, A.B., of &c. minister (or deacon &c. as the case may be) of the sect or denomination of christians known and distinguished by the name and appellation of congregationalist (or episcopalian, baptist, &c. as the case may be) do hereby certify that C. D. of _____ is of the same sect or denomination of the subscriber and that I, the said, A.B., a minister (or deacon &c. as the case may be) of the said sect of denomination in the town of _____ in the county of _____ and the state of _____ Attest A.B. minister &c. Dated at _____ this _____ day of _____ A.D.

There is no record of particular protests or petitions against the system at this time. But subsequently some petitions were presented, and in 1800 the Council of Censors declared the act of 1797 "Repugnant" and recommended that it be altered or abolished.[29] In 1801 the legislature amended

28. Backus, *History,* II, 548.
29. Ludlum, *Vermont,* p. 46.

the act by liberalizing the certificate along the same lines as those proposed in 1794 i.e., allowing dissenters to write their own certificates:

> Whereas many of the good citizens of this state have represented to the general assembly that the aforesaid act appears to them a direct violation of the third section of our bill of rights an infringement of those inalienable rights which the good of society never requires to be resigned, and a compulsion of conscience in religious worship, Therefore [be it enacted] . . . that every person of adult age being a legal voter in any town or parish shall be considered as of the religious opinion and sentiment of such society as is mentioned in said act and be liable to be taxed for the purposes mentioned in said act unless he shall previous to any vote authorised in and by said act deliver to the clerk of said town or parish a declaration in writing with his name thereto subscribed in the following words, viz. 'I do not agree in religious opinion with a majority of the inhabitants of this town (or parish as the case may be) L. R.' Which declaration it shall be the duty of the clerk of said town or parish immediately to enter on record in his office which declaration, recorded as aforesaid, shall exempt such person and his property from being taxed for the purposes mentioned in said act.[30]

By allowing each dissenter to write his own certificate and to sign himself off from the established system in his parish, the legislature of Vermont took the same stand which Connecticut had taken ten years earlier.[31]

Some credit for this liberalization of the ecclesiastical system must go to the Democratic-Republican Party which that year for the first time captured control of the Vermont legislature. Vermont, due largely to its frontier radicalism and its high proportion of dissenters, was the first of the New England states to abandon the Federalist Party which always maintained that the Standing Order of church and state was the only true bulwark of good government. But note that the Democratic-Republican Party in Vermont, as in the other New England states, did not consider itself committed to a policy of complete separation of church and state. No doubt the dissenters in Vermont, as elsewhere, recognized that their claims for religious liberty and equality would receive more sympathy from a legislature dominated by the party of Jefferson. But the party itself did not utilize the movement for disestablishment as a vehicle for obtaining votes — at least not in any direct, overt form of campaign promise or platform plank.

30. Ms. Laws of Vermont (1797–1805), IV, 305–306, November 3, 1801, Vermont State Archives.
31. See Crocker, *History,* p. 175. Crocker, writing as a Baptist minister in 1913, said that it was "over scrupulous" of the Baptists to refuse "to comply" with this minimal form of certification. Another section of this amendment stated that any one moving into a town was considered to be of the majority view unless he made out a certificate, and anyone who was already a member of the majority sect who wanted to leave it had to pay the prevailing taxes that had been levied before he could fill out a certificate and be exempted.

The Jeffersonians recognized that the dissenters were a minority in Vermont and that consequently the Congregationalists could not be ignored or alienated. There was more to be gained by treating the liberally inclined among the Congregationalists complaisantly than by coming out entirely for the dissenters. Hence the victories of the Jeffersonians in Vermont, as elsewhere in New England, were not indications that the fight for disestablishment had been won. The dissenters sometimes found it even more difficult to persuade the Democratic-Republicans than the Federalists to mix politics and religion. The Democratic-Republicans, apart from their desire not to alienate their Congregational supporters, considered it a matter of principle that politics and religion should be kept separate — a convenient excuse for claiming that the issues should be settled at the local level, in the towns and parishes, rather than disrupting the intricate balance of political and economic alliances at the state or national levels.

In Vermont, however, the Republican Party was in a less precarious position than it was in other New England states — less dependent upon placating a hostile alliance of established clergy and entrenched Federalists. Moreover, the Baptists, who had won early acceptance in the power elite were themselves prominent in the ranks of the new party (as they were not in other New England states). Two of the leading figures in the Republican Party in these years were Baptist elders — Aaron Leland of Chester and Ezra Butler of Waterbury. Ezra Butler was born in Lancaster, Massachusetts in 1763; he was raised by an elder brother who left the Congregational church in 1780 to become a Baptist and later an elder. At the age of sixteen Butler enlisted in the Revolutionary Army and when he was twenty-one he moved to Waterbury, Vermont. At that time, in 1785, there was only one family living there and only half a dozen dwellings within twenty-five miles. Here he built a home, married, and began carving a farm out of the forest. In 1787 he was converted through the efforts of an itinerant Baptist minister from Woodstock. But there was no Baptist church within forty miles of Waterbury, and it was not until the following year when Elder Joseph Call of Woodstock again passed through the area that Butler was immersed. Eventually he joined the Baptist church in Bolton, and in 1800, when a Baptist church was finally formed in Waterbury he was chosen as its pastor.

Meanwhile he had already entered politics, beginning as Town Clerk and Justice of the Peace in the early 1790's and then being elected to the lower house of the General Assembly in 1797. He served many terms here and was also appointed Chief Justice of the County Court. Later he was chosen to the upper house of the legislature; he served a term in Congress (1813–1815) and climaxed his career as governor of the state from 1826 to 1828. As governor his principal contributions were his efforts to suppress lotteries and to improve the public schools. During all of these years, however, he remained a regular and faithful pastor of his church in Waterbury from which he received no stated salary and very little in voluntary gifts.[32]

Aaron Leland was born in Holliston, Massachusetts in 1761. He became a Baptist in 1785 and shortly thereafter was granted a license as an itinerant preacher by the church in Bellingham. After several visits to Chester, Vermont he made enough converts to form a church over which he was settled as pastor in 1789. He continued to itinerate and at least half a dozen churches in the neighboring areas owed their existence to his preaching. His parish was too poor to give him any salary and he supported his family by farming. Like Butler, he entered politics as a Jeffersonian in the 1790's and after serving at the town level was elected to the legislature in 1801 where he served nine successive terms. For three of these terms he was Speaker of the House and for four a member of the Governor's Council. Also like Butler he was appointed to the bench and served eighteen years on the County Court. In 1822 he was elected lieutenant governor of the state and after serving in this office for six years he was proposed as a candidate for governor in 1828. He is reported to have turned down this nomination because "the claims of that high station seemed to him incompatible with the duties of the Christian ministry." His principal efforts in office were to promote the temperance movement and to improve ministerial education. For his efforts in the latter field he was made a fellow of Middlebury College (a Congregational institution), and he received honorary degrees from both Middlebury and from Brown University. Like Butler, he continued to minister to his church throughout his life, and at his death in 1833 he was engaged in a vigorous revival meeting in his church.[33]

The effort to repeal the ecclesiastical law of 1797 began in the session of 1806, but despite Butler's and Leland's vigorous support of the repeal, the legislature refused to take any action. In 1807 the Council of Censors once again declared the law repugnant to the constitutional guarantees of religious liberty and finally, in that session, with the help of Leland as Speaker of the House and Butler in the Council, the Assembly passed the following act which put an end to the system of compulsory tax support for religion in Vermont:

> Whereas the late Council of Censors have recommended to the legislature to repeal an act entitled 'An Act in addition to and alteration of an Act for the support of the Gospel' passed on the third of November 1801

32. William B. Sprague, *Annals of the American Pulpit* (New York, 1860), VI, 411–416. As noted above in Chapters 39 and 40, the Massachusetts Baptists tended to withdraw from political activity after 1800 and Leland's and Butler's careers were something of an embarassment to them. David Benedict, writing in 1812, felt it necessary to apologize for them: "It is generally thought that our ministering brethren had better keep at home than to engage in the bustle of political affairs. But on this occasion [in Vermont in 1807] these two ministers did much good." *History*, II, 352–353.

33. *Ibid.*, VI, 240–242.

and the second, third, fourth, fifth, and sixth sections of an Act entitled 'An Act for the support of the gospel' passed October 26th 1797 and Whereas it appears to this assembly that the said act and sections, the better to promote harmony and good Order in civil society, ought to be repealed, therefore, It is hereby enacted by the General Assembly of the State of Vermont that the Act and sections aforesaid be and the same are hereby repealed.[34]

Although the Baptists took the lead in this effort, as the Baptist historian, David Benedict said, "They were seconded by many gentlemen of different persuasions." Many of the Congregational clergy and Federalist politicians considered this act a horrendous mistake which would loose the forces of anarchy and lead to the withering away of the churches. The *Dartmouth Gazette,* a staunch Federalist journal, stated on November 18, 1807 that this was "another striking instance of the pernicious, the direful, the infernal consequences to which the leveling spirit of democracy must inevitably tend. It discloses at once its great and only object, viz. the eradication of every moral, virtuous, and religious principle from the human heart." [35] And the Rev. Thomas Robbins of East Windsor, Connecticut, noted in his diary on November 24, 1807: "The Legislature of [Vermont] have lately annulled all their laws for the support of the gospel. We have almost ceased to be a Christian nation." [36] But Benedict, writing four years later, made a more judicious estimate and held up the example of Vermont as one which Massachusetts, Connecticut, and New Hampshire should emulate:

> Many had very alarming apprehensions of the levelling consequences of this law; none of them, however, have been realized. There were at this time about a hundred Congregational ministers settled in this State, but not one of them was displaced in consequence of this law. They were a worthy set of men, and as soon as their churches and congregations saw the law was repealed which empowered them to raise money for their support, they set about raising it in other ways, and all of them were supported as well without law as they had been with.

This, said Benedict, would doubtless be the case generally in other New England states:

> But the ministers there have so long been accustomed to lean on the strong arm of the civil power for their support, that they are afraid to stand up and trust to the voluntary contributions of their flocks. And it is highly probable that many of them would make out poorly indeed. But those who are worth having would be supported, and those who are

34. Ms. Laws of Vermont (1805–1810), V, 150, Vermont State Archives. Ludlum, *Vermont,* pp. 46–47; Benedict, *History,* I, 351–353.
35. Ludlum, *Vermont,* p. 47.
36. Thomas Robbins, *Diary,* ed., I. N. Tarbox (Boston, 1887), I, 340

not, ought to dig for themselves, and it is no matter how soon they are displaced.[37]

Benedict displayed quite frankly here the nineteenth century competitive individualism in religious affairs which the Puritans had always viewed with alarm and which amounted to a policy of survival of the fittest among the ministerial profession — a fitness determined all too often by the preacher's ability to be pliant, popular, and patronizing toward his parishioners. The Baptists were clearly looking to the future. They displayed a faith in the wisdom and pietism of the common man which the Congregational-Federalists still lacked.

37. Benedict, *History*, I, 353.

Chapter 42

The Baptists and the Vermont Glebelands, 1790–1820

In the act of the legislature passed in 1794, appropriating the rents and profits of the Glebe rights for the support of religious worship, they were to be distributed, when there was more than one religious teacher, in proportion to the number of rateable polls belonging to the respective congregations resident in the town.

Supreme Court of Vermont, 1839 (Gardiner *v.* Rogers)

Considering that Vermont operated under a system of compulsory religious taxation for over half a century and that in the majority of the state's 259 towns the Congregationalists were dominant, it is surprising how few cases of actual prosecution of dissenters occurred. But even admitting that the frontier produced, through selectivity of inhabitants and circumstances of environment, a tendency toward equalitarianism and toleration, religious animosities were still there, as were the stubborn intransigence of individuals who believed either that laws were meant to be obeyed or that the higher law was superior to man-made law. While the Baptist associations in Vermont, as others elsewhere in the 1790's, exhorted their members not to give certificates to the assessors most Vermont Baptists did so — though in some cases they were granted exemption by the Congregationalists even when they did not.[1] Despite what would appear to be the higher proportion of radical pietism in Vermont, both quantitatively and qualitatively, the question of religious taxation seems to have followed the same pattern there after 1790 that it did elsewhere in New England. Pietists on both sides preferred to compete with each other in saving souls and building new churches rather than in quarreling over a decadent ecclesiastical system.

During the period from 1725 to 1807 when Vermont lived under an established church system, only two cases are recorded in which Baptists were, or claim to have been, persecuted for failure to pay religious taxes.

1. Isaac Backus, ms. "Diary," XII, 117 (September 16, 1794), in the BP(AN).

One of these occurred in Hartford in 1795, the other in Bethel in 1796. Doubtless there were other cases, but there is no record of them, even by allusion. All that is known of the Hartford case comes from a letter which Elder Elisha Ransom of Woodstock wrote to Isaac Backus on March 23, 1795:

> A brother living in Hartford, in Vermont, belonging to Elder Drew's church, has suffered much about rates from another denomination. He was first carried to gaol, and then came out by paying the money, and prosecuted them in vain, for he was beat three times. I cannot ascertain the costs, for his last trial was the last day of February past; but it is supposed that his costs will be above fifty pounds.[2]

Backus made a trip to Woodstock in September 1796, to attend the meeting of the Woodstock Association and noted in his diary that there he met John Bennet, the man who had been carried to gaol for not paying his religious tax in Hartford. But he noted, "Mr. Gross, the [Congregational] minister of the town has since given up the practice of being supported by tax and compulsion." [3] Thus, despite the courts, the episode concluded with a local victory or concession to the Baptists.

The Bethel incident is known only through a petition made to the General Assembly in 1802 by Baptist Amasa Green. Green claimed that he had given in a certificate as a Baptist to the town clerk in Bethel in 1792. But in 1796 the Rev. Thomas Russell, the Congregational minister of the town, won a suit against the town for arrearages in his salary. The town therefore levied a tax on all its inhabitants to raise the unpaid salary and Green, among other dissenters, was asked to pay his proportion. When he refused to do so, he was distrained of two steers which were sold at auction to pay his tax. He then sued the town selectmen, Simeon Chase and Stephen Cleaveland, to regain his money. He lost his case before a Justice of the Peace and he lost his appeals before the County Court and the state Supreme Court. But he had reason to hope for some success from his petition to the General Assembly not only because it was controlled by the Democratic-Republicans but because the Supreme Court judges were split in their decision, two to one; the one who favored Green was Chief Justice Jonathan Robinson. Green claimed that by ruling that "all the certificate men" were required to pay the tax for Russell's salary, the court "necessarily involves the ruin of our liberties and rights of conscience and establishes a precedent for every town in this state to compel the Quakers and every denomination of Christians within such town to pay a proportion of past expenditures in settling and hiring ministers and [it

2. Isaac Backus, *History of New England,* ed. David Weston (Newton, 1871), II, 548.
3. Backus, ms. "Diary," XII, 152 (September 28, 1796).

has done] that by a wicked evasion of the statute and constitution made to protect the rights of conscience . . ." [4] The Assembly appointed a committee to look into the matter, but the committee ruled that "the matters therein stated are not supported and that the prayer thereof ought not to be granted." Thus the matter ended. Whether the committee discovered that the facts were not as Green had presented them or whether they believed that because the tax was levied to pay off a judgment of a suit against the town rather than specifically to pay the salary of Russell, was not clear. Green's fear, however, was not realized since the Supreme Court's decision did not abrogate the certificate system and subject all "certificate men" to religious taxation.

Absence of any other evidence of persecution of Baptists, either in extant court records or petitions or in general statements of opposition to the established system, would seem to indicate Backus was correct that such incidents were relatively rare and unimportant in Vermont. Thus it does not mean that Baptists in some towns and parishes never resented the certificate system and never refused to pay taxes levied on them when they failed to give in certificates. Rather it indicates that when this happened the towns and parishes did not usually press the point and take advantage of their legal right to distrain or imprison the delinquent. For example, the Congregational majority in Woodstock North Parish levied taxes for the support of their ministers from 1776 to 1792, and the Baptists appear not only to have refused to pay them but also to have refused to give in certificates. No evidence exists that they were ever distrained or jailed but as the constitution of their United Baptist Society stated in its preamble in 1793, "our Congregational Brothers have often called upon some of us, wishing to know our sentiments respecting supporting the gospel." [5]

The town of Pomfret began levying ministerial taxes in 1774, but after it met with resistance from some non-Congregationalists it voted in 1781 "that the stiddy herers Bee taxed for the last year's Servis." [6] By this the town meant to exclude those who were not "steady hearers," at least for that year. Taxes continued to be levied, however, "on the Grand list," and not until 1787 did the town clerk record the first certificate. For those who did not file certificates but who nevertheless refused to pay their religious taxes, the town voted in 1790, 1792, 1793, and 1794, to "abate" or

4. Ms. petition in Vermont State Archives, Volume 43, Vermont State Papers, Petitions, October 1800–October 1802.

5. H. S. Dana, *History of Woodstock* (Boston, 1889), pp. 373–377. That the Woodstock Baptists refused to give certificates is unknown, but it seems likely.

6. For this and other details regarding Pomfret, see H. H. Vail, *Pomfret, Vermont* (Boston, 1930), I, 212–230, and R. A. Perkins, "Early Relations of Church and State in Vermont," *The Republican Observer* (White River Junction), January 31, 1879.

rescind their taxes. This left the Rev. Elisha Hutchinson considerably deficient in his pay, but for various other reasons the town decided to dismiss him in 1794.[7] Meanwhile the number of "certificate men" in the town had increased to a total of 76 by that year. The town had only occasional preaching thereafter until in 1802 it voted "not to raise money by tax" for ministerial purposes but "to raise money by Covenant" or subscription.[8] Despite the town's obvious need for the money and its legal right to tax those without certificates, it appears to have acted typically in refusing to press the issue to the point of prosecution.

Although religious taxes were not a serious problem in Vermont, another church-state issue frequently did involve the Baptists in quarrels with the Congregationalists. These arose over their conflicting claims to the "minister's right" and the "ministry lands," or what were popularly called the "glebe lands" in the various towns. The significance of these disputes lies not so much in the realm of persecution or prejudice as in the inconsistency of the Baptist position toward separation of church and state. For the Baptists were not only willing but eager to obtain land from the towns to aid them in the support of their ministers and churches and in certain cases they claimed it as their right. This issue underscores again the New England Baptists' belief that the state had a duty to encourage religion rather than to maintain a high wall of separation which might encourage secularism.

Of the 128 town charters in Vermont which Governor Benning Wentworth issued as "the New Hampshire grants" between 1741 and 1764, almost all of them set aside four "shares" of land (about 250 acres constituting a share) for public purposes: one share was to go to the SPG; one was to support the Church of England in the town; one was to support the town school; and one was to be given to "the first settled minister" in the town. And in the 131 town charters which the state of Vermont issued (mostly between 1779 and 1782) five shares or "rights" (also of about 250 acres each) were set aside for public purposes: one for a state college (ultimately the University of Vermont, founded in 1791); one for the county grammar or Latin school; one for the town common, or English, school; one for the support of "the social worship of God" (sometimes phrased "for the support of the preaching of the gospel" or "support of the ministry"); and one to be given to "the first settled minister" as his "settlement" or "encouragement" to settle in the wilderness. The Baptists became involved in quarrels over the share for the first settled minister

7. Hutchinson, who had moved to Zoar, Massachusetts, became a Baptist, Vail, *Pomfret*, I, 222.

8. *Ibid.*, I, 223. Some of the certificate men were Congregationalists who, from dislike for Hutchinson or because of the bitter local feud over a meetinghouse site in these years, preferred to join the Congregational church in Woodstock.

(usually referred to as "the Minister's right") in many towns as well as over the share for the support of the ministry (the glebe land).[9]

The courts of Vermont took a peculiar view concerning all of these "lease lands" in claiming that except for the minister's right, all of them were to be held in permanent trust by the towns (or their selectmen) for the benefit of living and future generations. Therefore the towns could not alienate or sell these shares (as they often did in Massachusetts and Connecticut); they could only lease them. However, regarding the minister's right, the courts held, as they had in Massachusetts, Connecticut, and New Hampshire, that this land could be granted by the town in fee simple to the first settled minister and that thereafter it was his private property to dispose of as he saw fit. The courts also ruled that all of the lease lands, as well as the minister's right, were forever tax exempt (although buildings on these lands were not). Thus the minister's right to 250 acres of tax-free land, especially if it were good farming or timberland, was an extremely valuable gift at the town's disposal and it is not surprising that the various denominations coveted it greatly. Similarly, any denomination which gained the right to the ministry land, or glebe lands, obtained a very valuable permanent endowment for its local church. We have noted that in Massachusetts, in the early decades of the nineteenth century, that although several Baptist ministers sued for a share of the income from the ministerial lands in their towns, they never won these suits. The Massachusetts courts ruled that the land was designed originally for the Congregational church, or rather for the parish and that it must remain theirs (unless the parish itself voted to divide it with other sects). Nor were the Baptists in Massachusetts ever able to obtain the right to the minister's lot, since they could not show that they were learned, pious, and orthodox settled ministers within the meaning of the law.

But the ecclesiastical laws in Vermont were not designed, either by Governor Wentworth (himself an Anglican) nor by the state, primarily to benefit the Congregationalists. And the town charters left the meaning of the designation "minister" purposely vague. Eventually, in the early nineteenth century, the courts decided that the decisions as to who was a minister of the gospel and what was a Christian church were to be left to the discretion of the town officers, the selectmen. But in the eighteenth century the town meeting made this decision, for it was assumed to be the right of each town to settle whatever minister it wanted on whatever terms it wanted. The courts generally required only that the minister be ordained

---

9. In some town charters not all of these rights were included. For these exceptions see Walter T. Bogart, *The Vermont Lease Lands* (Montpelier, 1950), App. A. Bogart provides a thorough and illuminating account of these "lease lands" and the quarrels concerning them. I have relied heavily on his book for these observations on the problem.

by the customary rites of his sect, that his denomination be a recognizably Christian (or Protestant) one, and that his choice be acknowledged by vote of the town for him to be qualified to receive the minister's rights and for his church to be qualified to receive the income from the ministry lands.[10]

Nowhere did any Baptist discuss why he or his ministers were entitled to these shares of land. They simply accepted them as their due. Some apparently had scruples about doing so, but there is no extant statement of these scruples. The closest approach to such a discussion occurs in Elias Smith's autobiography. Writing in 1816 and looking back to his early years as an itinerant Baptist preacher in Vermont, Smith said that in 1791 he received a call from the people of Danville "to settle with them as the minister of the town and to give me the land which was designed for the first settled minister." Smith refused the call because, "I had left all for Christ and thought it wrong and contrary to the new-testament to accept of such an offer [of 200 acres]." Besides, he said, he felt that he had a call to be an itinerant evangelist and preferred not to be bound to one township.[11] Smith's reaction was apparently unusual and the town of Danville soon found another Baptist willing to accept the position and the land. There is no record of how many towns did settle Baptist ministers or of how many of these ministers received the minister's right as the first settled minister; it would probably be a fair estimate to say that this happened in at least a score or more places.

More common, however, was for a town to have such a divided population by the time it was ready or able to settle a minister that the Congregationalists and the Baptists (and occasionally other sects) agreed to split the ministerial lands (or rights) and minister's rights between them. In some towns the people were so loathe to see this tax-free property in the hands of an individual who might sell it and leave town, keeping the money for himself, that they stipulated with the minister who first settled there that he must deed the property back to the town either at his departure, or at his death, or, in some cases, immediately. At the same time, since most towns were too poor to support the building of two or more meetinghouses in addition to supporting two or more ministers, existing denominations often made arrangements to share the use of the meetinghouse between them, thereby preventing the dilemma which occurred so often in Massachusetts in which the town levied taxes on all citizens for building what

10. The absence of court records before 1806 — or really before 1826 — makes it impossible to say precisely how the courts did define these terms, but from the actions in town meetings it is possible to surmise what the courts expected in this matter, assuming the towns were trying to meet the legal criteria. Bogart, *Lease Lands,* p. 308.

11. Elias Smith, *The Life, Conversion, Preaching, Travelings and Sufferings of Elias Smith* (Portsmouth, 1816), I, 205. In 1792 he again turned down an offer from the town of Stratham to become "the town's minister"; p. 206.

was considered a town hall and then used this building as the place of worship of the Congregational church. Eventually here, as elsewhere in New England, the people of Vermont separated the function of the town hall from that of the "social worship" of the parish majority — partly to separate church and state more effectively, but partly also because increasing prosperity and denominational rivalry dictated the policy of having a separate meetinghouse with regular Sunday services for each denomination.

In recognition of the multiplicity of sects in the various towns and the consequent struggles over the distribution of the ministerial lands and the income from other lease lands, the legislature passed several acts over the years designed to encourage the division of the land and the money among the various denominations and to provide general regulations for this purpose. These were summarized by a court decision in 1839:

> In the act of the legislature, passed in 1794, appropriating the rents and profits of the Glebe rights for the support of religious worship, they were to be distributed, when there was more than one religious teacher, in proportion to the number of rateable polls belonging to the respective congregations resident in the town. The rents of the ministerial lands, by another act passed in 1798, were to be applied to the use of the several settled ministers, in proportion to the number of their several congregations. By an act passed in 1818 the rents of the same lands were appropriated to the use of the religious society or societies in such towns in proportion to the number of which said society consists . . . [and] it must be to some society or association where there is a minister officiating, and it must be contributed to the support of the gospel.[12]

Neither the legislature nor the courts were consistent in their approach to these problems, however. Much legislation concerning the glebelands was repealed or revised or declared unconstitutional, and over the years many court decisions were reversed and practices modified. In most cases, however, the issue was settled in the first, and often in the final, instance by the towns themselves. Some examples will illustrate the varied aspects of and solutions to the problems these lands raised.

The town of Wallingford was settled in the 1770's and in February 1780, twenty-two persons (some of whom lived in Clarendon) joined in organizing a Baptist church which grew steadily until it had 225 members in 1805.

12. Bogart, *Lease Lands,* pp. 190–191, quoting the court in Gardiner *v.* Rogers, 11 Vt. 334, 337 (1839). In 1794 and 1805 the legislature passed acts declaring that the rights which had been set aside for the Church of England should be used for the public schools or else shared among all religious sects. Though the Episcopalians sued to have these laws set aside the court upheld them. However, when the legislature tried to divest the SPG of its rights by giving them to the towns, the courts declared the law unconstitutional because it was contrary to the Treaty of Paris (which guaranteed rights to legal corporations in Britain). See Bogart, *Lease Lands,* pp. 72, 216–220, 245, 261, for discussions of these issues. For interesting reactions to the law of 1794 by Episcopalians see *Connecticut Courant,* July 18, 1796 and September 19, 1796.

A Quaker group was formed in the town in 1777, but no Congregational church was organized until 1792. For the first seven years of its existence the Baptist church had no pastor, but in 1787 Henry Green was ordained; he remained over the church until 1807. The town meeting concurred in the choice of Green in 1787. This constituted legal recognition that he was the first settled minister of the town and that therefore he was entitled to the minister's right. (Wallingford as a Wentworth grant had no right set aside for the support of the ministry.) However, some of the Congregationalists in the town protested against Green's receiving the grant on the grounds that they were planning to form a church soon and that they would need some help in obtaining a minister. The town compromised by appointing a committee to suggest some form of division of the land. On October 3, 1787 this committee reported "That the right of land for the first settled minister in town be equally divided, in quantity and quality, between the Presbyterian [i.e., Congregational] and Baptist churches. The two groups agreed to this and the town so voted.[13] Green, however, remained the official minister of the town and in 1793 the problem of levying taxes for a meetinghouse for the town arose.

At first the Baptists planned to build the meetinghouse from their own subscriptions, though the church voted that it would permit Congregational or Presbyterian ministers to preach in it after they were approved by a Baptist committee. The Baptists asked the town, which needed a meetinghouse for its secular business, to concur in this arrangement in exchange for being allowed to use the Baptist meetinghouse for town meetings. On December 24, 1793, the town confirmed that Elder Green was "a minister for the town of Wallingford" and officially made him a member of a committee "for the examination and approbation of regular ministers of the Baptist, Congregational, and Presbyterian orders to preach with us occasionally." But after the town agreed that the Baptist meetinghouse would be the official meetinghouse for town affairs, they then began to dispute its site. To persuade the Baptists to build the meetinghouse where it would be most convenient for the town rather than for the Baptists, the town reached an agreement to raise at least part of the cost of the building by levying a general tax on all inhabitants. The Congregationalists evidently concurred in this, for thereafter both denominations met in the same building.

Although Elder Green was the legal minister of the town, however, and although they were entitled to do so, the Baptists never tried to raise his salary by taxation. Instead, the deacons of the church assessed the Baptists according to their property valuation and subjected to church censure (for covetousness) any member who failed to pay the annual amount he was assessed. Green's salary was forty dollars a year until 1805, when it was

13. S. H. Archibald, *Historical Sketch of the First 100 Years of the Baptist Church in Wallingford, Vermont* (Rutland, 1880), pp. 12–13.

raised to one hundred dollars. But this sum proved to be too much for the Baptists to raise and in 1807 Green left the church for its failure to keep its promise.

A less amicable compromise was tried unsuccessfully in Poultney. Poultney was settled in 1771, and several Baptists from Canaan, Connecticut, were among the early settlers. They organized a Baptist church of ten to twelve members in 1782, but instead of trying to find an elder of their own, they united with the Congregational church in the town. The Congregationalists were willing to have open-communion with the Baptists, though they agreed to disagree about infant baptism. The Baptists also agreed to pay the religious taxes levied for the support of this open-communion Congregational minister, a man named Ithamar Hibbard who had formerly been a member of the Separate church founded in Bennington. In 1782 the town voted to erect a meetinghouse financed partly by voluntary contributions and partly by taxation. In 1785, however, some of the Congregationalists withdrew from the church after disagreeing with Hibbard. The Baptists, fearing that this group would try to deprive Hibbard of his right to the minister's land on the grounds that he had never been formally ordained, called a council of Congregational ministers who formally installed him in 1788. Then in 1795 the Baptists gave up the practice of open-communion and left Hibbard's church to become members of the Baptist church in Middletown. The following year Hibbard was dismissed from the church and for four years the Congregationalists tried unsuccessfully to find a replacement for him. Rather than see the town go without preaching, the Congregationalists asked the Baptists to find a minister for the town. The Baptists agreed and called Elder Clark Kendrick who was then preaching in Salem, New York. The town officially concurred in this call to Kendrick to be its minister and he accepted. However, Kendrick was opposed to open-communion with pedobaptists, and although he had no objection to their attending his services, he felt they should not be acknowledged as members of his church. His solution was to transform the town church into a closed-communion Baptist church and to force those Congregationalists who would not become Baptists to form a church of their own. About thirty Congregationalists became Baptists and joined the thirty-four Baptists who ordained Kendrick in 1802 over the newly constituted church. The other Congregationalists called a minister for themselves, the Rev. Samuel Leonard. Since Kendrick no longer claimed to be the minister of the town, a dispute at once arose over the use of the town meetinghouse. But this dispute was settled in 1803 by the Congregationalists' decision to build their own church. Animosity still remained. In 1807 some disgruntled Congregationalists, who disliked both Kendrick's Jeffersonian political views and the Baptists, accused Kendrick of certain misdemeanors which were discussed in the newspapers and then tried in the courts. A Baptist council investigated the charges and exonerated

Kendrick, as did the courts. After his acquittal, matters became peaceful and he remained as elder in Poultney until his death in 1824. In 1817 he was honored by being appointed chaplain to the Vermont legislature.[14] This sequence of events could never have happened in Massachusetts or Connecticut.

The Baptist minister of Hardwick, who took the opposing stand on open-communion from Kendrick, found himself in an even more anomalous position. Elder Amos Tuttle had been pastor of a Baptist church in Litchfield, Connecticut before he moved to Hardwick in 1795. Here he formed a church of Baptists from Hardwick and from the neighboring towns of Walden and Greensboro. In April 1796, the town voted that Tuttle should obtain the minister's right as the first settled minister; his services were attended by all inhabitants, Congregational as well as Baptists. When the Baptists decided to practice closed-communion, they could not persuade Tuttle to join them, so they left his church. Tuttle thus remained until 1806 as the Baptist elder of a church made up almost entirely of Congregationalists. Then he left Hardwick to accept the pastorate of a Baptist church in Fairfax.[15]

A case where a Baptist minister sued for a ministerial right and won happened in Pownal in 1789. Elder Benjamin Garner (Gardner) had been ordained over a Baptist church in West Greenwich, Rhode Island in 1751, but he moved to Pownal and gathered a Baptist church there in 1772. A revival meeting following an epidemic of sickness in 1773 increased the membership by sixty under Garner's fervent preaching. According to a contemporary account "He has been variable in his Sentiments: Some part of his Life he has been a high-flying Calvinist; but for a Number of years past he has opposed the Doctrine of Election with all his Power, declaring that the Doctrine came from Hell and was a damnable Doctrine." [16] In addition to wavering in his doctrinal principles, "Elder Garner's conduct was not as savory as could be wished for." Soon after the great revival in Pownal "Elder Garner's Sin which easily beset him (Freedom with Women)'" led to a scandal which disorganized the church for some time. Garner was dismissed. In 1782 the church was reorganized by another Rhode Island minister, Francis Bennett. In 1788 Elder Caleb Nichols was

14. William B. Sprague, *Annals of the American Pulpit* (New York, 1860), VI, 381–382; John Goadby, *Remembrances of Past Years* (Rutland, 1852).

15. Henry Crocker, *History of the Baptists in Vermont* (Bellows Falls, 1913), p. 341.

16. See ms. accounts of the histories of the Baptist churches in Stephentown, Petersbury, Pownal First and Pownal Second among the BP(AN). This 26 page ms. is unsigned and undated but it has all the earmarks of being written by John Leland and was obviously sent to Backus for use in his *History*. Also Backus, *History,* II, 547. David Benedict, in his *A General History of the Baptist Denomination in America*, 2 vols. (Boston, 1813), I, 337–338, attributes this ms. to Leland. Crocker, *History,* p. 23.

chosen as pastor.[17] Garner remained in Pownal, however, and in 1789, he sued the town for the minister's right because he claimed that he was the first settled minister in the town. Though he had never been officially chosen as the town's minister this was not considered necessary (as it was in Massachusetts) for him to claim the minister's lot. Garner won his suit, but in an unexplained gesture of magnanimity he deeded it to the town to be used for the support of the town minister.

Another instance of this kind involved Elder Isaac Sawyer of Monkton who was ordained over the Baptist church in that town in 1799. When the town refused to grant him the minister's right he brought suit against it. He began his suit in 1805 but did not succeed in winning it until 1812. By then he had become so engrossed in the pursuit of the land that his congregation began to accuse him of covetousness, and he gave up his pastorate soon after he had won what he coveted.[18]

But in most cases no suit was necessary and the Baptist elders showed little covetousness. Elder Isaac Webb was the first settled minister in Brandon, in 1789, but he generously agreed to accept only half of the land to which he was entitled so that the Congregationalists in the town could have the remainder for their minister when they got one.[19] Elder Simeon Coombs became joint pastor over the churches of Jamaica and Wardsboro in 1793, and when he became the full-time pastor in Jamaica in 1803 he was given half of the minister's right in the town. When he left the town two years later for another pastorate he deeded to the town those parts of his land on which the Baptist meetinghouse, parsonage, and cemetery were located.[20]

On the other hand, Elder Hezekiah Eastman, who gathered a small Baptist church in Danby in 1780, left the town within a few months after he had been given the minister's right as the first settled minister. He caused considerable bitterness both among his followers and with the rest of the town because he simply sold his land to the highest bidder, even though he had every legal right to do so.[21] Baptists in the town of Bradford formed a church in 1795 at just about the same time as the Congregational

17. The ms. history of the Pownal church mentioned in note 16, above, contains the following noteworthy description of Caleb Nichols: "his Preaching is spiritual and animating, pretty full of the musical New-Light Tone which the Rev. Gentlemen of Connecticut call the *Rhode Island Wind-preaching,* and which young struts of starched collegiate cadence are prone to sneer at."

18. Sprague, *Annals,* VI, 371. Sprague also notes that "the influence of party politics" had something to do with his leaving.

19. Crocker, *History,* p. 89.

20. *Ibid.,* p. 205.

21. *Ibid.,* p. 116. Bogart points to cases where Congregationalist ministers made a business of going from one new town to another getting ordained and acquiring the ministerial right; he cites the case of one minister who obtained the rights in seven different towns (1,750 acres) by this procedure; *Lease Lands,* pp. 303–309.

church was formed. Much discussion resulted over which church should have the right to the ministerial lands. The town resolved the problem by voting to give 200 acres of the land for the support of the Congregational church and 100 acres for support of the Baptist church, presumably in proportion to the relative size of their membership.[22]

Examples are numerous of towns in which Baptists and Congregationalists shared the use of the meetinghouse built from taxes levied on all inhabitants. In Middletown, a Baptist church was formed in 1784 and the Congregationalists permitted its pastor, Elder Sylvanus Haynes, to conduct the service in the meetinghouse on alternate Sundays. Members of both churches attended every Sunday but apparently the two churches took communion separately. In 1804 the Congregationalists voted to give the Baptists a stipulated sum of money as their share of equity in the meetinghouse if they should decide to build a meetinghouse of their own and leave the town's meetinghouse to accommodate the growing Congregational adherents. The Baptists voted to do this in 1806, and on January 9 of that year they voted "to call upon the Cong. society to refund to this Church their property in said meeting-house agreeable to their vote in March, 1804." Presumably the agreement was carried out, for the Baptists proceeded to erect their own building. Elder Haynes was so well considered that in 1809 he was invited to give the election sermon to the state legislature.[23]

A similar cordial relationship existed between the Baptists and Congregationalists in East Swanton where, according to the Baptist historian of Vermont, "preaching was supported on the grand list" by regular taxation.[24] This is particularly significant since the Baptists were the established church in that town. The Baptist church was formed here in 1803, and since there was no Congregational church the Congregationalists joined the Baptists in worship, making this church the standing church for the town. Elder Jesse Smith, ordained in 1804, was the town minister; even after 1814, when the Baptists built a new meetinghouse, the Congregationalists shared in its cost and attended its services.[25]

---

22. Crocker, *History*, p. 305. Another case in which two churches were founded almost simultaneously occurred in Sunderland in 1790. After considerable litigation the court awarded the right to one of the churches on the grounds that its minister had been ordained *two minutes* before his rival. Both ministers in this instance were Congregationalists. Theophilus Packard, Jr., *A History of the Churches and Ministers and of Franklin Association* (Boston, 1854), p. 11.

23. Crocker, *History*, p. 87; H. S. Davis, *History of the Baptist Church in Middletown, Vermont* (Middletown Springs, 1884), pp. 49–50.

24. Crocker, *History*, p. 363.

25. It is not clear whether open communion was practiced here or not. One of the most famous of the Baptist elders in Vermont, Roswell Mears, who preached in Fairfax and then in East Swanton (from 1815 to 1820), reported that the Baptists and Congregationalists in the town of Cambridge also amicably joined a common worship: "The Church in Cambridge though composed partly of Baptists was called Congregationalist" in 1793, he wrote, but "About this time a Baptist church was

In Woodstock, where the Congregational church lost one-third of its members to the Universalists in the early 1790's and lacked the money to build a badly needed new meetinghouse, the church proposed to share with the Baptists the cost and use of a meetinghouse which the Baptists had started in the western part of the North Parish. The Baptists, having dismissed their pastor, Elder William Grow, in 1794 for "his misbehavior and chicanery" were in too divided a state to complete the building themselves so they voted "to chuse a committee to confer with and make proposals to our congregational Brethren in the vicinity of the Society respecting their agreeing with us to come in on an everage [i.e., by proportionate assessment] to compleat the furnishing [of] the meeting house and have an equal privilege with us in regulating the religious worship." [26] They agreed to do so, and the meetinghouse was finished by joint contributions, with members of both denominations united for two years under the preaching of the Congregational minister, the Rev. George Daman. After his death in 1796, this mixed church ordained Elder Ariel Kendrick as its pastor. He ministered to both denominations and waged a pamphlet war with members who began defecting to the Universalists until 1800, when the lack of voluntary support for his salary forced him to give up the task and move to New Hampshire. The church continued under the joint eldership of Aaron and Nehemiah Woodward. For a time it joined the Woodstock Baptist Association to which it reported 79 members in 1806. But in 1809 it was dropped from the Association because most of its members had defected to the new Christ-ian denomination led by Elias Smith. From 1809 to 1839 there was no Baptist church in Woodstock.

The lack of Baptist church records for these early years makes it difficult to be precise about these matters, but there is evidence that Baptists and Congregationalists joined in building meetinghouses and shared in their use in the towns of Pittsford, Bridgport, Windsor, and Ludlow in the years 1788 to 1820.[27] Such arrangements, however, often led to bitter disputes. In the town of Georgia a vote was taken to levy taxes on all inhabitants for erecting a meetinghouse, but since the Baptists realized that the Congregational majority would assume the use of it for their church they vigorously opposed the tax. The town reconsidered its vote and then voted instead to erect the meetinghouse by voluntary subscription. This was done and the Baptists subscribed one-sixth of the costs. At that time they had no pastor for their church, but when they ordained Roswell Mears

---

constituted in Cambridge and Rev. Joseph Call became their pastor. A large portion of the Congregational church united with it." L. A. Dunn, *A Brief Sketch of the Life and Labors of Roswell Mears* (Burlington, 1856), p. 8. The town of Halifax asked Elder William Ewen to serve as town minister in the late 1780's and the town of Cavendish employed a Baptist elder named Pierce to supply its pulpit at one time. Crocker, *History*, pp. 180, 262.

26, Dana, *Woodstock*, pp. 380–382.

27. Crocker, *History*, pp. 106, 152, 241, 271.

in 1807, they claimed the right to share in the use of the meetinghouse on the basis of the money they had subscribed to its building. The Congregationalists denied that they had any right to use it for religious purposes, and for four years a fierce dispute raged in which the two groups almost came to blows. Finally in 1811 both parties agreed to submit the matter to arbitration and the arbitrators decided:

> Agreeable to the exhibition made to us by the contending parties of the Meeting house in Georgia according to our Award in the Case one Sixth part of the time is to be improv'd by the Baptist order and the remainder to the Congregational order the Baptist to Commence on the 21st day of Instant July.[28]

In Westford the Baptists met even more intransigent opposition from the Congregationalists. Here they applied in 1821 for part-time use of the meetinghouse which they had helped to erect, presumably through taxes. The Congregationalists voted that they could use the meetinghouse on any day but Sunday. The Baptists found this unsatisfactory and united with the Methodists to erect a new meetinghouse directly across the green. These two sects thereafter shared the use of this meetinghouse.[29]

All of these aspects of interdenominational sharing, harmony, and quarreling illustrate the highly unstable and unsettled quality of the Vermont frontier during its transition from a raw wilderness to the early stages of community organization. The pietism of the various denominations produced a keen desire for the creation of religious institutions, but the prevailing poverty of the frontier compelled a general sharing of the expense of supporting them. As the population increased, and with it the wealth of the communities, the early phase of ecumenicalism gave way to an intense evangelical competition for converts. But that did not happen before the frontier climate and the spirit of the natural rights philosophy had put an end to the old tradition of compulsory religious taxation.

The Baptists' steady growth in Vermont from a single church in 1768 to a total of eighty to ninety by 1810 led to the creation of six Baptist Associations to integrate, direct, and stabilize the denomination: the Shaftsbury Association, founded in 1781; the Woodstock Association founded in 1783; the Manchester Association, 1785; the Vermont Association and the Leyden Association, 1793; and the Richmond Association, 1795. From the records of the minutes of these associations (and deducting the figures for member churches outside of the state of Vermont) it would probably be safe to estimate that in the year 1810 the denomination had 4000 members and 20,000 regular attendants. With the exception of the eccentric Vermont Association, these associations patterned themselves directly after the Warren Association. Their delegates regularly attended the meetings of

28. Ms. in the Vermont Historical Society. Also Crocker, *History,* p. 358.
29. *Ibid.,* p. 366.

all the other New England Associations, and occasionally they attended those in the Middle Colonies as well.[30]

The history of the Vermont Association deserves special mention for the trend it displayed toward a more rigid control of its members. This association was formed by delegates from five churches who met in Elder Joseph Cornell's barn in Manchester in May 1785. The constituent churches were those of Manchester, Clarendon, Danby, and Middletown, Vermont and of Granville, New York. They had a total of 213 members in 1785 but by 1791 there were fifteen churches with 485 members. For its first ten years it followed the plan of the Warren Association, but in 1795 the growth of Methodism, Universalism, the Congregational counter-reformation, the Freewill Baptists, and the Christ-ians seemed to be making such inroads into the Vermont Baptist churches that the Association voted to revise its constitution to provide a closer watch and care over the member churches. They held a meeting in January 1796 to institute the new constitution, primarily the work of Elders Isaac Beals, Caleb Blood, and Obed Warren. This constitution required any pastor who was sent as a delegate to the Association to undergo an examination respecting a "work of grace upon his soul, ministerial qualifications, principles [in] the Christian religion." If he did not pass this examination not only was he not admitted to the Association meeting but his church was to be expelled from the Association unless it dismissed him. The constitution also provided carefully constructed rules for adjudicating disputes among member churches and gave the Association the right to "pass judgment upon churches and associations [with] which they were in correspondence." [31]

This interference with the traditional Baptist belief in the congregational autonomy of the individual church aroused considerable dissension within the Association. The majority of member churches ratified the new constitution, but a minority refused to do so.[32] For ten years the Association was split over the matter, each group meeting separately and claiming to be the true Vermont Association. The other Baptist Associations tried to placate the disputants and temporarily declined to admit fraternal delegates from either of the factions. Eventually the matter was settled by revoking the more rigid presbyterian aspects of the new constitution and returning to the older and looser form of association. When the factions reunited in 1806, the Association had 19 churches and 1300 members.

30. The published minutes for these associations are among the papers of the Baptist Historical Society of Vermont in the Vermont Historical Society. See also Benedict's and Crocker's histories for general accounts of the founding and growth of these associations. These were all closed-communion, Calvinistic Baptists and their churches usually had Separate-Baptist backgrounds.
31. Crocker, *History*, pp. 72–73. This constitution was proposed as early as January 1795. Also Benedict, *History*, II, 347–348.
32. See ms. records of the Shoreham Baptist Church for January 1, 1795, which voted at this time to reject the new constitution. This record attributes the new constitution to Isaac Beals. These records are at the Vermont Historical Society.

The principle work of all the associations was to uphold and strengthen the denomination by settling disputes, by providing pastoral supplies for vacant churches, by ordaining evangelists, and above all by providing encouragement for missionary activity throughout the state and in adjoining areas of New Hampshire, New York, and lower Canada. Like the Massachusetts associations, most of them opposed in principle both the incorporation of churches by law and the giving of certificates.[33] They exhorted their member churches to give liberal voluntary support to their pastors and to beware of imposters and false preachers.[34] They warned their ministers not to enter into "merchandize, trade, or hard labor" which might embarrass their mind, destroy their usefulness, and "spot their garments." [35] They thought it was not "expedient or for the honor of religion to ascribe the title of Reverend to our Elders." [36] After 1800 they became

33. The Woodstock Association minutes for 1786 contain this query: "The Church in Windsor proposed the following question, viz. Whether it can be profitable to Zion's cause for us to give the world certificates of our being Baptists? Answered in the negative." In 1803 the Shaftsbury Association considered the query "Is it agreeable to the Gospel, for a church of Christ to petition the civil power to incorporate them into a religious society?" To which it answered: "We view it as derogatory to the dignity of Zion's King, and undervaluing his ample code of laws, for christian churches to apply to civil authority, to be incorporated as bodies politic, for the purpose of regulating their ecclesiastical concerns, or forcing their members to support their preachers, or even for the sake of getting exemption from religious oppression; believing religion (in all its branches) to be no object of civil government, nor any wise under its control. It may, nevertheless, be proper, in some of the states, for churches to avail themselves of the act of incorporation for the sole purpose of holding social property." Also Backus ms. "Diary," XII, 117.

34. Stephen Wright, *Shaftsbury Association* (Troy, 1853), pp. 48, 129. The circular letter of the Leyden Association in 1804 contains an interesting comment on the dangers lurking in efforts by Congregationalists to seek open-communion with the Baptists: Formerly, said the letter, the Baptists were persecuted and thrived on it, but

> The Devil then turned his coat and brought up the war in a more soft but more fatal way: he began to flatter and offer rewards to those who would embrace christianity. Upon persecution ceasing and religion growing popular, gentlemen and ladies (more for pride and vain glory than real piety of heart) embraced it . . . carnal Ministers soon began to contend for power and superiority . . . Those who once held us at the greatest distance and held our faith to be dangerous, have changed their language and are trying the old art of flattery: come, say they, let us meet together in some one of the villages on the plains of Ono, that is in a half way place: — let us meet at the Lord's table: you must not be so bigoted in sentiment and strenuous about non-essentials — if conscience is answered that is sufficient. Here observe the different language. Once the sprinkling of infants was essential — now Baptism itself is non-essential. Observe brethren, which of the commands of God are non-essential? Choosing some of the commands to follow and refusing the rest is to destroy the whole . . . What is this but to slip our necks out of the yoke of Christ and cast off his government, and virtually to say to the Almighty, thy government is not good, thy rules tend to make schisms in the church . . . never give up our truth for the mere name of union.

35. Wright, *Shaftsbury Association,* p. 48.
36. Woodstock Association Minutes, 1790.

intensely interested in foreign missions to bring the gospel to the "benighted heathens" of Africa and Asia.[37] But they showed almost no interest in education and made no attempt to form a Baptist college or seminary; there was marked anti-intellectualism among them, carried to such an extent that several members of the Baptist church in Georgia withdrew when they discovered that their pastor, Alvah Sabin, had spent some time studying at a theological seminary.[38] Nor did the Baptist Associations of Vermont engage in any of the political activity for disestablishment which the Grievance Committee of the Warren Association undertook in Massachusetts. The minutes of the associations indicate no problems of persecution and no attempts to petition or lobby either singly or jointly for separation of church and state.

In social outlook the Baptists of Vermont were similar to those elsewhere in New England. The Shaftesbury Association proclaimed in 1792 its "hearty detestation" of the slave trade." [39] Several associations and churches expressed equal opposition to the Masonic movement in the 1790's.[40] They warned members about the great "impropriety of Christians running into debt" or refusing to pay their honest dues.[41] The Baptists of Middletown voted in 1801:

> that we utterly disapprove of every species of gambling: that is any kind of play for any kind of property . . . viz., card playing, horse racing, pitching dollars &c. turning dollars &c. pitching quoits, playing ball, &c. &c.[42]

They warned the young about the dangers of "frolicking with wicked youth," and by 1830 they were ready to join in the incipient temperance movement.[43] When Elder Caleb Blood of Shaftesbury was given the honor of preaching the election sermon in 1792, he used the opportunity to lec-

---

37. Wright, *Shaftsbury Association*, pp. 78, 114. They were also anxious to send missionaries to the American Indians; see Crocker, *History*, p. 49.

38. Crocker, *History*, p. 359. This occurred in 1817. Also Sprague, *Annals*, VI, 270; David Ludlum, *Vermont in Ferment: 1791–1850* (New York, 1939), p. 45.

39. Shaftsbury Association Minutes, 1792. The grounds for opposing slavery as stated here were that it was hostile to "that freedom which every child of Adam is entitled to by nature." The Association went on to recommend "to all our brethren to pray Almighty God to hasten the auspicious day when the Ethiopian, with all the human race, shall enjoy that liberty due to every citizen of the commonwealth; and the name of 'Slave' be extirpated from the earth." This was a more forthright public stand than any of the Baptist associations in Massachusetts, Rhode Island, or Connecticut took at this time, and may again be attributed to the radical individualism of the frontier and the more radical pietism of those who settled it.

40. Wright, *Shaftsbury Association*, pp. 57, 352; Davis, *Middletown*, p. 40; Crocker, *History*, pp. 45–46; Benedict, *History*, II, 340–341.

41. Wright, *Shaftsbury Association*, p. 180.

42. Davis, *Middletown*, p. 4.

43. Archibald, *Wallingford*, p. 5; Crocker, *History*, p. 47; Wright, *Shaftsbury Association*, p. 195. The temperance movement did not begin among the Baptists until the late 1820's.

ture the frontier legislators on the evils of profanity: "A magistrate who is rough and profane in his language is a monstrous character . . . He is not the gentleman; for any person of sense knows that a rough, profane way of treating mankind better fits the character of a clown than a gentleman." [44] As for the role of women in the churches that was left precisely where the apostle Paul had left it: "We conclude," said the Woodstock Association in 1789, "that the Holy Spirit does not in this or any passage of Scripture [I Cor. 14:34] prohibit women in the Church to speak on all suitable occasions respecting Gods kind and gracious dealing with their souls; but forbids them to usurp authority as public teachers, or to take upon them in any respect the government of the Church." [45]

But there were two features of the Baptist outlook in Vermont which appeared to be different from that of the Massachusetts Baptists. First was the tendency of some Vermont churches to censure their members for holding unpopular political beliefs; second was the practice of voting resolutions in church meetings on political issues. For example, on March 23, 1774, the First Baptist Church of Shaftesbury, became involved in one of the perennial disputes between Yankees and Yorkers. The church records read:

> Considered a difficulty that Br[other] William Fareman and Amaziah Martin Brought into the Chh, which they had with some of the Brethen, Because they have assisted the Mobb against the Yorkers . . .

> 2ly the Chh Concludes that agreeable to the advice of the Governor and Council of New York, it Is Right for Every man to keep his Possession and not to be Turned out of it as things are now Circumstanced.

> 3ly the Chh Doth wholy Renounce Resisting the authority, or opposing any office, in Bringing any man to Justice for any Crime that he hath Committed or from bringing any to Pay his Lawfull Debts.[46]

Why the church felt it had to take sides with the Governor of New York is not clear, except as a means of preventing disputes among the brethren.

The Church took a similar action in Halifax in October 1788 when it saw fit to hear a case brought by one of the brethren against the pastor, Obed Warren, and others of the church. Warren was accused of the sin of joining "a Society called the Directorenes." Whether this group was for

44. Backus, *History*, II, 547.

45. Woodstock Association Minutes, 1789. The Baptists in Vermont also suffered from some of the more eccentric doctrines of pietistic-perfectionism, as one can see in the church records of the Orwell Baptist Church. Here a schism occurred in the years 1792–1798 in which the pastor, Elnathan Philips sided with those accused of favoring "a plurality of wives." These records are in the Vermont Historical Society.

46. Crocker, *History*, p. 20. Party politics also led Elder Isaac Sawyer to leave his pastorate in Monkton in 1812 — though his parishioners were also dissatisfied with his covetous efforts to sue the glebeland away from the town. Sprague, *Annals*, VI, 371.

or against the Allen brothers is not clear, but on March 5, 1789, the church voted that it was wrong for any member of the church to belong to this political organization.[47]

The War of 1812 brought new political complications. Although the Baptists of Vermont were as staunch supporters of Jefferson's party as were the Baptists elsewhere in New England, some of them, especially among the more conservative elders, did not like the policies of Jefferson and Madison concerning the Embargo. When Elder Amos Tuttle of Fairfax took a public stand on the matter, the church censured him in April 1809 "for speaking publicly in a manner that implicated his rulers." According to the church records, "Elder Tuttle, speaking on government affairs, said our rulers have brought difficulties on us, and if they do not immediately remove them they will bring down the judgement of God upon us."[48] No doubt the vote was taken (ostensibly) on the ground that a minister should not meddle in politics and should show respect toward the governing party, but the political animus in the affair is apparent.

In 1812 the same church in Halifax excommunicated ten of its members who had joined a conservative Federalist organization called the Washington Benevolent Society. The members were later restored, but it is not clear whether they had to leave the organization in order to be forgiven.[49] The Baptist church in Wallingford became involved in a serious dispute on this same question in 1812 when it was proposed at a church meeting to exclude any member of the Federalist Party from church membership. The vote failed to carry by a slim margin.[50]

This tendency to equate religious orthodoxy with certain standards of social and political conformity increased as rapidly among the Baptists as it did among other evangelicals in the nineteenth century. By the 1830's a church member could be excommunicated or a candidate for admission to a church turned down for failure to meet any of a host of rules on moral or social behavior which came to be equated with respectable, church-going Christianity. In 1837, for example, the Shaftesbury Association voted:

> That this Association recommend this subject ["of Temperance"] to the attention of the churches and individuals to abstain from the use and traffic of all intoxicating drinks, believing that it is the duty and privilege of all professing godliness to stand aloof from such drinks.[51]

47. Ms. church records of the Halifax Church in the Vermont Historical Society. I have been unable to locate any group called by this name in 1789. It does not seem likely that it relates to Ira Allen's conspiracy with the French Directory in 1796. Chilton Williamson, *Vermont in Quandary* (Montpelier, 1949), pp. 229–235.
48. Typescript of the church records in the Vermont Historical Society; Crocker, *History*, p. 353.
49. Ms. church records in the Vermont Historical Society; Crocker, *History*, p. 354.
50. Archibald, *Wallingford*, p. 22. For a similar case in Templeton, Massachusetts, see Sprague, *Annals*, VI, 272.
51. Wright, *Shaftsbury Association*, pp. 216–217

The Association even went so far as to insist that it was "just and right in a church to require of all of its members a pledge of entire abstinence from all drinks that are intoxicating as a condition of membership of good standing." [52] That same year the Association declared slaveholding to be a sin and voted that "the churches of this body record their testimony against this sin most decidedly and cooperate in sending letters of admonition to their Southern brethren" who are "implicated in this sin."

The indiscriminate equation of the prevailing contemporary and regional mores with the divine will could hardly have been avoided. It was implicit in the pietistic aspects of the Calvinist ethic. It was sharpened by the radical perfectionist zeal which gave the cutting edge to the Baptists fight against the Standing Order. And it was heightened by the recognition that with the breakdown of the elitist, clerical, corporate system which had hitherto dominated New England, the only available new criteria for fashioning a social ethic in an individualistic, democratic society was the majority consensus of godly (i.e., converted) evangelical churchgoers. Thus a new kind of voluntaristic national establishment based on the will (or the tyranny) of the majority emerged to replace the old. At the same time that the evangelicals maintained a specious concern for separation of church and state (a concern which led the Baptists of Vermont to censure Aaron Leland because he ran for office while continuing to retain his eldership over a church), they worked to reestablish on their own pietistic terms, the conception that America was a Christian commonwealth in which any sinner against the divine ethic upheld by the evangelical (that is, the Protestant) churches was a sinner against society and must be punished both by the church and by society. If society had no laws by which to punish these outcasts, the churches would either lead in the effort to create laws, or they would wink their eyes while godly vigilantes administered tar and feathers or rode the culprit out of town on a rail.

In Vermont in the half century between 1780 and 1830, the entire history of the Baptist effort to overthrow the Puritan system was telescoped and heightened by the frontier conditions and Revolutionary mood in which it took place. The result reflected both the virtues and the failings of the unique American character which resulted from the combination of pietistic-perfectionism and the frontier.

52. Crocker, *History*, p. 47. See also Ludlum, *Vermont*, pp. 55 ff. on the rise of evangelical "ultraism" in Vermont after 1830.

Chapter 43

Dissent in New Hampshire,
1640–1792

As morality and piety, rightly grounded on evangelical principles, will give the best and greatest security to government and will lay, in the hearts of men, the strongest obligations to due subjection . . .

New Hampshire state constitution, explaining the need for compulsory religious taxes, 1784

The dissenters in New Hampshire, like those in Vermont, encountered less difficulty than their brethren in Massachusetts and Connecticut. Religious liberty in that area of New England evolved from very different circumstances and in a very different way. First, New Hampshire was settled almost as early in the seventeenth century as Massachusetts. Though the greater part of it remained a wilderness, those areas which were settled established strong precedents for the same system of church-state relations which existed in Massachusetts. The dissenters benefited, as they had in Vermont, from the frontier situation and tended, after 1740, to see New Hampshire as a haven from oppression and for new social and economic opportunities. But by the time the first Baptist church was founded in the colony in 1755 the ecclesiastical pattern was already well established. The close ties between New Hampshire and Massachusetts from the earliest days made this colony much less tolerant of dissent than Vermont. In the seventeenth century dissenters from Puritan orthodoxy were harassed out of the colony and Quakers were whipped. However, by the end of the 1680's the Quakers were obtaining exemption from religious taxes, and the Anglicans and Presbyterians obtained it soon after. The Baptists found when they arrived in large numbers that their reception varied greatly from town to town, and they faced many of the same problems of certification, incorporation, and social ostracism which had led them to emigrate. New Hampshire never enacted laws similar to those enacted in Massachusetts and Connecticut in 1727–1734 designed expressly to grant dissenters exemption from religious taxes. But in 1693 it did adopt almost the same law for ministerial support as had been adopted in Massachusetts, and the New Hampshire State Constitution of 1784 incorporated almost all of Article Three of the Massachusetts Constitution. So that despite a frontier climate which encouraged egalitarianism and toleration, the dissenters were never sure what their status was in New Hampshire. Such freedom as the Baptists acquired was primarily the result of local town meeting decisions and not of legislative or constitutional guarantees or of judicial decisions. In 1817–1819 it was to the pragmatic expediencies of party politics rather than to any triumph of principle that the dissenters owed their final victory over compulsory religious taxes. Even this occurred only after Connecticut had set the precedent in 1818. It was disestablishment in Connecticut, not in neighboring Vermont, which provided the catalytic stimulus to end the established system in New Hampshire.

The New Hampshire dissenters' ambiguous position was the direct result of the political ambiguities in the conflicting claims of the Mason and Gorges proprietors, the Massachusetts authorities, and the King for control of the colony. Though the Puritans of Massachusetts Bay asserted practical control over the colony from 1641 to 1679 and again from 1689 to 1692, they did not found the colony nor were they ever certain of permanent control over it. In the 1640's they had to uproot some strongly entrenched Anglican groups (especially in Portsmouth and Dover) which had been established in the 1630's. When Governor Edward Cranfield was appointed over the colony by the King in 1682 to reestablish the proprietors' claims, he nearly succeeded in ousting the Puritan ministers from New Hampshire. When the Antinomians were driven out of Boston in 1638 they thought at first that the New Hampshire frontier would provide a haven for them. Two men who later became prominent Baptists (Hanserd Knollys and John Clarke) spent some time trying to establish themselves here at that time. Clarke left for Rhode Island after one cold winter and Knollys returned to England in 1641 after a division in his church at Dover.[1] The same year (1639) that John Wheelwright and the Antinomians were setting up a church in Exeter and Knollys was establishing one in Dover, a group of Anglicans formed a church in Portsmouth and a group of orthodox Puritans settled in Hampton and three other New Hampshire towns. But when Massachusetts asserted control over the colony in 1641 (with the consent of most of the settlers there) all dissent was rooted out, including the Anglican rector in Portsmouth.[2] During the next forty

1. There has always been some doubt as to whether Knollys became a Baptist while he was in Dover, New Hampshire from 1638 to 1641. The best evidence indicates that he did not. But he did become one shortly after his return to England. Isaac Backus, *History of New England,* ed. David Weston (Newton, 1871), I, 81–83; Henry S. Burrage, *A History of the Baptists in New England* (Philadelphia, 1894), pp. 65–66.

2. Jeremy Belknap, *History of New Hampshire* (Boston, 1792), I; Charles B. Kinney, Jr., *Church and State: The Struggle for Separation in New Hampshire* (New

years all the New Hampshire towns settled able, learned, orthodox Harvard graduates and levied taxes for their settlement and support according to the ecclesiastical laws of Massachusetts. The complaints of the Anglicans, the Baptists and the Quakers went unheeded until 1679.[3]

That year New Hampshire was made a royal province. The King appointed John Cutt, a leading Portsmouth merchant, "President" of the colony with instructions in his commission that "liberty of conscience shall be allowed unto all protestants; yet such especially as shall be conformable to ye rites of ye Church of England shall be particularly countenanced and encouraged."[4] The Anglicans now looked forward to becoming the established church of the colony, but the effort to oust the Puritans came too late. President Cutt made no effort in this direction. His successor, Lt. Governor Edward Cranfield, worked hard at it for three years, even jailing Joshua Moody, the Puritan minister of Portsmouth, for refusing to follow Anglican practices. From 1682 to 1685 the Puritans were in the anomalous position of pleading for liberty of conscience in New Hampshire — though this seems to have no direct relation to the granting of toleration in Massachusetts at this same time. Cranfield received no help from England and his efforts to enforce his commission by establishing the Church of England in New Hampshire failed. Moreover his attempts to collect quitrents for the Mason heirs did not generally endear him to the inhabitants.[5] Cranfield's successors, Joseph Dudley and Edmund Andros, left the Puritans in peace. Under Andros the New Hampshire legislature passed a law in 1686 which confirmed for the Puritan ministers settled in the various towns the salaries which had been voted for their support.[6] When James II was overthrown and Andros fled, most of the people in New Hampshire welcomed the opportunity to put themselves again under the government of Massachusetts. But in 1692 William and Mary appointed Samuel Allen governor of the colony and (although Massachusetts and New Hampshire shared the same royal governor from 1699 until 1741) after that period the laws and practices of New Hampshire took a separate and distinct course of their own.[7]

Governor Allen sent his son-in-law, John Usher, to act as his deputy in the colony and under Usher the New Hampshire legislature passed its first

---

York, 1955), pp. 13–22. I should like to thank Professor Charles E. Clark of the University of New Hampshire for commenting on this chapter in manuscript.

3. For documents concerning persecution of Anabaptists and whipping of Quakers see *Provincial and State Papers of New Hampshire,* ed. Nathaniel Bouton *et al.,* 30 vols. (Concord, 1867–1910), I, 191, 243–244.

4. *Ibid.,* I, 375.

5. Kinney, *Church and State,* pp. 23–30.

6. *Provincial Papers,* I, 600.

7. While the royal instructions to the governors from 1679 to 1688 had included directions to encourage the Church of England, William and Mary omitted this clause in their instructions to Allen. *Laws of New Hampshire,* I–III ed. Albert S. Batchellor *et al.* (Manchester and Concord, 1904–1915), II, 64–65.

and most comprehensive act dealing with the support of religion. This act of 1693 was reenacted in 1714, revised in 1719, and incorporated in the state constitution of 1784. The act of 1719 was reenacted verbatim by the state legislature in 1791. It was essentially this act that was amended in 1819 to put an end to the system of compulsory religious taxes. Although it was modeled on the ecclesiastical laws of Massachusetts (passed in 1692 and 1693), the New Hampshire law of 1693 differed from them in several important respects. "An Act for Maintinance & Supply of the Ministry within this Province," it began by asserting "it shall & may be Lawfull for the freeholders of Every respective Towne Convened in Publik Towne meeting" to choose and "agree with a Minister, or Ministers, for the Suppley of the Towne." The freeholders also were to decide "what Annuall Sallery shall be allowed him" and the selectmen of the town "Shall make rates and Assessm'ts upon the Inhabitants of the Towne for the paym't of the Ministers Sallery." However, this act was not to "Interfere with their Majesties grace & favour in Allowing their Subjects liberty of Contience [conscience]." Persons who were "conscientiously" "of a different perswassion" from the majority of the freeholders in any town and who "Constantly attend the publick worship of God on the Lords day according to their owne p'rswassion" were to be "Excused from paying towards the Support of the Ministrey of the Towne." [8] The act did not specify how this exemption was to be administered, but it specifically forbade exemption to any person who refused to pay religious taxes merely on "pretence of being a different perswassion." Obviously some administrative procedure was required, and it is not surprising that the province developed the same certificate system as prevailed in Massachusetts even though no specific procedure for certification was ever embodied in this or any other colonial or state statute in New Hampshire.

There were significant differences between the ecclesiastical system established under this law and that established in Massachusetts. First, the law did not specifically require every town or parish to hire a minister; it simply said that it "may be Lawfull" for a town to do so. Consequently no machinery was imbedded in this act or in any subsequent act to enforce towns to maintain such a minister (though the act did in other clauses enforce the hiring of school master). Second, the act did not define the ministers' qualifications as being "Able, Learned, and orthodox," thereby leaving the possibility open for each town to set its own qualifications and, by implication, permitting a town to support an Anglican, a Baptist, or a Quaker if it so chose. Third, the act had imbedded in it the important right of exemption from compulsory religious taxes which Massachusetts and Connecticut did not acknowledge until thirty-five years later. This provision was a landmark in the history of religious liberty in New Eng-

8. *Laws of New Hampshire,* I, 560–561.

land. It set a precedent for toleration in New Hampshire which, despite numerous infractions of its spirit, made that province the freest of the Puritan colonies before the development of Vermont.[9]

This spirit of toleration and tax exemption was confounded by several subsequent actions by the state which considerably narrowed its liberal intent. For though this law was reenacted without change in 1714,[10] an act of 1716 required all towns and parishes to settle a minister within six months of their incorporation or else to pay toward the support of the ministry in the town or parish from which they had been set off.[11] This denied the implicit option of the law of 1693 that a town did not have to settle a minister and to levy taxes for him if it did not choose to do so. Perhaps this original option meant only to permit voluntarism, and the increasing number of towns and parishes without settled ministers was producing a total neglect of religion in some of them. Poverty and a general dislike for taxes of any kind may have encouraged some persons to request to be set off as a new town or parish primarily to escape such religious taxation. This was what the law of 1716 was designed to prevent.

"An Act for Regulating Townships, Choice of Town Officers & Setting Forth Their Power," passed on May 2, 1719, was a more serious revision of the ecclesiastical system. This elaborate act detailing the regulation of town government contained a section regarding religious taxation that may have been construed by some persons to revise and supersede the act of 1714 regarding support of the ministry. Probably it was meant to clarify that act; some statement regarding ecclesiastical procedures could hardly have been omitted from a comprehensive act on town government. Because it confirmed the right of compulsory taxation and omitted any statement regarding the right of tax exemption, it considerably weakened the dissenters' position. This section of the act read:

> And be it further Enacted by the Authority aforsed that the Selectmen or townsmen . . . are Impowered to assess the Inhabitants & others Resident within Such Town & the Precincts thereof & the Lands and Estate lying within the Bounds of Such Town in just and Equal proportion as near as may be unto all Town Charges each Particular Person according to his known Ability & Estate Such Sum & Sums of money as hath or

9. In July 1706, the Lord Commissioners for Trade and Plantations described the Act of 1693 to the Privy Council: "The Act leaves the Ministry perfectly at the Will of the people, and also leaves it wholly in the People's Choice whether they will have a Ministry or no and exempts all persons who shall serve God Separately according to their own perswasion from contributing to the Minister." *Laws of New Hampshire*, I, 861. Another significant difference from the Massachusetts Act was that this act failed to grant the church a concurring voice or veto in the choice made for the Standing minister of the majority. From the outset the town was superior to the church in this respect, thus making a much more clearcut case for the claim that the town minister was a civil and not a spiritual officer of the state.

10. *Laws of New Hampshire*, II, 143–144.

11. *Provincial Papers*, XIX, 92; Kinney, *Church and State*, p. 47.

> Shall be ordered, granted and agreed upon from time to time by the In-
> habitants in any Town meeting regularly assembled or the Majr part of
> those present in Such meeting, for the maintinance and Support of the
> Ministry, Schools, the poor & for the defraying other necessary charges
> arising within sd Town.[12]

Since it was this act (reenacted in 1791) — and not a constitutional
amendment — which was amended by the legislature in 1819 to end compulsory religious taxes, it would appear that legally this was the operative
enactment of New Hampshire's established ecclesiastical system. Apparently the courts considered the general provision for the support of the
ministry which (as Article Six of the state's Bill of Rights) became part of
the New Hampshire constitution in 1784 merely as a general confirmation
of this act.

The third factor which decreased the possibility for voluntarism (and
the neglect of compulsory religious taxes) was the wording of the legislative grants to the proprietors of new towns. Like the grants in Massachusetts and Connecticut, those in New Hampshire contained stipulations
requiring the building of a meetinghouse and the settling of a minister
within a specified period (usually three or four years) after the enactment
of the grant or forfeiture of it. Although the time limit in these stipulations
was seldom met, the town proprietors never failed to try to comply with
them as soon as possible, and they were granted extensions when their
efforts failed. The proprietors recognized that the real estate values increased considerably once a meetinghouse was built and a minister settled;
new settlers not only desired religious services but they were happy when
the earlier settlers or proprietors had borne the initial burden of establishing
them. The grants did not specify, as the ministry act did not, that the ministers should be able, learned and orthodox. If dissenters were sufficiently
numerous they could have elected a minister of their own denomination and
have obtained the minister's right and the ministry plot for his support.
But seldom were the dissenters that numerous; before 1770 almost every
town in New Hampshire not only settled a Congregational minister but
supported him by the traditional system of compulsory taxes.

As a result of these ambiguities the dissenters in New Hampshire frequently had to fight for the religious toleration which they thought was
legally theirs. For the Quakers the fight seems to have been relatively simple. Despite their persecution in the middle of the seventeenth century, by
1687 they had established a sizable congregation in the town of Dover.
That year one of them, Edward Wanton of Scituate, complained to the
legislature that he had been unjustly taxed and distrained for the support
of the Congregational church. After they received his petition, the legislature

12. *Laws of New Hampshire*, II, 342. This act merely "empowered" but did not
require the levying of religious taxes. It presumably superseded the law of 1716.

"Resolved that the said Wanton, being a Quaker and attending other Worship than the Ministry of the Towne and the Distresse made since his Mj'ties gracious indulgence, the same is not approved off, but the Goods Distreyned and now in the Constables hands as by his returne to be restored." [13] Governor Andros may have forced this decision on the legislature, for it was not in any of the statutes of the time.

The Quakers assumed thereafter that they were exempt from taxation. In 1729 they went a step further in petitioning that they no longer be required, if they were chosen as constables, to collect religious taxes from others. The petition, restated in 1731, indicates the Quakers' assumption that they were exempt:

> Whereas we ye people Comonly Called Quakers did in ye 2d mo. 1729 offer a petition to ye Govener humbley Requesting that we might not be imposed upon when we are Chosen Counstables to gather the taxes or assessments that are from time to time assesed upon the inhabitants for ye support of prisbetrian [i.e., Congregational] minestry and did not mention the Councel and house of Representatives in sd petition for which Reason the Genl Court would not act thereon — we do therefor humble [humbly] Crave that you would be pleased to considered of this matter for altho we are exempted in ye Law from paying any part or proportion of such taxes or assessments yet nevertheless we are Required when we are Chosen Counstables to Leve and Collect ye same of others which is contrary to our principles to pay such taxes neither can we gather ye same of others: where upon we have been and are Likely to be under great sufferings notwithstanding we Refuse not neither do we desire to be excused from serving [as] Counstables in any other part of the office whatsoever.[14]

The petition did not say by what law they were made exempt, but presumably they understood the law of 1693 (reenacted in 1714) to assert this right. The legislature did not challenge the statement; it granted the petition and on May 10, 1731, enacted a law exempting Quakers from collecting religious taxes.[15] It was a privilege they never obtained in Massachusetts, Connecticut or even in Vermont.

The Anglicans had a slightly more difficult time obtaining exemption. In 1732 the Anglicans in Portsmouth revived their church (then called Queen's Chapel but later St. John's Church) with the help of the Society for the Propagation of the Gospel. Though Governor Belcher refused to become

13. *Laws of New Hampshire,* I, 252
14. *Provincial Papers,* XVIII, 40–41.
15. *Laws of New Hampshire,* II, 530. This may have been another of Governor Belcher's actions on the Quakers' behalf. The claim that the Quakers were not subject to any difficulties after this date is disproved by a petition of 1745 to the legislature from "Joshua Purrington & others Quakers in behalf of Daniel Sawyer about some Land Distrained from him by the Constable of Nottingham for ministers rates." *Provincial Papers,* V, 781.

a member of it, he did agree to purchase a pew.[16] For the first few years members of this church were required to pay religious taxes to the Congregational church as well as to pay their own minister (the Rev. Arthur Brown who was installed in 1736), partly by subscription and partly through a donation from the SPG. By 1740, however, the Anglicans in Portsmouth were being exempted. In February 1739/40 the clerk of the parish of Greenland, where several members of this Anglican church lived, made the following entry in his papers: "These may Certify yt Mr. Thomas Packer, Mr. Thomas Marston, and Willm Simppson Are Cleared from paying Rates to the Minister of this Perish By atending devine Worship at the Church in Ports^mh. And likewise Willm Jenkins is Exempted being a quaker." [17] Records do not reveal whether the Greenland parish passed a vote to exempt Anglicans at this time, or whether the clerk decided independently that they should be grouped with Quakers, or whether the Anglicans presented a petition or certificates or threatened to go to the legislature. But presumably other parishes began at about this same time to excuse Anglicans from religious taxes if they regularly attended a duly constituted church of their own.

Tax exemption was not automatic for non-Congregationalists. That the Presbyterians had to obtain the legislature's assistance to win it indicates this. The Scotch-Irish Presbyterians came to New Hampshire in large numbers after 1719. They settled in the towns of Londonderry, Chester, Bedford, Hampton Falls, Pembrook and Goffstown. At first Presbyterians attended the Congregational churches and made no objections to paying for their support. But as they became more numerous they founded their own churches and brought over their own ministers from northern Ireland. Then the conflict began. After the Rev. Moses Hale (Harvard, 1722) was dismissed from the Standing Church in Chester in 1734, the Presbyterians brought over the Rev. John Wilson to preach to them. In the absence of an immediate replacement for Hale the town levied no taxes on the Presbyterians during the next two years. However, in 1736 the Congregationalists settled the Rev. Ebenezer Flagg over their church and the question arose whether the Presbyterians were entitled to exemption. The majority of the town thought they were not; taxes were levied on them to support the Rev. Mr. Flagg. The Presbyterians petitioned the legislature. At first they were dismissed, but the Governor and the Council informed the House of Representatives that they were "of opinion that Petitioners are within the Saving of the Act of this Province" concerning ministerial support. The House did nothing about this but the voters of Chester accepted it and thereafter

16. *Provincial Papers*, IV, 837; Kinney, *Church and State*, pp. 58–59, 69. There was, however, no specific legislative act passed to exempt Anglicans.

17. *Provincial Papers*, XII, 67. Despite strong support of Anglicanism by the Wentworths and other leaders of the colony, the church did not thrive in New Hampshire. Only three other Anglican churches had been formed by 1776.

permitted the adherents of each church to levy their own taxes for their own minister on their own members.[18]

The Scotch-Irish Presbyterians, who considered themselves part of "the Establist Church of North Britain" (i.e., the Church of Scotland), in principle had no objection to religious taxes, any more than did the Anglicans. In the town of Londonderry, which they founded in 1719 and where they always constituted the great majority of the inhabitants, there was no other church; the Presbyterian church became the established church in Londonderry. They chose their own ministers (brought over from Ireland) and taxed the pews of their church for his support. When the town was divided into two parishes in February 1739/40, both of them installed Irish Presbyterian ministers and the legislature empowered both parishes to levy taxes on polls and estates for the support of the Presbyterian minister in each. If any Congregationalists or other "dissenters" from Presbyterianism lived there, they never complained of being unjustly taxed; probably these parishes taxed only their own Scotch-Irish adherents.[19] The same situation prevailed in the town of Bedford where the predominant Scotch-Irish maintained the established (and the only) church.

The Presbyterians in Hampton Falls and Pembrook, however, fought long before they were freed from supporting the Congregationalists. The legislature made the Pembrook Presbyterians a separate poll parish in 1763 and the Hampton Falls Presbyterians a poll parish in 1765.[20] In Goffstown they waited until 1781.[21] As in Londonderry, the Presbyterians had no objection to incorporation by the state and willingly used the powers granted thereby to levy religious taxes on their members. This attitude toward the relationship between church and state made the Scotch-Irish Presbyterians here, as elsewhere in America, generally unsympathetic to the efforts of Baptists and other sects toward disestablishment and voluntarism.[22]

The Great Awakening produced some Separate dissenters in New Hamp-

---

18. See Kinney, *Church and State,* pp. 55–56, who quotes the vote of the House of Representatives in 1740 which ratified this local arrangement in Chester in the following resolution: "[those] that are called Congregationalists and those that are called Presbyterians have power to act separately in Raiseing money for Support of yr Ministers Respectively for Defraying the Charges of building & Repairing their meeting houses and that they have power to chuse Wardens Separate to assess all persons and their Estates belong to their Respective Congregations" (*Provincial Papers,* IX, 105–106; IV, 725 ff).

19. *Provincial Papers,* IX, 480–481, 495–503; Edward L. Parker, *The History of Londonderry* (Boston, 1851), pp. 129–179.

20. *Provincial Papers,* VII, 95, 163. Kinney, *Church and State,* pp. 74–75.

21. *Provincial Papers,* XII, 28. A petition for this was dismissed in 1772; VII, 304. For a request by a Quaker congregation in 1768 to be incorporated as a poll parish see VII, 163.

22. While the Presbyterians had no quarrel with the Calvinistic doctrines of the Baptists, they disagreed with their congregational polity, their antipedobaptism, and their lay ordination of unlearned ministers.

shire who suffered the same kind of oppression as did dissenters in Massachusetts and Connecticut. But only half a dozen Separate churches were formed in the colony and by 1755 the legislature was willing to extend to at least one of these the same privilege it granted the Presbyterians and Anglicans — the right to become a poll parish with power to tax its own members and exemption from supporting any other.[23] Perhaps the generally more tolerant climate in New Hampshire not only produced fewer Separate schisms but also led to almost no Separate-Baptist churches formed as a direct consequence of the Awakening. Not until after 1765, when the evangelistic thrust of the Separate-Baptists in Massachusetts became strong, did the Baptists become sufficiently numerous to form any churches.

The first and only Baptist church formed in New Hampshire before 1770 was in Newton.[24] Its adherents were not Separate come-outers from the Congregational church but Calvinistic Baptist immigrants from the Westerly and Kingston areas of Rhode Island. Under the leadership of Elder Thomas Walter Powers this church had a short and stormy career; it dissolved in 1768. But before its dissolution it was able to set a valuable precedent for tax exemption. This church was formed in the spring of 1755. On June 10 of that year four elders from Rhode Island and one from eastern Connecticut traveled to Newton to ordain Powers over it. They were Stephen Babcock of Stonington; Thomas Wells of Westerly; James Rogers of South Kingston; Benjamin Pierce and Peter Werden of Warwick.[25] At this time the town had not yet settled a minister, but as soon as they did so, they levied taxes on the Baptists. The Baptists refused to pay and in a petition to the town on March 28, 1764, requested that

> you would Exempt us from being taxed for the Support of the Congregational minister in this town for as much as we have attended the worship of God and the preaching of the Gospel in the Baptist Society and Paid our part for the Support of the Gospel there for a number of years Even from before the time that any Congregational Minister was Settled in this town and are Still bound in concience to do the same.[26]

23. This privilege was granted to the Separates in Exeter in 1755; *Provincial Papers,* IX, 275–298; Kinney, *Church and State,* p. 61; Robert F. Lawrence, *The New Hampshire Churches* (Claremont, 1856), pp. 50–51. For a list of the Separate churches in New Hampshire see C. C. Goen, *Revivalism and Separatism in New England, 1740–1800* (New Haven, 1962), pp. 246–248, 256, 319–321. As Goen's tabulations show, only two of these were formed in the 1740's. The only Separate church to adopt Baptist principles was the one in Portsmouth, and this did not occur until 1826. Lawrence, *New Hampshire Churches,* p. 99.

24. There is some evidence that a short-lived Separate-Baptist church existed in Durham, New Hampshire in the early 1750's. It was led for a time by William Odiorne, Esq. but evidently never ordained a pastor. Backus mentions a visit to it in his diary on February 1, 1752. See also the letter to Backus from Odiorne, April 27, 1752, BP(AN).

25. *Provincial Papers,* XIII, 53–54; Backus, *History,* II, 534. Elder Pierce was the man who had baptized Isaac Backus by immersion in August 1751.

26. *Provincial Papers,* XIII, 60. There are several letters and other papers relating to Powers's church among the BP(AN).

The town dismissed the petition, and the tax collectors distrained the Baptists' goods. The Baptists brought suit for recovery and simultaneously joined a sizable body of Quakers in the town to gain control of the town meeting. On March 29, 1769 these dissenters, in an unruly town meeting, passed a vote granting exemptions to themselves. The town appealed the vote to the legislature. The legislature declared the vote void because of the circumstances under which it was passed. In 1770, a number of the more respectable Congregationalists in Newton, exasperated with the quarreling, petitioned the legislature "that the said Baptists may be set off entirely from said Town and have nothing to do with them or that they may, by a Law for that purpose, be rated according to their abilities to all charges as well to the support of the Minister as any other and the part they pay to the latter be given to them to support their own mode of Worship." [27] There is no record that the legislature took any action to clarify the Baptists' status as dissenters at this time. Significantly, the Baptists refused to accept the town's offer to be set off as a separate parish. They would not, like the Presbyterians, accept this legal incorporation as a basis for their exemption. In this case, the matter was settled by the dissolution of the Baptist church as the result of internal quarrels. Apparently, however, those of its members who joined Hezekiah Smith's Baptist church in nearby Haverhill, Massachusetts, were granted exemption by the town after 1770.[28]

After 1770 the Baptist movement in New Hampshire underwent a rapid growth; from the two churches founded in that year it increased to a total of forty-one churches by 1795. Chief evangelists of the Baptist cause in New Hampshire were Samuel Shepard, William Hooper and Hezekiah Smith. But just as this Baptist growth began to produce problems, the Revolution put an end to colonial laws and required reformulation of them in a new state constitution. It was under the constitution and the subsequent ecclesiastical laws which implemented it that the Baptists waged their fight for religious freedom.

The constitution-making process in New Hampshire extended over seventeen years, from 1775 to 1792, before the people were satisfied. It began when the New Hampshire provincial assembly, following Governor Wentworth's flight to Boston in August 1775, took the suggestion of the Continental Congress and constituted itself as a convention. As such, it drew up and published in January 1776 a plan of government under which the new state was governed for the next eight years. This brief document can scarcely be called a constitution. It was designed only as a temporary set of rules to govern the election of and limitations upon provincial assemblies. It made no provision for the basic institutions of a judiciary or an executive

---

27. *Ibid.,* XIII, 62–65, 67.
28. Backus, *History,* II, 534. There is no record of the disposition of the court cases brought by the Baptists in Newton in 1764–1769, but presumably they did not win them or the matter would have been settled more easily.

branch of the government, and it contained no bill of rights.[29] This "constitution" was not ratified by the voters and was considered only as a temporary expedient until the situation was sufficiently stable to elect a full-fledged constitutional convention. This happened in June 1778, when ninety towns sent delegates to a convention called by the provincial assembly. The document which this convention submitted to the voters on June 5, 1779 contained only one reference to religion. Its Declaration of Rights stated: "The future Legislature of the State shall make no laws to infringe the rights of conscience or any others of the natural, unalienable rights of men or contrary to the laws of God or against the Protestant religion." [30] For reasons not religious the voters rejected this constitution and the state continued to operate under the plan of 1776. A new constitutional convention was called in June 1781; this convention drew up the bill of rights which the voters accepted three years later. Its fourth, fifth, and sixth articles concerned religion and were modeled on Articles Two and Three of the Massachusetts Constitution. However, the differences from the Massachusetts articles are significant:

4. Among the natural rights, some are in their very nature, unalienable because no equivalent can be given or received for them. Of this kind are the Rights of Conscience.
5. Every individual has a natural and unalienable right to worship God according to the dictates of his own conscience and reason: and no subject shall be hurt, molested, or restrained in his person, liberty, or estate for worshipping God in the manner and season most agreeable to the dictates of his own conscience or for his religious profession, sentiment, or persuasion; provided he doth not disturb the public peace or disturb others in their religious worship.
6. As morality and piety, rightly grounded on evangelical principles, will give the best and greatest security to government and will lay, in the hearts of men, the strongest obligations to due subjection; and as the knowledge of these is most likely to be propagated through a society by the institution of the public worship of the Deity, and of public instruction in morality and religion; therefore, to promote those important purposes, the people of this State have a right to empower and do hereby fully empower the Legislature to authorize from time to time the several towns, parishes, bodies corporate, or religious societies, within this State, to make adequate provision, at their own expense, for the support and maintenace of public protestant teachers of piety, religion, and morality.
   Provided notwithstanding, That the several towns, parishes, bodies corporate, or religious societies shall at all times have the exclusive right of electing their own public teachers, and of contracting with them for their support and maintenance. And no person of any one par-

29. James Colby, *Manuel of the Constitution of the State of New Hampshire* (Concord, 1902), pp. 71–73.
30. *Ibid.,* p. 81.

ticular religious sect or denomination shall ever be compelled to pay toward the support of the teacher or teachers of another persuasion, sect, or denomination.

And every denomination of Christians, demeaning themselves quietly, and as good subjects of the State shall be equally under the protection of the law: And no subordination of any one sect of denomination to another shall ever be established by law.

And nothing herein shall be understood to affect any former contracts made for the support of the ministry; but all such contracts shall remain and be in the same state as if this Constitution had not been made.

Comparison of these articles with those of the Massachusetts Bill of Rights reveals three significant variations. The first and most obvious is the omission in the New Hampshire articles of the important paragraph dealing with right of dissenters to have their religious taxes paid to the teacher of their own sect; instead the omission seems clearly to grant to dissenters the right of exemption from paying religious taxes at all. Second, and equally important, where Article Three of the Massachusetts Bill of Rights gave the legislature the power "to authorize and require" the towns and parishes to make suitable provision for public worship, Article Six of the New Hampshire Bill of Rights gave the legislature only the right to "authorize" such action; by explicitly omitting the word "require" it granted the towns and parishes the right of local option in levying religious taxes. Third, the New Hampshire Bill of Rights did not contain any clause authorizing the legislature to require the inhabitants to attend public worship.

Obviously all three of these variations indicate a conscious attempt by the framers of the New Hampshire constitution to expand the conception of religious liberty beyond that which existed in Massachusetts. But these variations do not indicate that the Revolutionary fervor over natural rights materially altered the outlook which already prevailed in New Hampshire. The Bill of Rights merely codified the slightly more liberal establishment which had already evolved in New Hampshire; it did not constitute a radical new step forward. No one in the state appears to have thought that under this Bill of Rights religious liberty was extended to deists, atheists or Nothingarians or even that it would apply to new sects like Universalists, Shakers, Christians or Unitarians which were beginning to arise. In 1803, Judge Jeremiah Smith of the New Hampshire Supreme Court stated that while Episcopalians, Presbyterians, Quakers, and Baptists "were at that time [1784] exempt" from religious taxation by virtue of the Bill of Rights, "atheists, deists, revilers and contemners of religion and persons of no religion at all" were not then exempt and should not be exempted in 1803.[31] He continued "Perhaps it would be going too far to say that these words

31. *Decisions of the Superior and Supreme Courts of New Hampshire*, (Boston, 1879), pp. 25, 30. Hereafter referred to as Smith, *Decisions*.

[in Article Six] shall not be construed to extend to sects that may spring up in future," but "When they arise and become distinctly marked, they will doubtless be entitled to claim the privilege of exemption." Before they could make this claim, however, they would first have to convince the courts both of their distinction from other sects and of their piety. In 1803 — and probably until 1819 — the New Hampshire courts were not willing to concede that any new sects beyond the original four had become sufficiently distinct to meet the requirements for exemption. However, as we shall see, the legislators circumvented the judges' more rigid views on this issue.

Significantly, too, because of the careful wording of Article Six, it was possible to alter radically or to amend the religious system of New Hampshire by legislative action — even to the extent of abolishing compulsory religious taxation — without, as in Massachusetts, requiring an amendment to the constitution.

In the absence of any journal of the debates of this constitutional convention and the even more important absence of any expressions of opinion in the newspapers or extant private papers by those who wrote the constitution or those who were asked to ratify it, it is impossible to state precisely what interpretations were placed on these articles at the time. We know the constitution was drawn up in September 1781, was rejected overwhelmingly by the voters and had to be redrawn twice more, in 1782 and 1783, before it was acceptable. We also know no alterations were made in these particular articles concerning religion from the time they were first drawn in 1781 until they were accepted as part of the third constitution drafted by this convention in 1784. This clearly indicates that the objections to the drafts did not stem from religious issues but rather from objections to certain political aspects.

Curiously, one of the few protests against religious taxes at this time came from a Congregational minister, the Rev. Eden Burroughs of Hanover, though he did not address himself specifically to the constitution. Burroughs was born in Stratford, Connecticut and graduated from Yale in 1757. After serving as pastor of a church in South Killingly from 1760 to 1771, he accepted the position as settled minister in Hanover Center, New Hampshire, where he remained until 1809. Burroughs's liberal views on religious taxation may have resulted from his years among the Separates and Separate-Baptists in South Killingly, but more likely they came from his association with Eleazer Wheelock, for Burroughs was a close friend of Wheelock's. He received an honorary A.M. from Dartmouth and was a trustee of the college. He may well have worked with Wheelock in drafting a tract entitled *Liberty of Conscience or No King but Christ in His Church* which Wheelock published in Hartford in 1775 to defend himself against charges of Toryism for his failure to observe a Thanksgiving Day proclaimed by the New Hampshire Provincial Assembly in November 1775. Wheelock's tract argued that while it was proper for legislatures to propose days of fasting they had no power to enforce their observance. For the State to force people to observe certain ceremonies of a religious nature was an encroachment on the spiritual freedom of the people and of the churches:

> When civil power encroaches an inch upon Christ's prerogative, a sanctified and enlightened conscience can never be compelled to a compliance; and if they are of the truth and hear Christ's voice, no instruments of cruelty will avail any thing in this attempt . . . The least yielding in this case is dangerous, and a direct and leading step to a flood of persecution, however remote it may seem at present.[32]

Eden Burroughs went beyond Wheelock in his tract, *The Profession and Practice of Christians . . . Appearing in the Neglect of Executing the Laws of Christ,* published in Hanover in 1784. He frankly took the Baptists' voluntarist view (he had preached it in his pulpit in 1783) that the state had no right to intervene or intermeddle in religious affairs at all, even by requiring compulsory support of religion. Burroughs had demonstrated his friendship with the Baptists before he published this work. Elder Jedidiah Hebbard of Lebanon, New Hampshire, wrote to Backus in 1784 praising Burroughs because "he has fellowship with the Baptists. He has Changed [exchanged pulpits] with Eld[r] [Thomas] Baldwin of Canaan on the Sabbath and the reason as he tells me is because the Baptists in their Disapline honour Christs Laws and Dont in so Dareing a manner Trample on Christs authority." [33] Hebbard also told Backus in 1783 that

> Several of ye Ministers of ye Standing order have Declared yt ye civil magistrate has no Right to enforce any of ye positive laws of Christ, and if he attempts to Do it he Touches Christs Kingly office — and [they] whooly Disapprove of Ministers support by civil law, for ye manner as well as the matter of the Duty is Directed by a positive law of Christ — also they say it is plain from Scripture that Brother Shall not go to law with brother. Mr. Boroughs of Hanover has wrote on ye Subject but it has not come from ye press.[34]

That Backus was pleased with Burroughs' book is indicated by the long quotations from it which he put in his *History.* He particularly liked

32. This passage was quoted approvingly by Backus in his *History,* II, 543. But Wheelock of course did not here or elsewhere ever publicly attack the system of compulsory religious taxation. For a very similar view of civil proclamations of fast and thanksgiving days see Elder Henry Grew's statements in Hartford in 1810, discussed below, Chapter 51.

33. Jedidiah Hebbard to Isaac Backus, October 11, 1784, in the BP(AN).

34. Hebbard to Backus, May 9, 1783, in the BP(AN). Hebbard does not identify the other Congregational ministers who took this stand, but from the attacks on Burroughs after he published his tract it appears that he was in a decided minority. Hebbard told Burroughs that he was sending Backus a copy of his book and Burroughs said that he would welcome Backus's frank comments on it.

Burroughs' statement that "it is absolutely impossible for professing Christians to have this mutual confidence towards each other, while they see that they are so commonly disposed to bite and devour one another, by seeking to get the advantage of each other in their commerce and dealings" and his warning that "Those corporations who call themselves churches of Christ, whilst they refuse to put the laws of his kingdom into execution, and will suffer them to be trampled under foot, are more awfully guilty of the blood of souls than every other set of men under heaven." [35]

Burroughs gave up the practice of religious taxation in Hanover after 1783. But whether his tract may be taken as a direct comment on the constitutional convention is unclear. He does not mention the constitution in the book, yet because he was first known to advance such views in 1783 seems indicative of some connection. It is also curious that neither Elder Hebbard nor Elder Baldwin made any known protest against the constitution in either public or private statements.[36]

The only other public comment on the religious aspects of the constitutions, drafted between 1781 and 1783, was a letter written to the New Hampshire *Gazette* by William Plumer (using the pseudonym "Impartialist"); it was published on February 16, 1782. Plumer was concerned, however, not about religious taxation but about the restriction of protection of the law only to "christians" and the requirement that only persons "of the Protestant religion" could hold state offices. Plumer urged that Article Six be changed "expressly to declare that the protection of the law shall extend to each individual, to all sects and denominations whatsoever, provided their conduct is moral." He urged that officeholding be open to anyone who "is a practiser of morality and the social virtues." Plumer was at this time in his long and varied career, an exponent of deism; it may well be that he spoke less on behalf of Roman Catholics and Jews than on behalf of persons like himself who might be denied office as "infidels" or "Nothingarians." [37] The people of New Hampshire were not unique in placing these restrictions on office holding but they were more dogged in their attachment to this belief than were most, for it was not until 1876 that they finally struck this restriction from their constitution. Plumer was unique in arguing for

35. Backus, *History*, II, 542. I have not been able to locate the 1784 edition but the introduction in the 1793 edition is dated January 10, 1784.

36. See Hebbard's letter of November 15, 1783, however, in which he did protest privately to Backus against the certificate law of Vermont. Hebbard's concern with Vermont's ecclesiastical laws rather than New Hampshire's was because the town of Lebanon was one which had in the past few years sought union with Vermont. The most recent union of these towns with Vermont had ended only a year before, on February 22, 1782, and Hebbard may well have felt that the union would revive again and that the Vermont laws would be applicable in Lebanon.

37. See the excellent biography of Plumer by Lynn W. Turner, *William Plumer of New Hampshire, 1759–1850* (Chapel Hill, 1962), pp. 10–11. Plumer's career as it relates to the history of separation of church and state in New Hampshire is traced in detail below.

the rights of minorities in such broad terms: "If [the majority] deny that liberty, which they enjoy themselves, to others because their ecclesiastical sentiment is different from their's, then their determination is partial & unequal. The ideas of power & equality are in their nature distinct, & ought not to be confounded."

Indicative of the conservative public temper on this question was the fact that Plumer had to pay the printer three dollars to have his letter published. It is also indicative that Plumer, who had recently been a Baptist exhorter and who throughout a long political career (which eventually led him to the governor's chair in 1812) claimed to be a staunch opponent of the union of church and state, said nothing in this letter about the right given to the legislature and the towns to maintain the old system of religious taxation. Plumer, and presumably the great majority of the inhabitants of New Hampshire, subscribed to the fundamental assumption of the Congregationalists in New England that "the best and greatest security to government" lay in "the institution of the public worship of the Deity" (as Article Six said), and therefore the State had a right to lend its support to the propagation of this worship by enacting laws "for the support and maintenance of public protestant teachers of piety, religion, and morality." That the Baptists of New Hampshire made no protest against the continuation of this system may be attributed to the failure of the very active protest Backus led in Massachusetts several years earlier, or it may be attributed to their hope that most towns and parishes would interpret Article Six freely to grant exemption to them. Or it may simply be that the Baptists were still so few and that they were too busy trying to maintain a bare existence to muster any effort to fight for the abstract principle of separation. David Benedict, writing his history of the Baptists in 1812, quoted Article Six and comments, "This article promises all that dissenters would ask . . . our brethren in this State (New Hampshire) generally enjoy all the religious privileges which they have ever asked from the civil power, viz. *to be let alone.*" [38] This negative and self-centered attitude toward religious liberty began to prevail among many Baptists toward the end of the century when religious oppression gradually disappeared.

Once the constitution and bill of rights were ratified in 1783 (they went into effect in 1784) the next step in sustaining the old system of church and state was to enact a law authorizing the towns and parishes to make provision for the maintenance of public Protestant teachers. For some reason this law was not enacted until February 8, 1791, though the towns continued to operate under the old system during the interval. The law itself was a verbatim reenactment of the act for regulating towns and the choice of town officers which had been in force since 1719. It entitled the majority of the inhabitants of any town to vote "such sum or sums of money as they

---

38. David Benedict, *General History of the Baptist Denomination in America*, 2 vols., (Boston, 1813), I, 332. The italics are his.

shall judge necessary for the settlement, maintenance and support of the ministry, schools, meeting houses" and these sums "to be assessed on the polls and estates" of all inhabitants. This act did not *require* towns to levy taxes for the support of religion; it simply said they might do so "agreeably to the Constitution." [39] Neither this act nor any other act said anything about how dissenters were to be exempted, as the Constitution required; no certificate system was spelled out and the decisions on exemptions therefore had to be resolved on an *ad hoc* basis in each town or through the courts.

Once again there is no evidence that any of the dissenters raised objections to this act. The only indication that any clarification was needed or wanted concerning its reinforcement of the practice of religious taxation occurred at the constitutional convention called in September 1791, regarding a requirement in the constitution of 1784 that a convention be called every seven years to consider needed alterations. According to the journal of this convention, on its second day "The 6th Article [of the Bill of Rights] was read & largely debated and some alterations proposed but no vote obtained in favour of the alterations. A motion was made to erase the 6th article in order to substitute another in its stead: on which motion the yeas and nays were called" and the motion was lost by the overwhelming vote of 89 to 15.[40] The journal of the convention gives no details concerning the debate, nor does it quote the proposed amendment to Article Six, nor does it even say who proposed the amendment. But from other evidence it appears certain that it was the work of William Plumer.

Plumer was unquestionably the most significant figure in the religious history of New Hampshire from 1780 to 1820 and he played a crucial role in almost all aspects of the controversy over the Standing Order. Yet strangely enough he began his political career as a Federalist. Plumer was born in Newburyport, Massachusetts in 1759.[41] His father was a New Light who became a Baptist in 1775 after he had moved to Epping, New Hampshire. Four years after his father joined the Baptists, William Plumer was converted in a revival led by Elder Samuel Shepard of Brentwood. Shepard, a practicing doctor of medicine, shared with Elder William Hooper of Madbury the leadership of the Baptists in New Hampshire in this period.[42] Under Shepard's inspiration young Plumer felt a call to preach during the summer of 1780. He itinerated throughout the state exhorting and making

---

39. *Laws of New Hampshire,* V, 592.
40. Nathaniel Bouton, ed. *Journal of the Convention . . . To Revise the Constitution of New Hampshire,* 1791–1792 (Concord, 1876), p. 41.
41. Turner, *Plumer,* pp. 10–11.
42. For Hooper, see William Plumer's ms. biographical sketches, V, 431–432. For Shepard see Backus, *History,* II, 168–169, 280, 535; also William Plumer's ms. biographical sketches, V, 73–75, in the New Hampshire Historical Society. Plumer wrote of Shepard in later years, "He did more than any other man in New Hampshire in building up the sect of which he was a member."

many converts. But in the fall he began to have doubts about the truth of evangelical Christianity. He read the rationalistic works of Addison, Sherlock, Akenside, and Cato which, he said later, caused him to abandon his religious faith.[43] He became a deist and remained one for the rest of his life. It was as a deist that he wrote his letter to the New Hampshire *Gazette* in 1782 protesting against religious restrictions for officeholding. It was as a deist that he attacked Article Six in the constitutional convention of 1791–92.

Among his papers are many relating to the convention of 1791 in which he played a dominant role. He was a member of the Grand Committee of Ten appointed by the convention to draft the amendments brought forward in the convention's debates. One of these papers contains the following proposal which, though unmarked, seems clearly to have been the amendment which was read and debated in September 1791. Had it been adopted, New Hampshire would have been the first of the Puritan states to separate church and state:

> That we are required by the benevolent principles of rational liberty to guard against that spiritual oppression & intolerance wherewith bigotry and ambition of weak and wicked priests & princes have scourged mankind: therefore the free exercise and enjoyment of religious profession & worship, without discrimination in preference, shall forever hereafter be allowed within this State to all mankind: Provided that the liberty of Conscience hereby granted shall not be construed to excuse acts of licentiousness, or justify practices inconsistent with the peace or safety of the State & That no person shall ever in this State be deprived of the inestimable priviledge of worshipping God in a manner agreeable to the dictates of his own Conscience nor under any pretence whatever be compelled to attend any place of worship contrary to his own faith & judgment; nor shall any person within this State ever be obliged to pay tithes, taxes, or any other rates for the purpose of building or reparing any other church or churches, place or places of worship or for the maintenance of any minister or ministry contrary to what he believes to be right or has deliberately or voluntarily engaged himself to perform.[44]

One can understand why the Congregational delegates voted down such a radical proposal. It is perhaps not so easy to understand why the two leading Baptist delegates at the convention also voted against it. One of these was William Hooper; the other Amos Wood. (Plumer, of course, was recorded in the journal of the convention among those in its favor.)

William Hooper was born in Berwick, Maine, and joined the first Baptist church there in 1763. A farmer and shoemaker by trade, Hooper felt the call to preach in 1776 and was ordained that year as the minister of the

43. Turner, *Plumer,* pp. 10–11.
44. Plumer, ms. "Repository," IV, 333, in the New Hampshire Historical Society. Also Turner, *Plumer,* pp. 44–49

church of which he was a member. It is said that one of the first persons he baptized was young Benjamin Randall, who, four years later, founded the Freewill Baptist denomination that caused so much difficulty for the Baptists in the ensuing years. In 1776 Hooper was called to settle over the Baptist Church in Madbury, New Hampshire. Here he remained, supporting himself by shoemaking and farming, until his death in 1837. He helped to organize the New Hampshire Association of Baptist churches in 1785 and was for twenty-five years the clerk of this association. One of the leading members of his denomination in the state, "He possessed," said William Plumer, "a strong mind, a retentive memory — great decision of character." He was "a man of inflexible character . . . universally esteemed." In 1788 he was elected a delegate from Madbury to the convention chosen to ratify the federal constitution. Like most rural Baptists he was anti-federalist and voted against ratification.[45] As a member of the constitutional convention of 1791–92, Hooper "was in general opposed to making changes in the original constitution," wrote Plumer.

Elder Amos Wood was born in Rowley, Massachusetts, in 1760 and graduated from Rhode Island College in 1786. The next year he settled as pastor of the First Baptist Church in Weare, New Hampshire, where he remained until his death in 1798. As a member of the constitutional convention he appears to have shared the conservative views of his colleague.

There are two explanations why Hooper and Wood voted against Plumer's proposal to end religious taxation. First, these elders may well have resented Plumer as an apostate, an infidel, a man who had turned against the Baptist faith and was not to be trusted or encouraged. Second, they may well have been antagonized by the anticlerical tones in which Plumer phrased his amendment. Both the man and his radical deism were anathema to the Baptists. The New England Baptists were always opposed to the kind of secular social order which the deists advocated and those in New Hampshire seemed generally content with their status under Article Six. A deist might fight for separation on principle; the Baptists preferred simply to be let alone.

Two days after Plumer's radical amendment lost, the convention considered a motion, also probably made by Plumer, "that the words 'Shall be of the Protestant religion' be struck out" of the requirement for office-

45. It is unknown whether Hooper favored the amendment to the United States Constitution Samuel Livermore proposed at the ratifying convention which stated that "Congress shall make no laws touching religion or to infringe the rights of Conscience." Anson Phelps Stokes, *Church and State in the United States* (New York, 1950), I, 315–316. Livermore was an Episcopalian and a member of Congress when it passed the First Amendment. He was also President of the constitutional convention of 1791–1792 in New Hampshire, but I have found no evidence that he ever took a strong stand to end religious taxes in New Hampshire. His efforts for the First Amendment in Congress seem to have been motivated by his desire to protect the Anglican Church since many thought it possible that Congress might try somehow to create a Calvinistic establishment led by Presbyterians and Congregationalists.

holding. This motion lost by a vote of 51 to 35. This time Plumer was joined in the minority by Hooper but not by Wood.[46] The convention later reconsidered this proposal, however, and agreed to include it among the amendments proposed to the people. The only other success in liberalizing the religious system Plumer had at the convention of 1791 was in formulating a clarification of Article Six which the convention also agreed to recommend to the people.[47] This concerned the system of certification for exemption from religious taxes. It would have enabled anyone who opposed the minister chosen by a town to enter his dissent and be excused from paying toward his support:

> And whenever a minister is settled by any incorporated town or parish, any person dissenting, shall have liberty either at the meeting or previous to the ordination of the minister, or within one month after the vote obtained for his settlement, to enter his dissent with the town or parish clerk against paying or contributing toward the support of such minister; & all minors, who after such settlement shall come of age, and all inhabitants of such town or parish who are absent from the same at the time of such meeting or settlement, and all persons who after such settlement move into such town or parish to reside, shall have three months from the time of their coming of full age, returning into town or moving in to reside, as aforesaid, respectively, to enter their dissent with the town or parish clerk as aforesaid.
>
> And all persons who do not enter their dissent as aforesaid, shall be bound by the major vote of such town or parish, & it shall be considered as their voluntary contract: But all persons who enter their dissent as aforesaid shall not be bound by the vote of such town or parish or considered as party to such contract, or in any way to be compelled to contribute towards the support of the minister, nor shall any person be compelled to contribue towards the support of a minister who shall change from the sect or denomination of which he professed to be when he settled, to any other persuasion, sect, or denomination.[48]

This alteration in the system was designed primarily to aid Congregationalists rather than to aid dissenters. The dissenters were already generally granted exemption, but a Congregationalist with Unitarian or deistic views had no way of avoiding payments to support whatever kind of Congregationalist the majority supported. By the same token, the final clause gave relief to an orthodox Trinitarian if a settled minister of a town changed his views from Trinitarianism to Unitarianism. This was the first of the seventy-two amendments which this convention proposed to the people on February

---

46. Bouton, *Journal of the Convention,* p. 46.
47. Plumer was sufficiently cautious to include as the first clause of this proposed amendment the statement that "this shall not be construed to free a person from the obligation of his own contract on his pretence of changing his religious persuasion after making the contract." Or possibly this was forced on him.
48. Bouton, *Journal of the Convention,* pp. 113–114.

24, 1792. When the votes were counted on June 1, 1792, the people rejected it by 3993 to 994 votes; they also rejected the amendment which would have ended the limitation on officeholding to Protestants.[49] The religious system of New Hampshire continued to operate under Article Six and the act of 1791 for another twenty-eight years. In the concluding pages of his exhaustive, three-volume history of New Hampshire, published in 1792, Jeremy Belknap wrote that there was "as entire religious liberty in New Hampshire as any people can rationally desire." [50] Belknap was, of course, a Congregationalist.

49. *Ibid.,* p. 141. The opposition to the amendment regarding certification for tax exemption undoubtedly arose from the fears of Congregationalists that it would seriously undermine the system of tax support, that it would encourage dissension, and that it would reward deists and tax dodgers. However, in 1793 the town of Epping allowed William Plumer to sign himself off as a dissenter from the Standing Church. Turner, *Plumer,* p. 11 note.

50. Jeremy Belknap, *The History of New Hampshire* (Boston, 1792), III, 325.

Chapter 44

The Dissenters and the Courts
in New Hampshire,
1792–1807

. . . a difference in government, discipline, and worship alone constitutes
the difference of sects and denominations.

New Hampshire Superior Court, 1803 (Muzzy *vs.* Wilkins)

The rapid growth among the Baptists in New Hampshire after 1770
stemmed from the itinerant evangelism of Elder Hezekiah Smith of Haverhill, Massachusetts. Largely through his efforts enough people were converted to form a Baptist church in Deerfield and another in Stratham in
1770; one in Exeter in 1771; one in Brentwood in 1772; and one in East
Northwood in 1773. The ministers ordained over these churches themselves practiced itinerant evangelism and in this way the movement spread.
By 1776 there were eleven Baptist churches in New Hampshire (though
only five of them had ordained ministers at that time). At the same
time there were eighty-four Congregational churches, fifteen Presbyterian
churches, four Quaker Meeting houses, and three Episcopal churches.[1] In
the 1780's Universalists and Freewill Baptists began to form churches, as
did Shakers and Methodists in the 1790's, and Christ-ians in 1803. But the
regular Baptists quickly became the most numerous and important dissenting
group in the state. Probably the Baptists made most of their converts from
nominal but non-churchgoing Congregationalists, from New Lights, and
from real or potential Separates, though there is no indication that any of
the five or six Separate churches in New Hampshire accepted Baptist views
en masse.[2] The Baptists continued rapid expansion through the rest of the
century: by 1790 they had formed thirty-one churches and by 1795, forty-

1. Charles B. Kinney, *Church and State: The Struggle for Separation in New
Hampshire* (New York, 1955), p. 83.
2. C. C. Goen, *Revivalism and Separatism in New England, 1740–1800* (New
Haven, 1962), pp. 246–248. By 1801 there were four Methodist churches, four Universalist churches and seventeen Freewill Baptist churches in New Hampshire.

one. The treatment which they received as dissenters varied greatly from town to town.

The fact that there were no laws in New Hampshire defining the proper procedure for a dissenter to obtain exemption appears to have posed no problem. From the outset the Baptists assumed they were by right and precedent entitled to exemption from religious taxes if they presented some form of certification that they were bona fide Baptists. When the Baptists of South Hampton and Salisbury united to form a church in 1780 over which Elder Samuel Shepard of Brentwood preached one Sunday out of four, all those who wished to join the congregation were required to subscribe to the following statement in the church records:

> We being conscious that the Anti-Pedobaptist Churches are most in ac-cordance to Scripture in their principles and way of supporting the min-istry of the gospel, have applied to the Anti-Pedo Baptist Church belong-ing to South Hampton and Salisbury to join them and being received by said church as members of said society we hereby sign their church book to signify our willingness, according to our ability, to assist in supporting their religious cause.

After they signed this book, those Baptists (even those who were not yet immersed but were only adherents who had volunteered to give financial support to the new Baptist church) were then given certificates signed by a committee of the congregation (or society) which read:

> We, the subscribers, being chosen a Committee by the Society of the people called Anti-Pedo Baptist who meet together for religious worship on the Lord's Day in South Hampton, to exhibit a list or lists of persons belonging to said Society or Congregation, do certify that A. B. and C. D. of Salisbury and inhabitants of the second parish in said town do fre-quently and usually when able attend with us in our meetings for re-ligious worship on the Lord's Day and we do verily believe are, with respect to the ordinance of baptism, of the same religious sentiments with us.
>
> Elder Samuel Shepard ⎱
> Deac. Barnard Curier ⎰ Committee[3]
> Jeremiah Flanders ⎰

Here the Baptists followed the Massachusetts system because the town of Salisbury was in Massachusetts; it therefore seemed logical to provide the same certification for those members who lived in South Hampton even though New Hampshire had no certificate law.

This kind of precedent, set by Baptists who came from Massachusetts and adopted by those Baptist churches formed on the border of the two

3. B. P. Byram, *History of the First Baptist Church of Salisbury and Amesbury* (Salisbury, 1860), pp. 20–21.

states, was followed by the churches formed farther north. Even the Free-will Baptist church records contain the same kinds of certificates. The Freewill Baptist church founded in New Durham by Benjamin Randall in 1780 issued this certificate in 1788:

> This May Certify all whome it May Consern that James Jewett has this Day met with the Members of the Baptist Church at New Durham at a Monthly Meeting and Declared that he has Been of the oppinion of the Baptist[s] for a Number of years Past and has this Day Joyn'd as a Member of the Society of Baptist[s] in sd town.
> Signed with the Consent and in the Behalf of the Chh By
>
> Benjn Randel, Clark at Monthly Meeting May 28, 1788[4]

Certificates like these, read in a town or parish meeting or entered by a clerk into the town or parish records were adequate in most cases to exempt a Baptist, or any other dissenter, from religious taxes.

But sometimes the towns themselves passed votes granting such exemptions en masse as a kind of local ordinance. The town of Cornish, for example, voted in 1793, "That from the 29th of September next, no person shall be held or bound by Civil Contract to pay any taxes for the support of the Gospel unless he shall previously consent thereto." [5] In Northwood the Baptists built in 1773 a church in the eastern part of the town whose eleven members were exempted without difficulty. As the church grew in size its additions were added to the list until by 1800 eighty-six of the 175 taxpayers in Northwood were exempted from religious taxes; all but eight of these (by a practice of self-segregation practiced throughout New England) lived in East Northwood.[6] The town of Littleton, which was not settled until late in the century, had so many Baptists in it from the beginning that it never levied a religious tax. When it began to build its first Congregational meetinghouse in 1811 it did so by subscription and the sale of pews. As the Baptists here had no meetinghouse, the Congregationalists voted that if any Baptists subscribed to the building of the meetinghouse, their denomination would be allowed to use the meetinghouse in proportion to the amount contributed.[7] In 1805 the town of Haverhill, New Hampshire, accepted the notice by sixteen persons that "We are not of the same sect or denomination on matters of religion with Mr. Smith, the minister of the Town. We do not attend on his ministry or meeting nor do we consider our polls or estates liable to be taxed to pay any part of his

---

4. Ms. church records of the New Durham Freewill Baptist Church in the New Hampshire Historical Society.

5. Kinney, *Church and State*, p. 88; Otis F. R. Waite, *History of the Town of Claremont* (Manchester, 1895), p. 85.

6. J. M. Moses, "Early Settlers of East Northwood," *The Granite Monthly* (Concord), XLIX (1917), pp. 37 ff.

7. James R. Jackson, *History of Littleton* (Cambridge, 1905), I, 235.

salary." [8] By 1810 there were so many dissenters exempted in Winchester that the town ceased voting religious taxes and voted to divide the use of the meetinghouse among all the sects in the town.[9] A year later the town of Hillsborough, where 153 of the 373 taxpayers were exempted, gave up the practice of voting religious taxes.[10] A contemporary observer claimed that by 1819 when the legislature finally put a formal end to compulsory religious taxes, the practice had already ceased in at least half the towns in the state.[11]

Most of the towns which granted exemption to dissenters or gave up religious taxation when dissenters became numerous did so either because they wished to maintain harmony in the town or because they believed Article Six required such exemption. But in some cases the dissenters had to wait until they were a majority before they could end the system. In Hampstead, by 1782, the Baptists and Nothingarians had increased to the point where they were able to prevent the town from passing a vote to settle a new minister to replace a deceased Congregationalist. After the Congregationalists had been thwarted for four years, the town finally settled the matter by inserting an annual vote in the town meeting to free all non-Congregationalists from paying religious taxes. After they had made this concession, the Congregationalists were permitted in 1786 to choose a new minister for the town. But the number who supported him was so small that in 1792 the church had to solicit voluntary contributions to make up for taxes which they could not collect from their congregation. By 1798 the Congregationalists in Hampstead stopped levying religious taxes.[12]

The turning point for toleration of dissent, especially of the Baptists, appears to have occurred in New Hampshire, as it did elsewhere in New England, during the Revolution. This toleration is evident from 1778 to 1783 in a letter which a former resident of Norwich, Connecticut wrote to Isaac Backus in November 1783:

> There is a Great fall of Bigitry Since I Came to this Town about five years ago when all [dissenters] was Reprobated that Did Not fall in with the Traditions of the Fathers and Believe in the Desent from Peter and ministers must be Licens[d] by those that had Regular ordination and that the Civil Law must be Exerted for the Support of their [Congregational] Teachers otherwise all Religion would fail and None may speak in a Congregation without License and a Baptist Elder ought Not To be heard by No Means and many more Erors that they Brought with them

---

8. J. Q. Bittinger, *History of Haverhill* (Haverhill, 1888), p. 219. Most of these, if not all, appear to have been Methodists.

9. Kinney, *Church and State*, p. 91.

10. *Ibid.*, p. 92.

11. The New Hampshire *Patriot* (Concord), June 22, 1819, p. 2.

12. John Kelly, "Historical Sketch of the Town of Hampstead," New Hampshire Historical Society, *Collections*, V (1837), 179 ff.

from Home &c but God in his Providence hath Confounded in some measure the Loftiness and Pride of men. A Partickelar Instance is one Thomas Baldwin some years since from Norwich, Now ordained at Canaan a Baptist Elder born out of wedlock Educated at Ames forge at New Concord who Caries Conviction in all that Hear him that he is a Sent [saint?] of God and hath a Great Gift in Doctrine Hardly his Eaquil To be found and Likewise Mr [Elisha] Ransom of Woodstock about Twenty miles from here who is a vire [very] Rare man a Baptist Elder and Now Heard and Estem^d by those that once was so Bigoted as afore Described. Sir, I am more and more Convinced of this Truth that it is the Holy Ghost that only Can Quallyfie and Prepare men for the ministry.[13]

Obviously the Baptists felt that their fervent though unlearned ministers were winning new respect for their denomination. These itinerant preachers did win a multitude of new converts in New Hampshire in these years. The same letter reported one hundred converted in Lebanon during the preceding two years.

After 1780 dissenters in several towns, now majorities, elected one of their own ministers as the established minister of the town, levied taxes for his support, and forced the Congregationalists to provide certificates or to pay to maintain him. The Episcopalians did this in the town of Holderness in 1783. The Methodists did it in South New Market in 1808. The Universalists did it in Langdon in 1804. The Baptists did it in New London in 1788. In some other towns where a dissenting minister became the town minister, he accepted the ministerial lot but would not allow taxes to be used to support him. He would, however, even if he were a Baptist, accept the income from the ministry lot.[14] The Baptists' use of religious taxes in New London was always an embarrassment to the denomination, but it explains much about the Baptist outlook in New Hampshire.

A large proportion of the early settlers in New London in the 1780's were Baptists from Attleborough, Massachusetts. Since New London had no settled minister, these Baptists voted to ask Elder Job Seamans of Attleborough to come north to join them and they offered as encouragement the ministerial lot set aside in the town charter for the first settled minister. Seamans came to investigate the situation in June 1787. While he was there he preached, to the town's general satisfaction, and on September 24, the town meeting "Voted to give Elder Seamans a call to settle," and "voted to give him forty pounds yearly" for his salary, three pounds in cash and the rest in labor and produce. The town also voted to give him not only the

13. This letter, among the BP(AN), is from Elihu Hyde, November 15, 1783.
14. For the Methodists in South New Market and the Episcopalians in Holderness see Kinney, *Church and State*, pp. 79, 90; for the others see Robert F. Lawrence, *The New Hampshire Churches* (Claremont, 1856), pp. 137, 602, 613, 348–349, 311–313, 449–450, 491, 395.

ministerial lot (of about one hundred acres) but also one half of the ministry or glebe lot.[15] On March 28, 1788 Seamans accepted this call to become the Standing minister of the town and in July he moved up from Attleborough with his family. He was formally installed a year later in a new meetinghouse (for which money was raised by subscription). The installation council were Elders Amos Wood of Weare, Thomas Baldwin of Canaan, and Samuel Ambrose of Sutton. They evidently found nothing to condemn in his acceptance of this connection between church and state. The church grew very slowly; by 1792 it had only eighteen members. But the results of a revival that year increased church membership to 115 by 1794.[16] Taxes were levied regularly for Seamans's salary but inevitably some of the inhabitants fell behind in paying them. The town had given Seamans a bond as security for annual payment of his salary; people began to fear he might have to use it against the town to collect his arrearages. In 1795, therefore, the town requested he yield the bond. He acceded to their request; thereafter, he was supported entirely on a voluntary basis.[17] But he still kept the land which had been given to him and he was still officially the Standing minister of the town; he remained so for forty years.

But despite a general spirit of toleration in New Hampshire, the dissenters did not always have an easy time. The Baptists in particular felt the same social prejudices existed against them among Congregationalists here that existed in the older states. James Chandler, the Congregational minister of Rowley, published a letter against the Baptists in 1781, when they first began to be numerous:

> Alas, the consequence of the prevalence of this sect! They cause division everywhere. In the State of New Hampshire, where there are many new towns, infant settlements, if this sect gets footing among them, they hinder, and are like to hinder, their settling and supporting learned, pious and orthodox ministers; and so the poor inhabitants of those towns must live, who knows how long? without the ministry of the gospel and gospel ordinances.

The Baptist ordinances did not count, because their "illiterate and unskillful preachers" taught only error and confusion.[18] Despite claims from

15. Edward and Myra Lord, *A History of New London* (Concord, 1899), p. 24.
16. Isaac Backus, *History of New England*, ed. David Weston (Newton, 1871), II, 538, 542. In 1793 this town consisted of fifty families.
17. Lord, *New London*, pp. 33–34. See Seamans' letter to Isaac Backus, December 1, 1794, complaining over "what confinement it is to be a town minister," because he could not itinerate, BP(AN).
18. *Continental Journal and Weekly Advertiser* (Boston), quoted in Backus, *History*, II, 533–534. Chandler also accused them of being Tories and of trying to hinder the war effort; he said they became Baptists "to save themselves from paying anything to support the gospel" and that their ministers were "young, illiterate, and bold itinerating preachers."

Backus, Benedict, and Belknap that a climate of religious freedom prevailed in New Hampshire, in towns where Congregationalists like Chandler prevailed, the Baptists had to fight hard for tax exemption. Backus noted, though he thought it exceptional, that the voters of Richmond, New Hampshire refused in 1771 to accept Elder Matturin (or Matturean) Ballou's claim to the ministerial lot as the first settled minister in the town; they also refused to accept his certificates to exempt his congregation from religious taxes.[19] In a letter to the Warren Association in 1771, Ballou asked for assistance against this oppression:

> for we meet with great opposition in our province, and the main point of their objection is, they say our settlement is not according to law, so that they threaten to pay no regard to our certificates given to our brethren lying in other towns. Another particular is, it is so ordered in our [town] charter by the king's grant, that one whole share of land shall be given to the church of England, one whole share to the incorporate society to propagate the gospel in foreign parts, and one whole share to the first settled minister of the gospel in said town . . . Our elder being the first, we think it belongs to him, but being opposed by the inhabitants of the town of other denominations we ask your advice what we had best do.[20]

How this matter was settled is unknown. In the same letter Ballou also mentioned a Baptist church in Rindge, New Hampshire, which "have suffered much by the inhabitants of their town who have taken away their cattle and sold them at the post for their ministers rates" even though they were duly organized into a church.

Members of the Baptist church of Elder Abel Webster in Plymouth, New Hampshire suffered taxation and distraint of goods in the years 1777–1780, until they were finally voted exemption in a town meeting.[21] The same thing happened in Hillsborough in 1790.[22] The town of Hollis voted in 1785 not to exempt the Baptists who petitioned that year for this privilege.[23] The Baptists and Methodists united to fight for exemption in the town of Lancaster and finally obtained it after giving in certificates in 1802.[24] Only through the kindness of the Congregational minister, David Sutherland, did the dissenters escape distraint and jail in the town of Bath. Sutherland personally told the tax collectors not to force anyone to pay for his support, thus accepting a loss in salary which the town would willingly have wrung from the dissenters.[25]

The Baptist experience in Hampton Falls was typical of the hard fight

19. Backus, *History,* II, 539.
20. *Ibid.,* 539.
21. Kinney, *Church and State,* p. 86.
22. *Ibid.,* pp. 86, 92.
23. *Ibid.,* p. 88.
24. *Ibid.,* pp. 89, 90.
25. *Ibid.,* p. 90.

which they were often forced to wage in those towns which did not see either the legal or the social impulsions of voluntarism. The Baptists first held services here in a private home in 1800. But the man in whose home they met forbade their meetings there after four of his windows were broken by a heckling mob. The Baptists petitioned the town meeting repeatedly "To see if the said meeting will agree to discharge the Congregational minister tax standing against the Baptist society" and "To see if the meeting will agree that the inhabitants each of them have liberty to attend any society they like best and pay their minister tax where they attend only." These petitions were turned down. In 1806 four of the Baptists were distrained for religious taxes. They brought suit against the assessors. The town voted to defend the assessors. But evidently it appeared the case would go against the town, for finally in 1809 the town "voted not to tax the Baptists who shall present certificates before assessment is made the present year for their ministers tax." Since this vote exempted those who filed certificates only for that year, it was necessary to pass a similar vote each year in town meetings until the Toleration Act was passed in 1819.[26]

Inevitably, as in Massachusetts, the problem of religious taxation had to be settled in the courts when the town meeting would not do so. The New Hampshire constitution was almost as vague and contradictory about the dissenters' precise rights as was the Massachusetts Constitution, from which its clauses on this subject were borrowed. As in Massachusetts, the courts were dominated by Congregationalists who were firmly convinced of the necessity for religious taxation and were determined that only the bona fide dissenters should be exempted from it. "Not only the judges of the courts were favorable to the dominant sect" said a writer in 1819, "but there was a combination among the lawyers against dissenters and it was even accounted disgraceful for a lawyer to advocate the cause of those persecuted." [27] William Plumer claimed that he was one of the few lawyers in the state who dared risk his reputation by defending the dissenters in religious tax cases. If so, the risk paid off handsomely.[28] Later Plumer wrote a biographical sketch of Paine Wingate, one of the three Justices of the Superior Court of Judicature between 1798 to 1809; it reveals much about the social prejudices of the defenders of the Standing Order. Wingate, born in 1739 and a Harvard graduate of 1759, had been ordained as minister of the Congregational church in 1763. But difficulties arose which led to his dismissal in 1771. He turned first to farming and then to politics. He married a sister of Timothy Pickering, was a member of the Provincial

26. Warren Brown, *History of the Town of Hampton Falls* (Manchester, 1900), pp. 92, 95, 96.
27. New Hampshire *Patriot*, August 3, 1819, p. 3.
28. Lynn W. Turner, *William Plumer of New Hampshire*, 1759–1850 (Chapel Hill, 1962), pp. 33–34. Unlike John Adams and James Sullivan who took cases for both sides, Plumer refused to defend assessors against dissenters.

Congress in 1775, served in the Continental Congress in 1788–1789, in the New Hampshire legislature in 1789–1793, and became a Superior Court Judge in 1798, even though he was not a lawyer and had had no formal legal training. Plumer, and other lawyers, did not consider him a very competent judge, especially on the finer points of jurisprudence. What particularly annoyed Plumer was that "As a judge he was uniformly and zealously in favor of making every man support the clergyman who was settled in the town whether they believed in his doctrine or not." Judge Arthur Livermore, one of Wingate's colleagues, once informed Plumer "that the other two judges [Wingate and Jeremiah Smith] had expressed a decided disapprobation of my conduct and zeal in supporting those who claimed exemption from ministerial taxes assessed for the support of Clergymen. I expressed regret that any of the judges were inclined to support a privileged order, but that circumstance instead of restraining, would increase my exertions." [29]

The most important of all the cases concerning religious taxation to come before the New Hampshire courts was brought by a Presbyterian. This was Muzzy *vs.* Wilkins, *et al.,* which was settled in 1803. John Muzzy lived in Amherst, New Hampshire; he was taxed seventy-five cents in 1795 for the support of the Congregational minister of the town. He refused to pay, claiming exemption as a Presbyterian. The collector took him to prison where he remained until he paid his tax. He then brought suit against the three assessors, Samuel Wilkins, Jonathan Smith, and Daniel Campbell, for trespass and illegal assessment. In a long and involved decision rendered by Chief Justice Jeremiah Smith, the entire context of church-state relations in New Hampshire was finally spelled out, though not with sufficient clarity to satisfy the dissenters. Smith maintained that "the only question referred to the decision of the court is whether Presbyterians are, within the meaning of our Constitution, of another or different persuasion, sect, or denomination from Congregationalists. If they are, the plaintiff is entitled to recover upon this court. If not, he was rightfully taxed." [30] Considering earlier legislative actions regarding the Presbyterians in Chester and Goffstown, it would seem clear that certain differences between these two denominations were already acknowledged by law. However, Smith's decision, argued from a variety of historical analogies and based on the wording of Article Six of the constitution, was one of the few original contributions to the question of church and state in the post-Revolutionary era. Smith defined sectarian differences in terms of polity not of theology. He offered a convincing argument for his view historically, however specious it was factually at the time.

After he quoted Articles Four, Five, and Six of the New Hampshire Bill

29. Plumer, ms. biographies, V, 605–607.
30. Jeremiah Smith, *Decisions of the Superior and Supreme Courts of New Hampshire* (Boston, 1879), p. 3. Hereafter referred to as Smith, *Decisions.*

of Rights, Smith praised them for prohibiting the civil magistrate from prescribing "to men what they shall believe and what they shall not believe . . . No human government has a right to set up a standard of belief, because it is itself fallible. It has not pleased God to enlighten by his grace any government with the gift of understanding of the Scriptures." Hence the New Hampshire constitution rightly prohibited laws of conformity and uniformity in belief. Moreover, "our Constitution goes further. It wholly detaches religion, as such, from the civil State." He asserted (in words with which any dissenter would have agreed): "By the mixture of civil and spiritual power, both become polluted." But under the Bill of Rights, "No such union, no such mixture" was permitted, and "No one sect is invested with any political power much less with a monopoly of civil privileges and civil offices . . . All denominations are equally under the protection of the law, are equally the objects of its favor and regard." But Smith was no secularist. No one could claim, he said, "that the civil magistrate may not lawfully punish certain offences against the unalterable and essential principles of natural and revealed religion" such as "blasphemy, reviling religion, profanation of the Sabbath, &c." "Nor are we to infer that religion is a thing of no consequence to society. The reverse is the case." For although "Religion, in the strict sense of the word, is a personal concern," still the open clauses of Article Six clearly showed that "morality and piety rightly grounded on evangelical principles . . . will give the best and greatest security to government." Hence the towns, via the legislature, were rightly empowered to "make adequate provision for the support and maintenance of public teachers of piety, religion, and morality."

This, Smith continued (in the language of Charles Chauncy, Samuel West, and the other Congregational clergy of Massachusetts), did not constitute an establishment of religion for "A religious establishment is where the State prescribes a formulary of faith and worship for the rule and government of all the subjects." But in New Hampshire, the state allowed each town and parish "not to prescribe rules of faith or doctrine . . . but barely to elect a teacher of religion and morality who is to be maintained at the expense of the whole." This "privilege is extended to all denominations," because the state views "them all as equally good for the purposes of civil society because they all inculcate the principles of benevolence, philanthropy, and the moral virtues." Smith even said that had the Bill of Rights not granted exemptions from religious taxes to the minority in a town who were of a different sect from the majority, they would still have no cause to complain of infringement of the rights of conscience, for the minority did not have to believe or worship with the majority. "Society has a right [in purely civil affairs] to judge what will promote the good of society and to provide for it at the expense of the whole. The minority must submit to the judgment of the majority." And "Public instruction in religion and morality, within the meaning of our Constitution and laws is to every purpose a civil, not a spiritual institution. The relation that subsists between a minister and the church is spiritual." He employed the standard analogies of the schools and the courts as civil institutions which minorities must support even if they do not use them. Smith would not accept any claim that a minister, because he preached about more than morality and because he preached it in a church during a worship service, was therefore involved in spiritual affairs which were not purely civil. Those who said that to support a minister in a civil capacity was also to support him in his spiritual capacity were making too fine a distinction. While dissenters saw the Standing minister as preaching erroneous religious views which would lead men down to hell, Smith saw them as preaching only benevolence and morality upon which all sects agreed. "In short, on this subject of conscience, there is no mistake more common than for men to mistake their wills and their purses for their consciences." Dissenting minorities were either willfully distorting the definition of conscience or maliciously trying to dodge their tax obligations to the community. "The question before the Court, therefore, does not involve it in a matter of conscience. It is a mere question of the extent of a civil obligation and a civil duty." On this issue there was no difference between the conception of an establishment in Massachusetts and one in New Hampshire.

For Judge Smith the nub of the issue was whether membership in a Presbyterian church exempted Joseph Muzzy from religious taxes under the clause of Article Six which said "No person of any particular religious sect or denomination shall ever be compelled to pay towards the support of the teacher or teachers of another persuasion, sect, or denomination." He asked, "What is the criterion" by which the court can decide whether a Presbyterian and a Congregationalist are of the same or different sects or denomination? "Is it a difference in faith, in doctrinal points; or is it a difference in the form of church government, discipline and worship . . . ?" To Smith it was obvious that "The Episcopalian, Presbyterian, and Congregational Churches agree in articles of faith and differ in government, discipline and worship . . . Presbyterians, Independents, Baptists in England, all subscribe [to the] doctrinal articles of the Episcopal Church." This was required by the Toleration Act and none of these sects ever scrupled at those parts of the Thirty-nine Articles to which they had to subscribe under that act. They were nonconformists only because they opposed "the peculiar rites, ceremonies, discipline, government and externals of religion as practised in the Episcopal Church" which they considered "unscriptural" and from which the Toleration Act therefore dispensed them.

However, Smith argued, *within* each of these sects or denominations their own adherents, though they agreed on polity and ceremony, "differ widely in faith and doctrine." For example, "In the Episcopal Church there are Calvinists, Arminians, Universalists, &c. The same may be said of the Presbyterian and Congregational Churches." And who could deny that the

Congregational churches of New England, especially in the vicinity of Boston, varied greatly in their interpretations of doctrine? This posed a problem. "If we say that articles of faith are what only distinguishes sects, then Episcopalians, Presbyterians, and Congregationalists are of the same sect" for all of them adhered to a loose formulation of evangelical Protestantism known as the Elizabethan Compromise. "If we say that doctrinal points enter into the discrimination at all, then individuals among Presbyterians, Congregationalists, and Episcopalians are of the same sect, for they are Calvinists, Arminians, Universalists, &c; and individuals in the Episcopal Church are of different sects, for some are Calvinists, some Arminians, some Universalists, &c."

Smith settled the problem by declaring that "according to the common and usual acceptation of the term sects, matters of faith are not considered. The Episcopalians are a sect; the Presbyterians are a sect, &c. The individual members do not agree in doctrine" within each sect but that does not mean that the various shades of Episcopalians or Congregationalists are of different sects: "though there is much diversity of opinion in articles of faith, and perhaps no two Episcopalians understand the Thirty-nine Articles precisely in the same sense; yet they are all one denomination." (Smith noted in a footnote here that Calvinists were never spoken of as a sect.)

The conclusion was obvious: "If therefore we allow doctrinal articles to enter into the definition of a sect, the term becomes immediately indefinite and uncertain in its meaning." One can see Smith's legal mind struggling to render the indefinite definite. "And what is more to our purpose, affixing this sense of the term will render altogether nugatory that clause in the Constitution which enables corporate bodies to support and maintain public instruction in religion and morality." At last he had reached his conclusion. In no way could a general system of tax-supported religion be maintained if the sectarians of all varieties were permitted to plead doctrinal differences as grounds for exemption. This would be ridiculous:

> To illustrate this idea, let us suppose a whole town or parish to be composed of Episcopalians. They elect an Episcopal teacher. An individual refuses to pay, because the majority or the parson is a Calvinist, and he an Arminian. How is the matter to be tried? Who shall determine as to the creed of the parson or the person claiming exemption? We must take the parties' word for it.

This was the position the dissenters took and the position of the certificate system Plumer had wanted as an amendment to Article Six in 1791: i.e., to let every dissenter sign his own exemption certificate. To Judge Smith the concept was unthinkable. If it carried,

Then the corporation may make a contract as a corporate body, and yet every individual upon his own declaration merely may be loosed from the bond. What is this but saying that the corporation may coerce all who choose to be coerced.

This "absurdity," he said, could be avoided by using his definition as the accepted criterion of a sect or a denomination, "namely, that a difference in government, discipline, and worship, alone constitutes the difference of sects and denominations." (Here he cited several religious histories which maintained that in the seventeenth century sectarian differences grew out of differences in the externals of religion.) If one accepts this simple criterion, "If an individual claims exemption on the ground that he is a Baptist &c. the truth or falsehood of his plea may be examined and tried by a jury" for all the jury needs is evidence that the plaintiff follows the forms and discipline of the Baptists. They need not, and must not, try to examine the man's conscientious beliefs on matters of faith and doctrine. "By their fruits ye shall know them," he said sententiously. "If he is really and truly a Baptist, as he professes to be, it will appear" by "overt acts." He will attend their meetings, "He will conform to their rites and ceremonies and submit himself to their government and discipline."

That this might produce hypocrisy or formal conformity was a problem which the churches must decide. All the law could do was to define the terms of conformity as the sects themselves wished to define them. But as for the differences between a Calvinistic and a Freewill Baptist, a Six-Principle and a Five-Principle Baptist, an Open-Communion and a Closed-Communion Baptist, these were all trifles with which the law was not concerned. Smith was repeating here what the courts in Connecticut had said less clearly from 1750 to 1770 in distinguishing between Separates and Separate-Baptists: the test was the external rite of immersion. His originality was the precision of his historical and legal definition of a point of view which before had been operative largely on *ad hoc* or unconscious grounds.

It was a neat rule, but it flew in the face of the passionate zeal of those who considered even the most minute differences of doctrine or practice to be of crucial importance and therefore justifiable grounds for separation or schism. While Smith was correct in stating that even "a jury of theological doctors" would have trouble deciding "who are Calvinists and who Arminians, who are Arians and who Socinians," he was wrong to think that these matters could be ignored by society and the law and that minorities could be rightly coerced into supporting any one of them so long as the mere external forms of religion according to "the common and usual acceptation" of a sect or denomination were maintained. For a liberal or Unitarian member of Congregationalism, such as Smith himself was, details of doctrinal difference within a denomination were not worth quarreling about. But for the increasing number of evangelical pietists in America, they were the heart and soul of religion.

Smith recognized that "Disagreement in opinion as to the doctrines maintained by sects may have many times occasioned new sects to spring up" but he felt that "even where it has occasioned a separation the dissenters generally, if not always, differ more in government, discipline and worship, that is in the externals than in articles of faith." (How little he understood the nature of evangelical pietism!) However, he said, it was immaterial to the law whether "doctrine or government and discipline" was of the greater importance. "The former does not and the latter do admit of being known and established by evidence," and therefore they are the criteria by which the law must judge. Applying this test made it easy to settle John Muzzy's case. Since Muzzy belonged to a clearly recognized and generally accepted denomination (and since the sincerity of his adherence was not questioned), he was entitled to exemption. "Presbyterianism" is "the government of the church by presbyteries or presbyters;" while "Independents are so called from their maintaining . . . that each congregation is a complete church and is in no respect subject to the control of others." This, he said, "gives us solid ground to stand upon." And from this solid ground he said in an *obiter dictum,* "as to atheists, it is not proper to consider them as a religious sect" any more than "Calvinists, Arminians, Hopkinsians, Universalists, &c." were "distinct sects." Among these only the Universalists had claimed to be a sect, though Judge Smith was no more willing to recognize them as such than he was to consider Methodists as separate from the Episcopal church. Just as he argued that Bishop Thomas Newton was a Universalist in the Episcopal church and Charles Chauncy was a Universalist in the Congregational church, so Elhanan Winchester would have seemed to him merely a Universalist in the Baptist church. Had the incipient Unitarians proclaimed themselves a denomination at this time, as they did twenty-two years later, he would still have maintained that they were no more distinct legally from other Congregationalists than were the English Presbyterians (who had become Unitarian seventy-five years earlier) from the Scottish Presbyterians.[31]

Because Judge Arthur Livermore agreed with Smith in this decision, Muzzy won the case. But the third Judge, Paine Wingate, dissented. In principle Wingate agreed with Smith:

> every variance in religious sentiment will not constitute a Sect or Denomination within the meaning of the Constitution. If it did, it must

31. Smith's distinction in this decision between a "persuasion" and a sect or denomination was uncommon. He defined persuasion as a variety of doctrinal beliefs within a recognized sect or denomination.

effectually destroy the main object of the salutary provision for the support of instructors in religion by incorporated Societies. For I believe there are scarce two Christians who examine and think for themselves who, while they agree in essentials, do not think differently in some points, more or less important in their own view . . . But where differences subsist, some are of magnitude enough to constitute a religious Sect or Denomination.

If Muzzy could prove that "a Presbyterian is of a Sect, Denomination, or Persuasion which constitutes a conscientious difference in religion from the Churches or Societies in this state which are usually known by the name of Congregationalist" then he would win his case. But while Wingate acknowledged that Episcopalians, Baptists, and Quakers had differences of sufficient magnitude from Congregationalists to be considered distinct sects, he could not agree that Presbyterians did.

. . . wherein does any material difference appear? In doctrines no difference is pretended. In ordination by Presbyters and in the ordinances of Baptism and the Eucharist, I know of no important variation. Upon the whole, no difference, I believe is insisted upon as worthy of notice, unless it be in the government and discipline of the Church. And herein do the Presbyterians and Congregationalists differ not more from each other, than both of them differ among themselves?

That "Presbyterians have their Ecclesiastical Judicatories" was also insignificant to him. Since the Presbyterians "in this country have no Hierarchy established, as in Scotland" while the Congregationalists had councils and consociations, the question of judicatories "amounts to very little." The ministers of Massachusetts and Connecticut often spoke of themselves as Presbyterians and were so called by the dissenters, and none of them would have hesitated, as Jonathan Edwards did not, to become pastors of Presbyterian churches. Wingate stated also "to my knowledge, no instance has yet occurred where a Court or jury [in New Hampshire] have exempted one from paying to the support of the teachers of the other on account of a conscientious difference in religion." He concluded, "I am bound to give it as my opinion that by the Constitution and laws of this state, a Presbyterian is not exempt from a liability to pay taxes for the support of a minister of the gospel who is usually known by the name of a Congregationalist." [32]

Obviously the criterion established by Judge Smith was not so clear and simple as he imagined. Learned men had to quibble just as much to distinguish a sect from a persuasion on external grounds as they did to distinguish them on internal or doctrinal grounds. Although clearly the

32. C. E. L. Wingate, *Life and Letters of Paine Wingate* (Medford, 1930), II, 486–491.

judges were convinced of the necessity for religious taxes and were therefore biased against those who would break down the system, the fact that they readily acknowledged Baptists and Quakers to be entitled to exemption but denied it to Presbyterians seems to indicate that prejudice did not operate on social or religious grounds.

In the absence of court records before 1803, it is difficult to know whether the case of Muzzy *vs.* Wilkins marked a sharp turning point in the ecclesiastical law of New Hampshire or whether it culminated a long and consistent evolution of policy. From the scattered references to previous cases available, the latter seems more accurate. Judge Smith cited as a precedent in the Muzzy case a case which had been settled in 1802 involving a Universalist named Christopher Erskine.[33] Erskine's difficulties went back as far as 1789 when he began shopping for churches to attend because his own town church in Claremont was without a pastor. "I attended on such Religious Meetings as happened to come my way," he wrote, "and after hearing diferent oppinions and diferent doctrines respecting Religion and due consideration had thereon, I joined myself to a Society of people in Charlestown known by the name of the Universal[ist] Society who held to the doctrine of Salvation for all men." Soon after he made this choice the town of Claremont settled a new Congregational minister and levied a tax for his support. "I tooke a Certificate from the Clerke of the society in Charlestown . . . to the Selectmen in order to give them a perfect knowledge that I co[u]ld not Join them," said Erskine. At first the town seemed willing to honor his certificate, but in the year 1799 they taxed him "& others that never did Join with them." When Erskine refused to pay the $4.49 assessed him "the Collector came & took my property & sold [it] to pay said Tax." Erskine brought suit against the selectmen, and he won the case in the Court of Common Pleas. But when the selectmen appealed the case to the Superior Court in May 1800, the jury could not agree. The case was held over to the October term, but, said Erskine, "when I appeared, ready for trial, by some means or other the Action was quashed and a Bill of cost recorded against me." Erskine then sent a petition to the state legislature in November 1800, in which he said, "If I am obliged to pay taxes to Support a Religion which I think it (wrong & Contry to the holy Scriptures, or the Doctrine contained in them), my Case is a hard Case & not the freedom which I served the United States for [as a soldier in the Revolution]."[34] The legislature ordered the trial to be heard again, evidently agreeing with Erskine that

33. Smith, *Decisions,* p. 22, note c. and p. 36, note 1. He identifies the case as Henderson & Peckham *vs.* Erskine in error, October Term, 1802. Kinney, *Church and State,* p. 94, refers to him as Christopher Erskine; so does Richard Eddy in his long discussion of the case, *Universalism in America* (Boston, 1886), II, 18–36; however, in a petition quoted in the *Provincial Papers,* XI, 384–385, his name is given as James.

34. *Provincial Papers,* XI, 384–385.

justice had not been done.[35] When the new case came before the Court of Common Pleas in April 1801, Erskine won, but the assessors, Henderson and Peckham, appealed to the Superior Court. Erskine's lawyer, Caleb Ellis, planned to defend Erskine on the grounds that the Universalists were a distinctly different sect or denomination, and therefore Erskine's membership in their society entitled him to exemption from support of the Congregational church. But the Chief Justice of the Superior Court at that time, Simeon Olcott, informed him

> that it has been settled by the Superior Court that persons called Universalists are not such a sect, persuasion, or denomination as by the Constitution of New Hampshire are exempt from the payment of taxes for the support of a regularly settled minister of a Congregational Society in the town where such persons live. And I think that in establishing this practice, the Court was unanimous.[36]

Ellis therefore argued his case on other grounds. But in October 1802 the case was decided against Erskine.

Olcott did not cite the case in which the unanimous decision had been made against the Universalists, but it may well have been the case which William Plumer described in his autobiography. Plumer noted that he had argued a case for a Universalist before Judge Paine Wingate in the 1790's. Wingate asked him before the trial if he thought he could prove that Universalists were a different sect from Congregationalists. Plumer said he thought that there was a great difference between a doctrine of universal salvation and doctrines of election and eternal hellfire. But after he had argued the case on these grounds Wingate turned the case against him.[37]

Whenever and however the precedent had been set, it did not differ much from that in Massachusetts law — or perhaps the confusion was similar in both states. As we have seen, James Sullivan and his partners in the Murray case were barely able to convince the Massachusetts courts in 1786 that the Universalists were entitled to exemption.[38] However, in 1796, in the case of Annan *vs.* Salisbury, the Massachusetts Supreme Court agreed

35. The case may have been turned against Erskine in this first instance because he had mistakenly brought suit against the selectmen instead of against the assessors as he says in his petition.

36. Smith, *Decisions*, p. 37, note 1.

37. Turner, *Plumer*, p. 34. In 1868 Judge Charles Doe of the Superior Court declared in a dissenting opinion in the case of Hale *vs.* Everett, that both the Erskine and the Muzzy decisions were unconstitutional. "Those decisions were manifestly wrong in this: they were based solely on the indisputable proposition that Universalists are Congregationalists, in disregard of the two other propositions, that Universalists are one of several Congregational sects, and that religious liberty is the object of the constitutional provision." New Hampshire *Reports*, LIII, 133–148, quoted in Smith, *Decisions*, pp. 36–38, note 1.

38. Nathan Dane, ed., *A General Abridgment and Digest of American Law*, 9 vols. (Boston, 1823–1829), II, 330. See also Chapter 34.

that Presbyterians were a different denomination from Congregationalists.[39] Although Massachusetts seemed more liberal in allowing exemption to Universalists and Presbyterians, its judges tried to make a similar distinction between a denomination or sect and a variation of doctrinal opinion within a sect. In 1822 Judge Parker of the Supreme Court stated that by Massachusetts law

> it was early decided [before 1804] that difference of denomination as the term is used in the Declaration [of Rights in the Massachusetts Constitution] consists in a difference of church discipline and mode of administering some of the Christian ordinances; not in difference of opinion in doctrines of theology. Episcopalians, Congregationalists, Presbyterians, Baptists, and others were each of different denominations; but Christians belonging to either of these sects were of the same denomination, however widely they might differ as to the essential or non-essential matters of faith or doctrine.[40]

The whole tenuous argument contained echoes of the original seventeenth-century debate between the Baptists and the Puritans concerning the evils of Separatism or, put another way, concerning the differences between a sect and a schism. And the whole history of dissent in New England may be seen as efforts by various groups of pietistic schismatics from Puritanism to achieve liberty of conscience (or soul liberty) by persuading their neighbors (and the courts) to accept them as distinct sects or denominations. Remnants of the Puritan concept of a Christian Commonwealth persisted, and had to persist, so long as a system of tax-supported religion existed. The result made it difficult to decide whether a man like Wingate was more intolerant because he denied (on good historical grounds) that Muzzy and the Presbyterians were a distinct sect in New England or whether Jeremiah Smith was more intolerant because as a liberal he ridiculed, or thought unimportant, the various sectarian differences which constantly agitated the pietists. Smith had been willing to let Muzzy off, but the general tenor of his argument looked forward to the day when all doctrinal variations would be viewed as mere variations in persuasion and the establishment could be made to include everyone. Smith actually implied this in his decision: "I should hope that discordant sects may in time be brought to assimilate, and then to unite." He preferred toleration (at least for Presbyterians and Baptists) on the long-range grounds that "we should not hurry" towards "the good work of catholicism and union of sects" by ignoring altogether contemporary

39. *Ibid.*, II, 335–336. However, in this case the Rev. Chester Annan lost his claim to the religious taxations of his congregation because the court ruled that he was not a *settled* minister. It did so on the grounds that his contract with the congregation called for him to preach only one Sunday in four.
40. Smith, *Decisions*, p. 38, note 1, from Parker's decision in Holbrook v. Holbrook, 1822, I Pickering, 248, 256.

differences of religious practice. He recognized that dissent often breeds upon persecution, while toleration makes fanaticism irrelevant if not ridiculous. This helps to explain the decline of Baptist militancy on church-state issues after 1790. But so long as the courts were willing to condone the taxation, distraint, or jailing of any groups who claimed freedom of conscience, the "good work of catholicism" was bound to fail. America only obtained a national establishment (albeit a voluntary one) after it ceased to levy religious taxes; the evangelical consensus of mid-nineteenth-century America succeeded in making a Protestant nation despite all sectarian differences.

Because the Baptists, at least the orthodox Calvinistic Baptists, were clearly accepted by the New Hampshire courts as a distinct denomination entitled to tax exemption, few cases which involved them could be characterized as religious oppression. But two questions about their status did arise. The first concerned the old problem whether all Baptist adherents were exempt or whether only full members who had been baptized by immersion were. The second, which grew out of this, involved the problem of incorporation which was, in one respect, a device for gaining exemption for adherents as well as for full members of a dissenting congregation.

The most notable case concerning the taxation of a Baptist who was only an adherent, not a full member, was that of Isaac Smith and his brethren in the town of Loudon. In 1802 Loudon levied a tax on all its inhabitants for the support of its Congregational minister. Four dissenters in the town refused to pay: Caleb Sleeper, Thomas Batchelder, John Carter, and Isaac Smith. All of them claimed to be Baptists by profession and three of them had produced certificates of their regular attendance at and support of a Baptist congregation. According to a report of the case in the New Hampshire *Patriot,* Caleb Sleeper was arrested and taken to jail where "after much difficulty and expense the tax [upon him] was settled" — presumably by abating it. Thomas Batchelder was also jailed; he paid his tax and then sued the assessors. When the trial reached the Superior Court, "Judge Smith decided against him and he was compelled to pay the tax and costs amounting to more than $100." John Carter, also jailed, "settled by paying the tax and costs." But the case of Issac Smith was more complicated.

Smith had been taxed only fifty cents, but it was a matter of principle with him. His family had been Baptists since his birth, but he had not been converted by grace and therefore had not been immersed. He had, however, on coming of age, declared "to the authority" (i.e., to the selectmen) that he was a Baptist in sentiment and he had presented them with a certificate of his membership in a Baptist congregation (or society) in or near Loudon, which affirmed his constant attendance and his participation in its support. He too was jailed after he refused to pay his tax and he too sued the assessors. His first trial, at a justice court presided over by

Michael McClary, Esq., went in his favor. The assessors appealed ultimately to the Superior Court where the case dragged on for four years. "Repeatedly the jury was culled and those who were dissenters from the Congregational order were taken off [presumably as prejudiced in Smith's favor]." Two Quakers were also removed from consideration for the jury which finally decided the case. Smith lost his case and was required to pay costs amounting to $100.

But he did not give up. He petitioned the legislature which was under Republican control and the legislature "restored him to law and a new trial ensued." The case dragged on for several more years until "Finally the action was discontinued; each party paying its own cost." Smith's total cost in order to save himself from the tax of fifty cents came to $1000. In addition, as a citizen of the town of Loudon, he was taxed to pay for the $1000 which was the town's share of the costs. At the final trial the lawyer for the town, Jeremiah[?] Mason, had argued that Smith was not exempt and was not a Baptist because he had not been immersed. "Mr. [George?] Sullivan, or Mr. Smith, answered that Mr. S. could not be a Congregationalist because he had never been *sprinkled*. But the court favoured the opinion that every person who had been neither *dipped* nor *sprinkled* was a Congregationalist!" Smith, who was well to do, but not wealthy "was nearly ruined" by this attempt to fight for his principles.[41]

Had Justice Jeremiah Smith's view in this case prevailed throughout the state, matters would have been hard for the Baptists. But because so few cases of this kind are known, presumably most towns accepted certificates from adherents without question. The small number of Baptist congregations which sought incorporation by the state also seems to confirm this. Although a total of twenty-six Baptist societies were incorporated by law between 1794 and 1819, only eight of these were incorporated before 1811. A few of the petitions requesting incorporation mentioned that the action was being taken to insure tax exemption. But most of them seemed to originate from the Baptists' desire to enable their congregations to levy religious taxes on their members which would be binding in law. The petition for incorporation from the Baptist Society in Deerfield, in June 1794 (the first such petition to be granted), stated that "They have labored under many inconveniences on account of their having no authority, by Law, to compell people to pay their Just proportion of the monies which the said Society have yearly raised" for the support of public worship.[42] Most of the Baptist congregations in New Hampshire, however, agreed with the decision of their brethren in the Warren Association that incorporation was against Baptist principles.

But neither court decisions nor incorporation was of assistance to dis-

41. New Hampshire *Patriot*, August 31, 1819, p. 3.
42. *Laws of New Hampshire*, I–III, ed. Allen S. Batchellor, *et al.* (Manchester and Concord, 1904–1915), VI, 194–195.

senters like the Freewill Baptists, the Methodists, and the Universalists whom the towns regularly refused to exempt; these sects found in the criteria of the Erskine and Muzzy cases reasons to fear for their right to tax exemption. To prevent towns from taxing these dissenters the legislature came to their rescue in a series of resolutions passed from 1804 to 1807. The first of these, passed in June 1804, was on behalf of the Freewill Baptists who apparently were not being recognized as a distinct sect by some towns, parishes, and lower courts. The Resolution read,

> Resolved that all people in this State known by the name of freewill antipedobaptists be and they are hereby recognized & considered as a distinct religious sect or denomination from any other and are intitled to all the priviledges and immunities which any other denomination is entitled to by the Constitution and laws of said State.

This resolution was passed by a Republican legislature but the Federalist governor failed to sign it so it was not included among the laws and resolutions when they were officially printed. In 1805 a similar resolution was passed for the Universalists and in 1807 one was passed for the Methodists.[43] Both of these were signed by Republican governors after they were passed by Republican legislatures. However, no such resolutions were passed for the Shakers or for the Christ-ians.

Whether these resolutions were binding in law may be doubted. At a much later date, in 1868, a judge of Superior Court declared the resolutions worthless: "Whether they [Freewill Baptists, Universalists, Methodists] were religious sects within the meaning of the Constitution or not was a judicial and not a legislative question; but by the unconstitutional and void resolutions of the Legislature, the erroneous decisions of courts, juries, towns, and town officers, were practically reversed." [44] But regardless of their constitutionality, these resolutions to circumvent the courts helped to cement the alliance between the rising Republican Party and the dissenters. Since these resolutions were never explicit challenged in the courts, they were probably effective in persuading towns and parishes to extend the privileges of tax exemption to these newer sects.

The Baptist churches grew from a total of forty-one in 1795 to over seventy by 1826. In addition the seventeen Freewill Baptist churches formed by 1800 had more than doubled by 1820.[45] Of all the dissenting denominations, the New Hampshire Baptists became, as they were in Ver-

43. *Ibid.,* VII, 417, 622; New Hampshire *Patriot,* November 2, 1819, p. 3, and November 9, 1819, p. 2.

44. Smith, *Decisions,* p. 37, note 1.

45. Lawrence, *New Hampshire Churches;* W. O. Hurlin, *et al., The Baptists of New Hampshire* (Manchester, 1902); David Benedict, *A General History of the Baptist Denomination,* 2 vols. (Boston, 1813), I, 315 ff.; and Norman A. Baxter, *History of the Freewill Baptists* (Rochester, 1957).

mont, the most respectable and attractive alternative to Congregationalism. So despite the constant warping off from their ranks of the more radical pietists or eccentrics into the ranks of competing dissenting groups, they more than held their own, especially when the Second Great Awakening evoked a renewed interest in evangelical religion after 1800.[46] Symbolic of the strong competition between the Baptists and the Freewill Baptists in New Hampshire during this period is that the regular Baptists of New Hampshire were the first in the nation to reject Calvinism openly in order to adopt a new confession of faith based on clearcut Arminian grounds. The New Hampshire Confession of Faith which was officially adopted by the regular or Calvinistic Baptists of the state in 1833 removed all the force from the doctrines of total depravity and election by asserting that "all mankind are sinners, not by constraint but by choice" and that "nothing prevents the salvation of the greatest sinner on earth except his own voluntary refusal to submit to the Lord Jesus Christ." [47] Thus did the evangelical Calvinism of the First Great Awakening become the Arminianized "Calvinism" of the Second Great Awakening.

Ultimately it was the Republican Party which ended the slowly declining establishment in New Hampshire. But despite the rapid growth of the Baptists (and other dissenters) there was no close alliance between the denomination as such and the party.

46. It is curious that at least five Congregational ministers in New Hampshire were converted to Baptist views in these years: the Rev. Eliphalet Smith of Deerfield in 1770; the Rev. Joseph Sanborn of Epping in 1770; the Rev. Peletiah Chapin of Rumney in 1806; the Rev. Jonathan Kittredge (a "licentiate") about 1806; and the Rev. Stephen Chapin of Mt. Vernon in 1817 — not to mention the Rev. Daniel Merrill of Nottingham West who had been a Congregational minister in Maine until 1805. Edmund Worth, *Annals of the Past* (Concord, 1852), pp. 23–24.

47. Goen, *Revivalism and Separatism,* pp. 286–287, 293–294. Also W. J. McGlothlin, *Baptist Confessions of Faith* (Philadelphia, 1911), pp. 302–305. McGlothlin comments on this Confession, "It is doubtful if it ought to be called Calvinistic, since it is non-committal on every point of difference between the Calvinistic and Arminian system."

Chapter 45

The Dissenters and the Republican Party
in New Hampshire,
1800–1816

The question between the parties at our next election is reduced to a much smaller compass than in past years. Formerly it was a question between federalists and republicans . . . Now . . . it is a question solely between the friends of religious toleration and universal freedom of conscience and a combination of men who are determined at all hazards to impose on the people a *law religion.*

Letter signed "A Baptist" in the New Hampshire *Patriot,* February 13, 1816

Why the New Hampshire Baptists did not take greater advantage of the possibilities for disestablishment the rise of the Republican Party offered is unclear.[1] Partly, perhaps, because, like Baptists everywhere, they became more interested in home and foreign missions, institutional development, and revivalism after 1800. Partly too they reacted against what seemed to be the intense political partisanship of the Congregational clergy in its alliance with the Federalist Party. If the Baptists were to be consistent in attacking the conception of a Standing Order, an alliance between church and state, they themselves had to maintain an aloofness from political action. Baptist ministers explicitly stated this on several occasions; in 1815 one of their associations issued a pronouncement on the topic which states the matter succinctly in pietistic terms:

> We believe that one of satan's most successful engines made to play on the cause of God to separate ministers and people and rend churches asunder is party politics. Do you wish to see the church flourish and the kingdom and coming of the Prince of Peace hastened? Do you wish as far as possible to imitate your glorious Exampler in being detached from

1. For an earlier version of this chapter see W. G. McLoughlin, "The Bench, the Church and the Republican Party in New Hampshire," *Historical New Hampshire,* XX (1965), 3–31.

the world? Then avoid political debates as a bane of the church and Christ. Keep yourselves unspotted from the world.[2]

Finally, the Baptists did not develop clerical or lay leaders comparable to Aaron Leland or to Ezra Butler in Vermont or to Isaac Backus and to John Leland in Massachusetts. To some extent this was because many of the better ministers were tempted to leave the state for more important posts in the wealthier churches of eastern Massachusetts. But it was more likely because of the ruling Congregational elite's inveterate disdain for Baptists. Unlike Vermont, where the rising Republican Party drew freely from the dissenters for its posts, the party in New Hampshire, as in Massachusetts and Connecticut, was made up of disgruntled Congregationalists who were willing to patronize the Baptists but not to include them as equals.[3]

After 1803 the Christian denomination joined the Baptists and the Universalists in the effort for disestablishment in New Hampshire. Elias Smith, leader of the Christians, was the nearest equivalent to Backus or to Leland in New Hampshire. Smith founded the first church of this denomination in Portsmouth, New Hampshire in 1803. Perhaps a half dozen other churches were formed in the state over the next fifteen years. Most of the converts came from the regular and Freewill Baptist churches. Although the sect remained small in numbers, its liberal views in theology, ecclesiasticism, and voluntarism reached a growing audience through the publications of Elias Smith who lived in Portsmouth when he was not itinerating. In addition to editing a number of anti-Calvinist, antiestablishmentarian, and anti-Baptist tracts, from 1805 to 1807 Smith edited *The Christian's Magazine* and then he edited *The Herald of Gospel Liberty*.

2. Minutes of the Dublin Association, 1815, p. 6.
3. The Baptists in their turn were not especially eager to accept Negroes as equals in their ranks. Records of the Londonderry Baptist Church offer a revealing picture of this. In 1806 a Negro member of the church felt the call to preach; he asked the church to license him or to ordain him as an itinerant. The first entry on this matter in the church records merely states that action was postponed on Benjamin Paul's request for ordination for "reasons too delicate to name." A month later, in November 1806, a council of Baptist elders and laymen put an end to the controversy by ruling that "it would not be expedient at the present time to Set apart Br Benjamin Paul by ordination." The real cause came out at the next church meeting when "Brother Benjamin Paul brings a complaint against Br. James Nut for objecting to his being Ordained on account of His Color and saying if the Church ordained him he would absent himself [i.e., Nut said this] from the Chh and his family should [also]." See the church records, pp. 45–51, in the New Hampshire Historical Society. Benjamin Paul may have been related to Thomas Paul who became pastor of the African Baptist Church in Boston in August 1805. Nathan E. Wood, *The History of the First Baptist Church of Boston* (Philadelphia, 1899), pp. 267, 297. Thomas Paul was received as a member of the Londonderry Baptist Church on April 11, 1805; he was ordained there as an evangelist on May 1, 1805. So perhaps Benjamin Paul's case was not entirely a matter of racial prejudice except on the part of a minority led by Brother Nut

The latter, founded in Portsmouth in 1808, was reputed to be the first religious newspaper in America. By 1815 it had 1500 subscribers. Smith was an ardent Jeffersonian and his paper was filled with incisive attacks on the Federalists and sharp criticisms of "law religion" and ecclesiastical priestcraft.

The paper also recorded the Christian denomination's early persecution by the established churchgoers. In September 1808, it told how a mob of fifty to sixty men broke up an open air meeting of the Christians, "firing their guns among the people and throwing potatoes, dirt, &c at the ministers . . . and striking one of them with a gun . . . when asked the reason of their conduct" the mob leaders "answered that they meant to defend their religion and their minister" from intruding itinerants.[4] A year later it told of Christians in Hampton Falls, who were distrained when they refused to pay religious taxes. They sued the town assessors. The town settled out of court and presumably exempted them thereafter.[5]

The Christians were congregationalists in polity and Arminians in theology; they differed from the Universalists by believing in hellfire and from the Freewill Baptists by opposing councils and associations. The regular Calvinistic Baptists deemed them heretics. Smith, though he was a brilliant journalist and fierce controversialist, was too unstable to provide significant organizational leadership (in 1816 he became a Universalist, then took up "Botanic medicine," and in 1840 returned to the Christians). The sect reflected the religious flux of the period, but it played no direct role in disestablishment or in New Hampshire politics.[6]

The Republican Party got a slow start in New Hampshire, stimulated more by the refusal of the legislature in 1799 to incorporate John Langdon's bank in Portsmouth than by any devotion to the principles of Thomas Jefferson. But by 1804 the Republicans had won control of both houses of the legislature; in 1805 they elected John Langdon governor. In 1806 Langdon was reelected by a total of 15,277 votes of 20,573 votes cast. That same year the first Republican Congressmen from New Hampshire went to Washington with four Federalist colleagues. The Republicans continued in power until 1809 when the reaction against the Embargo put them temporarily out of office. But Langdon won again in 1810 and in 1811. In 1812, William Plumer, Langdon's successor as party leader, won the governorship by a narrow margin. Then followed three years out of power during the war. But in 1816 Plumer was reelected; he remained governor until his retirement in 1819 when he was succeeded in office by another Republican governor, Samuel Bell. Between 1800 and 1820 the Republicans were

---

4. *The Herald of Gospel Liberty* (Portsmouth), September 5, 1808, p. 7.
5. *Ibid.*, November 10, 1809, p. 125.
6. Elias Smith, *The Life, Conversion, Preaching, Travels, and Sufferings of Elias Smith* (Boston, 1840).

in power twelve out of twenty years; after 1805 they were in power eleven out of fifteen years.

Yet despite this successful effort, the Jeffersonian party took longer to accomplish the separation of church and state in New Hampshire than it did in Connecticut. Unquestionably the dissenters (except possibly the Episcopalians) gave their votes overwhelmingly to the Republicans. But the Republicans felt no strong urge to alter the existing ecclesiastical system despite their repeated attacks upon the Congregational clergy for injecting politics into the pulpit. One might argue that the principle of decentralized government so fundamental to Jeffersonian political theory in this case played into the hands of those local town and parish units which wanted to maintain the establishment. But Jefferson's own willingness to utilize the state government to strike down institutional vestiges restricting individual freedom would negate this.

The Republicans of New Hampshire felt no strong urge, either from principle or from political expedience, to alter the existing ecclesiastical system. Quite the contrary. Despite their repeated attacks on the Congregational clergy for injecting (Federalist) politics into the pulpit, they recognized that the existence of the Standing Order was an asset in maintaining the political loyalty of the dissenters. Simultaneously, it made it easier for Congregationalists who liked the establishment but were disenchanted with Federalist politics to shift their loyalty to the Republican Party. Instead of disestablishing the churches, the Republicans preferred to give the dissenters every possible assistance short of disestablishment. This was the policy behind the resolutions of 1804, 1805, and 1807 designed to thwart the court's decision in the Muzzy and Erskine cases. This was the policy behind the Republicans' willingness to incorporate any and all dissenting bodies which applied for incorporation. The Federalists often refused such requests when they were in power and voted against them when out of power because they considered them evasions of the system. This was also the policy behind the Republicans' refusal to appropriate money for an election night banquet after 1808 — a banquet at which the Standing Clergy traditionally dined with the legislators at state expense after the election sermon.[7] Doubtless also this explains why during all their years in power the Republicans chose only one dissenter to deliver an election sermon — Elder Daniel Merrill in 1817.[8] They did, however (again ignoring Jefferson's precepts), choose many legislative chaplains from among the dissenters.

7. *The Herald of Gospel Liberty* (Portsmouth), June 23, 1809, p. 85. Baptists and other non-Congregationalists who were offered official town positions were entitled to attend such banquets, but they seldom did. They were considered Congregational affairs just as the Congregationalists were considered the Standing Church.

8. For Merrill's role in disestablishment see below. Merrill was born in Rowley, Massachusetts in 1765; he graduated from Dartmouth in 1789. He began to preach as a Congregationalist in 1791 and formed a Congregational Church in Sedgwick,

So little were the Republicans interested in raising the religious issue that even when Judge Jeremiah Smith left the Superior Court to run for the governorship in 1809 (and for several years thereafter) the Republicans never once attacked him for his defense of the establishment, though they attacked him for almost everything else he ever did and for some things he had never done. But in New Hampshire, as in Massachusetts and Connecticut, the leadership and the bulk of the votes in the Republican Party came from Congregationalists who saw nothing wrong with the established system. Not until 1816, when the dissenters were sufficiently numerous to give the Republicans a near majority and when the Federalists were badly demoralized, did the party feel justified in making disestablishment one of its campaign promises. Even then the matter was handled gingerly compared to other issues of the day.

One can see the measure of Republican reluctance on this issue from 1800 to 1816 in the New Hampshire *Patriot* and in William Plumer's speeches. The New Hampshire *Patriot* was the official organ of the Republican party in the state and its editor, Isaac Hill, was as radical an anticlerical as was Thomas Jefferson or Thomas Paine. Yet through all these years there are only four or five instances in which religion in any form was mentioned in Hill's paper. In 1811, Hill noted with approval the passage of the Religious Freedom Bill in Massachusetts and hinted that New Hampshire should "Go thou and do likewise." But of course this bill was not disestablishment and Federalists could well argue that New Hampshire already had granted as much freedom in this matter as this bill brought to Massachusetts. That same year Hill praised Jefferson and Madison for the "new light" which they had thrown on religious liberty, but he did not specify what it was. As the war of 1812 approached and the Federalists in opposing it heaped praise on Great Britain, Hill printed a long editorial denouncing the Church of England and the tithing system which supported it by $600,000 a year: "These evils do not arise so much from the natural wicked disposition of the clergy as from the provision made by the government to pay them for labor whether they labor or not. And yet we find a proportion of the clergy in this country warm advocates for compelling the people to pay them whether they derive benefit from their preaching or not." [9] But he did not specifically apply the case to the New Hampshire system. When the war came, Hill's paper roundly de-

---

Maine in 1793. It was the largest church in that province by 1805. But in 1805 Merrill became a Baptist and founded a new church on those principles in Sedgwick. In 1814 he moved to Nottingham, New Hampshire, where he remained until 1821. Then he returned to Sedgwick where he died in 1833. William B. Sprague, *Annals of the American Pulpit* (New York, 1860), VI, 507–511.

9. New Hampshire *Patriot,* July 2, 1811, p. 3, and July 23, 1811, p. 4, June 11, 1811, p. 3, November 12, 1811, p. 5, February 25, 1812, p. 1; October 27, 1812, p. 2. For Hill's praise of Madison see Elias Smith, *Madison and Religion* (Philadelphia, 1811).

nounced the Congregational clergy for siding with the Federalists in opposing it and in thwarting the war effort. But even then he made no statement calling for disestablishment.

Plumer, who became the leading figure and spokesman for the party after he left the Federalists in 1808, made no speech in which he raised the issue of disestablishment. Despite his ardent espousal of religious liberty in his early years, Plumer was conservative in his political outlook. This conservatism led him to try to strengthen the state constitution in 1791–92 by granting more power and independence to the Executive and to the Judiciary branches. In 1799, the rising tide of Jeffersonianism alarmed him by its radicalism; he therefore not only became a staunch Federalist but he returned to nominal adherence to the Congregational church, even willingly paying his religious taxes in support of it. As a member of the New Hampshire House of Representatives in 1800 and 1801, he also voted against the petitions from Baptists and other dissenting groups seeking incorporation. In his autobiography, which was never published, Plumer stated "I was against these sectaries because they were hostile to the federal interest & opposed to the congregational and presbyterian clergy who in general were zealous federalists." [10] In 1802 he was elected to the United States Senate as a Federalist and for the next three years he was one of Jefferson's most determined opponents. At this time he became one of the willing conspirators who plotted for secession of the New England states. He published in 1804 one of the most bitter denunciations of Jefferson as an infidel and enemy of American liberty that appeared in New England, *An Address to the Electors of New Hampshire*. He wrote prolifically for the Federalist newspapers denouncing vindictively every action of the Republicans, state and federal. Although he relaxed considerably after 1805, when he felt that Pickering was carrying matters too far, and although he even managed to let himself be won over by Jefferson's overtures of friendship, it was not until 1808 that he finally broke with his party and joined the Republicans. Even after he was elected governor in 1812, the closest he came to espousing disestablishment was in a series of letters which he wrote for the New Hampshire *Patriot* in 1813 — but he signed them with the pseudonym, "A Layman." In these he denounced the Standing Clergy for having tried over the preceding twelve years "to traduce and vilify the government [of Jefferson and Madison], to counteract and enfeeble its measures." Out of fear "from numerous sectaries who pervade the country," Plumer claimed, the clergy had "publicly avowed the object" of obtaining "a religious establishment" throughout the nation. He considered the work by Timothy Dwight, Jedidiah Morse, Lyman Beecher, and Nathaniel W. Taylor in organizing and promoting the Second Great Awakening (or the Protestant Counter-Reformation) in New England a reactionary plot of

10. For the quotation from his unpublished "Autobiography" see Lynn W. Turner, *William Plumer of New Hampshire, 1759–1850* (Chapel Hill, 1962), p. 75.

the Federalist Party.[11] But nowhere in this series of letters did he descend from general denunciation to specific arguments for ending the system of religious taxes in New Hampshire.

Were it not for the Dartmouth College affair, religion might never have become a party issue in any specific way in New Hampshire. But when in 1815 the trustees of Dartmouth fired John Wheelock, the son of founder Eleazer Wheelock, as President of the college, the Republicans found an issue which might bring them back to power after three years. They decided to use it in every possible way. Like all good political issues, it provided a convenient focus for a number of different grievances, fears, and discontents. It could be used to emphasize the Republicans' concern for the extension of public education, just becoming a popular issue, which the Federalists had shown no interest in promoting. It could be used to attack the aristocratic and monopolistic machinations of the college trustees and their Federalist defenders who were subverting a public institution for factional and upper-class purposes. It could be used to arouse the dissenters against a clerical "plot" to keep their children out of Dartmouth (supposedly a part of the Congregational counter-reformation against "the sectaries"). It could even be used to arouse those Congregationalists who disliked what was considered the high-flown theology of the Hopkinsian Calvinists — Hopkinsianism too was part of a clerical plot by this wing of the Congregational denomination to seize control of the ecclesiastical institutions of the Standing Order.

The arguments were largely specious on all of these grounds. A possible exception was the Republican claim that the state had the right to control the college because its charter made it a public, not a private, corporation — though eventually the United States Supreme Court denied this claim. However, the religious aspect of the issue was heightened in December 1815 when a decision of the Superior Court interpreted the law exempting settled ministers from civil taxes in such a way as to make only Standing (or official parish) ministers entitled to this privilege. This seemed to be a clear case of discrimination in favor of the Congregationalists who constituted the bulk of the official town and parish ministers. At least the Republicans portrayed it this way. But it was not a new decision at all. Precedents for it went back to 1798, and an equally important case on the same subject in 1807 had aroused no discussion or resentment at that time. Still, the light this matter threw on the legal rationale for the establishment as well as the emotional excitement aroused by the political repercussions makes it worth examining.

The decision in the case of Moore *vs.* Poole in 1815 rested on the decision Judge Jeremiah Smith rendered in Kidder *vs.* French in 1807. The Rev. Joseph Kidder of Dunstable, a Congregationalist, brought suit against

11. Vernon L. Stauffer, *New England and the Bavarian Illuminati* (New York, 1918).

the assessors of Dunstable for levying a civil tax of $8.51 on his real and personal estate in 1804. Kidder claimed that as an ordained minister he was entitled to exemption from civil taxes. His claim, however, as Judge Smith pointed out, could be based only on common law through long custom and usage, for there was no statute which expressly granted to ministers exemption from civil taxes on real and personal estate.[12] Kidder could, however, prove that since 1798 the annual tax laws for the state had specifically exempted the polls of "ordained ministers" from taxation.[13] But the assessors had not taxed his poll. One of the questions in the case therefore became whether the express exemption of his poll did or did not imply exemption of his real and personal estate.

The case was complicated, however, by two other questions: first, the legal definition of an "ordained minister" or "minister of the gospel"; second, Kidder's own status as a minister. Kidder had been the settled minister of Dunstable from 1767 to 1796, but in 1796 his official pastoral relationship with the town had been dissolved by a mutual council (presumably because age and illness incapacitated him). Under the common historical interpretation of New England Congregational polity, a minister ceased to have the rank of an ordained clergyman once he was no longer the pastor of a specific church.[14] However, this council had made an exception in Kidder's case and had specifically granted him the right to continue to baptize children and perform the Lord's Supper in Dunstable from time to time, which he had done regularly. Consequently the court conceded that Kidder was still an ordained minister though he was no longer a pastor. He was, like an evangelist, a minister to the world at large.

But what, in the eyes of the law, was the definition of a minister? Judge Smith stated that there seemed to be three kinds of ministers: "1st. Those who officiate in public teaching &c. who are neither ordained nor settled [such as licensed exhorters]. 2d. Those who are or have been ordained but not connected with any particular church or society [such as evangelists]. 3d. Those who are ordained and settled in a particular town or parish, connected with a particular church and congregation." And by "settled in a particular town or parish" Smith meant a minister "chosen by the freeholders of the town, convened in public town meeting, as a minister for the supply of the town at a certain annual salary." [15] (This seemed to rule out from consideration all dissenting ministers, but perhaps Smith was merely considering Puritan or Congregational ministers in this discussion.)

---

12. Jeremiah Smith, *Decisions of the Superior and Supreme Courts of New Hampshire* (Boston, 1879), p. 164. Hereafter referred to as Smith, *Decisions.*

13. *Ibid.,* pp. 156–158.

14. Williston Walker, *The Creeds and Platforms of Congregationalism* (New York, 1893), pp. 142, 143, 145, 217

15. Smith, *Decisions,* p. 159.

Smith then went into a long historical account of the origin of ministerial support by taxation and of the development of the tradition of exemption from civil taxes for the Standing or settled ministers. He proved, no doubt correctly, that the custom of exempting ministers arose because it would be foolish to tax a minister for his own salary. Furthermore, "as a further encouragement for his services to the State" the towns and state excused ministers from taxes for other civil purposes. This was the heart of the matter. Tax exemption for ministers was a *quid pro quo* on the part of the state. The minister was a civil officer providing certain services and tax exemption was conceived of as a perquisite, a part of his salary, a fringe benefit. But when Kidder ceased to be a civil officer "neither the town of Dunstable nor the public have any further claims on Mr. Kidder. He has, therefore, no claim on them." Because he was free to "labor in word and doctrine just as he pleases and when and where he pleases" he must now be considered a free agent; "He may preach only once a year or every day in the year just as he pleases or he may rest from his ministerial labors altogether" and no one can legally or morally require any service of him which he does not choose to give. Therefore, the town was no longer obliged to exempt him from taxes on his real and personal estate as it did when he was their legal teacher of piety and morality.

Judge Smith might have rested his case here, but he went on to discuss the obvious question bothering dissenters: did not all ministers, whether settled over a town or not, perform some service to the state, and were they not all therefore entitled to be regarded to the extent of exemption from civil taxes to the state as an encouragement to religion? Or, as Smith himself stated it, to explain why he could not help Kidder: "If any preachers are exempt except settled ministers why should not all who go about doing good in this way be exempt?" And he answered simply, "We must draw the line somewhere." To him it seemed too much to permit all the varied ministers ordained by all kinds of dissenters the privilege of tax exemption, and he could not see how he could honestly grant exemption to Kidder without granting it to all dissenting ministers. He recognized that this left him open to charges of prejudice against dissenters, but he denied this:

> If any preachers are exempt except settled ministers why should not all who go about doing good in this way be exempt? A Methodist itinerant preacher, or a Baptist, have the same claims in law as a Congregational preacher. Shall it be in the power of a presbytery at Philadelphia or in Scotland, or a Methodist bishop who made himself such, by ordaining a man to the church universal, as the practice is, to exempt that person's property from paying taxes? This would be enabling such men, or bodies of them, to confer civil privileges. The venerable council who ordained Mr. Kiddler, or that which loosed him and declared that he was still an ordained minister, are of no greater consideration in our law than a

Methodist bishop or Baptist association. I would not be understood to speak slightly of councils or of denominations. But I speak of them as they are viewed by the equal eye of the law — as all upon a level.[16]

Smith, though he was a defender of the established church system, was being more consistent in this decision than were those dissenters who protested against state aid to the Congregational churches and yet who accepted ministerial lots and who demanded the right of exemption from civil taxes for themselves. The dissenters may have been drawing the line somewhat less rigidly than was Smith, but they were certainly not being consistent in their demand for separation of church and state.

During the course of this decision in the Kidder case, Smith referred to the precedent set by Kelley *vs.* Bean in May 1798 when the court ruled "that a minister of the church and congregation in a town" was not liable to pay civil taxes.[17] The absence of a report giving the grounds for the decision forced him to review the case. But he came to the same conclusion. "The clergy not taxable are those whom the people, i.e., a particular town or society, are bound to support and who on their part are bound to minister in holy things. But where a clergyman does not depend on the people for support; where he is not the minister of any particular town or society, bound to preach to them, and they bound to support him — the reason for exemption fails."

Another case which he cited to support his conclusion in the Kidder case was Hampshire *vs.* Taylor (1797) in Massachusetts. In this case a Baptist elder of a church in Chester, Massachusetts claimed exemption from civil taxes in the town of Buckland, where he lived. The Massachusetts court ruled in this case that "a man's being ordained over a voluntary association formed by no act of government and bound by no law, could not be a settled minister."[18] Therefore Taylor did not come under the meaning of the law which exempted settled ministers from civil taxes in Massachusetts. But the real issue in the Taylor case was not whether he was settled over a town or parish as a Standing or settled minister, but whether or not his church was incorporated. In New Hampshire, the incorporation issue was never raised.

From Judge Smith's point of view, Moore *vs.* Poole, eight years later, was a routine confirmation of these earlier cases. The Rev. Humphrey Moore was the officially settled (Congregational) minister of the town of Milford. He brought suit against Poole, who was an assistant assessor of the United States direct tax. The federal tax law stated that "lands permanently or specially exempted from taxation by the laws of the State wherein the same may be situated" were not to be assessed by the federal govern-

16. *Ibid.*, p. 165.
17. Ibid., p. 157, p. 162.
18. MHS *Collections,* V (1798), 48–49. For discussion of this see Chapter 54.

ment. Moore claimed that as a settled minister he was exempt in New Hampshire from civil taxes and therefore he should be exempt from the taxes of the federal government under this act. Judge Smith, following the precedent in the Kidder case, found for Moore. The only possible claim Poole could make was that there was no express statute in New Hampshire granting exemption to real and personal estate of settled ministers. But as in the Kidder case, Smith considered the exemption a part of the common law established by custom and usage.[19]

Perhaps the furor aroused over this issue in 1815, unlike the silence in 1807, may be attributed to a change in the social climate and to the dissenters' rise over the years. All indications are, however, that it was primarily a product of political manufacture. Jeremiah Smith had left the bench in 1809 to become a Federalist candidate for the governorship and had served in that position in 1809–1810. He was the chief architect of a new Judiciary Act which the Federalists had passed in 1813 and which the Republicans had denounced as partisan in its aims and construction. Under this act Smith had been returned to the bench as Chief Justice in 1813 after he left the governorship. Finally, Smith, along with Daniel Webster, was one of the Federalist lawyers defending the trustees in the Dartmouth College case. It is not surprising, therefore, that two months after the decision a series of letters in the New Hampshire *Patriot,* signed "A Baptist," attacked the decision as part of a Federalist and Congregationalist plot to establish "a law-religion" on New Hampshire which would require uniformity and conformity of belief and practice from all.[20] On March 25, 1816, Isaac Hill in an editorial denounced "the unconstitutional Superior Court of this State" for deciding "that the property of the Clergy of the dominant sect is exempt from taxation and by a necessary consequence that the Baptist, the Quaker, the Methodist, the Universalist, &c. living in the town where such Clergy reside shall, contrary to the constitution, 'be compelled to pay towards the support of the teacher or teachers of another sect or denomination' " (because all inhabitants would have to pay higher civil taxes to make up for the exemption of the Standing minister).[21]

However, Judge Smith's "partisan decision" in Moore *vs.* Poole constituted only a small part of the political attack which the Republicans launched against the Federalists in the six months preceding the election of April 1816. The central feature of the attack was the Dartmouth College issue which Isaac Hill and William Plumer decided to use as a lever for overthrowing the entire established system. To accomplish this they copied the Federalists. Just as the Federalists of New England in 1798–1800 had concocted the plot of the Bavarian Illuminati to frighten voters against supporting Thomas Jefferson's new party, so the Republicans in New Hamp-

19. Smith, *Decisions,* pp. 166–168.
20. New Hampshire *Patriot,* February 13, 1816, p. 3.
21. *Ibid.,* March 25, 1816, p. 3.

shire in 1815–1816 concocted a plot against civil and religious liberty to frighten voters against supporting the Federalists. The plotters in this case were the right wing of the Standing Order — the pro-British or Tory Federalists or aristocrats in the secular sphere and the high-flown Hopkinsian Calvinist clergy or priestcraft in the religious sphere. The popular reaction against the Hartford Convention provided the general background for the political credibility of the plot; the widespread dislike for the aggressive but unpalatable doctrines of Hopkinsianism (as spread by the home missionary agents of the Connecticut and Massachusetts Congregational associations) provided the general background for its religious credibility.[22]

Hill's first outburst against the Dartmouth trustees appeared on September 19, 1815 in the New Hampshire *Patriot*. He printed a letter in his editorial column signed "Dartmouth" which said that the actions of the trustees "shock public feeling and call loudly for public reprehension." They were engaging in "a system of persecution" against Wheelock and "their insidious attacks upon religious liberty" had far reaching designs.[23] In many articles during the next few months the *Patriot* proceeded to show that the Dartmouth trustees were Hopkinsians and that they considered all non-Hopkinsians as heterodox. "These men stand at the head of a sectarian combination which intends to overrule, bear down, and crush all denominations of more liberal principles." [24] President Wheelock, on the other hand, was a good, old-fashioned kind of Calvinist "and as such is opposed to the Hopkinsian improvements and innovations." [25] On October 10, 1815 a letter signed "Junius" asked rhetorically what was behind the Dartmouth affair? "Lift the curtain and you will behold a monster, horrid to the sight, grasping in his right hand the Crown and Mitre — his left hand pointing to the Inquisition — trampling under foot *Religious Freedom* — and on his forehead labelled UNION OF CHURCH AND STATE!" [26]

At first Hill simply printed these accusations — directed primarily against the trustees — in the form of anonymous letters or pseudonymous ones. But as election time approached he shifted the argument to a direct attack upon the Federalist Party and, having endorsed Plumer's candidacy for the governorship on January 23, 1816, proceeded to make disestablishment the central issue of the campaign: "Our Constitution guarantees to us RELI-

22. For a general discussion of Hopkinsianism and the popular reactions to it see Williston Walker, *A History of the Congregational Churches in the United States* (New York, 1894), pp. 280 ff.

23. New Hampshire *Patriot*, September 19, 1815, p. 3.

24. *Ibid.*, September 26, 1815, pp. 3–4. An unsigned letter printed November 14, 1815, p. 1, said the Trustees "hold themselves up as Calvinists persecuted by an abominable combination of Deists and Sectarians;" but "The Eight Trustees have the reputation generally of being Hopkinsians" who consider all but themselves to be heterodox. November 14, 1815, p. 1, October 10, 1815, p. 1.

25. *Ibid.*, November 14, 1815, p. 1.

26. *Ibid.*, October 10, 1815, p. 1.

GIOUS LIBERTY, however the machinations of a party may be directed to its destruction." [27] This was designed, among other things, to arouse the Baptists and other dissenters to support the Republican Party as the party of religious liberty. A series of letters addressed "To the Members of the Baptist Societies throughout New Hampshire" which began appearing in the *Patriot* on February 13 was evidence of this. They were signed "A Baptist," though whether they were written by someone like Elder Daniel Merrill or by Hill himself is unknown. Their significance is that for the first time the Republican Party was openly making an appeal for Baptist votes on the issue of disestablishment. The party managers had decided that the dissenters and their sympathizers did constitute a majority of the voters.

According to "A Baptist," "a deep and dark plan has been secretly laid and artfully carried on to subvert religious Freedom and establish on its ruins a religious order 'Who will lord it over God's heritage.' " As a result of this plot

> The question between the parties at our next election is reduced to a much smaller compass than in past years. Formerly it was a question between federalists and republicans. . . . Now . . . it is a question solely between the friends of religious toleration and universal freedom and conscience and a combination of men who are determined at all hazards to impose on the people a *law religion* — who are determined to make the tenets of one sect the only standard of orthodoxy and that orthodoxy the sole qualification for office.[28]

One aspect of the plot was the continued efforts among the Congregationalists to promote revivals and missions and to raise vast sums of money to finance their hydra-headed philanthropic organizations. Another was "the late decision of the Supreme Court which exempts teachers of that denomination from contributing any share in support of the public expenses while the humble Quaker, the devout Baptist, the fervent Methodist and teachers of other denominations are compelled even to pay a share of the very salaries of those exempted." Third, the most sinister of all, was the "persecution of President Wheelock for the sole purpose of converting the Literary Seminary of New Hampshire into a potent engine for the building up a law religion." How long will it be, asked this tribune of the people, "ere we shall have the Inquisition and the hellish persecutions of Spain transplanted

---

27. *Ibid.,* January 23, 1816, p. 3. For a full and fair and fair discussion of the Dartmouth College affair see Leon R. Richardson, *History of Dartmouth College* (Hanover, 1932), I, chapter 7. Although there was some antagonism between Wheelock and the Hopkinsians, there was no substance to "the plot" which Hill and the Republicans developed. For Wheelock's paranoiac version of the affairs see his *Sketches of the History of Dartmouth College* which he published anonymously in 1815. For an earlier claim that Wheelock himself was converting Dartmouth into a "Hopkintonian" stronghold, see the *Connecticut Courant* (Hartford), September 19, 1796, p. 1.

28. New Hampshire *Patriot,* February 13, 1816, p. 3.

to this country?" He then launched into a defense of William Plumer, acknowledging that Plumer was once a Federalist but asserting that "In one thing we affirm that William Plumer has never changed — he has always been the undeviating advocate for religious freedom. Those who are acquainted with his practice at the Bar can testify that he always engaged on that side which was averse to compelling citizens of one religious denomination to pay for the support of another denomination whose tenets they did not approve." This he did while a Federalist and often "without a fee." And why did he leave the Federalists? "Because he had obtained good evidence that there was a combination among the leaders of that party with many of the Clergy to build up a law religion — to render the Clergy independent of the good will of the people by providing their salaries out of the public chest." [29]

On February 20, "A Baptist" revealed more clearly the details of the conspiracy against religious liberty. The design of the plot, he said, was "to build up a religious Aristocracy of the standing orthodox order and to batter down christians of every other denomination." One of the key instruments in this plot was Andover Seminary whose endowment was "worth a million dollars or more" and whose one hundred students were made to swear allegiance to the orthodoxy of the Hopkinsian clergy. Though it seemed incredible, it was true, said the "Baptist" that "the government of nearly every College north of the Delaware . . . is connected with or under the influence of the Andover Institution." It was Andover men who forced the resignation of Dr. Ebenezer Fitch as President of Williams in 1815 and of Dr. Daniel C. Sanders, the President of the University of Vermont in 1814. An Andover divine publicly stated that the Hopkinsian Calvinists should do everything in their power to keep students from entering the University of Vermont (which by an act of 1810 was put under the control of the legislature) and steer them instead to Middlebury College. And it was true that orthodox Calvinists (presumably with Hopkinsian leanings) replaced both President Fitch and President Sanders. [30]

On February 27, 1816, "A Baptist" uncovered the remaining details of the plot. "We have already seen this aspiring and successful Hierarchy seize on the government of Williams College in Massachusetts and the University of Vermont. Of Harvard University they despaired at present, but Dartmouth College they consider within their grasp." But fortunately for religious liberty "the sagacious Wheelock . . . saw their dark designs" and refused to yield. "He knew their deep malignity" and because he would not resign "he was hurled from office without notice . . . to make room for one who had given full proof of his attachment to the orthodox Hierarchy." One aspect of the plot which Wheelock had opposed was that the trustees wanted "the funds of the College to be exclusively extended to [aid] the

29. *Ibid.*
30. There is no substantial evidence for any of these allegations.

pious young men of Union Academy and of orthodox sentiments." [31] But Wheelock refused to see young men of other persuasions debarred from entering the state's — the people's — college. The plot was simple: An estimated three hundred young men graduated from New England colleges each year. Of these one hundred entered the ministry. If Andover controlled all of the colleges and if it enrolled all one hundred of the ministerial candidates each year in its seminary, soon every pastorate in New England would be filled with Hopkinsians. What was more, these Hopkinsians would be closely allied in a master plan to establish by law an independent (i.e. tax-supported) hierarchical clergy. They would start with the New England states and ultimately force this establishment on the entire nation. The sympathy and support which the Federalist Party was demonstrating toward the trustees of Dartmouth, which they had always shown toward the clergy of the Standing Order, made the decision of the voters at the next election crucial. Each voter had only to ask himself, "Does the candidate scrupulously regard the rights of conscience? and will he oppose a religion established by law?" By this test the decision between William Plumer and James Sheafe, the Federalist candidate (a wealthy Portsmouth merchant and lifelong Tory Federalist) was clear and simple.

William Plumer himself did not make any overt references to the plot. This was before the days of political campaigning by the candidate. Plumer therefore stood on his record and let Isaac Hill and his anonymous letter writers speak for him and for the Republican party. His only published essay in this area had been a series of letters published in the *Patriot* in 1813–1814 addressed to "The Clergy of New England and particularly those of New Hampshire" and signed "A Layman." These were later issued as a tract entitled *An Address to the Clergy,* and they were designed primarily to rebuke the Congregational clergy for siding with the Federalist Party in opposing the war. But in one passage he also foreshadowed the basic theory of "the conspiracy":

> Our Constitution has established perfect liberty to every man not only to worship God according to the dictates of his own conscience but the right of paying or not paying for the support of religious teachers as he may judge proper. This perfect law of liberty alarmed you [the Congregational clergy] . . . it left you dependent on your own merits and the good will of the people for subsistence. To relieve yourselves from this state of uncertain dependence many of you have been anxious to obtain a religious establishment . . . In Massachusetts some of you have publicly avowed the object. The *Panoplist* of July, 1812, contends for the

31. An anonymous earlier letter to the *Patriot* attacked Union College because its act of incorporation in 1813 "required that no man should be elected a Trustee of Union Academy till he had subscribed to the Hopkinsian creed." September 26, 1815, pp. 3–4. It was true that creedal affirmations were required at both Union and Andover to prevent the inroads of Arminianism, and it is generally held that the one at Andover was Hopkinsian.

establishment of a permanent tribunal with power to ordain and depose ministers as they should judge proper — and in fact establish articles of faith and practice.

It was because the Republicans opposed this while "by many federalists your [the Congregational clergy's] pretensions have received countenance" that "you have attached yourselves to them as political partizans." [32] Although the general public may not have been aware that Plumer was the author of these letters and the subsequent tract, there was no doubt that he lent his support to Hill and the other party leaders who were determined to wage his campaign in 1816 on the basis of religious liberty.

On March 5, a month before the election, the *Patriot* appeared with a huge cut of a ship which filled most of the front page. From the ship's rigging numerous flags were unfurled in each of which was written some campaign slogan. And above the ship in large headlines was the by-word of the election: "Religious Freedom, the Rights of the Baptist, Quaker, Methodist and of all denominations — in room of a Law Religion imposed by an intolerant sect who boast they 'will manage the Civil Government as they please.'" Underneath the ship was the "Whig Ticket" headed by the Hon. William Plumer for Governor. There were other issues, notably the Republicans' desire to repeal the Federalist Judiciary Act of 1813, by which the entire judiciary system of New Hampshire had been revised to remove a number of unpopular Republican judges as well as to make needed reforms in the system.[33] But the religious issue predominated. It was particularly important for disestablishment that in this campaign the Republicans not only made generalized statements about religious freedom and liberty of conscience but that they specifically called attention to the iniquities of religious taxation as they had never done before.

The same issue which contained the large picture of the ship of state also contained a letter signed "Luther," which described recent instances of distraint and imprisonment for failure to pay religious taxes:

> A good [dissenting] citizen of the neighboring town of Marlow once felt the grip of the officer because he presumed to rely on the strength of the constitution [and refused to pay religious taxes to the Standing Order]. Amos Heald, Esq. of Packersfield, who is a Baptist and who attended public worship with the Baptist Church of Dublin was taxed by the selectmen of Packersfield who were of the standing order; and because he refused to pay, his property has been distrained and sold by the constable. He appealed to the laws of his country for redress and a jury of his peers have determined in his favor. And lately a Mr. Sumner of Keene, a

32. New Hampshire *Patriot,* December 6, 1813. For answers to this by the Rev. Asa McFarland, who signed himself "W." see the Concord *Gazette,* December 28, 1813 to February 22, 1814. Probably McFarland knew Plumer was the author, but it is uncertain whether the general public knew this.

33. Turner, *Plumer,* pp. 225–226.

Methodist, has been taxed to the support of a Congregational teacher, HAS BEEN COMMITTED TO GAOL, and in order to procure his liberty has been *'compelled to pay'* the tax. These men are republicans.

Another article in the same paper entitled "Subordination of Religious Sects" pointed out that in the preceding June session of the legislature the Federalist majority had refused to grant incorporation to any of the Baptist churches which petitioned but that they did grant incorporation to all the Congregational societies which applied. A third article in this issue, signed "Leonidas," was addressed to the Quakers; it told them to beware of the Federalists who were out to destroy all religious freedom.

The Superior Court was attacked again in subsequent issues for its refusal to exempt from civil taxes any ministers except ministers of the Standing Order, and a number of instances were described in which these tax-exempt Congregational ministers had cast the deciding votes in town elections which sent Federalist representatives to the legislature.[34]

When the election came in April, Plumer defeated Sheafe by 2300 votes. The Republican campaign for religious liberty had succeeded. But, as in many elections, the voters had some difficulty in persuading those they had elected to keep their preelection promises.

34. For an example, see the *Patriot* for March 25, 1816, p. 3.

Chapter 46

Disestablishment in New Hampshire,
1816–1819

No person shall be compelled to join or support nor be classed with nor associated to any congregation, church or religious society without his express consent first had and obtained.

New Hampshire Toleration Bill, 1819, ending the territorial parish system

In June 1816 William Plumer delivered the Governor's message to the legislature. This message was usually the basis upon which the party enacted its program for the session. The state's taking over of Dartmouth College received primary consideration; the repeal of the Judiciary Act received considerable attention; and there was a short paragraph on religious freedom. It urged the legislature to grant incorporation to any groups which applied for it, and it urged unremitting vigilance to protect the rights of conscience, but it said nothing about repealing the system of religious taxation:

> The rights of conscience and of private judgment in religious matters are not only secured by our constitution to all men but are in their nature unalienable. Civil and religious liberty have usually flourished and expired together. To preserve their purity requires the constant unremitting vigilance of the people and their legislators. If any religious associations request acts of incorporation to enable them more fully and securely to enjoy their religious privileges it appears to be our duty to grant them. The correctness of their tenets is a subject that lies between God and their own consciences and is one that no human tribunal has any right to decide.[1]

The Republican legislature did grant a large number of acts of incorporation to dissenters at this session; the only other action it took on their behalf in 1816 was a bill to overrule Judge Smith's decision in the Moore case. But this act, instead of granting exemption from civil taxes to ministers of

1. New Hampshire *Patriot,* June 11, 1816, p. 2.

all denominations, took precisely the opposite tack. It denied exemption from civil taxes to any minister. The Standing ministers thereby lost their advantage. There was a more consistent line drawn between church and state on this issue, but it was scarcely more than a moral victory for the dissenters.[2]

The administration did, however, make good its pledge to repeal the Judiciary Act of 1813, thereby removing Judge Smith from the court. It also passed an act to bring Dartmouth College under state control. The Republican legislators took seriously at least some aspects of the "religious conspiracy" story because they inserted a religious freedom clause in the new Dartmouth charter: "Perfect freedom of religious opinions shall be enjoyed by all the officers and students of the university and no officer or student shall be deprived of any honors, privileges, or benefits of the institution on account of his religious creed or belief. The theological colleges which may be established in the university shall be founded on the same principle of religious freedom." According to the *Patriot,* this part of the new charter aroused the most opposition from the trustees and their friends. The old charter "enables the old Trustees to patronize and build up one sect in religion" and to establish creedal tests for officers and students. "Distort the case who will, it cannot be longer concealed that the question between the old Trustees and the people is, Shall there be 'perfect freedom of religious opinions' or shall there be freedom for only one sect?"[3]

In the election of November 1816, Judge Jeremiah Smith was the Federalist candidate for Congress. The *Patriot* used the religious issue against him: "All Baptists, Methodists, Quakers &c. who wish to be compelled to support the Clergy of the Standing Order will next Monday give their votes for . . . Jeremiah Smith . . . We would refer them to his decision in the case, *Humphrey Moore vs. Benjamin Poole.* By that decision many of the good people of New Hampshire are COMPELLED to contribute to the support of a religious denomination to which they do not belong."[4]

But Plumer's message to the fall session of the legislature ignored religion and nothing was done in that session on ecclesiastical matters except to incorporate more dissenting societies. In the spring campaign of 1817 the Republicans made only one brief reference to religion when the *Patriot* noted that the Standing Clergy disliked Plumer because "They know him to be a friend to those hitherto persecuted denominations, the Baptists,

---

2. Lynn W. Turner, *William Plumer of New Hampshire* (Chapel Hill, 1962), p. 290; *Laws of New Hampshire,* vols. IV–IX, ed. Henry H. Metcalf (Bristol and Concord, 1916–1922), VIII, 582: "Be it enacted by the Senate and House . . . that the real and personal estate of all ordained ministers of the Gospel of every denomination within this state shall hereafter be assessed and taxed in the same way and manner as other estates are now or hereafter may by law be taxed, any law or custom to the contrary notwithstanding."

3. New Hampshire *Patriot,* September 17, 1816, p. 2.

4. *Ibid.,* November 2, 1816, p. 2.

Methodists, Quakers &c. — they know that long as he shall remain Governor those decided denominations will enjoy the rights of conscience . . . they know that he will never place his name to the law [i.e., to any law] which shall compel these denominations to pay for the support of the self-styled 'orthodox order'." [5] This seemed to indicate clearly that Plumer and the Republicans felt that they had done all they could for these sects and that holding the line against potential oppressive acts by the Federalists was their only task in religious affairs. A cynic might almost conclude that the Republicans did not want to disestablish the Standing Order for fear that it would remove the bond of anxiety which tied the dissenters to the party. The truth appears to be that however strongly Plumer and Hill personally may have felt on this issue, they knew that their party was not yet ready to vote for disestablishment. This became clear when a bill, forerunner of the so-called Toleration Act which finally put an end to religious taxation, was brought forward in June 1817.

How or why this bill was brought up at this time is not clear. Certainly it was not a party measure. Nor do there appear to have been any petitions or other actions by any of the dissenting sects or their ministers which stimulated it. The only incident preceding the bill which even hinted at its appearance was the election sermon Elder Daniel Merrill of the Nottingham West Baptist Church delivered on June 5. In this sermon Merrill discussed religious liberty at length; among other things he stated, "It belongs to every wise legislature to rescind all those laws which their erring predecessors have sacrilegiously enacted" contrary to the unalienable rights of conscience. "May it be the honor of the present legislature to occupy the first rank in acts so just to God, so safe to man." [6]

Four days after this the Senate *Journal* records that "an act securing equal rights and privileges to Christians of every denomination in this State" was presented and sent to a committee for consideration. On June 24, "A bill entitled 'an act to repeal a certain part of an act entitled "an act for regulating towns and choice of town officers"'" was introduced by the hon. Mr. Young, read a second time and on the question shall this bill pass to a third reading the yeas were called for." [7] This seems to indicate that Dan Young, the senator from the twelfth district, introduced the bill to abolish religious taxes as a separate bill but that it emerged from committee as an amendment to the act of 1791 which granted towns and parishes the right

5. *Ibid.*, March 4, 1817, p. 2.
6. Daniel Merrill, *The Kingdom of God* (Concord, 1817), delivered June 5, 1817, p. 35. See also Merrill's attack on the Standing Order in his Thanksgiving Sermon, *Balaam Disappointed* (Danville, Vermont, 1816), in which he said that the clergy and the Federalists were attacking the Republican Party and had sided with Britain in the war because they saw "that our excellent Constitution must be altered and the present administration [Madison's] put down or the dominant, the law-favored religion of New England will be in danger." pp. 9–10.
7. *Journal of the Honorable Senate of the State of New Hampshire* (Concord, 1818), June session, 1817, pp. 54, 157.

to levy religious taxes. The amendment would have taken this right from the towns and parishes and thus effectively ended the establishment.

Dan Young, according to his autobiography, was born in Grafton County, New Hampshire, in 1783, son of a well-to-do miller and tavern keeper who had been an officer in the Revolution. Raised a Congregationalist, Young first heard Jesse Lee preach in 1798 when he, his brother and his sister were converted to Methodism. He attended an academy in Haverhill, taught school, toyed for a time with Universalism, but finally in 1803 joined the Methodists — over the objections of his parents. A year later he felt called to preach, was licensed, and assigned to the Grantham circuit. Over the next fifteen years he preached in various circuits in New Hampshire, Vermont, and Ohio, taking particular interest in converting Universalists, Calvinists, and Roman Catholics. He returned to New Hampshire in 1816, settled in Lisbon and was elected to the state Senate where he served until 1821. At first he sponsored temperance legislation and then, in 1817, decided to introduce a bill to end compulsory religious taxes.

He undertook this effort entirely on his own initiative. He neither consulted nor sought the support of the Republican Party leaders. Young never thought of himself as a party man, though he makes it clear that like most Methodists he always voted for the Republicans. The first time he introduced his bill in 1817 he did not speak extensively in its favor. Although nine of the twelve senators at this time were Republicans, the bill received only four votes, including his own.

> I knew well that at first this measure would receive but a very meager support, and I said very little on the subject, merely to explain it . . . The enemies of religious liberty chuckled and congratulated themselves that this would be the last of Mr. Young's new-fangled notions about religious liberty. It was rumored that I was a deist . . . The friends of religious liberty hung their heads in despondency, and said to me, "We shall never succeed and may as well give up the controversy." [8]

The *Patriot* made no mention of the bill in 1817. Obviously the Party did not care to discuss the matter. Nor is there any other mention of it outside the Senate *Journal,* not even in the papers or autobiography of William Plumer. The only item on religion which the *Patriot* printed during the next twelve months was an excerpt from a letter Plumer wrote on January 31, 1818, which someone requested be printed. It concerned Plumer's views on religious freedom:

> My sentiments on that subject have not changed with time; but every

8. Daniel Young, *Autobiography,* ed. W. P. Strickland (New York, 1860), pp. 280–297. Also James O. Lyford, *History of Concord* (Concord, 1903), I, 357; M. V. B. Knox, "Intolerance in New Hampshire," *The Granite Monthly,* X (1887), pp. 326–330.

revolving season has added new proofs, in my mind, to the fitness and propriety of leaving every individual at full and entire liberty of choosing his own religion and of giving or withholding his property as he pleases for its support. Human laws cannot make men religious, but they may and often have made bad men hypocrites.[9]

While this might be considered as an implicit endorsement of the movement for disestablishment, it constituted the only effort which Plumer, as head of his party, made to support it. Nor did the *Patriot,* in subsequent issues, give the supporters of the bill any comfort.[10]

Early in June 1818, Dan Young again brought into the Senate a bill to abolish religious taxes. This time the Senate voted on June 13 to pass it and sent it to the House for concurrence.[11] Two weeks later the House voted on the second reading of the bill to postpone consideration of it until the next session. Although the Republicans had a large majority in the House at this time, the vote was 113 to 69 for postponement.[12] Again the *Patriot* gave the bill no publicity and made no comment about it. Nor did any letters appear in any of the New Hampshire newspapers on its behalf.

Plumer decided to retire from politics in 1819. The Republicans nominated Samuel Bell to succeed him. During the campaign in the spring of 1819 neither Bell nor the *Patriot* made any statements concerning disestablishment in general or Young's bill in particular. Bell won the election, however, and early in June 1819, Dan Young brought up his bill for the third time.

Once again it passed the Senate and went to the House for concurrence. When it was introduced into the House by Dr. Thomas Whipple, Jr., of Wentworth, the bill passed its first reading and was sent to committee. Only then did the *Patriot* break its long conspiracy of silence on the issue. On June 22, Isaac Hill printed the three sections of the bill and endorsed it in a strong editorial. Obviously he had been counting votes and foresaw a victory for which he wished his party to get credit.

The first section of the bill, which was still designed as an amendment to the act regulating town government of February 8, 1791, reiterated the right of the towns to maintain the public school system by taxation and to vote money for highways, bridges, and the care of the poor. The second section repealed Section Ten of the act of 1791 which granted towns the

9. New Hampshire *Patriot,* February 2, 1818, p. 3.

10. Plumer's biographer says of Plumer's silence on the issue, "For strategic reasons he had been content to remain in the background of this campaign." This presumably means that for him to have taken a stand might have split his party, and he therefore preferred not to make it a matter of party discipline. Turner, *Plumer,* p. 291.

11. *Senate Journal,* June session, 1818, p. 110. In his autobiography, p. 298, Young says (erroneously) that in 1818 the Senate vote "was tied, and thus [the bill] laid over until the next session."

12. *House Journal,* June session, 1818, p. 301.

right to levy taxes for support of public worship. The third section granted automatic corporate powers to all religious societies in the state and said that no persons could be associated in law with any religious society (i.e., with a parish) without his express consent. This third section of the bill was called "The Toleration Bill":

> And be it further enacted, That every religious sect or denomination of christians in this state, may associate and form societies, may admit members, may establish rules and by-laws for their regulation and government, and shall have all the corporate powers which may be necessary to assess and raise money by taxes upon the polls & rateable estates of the members of such association, and to collect and appropriate the same for the purpose of building and repairing houses for public worship, and for the support of the preaching of the gospel. And the assessors and collectors of such association shall have the same powers in assessing and collecting said monies, and shall be liable to the same penalties, as similar town officers now have, and are liable to — *Provided,* That no person shall be compelled to join or support nor be classed with or associate[d] to any congregation, church or religious society without his express consent first had and obtained. *Provided also* if any person shall choose to separate himself from such society or association to which he may belong and shall leave a written notice thereof with the clerk of such society or association, he shall thereupon be no longer liable for any future expenses which may be incurred by said society or association.

That no person could be automatically classed as belonging to the territorial parish in which he was born or into which he moved as a resident without his permission meant that all religious societies, all parishes, were henceforth on a voluntary basis. Of course, from the dissenters' point of view, the requirement that a man leave a written notice with the parish clerk when he left a society was a remnant of the certificate system, but at least the man himself could write it.[13]

Hill's endorsement of the bill tried to take into account the kinds of objections he knew would be raised against it. He feared any further silence would be more harm than help to the party and he therefore hoped to swing a majority of votes in its favor and prevent a bitter fight.

> It is difficult to perceive what objections can be made to this bill unless we supposed that some people are so in love with liberty of conscience that they want not only that to which they are constitutionally entitled but also all that belongs to their neighbors.

This was designed to restrain the more radical separationists who did not

13. The two provisos in the bill were copied verbatim from the new constitution which Connecticut had adopted the year before. By coupling disestablishment of territorial parishes with a general incorporation act, New Hampshire in effect transferred the taxing power from the state to the voluntary religious society.

even want to concede corporate taxing powers to those religious societies (like the Congregationalists) who wished to retain them. But most of Hill's arguments were directed against those who wished to maintain the prevailing system.

> This bill disturbs no existing contracts between ministers already settled and their people — it disturbs no property in meetinghouses erected by towns — it gives every religious denomination equal privileges such as are guaranteed to them by the constitution; it gives every religious society or sect the right to support their own teachers in the manner most agreeable to their own ideas of propriety; it gives every man a right when his conscience shall dictate to leave any sect to which he has belonged and unite himself with any other which he may deem more virtuous or more correct in its religious principles. Its tendency will be to make men sincere and honest in their religious profession — to make public teachers diligent and assiduous in the discharge of their important duties. It will render it necessary that they should deserve public confidence before they can receive it. *It takes no man's property to pay a teacher without his consent.* Not so with the present law on this subject. That first taxes and takes the citizen's property & then turns round to him in a tantalizing manner and says 'now submit the decision of your *conscience* to a jury of twelve men, perhaps a jury too, of men under strong religious prejudices (for who is free from bias on matters of this kind?) and if on proper inquisition they shall say you are not of the dominant sect, you may have your money again!' . . . It is to be hoped that this bill will become a law, that every member of the Legislature will consult the future good of his constituents, nor be terrified from his duty to posterity, his country and his God, by the designing and hypocritical cry, *the church is in danger! — the interests of religion are to be sacrificed! —* and such like senseless insinuations. Let this bill be brought to the test of reason, of the Constitution, of equity and justice; — and if any incongruity with these great principles can be discovered let it be rejected; but if not, let no interested motives, no desire for popularity with the advocates of religious tyranny, draw the representatives of the people from their duty.[14]

But despite Hill's plea, the fight was long, hard, and bitter. A shift of five votes would have defeated the bill, even though the Republicans had a much larger majority than that.

The arguments proposed for and against the bill are revealing for the kinds of issues which seemed important to both sides. They were not the same issues raised in the debates in the other New England states. On June 22, the day that the *Patriot* first endorsed the bill, it came before the House for its second reading. Whipple made a minor amendment to it from the floor and then gave a strong speech in its favor. John Pitman of Portsmouth answered him, saying that although he had no objection to the clauses incorporating all dissenters, he did object to the rest of the bill. Whipple's

14. New Hampshire *Patriot*, June 22, 1819, pp. 2–3.

amendment passed by a vote of 96 to 88.[15] On June 23, Pitman moved to amend the bill by striking out the first two sections (thus retaining Section Ten of the act of 1791 as it was) and revising the third section so as to provide "that a citizen who is of a different sect from the minister and majority of a town shall leave a certificate with the town clerk making declaration to that effect; and shall not thereafter be compelled to pay

15. *House Journal,* June session, 1819, pp. 222–228, 239–242. The bill, amended by Whipple, finally passed:

An Act in Amendment of An Act Entitled An Act for Regulating Towns and the Choice of Town Officers, Passed February 8th, 1791.

Section 1st. Be it enacted by the Senate and House of Representatives in General Court convened, That the inhabitants of each town in this State, qualified to vote at any meeting duly and legally warned and holden in such town, may grant and vote such sum or sums of money as they shall judge necessary for the support of schools, school houses, the maintenance of the poor, for laying out and repairing highways, for building and repairing bridges, and for all the necessary charges arising within said town, to be assessed on the polls and estates in said town as the law directs.

Sec. 2nd. And be it further enacted, That the tenth section of the Act to which this is an amendment, be and the same is hereby repealed. Provided that towns between which and any settled minister there is prior to or at the passing of this act a subsisting contract, shall have a right from time to time to vote, assess, collect and appropriate such sum or sums of money as may be necessary for the fulfilment of such contract and for repairing meetinghouses now owned by such town so far as may be necessary to render them useful for town purposes — Provided that no person shall be liable to taxation for the purpose of fulfilling any contract between any town and settled minister who shall prior to such assessment file with the town clerk of the town where he may reside a certificate declaring that he is not of the religious persuasion or opinion of the minister settled in such town.

Sec. 3d. And be it further enacted that each religious sect or denomination of Christians in this State may associate and form societies, may admit members, may establish rules and byelaws for their regulation and government, and shall have all the corporate powers which may be necessary to assess and raise money by taxes upon the polls and rateable estate of the members of such associations, and to collect and appropriate the same for the purpose of building and repairing houses of public worship, and for the support of the ministry: and the assessors and collectors of such associations shall have the same powers in assessing and collecting, and shall be liable to the same penalties as similar town officers have and are liable to — Provided that no person shall be compelled to join or support, or be classed with, or associated to any congregation, church or religious society without his express consent first had and obtained. — Provided also, if any person shall choose to separate himself from such society, or association to which he may belong, and shall leave a written notice thereof with the clerk of such society or association, he shall thereupon be no longer liable for any future expenses which may be incurred by said society or association. — Provided also that no association or society shall exercise the powers herein granted until it shall have assumed a name and stile by which such society may be known and distinguished in law, and shall have recorded the same in a book of records to be kept by the clerk of said Society, and shall have published the same in some newspaper in the County where such society may be formed if any be printed therein, and if not then in some paper published in some adjoining County.

Laws, VIII, 820.

towards the support of a denomination different from himself." [16] The Federalists were willing to concede that a dissenter might write his own certificate, but they did not want to abolish the system of territorial parishes and compulsory taxation of those who did not sign off. This amendment was vigorously debated and defeated by a vote of 96 to 87. The next day, June 24, the bill passed the second reading in its form as amended by Whipple by a vote of 95 to 88. On June 25 the bill came up for its third and final reading. The Federalists moved to postpone consideration of the bill until the next session. This lost by 103 to 79. The motion was then made to pass the bill; it carried. Though no tally was recorded, the figure was probably close to that of 96 to 87 which defeated Pitman's amendment. [17]

When the next issue of the *Patriot* appeared on June 29, the matter was over. But Hill did devote several issues to reprinting the debates in the house. Opposition from the Congregational clergy and from the Federalist newspapers was so bitter that it was not until July 20 that Hill wrote another editorial defending the act. This was merely a short attack upon the Standing Clergy because they "fear that a voluntary support of the people will be to them a loss of support."

Thomas Whipple, who led the fight in the House, received so much publicity from his support of the bill that some historians have credited him with its origin, and some contemporaries, forgetting that Young had introduced it first in the Senate, referred to it as "The Whipple Bill." Whipple was a physician, not a minister. He appears not to have been a dissenter. Nor was he an orthodox Congregationalist. From his defense of religious liberty he appears to have been a rather romantic liberal Unitarian, a man whose views were similar to William Cullen Bryant's. He spoke of the right of every man to worship God in the manner most agreeable to his conscience,

> in public or in private; in his own closet, or in temples dedicated to the worship of God; in the street or in the field, or in "The same temple, the resounding wood," where "All vocal beings hymn their equal God," by day, while the sun pours knowledge on his golden ray, or in the silence of the even,

> > "While the moon takes up the wondrous tale,
> > And nightly to the list'ning earth,
> > Repeats the story of her birth," [18]

Whipple vigorously repudiated the claim that the advocates of the bill were "deists, atheists, men of no religion." But his anticlericism was evident in

16. New Hampshire *Patriot,* June 29, 1819, p. 3.
17. *House Journal,* June session, 1819, pp. 239–242, 286–288, 293–296.
18. New Hampshire *Patriot,* June 29, 1819, p. 2.

his castigation of the spirit of persecution to which "Servetus was sacrificed as a burnt offering" and "which caused the bloody Mary to sacrifice her hecatombs of human victims." "This spirit, sir, caused our forefathers, who themselves fled from persecution, to banish Quakers, whip dissenting females, persecute baptists, and to other enormities which has stained the pages of our history."

But most of his arguments were directed to the charges that the bill would abridge the constitutional rights given each town to manage its religious affairs as it saw fit; that the constitution already granted exemption from religious taxes to all honest dissenters; and that liberty of conscience was not at issue in New Hampshire because the support of public worship was a purely civil affair. On the first point, Whipple reasoned:

> It is, however, objected that the amendment by requiring the express consent of the individual as a prerequisite to taxation for the support of the ministry and for the building and repairing houses for public worship, abridges the right intended by the constitution to be given to towns enabling them to provide for these objects. I would inquire of gentlemen, what evidence they would demand of a man's principles in religion beyond his own declaration or what beyond that they have a right to require by our constitution? Have we, sir, any tribunal to whom as a standard of faith, men's consciences can be referred to decision or regulation? . . . And, sir, do not your existing laws in effect establish such an inquisitional tribunal?

Whipple had struck at the heart of the problem. Although Judge Smith had provided what seemed a simple criterion for determining which sects were entitled to exemptions and which were not, neither he nor anyone else had found a way to determine the sincerity of a particular individual's claim that he really was an adherent of that sect. Smith had acknowledged in a footnote to the Moore case that it was the jury's task to determine sincerity of conscientious belief. He cited the case of Steele *vs.* The Assessors of Hillsborough in which the court had ruled that if Steele were really a Presbyterian, he was entitled to win his case against the assessors. But, said Smith, "The jury found for the defendants; it is presumed in the ground that Steele was not a real Presbyterian, but a pretended one." [19] A similar case had occurred in Holderness in 1816 involving an Episcopalian. The plaintiff had joined the Episcopal church after a quarrel had disrupted the Congregational church in the town, but the assessors had taxed him anyway. Judge Smith instructed the jury that the lawyers in the case must show that the plaintiff had become "a bona fide Episcopalian" for conscientious reasons and not simply out of a desire to escape paying religious taxes or "from a personal dislike to the Congregational society." The lawyers were

19. Jeremiah Smith, *Decisions of the Superior and Supreme Courts of New Hampshire* (Boston, 1879), p. 30, n.a.

unable to prove this to the jury's satisfaction, and the jury decided the case against the "pretended" Episcopalian.[20] The problem was the old one of distinguishing a mere cranky schismatic (who was not entitled to claim liberty of conscience) from a sincere sectarian (who was).

Because of this weakness in the law, the assessors, said Whipple, had the power to "exercise their judgments and assess those whom they may deem liable," while "the arbitraments of jurors," who were often "under the influence of strong religious prejudices" was hardly, he felt, a fair method of settling the rights of conscience.

> After struggling for years against the combined influence of the town, the prejudices of the jurors, the corruption of witnesses, the ingenuity of counsel disposed to perpetuate the oppression & the "glorious uncertainty of the law," after spending the means on which his family depend for support, ruining his fortune, and reducing himself to beggary, he *may* recover the amount of tax and costs. For, sir, let it be remembered, that unless he shows corruption in the selectmen or assessors or a design to tax wrongfully, he can recover no exemplary damages.

In addition, the dissenters who won such cases might be taxed by the town to pay the town's debts in the case. In cases where a Standing minister sued a town for failure to pay his salary, the dissenters as citizens were subject to taxation to pay the town's civil debts in such lawsuits. Dissenters also paid as part of their civil taxes the wages given to the collectors of religious taxes, and thus indirectly helped to pay for the support of the parish church. That the laws operated almost entirely to support the Congregational churches was contrary to the constitutional provision prohibiting subordination of one sect to another; it gave the Congregationalists a tremendous advantage, even though they were not mentioned by name in the law.

But Whipple's most subtle argument answered the charge that the towns had a constitutional right to manage their own religious concerns and therefore the Toleration Bill, as a legislative act, was unconstitutional. Only a constitutional amendment, said many opponents, could legally alter the ecclesiastical system. Here was one of the unique aspects of the New Hampshire situation. Whipple pointed out, however, that Article Six said the legislature may empower "the several towns, parishes, bodies corporate *or* religious societies" to make provision for the support of public worship. This Toleration Bill simply shifted the power from the towns and parishes to the religious societies (and it also made them bodies corporate). The constitution permitted the legislature to make this choice, for by the constitution either the territorial parish or the religious society (such as a poll parish) could be the basis of taxation. Thus it was not a constitutional issue but a question of legislative prerogative. If the religious societies which were

20. New Hampshire *Patriot,* August 3, 1819, p. 3.

given the power to maintain public worship by taxation did not choose to exercise it, that was their privilege. As it was, many towns and parishes, perhaps more than half, no longer exercised the power given to them by the legislature under the act of 1791. No one claimed that the state should or could compel these towns to do what they did not want to do:

> The provisions of the constitution in this respect are in the alternative. If, sir, you can impower the towns to provide for the object in this section contemplated and infringe no rights, impair no immunities, secured to the dissenters, you may so impower them; if you deem it more expedient to authorize the parishes, bodies corporate, or religious societies to provide for the maintenance of public worship, you may so impower them. The Legislature is not imperatively ordered by the constitution to impower all of them conjunctively, but may impower one or more of them separately as it may be deemed most expedient.

Whipple concluded his speech by answering those who said "that the foundations of the great deep will be broken up, and disorder and moral ruin will follow, if religion be left to its own uncontrolled and free exercise." To refute this, he cited "the experience of other states" — Vermont, "Connecticut, that land of steady habits," Pennsylvania. But not Rhode Island.

In answering Whipple's arguments, Pitman stated that the toleration bill did not embody the conception of freedom of conscience the people of New Hampshire had when they wrote their constitution. The passage of the bill would make a new and revolutionary alteration in the whole civil and social order of the state. The Constitutional Convention of 1791 had confirmed the constitution of 1784 in maintaining a tax supported territorial parish system. If dissenters were being unfairly taxed under this system, he was willing to consider a bill which would save them from having to go to law to recover their religious taxes. But he could not accept the complete overthrow of the old system and the establishment of a voluntary system which the bill proposed. Not only was it contrary to the wishes and traditions of the people but it would involve the impairment of "subsisting contracts" between ministers and parishes.

Henry Hubbard of Charlestown made a much more impassioned speech against the bill at its second reading. Hubbard, who in 1842–43 became the governor of the state, was a Congregationalist and a Federalist in 1819, though he later became a Democrat. He said in his speech that the bill would "disturb the public order" and "endanger public morals." It would "multiply and increase religious associations" so that "the flock should be dispersed" in every parish. This was not a question of intolerance but of "public order." Hubbard was surprised to hear that dissenters were being taxed and jailed and having to bring suits. That was not his understanding of Article Six. "It could not be supposed that all the members of town corporations can be legally assessed for this purpose unless they are all of the same religious sect or denomination," he said. For the Article clearly said that no one should be compelled to support teachers of another sect. "No language could be more definite, no expressions more direct. Those and those only then it would seem who are of the same persuasion can be assessed for the support of these teachers of morality and religion" hired by the parish or town. "Selectmen are not at liberty to assess the conscientious baptist for the maintenance of a congregational teacher."

Hubbard admitted that some assessors may have made errors in this regard, but "because there might have been a few instances of this kind should we break down the law? . . . would not the remedy be worse than the disease?" What was more, he had never heard anyone complain about the law and he knew of no general concern for the matter at the moment. "Does the public call loudly for the repeal of the law now in force and for passing the act now on the table?" He did not think so. "We have had these statutes in operation for nearly thirty years and no very serious evils have arisen." The courts were perfectly competent to deal with those few illegal assessments which had been made or might be made in order that dissenters might have justice. As for cases in which a dissenter was assessed to pay the salary of a settled minister who had sued the town for arrearages, he was certain the courts would exempt any dissenter from such a tax if he brought a case.

Hubbard also took a novel stand on the question of contracts entered into between a town and a minister. "Clergymen who are settled in our towns are settled on the implied condition that whenever a majority become conscientiously of a different persuasion from them in opinion and vote not to raise the salary, it is apprehended that under such circumstances such a contract between the clergyman and the town would necessarily be dissolved." If a town refused to vote the annual tax for his salary, the contract was *ipso facto* dissolved and no minister, he thought, could collect it. Hubbard assumed of course that the majority which refused to pay one minister would immediately choose another whom it preferred. But no court ever held this conditional view of ministerial contracts. It was sufficiently difficult to discern the conscience of one man without having to evaluate the conscientiousness of a majority which might become displeased with a minister.

As for Whipple's claim that Vermont had suffered no deterioration in religion or morals since it disestablished its churches in 1807, Hubbard offered evidence which seemed to him to show that Vermont had very definitely retrogressed in both areas since that time. If this bill were enacted, the churches of New Hampshire would "soon be deserted and forsaken." From this would follow the neglect of the Sabbath and the decline of all public morality.

Whipple answered Pitman and Hubbard by saying that he could not agree with their definition of liberty of conscience. He did not believe that it concerned only how, when, and where a man worshipped, but also "the means to be used for its propagation." There was a question of property rights involved, for even a man of no religious sect had a right to keep his property from being taxed to propagate beliefs he did not hold. If Hubbard was worried over the multiplication of sects which might follow, did he not thereby imply that "uniformity in religion" was his ideal system? This was precisely the trouble with established religions. Whipple said he had nothing against the clergy as ministers of the gospel, "But when we see them anxious to amass power, wealth, worldly honor . . . when like Thomas A. Becket [sic] they are aiming at the control of the civil authority" then it is necessary to oppose them. Here he brought up the recent enmity to government the clergy had evidenced "in the late struggle for the rights of our country" against Britain. He considered the multiplication of sects a positive benefit for society: "They act as *'censoris morum'* upon each other, correct the public morals and those of other sects. They divide and scatter that influence which when brought to a single point endangers government and depraves public morals." A nice bit of anticlericalism. As for the enthusiasm of the sectaries, he was sure that in the past twelve years "a greater portion of the reclaimed [sinners of New Hampshire] owe their moral improvement to these sectarian instructors" than they did to the established clergy. This was a curious use of the Second Great Awakening by an anticlerical in the defense of disestablishment.

William Butters of Pittsfield, speaking in favor of the bill, rebutted both Pitman and Hubbard. Hubbard might claim that assessors ought not to levy taxes on all inhabitants of a parish, but this was done regularly. At that moment Baptists, Episcopalians, and Quakers were being compelled to pay part of a tax of $700 levied by the town of Concord for the repair of the Congregational meetinghouse. As for impairment of contracts, he believed the bill would have no effect upon them. "Where such contracts now exist, however improper and burthensome in their operation, they must be borne. The object of this bill is to prevent the future occurrence of such contracts." [21]

Edmund Parker of Amherst attacked the bill not only because, as in revolutionary France, it would "let loose from all restraints of morality, piety and religion" and "unloose the chains with which our forefathers sought to bind" vice and wickedness but also because the dissenters were inconsistent in opposing the use of the state to maintain religion while at the same time frequently petitioning the legislature for the powers of incorporation to support religion. He admitted that the constitution was merely permissive and not obligatory in calling upon the towns to promote religious worship, and he admitted that "Nearly one half of the towns in this State are already freed from the operation of the law" by votes of the

21. *Ibid.,* July 13, 1819, p. 2.

inhabitants. But if the other half of the towns wished to maintain the traditions of their forefathers, what right had the state to prevent them? Let each town judge for itself. "They are the best judges of their own business." He even went on to make the strange observation that "The law [requiring tax support] will probably die a natural death in a few years" so that it seemed unnecessarily harsh to impose disestablishment now. "Suffer them still to go on and a few years will make that alteration in peace and quietness which would cause confusion and difficulty if done at once." [22]

Ichabod Bartlett, a prominent Republican lawyer of Portsmouth, concluded the debate with a strong argument for the bill and an ironic plea that they were all friends of order and of religion and that they all acknowledged the importance of religion to civil government. "We differ only as to the mode of accomplishing the great object which all must desire, the diffusion of the glorious Gospel of our Saviour." He agreed with Whipple that this bill merely transferred the support of religion from the towns to the religious societies. He said he thought Article Six could be read to say "The Legislature may empower each sect or persuasion to tax those who belong to them and no others." If the people had meant to give this constitutional right to the towns and only to the towns, why did they not say so? No, the people had wisely left the choice up to the legislature and after they had tried one system for thirty years and found it entailed many difficulties and hardships, the people now had the right through their legislature to try an alternative which the Constitution described. By this bill, he said, we are not "acquiring any new right in favor of religious freedom but are defining a right already granted by the constitution — to prevent the abuse of that right." He cited the case of a man who had been taxed to the Standing church after he was for ten years an adherent of another denomination. When he brought suit to regain the tax money the jury divided "and the sufferer is yet without remedy." [23]

It is impossible to know exactly what the constitutional convention had in mind in 1781 when it first drew up Article Six. If the delegates were copying the Massachusetts Constitution they certainly did not intend to leave an alternative choice to the legislature. On the other hand, if they were trying to be somewhat more liberal than Massachusetts, or to be more exact, if William Plumer's influence in drafting this article aimed to leave as many loopholes as possible, perhaps the ambiguity was intentional. That the convention or the people at large ever considered in the 1780's or 1790's that they had written a constitution which gave them the alternative of voluntarism (that is, the alternative of disestablishment) is entirely unlikely. For this imaginative stretching of constitutional interpretation to fit a changing social and intellectual climate, the credit must go to Whipple

22. *Ibid.*, July 20, 1819, p. 2.
23. *Ibid.*, July 27, 1819, p. 1.

and Young. Although the Baptists accepted it, it does not appear that they played any part in making it a reality.

However, the Methodists' motives differed little from those of the Baptists; nor does the speech Dan Young made in favor of his bill offer any argument which the Baptists and Universalists had not used before. Young began by comparing his fight against a corrupt church to Martin Luther's fight and then said "false systems of religion have always needed the strong arm of human laws to sustain them. Not so, however, with the pure and holy religion established by the Gospel." For Young, of course, the religion of the Gospel was Arminianism and hence the corruption he disliked most in the establishment was its Calvinism. But the Baptists would have agreed with his argument that "the religion of the heart," i.e., experimental religion, is a private, not a public, matter.

Young also said in his autobiography that there was much of the same anticlerical resentment present in New Hampshire at this time as there had been during the Separate movement of the First Great Awakening (pietism had perennially a large amount of levellism implicit in its doctrine of the priesthood of all believers). Young quotes a speech in the House of Representatives in favor of his bill which lashed out at "those [established] clergy who, snugly moored in stylish parlors, have their tables loaded with luxuries and their curtained beds of ease; who spend their leisure hours in visiting the wealthy, the fashionable, the gay . . . and who seem never to think of the condition of the poor."

And finally, the Methodists shared the general sectarian view that disestablishment would clear the way for the triumph of his own particular denomination. "The Methodist Church, being released from this yoke, now shot ahead with great success and cheering prospects." Methodist "doctrines are highly pure and evangelical and as such will have the approbation and support of God," wrote Young. "May we not then confidently trust that God will add to our numbers and graces and . . . that our banners . . . will be unfurled in every land and every clime . . . that Methodism will be the happy instrument, in the hand of God, of spreading Scripture holiness . . . through all the world."

In the months that followed the passage of the Toleration Act the Federalists tried to make an issue of it. Their newspapers were filled with bitter prophecies, lamentations, and recriminations. On August 3, 1819, Isaac Hill wrote an editorial protesting that "a senseless outcry is raised in the State on account of the toleration law. One calls it a repeal of the Christian religion; another says the Bible is abolished." But "The real truth lies here, a certain dominant sect can no longer make use of extortion and oppression to support *their* system." The Republican Party no longer felt that it had to cater to the Congregationalists. The dissenting sects, said Hill, "have become now probably more numerous than the Congregationalists." For those who claimed that the number of injustices done under the tax system was inconsequential, Hill offered to print a history of all such instances which any dissenters would care to send him.[24]

Three days after this editorial, William Plumer, now in political retirement, wrote to Hill explaining his views of the act: "The law upon religious freedom meets my entire approbation; it reflects honor upon each branch of the legislature. It is a monument proclaiming the rights of man & the progress of liberal sentiments. I wish some gentleman of talents and information would write & publish a series of numbers not simply vindicating that law, but stating & explaining the natural and unalienable rights of conscience & freedom of opinion." [25]

Fears that the Federalists would seek to make a campaign issue of the bill in 1820 and that there was a plot to repeal it were groundless.[26] The issue was settled once and for all. Though the fight to abolish the religious test for officeholding lasted until 1876, the major aim of the Baptists and other dissenters in New Hampshire had been satisfactorily accomplished.

The Toleration Act put an end to a system of compulsory religious taxes by which a man could, against his will and his conscience, be forced to pay to support a minister whom he never heard and to maintain a church which he never joined and with which he did not want to be associated. It thus ended the certificate system and the responsibility placed on juries for deciding the honesty of a man's claims to be a member of a sect distinct from that of the majority in his town or parish. But the Toleration Act did not draw a clear line between church and state in New Hampshire. It implicitly, if not explicitly, maintained the conception that New Hampshire was a Christian — in fact a Protestant — commonwealth. It clearly acknowledged that the Protestant religion was so essential to the welfare of the civil state that in certain respects the state should encourage and support it.

The means by which this support continued beyond 1819 lie outside the scope of this study, but they may be listed briefly: The most obvious legal sanction for Protestantism remained in the religious test which limited officeholding to members "of the protestant religion." This requirement was not abandoned until 1876.[27] Another form of support for religion was the exemption of church property from civil taxes, a system which is still retained. In addition, the towns also retained the power to dispense the income from

24. *Ibid.,* August 3, 1819, p. 3. For a series of eight articles signed "Alcibiades" and another series of ten articles signed "Gracchus" both defending the act, see *ibid.,* August 10, 1819, and succeeding issues. "Alcibiades" wrote to refute a series of attacks Thomas G. Fessenden of Vermont made on the act in the Dartmouth *Gazette.*

25. Turner, *Plumer,* p. 291.

26. New Hampshire *Patriot,* November 23, 1819, p. 3.

27. For the abolition of the religious test in 1876 see Charles B. Kinney, *Church and State: The Struggle for Separation in New Hampshire* (New York, 1955), p. 127.

ministry lands to support religion within the town. Some towns did not observe this and simply transferred this income to civil purposes. But some sought to divide it among the various denominations in the town proportionally, while others gave it to the majority sect.[28] Furthermore the Toleration Act explicitly required all religious societies which wished to obtain its privileges and benefits to be incorporated by law, even though this process was made a simple matter of formality. Finally, in the famous case of Hale vs. Everett in 1868, the Superior Court upheld the state's right to determine who was and who was not a Christian minister. The court declared in this case that the Rev. F. E. Abbott of Dover, who had abandoned his Unitarian faith to espouse what he called "Free Religion," had no right to be chosen to use the town meetinghouse even though the majority of the incorporated town parish had voted for him to be their minister.[29]

The unwillingness of the people of New Hampshire to yield to the Jeffersonian conception of a secular state was consistent with the pattern of the other former Puritan colonies, Connecticut and Massachusetts. In these states the fight to end the system of compulsory religious taxation was far more bitter and difficult, but the outcome was no less inevitable in the rising tide of Jeffersonian democracy.

28. For a brief discussion of this see *ibid.,* pp. 108–113.
29. For the 270-page opinion of the Superior Court (both majority and minority decisions) in this case see vol. 53, the New Hampshire *Reports* of the Supreme Court, pp. 9–276.

PART XI

Disestablishment in Connecticut,

1776–1818

"Truth has ever been most successful when left to combat error in the open field of argument and free discussion."

The Baptist Petition, 1803

Chapter 47

John Leland and the Era of "Modern Liberality" in Connecticut, 1776–1800

As to Christians of other denominations, labour to shun that narrow bigot principle which prevents some from either thinking or hoping well of them who do not believe and practice according to their views of what is right and scriptural in matters of religion. Dare we say we are right in everything . . . ?

Statement of Stonington Baptist Association, 1793

After the Revolution New England entered into a revival of the mood of "catholicity," "candor," and "toleration" which had characterized the early decades of the eighteenth century after the Glorious Revolution. The dissenters and Congregationalists still disagreed over religious taxes; the orthodox Calvinists deplored the rise of Arminianism, deism, and a host of new unorthodox sects. But the mood of the people generally was a broadly tolerant one. Development of this era of religious good feeling from 1776 to 1800 had many causes. Most significant were the influx of Enlightenment philosophy and science from Europe; the mutual camaraderie of the shared Revolutionary experience; the reaction against the religious fanaticism of the Great Awakening (and its divisive aftermath); the gradual shift of the Standing churches to New Light evangelical doctrines and practices; and the tremendous concentration of public effort on organizing, uniting, and strengthening the institutional structures of the new nation. To the Revolutionary generation the optimistic concept of inherent, inalienable natural rights implanted in a rational human race by a benevolent Governor of the Universe seemed more meaningful than the pessimistic "Five Points of Calvinism" with emphasis on the mystery of the universe, the depravity of man, and the wrath of God. How could a people who triumphed over the power of Britain and erected a free new nation out of a howling wilderness be mere worms?

Considering the unity of Americans of all faiths in overthrowing tyranny, it seemed petty to continue to label people by their creeds rather than by their deeds. Ezra Stiles lamented in 1783 that it began to appear less important what creed a man believed in than whether he was honest, upright, and dedicated to the republic. A poem in the Danbury (Connecticut) *Farmer's Journal* of September 26, 1791 captured the spirit of this antisectarian view:

> Sectarians fierce for systems fight,
> *Each* can demonstrate that he's right;
> And prove by scripture, blocks, and knocks,
> That every other is heterodox.
> *Each* claims a right to judge his brother,
> And by that right to damn each other, —
> Pray God to vindicate their sentence
> And smite all others with repentance.[1]

Zephaniah Swift, prominent lawyer and member of Congress from Windham, wrote in 1795, "It is a pleasing consideration, that pure religion and moral virtue have augmented in proportion to the progress of liberality of sentiment and that every relaxation of the severity of the ecclesiastical establishment has contributed to the stability of government and the happiness of the people." Swift was a Federalist and later a member of the Hartford Convention; he was also a spokesman for the new religious liberalism of the post-Revolutionary period. In his famous *System of the Laws of the State of Connecticut* published in two volumes in 1795 and 1796, he noted approvingly the increasing relaxation of theological and ecclesiastical uniformity and conformity in the state since the seventeenth century; particularly he approved the abandonment of the Saybrook Platform:

> This opens the door for the progressive improvement of religion unshackled by human laws. Many of the absurd and irrational doctrines which have so long disfigured and disgraced christianity are already exploded, and there is a prospect that many more will soon meet the same fate. Mankind are rejecting those false appendages of religion which have so long imposed upon them penance and restraints . . . They begin to entertain an idea that religion was not instituted for the purpose of rendering them miserable but happy, and that the innocent enjoyments of life are not repugnant to the will of a benevolent God. They believe there is more merit in acting right than in thinking right; and that the condition of men in a future state will not be dependent on the speculative opinions they may have adopted in the present.[2]

1. The poem was unsigned. For another poem in this vein see the *American Mercury* (Hartford), February 9, 1795, p. 3. The Rev. James Cogswell, the Standing minister of Scotland parish said in his diary, July 2, 1789, that many people in his parish told him that they did not attend church regularly because they did not want to seem too "pious." This ms. diary is in the Connecticut Historical Society.

2. Zephaniah Swift, *A System of the Laws of the State of Connecticut* (Windham, 1795–1796), I, 145. Swift did not, however, favor abandoning religious taxation. See Chapter 48.

Similar expressions of religious liberalism were numerous. Moreover, they were matched by concrete action on the local level. Many towns and parishes in Connecticut voted in these years to open the meetinghouse to speakers of all denominations. A few towns (which found the burden of maintaining several churches too great) tried to overcome the growing religious diversity by forming what were called "Catholic" or "Union" churches of members of all denominations. Pomfret and Windham, Connecticut both formed such "Independent Catholic Christian Societies" in the 1790's and in Windham the members of the first parish agreed in 1797 on the following articles to govern the Congregational meetinghouse:

> Article I. Charity, which is so strongly inculcated in Divine Revelation, and declared to be an essential christian duty, teaches us at all times to concede towards each other in our religious associations. We will therefore never withhold from each other a convenient and proper opportunity of receiving such different christian instructors as may be agreeable to their conscience — paying at all times a decent regard to engagements and priority of appointments.
>
> Article II. Whenever it shall be judged prudent and best to build a meetinghouse or procure instruments of music that will render the worship of God decent, orderly and graceful, the same shall be done by free and voluntary donations and used for the purposes assigned by donors.[3]

Even the Baptists shared something of this temper. The Circular Letter authorized by the Stonington Baptist Association in 1793 read:

> As to Christians of other denominations, labour to shun that narrow bigot principle which prevents some from either thinking or hoping well of them who do not believe and practice just according to their views of what is right and scriptural in matters of religion. Dare we say we are right in every thing; that we understand and obey every scripture exactly according to the design of its divine author? such confidence would not become us; shall we presume to say that professors of other denominations are right in nothing? God forbid: let us exercise more of that Charity which hopeth all things &c.[4]

However, all did not share this mood of benevolent unity and charity. The dissenting sects were proselyting at a vigorous rate and the neo-Edwardsian or Hopkinsian Congregationalists (sometimes called "hyper-" or "high church" Calvinists) were stoutly maintaining "orthodoxy" against rationalism and Arianism. In 1793 Samuel Hopkins published his famous *System of Theology* which put into its final form the *summa theologica* of "the New Divinity." Two years later Timothy Dwight began his vehement

---

3. Ellen Larned, *History of Windham County, Connecticut,* 2 vols. (Worcester, 1880), II, 313–314.
4. Minutes of the Stonington Baptist Association, 1793, p. 7.

attack on deism and infidelity at Yale. Before the decade was out the hysteria over Jeffersonian Jacobinism, the Democratic Clubs, and the Bavarian Illuminati had virtually put an end to the era of catholicity. By 1800 the Protestant Counter-Reformation (which came about in New England with carefully engineered revivalism by Dwight, Lyman Beecher, and Nathaniel W. Taylor) had begun. The Second Great Awakening shattered the hopes of religious liberals from Jefferson in Virginia to Channing in Boston. The leaders of this new reformation, however, were not nearly so concerned about the radical atheism of d'Holbach or the profane deism of Thomas Paine as they were about a general trend toward secularism posing as toleration. Timothy Dwight's retrospective sermon in 1801, *A Discourse on Some Events of the Last Century,* made the point clear:

> The religion of the country has exhibited a very commendable spirit of catholicism and moderation during the past century, a spirit extended perhaps as far as can be reasonably expected from men . . . Indeed, the existing error appears to be a tendency in many persons toward what is emphatically called *modern liberality;* which is no other than mere indifference to truth and error, virtue and vice: a more dangerous and fatal character than the most contemptible enthusiasm of the most odious bigotry.

A more vehement diatribe against liberalism appeared in the *American Mercury* in 1791 by a man who signed himself "Senex, M.A.":

> I am a friend to true liberty of a good conscience, but we hear of some having an evil conscience. What is liberty of conscience but a freedom from sin and error; and what is liberty of error but a prison for conscience. Suppose our present Congress in their present session pass a declarative resolve granting universal toleration to all opinions and free liberty to Familists, Libertines, Erastians, Anti-trinitarians, Anabaptists, Antinomians, Arians, Sabellians, Montanists, Arminians, Socinians, Deists, Mortalians, Gnosticks, Fatalists, Atheists, Universalists, Romanists, Sandemonists, Seekers, Shakers, &c., &c. In a word, room for Hell above ground. What can be expected but that such Gehenical errors will turn Christ's Academy into the Devil's University.[5]

This echo from the seventeenth century was not an isolated one. Connecticut's legislature declined to ratify the First Amendment to the federal Constitution,[6] and the Jacobin's Reign of Terror in France in 1793 produced an almost hysterical reaction in New England against the dangers of too much religious liberalism.

These attacks on liberalism did not stifle it. For many the attack merely

5. *American Mercury,* January 31, 1791, p. 2.
6. For discussion of this failure see the Introduction to vol. 7 of Conn. State Rec., esp. pp. ix–xi.

heightened a strong anticlericalism underlying their rationalism and their latitudinarianism. When the Standing ministers, out of fear for their status and prestige and, too, from a sincere dedication to their conception of the Christian faith, raised the cry of "The Church in danger" — suitably modified to "Religion and the general welfare of New England in danger" — the liberals reacted with the cry of clerical tyranny and ecclesiastical oppression. Besides the rationalists, there were many pious dissenters who feared the priestcraft as they did the deists. As religious historians have indicated, the movement for separation of church and state in America was a fortuitous and ambivalent combination of pietism and rationalism. Nowhere was this ambivalence more evident than in Connecticut.

The Baptists, for example, could readily sympathize with the liberal rationalists' efforts to extend liberty of conscience by weakening the established system, just as they sympathized with the attempt of the French Revolution to overthrow the Papal establishment. But as Christian pietists they shared with the Standing ministers a fear of increasing secularism and irreligion. Yet to choose either side in the debate would have been inconsistent. To aid the Congregational clergy was to bolster the Standing Order. To aid the rationalist would prevent creation of a Christian nation. This dilemma goes far to explain the Baptists' desperate effort (and that of most other evangelical dissenters) during these years to stand outside of party politics. Their future lay in a middle way between liberal secularism and an establishment. But not until the Standing Order was overthrown did their alternative — evangelical voluntarism and rule by the Christian majority — emerge clearly in New England. Meanwhile the dissenters had to consider both sides. In the post-Revolutionary generation liberalism offered the most benefits to dissent. By concentrating on evangelistic efforts, the Baptists increased their political leverage as they increased their numbers.

In 1760 there had been only nine Baptist churches in Connecticut with a membership of perhaps 450 (compared to 151 Congregational churches). By 1784 there were thirty Baptist churches with 1800 members; by 1795, fifty-five churches with 3200 members; in 1810, sixty-five churches with 5700 members; and in 1818, when the Standing Order was finally disestablished, eighty-five churches and 8000 members. For comparison, there were in 1792, 168 Congregational churches, thirty Episcopal, ten Separate, and one Methodist; in 1818, 204 Congregational, seventy-four Episcopal, fifty-three Methodist, two Separate and one Sandemanian churches. By 1818, the dissenting churches outnumbered the Congregational.[7]

7. This does not indicate that dissenters had more voters. These statistics have been gleaned from the works of Isaac Backus, David Benedict, and A. H. Newman on the Baptists; from the minutes of the various Baptist associations; and from Richard J. Purcell, *Connecticut in Transition, 1775–1818* (Washington, 1918), pp. 63, 69–70, 80, 83, 89, 91. Statistics vary widely for all denominations. In 1818 the Congregational churches were estimated from 210 to 228; the Baptists from 62 to 97,

Most of this Baptist growth in Connecticut resulted from itinerant evangelism by elders and exhorters. Some of these itinerants came from across the border in Rhode Island. Most notable was James Manning, President of the Baptist College in Providence, who, like many of his pious students, frequently devoted the summer months to itinerating when the college was closed. So successful was Manning in winning converts from the Standing churches in Windham county that the Rev. Aaron Putnam of Pomfret challenged him to a public debate on the validity of infant baptism. According to Ellen Larned, the local historian, "The result was precisely contrary to what was intended. Mr. Manning had greatly the advantage of his opponent in vigor and eloquence if not in argument, public interest was heightened and Baptist sentiments far more widely disseminated and embraced."

With growing size came growing organizational unity. The first Connecticut Baptist Association was the Stonington Association in 1772 which included churches in eastern Connecticut, Massachusetts, and western Rhode Island. In 1785 the Groton Union Conference was formed; it also included churches from the same three states in the same areas, but the churches of this association practiced open-communion with Separate churches, as they had done since the days when the Separates first emerged. The Stonington Association and its closed communion Baptist churches established fraternal ties with the Warren Association in 1782, but attempts by Backus, Manning, and others to persuade the members of the Groton Association to abandon open-communion and conform to the principles of the Warren Association failed. However, individual churches of this association gradually abandoned open-communion, especially as the Separate movement died out. Finally in 1817 it merged with the Stonington Association. The following year, 1818, the New London Association was formed by the Baptist churches west of the Thames River in eastern Connecticut; the Stonington Association retained the Baptist churches east of the Thames.

In 1790 the Danbury Baptist Association was formed to take care of the churches in western Connecticut; it also included three churches in eastern New York. In 1801 an association formed in Sturbridge, Massachusetts included those Baptist churches in the middle of Connecticut which were too far from either the Danbury churches on the west or the

---

and the Methodists from 50 to 60. The smaller sects in 1818 have been variously estimated at two to seven Quaker congregations; one or two Sandemanian; one to six Separate; one Shaker; one Rogerene; one to four Universalist. Among the Baptists in 1818 there were at least two Freewill Baptist churches, one or two Christ-ian churches, and one or two Seventh Day Baptist churches. For John Leland's estimates as of 1791, see *The Writings of Elder John Leland,* ed. L. F. Greene (New York, 1845), p. 186. Hereafter referred to as Leland, *Works.* For a claim that there were ninety Baptist churches in Connecticut in 1818, see Asa Wilcox, *A Plea for Baptist Petition* (Hartford, 1818), p. 12.

Stonington churches in the east for frequent fellowship. In 1818 the Danbury Association became too large; part of it split off to form the Hartford Association. The actions, purposes, and attitudes of these associations did not differ significantly from those formed in Massachusetts. Like them, the Connecticut associations were primarily concerned with preserving good church order and with stimulating institutional unity and growth. Like them, they tried to resolve questions of doctrine and practice raised by their members, and they opposed the giving of certificates and the seeking of incorporation.[8] But, unlike the Massachusetts Baptists, Connecticut Baptists did not form a statewide grievance committee or take concerted action against instances of local oppression by petitioning the legislature until after the turn of the century. This was partly because there were so few Baptists in Connecticut before 1790 and the majority of these were in the eastern counties where they generally had good relationships with their Congregational neighbors. It was also partly because tax exemption laws in Connecticut were not of temporary duration, as were the Massachusetts laws. They were therefore not periodically revised; their administration was relatively consistent. Nor did Connecticut go through the turmoil of writing a constitution after independence was declared. It merely made a few minor revisions in its royal charter and continued the rest of its laws without alteration. Thus there was no constitutional convention on which the dissenters could focus their reform efforts.

The forces of liberalism were nonetheless working in their favor after 1776. Four specific modifications of the Connecticut established system resulted from "modern liberality." First was the legal recognition of the Separates in 1777; second, the revision of the certificate system in 1784; third, the abrogation of the Saybrook Platform in 1784; and fourth, the liberalized certificate law of 1791. Each is discussed below.

The Separates, though they were declining in numbers, took new initiative on their own behalf in 1777. Eleven of their churches presented a petition to the General Assembly on May 14, 1777 which called for relief from religious taxation and threatened to carry an appeal to the Continental Congress if the state refused:

> We apprehend it would tend much to promote peace and harmony in the State in all civil matters, and union, especially in the common cause of America so much needed in the present day, when we are so much weakened by tories and neuters and have such a formidable enemy to encounter . . . But yet we pray your Honours to consider whether it is not discouraging to your Memorialists, when they are held under oppression themselves. For a fact it certainly is, that some of our brethren who have been the two summers past in the defence of their country against foreign

8. For actions against certificates see the Minutes of the Danbury Association, 1801, p. 4. For actions against incorporation see *ibid.,* 1802, p. 2, and the Minutes of the Sturbridge Baptist Association, 1812 and 1813.

tyranny and oppression, have been this winter past hardly assaulted by this domestick tyranny and oppression at home. Collectors have threatened them severely to committ them to Goal if they would not turn out estate to pay a rate to support a worship that they stood in no connection with nor received any benefit by.[9]

So vehement was the petition in comparing the tyranny of Connecticut to that of Great Britain that the General Assembly not only refused to hear the agent who presented it (Eliakim Marshall, a deputy from Windsor and a Separate lay exhorter who in 1786 became a Baptist) but also threatened to censure those who had signed it. Nonetheless the law exempting the Separates was passed. This considerably mollified most of them.[10]

One of them, however, Elder Israel Holly of Suffield, published a bitter attack on the exemption law of 1777 as a feeble palliative, "a miserable narrow grant of freedom" or rather an "altered oppression." [11] He disliked particularly that certificates could only be granted to persons who lived "near" a Separate place of worship which they "constantly attend;" that the act did not specify whether adherents or only full members were entitled to certificates; and that since the certificates had to be signed by the minister of the church, those churches which had not yet found a minister or were temporarily without one could not produce valid certificates for either their adherents or for their members.

Several of Holly's objections were remedied in 1784 by a new certificate act which applied not only to Separates but also to all denominations. This act was significant not only because it specifically included dissenting adherents as well as church members among those eligible for certificates and because it permitted dissenting deacons or church clerks as well as ministers to sign the certificates, but also because, like the Vermont exemption act of 1783, it extended the tax exemption to "all persons" of "any" denomination of Christians:

> And be it further enacted . . . That all denominations of Christians differing in their religious sentiments from the people of the established societies in this State, whether of the Episcopal Church or those Congregationalists called Separates, or of the people called Baptists or Quakers or any other denominations who shall have formed themselves into distinct churches or congregations, and attend public worship and support the gospel ministry in a way agreeable to their consciences, and respective professions; and all persons who may adhere to any of them and dwell so near to any place of their worship that they can and do ordinarily attend

9. Israel Holly, *An Appeal to the Impartial* (Norwich, 1778), pp. 6–7. Holly points out here how differently the act was interpreted by various of the legislators who voted for it.

10. See *An Historical Narrative and Declaration . . . by a Number of Strict Congregational Churches* (Providence, 1781) in which they assert that they are reasonably satisfied by this act.

11. Holly, *An Appeal*, p. 14

the same on the Sabbath and contribute their due proportion to the support of the worship and ministry where they so attend, whether such place of worship be within this or any adjoining State, and produce a certificate thereof from such church or congregation, signed by their order by the minister or other officer thereof, and lodge the same with the clerk of the society [parish] wherein such person or persons dwell, every such person shall be exempted from being taxed for the support of the worship and ministry of said society, so long as he or they shall continue so to attend and support public worship with a different church or congregation aforesaid.[12]

Before this only Episcopalians, Baptists, Quakers and Separates were eligible for exemption from religious taxes in Connecticut; by this act, however, Universalists, Methodists, Shakers, and any other Christians, presumably even Roman Catholics, were eligible.

This expansion of the principle of exemption did not come as the result of concerted action by any dissenting group. It grew from the climate of liberality which prevailed at this time when the laws of the state were undergoing a general revision. An even more important by-product of this climate which emerged from this revision of the laws was the unannounced, unheralded, and apparently unlamented dropping of the Saybrook Platform from the state laws.[13] Judge Zephaniah Swift, writing on the laws of Connecticut in 1796, declared that the omission of the Platform in this revision of the laws in 1784 constituted "the rejection of our ecclesiastical establishment." [14] For by this omission the state no longer gave its civil support to the actions of the various Congregational associations and consociations nor any civil endorsement to the Savoy Confession of Faith which was imbedded in the Platform.

Swift took the usual New England view that an establishment of religion was defined specifically in terms of a legally required uniformity and conformity of belief and practice — the state enforcement of religious creeds

---

12. This act also specifically freed all dissenters from the law fining those who did not attend the parish church on the Sabbath and explicitly ended the old requirement that new churches of any denomination must be licensed by civil authority: no Christian dissenters, it said, who "attend public worship by themselves shall incur any penalty for not attending the worship and ministry so established on the Lord's day, or on account of their meeting together by themselves on said day for public worship. *Acts and Laws of the State of Connecticut, October Session* (New London, 1784), pp. 21–22.

13. I have been unable to find any comment in any newspaper or from any Congregational minister at the time about the demise of the Saybrook Platform. However, Joseph Bellany, Nathanael Emmons, and other neo-Edwardsians had made attacks on associationism before 1784. Emmons is noted for his remark, "Associationism leads to Consociationism; Consociationism leads to Presbyterianism; Presbyterianism leads to Episcopacy; Episcopacy leads to Roman Catholicism; and Roman Catholicism is an ultimate fact." Williston Walker, *A History of the Congregational Churches in the United States* (New York, 1894), p. 307.

14. Swift, *System of the Laws*, I, 145.

923

and modes of worship on all its citizens. In the 1740's the state had used its power in ecclesiastical affairs to discipline ministers and churches which became involved in Separatism, itinerant evangelism, and other disturbances. It deprived ministers of their salaries and it defined which groups were the established churches in divided parishes — sometimes recognizing a minority party within a church or parish as the established society. It also deposed judges and deputies from their elected posts for religious nonconformity and required Yale College to enforce religious conformity among its faculty and students.

But these ecclesiastical actions had been few in number and limited in scope. The most far-reaching of these were the laws regulating itinerant evangelism; these were repealed or allowed to lapse in 1750. Since then the state had taken only such actions in religious affairs as it could justify in terms of civil order and stability; it retained that power after 1784. The dropping of the Saybrook Platform from the lawbook did, however, take the force of law from the hands of the ecclesiastical bodies of the congregational churches (though their power had never been any stronger than what the legislature wanted to give to it). After the famous dispute in Wallingford in 1760 when the New Lights and Old Lights fought so bitterly over precisely what the power of the Saybrook Platform was, its authority had been thoroughly undermined. The New Lights' attempt to use the Saybrook Platform to enforce creedal tests on those colleagues suspected of Arminianism after 1756 gave the state the choice of moving back toward the kind of conformity characteristic of the seventeenth century or of abandoning the principle altogether.[15] After twenty-five years of masterly inactivity the state's choice was clear. The omission of the Platform from the laws did not end the system of associations and consociations among the Congregational churches. These continued to exist and to function among almost all of the Congregational churches. But after 1784 their actions had no more significance outside the Congregational denomination than did the actions of Baptist associations or of Presbyterian presbyteries. After 1784, Connecticut, like Massachusetts, New Hampshire, and Vermont, had in effect a system of general establishment for the Protestant religion which gave certain privileges, *de facto* and by tradition, to the Congregational churches.

In the seven years which followed, both the dissenters and the deists flourished in Connecticut. The Rev. James Cogswell of Scotland parish, an Old Light of the same moderate temper as Ezra Stiles, noted with alarm in 1789 that his parishioners were running off after "strolling Teachers" of all kinds — Separates, Anabaptists, Universalists, Methodists, Wilkinsonians, Sandemanians. At the same time they were electing to pub-

15. For the mounting opposition to the Platform within the Standing Order after 1780 see M. Louise Greene, *The Development of Religious Liberty in Connecticut* (Boston, 1905), pp. 336–338

lic office irreligious men like Zephaniah Swift and Hezekiah Ripley. After the town meeting on September 8, 1789, Cogswell noted that the voters of Scotland "have chosen Swift and Ripley again for Deputies — they neither of them make a profession of Religion and Swift is a Man that totally disregards Religion — profligate, irreligious Persons, Baptists, and Separates are all very fond of such men for Deputies chiefly because They are inimical to the Standing Ministers and Churches." [16] Cogswell did his best to keep his people faithful to the church, but he admitted that he himself was often "skeptical" about certain aspects of religion and that his people told him they ran after other preachers because they got more spiritual satisfaction from them than they did from him.[17] He had trouble collecting his salary and regretted that the tax collecters were so persistent in dunning the delinquents that it turned many people against him and the Standing church: "were I affluent," he wrote, "I would give them the Arrearages — but I cannot think it my Duty in present Circumstances." One of the most prominent pillars of his church, Colonel Eliphalet Dyer, told him in December 1789, "that Connecticut is making the most rapid progress to Infidelity of any of the States in the Union." On April 12, 1790 Cogswell wrote in his diary,

> Went to freeman's Meeting and voted according to the Dictates of my Conscience, but could not succeed to keep Capt. Swift from being chosen Representative; however, I believe my preaching yesterday [the Sabbath] did Good for Mr. [Ebenezer] Devotion [Cogswell's Federalist son-in-law] had almost as many votes as Swift. It is a lamentable Consideration that Men have no Regard to Religion.

Cogswell was not surprised therefore when, while he was visiting his other son-in-law, Governor Samuel Huntington on June 17, 1790, Huntington told him that at the recent session of the legislature "the Gen[ll] Assembly had a good deal of talk about altering the Law which gives too much Latitude to opinionists and antiministerial persons with Regard to the Support of Ministers."

The General Assembly did nothing about this in 1790 but the next year it passed a bill which placed such serious restrictions on tax exemption

16. Cogswell, "Diary," September 8, 1789. See also the entries for April 7, 1788, and April 13, 1789, for remarks about Swift.
17. *Ibid.*, April 4, 1788. "Troubled with Sceptical, discouraging Thoughts." October 26, 1790: the widow Burnham "is loath to be convinced that she had done wrong in Separating — insists upon it that she can be more edified by Jn° Palmer's preaching than mine" (March 12, 1788). Year after year the parish failed to fulfill its promise to deliver him his firewood as part of his salary so he went out and got it himself from the common woods (December 23, 1789). "Govr H. . . . fears that a Spirit of Scepticism and Licentiousness will Spread and prevail throughout the United States. I fear so too" (March 26, 1790). One speculates that perhaps Cogswell's fears of spreading skepticism grew out of guilt-feelings over his own skepticism (June 17, 1790).

that it aroused a storm of protest. By this new act, the dissenter who wished to be exempt from ecclesiastical taxes had to appear before "two of the Civil Authority living in the Town" and prove to the authorities' satisfaction that he had "joined" a dissenting congregation and that he "ordinarily" attended worship with that congregation and contributed "his share" toward the support of that congregation. When and if he obtained the certificate he had to deposit it with the society (i.e., parish) clerk where he resided.[18] The law was defended on the grounds that too many new dissenting churches had been formed which were willing to grant certificates to persons who were not bona fide adherents of their persuasion but who were only tax dodgers or enemies of the Standing Order.[19] The requirement that it be signed by a Justice of the Peace was defended on the ground that since signing a certificate was a civil act granting a civil privilege (tax exemption) it should be signed by a civil officer not by a minister.

The law was attacked on the grounds that the Justices of the Peace, almost all Congregationalists, would be prejudiced against granting certificates, and that subjecting a man's religious beliefs to the scrutiny of a civil officer was a gross invasion of liberty of conscience. The protests which filled the newspapers and the debate which eventually led to the repeal of this act in October 1791 are significant for what they reveal of the liberal climate of the time and the attitude among Baptists and other dissenters toward the general establishment as it then existed.

A letter signed "Pandor" (probably a misprint for "Candor") in the Connecticut *Courant* on May 23, 1791, denounced not only the certificate system but the whole principle of a religious establishment in Connecticut. The style and arguments used in the letter closely resemble those used by Elder John Leland in his tract, *The Rights of Conscience Inalienable,* which was published in New London on August 9. A good guess would be that he wrote this letter. It displayed the dissenting mind in its most Revolutionary mood. The writer began by asserting that in the Revolution the patriots were "greatly strengthened by the prospect of liberty of conscience (dearer to the sincere than property and life). Without this idea the dif-

---

18. Conn. State Rec., VII, 256. The form of the certificate prescribed by the law read:

> We having examined the Claims of _____ who says he is a Dissenter from the Established Society of _____ and hath joined himself to a Church or Congregation of the Name of _____, and that he ordinarily attends upon the Public Worship of such Church or Congregation; and that he contributes his share or proportion toward supporting the Public Worship and Ministry thereof, do upon examination find that the above Facts are true.
>
> Dated _____   (Signed) _____
>   Justice of the Peace

19. For a typical statement to this effect in the Connecticut *Courant* in 1788, see Greene, *Religious Liberty in Connecticut,* p. 353.

ferent sects would never have cemented together to withstand the common foe." But unfortunately after the war Connecticut did not follow the example of the other states (notably Virginia) and create a new constitution with a bill of rights establishing religious liberty on a firm basis. Instead the people of Connecticut continued to believe the "absurd" argument that "religion cannot stand without the aid of civil law." In Connecticut, therefore, dissenters were still required to give in certificates or else be forced to support a church they did not attend:

> Preachers that will not preach without a salary found for them by law are hirelings who seek the fleece and not the flock. But if one religion must be dandled on the knees and fostered in the arms of civil power and all the rest pay obeisance, what one must it be? The greatest man in America [George Washington] is an Episcopalian; should the Episcopal religion be established in the continent would the people of Connecticut who plead for a certificate law be willing[ly] submissive to such a law?

The writer pushed his argument to the point of civil disobedience: "if legislatures make laws contrary to the constitution of the sovereign people those laws are not binding;" he saw nothing in the Connecticut charter or the United States constitution which would support a certificate law. "It is sometimes said that giving a certificate once a year or once in a man's life is but a trifle . . . The *three penny act* on tea was but a trifle, why did the good people of Connecticut make such a noise about a trifle?" The writer also proposed that "If certificates must be given, pray let those give them who chuse to be taxed by law: let all the friends of the standing order carry certificates to the rate makers in these words, 'This is to certify that A.B. wishes to be taxed by law to support his preacher (Rev. Mr. Lovemoney).'" Pandor's letter concluded with the forthright assertion that "the certificate law must be held in contempt and called by the name *Antichristian*."

In the next issue of the *Courant* an unsigned letter answered Pandor's arguments in the tones of the ardent supporters of the establishment. Pandor's letter, it began, was "full of false reasoning, evil insinuations, squeamish cants and infidelity . . . calculated to inflame the evil passions of the undiscerning and factious part of society . . . like a Fanatic's sermon." The certificate law, it continued, was passed from "pure lenity, candor, and benevolence" on the part of the Standing Order; it was they who ought to complain of it since it caused them great damage. He noted that dissenters in England still had no way to avoid paying taxes to support the established church. "The [certificate] law originated in a sense which the Presbyterians [i.e., Congregationalists] entertained of the justice of liberating Dissenters from taxes to support a religion disagreeable to them" and "all the thanks we get for it are deceitful evasions of the law and the scurrilous sauciness of Pandor." To compare this trifle, "a little certificate," to the tyranny of

Britain in 1775, was ridiculous. "The state have a right to regulate the temporal things necessary for the support of the Ministers in the state." As for Pandor, "He is plainly a *Nothingarian,* and the most of Deists are no more." [20]

But the outstanding document in this controversy was Leland's tract (published in New London in midsummer 1791), *The Rights of Conscience Inalienable, and Therefore Religious Opinions Not Cognizable by Law or, The High-Flying Churchman Stripped of His Legal Robes Appears a Yaho[o]*. Leland, born in Grafton, Massachusetts, was brought up a Strict or Separate Congregationalist. He spoke of his mother as "a high-flying separate" and his father as a Presbyterian who for a time doubted the validity of infant baptism. In 1772 Leland was baptized by immersion by Elder Noah Alden of Bellingham — though he stated in his autobiography that he was not then quite certain whether or not he had been converted. In 1775 he received a call to become a preacher; he at once began his long career as an itinerant. Six months later he was licensed to preach by the Bellingham Church, which he had joined. But he married in September 1776 and moved to Virginia where he lived until 1791.

Leland's fame as a protagonist of religious freedom is second only to Backus's fame among the Baptists. Among the public he is probably more famous. He worked with the Baptists of Virginia to petition the legislature for the passage of Jefferson's bill for religious freedom. He became one of the foremost lobbyists for a bill to end the incorporation of the Episcopal church and to dispose of its glebe lands. It is said that James Madison personally sought his aid in support of the federal constitution which Leland at first opposed.[21] In April 1791 he returned to New England, settling for two months in New London before moving to Cheshire, Massachusetts where, for the rest of his life, he was one of the outstanding leaders in the fight for disestablishment in Massachusetts as well as in Connecticut. He was also one of the leading Jeffersonian Republicans in Massachusetts; he often spoke at party rallies and served two terms in the legislature. But he devoted most of his time to preaching and itinerant evangelism until he died in 1841.

Because of the importance of his career as Backus's successor and because of certain misunderstandings about his position among the Baptists, we digress here to set the record straight. Most writers have failed to make any distinction between his views and Backus's views. They were different in their outlooks on this issue. It is Backus, not Leland, who was the more

20. The writer evidently assumed that "Pandor" was Zephaniah Swift and attacked him by name. Swift later said he found the anonymous writer of this answer to Pandor was a dogmatic, narrow clergyman. Connecticut *Courant* (Hartford), June 6, 1791, p. 2.

21. The best account of Leland is by Lyman Butterfield, "Elder John Leland, Jeffersonian Itinerant," American Antiquarian Society *Proceedings,* LXII (1952), 155 ff.

representative of the Baptists in this period. Leland was considered a scandal within the denomination both for the eccentricity of his language and for his behavior. He was admired as a dedicated preacher and opponent of religious tyranny, but his views on theology, church discipline, Baptist institutional aims, and church-state relations were often deplored by his brethren. His years in Virginia had put him out of touch with most of his New England brethren. Although they welcomed him back as an ally in their efforts after 1791, he was always considered a prodigal son rather than a distinguished spokesman or leader. However much of a hero he was to Virginians and to his local partisans in western Massachusetts, he was a distinct embarrassment to most of the denominational leaders in New England.

Three things distinguish Leland's outlook from that of Backus and the other Baptist leaders. First, he was born a generation after Backus; he therefore did not share the religious intensity of the Great Awakening and its aftermath. Second, he was more interested in saving souls than he was in doctrinal purity or the Calvinistic integrity of the Baptist faith. Third, regarding separation of church and state, he, like Roger Williams, favored total separation, not sweet harmony, like Backus. Effectively, Leland was more pragmatic, more liberal, and less sectarian than was Backus, though they knew and respected each other. Backus was widely read in the Calvinistic theology of his day and he wrote extensively on theological problems. Leland found himself confused and ill at ease in theological discussions and his religious works were primarily exhortations to salvation or attacks on those who tried to confuse the simple fundamentals of the gospel by doctrinal metaphysics. Backus read Jonathan Edwards with pleasure and felt capable of arguing with his conclusions. Leland probably never read two pages of Edwards and would not have understood him if he had. Backus never doubted that he was a Calvinist, but Leland was never sure that he was. When he was asked at his baptism whether he believed in "the Calvinistic doctrine" (as he reported in his autobiography), "I replied that I did not know what it was." [22] Although Leland believed in "free grace" and disagreed with those who taught that men could be saved through their own exertions, he admitted that he was never able to reconcile the problem of predestination and free will. He certainly never said, as Backus did, that Jonathan Edwards had solved that problem.

Leland's whole career among the Baptists was controversial, not only in theology but also in church practice. Because he accepted ordination over his first church by the members only, without any assistance from other elders, he was denied fellowship with most Baptist ministers for nine years until he allowed himself to be properly ordained. In the great disputes between the Regular and Separate Baptists in Virginia, and between the

22. Leland, *Works,* p. 16.

predestinarian and freewill Separates, he took no sides but urged them to compromise and be reconciled. He was sorry that they felt they had to unite on some agreement as to a confession of faith:

> Had they united without any confession of faith, as they did in Georgia, perhaps it would have been better. . . . Had a system of religion been essential to salvation, or even to the happiness of the saints, would not Jesus, who was faithful in all his house, have left us one? . . . Confessions of faith often check any further pursuit after truth, confine the mind into a particular way of reasoning, and give rise to frequent separations.[23]

When Leland visited Philadelphia in 1784, he did so with Elhanan Winchester, who had recently left the Baptist faith for Universalism. As a result the Philadelphia Baptists denied him fellowship because they feared he too was leaning toward Universalism.

When, in 1792, he became pastor of the Baptist church in Cheshire, Massachusetts he did not think it necessary to write any articles of faith for the church. He did join the Shaftesbury Association which presumably would not have accepted him had he not been considered Calvinistic. In 1798 he developed scruples about the administration of the Lord's Supper. For the next twenty years or more he refused to perform that ordinance, though he continued to preach and act as a pastor to the Cheshire church for most of that time. When a dispute arose in the church over this problem, he left the town for two years rather than argue over it. He returned only when the church decided to accept him on his own peculiar terms.[24] Like most Calvinists in this period of transition to a more Arminianized version of its tenets, he did not really know where he stood: "It has always been a question with me of great importance to know how to address a congregation of sinners, as such, in gospel style. . . . Neither Gill, Hopkins, Fuller nor Wesley could remove my difficulties." [25] In his old age he admitted, "I have never labored hard to support the CREED of any religious society; but have felt greatly interested that all of them should have their RIGHTS secured to them beyond the reach of tyrants." [26] Leland was a Baptist liberal, a child of an anticreedal, antisectarian era. He summed up theology once by saying, "What I cannot spell out, I must skip." Nehemiah Dodge, not Backus, was his closest parallel in New England in this era. Dodge was a Baptist elder in Connecticut who fought vigorously for disestablishment and then, in 1820, became a Universalist. Dodge had much in common with Elias Smith, the founder of the Christ-ians.

23. *Ibid.,* p. 114, note.
24. Cooke transcript of the records of the Second Baptist Church of Cheshire in the Berkshire Athenaeum, Pittsfield, Massachusetts.
25. Leland, *Works,* p. 33.
26. *Ibid.,* p. 39.

Leland, it has usually been said, based his attitude toward disestablishment on "rationalist principles" because his views of separation were so similar to Jefferson's and Madison's and because he hated all theological controversy.[27] But Leland was not a reationalist. He preached fervently "the great doctrines of universal depravity, redemption by the blood of Christ, regeneration, faith, repentance and self-denial"; he favored revival meetings which were full of the power of the Holy Ghost and "great emotion in the heart"; he was a staunch defender of the necessity of adult baptism by immersion. Far from exalting human ability, he said "I know myself to be a feeble, sinful worm." [28] He never approved of dancing, gaming, theatre-going, and gambling. His church records show that he was ready to excommunicate any church member who indulged in excessive drinking, abusing his wife, being in loose company, frolicking, or sharp horse trading. He once reported that the voice of God spoke to him and that on another occasion some devilish ghost approached his bed one night with such horrid groanings that Leland was able to vanquish him only by hiding under the bedclothes and praying to God for help.[29] Here there was little to distinguish him from any other uneducated frontier evangelist.

What has misled some people into calling him a rationalist was his obvious anticreedalism and anticlericalism, his dislike for "the priestcraft," his disdain for institutionalism and ritualism, his belief that religious convictions were merely "opinions," and his radical doctrine of separation of church and state. In this he was like Jefferson and Madison and differed from Backus and from most of the New England Baptists. Where Backus and the New England Baptists carried into their views many aspects of the Puritan belief in the necessity for a Christian commonwealth, Leland utterly repudiated that notion: "The notion of a Christian commonwealth should be exploded forever," he said, "without there was a commonwealth of real Christians." [30] He meant by this that the only way to have a Christian society was to convert all the people in it. His radicalism here made him agree with Madison and Jefferson that the government ought not to use public tax money to pay for chaplains in the Congress or for the armed forces. He also agreed with them that no magistrate had the right to proclaim days of thanksgiving or fasting (the state had no right to make any one day more holy than another). Both of these views went beyond those of Backus. True, Backus in one tract mentioned his opposition to paying Episcopalian chaplains for Congress, but that was because they were Episcopalians. When Baptists were appointed chaplains to the various New England legislatures (as was the case with increasing frequency after 1790), they thought it a great honor to themselves and to their denomination. No Baptist associa-

27. Butterfield, "Leland," p. 159.
28. Leland, *Works,* pp. 108, 115, 173.
29. *Ibid.,* p. 44.
30. Butterfield, "Leland," p. 163; Leland, *Works,* p. 107.

tion ever found the practice offensive, and I have seen no Baptist opposition to it in New England in this period except Leland's.

But what really shocked and embarrassed the New England Baptist leaders, who after 1800 sought to make themselves indistinguishable from other denominations on these points, was Leland's opposition to missionary activity, to the creation of theological seminaries, and to the Sunday School movement. When the Baptists joined the Congregationalists and others in petitioning Congress to abolish the delivery of the mail on the Sabbath, Leland joined the anticlerical Jacksonians in praising Col. Richard M. Johnson for his masterful rebuke to such clerical meddling in the secular affairs of the state.

Although it is possible, therefore, to admire Leland for his consistency in these matters and although it is correct to say that he belongs in the Jeffersonian tradition of separation, it is a serious mistake to classify him among contemporary rationalists or to imply that his views were representative of the Baptists of his day — especially of the New England Baptists. His official biography in the history of the Shaftesbury Association is more accurate when it refers to him as "this eccentric but useful minister" whose "peculiarities" were such that they "too much alienated the venerable Leland from many of his brethren." [31]

Apart from his radical consistency, Leland's redeeming feature in fighting for separation of church and state was his colorful, forceful style. In his attack upon the Connecticut certificate law of May 1791, he used his sharp wit and sardonic ridicule advantageously. Carrying the letter of Pandor one step further, he emphasized in his tract on the *Rights of Conscience* that if George Washington, whose name "fills every heart with pleasure and awe, should remove to Connecticut for his health, or any other cause, what a scandal would it be to the state, to tax him to support a Presbyterian minister, unless he produced a certificate informing them that he was an Episcopalian." [32] Pointing to the disestablishment of religion in the states outside New England (including Rhode Island) Leland said that "if the principles of religious liberty contended for in the foregoing pages are supposed to be fraught with Deism, fourteen states in the Union are now fraught with the same." And "If the citizens of this state have anything in existence that looks like a religious establishment, they ought to be very cautious; for being but a small part of the world, they can never expect to extend their religion over the whole world, without it is so well founded that it cannot be confuted." To him the clearest confutation of the Connecticut system was "that in the southern states where there has been the greatest freedom from religious oppression, where liberty of conscience is entirely enjoyed, there

31. Stephen Wright, *History of the Shaftesbury Association* (Troy, 1853), pp. 329–332. Wright claims that Leland so disliked religious institutionalism that for years he opposed the formation of Baptist associations lest they become spiritual despotisms.
32. Leland, *Works,* p. 191.

has been the greatest revival of religion." But most characteristic of him was his willingness to argue not only for his own sect or for other dissenters, but for all men:

> This certificate law is founded on this principle, "that it is the duty of all persons to support the gospel and the worship of God." Is this principle founded in justice? Is it the duty of a deist to support that which he believes to be a cheat and imposition? Is it the duty of a Jew to support the religion of Jesus Christ, when he really believes that he was an impostor? Must the Papists be forced to pay men for preaching down the supremacy of the pope, who they are sure is the head of the church? Must a Turk maintain a religion, opposed to the Alkoran, which he holds as the sacred oracle of heaven? These things want better confirmation.[33]

This was not the style the New England Baptists used on behalf of voluntarism.

More important than Leland's critcism of the certificate law was this willingness to acknowledge that even non-Christians had rights of conscience which must be respected: the right to support non-Christian religions or to give no support whatever to religion. This was a right which few Baptists in New England ever acknowledged — nor especially espoused in print. True, one could so interpret broadly their demands for complete liberty of conscience and for religious equality, but the Baptists' fight against the Standing Order was always waged within a much narrower and self-interested compass. They fully shared the belief of their Puritan forefathers and of their Congregational neighbors that in a Protestant nation, non-Protestants existed merely on sufferance, benighted objects of evangelism for whom *the* truth would dawn in due time.

Leland made a major contribution to the fight for religious liberty (after 1776, for religious equality) in New England by forcing the Baptists to acknowledge — or at least not to disown his publication of — the radical implications of their own premises. Leland rebuked his brethren of the Baptist ministry when he denounced those who kept civilly appointed fasts and thanksgivings, those who accepted minister's lot, those who sought exemption from civil taxes or even from military service as clergymen. His radical egalitarianism was consistent to the final full measure. He wanted no "sweet harmony" between church and state; no "general encouragement" for the Christian religion or its ministers: "The law should be silent about them [ministers], protect them as citizens, not as sacred officers, for the civil law knows no sacred religious officers." This was taking spiritual laissez-faire pretty far; it was difficult for the Baptists to accept; few ever did. But they could not continue, as Leland saw, to push the Congregational establishment further and further toward yielding its own privileges without

33. *Ibid.*, p. 187.

admitting that the Christian religion required no privileges whatsoever. Just where was the line between a "mild establishment" granting equality to all Christian sects and "sweet harmony"?

Leland frankly admitted that there was something dishonest about that Rhode Island law of 1716 which prohibited any minister from suing members of his congregation who failed to fulfill their written subscription or contract for payment of his salary. "If a number of people in Rhode Island, or elsewhere, are of opinion that ministers of the gospel ought to be supported by law and choose to be bound by law to pay him, government has no just authority to declare that bond illegal; for in doing so they interfere with private contracts and deny the people the liberty of conscience." This was a more consistent answer than Backus gave to the claim that disestablishment in New England would constitute impairment of contract. But, said Leland, the contract must be privately and voluntarily entered into. Let the Congregationalists make contracts and collect salaries by law if they felt obliged in conscience to do so, but let them not bind a minority to pay religious taxes by a majority vote of town or parish: "it is no abridgment of religious liberty for congregations to pay their preachers by legal force" if they voluntarily agree to it. But, he continued, this is "anti-Christian; such a church cannot be a Church of Christ;" there is no question of religious liberty involved. No wonder Backus and his New England brethren never quoted nor associated themselves with Leland. They wished to dictate to other men, even in a private capacity, what their rights of conscience were and what rights as ministers they could demand from the state. If the Standing Order "hypocritically" claimed the right of conscience to bind the minority, the Baptists hypocritically used this claim to bind their own members from entering into the kinds of voluntary association they wanted (viz. the association votes to censure churches which sought incorporation and the church votes to censure members who joined the Masons, Washingtonians, Directorenes, or other secular societies).

One other important aspect of Leland's liberal pietism pointed directly toward the increasing disintegration of the corporate or organic social theory of the seventeenth century and the rising individualism, atomism, and secularism of the nineteenth century. The logical consistency with which he applied the argument that infant baptism was a means of binding citizens to the state without their consent illustrates this.

> But supposing it was right for a man to bind his own conscience, yet surely it is very iniquitous to bind the consciences of his children — to make fetters for them before they are born, is very cruel. And yet such has been the conduct of men in almost all ages, that their children have been bound to believe and worship as their fathers did, or suffer shame, loss, and sometimes life, and at best to be called dissenters, because they dissent from that which they never joined voluntarily. Such conduct in

parents is worse than that of the father of Hannibal, who imposed an oath upon his son, while a child, never to be at peace with the Romans.

Backus and other Baptists had argued this before, but never in such stark terms. A whole new concept of the family, of the education or nurture of children, and of the mutual obligations (or interdependence) of the young and the old, is imbedded in this statement. For Leland's view atomizes the family by exalting the rights and independence of conscience of children. A good parent is not a nursing father to his children, inculcating in them for their own good the faith and practices of the church which the father believes to be the true religion. If "religion is a matter between God and individuals" then the child must maintain his own independence from parental control, from imposition on his heart, soul, and mind until he is old enough to judge for himself. "It would be sinful for a man [even as a child, a potential man] to surrender that to man [even to his father] which is to be kept sacred for God. A man's mind should be always open to conviction, and an honest man will receive that doctrine which appears the best demonstrated."

This is embryonic nineteenth century laissez-faire and pragmatism. This is what the Standing Order — clergy and Federalist laity — correctly interpreted as "the loosening of the bonds of society" and of the family. It advocated the rebellion of willful children (or citizens) against the lawful authority of their fathers. Here the test of empirical demonstration — judged by each man, woman, and child for himself — replaces the traditions and faiths of the ancient and honorable, the wise and the learned, the church and the state. The individual is supreme, and his own heart is the measure of all things. To be true to the commands of one's own conscience is to be true to God. Leland's liberal pietism is a link in the chain between Edwards and Emerson which Perry Miller noted in very different terms years ago.

But antagonism of the dissenters to the certificate law of May 1791 was not limited to Leland's words. They took action. A defender of the establishment who called himself "Hushai" wrote in the Hartford *Courant* on August 29 that the new certificate act had "created a very considerable agitation amongst all the various sects of Dissenters" who had now organized "corresponding meetings . . . throughout the state to devise ways and means" to get it repealed. The method they chose was "to get elected such representatives as will best serve their wishes." Although the dissenters "have acted with the greatest secrecy" so far, they would very soon hold "a convention of delegates from their several meetings" to influence the election of deputies in September. Hushai warned the freemen to beware of these activities and not to let the dissenters gain control of the town meetings for "Should that be the case . . . we may the next session see the Legislature filled with those (perhaps separate priests) who may give a loose to

935

every kind of irregularity to destroy every law made for the support of religion and the rights of conscience." He believed that opposition to this law arose because it "has rendered the act [i.e., religious taxation] less liable to be evaded."

But Hushai was answered on September 12 by a Quaker, "Plain Dealer": "If thou wilt travel out of Hartford thou wilt find more against thee than for thee." The new certificate law was "a law made to punish" those who dissent from the Standing Order. To prove that there was nothing secretive in the opposition to it he said "It is therefore hoped . . . that every dissenting freeman will meet on freeman's meeting and give their vote for persons of no particular sect but for men only who are willing [that] equal religious liberty should be established without a law-established religion and will take care not to choose narrow-minded bigots who think their interest is the chief good." [34]

Tension mounted in Hartford as the opening of the sessions of the General Assembly began in the fall of 1791. On October 23, the baptists held a large mass meeting in the courthouse; among the speakers they invited the venerable Isaac Backus of Middleborough, Massachusetts. Long the champion of religious liberty for his denomination in New England, Backus was now sixty-seven years old. But he spoke his mind as forcefully as ever: "preacht twice in the Hartford courthouse" he noted in his diary on that date; and "I plainly held it to be *heresy* for any men to make any laws to bind others in religious matters or to loose any from the laws of Christ in the government of his church." [35]

Exactly what happened in the legislature when this matter came up in October is unclear, for the legislative journal for 1791 gives no details. However, a letter in the Connecticut *Journal* on November 9, 1791, provides what seems to be an informed account of the proceedings:

> The house of representatives at an early period in the session repealed the law passed last May obliging dissenters to apply to justices of the peace for a certificate &c. Upon the question whether this law should be repealed the yeas and nays were taken [these were published in the *Journal* of October 26 as 104 yeas and 57 nays] . . . This bill [for repeal] went into the council and was there dissented to and a new bill sent down entitled "An Act to secure equal rights to christians of every denomination" which contained among other things a repeal of all former laws on the subject [specifically the act of 1784]. This new bill was debated in the house of representatives by paragraph and the several paragraphs were finally passed by a majority of ten or eleven but the yeas and nays were never taken upon any one paragraph nor on the whole bill. Afterwards it was moved, previous to taking the question on the whole bill, to amend the bill

34. The Methodists too were aroused. See the letter in the Windham *Herald*, September 10, 1791. In this same paper a defender of the laws compared religious taxes to school taxes as purely civil in nature.

35. Isaac Backus, "Diary," BP(AN).

and the house amended it by inserting an entire new clause which materially altered the spirit of the bill, and the question was then put on the
bill thus amended. . . . [the amended bill passed 124 to 33]. This bill
thus amended was sent into the council; but the amendment was totally
rejected by the council and a committee of conference appointed on the
differing votes of the houses. The bill was transmitted to the house of
representatives with the appointment of this committee of conference, and
the house instead of joining a committee concurred on the bill without the
amendment . . . but the yeas and nays upon this law were never taken.

By this account the Council initiated the new bill and then saved it from a
crippling amendment in the House. But what the nature of the amendment
was or what the arguments were in debating it are unknown. Obviously,
from the size of the vote to repeal the measure (which had been adopted in
May by a large majority), the dissenters had made a convincing argument about the oppressive aspects of the bill. And from the terms of the
new bill it also seems that the liberal sentiments of men like Zephaniah
Swift predominated over those of Governor Huntington and Col. Dyer. The
bill was the most liberal certificate act ever passed in New England. By it
the legislature said that every dissenter could write his own certificate and
no one needed to attest to the certificate's validity. It was the highpoint of
Revolutionary liberalism in Connecticut:

> That in future, whenever any person shall differ in sentiments from the
> worship and ministry in the ecclesiastical societies in this state constituted
> by law within certain local bounds, and shall choose to join himself to
> any other denomination of christians, which shall have formed themselves
> into distinct churches or congregations, for the maintenance and support
> of the public worship of God, and shall manifest such his choice by a
> certificate thereof, under his hand lodged in the office of the clerk of
> the society to which he belongs — such person shall thereupon and so long
> as he shall continue ordinarily to attend on the worship and ministry in
> the church or congregation to which he has chosen to belong as aforesaid,
> be exempted from being taxed for the future support of the worship and
> ministry in such society.[36]

36. Conn. State Rec., VII, 311–313. The form of the certificate required by this
law was not stated in the act but thereafter certificates were generally written:

> I certify that I differ in sentiment from the worship and ministry in the ecclesi-
> astical society of ————— in the town of ————— constituted by law
> within certain local bounds and have chosen to join myself to the (Insert here
> the name of society you have joined) in the town of —————.
>
> Dated at ————— this —— day of ————— A.D.

Greene, *Religious Liberty in Connecticut*, p. 378. The Baptist historian, David Benedict, writing in 1812, commented on this procedure: "This law is probably as favourable as any one of the kind can be framed. A dissenter has nothing to do but write
his own certificate" (David Benedict, *A General History of the Baptist Denomination in America*, 2 vols. [Boston, 1813], I, 535).

This act came as close as it was possible to come to disestablishment without actually altering the basic structure of the ecclesiastical system. The dissenters' objections were now reduced to whether a certificate itself constituted some kind of implicit discrimination and whether the taxing privilege gave the Congregational churches an unfair advantage.

For most dissenters, the law (though it was a great victory for liberalism) did not go far enough. For the Congregationalists it was a disaster. This law effectively made total disestablishment inevitable in Connecticut, for thereafter, it proved impossible for the parish system to maintain itself.

Chapter 48

The Decline of the Parish System
in Connecticut,
1784–1800

There are some who are inimical to the public worship, and many who had rather have none than pay anything for its support. Many others are in principle against all support of public worship but what arises from the private donations of the people . . . From these sources the upholding of public worship is become already unpracticable in some places and extremely difficult in others. As selfishness and disregard to religion increase this will become more and more the case.

Letter to the *Connecticut Courant,* April 14, 1794

The Connecticut supporters of the establishment, though defensive after 1776, were not silent or inactive. Seeing in the certificate law of October 1791 a vital, if not mortal, wound to their system, the Congregationalists raised some telling legal and constitutional questions regarding its validity. They also emphasized its obvious conflict with the traditional conception of parish unity and loyalty. A letter to the Hartford *Courant* in April 1792 discussed how acutely the law could affect a struggling country parish and asked the voters whether they were fully aware of the consequences of the new liberality. Signing himself "Plain Man," the writer noted that a few years before the certificate act his parish had amicably settled a minister and voted him a good salary;

> and till lately we have gone along well agreed. But finding we were not bound to maintain him according to bargain [by virtue of the new certificate act], and finding ourselves burdened with rates, a great number of our people have got certificates, and besides, they say, it is a dull business to go to meeting and hear nothing but the old story; and then again, they can have much better preaching [they say] without any rate; and since the Assembly have given them the chance to get free they think it a lucky opportunity to slip their necks out of the collar; and had this been the

case before we settled our Minister, I believe we never should have settled him, and so should not have got into the hobbles.

Now the pinch of the matter comes to know what those few of us shall do who can't in conscience leave the meeting and go to the four winds. Above half our people [in the parish] are Shakers, Methodists, Baptists, Separates, and Nothingarians — and now the whole burden of making good the bargain which the parish made falls upon one third of the whole. By what right am I compelled to pay my neighbor's engagement merely because he says *he wont pay it? Must* I be punished or burdened for honestly keeping to the bargain? Shall a few individuals be called the society in law, and be liable to be sued to make good the failure of others?

And what will our Minister do, in case the few that remain should all leave him? As the law now stands, can he in that case, sue the parish? and yet are not the parish to pay the Minister according to bargain and another law excuse them from it? [1]

The letter explained the traditional conception of the mutual bond of obligation between pastor and people which had constituted the corporate spirit of New England's territorial parish system: "Don't we suppose that a Minister is bound to a people? and that he would do wickedly if he should leave them, of his own head, without and even contrary to their consent?" It was like the marriage bond; a mutual pledge of loyalty, support, and bearing with one another was involved when a parish chose a pastor. But the new spirit of the times, whether from excessive liberality or excessive selfishness, was rapidly changing the old pastoral relationship. The individualistic and atomistic conception of society was destroying the traditional bonds of love and loyalty between pastor and parish, between the upper orders and the lower, between magistrates and people. Society was coming unglued, and this act served as a solvent.

As "Plain Man" plainly saw, the new certificate law made the parish system anachronistic. If it did not contradict the law which required every parish or society to support a learned, pious, and orthodox minister, it certainly removed support from it. This contradiction bore most heavily, as "Plain Man" said, against those who were conscientiously loyal to the minister, to their contractual obligations; it bore against the minister himself. Legally the minister could sue those few who remained loyal to him if his salary fell behind, for they alone were still bound in law to pay it; but this would be unfair. Yet was it right for the law to demand that the minister maintain his loyalty to the parish as a geographical unit when the people of the parish took so lightly their loyalty to this system and to him? "Is he bound to a people, if they an't bound to him? Or must he tarry till the major part or even the last man has left him, and then not be able to

---

1. *Connecticut Courant,* April 30, 1792, p. 2. This was the problem Judge Jeremiah Smith faced in Muzzy *vs.* Wilkins when he concluded that the fewer persons permitted tax exemption the better and so defined a sect as to permit very few exemptions. See Chapter 44.

recover his dues? Does not the law [the new certificate law] give him the same liberty by plain implication, which it gives to his people explicitly?" Isn't the minister now as free to seek the best bargain he can find for remuneration, just as the Nothingarian or tax dodger who is bored by Hopkinsian sermons or who feels that his taxes are too heavy is free to leave? Would not this debase the whole profession of the ministry? Thus the old system of mutual loyalty and affection which produced pastoral relations which throughout New England history had lasted for scores of years despite the inevitable quarrels and bickerings was bound to end.

But "Plain Man" did not rest his argument on sentimentality, though it is implicit. Like every Yankee, he was concerned with the law and particularly with the law of contracts or covenants.

> Is not every bargain or covenant mutually binding upon the parties? and can the Assembly break in upon particular bargains, and set the Parties obliged at liberty from each other; and say you are no longer obliged to perform those duties which you solemnly engaged to perform, and under the sanction of law too? In a word, are not all the covenants between Ministers and people in this state already dissolved, so far as the Assembly can dissolve them? Does it not now lie wholly with either of the parties to turn his back upon the other — and if they don't do it, is it because they are holden in justice or conscience, if the law as it now stands, is a righteous law? But I don't mean to say tis unjust — only wish you to tell the world what difficulties a few of us are in, in our parish.

One of the first supporters of the Standing Order to raise the question of the constitutionality of disestablishment under the federal Constitution, did so in an anonymous letter in the American *Mercury*. In 1793 this man stated that disestablishment would be contrary to the constitution of the United States because it would be an action by a state government which permitted "impairing the obligation of Contracts." [2] Another letter writer who called himself "Argus" also wondered in the Windham *Herald* that same year "Whether the operation of this law upon those contracts which are [or were] made previous to its existence will not be controuled by that article of the constitution of the United States which enacts that no State shall have power to make any ex post facto law or law impairing obligation of contracts." [3] Had some Congregationalist brought this case before the Supreme Court, might John Marshall have ruled that disestablishment was unconstitutional?

Because this question of contractual obligation was to be debated continually regarding disestablishment until 1818, it needs explanation here. Both Pandor's anonymous opponent and Hushai mentioned that the new

2. American *Mercury*, September 2, 1793, p. 2; *Connecticut Courant*, May 30, 1791, p. 2.
3. Windham *Herald*, November 23, 1793, p. 1.

certificate law would "place us in the enviable and blessed condition of Rhode Island where obligations given for the support of the gospel and gambling debts are on the same legal footing, being equally void." [4] Rhode Islanders denied that they ever equated the two forms of debt, but there was a law in the Rhode Island statute books dating from 1716 which declared that to prevent any church or sect

> Their Endeavouring for preheminence or Superiority one Over the Other by making use of the Civil Power for the Enforcing of a maintenance for their Respective minister — Be it Enacted . . . that what maintenance for Sallary may be Thought needfull or Necessary by any of the Churches or Congregations or Society's of People now Inhabiting or that hereafter may Inhabit within any part of the Goverment for the Support of their or Either of their Ministers may be raised by a free Contribution and no Otherways.[5]

Since no laws were ever enforced in Rhode Island making ministerial contracts legally binding, this act hardly could be construed as an ex post facto law impairing obligation of contract. John Leland was correct in saying that the law was "only cast upon them as a stigma because they have ever been friends to religious liberty." [6] But the contractual argument deserved an answer. We have already discussed Leland's eccentric view.

The most authoritative and forthright rebuttal to the claim that the certificate law of October 1791 was unconstitutional Zephaniah Swift made in his *System of the Laws of Connecticut* in 1796. Swift said that the ecclesiastical system was a political act and therefore a public contract and not a private contract. It involved majority votes and it involved liberty of conscience. It was a matter of the general welfare and was therefore subject to change by legislative action without consideration of the ordinary impairment of obligation of civil contract. (By the same reasoning the New Hampshire legislature had a right to alter the charter of Dartmouth College.) Swift said:

> The agreement of settling a minister, tho binding on the [religious] society, is merely a corporate or political transaction, and by no means involves a personal obligation upon the honor and consciences of men, like a private contract, because the majority governs, and a man may be legally subjected to a contract to which he never assented. The law [governing ministerial contracts] was passed for the purpose of promoting the

4. *Connecticut Courant*, August 29, 1791, p. 3; May 30, 1791, p. 2. Even Leland referred to this Rhode Island law as dangerous and apt to "interfere with private contracts." *The writings of Elder John Leland*, ed. L. F. Greene (New York, 1845), pp. 188–189. Hereafter referred to as Leland, *Works*.

5. Rhode Island Colony Records, ms. vol. IV (1715–1729), May 1716, p. 146, in the Rhode Island State Archives.

6. Leland, *Works*, p. 188, note. Leland also said that well-informed people in Rhode Island had told him in 1791 that this law was no longer in effect.

public good, and whenever an alteration became necessary for the same purpose, there must be an inherent right in the legislature to make the alteration. It would be the highest absurdity to pretend that when the legislature had once adopted a regulation, they could not vary it according to the varying circumstances of the people.[7]

Swift took the accepted New England view that "The settlement of ministers is merely a civil regulation, and in that point of view must be always under the power and controul of the legislature." Consequently, "there is no contract of settlement with any minister but that was made at a time when the parties concerned knew of the existence of such a power." No one should therefore claim injustice if the legislature chose to exercise that power in 1791. Thus Swift denied the charge that the exemption act was "an ex post facto law" constituting "a breach of contract and destroying the faith of government" regarding ministerial contracts. For this act employs "only the exercise of that power which the legislature has always exercised in altering and explaining the mode by which dissenters may attain that privilege, which had long before been granted to them [by the exemption acts of 1727–1729] and to which they have been forever entitled by the laws of nature and the principles of justice."

John Marshall probably would not have been impressed by the argument that the laws of nature provided a ground for altering contractual obligations. Even if the Connecticut charter of 1662 explicitly granted liberty of conscience to dissenters (which it did not), the United States Supreme Court might have assumed, as the laws of England did, that liberty of conscience was perfectly compatible with religious taxation and that Swift's distinction between a public and a private contract in this sense was invalid. But fortunately for the disestablishmentarians no one in those days thought of yielding state sovereignty in religious affairs to decisions of the United States Supreme Court; no one — the dissenters, the Standing Order, or the liberals — ever gave serious consideration to testing the Connecticut ecclesiastical laws in that Court.

The religious liberals or rationalists, men like Zephaniah Swift, did not dissociate themselves from the Standing Order. Like the Unitarians in Massachusetts, the liberals in Connecticut were in some ways the most vehement defenders of the Standing Order and the most obdurate against the Baptist demands for disestablishment. What they wanted (like Judge Jeremiah Smith in New Hampshire) was "catholicity" within the establishment, a broad-church, latitudinarian system of "comprehension." The established system should be sufficiently flexible to comprehend many forms of Christianity within it. Swift, though he was denounced by the Standing clergy for his "infidelity" or deism, was always a staunch Federalist

---

7. Zephaniah Swift, *A System of the Laws of the State of Connecticut* (Windham, 1795–1796), I, 141–142.

politically. He was admired in the 1790's by the dissenters for his anti-clericalism, just as Thomas Jefferson was, but Swift made it very plain in his *System of Laws* that he thought the certificate act of October 1791 granted all the liberty of conscience that any dissenter could reasonably desire; he had no intention of adopting the Baptists' arguments for complete disestablishment. He stated that he did not think a certificate given by a dissenter was in any sense "a mark of degradation" or "an act acknowledging any superiority in the located [i.e., the Standing] society . . . It is only a legal mode of evidence to ascertain to what society the people belong." He felt that "the sect in the located societies [i.e., the territorial parishes] which have considered themselves established [i.e., the Congregationalists] may cease to be the major part and become the minor and be obliged to give certificates to them whom they now call dissenters." [8] (This had happened in Vermont and New Hampshire but it had never happened in Connecticut.) He refused, he said, to make any distinction between dissenters and established sects because he felt no distinction existed; the old establishment had favored one denomination but as a result of the new certificate act no sect was favored: "This is levelling all distinctions and placing every denomination of christians equally under the protection of the law . . . I consider the inhabitants of the located societies to be as much dissenters from other societies [i.e., the poll parishes and the voluntary congregations] as I do them from the located societies." He did concede that he believed it an "important truth, that a religious establishment is not necessary to the support of civil government and that religion left to itself will produce the happiest influence on civil society."

Swift of course insisted that the new certificate act (and the repeal of the act of 1784 and the dropping of the Saybrook Platform) had disestablished the Congregational churches in Connecticut:

> No mode of worship is prescribed, no creed is established no church discipline enforced. In point of principle there is no coercion. In point of support there is no compulsion, only in such manner as by their own acts all have acknowledged to be right and to which they have agreed to submit. A Jew, a Mehomatan, or a Bramin, may practice all the rites and ceremonies of their religion without interruption or danger of incurring any punishment. A fair construction of the law will give to every person that religious liberty which leaves no ground for complaint or dissatisfaction.

However, Jews, "Mehomatans," and "Bramins" were not exempt from religious taxes. Swift said this clearly when he added the point on which he differed from John Leland (though perhaps not from all New England Baptists): "Every christian may believe, worship, and support in such man-

8. *Ibid.*, I, 144–145.

ner as he thinks right, and if he does not feel disposed to join public worship he may stay at home and believe as he please, without any inconvenience but the payment of his tax to support public worship in the located society where he lives." [9] Atheists, Jews, Muslims, and Nothingarians could worship (or not worship) as they wished, but they must pay to support Christianity in a Christian nation.

Swift made only one concession to the Baptists' complaints about the certificate requirement. True, he said, "Courts and juries have usually been composed of what was considered the standing church and they have frequently practiced such quibbles and finesse with respect to the forms of certificates and the nature of dissenting congregations as to defeat the benevolent intentions of the law." This was "illiberal prejudice" which he found "repugnant to the genuine spirit of christianity." But without questioning the right of the courts and juries to judge the honesty of a certificate man's profession of faith, Swift offered as his only solution to this difficulty the hope that when a dissenter was "brought to trial before a court of law, the triers should be extremely careful to strip themselves of all the prejudice which different sects are apt to feel toward each other." As a rational man, Swift thought others were as rational and unprejudiced as he. As a man of the Enlightenment he believed that men could learn to act without prejudice.

Swift revealed his conservative attitude toward religious enthusiasm in a statement similar to the views of Judge Jeremiah Smith of New Hampshire (also a religious liberal). "Christians," he said, "ought not to separate from each other on slight grounds." This conservatism was also revealed in his general view that religion "cultivates and enlivens all the social feelings" while public worship is "a noble source of useful improvement and rational entertainment." [10] As a liberal, Swift could be ecumenical toward all Christian denominations, but he did not understand either the intensity or the dedication of the high church Hopkinsian Congregationalists or the low church pietistic Baptists when he expected them to sit down together in the same meetinghouse in open-communion. A sophisticated and conservative man, he disliked the fanaticism of zealots on both sides; he also disliked the individualism implicit in the new evangelicalism. Religion for him, as for the Unitarians of Massachusetts, was a community endeavor; it enlivened the social feelings, "It smooths the asperities of temper and polishes the roughness of disposition; It refines the manners and liberalizes the sentiments." Swift belonged to that group of educated, urbane liberals (a rapidly diminishing number in Connecticut after 1796) who thought that the best way to conserve the old ideals of the corporate state was by avoiding partisanship toward the Standing Clergy or toward the sectarians — to maintain a system of harmonious religious worship devoid of creed and

9. *Ibid.*, I, 146.
10. *Ibid.*, I, 144, 156.

bathed in "benevolence and brotherly love." For him Christ brought not a sword, but peace.

Despite the Baptists' concerted effort to have the Connecticut certificate law abolished in the early years of the nineteenth century, it remained on the books unchanged until the charter government ended and the new constitution put an end to compulsory religious taxes in 1818. Throughout all of this period towns and parishes regularly levied religious taxes, and records show that Baptists and other dissenters regularly turned in certificates. In a few cases the Baptists refused to do so and were exempted anyway by their neighbors. One reason the system worked more smoothly in Connecticut than it did in Massachusetts was that most places accepted one certificate as sufficient for the lifetime of the dissenter. Annual renewal was unnecessary. Nor was there ever any legal fuss in Connecticut over the incorporation or nonincorporation of the dissenting societies. The courts accepted the right of voluntary religious congregations to exemption without legal recognition.

In two particular situations, however, the dissenting ministers in Connecticut had clearer privileges than did Massachusetts ministers. First was exemption from civil taxes; second was the right to perform marriages for members of their denomination. The dissenters in Massachusetts, as the result of several lawsuits, had acquired both of these privileges by 1770. In Connecticut, a law passed in October 1770 specifically exempted "all ministers of the gospel that now or hereafter shall be settled in this colony" from civil taxes, thereby putting dissenters in the same category as Standing or parish ministers and enabling them to perform marriages. But even under this law, there were problems.

One of the few documented cases of a claim for exemption from civil taxes was that of Eliakim Marshall in 1782. Marshall, a Separate exhorter, petitioned the General Assembly in October 1782 (when he was serving as a deputy from Windsor) for exemption from civil taxes as a preacher who "constantly preached the Gospell on the lord's day and occasionally at othertimes to a very considerable number of sober and orderly people, chiefly at his own dwelling house and spent a very great part of the week time in that momentous work." His petition was rejected in January 1783. Marshall was not the best candidate to test this policy, however, for he admitted that he had not been formally ordained over the congregation to which he preached.[11]

There were several cases prior to 1770 involving dissenting ministers who presumed to have the right to perform weddings for members of their congregations. The earliest of these concerned Elder Solomon Paine, the Separate minister in Canterbury. He was prosecuted in the county court in Windham in December 1748

11. CEA, 1st ser., XV, 276.

for marrying a couple of his own people. His brother [Elisha] came and pleaded his cause. The king's attorney, in pleading against Solomon, allowed that he was ordained the pastor of a church of Christ in Canterbury, in as solemn a manner as could be; but then pleaded that he was not a civil officer, because not chosen by the majority of the parish, which was the thing which made their ministers civil officers; and he said it was in that capacity that they were supported by tax, and had power to marry persons. And upon this plea the case was turned against him.[12]

Paine's case may have been turned against him because at that time the Separates were not a legally recognized sect.

The case which seems to have precipitated the law of 1770 occurred in Enfield in the 1760's, and it concerned the Baptists. When Elder Joseph Meacham married a couple who belonged to his Baptist church in Enfield in October 1764, he too was found guilty. He appealed to the General Assembly to be released from his fine of twenty pounds. In 1769 the General Court did so, but only "on consideration of the memorialist's innocency as to his design in transgressing ye law." [13]

Abel Stevens, the historian of the Methodists, reported that George Roberts, who preached to a Methodist congregation in Windsor in the 1790's was prosecuted and fined in Middletown for assuming the right to perform marriages.[14] There were probably other cases like this involving itinerant preachers, but no dissenter is ever known to have won one.

From all the available accounts and records there appear to have been only about a dozen to fifteen incidents between 1770 and 1818 in which Baptists were oppressed for refusing to pay religious taxes; most of these occurred before 1800. Unfortunately the dearth of legal records dealing with ecclesiastical law in Connecticut leaves many of these cases in doubt. But for the many settled by the General Court we have ample records. A few examples illustrate the kinds of problems involved and their solutions.

The persecution of Nathaniel Drake, Jr. and the Baptists in East Windsor was one of long standing. Drake and his brethren had originally been Separates but they became Baptists in 1762 and were granted exemption by the General Assembly at that time. Drake was first imprisoned in

---

12. Isaac Backus, *History of New England,* ed. David Weston (Newton, 1871), II, 80–81.

13. Conn. Col. Rec., XIII, 160–161, and CEA, XV, 292. Meacham's case is also mentioned in the ms. minutes of the Warren Baptist Association for 1768 in the Brown University Library. See also a letter from Meacham to Backus, dated September 26, 1774, in the BP(AN). See Conn. Col. Rec. XIII, 360 for the law.

14. Abel Stevens, *Memorials of the Introduction of Methodism into the Eastern States* (Boston, 1848), p. 119. A new act regulating marriages in Connecticut was passed in 1783 which reaffirmed the law of 1770: "the Power and Authority of ordained Ministers by Law authorized to Join Persons in Marriage shall extend through the County to which they severally belong during the Time they respectively continue the regular Ordained Ministers of any Ecclesiastical Society or Town within this State." *Connecticut Public Records,* V, 116.

1765 for refusing to pay a meetinghouse rate levied by the second parish. He was kept in jail for twelve months. Then he gave a note of hand for the rates and costs and was released. But he refused to pay the note. Judgment was obtained against him in the courts and in 1771 he was back in prison again — this time for failure to pay his note. His petition to the General Assembly in 1771 brought an investigating committee to East Windsor which recommended in his favor. In May 1771 the General Assembly voted "that the said Nathaniel Drake ought to be exonerated & discharged from said Judgment and Execution and it is hereby Enacted and Decreed that he be discharged therefrom and from his Imprisonment." [15] A year and a half later Drake and five other Baptists in East Windsor petitioned the General Assembly saying that the Congregational society (or parish) "persist in taxing [and distraining] your Mem^lts for the building of meeting House and for the support of their ministers . . . even tho they know them to be Baptists." [16] The General Assembly asked the parish officers to explain their position. In January 1774, the parish stated that if the Baptists felt abused they should take their case to the courts and not to the General Assembly. The General Assembly agreed and dismissed the petition. There is no record of the courts' disposition of the case.

Six members of Joseph Hastings' Baptist church in Suffield petitioned the General Assembly on May 6, 1772, saying that they were all "Anabaptists both by Profession and Practice" yet we are "Continually obliged to Contribute to the Support of the Reverend Mr. John Graham" and to pay for meetinghouses and repairs and "have had their Estate taken for these purposes by Distress and Sold for but a Small part of the value thereof" at public auction. They said they had "frequently petitioned said Society for Relief" but had been denied. They asked that the Society (i.e., the parish) be required to restore "not less than fifty pounds lawfull Money" taken from them and to exempt them in the future. The legislature appointed a committee which investigated and recommended in their favor. In May 1774, the General Assembly voted that "for the future [the petitioners] shall and they are hereby Exempted from all Rates for the Support of the Ministry and building of meeting Houses in sd Society so long as they continue to attend public worship with the Baptists agreeable to Law." [17]

Although the parishes appear to have flouted the exemption laws in both these cases, the General Assembly assessed no penalty on them nor did it require that the parishes restore the taxes which had been unfairly taken. Even assuming that there may have been some dispute over the certificates

15. CEA, XV, 298, CSL.
16. *Ibid.*, XV, 299 b,c. Greene erroneously states that Drake was "branded in the hand" for his refusal to pay. M. Louise Greene, *The Development of Religious Liberty in Connecticut* (Boston, 1905), p. 278.
17. CEA, XV, 303.

or over the status of the petitioners which made the error forgivable, it seems strange that no compensation was offered to the Baptists once the injustice was admitted. The crux of the matter seems to have been that these were Separate-Baptists whose status the asssessors questioned as bona fide Baptists under the law. But they were able to prove that they practiced adult immersion and therefore the General Court accepted them as Baptists.[18]

The persecution of the Baptists of West Woodstock has a more complicated history. This was the first Baptist church formed in Windham County; it began under the itinerant preaching of Elder Noah Alden of Bellingham in December, 1763. One of Alden's converts, a young man named Biel Ledoyt (or Ledoit) began exhorting in 1763; he denounced the Rev. Stephen Williams of the Standing church as dead, cold, and formal. In February 1766, fifteen persons in West Woodstock formed a Baptist church; on May 26, 1768 they chose Ledoyt as their pastor. Their certificates were not accepted because when the parish sent a committee to look at their church records to make sure they were a bona fide Baptist church they could find no record. The Baptists complained bitterly and refused to pay the taxes levied on them. On January 10, 1771, the parish met and

> put to vote whether or no ye society would prefer a Petition or memorial to ye Gen[ll] Assembly to be Holden to Hartford in May Next In order to get some further light Concerning ye people who call themselves Baptist or anny Baptist amongst us, and the vote past in the Negative; the moderator Then put to vote to see if the society would take the advise of the Hon[ll] Jonathan Trumbull Esqr. In the affair . . . and his ye sd Governors advis should Determine ye matter how ye said society should proceed.[19]

This passed in the affirmative, 17 to 6, and Deacon Ebenezer Corbin was appointed to write to the governor and to request an answer by March 1. On March 21, Governor Trumbull replied in a very interesting letter interpreting the law of 1770 regarding dissenters:

> it is my oppinion that a Baptist is Known in Law so as to be Excused from paying any Tax levied for the Support of ye established ministry In the society where he dwells when he dissents from ye same, attends the worship of God in such a way as it is practised By the Baptists and Joins himself to them. Whereby he becomes one of their society. That the

18. For instances where the General Assembly decided that the petitioners were really Separates, see CEA, XV, 306a, concerning the Separate-Baptists in Enfield and CEA, XV, 307a, concerning the Separate-Baptists in Somers.
19. Report of the committee in the West Woodstock Ecclesiastical Society Records, January 29, 1770, p. 140 and January 10, 1771, p. 145. It was less expensive to write to Trumbull than to petition the General Assembly, CSL.

Baptist Churches in this Colony Are no otherwise known in Law Than that Church of Baptists in Your society is, that those people having formed themselves into a Baptist Church or Society, They and the particular persons who hereafter do attend their meeting for the Worship of God and Joyn with them in their profession, are Excused from paying Any part in Your Society Tax for the support of your Minister — The Certificate Mentioned in the Law is to be produced from such Baptist Church signed by ther Elder or other Known proper officer among them Directed to your society Committee or Clerk — That the Law doth not oblige those people to make Application to the General Assembly or County Court to be Q[u]alifyed for such Exemption, which was formerly the Case and is probably the Occation of your Preasant difference in Sentiments.[20]

After they received this letter the parish voted to record Gov. Trumbull's advice and "to abat[e] all such Taxes that the Baptist[s] is wrongfully taxed with according to his Hon.[rs] Advice" and to give Ebenezer Corbin fifteen shillings for his trouble. The significant aspect of this dispute was that the Governor's interpretation of the law was accepted without question although the law itself did not mention that dissenting churches need no longer apply to the General Assembly for licensing.[21] This assumption made it unnecessary for dissenting congregations in Connecticut to obtain incorporation to be eligible for exemption from religious taxes. The Baptists in Suffield and Windsor obtained even more dramatic and positive results in 1785 when they petitioned the General Assembly because they were once again being unfairly taxed. They had, they said, long been Baptists

But many of us who Joined the said Churches and Congregations during the late War and amids the Distresses and Confusions thereof did not immediately procure certificates of our joining . . . and no advantage was then taken of our neglect in the time of it and disputes now arise whither we can derive any advantage from our certificates in the Meeting of said Societies previous to the Granting of the Tax or not, by means where of our estates are daly Threatned to be sold for the payment of the Taxes that have been laid . . . some of us have our Estates already sold for the payment of said Taxes — Lawsuits have been Instituted and many more are daily Threatned, and much ill-will, Injustice, and expense will ensue unless your Honors by some timely Provisions put an end to the Disputes.

Permit us to say that during the War our minds were so taken up with the affairs thereof, so much ingaged in Defending the Cause of our Country to which we were ever sincere and warm Friends, and at the

20. *Ibid.*, p. 146.
21. In the late 1780's the Baptist church in Woodstock refused to turn in certificates any more and sent a memorial to the First Parish demanding that they exempt the Baptists on the basis of a list of the names supplied but not certified by the church. After some quibbling the parish agreed. Ellen Larned, *History of Windham County,* Connecticut (Worcester, 1880), II, 373; Clarence W. Bowen, *The History of Woodstock,* Connecticut (Norwood, 1926), p. 305.

same time there was such apparent Friendship and Charity subsisting between the several denominations of Christians embarked in one General Cause and such an eager desire of Liberty Civil and Religious that we did not attend to lesser Circumstances, and that too which we did not consider as material. For we were ever informed and fully believed that nothing more was Necessary for us to do than to produce our Certificates when we were called upon for the payment of Taxes; and that is our present Opinion. But as there is a Diversity of opinions and for want of having that matter ascertained by some express Law the aformentioned evils will unav[o]idably be the Consequences.[22]

The problem, therefore, was whether a Baptist had to obtain and file a certificate before a tax was levied or whether he could obtain one and present it when the tax collector came to his home to collect the tax. The law was not specific about this, but it was not likely that the courts would allow Baptists to certify themselves retroactively. The petition concluded therefore by asking the General Assembly to amend the certificate act of 1784 to make all certificates valid retroactive to "the commencement of the late War." This memorial was signed by thirty members of the church formerly led by Joseph Hastings, now led by his son John.[23]

As a result of this petition the General Assembly passed an amendment to the certificate act of 1784 in May 1785: "Whereas there is no time limited in said Act or before the making thereof when or wherein certain denominations of Christians should lodge their Certificates with the Society Clerk . . . Be it enacted that all certificates registered by January 1, 1786, shall be effective as of the date they were obtained." [24] This was not precisely what the petitioners wanted, but it was probably effective since they did not complain further.

One of the few court battles involving certificates in the 1780's of which there is any record was waged by the Baptists of Stafford. The Separate Baptist church founded there by Noah Alden had fallen into disarray after his departure in 1765, but enough Baptists remained that when David Lillebridge became pastor of a new Baptist church in nearby Willington in 1780, these Stafford Baptists began attending his services. After the certificate law of 1784, these Baptists requested exemption from parish taxes in Stafford on the grounds that they were now members of the Willington

22. CEA, XV, 308a–c.
23. One interesting aspect of this case occurred when the tax collector from the North Parish of Windsor tried to distrain Eliakim Mather (one of the memorialists) on May 12, 1785; he wanted at first to take a horse cart to be sold at auction. Mather, however, persuaded the collector to take instead some Bibles, New Testaments, and Hymnbooks which he had in his house (presumably for sale). This gave the Baptists the opportunity to claim that the tax collectors were sometimes so mean that they took people's Bibles from them to pay their religious taxes. The note in BP(AN) relating this incident adds that Mather had a certificate from Elder Hastings dated November 1779 but that the collector refused to honor it.
24. CEA, XV, 309a.

congregation. But "the distance being great and the way rough, they did not meet with the church so often as they could have wished." The parish refused to accept their certificates; the law specifically exempted only members of dissenting congregations who live "so near to any place of their worship but that they can and ordinarily do attend the same on the Sabbath." When the tax collectors distrained their property to pay these taxes, the Baptists of Stafford brought suit against the parish assessors. They lost their case in the justice court but after appeal to the county court they won. David Benedict wrote:

> the counsel for our brethren plead [pled] that they were Baptist *sentimentally* [in sentiment,] *practically*, and *legally*. To this statement the counsel on the other side acceded, but still continued his plea against them because they did not *ordinarily* attend their own meeting. While the lawyers were disputing, the Judge, who was an Episcopalian, and not very well affected towards the predominant party, called the attention of the court by inquiring how long a man who was a Baptist *sentimentally*, *practically* and *legally* must stay at home to become a Presbyterian [i.e., Congregationalist]? His Honor's logic produced the same effect upon the whole court as it must upon the reader and the Baptists easily obtained the case.[25]

There were other instances of prosecution or persecution through misunderstandings or stubbornness during these years,[26] but the most serious, the most confusing, and at the same time the most revealing, occurred in New Salem from 1789 to 1795. This was a classic example of the irreconcilability of the conception of a tax-supported established church in every parish with the conception of permitting each parish, even if it were dominated by a majority of dissenters, to choose its own minister. Try as it would, the General Assembly could not find a compromise for New Salem which would satisfy both the Congregationalists who wanted to maintain a tax-supported church and the dissenters (and Nothingarians) who opposed it. The case is well-documented by the numerous petitions, counter-petitions, committee reports, depositions, and draft legislation in the state archives; these provide a vivid account of the confusions and perplexities of the established system during this period of transition. New Salem was New England's moribund parish system in microcosm.

The problem arose in 1789 when a group of Congregationalists, led by Zebulon Waterman, Jr., decided that the parish of New Salem, which had been without a Congregational minister for over forty years, should have a new meetinghouse and should levy taxes to build it and to install and

25. David Benedict, *A General History of the Baptist Denomination in America,* 2 vols. (Boston, 1813), I, 534.
26. For reference to a Baptist jailed in Tolland in 1792 see George Roberts, *Strictures on a Sermon Delivered by Mr. Nathan Williams* (Philadelphia, 1794), p. 22.

support a regular minister of the Standing Order. Waterman claimed he and those who acted with him never intended to levy any taxes on the Separates and Baptists who lived in the parish. Probably they did not. But the difficulty arose in deciding who was and who was not a Separate or a Baptist. According to the law this was a very simple matter, for all those who gave in certificates were Separates or Baptists and all who did not were to be taxed as Congregationalists. But instead, many Baptists and Separates, as well as some nominal Congregationalists (the Nothingarians) neither wanted to nor would turn in certificates. And there was no way to make them do so without threatening them with taxation if they did not. It turned out, however, that these dissenters and Nothingarians were a majority of the parish (at least when they combined and attended the meetings together). They were therefore able to prevent Waterman's group from using the parish machinery and to frustrate that group's honest efforts to follow the traditional procedure of establishing a Congregational church in the parish. The simple solution to this would have been for the General Assembly to incorporate Waterman's group as a poll parish and let them proceed independently of the old parish system. But apparently Waterman's group was neither large enough nor wealthy enough to sustain a church by taxing only its own members. Besides, they were convinced that the opposition to their efforts was not from honest dissenters but from tax-dodgers who had personal malice against Waterman and his friends. Therefore, it became a matter of principle for Waterman, and for the General Assembly, to determine whether there was any way in which the system could be made to work despite efforts by a malicious group of nominal Congregationalists who, for selfish and spiteful reasons, were able to ally themselves with and to play upon the fears of honest dissenters in the parish. The tax dodgers here held a balance of power in the parish and the supporters of the old Standing Order (in the town and in the legislature) did not want to permit them to wreck the system. It was a typical small-town New England fight which to outsiders seemed a petty, spiteful feud. To insiders, however, it was a matter of principle.

To grasp the fundamental issues and comprehend their complexities one must refer to what happened in New Salem during the Great Awakening. In a deposition given to an investigating committee of the legislature on May 12, 1792, Col. Elias Worthington of the nearby town of Colchester, one of the oldest and most respected inhabitants of the area, told how the parish had become divided and the Congregational church defunct. Worthington was a Congregationalist with Old Light, but generally liberal, views; his prejudices showed occasionally, but his story rang true.

In 1742 when "the time of the great Religious Commotion prevailed," said Worthington, the Rev. Joseph Lovett was the Standing minister of the parish (he had been installed in 1719 when the parish church was first organized). New Salem had been incorporated in 1726 as the second parish of Colchester. It included within its boundaries sections of Lyme and Montville as well as Colchester, and it was located in the northwest corner of what had formerly been the large township of New London. In 1742, Worthington claimed, there were only three dissenters officially registered in the parish: Josiah Gates, Jonathan Rathbun, and James Welch who were "Baptists or Quakers." But when the Awakening began a New Light resident of the town, Jabez Jones, Sr., "headed a party that opposed Mr. Lovett" and accused Lovett "in the Common Court of the times" of being "an unconverted man." Jones began holding Separate meetings in his home with "warm and Zealous Exhortations" which often lasted most of the night. Jones "so inflamed the minds of the people against Mr. Lovett that he [Lovett] sought for & obtained a Dismission" in 1745. No parish minister had been installed since that day. Jones, who continued to exhort in his house in the northwest corner of the parish, attracted New Light radicals from Colchester who were dissatisfied with the Rev. Ephraim Little of the Standing church there. Soon they had enough members to build a Separate meetinghouse and Jabez Jones, Sr. continued to preach there until 1768. Then Jones became involved in moral difficulties, and many of his hearers left. In 1775 Barnabas Silas, "an illiterate & separate preacher, for about two years," replaced Jones as pastor of this Separate Church. Then the church was vacant for a year. Subsequently the Rev. Timothy Wood, a licensed Congregationalist, preached in the church for a year. Next followed "Gilbert Smith, an illiterate & unlearned preacher" against whom the county ministerial association took action (presumably on the ground that Wood's preaching in the church had brought it back into formal fellowship with the Standing association of Congregational ministers of the county). After Smith left, the pulpit was vacant for a decade or more. Then Zebulon Waterman's Congregational group began in 1789 to plan a new meetinghouse. In 1792, when it was built, they hired James Treadway to preach for four months by subscription.

Worthington's deposition continued that a similar Separate schism took place in Colchester in 1742, led by Zebulon Waterman, Sr., father of the man who in 1789 wanted to resurrect the New Salem Standing church. (Waterman, Sr., was the brother-in-law of Jabez Jones, Sr.) But in 1743 he became a Baptist,[27] and the Separates in Colchester made Thomas Denison their minister. Waterman, Sr. then moved to the eastern part of New Salem where he founded a Baptist church which soon built its own meetinghouse in the parish. For many years the only preaching in New Salem was by Jabez Jones in the New Salem Separate meetinghouse and

---

27. Backus says that Waterman, Sr., after he became a Baptist, itinerated for a time and was arrested and imprisoned in Hartford for exhorting in Colchester by Judge John Bulkley. (Bulkley had replaced Col. Hezekiah Huntington as Justice of the Peace in Colchester when Huntington was ejected from the Council for New Light sympathies.) Backus, *History*, II, 58.

by Zebulon Waterman in the New Salem Baptist meetinghouse. The remnants of Lovett's Standing church were unable to hire a new Congregational minister.[28]

"As those that were neither separates nor Baptists," said Worthington, "liked Mr. Waterman & his Baptists better than Mr. Jones & his separates, more attended with the Baptists than with the Separates, which distinction still continues." [29] Worthington himself, however, sided with Zebulon Waterman, Jr. in 1789 in wanting to reorganize the Standing church. He thought this would help reunite the parish (this is the typical liberal quest for unity sought by Zephaniah Swift and Jeremiah Smith of New Hampshire). Worthington's deposition did not mention that Zebulon Waterman, Sr. was replaced as Elder by Ichabod Allen in 1751 and that Allen himself proved unstable and scattered the flock until Elder Abel Palmer was ordained by the Separates in 1784. Nor did Worthington note that in 1783 a Baptist church had been formed in Colchester near the border of Lebanon over which Christopher Palmer, Abel Palmer's father, was minister. Both Palmers came from Stonington.[30] Thus, in 1791 there were four competing churches in the area of New Salem — the two Baptist churches of the Palmers; the Separate church founded by Jones (but which currently had no pastor); and the new Standing church which Waterman, Jr. was reviving.

The religious situation was further complicated by a quarrel over the proper use of a forty-acre plot of land which Col. Samuel Brown had given to the Standing society in about 1726 to be used by the Society as long as it had a lawfully settled minister. (The deed to the land was lost but no one disputed the details.) When Waterman, Jr. and Worthington decided to revive the defunct parish in 1789, they first got permission from the County Court to build a meetinghouse and to levy a tax for it. They then decided to vote that the income from this plot of land (about six pounds per year) be applied to use by the Society. But the Baptists had settled their minister on this lot and although he paid rent for its use, they felt that since the Baptist church had supplied public worship for most of the parish for so many years, it was not unfair that they should have a vote in the use of the income. Col. Worthington, who acted as Moderator of the Society's meeting, thought otherwise and asked all of those who were Baptists to withdraw from the meeting. Apparently about twenty persons did withdraw, but many others who were Baptists (in practice if not by certificate) remained. The

---

28. A petition in the CEA, IX, 215, dated May 14, 1747, reports the difficulties of the remnants of Lovett's Standing Church. In May 1747 the petitioners said that of the £4140 of rateable property in the parish at the time, £1005 belonged to Baptists and £640 to the Separates, so it seemed impossible to raise enough from the rest to support a Standing minister.

29. For Worthington's deposition see CEA, 2d ser., I 128a–d. For the other documents quoted below in this case see *ibid.*, I, 103–142.

30. See Backus, *History*, II, 520 for information about the Palmers.

vote taken on January 27, 1791 went against the Congregationalists and in a compromise gesture the income from Brown's plot was voted to be used for the support of the parish school. The Congregationalists opposed this and considered it a misappropriation of the funds. The Baptists grew angry and on December 27, 1791 they obtained a majority vote at a Society meeting that the income from the land should be given directly to Elder Palmer, thereby declaring that he was somehow the lawfully settled minister of the parish (i.e., they effectively took over the parish from the Congregationalists). It was not a vote which generally accorded with Baptist principles, but it is understandable in that situation.

As for the taxes levied for the new Congregational meetinghouse, the Society's collector, John Douglas, Jr., testified that he had been given instructions "not to collect of any persons who should Evidence to me that they were Baptist or Baptist adherents by a Certificate or any other means." He said because of this "a larg number of sd persons named in sd Rate bill" were not required to pay. The Congregationalists therefore claimed that they had raised their new meetinghouse "by free donation." But when, on January 27, 1791, they came to levy a second tax, two pence on the pound, to finish the meetinghouse, they found the Baptists were beginning to be alarmed and they feared that the "voluntaryism" of the Congregationalists might eventually disappear as the Standing Order became stronger and the ecclesiastical expenses grew larger. The Baptists therefore began to attend the Society meetings in large numbers to obstruct further action by the Congregationalists. In this way they rescinded the tax vote of January at a meeting on April 7. The Congregationalists then turned to the legislature for help. On September 26, 1791 they complained in a petition that as a parish they

> were divided and very much troubled with persons who do not belong to said Society but are Babtists or adhere to the Babtists & are taking Subtil and cunning methods to defeat the designs of sd Society in finishing their Meeting-House and Settling a Minster and Obtrude themselves into all Society Meetings warned for the purpose of Laying a Tax to finish sd House or Settle a Minister agreble to the Laws of this State . . . [we] having no power to discriminate between Baptists and &c. as they refuse to take Certificates on purpose to defeat and prevent sd Society from finishing sd House or Settling a Minister.[31]

The Baptists and Separates knew if they took out certificates they would then be prevented by law from voting in the Society meetings, and although the law might assume that the certificates protected them from oppression, the Baptists had reason to doubt this. Certainly some of the Baptists' certificates would have been challenged. They refused, therefore, to get certifi-

31. CEA, 2d ser., I, 110a–d.

cates, retained their votes in Society affairs, but voted against the Society's interests and for their own. Moreover, they were determined to keep the income from Brown's plot for their own minister. At a meeting of the Society (that is, parish) held October 13, 1791, the Baptists and their friends voted a resolution stating their opposition to the petition which Waterman, Jr., had made to the legislature. The vote, 57 to 29, favored censuring the petition, but whether all of the supporters of Waterman attended the meeting is not known.

The legislature sent a commission to New Salem in May 1792, where it heard testimony from both sides. Thomas Avery, a Baptist sympathizer, told them that the Baptists never interfered with or objected to any society votes which applied only to the "Presbyterians" (that is, the Congregationalists) but that they did object to the Congregationalists' claim that they had the right to levy taxes on the entire parish (and then to exempt the certificate men). Avery freely admitted that many Baptists had refused to turn in certificates and that he believed "those that now call themselves the parrish [i.e., Palmer's interlopers in the Society meetings] to be Chiefly babtists & their adherents." [32]

The legislative committee, having gathered copious testimony and statistics, submitted its report to the General Assembly in May, 1792. It declared it had found those who claimed to be of the established church "to be inferior in Numbers to the Baptists and their Adherent[s]." Also the committee had "found it utterly Impossible . . . to Effect a Reconciliation between the Parties."

> The Baptists utterly disown any Persons to be Baptists but such as have been baptized by Immersion as a Characteristic of their Members. This leaves a large Number of their Adherents or attendants on their Meeting who will not designate themse[l]ves by Certificates and Challenge a Right to Vote in Society Meetings & Many Acknowledged Baptists and officers in their Churches also Refuse to Designate themselves in the above mode and also appear & vote in Society Meetings with the Memorialists [i.e., Waterman's group] and form a large Majority by which they wholly Obstruct the Memorialists [in establishing a Congregational church].[33]

The commissioners also stated that some disaffected Congregationalists attended the Baptist church and voted against Waterman's group because they disliked the location of the new Congregational meetinghouse.

The crux of the committee's report was the statement that the committee tried "to find by the List of the Inhabitants of said Society [i.e., the parish]

---

32. From the depositions and petitions it appears that the leaders of the Baptist faction were Captain Stephen Billings and Joshua Rathbun. Seven members of Elder Christopher Palmer's church in Colchester lived in New Salem and lent their weight to the Baptist faction there.

33. CEA, 2d ser., I 131 a. The Committee were Benjamin Huntington, Elijah Hubbard, and Thomas Avery. Conn. State Records, VII, 357–358.

who belonged to Each Denomination . . . But in this Inquiry such wide Disagreements and Sharp altercations took Place among the Parties as Convinced your Committee of the impropriety of any further Inquiry on that head." But they added that the Baptists appeared not to object to the Congregationalists forming into a distinct society or poll parish of their own, if they filed certificates with the parish clerk of their signing off (another indication that the Baptists considered themselves, as the majority, to constitute the true parish society in New Salem). Zephaniah Swift and others had said that this was not only possible but also entirely legal under the act of 1784. When the dissenters became the majority in a parish it was the Congregationalists who had to produce certificates to gain tax exemption or to form their own society.

But when the legislature was faced with the possibility that Elder Abel Palmer would officially have to be recognized as the Standing minister in New Salem and that the Congregationalists be designated as dissenters, it boggled. The Standing Order could not face the possibility of admitting that the Congregationalists were not the established church throughout Connecticut, no matter what the law implied. The legislators stalled for several weeks trying to find some way out of the dilemma. The archives contain three different draft bills which were drawn up to solve the problem. The first of these declared "the Memorialists [Waterman's group] and their adherents and those who may hereafter join them, be and they are hereby declared to be the *only* Ecclesiastical Society within the bounds of sd Society [parish] of New Salem . . . and no person shall have [a] right to vote in any Society meeting of the Memorialists until he have first enrolled his name with the Mem[sts] . . . [and] a Tax [shall] be laid on the polls and rateable estates of the *members* of sd Society" to raise two hundred pounds for a meetinghouse and this shall be "collectable of all such *inhabitants* in sd *Society*" who do not sign off from it by certificates.[34]

The difficulty here lay in the ambiguities in the words "only," "member," "society" and "inhabitants." Why should the Congregationalists be the only society in New Salem? This was doubtless intended to invalidate the Baptist majority's claims to be the Standing society. But did "society" mean the territorial parish or did it mean the poll parish of the Congregational memorialists? Who were the "members" of this society to be? If they were only the memorialists and their adherents and those who voluntarily joined them, then this bill's purpose was clearly to create a poll parish. Yet the tax was to be collectable of all "inhabitants" in the society. The word inhabitants implies residents in a territorial parish. If this were to be the case, then the Congregational poll parish could tax all the inhabitants or residents in the territorial parish of New Salem.

The upper house tried to clarify this draft bill first by deleting the word

---

34. CEA, 2d ser., I 134a–d. The italics in the quoted passage are mine.

"only," thereby leaving room for other societies within the territorial parish. It also added a clause that those who did not enroll in the society of the memorialists should not be "liable to be taxed by them," for religious purposes. This would have settled the matter satisfactorily, though it was still unclear what the difference was between the territorial parish and the poll parish. But the archives contain still another draft of this bill which retained the word "only" and omitted the statement that those not enrolled should not be liable to be taxed. It continued that the tax of £200 was "to be levied on the Inhabitants of sd Society which do not discriminate themselves by Lodging of Certificate[s] with the Clerk of sd Society by the first day of October next." This version was worse than the original one, for it clearly gave the Congregationalists the right to be the only parish and to levy the tax on all inhabitants of the territorial parish who did not file certificates. It was a legislative fiat stating that even if the dissenters were a majority, the Congregationalists would not be the ones to give in certificates.

But the final version of the bill, enacted into law, adhered more closely to the wishes of the upper house.[35] The word "only" was omitted, as was the clause stating that those who did not enroll with the society of the memorialists should not be taxed. The bill read that this society "shall exercise all Rights of an Ecclesiastical Society except Taxing those that have not joined and shall not Join the Mem^{ts} by enrolling." The act did not mention levying a tax of £200, nor did it say anything about filing certificates by the first of October. The Congregationalists became effectively a poll parish for religious purposes. The act did say, however, that all inhabitants were to be permitted to vote on school issues. This seemed to indicate that to the legislature the Congregational society was effectively the official society of the parish in everything but the right of religious taxation.

Thus, the society or parish of New Salem was to be considered in its territorial entirety a civil unit, but the Congregational memorialists were to be a poll parish within that civil unit and as such they were to constitute the established church, thereby entitling them to Brown's ministry lot. As an established society the Congregationalists could levy taxes on their members and collect them by means of the civil law. But the legislature did concede that the memorialists, as a minority, did not have the right to levy a tax on all the inhabitants of the civil parish nor did they have the right to excuse or exempt only those inhabitants who provided certificates. The compromise was neat, if unfair. It granted exemption to all inhabitants *not* mentioned in the memorial regardless of their reasons for not wanting to join in reviving the ecclesiastical parish; and it saved the Congregationalists the ignominy of having to file certificates with dissenters. But it was unfair in

35. *Ibid.*, 2d ser., I, 136 a, and Conn. State Rec., VII, 423–425. Also *ibid.*, VIII, 220–221, 337–338.

its outright refusal to acknowledge that this minority, because it was a minority, was not justified in calling itself the established church. As for Samuel Brown's ministry lot, the exact wording of the deed was unknown, but it was probable that he meant it to support the Congregationalists in the parish. In any case, Elder Abel Palmer, who lived on the Congregational ministry lot was required to pay his rent to the Congregational society.

But the matter did not end here. The problem of how to pay for the extensive costs of the petitions, for the committee of inquiry, and for the other expenses in settling the dispute remained. On April 29, 1794 Zebulon Waterman, Jr. and his new Standing society petitioned the legislature that it was unable to pay all of the costs of the dispute since its membership was too small. Waterman complained that many of those who had originally petitioned with him and been incorporated as the society had since moved away and that while many wealthy persons attended the new Congregational church regularly, they refused to enroll officially as members of it because they did not want to become liable to pay taxes to support it. Waterman declared that unless the legislature did something more to help them the society would soon sink back into decay. The legislature at first declined to reopen the matter. On September 30, 1794 the Congregationalists again petitioned (this time through Jabez Jones, Jr.) that although they had paid forty pounds of the costs they felt the dissenters should pay fifteen pounds of this and had therefore sued them in court to enforce this. The court had ruled that the society was responsible for its own religious debts. This time the legislature did something: it appointed an investigating committee. The committee found remaining a debt of £121.0.5½ which was to be paid by the Standing parish; it resolved that a tax of five pence on the pound should be levied on all the polls and rateable estates within the territorial bounds of the parish of New Salem. The legislature instructed the committee to make out such a rate using the tax list of 1794 and to appoint a collector to collect it. Ultimately, therefore, the Baptists and other dissenters paid the major part of the dispute costs. It may well have been this dispute, or similar ones arising elsewhere in Connecticut, that led to the passage of the new certificate act of October 1791 and made such quarrels unlikely thereafter. As a fitting postscript, in 1793 the Congregationalists hired and installed the Rev. David Huntington as their minister. But he left within three years because they were unable to keep up his salary. The Congregationalists then remained without a minister until 1813.

New Salem was not the only parish or town in these years in which the Congregationalists found themselves unable to sustain a ministry either because of the dissenters' aggressive competition or because of the apathy of the nominal Congregationalists. The Second Parish of Voluntown (Nazareth) had so many dissenters in it from its incorporation in 1734 that it was never, throughout its history, able to get a vote to levy religious taxes. It had a Congregational minister on voluntary support only from 1772 to

1782. Of the $12,357.80 in its tax list as of May 3, 1807, two-thirds was owned by dissenters.[36] The Congregational church in Newent parish (Norwich) finally united with the Separate church in the town on terms acceptable to the Separates in 1770. A minister, Joel Benedict, was chosen by the two groups who agreed to take his support only by voluntary contributions. After eleven years he found that this was insufficient and left. No religious taxes were levied in Newent after 1770.[37] The town of Goshen petitioned the General Assembly in 1772 that with £900 of its tax list in the hands of the Baptists it was unable to raise sufficient taxes to support its minister.[38] On May 10, 1774 the Congregationalists of the fishing village of Long Point in Stonington told the legislature they were too poor to build a meetinghouse, adding that "the various & Different Sentement[s] in the Religious Denomination[s] of Christians Among them Vizt. First day Babtists, Sevenday Babtist, and the Quakers or those Call'd friends are such real Grief and Great Discouragement to your Memorialists" that in view of the low market for fish if a church were to be built the legislature would have to help.[39]

Faced with the declining feasibility of maintaining the Congregational churches and clergy by parish taxes, the defenders of the Standing Order had to find some supplementary means of support — some expedients by which the legislature itself could come to the aid of the beleaguered parishes. Ecclesiastical history in Connecticut after 1780 is the history of how the legislature tried, one way after another, to prop up the failing system. Or, in their terms, it is the story of how those descendants of the Puritans who were still dedicated to the principle of state support for the Christian religion tried to preserve that practice and yet grant as broad and free a toleration as possible to those Christians who dissented from that tradition.

36. CEA, 2d ser., IV, 119; Larned, *History*, II, 385–386.
37. Newent (Lisbon) First Congregational Church Records, mss., I, 127–136, and First Society Records, mss. II, 132–143, CSL. Benedict was a graduate of Princeton, 1765. William B. Sprague, *Annals of the American Pulpit* (New York, 1858), I, 682–685; C. C. Goen, *Revivalism and Separatism in New England, 1740–1800* (New Haven, 1962), p. 84.
38. CEA, XIV, 207.
39. *Ibid.*, XIV, 181. The North Stonington Congregational Church, according to its records, was unable to support a minister after 1783. The ms. records are in the Connecticut State Library.

Chapter 49

Expedients to Prop Up the Establishment in Connecticut,

1780–1800

By the appropriations act the burdens of small and poor parishes, the inhabitants of which are obliged to pay six pence or eight pence on the pound to support the ministry, will be greatly eased, and they will be confirmed and prevented from scattering and breaking to pieces in the consequence of the burthen of supporting public worship.

Letter in the Connecticut *Courant,* April 14, 1794

One of the first ways in which the Connecticut legislature tried to help needy parishes after 1780 was to grant them the right to conduct a lottery to raise the funds which they could not obtain by religious taxation. From the various petitions requesting permission to conduct lotteries one can derive considerable information about the decay of the parish system. The First or Middle Society in Killingly petitioned in 1783 for permission to raise £300 by lottery to buy a parsonage because

> Soon after the Commencement of this distressing & unnatural War with Great Britton, Just at a time when the Sectaries began to creep in among us, Many immigrations from a Sister State [Rhode Island] not friendly to our Religious Constitution has taken Place; and Sundry of our most Valuable settlements are now in the Possession of those People who Stile themselves Baptists.

Moreover, said the petitioners, the Standing minister left after one year and took the £300 they had given him for a settlement (or encouragement) with him. Unable to obtain another pastor because of its lack of taxable property, this society petitioned the legislature again in 1805 saying that it had been destitute of a pastor for thirty years: "almost all the Inhabitants living in the easterly half of sd Society are dissenters and as such they have for a long time withdrawn from your Petitioners . . . & about twenty five years ago erected a meeting house . . . & have formed a Baptist Church."

Others in the parish have "become wholly indifferent to the preservation of Society order or public worship." In 1798 some of the Congregationalists raised enough money to hire a minister and build a meetinghouse, but they were unable to levy a tax even on themselves for "the Dissenters never have availed themselves of the Law authorizing them to form themselves into a Distinct Society nor have they lodged Certificates, being able, united with those desirous of supporting no mode of public worship, to pass [or prevent] any vote in said Society." In October 1805, the legislature granted both the Congregationalists' requests: first, to hold a lottery; second, to divide the Middle Society into two parishes, leaving the eastern half to the Baptists.[1]

The Congregationalists of Preston were granted a lottery in May 1803, to raise money for their meetinghouse. The petitioners noted that they had lost a large part of their voters to the Separates in 1744 and that since 1781 they had had to raise their religious funds by voluntary methods because "so many persons have forsaken the Society & joined to other denominations of Christians or become indifferent or averse to public worship that an attempt to raise money by tax to build a meetinghouse, would wholly break up sd Society; an attempt to repair the present meetinghouse occasioned the lodgement with the Society Clerk of thirty nine certificates" by persons (largely Congregationalists) who refused to be taxed.[2]

The Congregational Society of West Britain in the town of Bristol petitioned the legislature on October 17, 1803, saying that despite several attempts "a vote either to repair or build by Tax [a meetinghouse] cannot be obtained in said Society — owing to the influences of the numerous sects among them embracing different religious Tenets — That nearly one half of their number & wea[l]th belong to Sectarians — And it is apprehended that their influence would destroy the Society should they attempt to build by the avails of a Tax." The total tax list amounted to $31,987.55 of which the dissenters held $14,676.20. The Congregationalists had raised $1600 voluntarily to build a meetinghouse but they requested a lottery to raise $2000 more to complete it.[3]

The Ellsworth Society in the town of Sharon petitioned on May 7, 1805 for a $1500 lottery to build a church because "there are some conscientious dissenters and others who have sheltered themselves under the Liberality of the Law" who will not contribute and "recourse to Taxation, which is extremely unpleasant and is attended with serious difficulties" is not desired. The legislature granted their request.[4]

1. CEA: XIV, 340. The war with Great Britain was "unnatural" because it was fratricidal or a war of a mother country against her children; *ibid.*, 2d ser., II, 159a,b.; *ibid.*, 2d ser., II, 160a–d.
2. *Ibid.*, 2d ser., IV, 22a–d.
3. *Ibid.*, 2d ser., I, 67–69.
4. *Ibid.*, 2d ser., IV, 52a,b. In 1808 the Congregationlists of the Fourth Society of Guilford petitioned to be joined to the First Society because they had been

But the Baptists as well as the Congregationalists were having trouble supporting their churches. The Congregationalists's losses were not the dissenters' gains. Records of the Baptists and other dissenters contain as many complaints about the neuters and Nothingarians and the "certificate men" as do those of the Congregationalists. Men who signed off from the Standing parish and called themselves Baptists (they had to call themselves something) were theoretically members of a Baptist congregation. But when the Baptists came to these alleged Baptists and asked them to contribute, they found them no more willing to aid voluntary religious worship than compulsory religious worship. There was as much contempt in the Baptists' use of the term "certificate man" or "certificate members" after 1791 as the Congregationalists had expressed earlier. Presumably a real Baptist did not use certificates.[5] Significantly, the Connecticut Baptists no longer felt a stigma attached to their sect, but this also indicated they felt there was less possibility of oppression. Before 1791 Baptists could rightly repudiate the charge that those who chose to join their congregations were tax-dodgers; but not after 1791. Like the Congregationalists in New Salem in 1794, the Baptists in many towns found men (with their families) sitting in the Baptist church every Sunday who made no effort to contribute to the support of the church, and who showed no interest in joining. Not surprisingly, churches of all denominations began to search for alternative ways of raising money. The most popular device quickly became the use of pew rents.

The trouble lay not only with the "certificate men" or Nothingarian tax dodgers. Even the bona fide Baptists who had been converted and baptized by immersion seemed unwilling or unable to provide much support for their elders and meetinghouses. If one reads the Baptist association records and

---

unable, since 1787, to obtain a minister and "a number of members of sd society have shifted their religious sentiments & joined the baptists." This petition was granted; *ibid.*, 2d ser., II, 86a,b. By 1782 the Baptists and Separates in East Lyme were a majority of the parish. This put an end to religious taxes there. There was no Standing minister in this parish from 1761 to 1823; D. Hamilton Hurd, *History of New London County* (Philadelphia, 1882), p. 562. The town of Montville had to give up religious taxes by 1791; Frances M. Caulkins, *History of Norwich* (Hartford, 1866), p. 605. Groton had so many dissenters that from 1798 to 1810 it had no Congregational minister; Charles R. Stark, *Groton, Connecticut* (Stonington, 1922), p. 120.

5. David Benedict, the Baptist historian, commented in 1812 that the ease with which Congregationalists could sign their own certificates and claim to belong to some other sect "has been the cause of multitudes leaving the established order who are of no use to any other denomination." *A General History of the Baptist Denomination in America*, 2 vols. (Boston, 1813), I, 535. Probably most of these tax dodgers claimed to be Baptists and thus brought disgrace to the denomination just when it was achieving some respectability. By contrast, in 1780, the Baptists in West Woodstock, Connecticut, voted never again to utilize certificates to obtain exemption from religious taxes; they won exemption by staking their property and liberty on the principle that certificates were unjust *per se*. Ellen Larned, *History of Windham County, Connecticut* (Worcester, 1880), II, 373.

church records in these years, he finds a constant stream of laments about the lack of ministerial support. Records of the West Ashford First Baptist Church from 1765 to 1818 exemplify how churches tried one expedient after another to cope with this problem.[6] When this church was formed in 1765 it adopted the usual view that the minister was worthy of his hire but that his support should be based entirely on free will offerings of the members and regular attendants. A committee was appointed "to Receive and pay all the money that shall be given towards maintaining and supporting a Baptist gospel minister or ministers." But by 1782 the members were giving so little that the elder, Ebenezer Lamson, requested a dismission. This was given reluctantly. The church then tried passing round "a Subscription Paper" on which each member and attendant would write down what he expected to give annually. But this method was also inadequate. So in 1791 the church voted to appoint "a Committee to Make assessments for . . . . the Purpose of Purchasing a farm" for the minister. They hoped that the minister could support himself if he had a farm, but this did not prove feasible. Finally the church adopted a system of assessing each member personally to obtain the additional funds needed each year. It is unclear what method the committee chose at first in making the assessments, but in 1797 the church directed the committee to make the assessments "according to our lists," that is, according to the legal tax rate. When a new minister was chosen in 1801 the congregation voted to give him a fixed salary of $170 a year. This was the first time this church imitated the Congregational system of "hireling ministry." But the Baptists were advancing beyond the primitive stage of pietism. In addition to the assessments, the church voted in 1801 to build pews in the meetinghouse and to auction them off to the highest bidders. This was partly to cover the cost of building them, partly to build up an endowment, and partly, perhaps, to get rid of "certificate men" who refused to pay their assessment. The best pews sold for $61, the cheapest for $10. But just as this transaction occurred, the meetinghouse burned. Earlier the Baptists might have seen this as a judgment of God for their use of unscriptural methods of raising money. But the only result in 1801 was to send the church to the legislature with a petition to grant a lottery to raise the money to build a new meetinghouse.

The lottery was not granted and although many other Baptist churches petitioned for this privilege in the early years of the nineteenth century there is no record that the legislature ever granted a lottery privilege to a Baptist church. This may have been simply prejudice against Baptists. But more likely it was the fear that granting lottery privileges to any and all dissenting churches would not only encourage dissent but also would produce an unending number of lotteries, thereby decreasing chances of success for the lotteries of the Standing churches. The decision may even

6. West Ashford Baptist Church Records, mss. in CSL.

have been rationalized because lotteries for a parish were a civil grant in aid, while lotteries to dissenting churches were direct state aid to religious bodies.

Incorporation and pew rents were two expedients which the West Ashford Baptists did not try but which other Baptist churches did. The First Baptist Church in Hartford petitioned for and received incorporation in 1811, but it does not appear to have used this power to bring suits against members who failed to pay their proportionate share of an assessment. Rather it used its corporate power to raise money in trust as an endowment fund which could be invested and the income used to support the ministry.[7] On the other hand, the Second Baptist Church of Groton wrote the following into its Articles of Faith in 1765:

> It is the duty of every member of the church to communicate willingly and cheerfully to the support of the gospel Ministry . . . according as God hath prospered each individual . . . [to refuse this is] covetousness which is idolatry, a disciplinable matter but in no case to be controuled by civil law, except where persons have voluntarily given their obligations. In that case where payment is refused or procrastinated if the church judge such person or persons, dishonest or wicked in their neglect (to an exclusion from church fellowship) we think it is not unrighteous to use the civil law in bringing the lawless and disobedient to a compliance with their own voluntary engagements.[8]

There is no record that this church ever sought incorporation from the legislature to obtained the legal right to sue delinquent members or proceeded to law against an excommunicated member who refused to pay. However, one can find in the Baptist church records in these years many instances of members censured for covetousness for refusal to pay their fair share of support. The use of annual pew rents became general practice for almost all churches in New England by 1810. Sometimes the annual pew rent was determined by auction, other times by assessments. But whatever method they used, the Baptists had a difficult time.

Unquestionably the chief reason for the dissolution of Baptist churches in these years was their inability to support a minister. If the Baptists had not been willing to have an unlearned ministry (before 1818, only one Baptist church in Connecticut ever had a college-educated minister) and if these ministers had not been dedicated men asking little from their congregations and working at other jobs during the week to support themselves and their families, the denomination would have grown much more slowly than it did.

7. Hartford First Baptist Church Records, mss., pp. 38–39, in CSL. The pastor of the church, Henry Grew, opposed this but the church received support for its action from two Massachusetts elders, Thomas Baldwin and Caleb Blood.
8. Second Baptist Church in Groton, ms. records in CSL.

Not surprisingly, however, the Baptist associations of Connecticut, as elsewhere in New England, considered it one of their primary and most difficult tasks to keep vacant churches supplied with competent ministers. Only the Baptists unequenchable enthusiasm for itinerant evangelism saved the churches in the more remote rural areas from dissolution.

Although the Baptists were able and ready for a new burst of evangelistic activity after 1791, the Standing Order continued to search for other expedients before it finally undertook to engineer a second Great Awakening. One plan suggested to help the ailing system appeared in the Connecticut *Courant* in 1788. The writer recommended that the legislature enact a general assessment tax to be "collected from all the rateable members of [the] state for the support of the public teachers of religion of all denominations within the state." This money would then be distributed by the state to the various denominations in proportion to their numbers and to the amount contributed by their members. The writer had obviously read about Patrick Henry's general assessment bill introduced into the Virginia legislature three years earlier, which had been barely defeated by efforts of James Madison. No action was taken on this proposal. Another suggestion — also with precedent in Virginia — was that the legislature fix a minimum level for the salary of parish ministers throughout the state at a given rate per hundred families. A minister with a numerous parish would receive a larger salary than one whose parish was small, but presumably the sum even for the smallest parish would be set sufficiently high by the legislature to guarantee a living wage. Parishioners would be encouraged to add to this sum by voluntary subscription or by the collection plate, thereby enabling some reward for merit.[9] This measure also fell. Perhaps these proposals failed to find support because both would have taken a large part of the control of the parish church out of the hands of local residents and put it under the centralized control of the state.

One plan, however, did meet with general favor from those in the establishment in the early 1790's. This one succeeded in obtaining enactment. The great virtue of this expedient was that it promised to raise the level of support for the Standing church without necessitating any new taxes on the people of the state and without diminishing the control and administration of the parish at the local level. This plan would use the large sum of money from the sale of Connecticut's western land as a permanent and statewide endowment fund for the churches of the Standing Order. But if the Congregationalists considered it a good expedient, both the dissenters and the anticlerical liberals were thoroughly opposed to it. Although these two groups opposed the new measure from different premises, doubtless

9. M. Louise Greene, *The Development of Religious Liberty in Connecticut* (Boston, 1905), p. 352; *ibid.*, p. 353.

this battle, waged so heatedly from 1793 to 1795, was one of the important preliminaries before the emergence of that alliance of Congregational malcontents and dissenting pietists which formed the basis of the Democratic-Republican Party in Connecticut.

The law establishing this state endowment of religion had several revisions. When it first passed the General Assembly in 1793 it was entitled "An Act Establishing a Fund for the Support of the Ministry and Schools of Education." But this bill, and its successors, were generally referred to as the Appropriation Act or the Western Lands Act. The original act did not say specifically how funds from the sale of the land were to be appropriated by the individual churches:

> That the Monies arising from the Sale of the Territory belonging to this State lying West of the State of Pennsylvania be and the same is hereby established a perpetual Fund, the Interest whereof is Granted and shall be appropriated to the Use and benefit of the several Ecclesiastical Societies, Churches, or Congregations of all denominations in this State, to be by them applied to the support of their respective Ministers or Preachers of the Gospel, and Schools of Education, under such Rules and regulations as shall be adopted by this or some future Session of the General Assembly.[10]

The bill, as it was originally designed in the Council, had appropriated this money solely to the support of religion, but this met such opposition in the House that it was revised to include support for public schools.[11] Even then the bill passed the House in October 1793 by only a small majority, 90 to 76, over vigorous opposition. Once published, it set off a chain of political and religious reactions which startled the bill's Federalist supporters and revealed dramatically the increasing social tensions.

At least ten towns, and probably many more, passed resolutions in town meetings opposing the bill, and numerous letters appeared in the papers attacking it. So strong was this opposition that when the General Assembly met next in May 1794, the House voted 109 to 58 for repeal of the act. But the Council stubbornly refused to yield to popular pressure and voted eleven to three not to concur with the House. The bill remained as it was. However, both houses did vote to postpone the actual sale of the lands.

The act had its defenders who believed that the parishes were rapidly decaying and that all religion soon would disappear. A series of letters in *The Phenix or Windham Herald* in November 1793 began by attacking the certificate act of October 1791 for having "by one sovereign stroke vacated" two hundred civil contracts between parishes and ministers in the state.

10. Conn. State Rec., VIII, 100–101. For a discussion of these various acts see the Introduction, VIII, pp. xiii–xix.
11. For this change see *Connecticut Courant,* May 19, 1794, and *American Mercury,* April 6, 1795.

Since then all attempts to maintain the parish system have been "perfectly vain and delusory and totally inadequate." The appropriations act was, said this writer (who called himself "Argus"), a necessary expedient to bolster the system. Arguing that he would never condone any "attempt to controul the consciences of men" whatever their persuasion (provided they attended worship under teachers who have "a salutary effect upon the morals of the people") and claiming that there was nothing unfair in an act which provided support for all denominations, Argus said benignly of the dissenters "Let them all stand on an equal footing and share equally the smiles of government." "Every other method which they [the legislature] have attempted, and they have for several years past been attempting almost every other, to have public worship and instruction supported . . . has failed." But this plan he thought both effective and inoffensive.

Opposition to the act nevertheless grew even more vehement during the summer of 1794; by the October session that year even the Council decided that some alteration should be made. The House again voted to repeal the act, this time by 110 to 51. The Council instead offered a revision of the act which stated more clearly the method by which the money would be appropriated.[12]

Under the terms of the revised act (in which the House concurred by the narrow vote of 83 to 78) each parish or school district was to have the right to vote whether its share of the annual income from the fund would go for the support of the ministry or for the schools in that district. But because the vote in the House was so close and so bitterly contested, the General Assembly voted to postpone putting the act into effect until it had been published in the newspapers and the people had had a chance to express their opinions. For the next six months the debate raged, but now public opinion seemed to shift toward support of the act. Town meetings in at least nine towns expressed their votes in favor of it, although at least two town meetings opposed it (Cheshire and New Milford).[13] However, the dispute in other quarters continued to increase in bitterness. Thus, when the Assembly met again in May 1795, instead of ratifying or putting into effect the act which was passed in October 1794, it appointed a committee of members of both houses which devised a further revision of the act. This revision, with some amendments from the floor, was the act which finally passed.[14] But it almost completely reversed the original intent of the first bill.

Instead of making support of the ministry of primary or even of equal concern, the bill supported the schools first. By this act the money was to go only to the schools unless the members of some particular school district or society should vote by a two-thirds majority to transfer the money to the support of the ministry. Even in that case, the school society's request had

12. *Connecticut Courant*, November 3, 1794.
13. Conn. State Rec., VIII, xvi.
14. *Ibid.*, VIII, 237–239.

to be approved by the legislature. Then, if and when it received the approval of the legislature, the money had to be divided proportionately among all of the denominations represented in the school district. But these obstacles were so great that no school district or society ever requested its share of the perpetual fund should go to the ministry. The income from the Western Lands thus became the basis of the Connecticut public school system, with both positive and negative results for the system which lie beyond the concern of this study.[15] This new act was passed on June 3, 1795 by a vote of 94 to 56 in the House. It became effective in October 1795, after the Western Lands had been sold to the Connecticut Land Company for $1,200,000. But the acrimony aroused by the debate continued to affect the state long afterward.

Although there were many arguments against this bill during the course of the two-year debate, Timothy Dwight only slightly exaggerated when he said in 1795 that "The debate, however disguised, respected ultimately nothing but parochial taxes." [16] True, some argued primarily on economic grounds that this was not the proper time to sell the lands to get the best price for them; others argued on political grounds that war with England was imminent and the money had better be set aside for military purposes; still others argued from utilitarian grounds that the money could better be spent to pay the outstanding state debt or to promote home manufactures or for internal improvement or a dozen different projects. But generally the arguments were concerned with religion, and particularly with the question of state support of an established clergy. Implicitly, and ultimately explicitly, the debate ranged over a much wider ground — the role of religion in the state; the comparative merits of the corporate state versus the atomistic state; the Puritan's organic view of social order and the Separatist-Baptists' individualistic view of personal freedom. For the Congregationalists the danger was "loosening the bonds of society"; for the dissenters it was tightening them. When the opponents of the bill began to assert that legislators who ignored the wishes of the people on such an issue should be summarily turned out of office, they touched on one of the most vital principles of the Standing Order — a principle of loyalty of the people toward their elected magistrates — which was central to the Puritan tradition of loyalty and mutual obligations between ruler and ruled, pastor and congregation, the general good and the individual's duty. One may correctly interpret this dispute as a crucial turning point in Connecticut political and social history, at least as it transformed what before had been a speculative debate

---

15. The positive result was provision of a secure endowment for schools' support. The negative result was that the people came to rely too much on the state fund for financing schools; to avoid additional local taxes the school committees declined to make any improvements in their district schools except those covered by these funds.

16. *Connecticut Courant,* March 16, 1795, p. 2.

over "factionalism" and "electioneering" into a very real and permanent political schism both in outlook and in political practice. In short, a direct continuity exists between the adherents and the arguments set forth in this debate and the rise of the Democratic-Republican Party.[17] Anticlericalism and republicanism were the issues.

The debate had two important features for the Baptists and other dissenters. First, it enabled them to demonstrate their views and exhibit their strength: second, it proved that because of the growing anticlerical or liberal sentiment in the ranks of the nominal Congregationalists it was now possible to thwart at the state level some of the Standing Order's more cherished ambitions. Equally important, however, the dissenters clearly played a secondary role in the debate, as they were to do for many years in the Republican Party. Most of the arguments against the Western Lands Act were not phrased in terms of the Baptist ideals, and the results, although gratifying in a negative way, were not necessarily a significant step toward disestablishment. Moreover, this defeat aroused the Standing Order to a more vigorous attack on all those who threatened their position and served as a prologue to the hysteria over the Jacobinial Jeffersonians which produced the Alien and Sedition Acts and the Bavarian Illuminati scare. The dispute therefore seemed to have made the New England dissenters' position worse rather than better. It produced what today we would call a backlash among establishment conservatives and it certainly forced the evangelical dissenters into an uncomfortable alliance with the rationalist deists and liberals from which, at first, they gained almost nothing.

True, in this dispute the anticlerical (but nominally Congregational) liberals sometimes expressed great sympathy with the Baptists and professed to speak in their behalf. But they did so in paternalistic terms, speaking as "candid," "catholic," "liberal" men of the Enlightenment who hated intolerance, rather than as sympathizers with the pietistic principles on which the Baptists based their objections. Both groups were united in disliking any measure which would strengthen the hand of the Standing clergy, but they were united neither in their reasons for disliking the clergy nor in the ultimate solutions they sought. The anticlericals attacked the grasping hand of the priestcraft in the guise of freeing the mind from superstition and political tyranny; except for the fact that they really did not oppose a

---

17. For the political overtones of this debate see Connecticut *Courant*, August 11 and 18, 1794; September 1, 1794, September 8, 1794, March 30, 1795; *American Mercury,* September 1, 1794, and August 14, 1794. The old-line Federalists expressed considerable shock at the demagogic demands by the opponents of the bill that the electorate rise up and throw out of office those who supported the Western Lands Act. It was revolutionary to talk as though the people should use their suffrage to put out of office men of experience and character just because they did not like some measure which the officeholders advocated. This factionalism for party interest and power was what the Federalists feared and deplored most among the incipient Republican leaders.

general establishment, they spoke with the accents of Thomas Jefferson and Thomas Paine (whose *Age of Reason* appeared in July 1794, in the midst of the struggle). Perhaps the liberal sentiment may be best compared to that of George Washington and Patrick Henry in their advocacy of a general assessment for religion as a middle way between the establishment of the Anglican system and the secularism of Jefferson and Madison. The Baptists and Separates and Methodists spoke in the pietistic tradition for freedom for the Truth of the Gospel to prevail without hindrance from the state.

The stand of the Baptists and other dissenters on the Western Lands Act was exemplified clearly in a letter signed "Farmer" which appeared in the Connecticut *Courant,* May 11, 1795. "Farmer" had, he said, no objection to a bill to aid the schools of the state, but he was convinced that the act's main design was to provide state aid to religion.

> It is not part of the duty or business of civil rulers acting as such to make provision out of the property of the state for the support of ministers and teachers of the gospel . . . The Christian religion was originally introduced and set up independent of and unconnected with civil government; the Divine Author and his inspired followers disclaimed interference in things of that nature.

One trouble with any bill which tried to give state aid to religion was that it permitted or required the civil magistrates "to designate who they are" who deserve support, and the Bible clearly stated that "it is not the duty of civil rulers . . . to judge and determine" who should and who should not be supported. In trying to aid religion, "they may, and frequently do, instead support its opposers." History was full of false religions supported by the state, and

> among all the various clashing and contradictory sectaries existing in this state all cannot be right; we are told that error and heresy already exist, they will therefore come in and participate in the liberal provision made in this act and should they, as is feared, greatly prevail, they will of course ingross this provision and it may hereafter most fitly be termed a provision for the support of error and heresy.

This is the argument of a pietist who fears that the state will promote, to the detriment of the true religion, the Unitarians, Universalists, Arminians, or some other heretical group.

"Farmer" continued that the whole process of an establishment with religious taxes would always "infringe on the right of private judgment and conscience." Moreover, the claim that "forming and guarding the manners and morals of men" is a part of the minister's duty and also "a necessary service incumbent on the state" (as the supporters of the bill argued) led to the false conclusion that ministers "are to be considered as the officers or servants of the state and as such entitled to support from thence." But ministers (as the pietistic opponents of the bill persistently argued) "being divinely called and devoted" wholly to the service of "their divine master," they cannot in any sense be considered "civil officers." "However eminently the christian religion of the ministers thereof may subserve the good of society, it is no reason why the support of it should be assumed by the state." History would show that state support hinders rather than helps true religion. State support would "enervate, adulterate, and destroy" the churches until they were "debased and made a mere tool of state wherewith to execute the vilest purposes." In the past "Even the good state of Connecticut was not wholly clear in these respects." This bill was "totally unnecessary," "Farmer" concluded. "I would," he said, "by no means oppose worthy provision being made for the encouragement and support of this order [the ministers] — I only contend that it is a duty to be performed by christians individually or voluntary societies combined to this end." To the pietist the conception of "perpetual support" for the clergy through this kind of permanent endowment, was far worse than the system of religious taxes voted by the individual parish majorities. It was reminiscent of the Anglican system of tithes and endowments. It left no hope that the establishment might wither away beneath the advance of gospel truth.

One possible answer which the defenders of the act could have made to this pietistic line of argument would have been that the endowment fund was a better system than taxation in that it obviated the possibility of distraints and imprisonments. But because the act did not specifically eliminate the power to levy religious taxes and because it was presented as a supplement to this means of support, they did not use this argument. However, one defender of the act did try to argue that the endowment system was not open to the same objections as were religious taxes and that therefore the Baptists should not oppose it:

> As to those denominations of christians whose principles forbid their having recourse to the civil arm to compel individuals of their communion to contribute to the support of religion, on the ground that such support must be obtained by free donation . . . I do not see that their principle would in the least prevent their taking complete benefit of their proportion of the interest [from the endowment fund] . . . the measure would, as far as I know, entirely coincide with their principles as the interest . . . would be a free donation from the state, and as it is not inconsistent with their principles or their practice to receive free donations occasionally from individuals who are not of their communion, so I trust it would not to receive such donations from the state; for it is the principle and not the person which shall make such donations, that is material in this case.[18]

18. *Connecticut Courant,* March 16, 1795, p. 1.

Given the fact that Baptists in Vermont and New Hampshire often accepted ministers' lots from the state, this was a good argument. Still the principle at stake was not *how* the state supported religion but that it supported it at all. One could argue that the money from the Western Lands was as much the property of all the people as was any direct tax money and that hence the legislators had no right to dispose of it in a way contrary to the fundamental principles of religious liberty and of conscience.

The heart of the debate was not the radical principle of disestablishment, which the Baptists and their friends espoused, but instead the more specific objections raised by the anticlerical liberals. These writers had no objection to the prevailing system of religious taxes, but they strongly objected to supplementing or replacing that system with a permanent endowment for the support of religion. This, however, was a somewhat awkward position. If they had no objection to an establishment as such, it seemed perverse to object to this means of supporting religion. The anticlerical arguments used by religious liberals can be grouped under four headings. First were claims that the act would make the clergy independent of the people and therefore encourage a "permanent sacerdotal order" and an ecclesiastical tyranny. Second was the claim that the act was unfair toward the dissenters in various ways. Third was that the act would increase rather than diminish religious strife and contention both within the Standing Order and between the Standing Order and the dissenters. And finally that it was doubtful whether the act would help to alleviate the problems it was designed to solve and that it was really unnecessary as well as misguided.

The bitterness of the anticlerical attack on the clergy is evident in a letter signed "Cato" in the *American Mercury,* April 6, 1795.

> That the appropriation of the avails of the Western Lands to the use of the Clergy was long since projected by the leading individuals of that order is scarcely to be doubted. The act of Assembly that adopted a majority of the Council into the Corporation of Yale College[19] afforded a happy opportunity of securing one branch of the Legislature in their interest. From this period [1792] the design began to unfold itself . . . The schools form the most prominent feature in the present bill. The ministers are placed in the background; but so disposed that in every parish where the ministerial influence prevails, they may easily step forward and take the front. It was calculated that this disguised arrangement would give the bill a currency . . . a wonderful display of the jesuitical talents of the

19. Although in Vermont and New Hampshire acts which placed elected officials on the boards of the state universities were considered attempts to bring these universities under public control, in Connecticut a similar act was considered another example of the aristocratic unity of the clergy and the upper house in the interest of preserving the Standing Order. The principle objection to the act was not the inclusion of the governor, lieutenant governor, and six senior state senators on the board of trustees, but the gift of $40,000 of the taxpayers' money to the university. For the act see Conn. State Rec., VII, 392–394.

draughtsmen [which] . . . will give full scope to ministerial intrigue . . . It is one of the links in the great chain formed to increase and establish the influence of the prevailing order of the clergy. . . . The clergy united to a man to carry the appropriation into effect. Preaching, praying, and scribbling in its defense . . . every clergyman's son and other family connection who has been a member of the legislature . . . has been uniformly in favor of the appropriation . . . [It is] a deeplaid scheme [based upon] . . . priestly pride and priestly avarice.

Major William Judd, a Congregational liberal from Farmington and later a leading figure in the Republican Party, stated this anticlerical argument more moderately. He spoke in the legislature for the repeal of the first Western Lands Act in May 1794. His speech was reported in the *Connecticut Courant.*

If we transfer the property from the state to the several ecclesiastical societies, will not the principle go through and induce the societies to grant larger salaries to their clergymen, and thereby render them in some degree independent of their people and in circumstances far more eligible than their parishioners in general and by this means destroy that equality which is said to be the basis of a republican government? . . . I revere the clergy of this state and freely pay my money for their support, as I do my daily bread, but am unwilling the churches and people in this state should be subjected to ecclesiastical tyranny.

This act, he continued, may well "establish a clerical hierarchy inconsistent with the spirit of toleration or the principles of republicanism." [20]

In the same debate, Charles Phelps, the representative from Stonington and later a Republican leader, favored repeal because

If we look into history we shall see the ill effects of enriching the clergy and making them independent. If the Clergy find themselves enriched by the funds which are provided for their support, they will not be faithful, diligent, and attentive to visiting their people; but they will become negligent . . . In some countries of Europe one third of their property is in the hands of the Clergy who are a dead weight on the community . . . They ought to be as dependent upon their people as the members of this house are upon their constituents . . . The Clergy have great influence . . . They will exert all their influence to have the lands sold in their time, so they may enjoy the avails.[21]

To the claim that the proposed legislation was far from the evils of European ecclesiastical establishments, it was easy to reply, as "Cassius" did in the *American Mercury,* "it is objection enough that it tends to an established provision for the sallaries of an established order of Citizens. Indeed

20. *Connecticut Courant,* June 2, 1794, p. 2.
21. *Ibid.,* May 19, 1794, p. 2.

. . . half the happiness of the human race has been blasted by establishments and perpetuities with as mild and plausible beginnings as this." [22] The spirit of Thomas Paine was evident in a letter signed "Terra Firma" in the Norwich *Packet,* April 2, 1795:

> If the western lands are to be sold by an act founded in despotic principles which takes away the citizens property without his consent; and the legislature still to be the disposers of the cash, I will venture to affirm that is a plan of clerical usurpation and aggrandizement designed for the use of a privileged order of men, that are unwilling to take their masters advice . . . and be content with their wages; And that it is a continuation of that systematic care adopted in Saybrook platform, wherein the reverend clergy have under taken to add betterments to divine revelation; and exend a system big with priest-craft to all succeeding generations.

The degree of anticlericalism is difficult to account for, but these quotations accurately reflect its intensity — and not only among dissenters. Perhaps the vehemence of the phrasing was for political purposes, but that it was effective in blocking this act indicates that many people of Connecticut disagreed greatly with their ministers. Doubtless this was to some extent a reflection of the antipathy toward the high-flown Hopkinsian divinity the ministers preached in the pulpit contrasted with the simple common sense Ethan Allen and Tom Paine preached. The groundswell against the fatalistic and aristocratic implications of Calvinistic predestination combined with protests against dull, dry preaching and snobbish, wealthy ministers. And it all contrasted sharply with the rising optimistic faith in the common sense and equality of all men. The spirit of the French Revolution exalted in the Democratic Clubs and liberty pole rallies and the frequently expressed desire to substitute "citizen" for "subject" were part of a restlessness and rebellion of many people in the state. They felt that the *ancien regime* was a closed corporation in which certain families tended to dominate the political, military, judicial, and economic life of the community and that the clergy, allied by learning, intermarriage and status with this ruling elite, were dedicated to uphold this Standing Order. The clergy, said one representative in the debate in the House in May 1794, "have sometime resolved among themselves whose election they would favor and whose they would oppose." [23] And another representative added, "The clergy are a discerning set of gentlemen, and look well for themselves as respects property and influence." [24]

But anticlericalism was only one aspect of revolt against the old order. In many of the letters in the newspapers and speeches in the legislature op-

22. *American Mercury,* September 1, 1794, p. 1.
23. *Connecticut Courant,* May 19, 1794, p. 2. The man who said this was Moses Cleaveland of Canterbury.
24. *Ibid.,* June 2, 1794.

ponents of the bill made an effort to push religion to one side by saying, "The clergy are all right in their place so long as they will keep out of political issues." But the quarrel was heated precisely because the clergy considered that they had every right — indeed that they had the duty — to assert themselves in the political life of the state. Anticlerical liberalism was sympathetic in this respect to the apolitical pietistic attitude of the dissenters. Deistic rationalists and pietistic evangelicals shared a republican theory of politics. Usually when the argument took this tack the liberals opposing the act argued as though they were simply concerned for the rights of an oppressed minority. One of the first letters to appear after the passage of the act of October 1793, signed "A Citizen," took this stand. It appeared in the *Connecticut Journal* (New Haven) on October 23, 1793: "How will you distribute these funds?" he asked, since the act did not specify this important detail.

> If you appropriate them only to support *one* denomination you will incur the charge of partiality, of bigotry, and you will *deserve* it. Nay more, you have no right to do this — every citizen, the baptist, the methodist, has a right, a property in these funds and you have no right to apportion them to any one or two sects of christians. To do justice to all sectaries even the smallest number must have their share according to their lists.

A writer in the Norwich *Packet,* on March 25, 1795, pointed out that "If the appropriation succeeds the dissenters must draw their proportion of the money by certificates only; this is rendering this yoke heavier and giving their presbyterian brethren a new opportunity of oppressing them."

Opponents of the bills were precise about how awkward and unworkable the bill would be when the time came to execute it. Gideon Granger, later a leading Democratic-Republican in Connecticut, said as representative from Suffield during the debate in May 1794:

> As it [the act] respects the societies of churchmen, baptists, and all who are called dissenters, it cannot be carried into effect. Suppose five citizens of Hartford belong to the baptists society in Suffield, it is clear they cannot derive any benefit from that part which is appropriated for education. They are not to be compelled to send their children from one town to another for schooling. This would increase the expenses of education . . . They are not enabled to draw their share, for the societies themselves are to make the application. They are not to deliver it to individuals to be by them applied. One of two events must take place; either the baptists at Suffield must gain to themselves the monies of Hartford baptists; or the money must be distributed to individuals contrary to the principles of the appropriation. The fact is, that the interests of all sects are intimately blended in our schools of education. From this it follows that the ecclesiastical societies [territorial parishes] cannot apply the school money.

977

Granger's argument was correct, and doubtless led to the revision of the bill so that in its final form the money was appropriated not to the ecclesiastical societies but to the school societies.[25] In the school societies all inhabitants of the territorial parish voted, dissenters as well as Congregationalists, whereas the official ecclesiastical societies consisted only of the Congregationalists. But even this did not overcome Granger's argument that dissenting societies (congregations) had no official bounds.

Another letter, signed "Senectus," in the *Connecticut Courant* of March 30, 1795, made an equally strong legalistic attack on the revised land Act then under discussion:

> There is no provision in the bill in favor of any located society that shall hereafter be established. The members of such society [i.e., parish] from the moment of its establishment, forever lose all right and title to the money . . . Whenever a new society is formed out of part of an old society, the old society retains all the powers . . . There is no provision for any new denomination of christians than now are, that are not already formed into regular ecclesiastical societies; for the monies are given to the present existing societies and to the present existing denominations only . . . There is no provision in the bill for the dissenters who do not pay their teacher or who have no regular appointed teacher — as Quakers, for instance.

The opponents of the bill were often castigated as a pack of scheming or ambitious lawyers, but as lawyers they were, from experience, aware (as were the dissenters) of the tangles which the administration of ecclesiastical laws could and would entail. And the history of New England ecclesiastical law bears them out.

It was a part of this argument and a separate argument in itself, that the Western Lands Act, in any form, would greatly increase the social contentions and civil quarrels in the state. "Senectus," emphasizing the bill's failure to state clearly what allowances would be made for new ecclesiastical societies, added he foresaw "perpetual discord" among the two hundred to three hundred ecclesiastical societies in the state over whether the money should go to the ministry or to the schools.[26] Evidently he believed that it would require an annual vote of each society to determine this question of choice. Ephraim Kirby, another incipient Republican leader in the House of Representatives, said during the debate in May 1794,

> If the distribution of the money is to be confined to the ecclesiastical societies now organized and established by law, it will be very unequal . . . If

25. This division of the parish into two separate units, one for ecclesiastical purposes and one for educational purposes, was a further important step in the breakdown of the Puritan corporate Christian commonwealth and a great step toward the secularization of the social order in New England.
26. *Connecticut Courant,* March 30, 1795, p. 1.

the distribution is to extend to all the religious persuasions now existing in this state or that may hereafter arise its effects will be still more injurious to the morale of the people. Every dissatisfied party will separate and form a new society until the whole state is subdivided into inconsiderable petty districts.[27]

Kirby, one of the liberal Congregationalists who favored a catholic and ecumenical religious system, revealed a typical bias against itinerant preachers (who were usually Methodists or Baptists) when he predicted that under the act "Itinerant preachers without either morals or ability will be employed for the small trifle of public money which the parish draws; a reliance upon the fund will in time produce inattention to all other provision; and the strong rooted habits of the people to provide for licensed and pious Clergymen will be overcome." He probably meant to say "learned" as well as licensed and pious. Moses Cleaveland said of the fund in the same debate, there would be "the greatest confusion in parting it out to all who will be from time to time entitled to it . . . it will be the cause of lawsuits and controversies to determine what description of persons are entitled to receive the funds." [28] A letter in the *Connecticut Courant* for April 6, 1795, gave further emphasis to this aspect of the problem:

> My reasons against applying the money to the support of the clergy are — The constant increase of some and diminution of other ecclesiastical societies within the same local [parish] limits, which will occasion forever an endless ro[u]tine of discriminations attended with conflcts of jarring interests. . . . An annual scrutiny and examination into the religious opinions of the citizens will become necessary — and the question whether a man belongs to this or that society will be determined by his having conformed or not having conformed to certain laws which now exist but which may and probably ought to be repealed. . . . Resort must be had to courts of law to settle the question — then commences what the dissenters call persecution.

And finally, many opponents of the act argued that the bill was unnecessary, irrelevant, and would never accomplish the purpose for which it was designed. This argument was in some respects an extension of the anticlerical outlook, for it was argued on one hand that the clergy were well enough off already and did not need any more assistance; on the other hand it was said that the reason so many parishes had trouble keeping their ministers was that the ministers were incompetent and that the remedy for this was to get more pious men and not to give more money to the current incompetents. William Edmond (or Edmonds) from Newton said, for example,

> Is there a single child in the state destitute of the privileges of a school?

27. *Ibid.*, May 19, 1794, p. 2.
28. *Ibid.*

. . . Is there a single town, is there a single parish, unprovided with a decent house for public worship? . . . Are they not for the most part in a prosperous and flourishing condition and well supplied with preachers except in a few instances . . . ? Are not the clergy in general and their families in affluence? They are. Where then is the necessity for this very extraordinary measure at this particular time? [29]

A writer named "Civis" in the *American Mercury* was more bitterly opposed:

> If the Clergy would pay more attention to the study of their profession, particularly to that simple elegance in composition and natural engaging delivery which is calculated to gain attention, we should find fewer disputes between ministers and people, less complaint of societies broke to pieces by different sectaries, and of the unwillingness of the people to support the preaching of the gospel.

He scornfully favored giving the money "to the education and better qualification of those who are candidates for the important work of the ministry," thereby improving the quality of the clergy to the point where people would be happy to support them.[30] John Allen, deputy from Litchfield, said frankly that "The curse upon us is that we have so many men in the pulpit who are so incompetent to the duties of their profession. It is not strange that the people should reluctantly pay their money for *chips and porridge* instead of the genuine milk of the word." [31]

To all of these arguments the proponents of the act had ready answers. They declared that there were forty to fifty parishes in the state which for years had had no pastor "for want of support." [32] They said that most ministers who were supported received barely enough to keep their families:

> The usual salaries of clergymen in this state are from sixty to a hundred and thirty pounds. In some instances they have a settlement, and in some not; in some instances they have a parsonage and in some not; in some instances they have their supply of wood found them and in some not; and averaging the amount of their salaries, they will not, I presume, amount to more than eighty or an hundred pounds. I would now ask my fellow citizens of this state, can a man with a family live on eighty or an hundred pounds, and live in the manner they all wish their Minister to live in? . . . but they are obliged . . . to live in a parsimonious manner . . . unless they, in defiance of the censures of mankind, engage in some emolumentary occupation which may serve as an auxiliary to their salaries . . . [and] the families of clergymen are commonly left destitute [when the minister dies] . . . We are all ready enough to complain of the dull,

29. *Ibid.,* May 26, 1794, p. 2.
30. *American Mercury,* February 24, 1792, pp. 1–2.
31. *Connecticut Courant,* May 26, 1794, pp. 1–2.
32. *Ibid.,* May 5, 1794, p. 3.

uninteresting, unentertaining and uninstructive preaching of our clergymen and how far that arises from a deficiency of support I will leave every person to reflect at his leisure.[33]

They argued also that the Western Lands Act would "ease the burdens of the poor" by relieving them of paying religious taxes each year. "Philanthropos" said in the *Connecticut Courant,* April 14, 1794,

> By the appropriation act, the burdens of small and poor parishes, the inhabitants of which are obliged to pay six pence or eight pence on the pound to support the ministry, will be greatly eased, and they will be confirmed and prevented from scattering and breaking to pieces in consequence of the burthen of supporting public worship. By the assistance this will give to parishes which are still less in number and ability to support the ministry and in which otherwise the public worship could not be kept up, it will be supposed, and there will be a more general diffusion and enjoyment of the means by which the citizens of the state may be made wise, useful, and good, than upon any other plan.

Proponents of the bill rejected the claim that this money would enrich the ministers on the grounds that it would go to the parishes; there would be no way in which the ministers could increase their salaries except by the vote of the parish. Therefore they rejected the objection that this act would make the clergy too independent — though one might assume that parishes would certainly be more lavish and salaries more secure when the money was so easily available.

A clearcut difference of opinion also existed between the opponents and proponents of the bill regarding the current difficulties over raising religious taxes. The proponents not only denied that all parishes were well provided for and that all ministers well paid, but they also denied that the people paid their religious taxes gladly and hence had neither need nor wish for an endowed system.

> There are some who are inimical to the public worship, and many who had rather have none than pay anything for its support. Many others are in principle against all support of public worship but what arises from the private donations of the people. . . . From these sources the upholding of public worship is become already unpracticable in some places and extremely difficult in others. As selfishness and disregard to religion increase this will become more and more the case. But the appropriation makes an easy provision in these cases.[34]

Several opponents of the bill claimed that people paid their religious taxes cheerfully Thaddeus Benedict of Reading argued in the legislature: "The

33. *American Mercury,* April 14, 1794, p. 1.
34. *Connecticut Courant,* April 14, 1794, pp. 1–2.

people are accustomed to the taxes which are necessary for the purpose of religion and pay them willingly." [35] One argument for using the appropriation money for highways and other internal improvements was that people could pay their ministers in food, clothing, or wood, but they had to pay other taxes in labor or money; therefore they were better able to pay their ministerial taxes than they were any other kind of taxes. Another opponent who wanted the money to be put in the Hartford or New London banks or in a state bank said "The clergyman depends for his support upon the rich and those of decent property, not upon the poor," and therefore had no trouble collecting his salary.[36]

To the opponents who said the act would increase schisms and separations, the proponents answered, "It ought to be considered that separations from motives of interest [rather than conscience] simply, which I trust none will deny have been very operative, will be greatly diminished. And this in proportion as the expenses of public worship are defrayed out of public funds." [37] In short, there would be less reason for dodging taxes. Moreover, "Because the larger the society the larger the funds for the support of public worship [and the lower the tax necessary]. So therefore as considerations of interest prevail, the proposed measure instead of causing separations will tend to consolidate the people into large bodies." [38] In this regard, the large city churches would undeniably get more money than would the small rural parishes which perhaps needed it more, but that problem was insoluble.

Also undeniable was that the Standing Order would definitely gain the largest share of the funds, but that too seemed only fair. What was most unfair was that the fund tended to freeze the proportion of members in each denomination or to attract persons having little faith to the largest denomination. New churches or societies would get such a small amount of money that their members would have to contribute more of their own funds. Logic suggests that this was the prime purpose of the act — to strengthen the Congregational churches and to prevent further growth of the sects. Timothy Dwight, in his sermon favoring the act, affirmed that most certificate men were tax dodgers and Nothingarians who would be regained to the Standing church under this act — or at least that the act would prevent any more of them from leaving.[39] The act's supporters also argued that it would improve the quality of the ministry because, by giving them better, more secure salaries, it would attract better men to the profession. This would then produce better preaching and more time for preparing sermons: "If we have poor preachers," said William Hart of Say-

35. *Ibid.*, May 19, 1794, p. 1.
36. *Ibid.*, April 6, 1795, p. 1. This same writer said that school teachers always demanded payment in specie while ministers accepted it in goods and produce. This is presumably because teachers were often non-residents and usually not married.
37. *Connecticut Courant*, April 6, 1795, p. 4.
38. *Ibid.*
39. *Ibid.*, March 16, 1795, p. 2.

brook in defense of the bill, "it is for want of ability to employ gentlemen better qualified. This act will remedy the difficulty and enable the people to place in the desk and in their schools, learned, able, respectable gentlemen." [40]

The arguments on both sides could be summed up briefly. The proponents of the bill agreed with "A Friend to Religion" that "Religion is indispensable to good government . . . [and] it is probable that this is the last and best opportunity that the state ever will have to put a helping hand" in its behalf.[41] The opponents of the bill agreed with the citizens of New London who voted in town meeting in March 1794, that they saw no reason why the legislators had a right "to sell our lands for preaching." [42]

The immediate result of the debate cannot be called a Baptist victory, though it was one in which they shared. The anticlerical or liberal Congregationalists (the incipient Democratic-Republican leaders) were the most articulate and forceful opponents of the measure. It was certaintly a defeat for one of the more original and imaginative attempts by an American state to cope with the problem of church and state during this period of transition from an establishment to voluntarism. It was a victory for republicanism. It is difficult to explain why the dissenters in general, particularly the Baptists, did not make a more vigorous attempt to organize their denominational voices and votes to defeat the bill. The minutes of the various Baptist associations make no mention of the debate. No one established special committees to prepare petitions. There is a tradition that at the May 1794 session of the legislature the Baptists and other dissenters staged a great rally on the steps of the Hartford State House and that John Leland addressed the throng with a stirring speech. But there is no record of this event in contemporary newspapers or any other source.[43] Doubtless, the dissenters made their opinions known in the various town meetings, however, and some of the anonymous letters to the newspapers bear their stamp. But since the Congregationalists were being attacked for intermeddling in politics, the Baptists no doubt felt that they should practice what they preached — and keep their churches out of politics.

The defeat of the Western Lands Act helped to embitter the Standing Order and to foment the Federalist reaction of the late 1790's. It also

40. *Ibid.*, June 2, 1794, p. 4.
41. *Ibid.*, May 5, 1794, p. 3.
42. *American Mercury*, March 31, 1794, p. 3.
43. Greene, *Religious Liberty in Connecticut*, pp. 388, 423. Greene says that at this rally the speech Leland delivered was later published as *A Blow At the Root*, but this is clearly a mistake. This tract was a fast day sermon given in Cheshire, Massachusetts, in 1801; it was wholly concerned with Massachusetts ecclesiastical affairs. Leland does not mention such a meeting in any of his writings. However, someone described as an eyewitness to the rally claimed that Leland did deliver such an address to a large and angry throng at that time: see E. H. Gillett, "Historical Sketch of the Cause of Civil Liberty in Connecticut, 1639–1818," *The Historical Magazine* (Morisania, N. Y.), IV (July 1868), 28.

helped to coalesce and define that political cleavage which produced the two-party system in Connecticut. Within the next few years, almost every important opponent of the act became a leading figure in the new party. For the Congregational clergy, the defeat led to the inauguration of an aggressive evangelistic campaign designed to outdo the dissenters and to put the deists on the defensive. Dwight and Beecher engineered a revival movement which successfully transcended the bitter theological cleavages within the denomination at the turn of the century; in the overarching desire to save souls (and to save the Standing Order), they produced a new theology (the New Haven Theology, "Taylorism," or "Beecherism") which subtly transformed Calvinism into nineteenth-century Arminian evangelicalism.[44]

Partly in self-defense against this so-called "Protestant Counter-Reformation" [45] in Connecticut, and partly from the hope that the election of Jefferson and the rise of the Republican Party had finally provided the environment for the final, complete overthrow of the established system, the Baptists made their last concerted effort as a denomination to engage in political action. This effort, "The Baptist Petition" movement, which began in 1800, symbolically launched the fight for separation in Connecticut into its final phase.

44. This story is brilliantly told by Sidney Mead in *Nathaniel W. Taylor* (Chicago, 1942); also Charles R. Keller, *The Second Great Awakening in Connecticut* (New Haven, 1942).
45. The term was coined by Evarts B. Greene in his essay, "A Puritan Counter-Reformation." American Antiquarian Society *Proceedings,* n.s., XLII, 17–46.

Chapter 50

The Baptist Petition Movement,
1800–1807

Feeling ourselves aggrieved with the laws establishing religion in this state, we beg leave to present ourselves before your honorable body to briefly state our ideas of sundry of those laws and to request complete relief.

Baptist Petition to the Connecticut legislature, 1803

One may compare the Baptist Petition Movement in Connecticut which began so hopefully in 1800 and ended so dismally in 1807 to the efforts of Isaac Backus and the Massachusetts Baptists from 1778 to 1781. The Connecticut movement attempted to arouse the conscience of the Congregational majority in the state to rectify the grievances of the dissenting minority. The mood of the petitioners was not one of fanatical or aggressive indignation. It was born of a serious and sober conviction that injustice and discrimination had continued long enough. The restrained but determined mood underlying the movement is evident in the address Elder Amos Wells of the Second Baptist Church of Woodstock delivered in April 1799 to the assembled voters of the town at their town meeting. He hoped the freemen of Woodstock "may be persuaded not to make use of the advantages put into their hands by civil law, to oblige their dissenting brethren to lodge certificates to pay taxes to support public worship where they do not belong." [I wish] those of the standing order or present establishment . . . to suppose themselves in the place of these dissenting brethren and see if they can find themselves willing to shift sides; not that I would wish for the change, for if there must be a law established religion I wish not to be included in it, for I had rather suffer wrong than do wrong." But "I ask for my freedom and the freedom of my brethren by virtue of our birthright." The text of his address was Acts 21:28, "But I was born free."

"How men of good sense and real abilities," said Wells, "can positively assert that there is no religious establishment in this state or law preference given to one sect above another is to me next akin to unac[c]ountable. . . . 1st None but the standing order have located parishes or societies" and are able to tax all within their territorial bounds. "2d All non-resident lands must pay to the standing order; certificates avail nothing in this case." And third, the necessity for the dissenters to file certificates gives a legally preferred status to the Congregationalists. And to justify this by saying that without compulsory taxes religion will disappear "is supposing that in order to flourish the rights of men born free must be [w]rested from them, which is an abhorrent idea and inadmissible in christian reasoning." Just as "To say others get more than we lose . . . & so on the whole it will be for the good of the community at large [if we are taxed], is as good as saying 'let us do evil that good may come.' " "As a freeborn citizen I revolt from the idea and exclaim from whence cometh this evil?" Wells and his fellow Baptists decided that the evil came from the laws which granted a privileged or favored position to the Congregationalists. On the ground that "A law preference is certainly a law establishment" they waged their petition campaign to disestablish the Congregational church by repealing all those laws which gave it a preferred position.[1]

So far as is known the petition movement originated at the annual meeting of the Danbury Baptist Association in October 1800. The association at this time consisted of twenty-six churches, most of them in the Connecticut Valley, stretching from Suffield to Middletown and including several as far west as Amenia, New York.[2] These twenty-six churches had a total of 1484 members but this number could be multiplied by five to include all the nominal adherents of these churches. At this meeting, according to a report of Elder Stephen S. Nelson of the Hartford Baptist Church,

> A number of our brethren stated and proved to us several late instances of unjust and unprovoked oppression; committed under the pretext of some of the existing laws of this state, and requested our council and assistance. In answer to their request the Association chose a committee to state and represent the case to the Stonington Baptist Association [which met the same month in Hampton] . . . a number of like instances of oppression were proved to exist in those parts also. That association then chose a committee to set jointly with ours to devise the best method of obtaining redress. The joint committee, wishing to act as good subjects of civil government and as became the religion they professed, chose two

1. Amos Wells, *The Equal Rights of Man Asserted* (Norwich, 1800). Wells gave an example of recent persecution in Woodstock involving a "Mr. C.," well-known as a leader in the Baptist church, who did not file a certificate. As a result he found himself taxed to the Congregationalists. For some reason the collector did not approach Mr. C. until three years of taxes had accumulated against him, and he was forced to pay them all at once.
 Wells felt it necessary to conclude his speech by declaring, "I would not be understood from what I have said to be an advocate for all kinds of religion and no religion, for it is foreign from my heart to harbour the idea. I contend for every man's right, not for every man's religion."
 2. Wells's church in Woodstock belonged to the Stonington Association at this time; there is no evidence that he initiated the petition campaign.

of their number to remonstrate and petition for relief. A petition was accordingly prepared and presented to the joint committee and received their approbation. From thence to the association[s] and received theirs. Several of our members were then chosen as a committee to superintend the printing and circulating said petitions and also the presenting and advocating them before the Honorable General Assembly.[3]

No record of this appears in the Danbury Association minutes of 1800, but the Stonington Association minutes that year report, "The committee appointed to examine the letter from the Danbury association after examining the same brought forward a petition to be presented to the general assembly of the State of Connecticut to be holden at Hartford . . . May, A.D. 1801 . . . which was read and received." The committee consisted of Elder Zadock Darrow (Waterford, New London); Elder Christopher Palmer (Colchester First); and David Bolles, Jr. (Ashford Third). After the Stonington Association voted to lend its support to the petition it approved of a committee to present the petition. Among those from the Stonington and Danbury associations who took the most active part in the movement at this stage were Stephen Nelson, Zadock Darrow, Simeon Brown, Daniel Bestor (Bester), John Hastings, Ephraim Robins (or Robbins), David Bolles, Jr., and John Bolles.

Evidently at first the petitioners had some difficulty in obtaining sufficient signatures for the petition in time for the meeting of the General Assembly in May 1801. Nelson stated in June 1801, "In behalf of the Superintending Committee," "we express our grateful acknowledgments to the public for the ample encouragement they have given the petitions the few weeks they have been in circulation. Some thousands of Freemen it appears have signed them already." However, there were, he said, three reasons why the petition had not been presented in June and could not be presented in October:

> 1st. Of more than 200 papers which were printed and sent out only about 70 or 80 have had time to be circulated and returned. 2d. Several of our friends to whose care some of them were committed have complained for want of time . . . 3d. Subsequent to our appointment so great and unhappy an increase of party spirit in political opinions took place as led us to fear that misconstructions would be made and a candid discussion could not be obtained at this May session. We therefore hesitated to publish and circulate them till a late period hoping the spirit of the

3. *American Mercury,* June 4, 1801, p. 2. Neither here nor in the petition did the Baptists give the details of the instances of "oppression" which instigated the movement. Whether these were efforts to harass dissenters as a result of the anti-Jeffersonian hysteria or whether they were simply the result of the difficulty decaying parishes found in making ends meet is unknown.

Stephen S. Nelson was a graduate of Rhode Island College (and later one of its trustees). He was one of the few college-educated Baptists in the state. He removed from Hartford to Mt. Pleasant, New York in 1801 to become principal of an academy. His departure was a serious loss to the petition movement.

times would become more favorable. At length we concluded that faithfulness to our care and trust would oblige us (at least) to prepare for a trial . . . But the present rage of party spirit and the advice of some of our most judicious friends and christian brethren, together with some other causes [perhaps lack of funds] . . . have convinced us it is best to suspend the business to some other session.[4]

Significantly, the Baptists, as this statement indicates, went out of their way to avoid becoming embroiled in the political disputes and heated dissensions over Jefferson's election and the emergence of the Republican Party in Connecticut. They recognized the danger of their petition's becoming stigmatized as a mere political maneuver by the Republicans. Not until the petition movement in its non-political form seemed doomed to failure in 1804 did the Baptists throw in their lot with the Republican Party; thereafter they campaigned as partisans for partisan ends. In 1801 the Baptists still hoped to gain the support of well-disposed Congregationalists and Episcopalians, as well as that of other dissenters, who might sympathize with their conscientious objections to the ecclesiastical system but who would not have supported a Republican Party measure.[5]

In the Danbury Association minutes for 1801 Nelson inserted the following note: "It is requested by the committee appointed to superintend the Dissenters' Petitions, that all persons who are engaged in circulating them and such as are friends to them should get as many of the Freemen of the State to sign them as they can, who have not set their names before and return them to Deacon John Bolles, Hartford, as early as the first of May, A.D., 1802." [6] Early in May 1802, the petition was presented to the General Assembly headed by the signatures of Zadock Darrow, Simeon Brown, and other members of the committee. The petitioners requested and were permitted to argue the merits of their case before the Assembly. The petition was then referred to a committee of eighteen for consideration.

The petition was a bold, root-and-branch plea for a complete repeal of all laws which in any way might be construed as establishing religion in Connecticut. It began by asserting that the subscribers, believing in freedom of conscience and opposing any system of supporting religion by taxation, and believing "that all religious establishments are opposed to the spirit of

4. *Ibid.*, June 4, 1801, p. 2. Nelson also added that perhaps the committee would have more petitions printed "for those who did not get a chance to sign." He asked those who were still circulating petitions in these towns to "be careful that no name may appear on them which is not under the freeman's oath."
5. See note 13, below.
6. While the Baptists preferred at this time to call it "The Dissenters' Petition" it was always referred to popularly as "The Baptist Petition." The Stonington Association Minutes of 1801 note the appointment of a committee "to superintend a Petition of the Freemen of the State to the General Assembly." The Episcopalians are not known to have given the petition any support, and the Baptists made no effort to include members of other denominations on the various committees to print, circulate and present the petitions.

pure Christianity," would humbly show "That some of the existing laws of this state do establish and invest the Presbyterian [Congregational] denomination so called, with many powers and claims over the other religious denominations." It then listed each of these acts and explained in what ways it gave the Congregational churches a privileged position. The acts listed for repeal were "An Act for the Settlement, Support and Encouragement of ministers and for the well ordering of estates given for the support of the ministry"; "An Act for Forming and Regulating Societies"; "An Act Securing Equal Rights and Privileges to Christians of Every Denomination in This State [the certificate act]"; and "An Act in Addition to the Aforementioned Act, passed May, 1786 [which concerned the payment of religious taxes by non-resident property owners]."

The petitioners then proceeded to "shew that under the influence and operation of the above acts and regulations many worthy citizens of this state have been thrown into prison, have been and now are harrassed with unreasonable returns at law, and unjustly deprived of their property and support." They concluded with a request to the legislature "so to repeal, alter, or amend the above-mentioned laws and regulations as not to interfere with the natural rights of freemen, nor the sacred rights of conscience, in any case whatsoever. And that the pure religion of Christ may be left alone in his hands to be governed entirely by his laws and influence." [7]

The joint committee which the General Assembly appointed to consider this petition consisted of three Democratic-Republicans (John T. Peters, Elijah Sherman, and Nathan Wilcox) and fifteen Federalists, headed by Governor Oliver Ellsworth.[8] According to one story, Ellsworth reflected the general contempt in which the committee held the petition when, at its first meeting, he took the petition, threw it on the floor under the table, and put his foot on it, saying "This is where it belongs." [9] Nevertheless the committee took up the petition point by point and their detailed report was published in several newspapers and quoted for years afterwards as the definitive answer to dissenters' complaints about the establishment. In answer to the objection

7. The petition was printed in the *Connecticut Courant*, June 7, 1802, and in John Leland, *The Connecticut Dissenters Strongbox* (New London, 1802). It was also printed in the Boston *Independent Chronicle*, June 29, 1801, p. 1, along with a letter from a man who had recently traveled through Connecticut who said that the petition "has caused an uproar almost equal to that we read of when Diana of the Ephesians was supposed to be in jeopardy . . . Church members [presumably Congregationalists] were greatly offended with the brethren who had signed it and threatened them with severe discipline. I heard a father declare that he would never speak to his son again, nor suffer him to enter his door, till he made a humble confession before the church and congregation for that . . . [It is called] 'the infidel petition.' "

8. It appears that Nathan Wilcox was a dissenter. The other members of the Committee were Noah Webster, David Daggett, Pliny Hillyer, Eliphalet Terry, Abraham Vanhorne, George Colfax, David F. Sill, David Burr, Lewis B. Sturges, Shubael Abbee, John Parish, James Morris, Jonathan Lay, Jonathan Barnes.

9. Ellen Larned, *History of Windham County, Connecticut* (Worcester, 1880), II, 296.

that the "Act for the settlement, support, and encouragement of ministers" was unjust, the committee reported that it was "an equitable principle that every member of society should in some way contribute to the support of religious institutions," and that therefore the state had a perfect right as well as a duty to require such support by law. Regarding the complaint that "An act for forming and regulating societies" prohibited the inhabitants of any town or society "from having the preaching of the gospel among themselves in their own private houses without special permission from the General Assembly," the report said there is "no such prohibition" in the present law. This complaint "is founded on a misapprehension, and . . . if such a law ever existed, it has been long since repealed." Concerning the requirement that wives and children were to be considered of the same denomination as the head of the family until they signed off (children could do so at twenty-one), the committee said it could see no harm in this. As for the certificate law, that "is as simple and liable to as few exceptions as any which hath yet been suggested." The complaint about taxing non-residents' lands for support of the Standing church in a town or society was also unfounded; the petition was apparently written before the General Assembly passed an act in May 1801, by which the taxes on non-resident lands were to be assigned to the denomination of the owner of the land. In conclusion, the committee said, "No legislative aid is necessary on any of the grounds of complaint specified in the Petition." The principle underlying the ecclesiastical laws was still valid: that the civil law concerns morals and "religious institutions are eminently useful and important" in promoting good morals. Therefore "the legislature, charged with the great interests of the community, may and ought to countenance, aid, and protect religious institutions"; on "the same principle of general utility" by which the legislature passes laws to support schools and courts of law, it "may aid the maintenance of that religion [Christianity] whose benign influence on morals is universally acknowledged." [10]

The committee's report was adopted by a large majority, the petition was dismissed, and as far as the Federalists were concerned this ended the matter. The Federalists did not alter their views on this question until they were forced to do so in 1818. The Baptists, however, did not give up. The Stonington Association minutes for October 1802, "Attended to the report of the committee appointed in October 1800, to prefer our petition. Voted to return the thanks of this association to them for superintending said petition to the General Assembly" and "Appointed a committee of brethren Asahel Morse, Daniel Bestor, David Boll[e]s, Jr., Amos Wells, Abel Palmer and Samuel West to meet brethren from the Shaftsbury and Danbury associations to consult means for the prosperity of Zion in reference to the interference of Civil Authority in matters of religion."

10. *Connecticut Courant,* June 7, 1802, p. 3. See also *Columbian Register,* March 22, 1817, p. 3.

The Baptists held a convention in Bristol on February 2, 1803 to decide on the next step. At this convention they chose a committee, headed by Daniel Bestor of Suffield, Rufus Babcock of Colebrook, and David Bolles of Ashford, to prepare a new petition in May. Before the convention adjourned it adopted the petition which this committee drew up. The petition was presented as "The Remonstrance and Petition of a Convention of Elders and Brethren of the Baptist denomination assembled at Bristol on the first Wednesday of February, 1803" — an indication that the attempt to include other dissenters had been abandoned. They made no attempt to circulate the petition for signatures, since the convention itself was considered representative of the denomination. Because the petition was never published, except in the newspapers, and because it represents the most detailed analysis available of the Connecticut ecclesiastical system as the Baptists saw it, it bears quoting here. The issue became at this point a matter of legalistic detail concerning how the inconsistent line drawn between church and state constituted an establishment of religion. The Federalists denied that their laws constituted an establishment, and the Baptists had to confute them by collecting proof of the continued constraints on their freedom which resulted from the remnants of the old Puritan system. This petition began, however, in broader terms of natural rights:

> Your petitioners believe that all mankind are entitled to equal rights and privileges, esp. the rights of conscience . . . and that all human laws which obliged a man to worship in any lawfully prescribed mode, time, or place or which compel him to pay taxes or in any way to assist in the support of a religious teacher unless on his voluntary contract, are unjust and oppressive. That all law made subordination of one or more denominations of professing christians to *another* is productive of evil . . . and that no such establishment has been nor can possibly be invented but what is contrary to the holy word of God . . . feeling ourselves aggrieved with the laws establishing religion in this state, we beg leave to present ourselves before your honorable body to briefly state our ideas of sundry of those laws and to request complete relief . . . *We ask only to be free.*[11]

The petition enumerated what in each of the state's specific ecclesiastical laws the Baptists considered evidence of an establishment. In this respect the petition of 1803 was much more precise than that of 1802.

It began: The "Act for the settlement support and encouragement of ministers" empowered "a majority of the inhabitants of a society who have a freehold estate therein, rated at nine dollars, or $134 in the common list, or persons in full communion with the church to *call* and settle a minister

11. *American Mercury,* July 14, 1803, p. 1. It was signed "Bristol, February 2, 1803, on behalf of the convention, Rufus Babcock, Moderator, David Bolles, Jr., Clerk."

among them and provide for his support." This embodiment of majority rule in the spiritual administration of Christ's church seriously injured the minority's spiritual rights; moreover, "said statute enacts that all such agreements shall be binding and obligatory on all the inhabitants of such society and their successors," thereby limiting the rights of new inhabitants or of a younger generation as to whom they wished to accept as God's minister to them. Anyone who moved into a town or parish was bound by the spiritual (ecclesiastical) contracts already enacted there. Furthermore, although it was true that "God requires all men to employ his ministry" it is manifestly contrary to God's will "to compel any man to become qualified with an estate, real or personal, before he is at liberty to obey such divine requirement. *Riches* are a legal not a scriptural qualification for the performance of religious duties; and to exclude a man from acting in the performance of such duties because he is poor, is wholly unprecedented in the annals of primitive christianity." This was a much more sophisticated, more Jeffersonian, approach to this issue than was that of the Separates in the 1750's, though in essence it echoed Solomon Paine's pietistic dislike for control of church affairs by the unwashed majority.

Next, the petition moved from the issue of choosing a minister to that of using civil taxes to support him. The "Act for forming, ordering, and regulating societies [parishes]" empowers the same money-qualified majority to tax the minority against their consciences: "Your petitioners have beheld with some degree of astonishment the clergy of the established order receiving monies that were *forcibly* collected from men who never heard, nor agreed to hear them preach, nor contracted to give them a penny."

Even the liberal certificate law of 1791, "An act securing equal rights and privileges to christians of every denomination," operated upon false premises; for under it "every person, whether citizen or alien, bond or free, if he dwells in this state, is presupposed to be presbyterian, or to belong to the established order" and therefore required to pay religious taxes to support that order "until he lodges his certificate." This was involuntary assignation of denominational affiliation by the state. "Your petitioners cannot conceive why such persons as have joined no sect whatever may not as well be presupposed to be baptists or episcopalians, as presbyterians." By what right did the state tell a man what sect he must belong to and attend worship at and support? Men thus became legally committed to one denomination before they heard the claims of any others.

The Baptists had to add that no matter how liberal the certification process was, "It is contrary to the dictates of conscience of many [but not all?] of our order to give certificates." We are told "that the giving such certificates is a *mere trifle:* if it be so we would desire that the law would not intermeddle with such a trifling business." It was no trifle to them.

In addition, "This statute requires the certificates to be lodged with and holden by the clerk of the established order, an officer not chosen by nor responsible for his office to the dissenters, and whose interest it is to depress or destroy the certificate that the dissenter may have no benefit of the same." There was also something Jeffersonian in this claim that all officers of the state must be responsible for their election or continuance in office to those over whom they officiate.

The Baptists also found it "unreasonable and unpleasant" that a Baptist who wished to change his membership from one congregation of Baptists to another — perhaps one nearer to him — "must, by a new certificate, give the established order notice of such alteration, or be taxed to their minister." That he remained a Baptist was not enough.

Without referring to the case in Stafford, the Baptists argued that "the word 'ordinarily' as used in this statute has no definite meaning or certain import, and thus the rights and property of the dissenters are rendered insecure." Which seems to indicate that the Stafford Baptists were not the only ones who had their certificates invalidated on this ground. What was more important, given the wide-ranging proselytism of Baptist (and Methodist) itinerants in the Second Great Awakening, "there are many persons of various sentiments scattered in several towns in the state whose local situation renders it extremely inconvenient for them to attend public worship weekly or even monthly, with the church or congregation of their own communion and faith." Why should these new converts (or old ones who had moved to frontier towns where there was no Baptist church nearby) be required to "pay taxes to support the worship and ministry of the established order or lodge a false certificate"? They were dissenters whether they had a church of their own nearby to attend or not.

The Baptists even insisted that the mere use of the term "established by law" in certain ecclesiastical statutes, to designate the Congregational churches, was offensive. Why should "one favoured or privileged order . . . be 'allowed' by the General Assembly or 'approved' and 'established' by law in contradistinction to all other denominations of christians who are declared [in these statutes] to be only 'tolerated' and whose difference of opinion from the 'approved' societies is termed 'dissenting' as from a given standard of faith in matters of religion"? No matter how the civil authorities might struggle to broaden toleration, the ancient predominance of the Congregational churches and parishes made it necessary to use them as the criteria or base-line from which newer denominations were to be differentiated. So fine had the Baptists' consciences become that even this was intolerable. It certainly was not equality if some were more equal than others.

The petition concluded with a request "to repeal all the laws of this state which form the religious establishment thereof" and leave religion purely a voluntary matter, unknown in the law. Yet recognizing that this was perhaps too much to hope for, "if our prayer in full cannot be granted, we request your honors to relieve us of the burden of giving certificates to be freed from taxes for ecclesiastical purposes." Or, "if certificates must be given, those who believe that religion ought to be supported by the energy of law . . . may be the men from whom certificates shall be required" — all others should be assumed to favor voluntarism. (That the state would thereby be making an assumption which probably only a minority held at this time, did not concern the Baptists.)

In probably the most revealing paragraph in this petition, the Baptists attacked the towns and parishes as soulless corporations: "Such a corporate body" as a town or parish "is not a moral agent." Ministers could not be called to their offices by a town meeting vote not only because the ministerial "calling" is "an act of divine power" but also because this is an action enjoined by God upon His people "as individuals." Here the Baptists denied both the claim that the standing minister of a town performed in a civil capacity and was therefore to be called in a civil election and the more far-reaching claim that the state and its constituent parts had a corporate essence which transcended the rights of individuals. It is no accident that at the same time the Baptists were petitioning on this basis the Republican Party was beginning its long effort to obtain universal manhood suffrage in Connecticut. Yet in fighting for the unalienable rights of the minority against the old corporate theory of society, the Baptists also expressed a healthy fear of the majority. A converted Christian majority might rule in church affairs, but an unconverted electorate should not legislate for the minority who were in the Truth. Though the Baptists here sounded like Jefferson when they said that "truth has ever been most successful when left to combat error in the open field of argument and free discussion," what they obviously believed was that if the Standing Order once lost its special privileged position it would soon wither away before the truth of the Baptists' arguments. What rights the majority of saints might have then was to become clear later in the century when the new evangelicalism became the unofficial national establishment and began to legislate the morality of the nation, using its own social ethic as the criterion for conformity.

Having presented their petition, the Baptists again requested the General Assembly to permit them to have legal counsel to plead their case before them. This time the Assembly refused. The petition was again referred to a committee. The committee reported that the petition was similar to the one rejected the preceding year and that no action was necessary on it. The house voted to accept this report by 131 votes to 45. The *Connecticut Courant,* now the organ of the Federalist Party, made some editorial "Remarks" on the petition (doubtless reflecting the opinion of the 131 legislators who dismissed it). The remarks acknowledged that although "many of the denomination of Christians called Baptists are entirely sincere in their endeavors" it seemed evident "that many have countenanced these Petitions as mere political engines." The question, "why in the midst of the strife of party, the subject of religion should constantly be brought into view by a denomination of Christians professing that 'Christ's kingdom is not of this world'?" was therefore fair. The *Courant* went on to point out that "a great majority of the citizens of Connecticut believe that their welfare is intimately connected with the preservation of our religious institutions, and that the Legislature, charged with the great interests of the community, would betray both weakness and wickedness in abandoning these strong bulwarks of society." [12]

In short, for both sides it was a matter of conscience (and democratic republicanism). But the *Courant* professed to be particularly disturbed by the new kind of factional tactics which the Baptists were using to influence the legislators. "It is well known that this Petition was printed and that each member of the Legislature was furnished with a copy at an early day of the session . . . such a measure is quite unprecedented, and it might be added, of a very suspicious aspect." This was pressure politics: one small group attempting undue influence on the legislators (who were duty bound to consider the general welfare at all times), simply for their own special advantage. Fortunately, said the *Courant,* the legislators chose to ignore and dismiss the petition: "A public discussion might have answered the purpose of inflaming passions already too heated but it could not have promoted either tranquility or religion." Some issues were best ignored by wise statesmen.

Not only were the Federalists revealing their own old-fashioned Burkean concept of a legislature, but they were also convinced that the Baptists, at best, were pawns of Jeffersonian politicians attempting to wreck the best of all governments. Why "should this subject be *pressed* at *this* time?" Obviously because Mr. Jefferson's party thought it had a chance to overthrow the Federalists in Connecticut. "Is it wise to embitter party spirit by driving men into discussions which are sure to be unprofitable, and to issue in nothing but a list of yeas and nays to be used for political purposes?" Clearly, this was not healthy for the party in power when it saw its control slipping. "Let candid and upright men who have only the public good in view answer these questions."

The Baptists' efforts to keep the matter out of politics failed. Feeling that they might as well be hung for sheep as for lambs, after 1803 they began to give up the hope of appealing to the conscience of the Federalist majority. The only possibility of achieving their goal seemed to be to side with the Jeffersonians to drive the Federalists out of power.

Probably at this time the Baptists also ceased trying to enlist the aid of other dissenters. Bishop Francis Asbury's reaction to their call for assistance from the Methodists gives sufficient indication of the continuing animosity

12. *Connecticut Courant*, June 1, 1803, p. 3. The *Courant* reported also that the petition as submitted in 1803 had three thousand signatures.

between the various evangelical denominations vying for converts as the Second Great Awakening got under way. Asbury in Connecticut, writing in his journal on May 27, 1803, said:

> The Baptists of Connecticut have sent their petition from the Assembly to the legislature of Connecticut to the bishops of the Methodist Church, that they may have their aid in obtaining toleration; what can we do, and how is it our business? We are neither popes nor politicians: Let our brethren assert their own liberties. Besides, who may now be trusted in power? The Baptists are avowed enemies to episcopacy, be the form of Church government as mild as it may be; now it seems popes, as they would otherwise term us, may be useful to them, nor are they too proud to ask for help; but our people will not be pushed into their measures; their bishops have no coercive power of this sort: if the Baptists know not what to do we cannot tell them.[13]

Asbury was correct; the Baptists had bitterly opposed them and had called them names. Both Backus and Leland had only a few years before published tracts against them. But Asbury's apolitical stand probably stemmed more from the small number of Methodists in Connecticut and from their lack of experience with the system. Ironically in the next entry of his journal he records ordaining Daniel Burrows of Hebron as a deacon; Burrows later became a leading figure in the final overthrow of the establishment in Connecticut in 1818.

At the meeting of the Danbury Baptist Association in October 1803, the delegates

> Heard the report of Daniel Bester, who was appointed [to] a Committee by the Baptist Conference at Bristol to superintend their petition and remonstrance which was carried into the General Assembly at Hartford last May: and as we could not be heard in said petition, we invest our delegates to the Stonington Association with power to meet any Committee which may be appointed by said Association to consult what further measures are necessary to prosecute the same. We also appoint our Brother Luther Savage of Hartford to be our Treasurer to receive such sums of money as may be collected to defray expenses which may arise from farther attendance to our petition and remonstrance. Also we appoint the following Brethren to be our Committee to make collection for the above-mentioned purpose and deliver the same into the hands of our Treasurer, viz. Daniel Bester of Suffield, Hezekiah West of Bristol, Peter Ambler of Danbury, and Abel Gregory of New Fairfield.

When the Stonington Association met,

> The committee appointed to confer with the committee from the Danbury

13. Francis Asbury, *Letters and Journals,* ed. E. T. Clark (London, 1958), II, 391–392.

Association respecting what further means are necessary to be attended in regard to our remonstrance &c. Reply, that they fully adopt the opinion of the brethren of the Danbury Association that it is our duty again to present our remonstrance and petition to the General Assembly and continue the same until we obtain a full redress of our grievances.

They also appointed a committee of twenty-three brethren in twenty-three different towns "to receive monies contributed to carry into effect the result of the committee" and to pay over any money they received to Luther Savage.

The petition, slightly reworded, was presented to the General Assembly for the third time in May 1804. Again the legislature refused to grant the petitioners the right to have counsel heard in support of their petition. But this time the vote to refuse the petition a hearing, passed by a much smaller margin, 106 to 77. A report on the petition, signed "A Baptist," appeared in the *American Mercury,* May 31, 1804. The writer was evidently a member of the committee which presented the petition. His letter revealed a growing indignation among the Baptists at the recalcitrance of the Federalists and a new readiness to accept and praise the support of the Republicans. The motion to allow the petition to be heard on the floor by counsel said "A Baptist" was earnestly opposed by the federal [Federalist] members of the house but ably advocated by several republican speakers of talents and eloquence." The Republicans pointed out that "this right had never been refused to anyone before . . . and that it was evidently improper to prejudge and condemn a cause before it was heard." But the Federalists argued "with a zeal that discovered a fixed determination against the motion." Their argument was "that the laws objected to in the petition were of a general nature and therefore the petitioners ought not to be heard, seeing they complained of their operation [rather than their content?]." "A Baptist" waxed indignant at this argument: "If this reasoning is just, let whatever general law be made, no person or persons are to have a hearing on the floor of the house who complain thereof." He devoted the remainder of his long letter to attacking the injustice of the certificate law and to the fact that certificates "prove a feeble defence in many instances" against the malevolence of assessors and tax collectors: "Some of the standing order are almost continually distraining in one place or another the property of dissenters who have given in certificates." He concluded,

How do the Baptists expect to get relief seeing they are the minority? They appeal with confidence to the candid part of that majority who have the power to oppress them, to consider of this thing: and to ask in their own hearts and conscience whether they would like to stand in the same situation in which they place their neighbours and brethren of other sects . . . you have fixed the laws so that no man can be taxed by the Baptist or Episcopalians &c. until he has said in a certificate that he belongs to the body that lays the tax? Be so kind as to fix the laws so as that no man can be taxed by 'presbyterian, congregational, or consociated' societies, until he has given in a certificate that he belongs to that body who lays that tax . . . give your own certificates to your own officers and then if any one of us is taxed by you, the cause can be very easily decided indeed . . . If you grant this, the petitioners are content . . . without this it is hardly to be expected that they will cease asking.[14]

Probably the views this letter presented were those of the Baptists generally. The action taken by the Danbury and Stonington associations the following October bore this out. What the Baptists did in effect was to decide to unite their denominational aims to the political efforts of the Republican Party. This meant that they were ready to join the movement to overthrow the Charter government of Connecticut and to call for a constitutional convention. They even appointed a committee to confer with the Republican leaders on the best means of achieving this revolutionary aim:

Whereas the Petition of the Baptists in this State to the Legislature for several years past praying for the free enjoyment of those religious rights which we conceive all men entitled to, has failed of success. And whereas the people of this State are without any specific Constitution of civil government which renders our religious liberty more and more precarious. And whereas a number of our fellow-citizens are engaged to obtain a Constitution of government; we have therefore thought it expedient to appoint Elders Wildman, Dodge, and Morse together with Deacon Jared Mills and Daniel Bester, as a Committee to concert measures with others of our fellow citizens in every peaceable manner that shall appear expedient to obtain a Constitution which shall draw the line between those rights which are alienable and those which are inalienable — define the powers of the several departments of government — mark out the lines of their respective operations and erect proper barriers to prevent one department from intruding on the other — secure the right of suffrage to all who contribute for the support of the law — which shall contain the means of peaceable amendments within itself; that when the time and experience discover defects, the people may remove them and be happier without the hazard of convulsion or war; and finally confirm unto us and our posterity all the blessing that can reasonably be expected from a free representative republic.[15]

Thus, in 1804, the Baptists deliberately endorsed the platform of the Republican Party, and the men they appointed to work with that party —

14. *American Mercury,* May 31, 1804, "A Baptist" said that the Baptists withdrew the petition when it was refused a hearing but that "The Petitioners have great reason to be encouraged" by the increased vote in their favor. For an answer to this letter in defense of the Federalists see the *Connecticut Courant,* June 6, 1804, p. 3.

15. Danbury Baptist Association Minutes, 1804, p. 3. For the concurrence of the Stonington Association see its minutes of 1804, p. 4. The committee appointed by the latter included Amos Wells, Reuben Palmer, George Gates, George W. Williams, and Jedediah Russell.

Wildman, Dodge, and Morse — were already active in its support. The Corresponding Letter of the Association this year was drawn up by Morse, Wildman and Nathan Bulkley in conjunction with John Leland who attended as a visiting messenger from the Shaftesbury Association. The letter was designed to arouse the members of the denomination to engage themselves in this political struggle to defeat the Federalist Party:

> The condition of the Baptists in this State is widely different from the condition of many of the Associations with which we correspond. From the first settlement of this State, *religion* has been considered as a principle of *state policy* under the notion of an *Abrahamic-Christian Commonwealth:* and the memorable revolution in 1776 had no constitutional or legal effect on the people of Connecticut to dissolve the *firm* of Moses and Aaron which many erroneously believe exists in gospel times between *rulers* and *ministers* — secure to us the liberty of conscience — confirm unto us the right of suffrage — define the powers of government — and guarantee unto us and our posterity the blessings of a free republic. As for any legal security (which indeed is variable and precarious) we have none that reaches our case in such a manner but what (unless we bow to a power which we believe the God of heaven never ordained for church and state) we are exposed to have our property taken from us by force, or our bodies cast into prison, if we do not pay the preachers which we never chose, never hear, and in whom we place no confidence as our guides to heaven. This is the truth of our case: and all our petitions to our legislature, for a repeal of these partial, cruel, illegitimate laws, have been treated both with neglect and contempt, and the petitioners have been accused of infidelity. But we have found that *Jehovah* is verily a God that regards the afflicted! Our churches do increase in numbers . . . and although they are not the learned and the wise of the world, yet they are such as God condescends to bless . . . The rights of men are better understood than they formerly were . . . we hope the Lord will deliver us from the manacles of religious establishments [and] . . . the dominion of sin.

This militant declaration of political war bears the indelible stamp of John Leland. It marks the high water mark of the Baptists' fight for disestablishment in Connecticut.

For some reason the joint committee of the Danbury and Baptist Associations failed to submit a petition at the May session of the legislature in 1805. The minutes of the Danbury Association for October 1805 simply state, "Heard the report of Brother Daniel Bester respecting his not carrying forward our Petition last spring to the General Assembly and voted unanimously that Brother Bester shall be our Agent in connection with the Agent from the Stonington Association to present our petition to the general Assembly of the State of Connecticut at their session in May next." The Stonington Association voted to continue its support of the petition and asked its members to "stand with our loins girt with truth" while the saints fight on against "the painted hypocrite with the veil of *State Religion* [who] attempts to wrest the government of the Church from the hand of Christ."

The petition was presented again in May 1806, but again the Federalist majority refused to give it a hearing. The Danbury Association in October "Heard the report of Brother Daniel Bestor who stated the treatment our petition met with last Spring in the General Assembly at Hartford; and as we obtained no hearing we still continue Brother Bestor our Agent and direct him to present our Petition to the General Court at Hartford at their session in May next." Again the Stonington Association concurred. But by May 1807 the Embargo question had arisen and the people of Connecticut were so stirred up about this that the Baptists decided not to petition that year.

> Brother Daniel Bestor reported that he had not presented our Petition to the General Assembly — Whereupon, *Voted,* That this Association view with deep concern and sincere disapprobation several of the Laws of this State relating to Religious Establishments; yet under existing circumstances they think it inexpedient to continue their exertions for redress by application to the Legislature for the present.[16]

Again, in October 1808, the Association "Voted — as the same reasons exist in the minds of the members of this Association respecting our Remonstrance to the Legislature against legal encroachments, that the case rest this year also." This proved to be the end of the Baptist Petition Movement. No further record of the committee or the petition is found in any subsequent minutes of any of the associations nor do the newspapers make any mention of the petition after 1806. The Stonington Association minutes reveal that these churches had given up the fight in 1807 when they voted "to discontinue our petition for redress of grievances and brother David Bolles from being our agent to the General Assembly."

The reasons for the failure are obvious. Insofar as the Baptists had appealed to the hearts and consciences of the majority, they had been unable to move them. Insofar as they had based their hopes on the Republican Party, they had advanced no further than did that party at the polls. Moreover, the Baptists undoubtedly found that the Republicans were more eager for Baptist votes than for Baptist principles. In any case, as the Republican Party went into a period of decline after reaching its peak in 1806, it seemed pointless to continue the petition movement. In their frustration the Baptists turned their attention to the new religious movements for home and foreign missions, for Sunday Schools, and for moral reform.[17] As in-

16. Danbury Baptist Association Minutes, 1807, p. 3.
17. Since the chief center and leaders for these activities were in Massachusetts, I have discussed them elsewhere in chapter 57. Not even John Leland's tract calling for a new constitution in Connecticut in 1806 succeeded in inspiring the Baptists to further action. *Van Tromp Lowering His Peak with a Broadside* (Danbury, 1806).

dividuals they continued to support the aims and leaders of the Republican Party, but as a denomination they reverted to their former apolitical outlook. Ultimately, however, it was through a political victory engineered by the Republicans that the Baptists achieved their goal in 1818. Because the dissenters played a large part in that political victory, it is relevant to examine how and why the two groups worked together.

From this point of view the diary of a Baptist who lived in Thompson, Connecticut during these years offers some interesting insights into the attitudes and behavior of a typical rural member of the denomination. Joseph Joslin, born in 1759, was the son of a poor Baptist farmer on Breakridge Hill in Thompson. His diary covers the period from 1777 to 1843, the year of his death.[18] It begins with his enlistment for one year in the revolutionary army with his brothers, Jesse and John. His dislike for the "diabolical" and "Damnabel torys" in Connecticut indicates the strength of his patriotism, but one year as a carter and driver for the commissary was enough for him. He then moved to Rhode Island where he worked near Smithfield as a stone mason, flax dresser, mill operator, and general farm laborer for the Arnold and Angell families and for others in the vicinity. In 1783 he married Lydia Bucklin of Smithfield in Elder Mitchell's Six Principle Baptist church. They rented a farm in Smithfield where they lived until 1796. At the time the federal constitution was to be ratified Joslin sided with the "Antifidrel" party against ratification.

After he returned to Thompson in 1796 he worked on his father's farm, served on the school committee, and attended Elder Parson Crosby's Calvinistic Baptist church, to which his father and brothers belonged. But he also enjoyed going to hear itinerant Universalist preachers like Hosea Ballou and circuit riding Methodist exhorters. In 1800 he and his family were among the few persons in Thompson to support Jefferson, and he continued to support the Republican Party faithfully. In November, 1804, he noted "I was to town meeting . . . 82 to 103 feds. So they go yet." On July 4, 1806 he and Elder Crosby "met a number of Republicans to Celebrate independence and there was a good entertainment — a good oration Delivered by Elder Amos Wells of Woodstock, John Nichols made a prayer and Read the Declaration of Independence and 5 musicians [provided music]." John Nichols was also a Baptist elder. That year Joslin noted that the Republicans received 96 votes to 109 for the Federalists.

In May 1808, Joslin helped "Asa Sheldon Raise a Liberty pole 60 feet

18. Most of the ms. diary of Joseph Joslin is in the CHS; the volumes for the revolutionary years have been published in the Society's *Collections,* VII, 297–369. For a free rendition of them see Ellen Larned, *Historic Gleanings of Windham County, Connecticut* (Providence, 1899), pp. 150 ff. Larned had access to some volumes of the diary which are not in the CHS but she took some liberties with what she transcribed. I have supplemented this diary with references to the Town Records and the ms. records of the Baptist Church in Thompson which are in the office of the Town Clerk in Grosvenordale.

high" and in September "drove to pomfret, 9 miles, to see a Methodist camp meeting" which lasted five days and nights. He helped to build a woolen factory near his home and thereafter he and his family wove wool into bed ticking for the factory. He noted with approval the election of James Madison, and his son fought in the War of 1812. In 1818 he was active in the first election of a Republican representative from his town to the General Assembly. He himself was rewarded by being elected selectman in 1818 and 1819. He found the constitution of 1818 to his liking and the town of Thompson ratified it by a vote of 174 to 95. He was now well enough off to buy two pews in the Baptist meetinghouse. In 1826 he was elected to the state legislature and went to Hartford to vote with the Republicans. There he met a Methodist who convinced him that Arminianism was closer to Biblical truth than Calvinism and along with many other Baptists at this time he switched his allegiance to the Methodist church. In the 1830's he voted for Andrew Jackson and Martin Van Buren, and regretted the "Tippecanoe craze" which elected the Whigs in 1840. He never doubted that the Jacksonian Democrats were the true heirs of Jefferson and he continued to call the parties by their original names. His entry after the election of 1840 read: "I went to town meeting; there ware more feds than there was Republicans" and the town went for Harrison. The year he died he still considered himself one of the "Republicans of the old stamp."

Joslin was not an especially religious man, though he often went to religious meetings and did his duty in his church. His formative years came in the Revolutionary Era when religious zeal was at a low ebb, and his diary throughout is concerned more with his personal problems as a farmer than with spiritual or political affairs. Yet his life reflects clearly the mainstream of Baptist adherence to the Revolutionary, anti-federalist, Jeffersonian, Jacksonian tradition.

Somewhat above the level of this common man and back country farmer, was David Bolles, Jr., who played such a prominent part in the Baptist Petition Movement. Bolles, born in 1765 (grandson of a Rogerene and son of a Separate), lived all his life in Ashford. He imbibed his hatred for the establishment in his childhood when he saw the tax collector distrain his mother's pewter (despite her tears) because his father — then a Separate — refused to pay his religious taxes. Like most Separates, his father later became a Baptist; he was ordained elder of the Baptist Church in Hartford in 1801. Young Bolles's brother Lucius graduated from Rhode Island College in 1801 and became a Baptist elder in Salem, Massachusetts. His brother Jesse was a Baptist deacon in Amos Wells's church in Woodstock and a deputy to the legislature, 1789–1791. David, himself a deacon in Wells's church, became a prominent lawyer and a leader in the Republican Party. As deacon of his church he led the movement in the 1780's which induced the members to give no more certificates and the Congregationalists yielded to their decision. In addition to promoting the Baptist Petition (which according to tradition, he drafted) for six years, he later served in the General Assembly as a Republican and was appointed Justice of the Peace. He published several tracts defending Republicanism and the Baptist faith and in 1819 he received an honorary degree from Brown University. He frequently attended the Methodist Church in his later years. He died in 1830.[19]

The complement to the Baptists' inherited antipathy toward the Standing Order (like the Bolles family) which led them to support the Republicans was the obvious scorn for the Baptists which the Congregational ministers who were attacking the Republicans expressed. Many passages in the diaries of ministers like James Cogswell and Thomas Robbins substantiate this.[20] This disregard, even contempt, for the dissenters was sometimes evident in the political actions of the ruling party. For example, the New London *Bee* reported on June 19, 1799, that a Baptist was deprived of a justiceship simply because of his denominational affiliation:

> The nomination of deac. Lemual Darrow, a reputable member of the Baptist church in this place [New London] having been agreed to by the assembly [as a Justice of the Peace] was sent to the Council for concurrence: but the Upper House negatived the appoint for the reason, as was declared in the committee of conference, that the candidate was a dissenter.[21]

There was an equal obtuseness in the Federalists' insistence that all admirers of Thomas Jefferson must be atheists and enemies of a Christian society: "Consider the effects which the election of any man avowing the principles of Mr. Jefferson would have upon our citizens," said a writer in the Connecticut *Courant* on September 8, 1800; "The effects would be

19. Larned, *Windham County*, II, 296, 303, 373, 376, 459; Clarence W. Bowen, *The History of Woodstock, Connecticut* (Norwood, 1926), pp. 311–312. About David Bolles, Sr., see William B. Sprague, *Annals of the American Pulpit* (New York, 1860), VI, 474, and about Lucius Bolles see *ibid.*, VI, 474–476.

20. The ms. diary of James Cogswell is in the CHS; it contains many unflattering references to the Baptists because they invaded his parish in 1788, converted many of his congregation, and founded a church there in the year 1788. Cogswell characteristically referred to them as "Separates" though they were antipedobaptists. One of his remarks indicates how deep-seated the social prejudices were against Baptists: "heard yt ye wid[ow] Bingham has refused to marry Eb[enezer] Burnham because he attends the Anabaptist Meetings." The widow later relented and became a Baptist herself, which is also significant. About Robbins see *Diary of Thomas Robbins, 1796–1834*, ed., I. N. Tarbox (Boston, 1887), I, 90, 343, 470. Robbins, the standing minister in Windsor, Connecticut (1808–1827) was equally contemptuous of Baptists and Methodists.

21. New London *Bee*, June 19, 1799. A similar report in the *Connecticut Courant*, February 9, 1801, p. 3, stated that at the preceding session of the legislature, the lower house had voted a commission in the militia to a Universalist but the upper house had refused to confirm it because he "was not orthodox in his religious sentiments."

to destroy religion, introduce immorality, and loosen all the bonds of society." What was more, since this was "a Christian nation," think of "the dishonor which would be done to God," and consider "the fear of his displeasure if an opposer of Christianity should be preferred" as President. That Jefferson had helped to separate church and state in Virginia was considered a prime argument against his election.[22]

But the Baptists did not become Republicans because Republican leaders in Connecticut went out of their way to seek or to encourage their support. Though one may trace the beginnings of Jeffersonianism to the early 1790's, if not earlier, not until 1802 did the party think the Baptists and other dissenters worth courting. Republican party leaders like Ephraim Kirby, William Judd, Pierpont Edwards, and Abraham Bishop, happy to attack the Standing Clergy, were equally ready to denounce the dissenters' fanaticism. Not once in the 1790's did any Republican or anti-Federalist argue either in Baptist or in Jeffersonian terms that the certificate system or compulsory religious taxes were unjust or discriminatory toward dissenters and should be abolished. Although the 1800 election campaign was filled with anticlerical speeches by the Republicans, none of them touched on the issues so important to the Baptists. Disestablishment simply was not an issue in Connecticut in the 1800 election. Not until the Baptist petition forced the Republicans to take a stand did they acknowledge it. And even then their commitment was vague. However, after 1802, when the Danbury Baptist Association elicited from President Jefferson his famous letter enunciating the doctrine of "a wall of separation between Church and State," the Republicans in Connecticut did begin to ask Baptist elders to participate in their annual Fourth of July celebrations.[23] There is some irony in that: to separate church and state, join the party.

22. See, for example, the *Connecticut Courant*, April 20, 1803, p. 2, where a writer notes "Mr. Jefferson has induced the Legislature of Virginia virtually to declare by law that it is as unimportant to society whether a man believes or disbelieves the existence of God and a future state of rewards and punishments as whether he is informed or uninformed of the principles which govern the movement of a Steam Engine or the act of surveying." In Virginia, "atheistical principles are as much protected as religious opinions" but "An Atheist would not be allowed to testify in our Courts."

23. Jefferson's famous letter came in response to an address voted by the Association in October, 1801, which is less well-known but relevant here: Here in Connecticut, it began "we have no constitution and religion is considered as the first object of legislation: and therefore what religious privileges we enjoy (as a minor part of the state) we enjoy as *favors granted* and not as *inalienable rights;* and these *favors* we receive at the expense of such degrading acknowledgments as are inconsistent with the rights of freemen." Your enemies reproach you here because you do "not assume the prerogatives of JEHOVAH and make laws to govern the kingdom of Christ. Sir, we are sensible that the President of the United States is not the legislature, and also sensible that the national government cannot destroy the laws of each state, but our hopes are strong that the sentiments of our beloved President . . . like the radiant beams of the sun, will shine and prevail thro' all those states and all the world, till Hierarchy and tyranny are destroyed from the earth . . . we have reason

The Baptists' efforts to use the Republican Party — or to persuade its leaders in Connecticut to make clearcut commitments to their goal of disestablishment — were fraught with frustration. The Party would not, and could not, move as fast and as directly in this matter as the Baptists wanted. But the Baptists had no alternative. The Federalists had slammed the door on their petition movement. So the Republicans opened their door a little.

to believe that America's God has raised you up to fill the chair of state." It was signed for the Association by Nehemiah Dodge, Ephraim Robbins and Stephen S. Nelson. I have not found this letter or Jefferson's reply printed in any of the Connecticut newspapers of the time. It did appear in the Boston *Independent Chronicle,* January 25, 1802, p. 2. Oddly the Danbury Association Minutes, although they mention writing to Jefferson, neither printed the letter to him nor mentioned his reply.

Chapter 51

The Dissenters and the Republicans
in Connecticut,
1800–1812

Among the various schemes which the enemies of our state government [the Jeffersonians] have adopted to promote their grand object, self aggrandizement, no one has been so successful as their attempt to enrol under their banners the minor sectaries of christians.

Connecticut *Gazette,* June 9, 1802

Apart from Abraham Bishop's brief and ambiguous reference to "intolerance" in his famous New Haven oration of 1800,[1] the first sign that Baptists and Republicans were about to avow their political unity came in the speeches two Baptist elders delivered at Republican Fourth of July rallies in 1801. Elder Nehemiah Dodge participated in the rally in Suffield; Elder Daniel Wildman participated in the rally at Bristol. Neither of their addresses was published, but the following year Elder Asahel Morse's *Oration Delivered at Winsted, July 5th A.D. 1802* was printed in Hartford. Undoubtedly it is typical of the genre. Morse was elder of the Baptist church in Suffield, a Republican stronghold from the outset. He was prominent in politics throughout his life; in 1818 he was sent as a delegate from Suffield to the constitutional convention. He began his oration in Winsted by pointing out that although the Puritans left England to get away from religious and political tyranny, "no sooner were our fathers

---

1. Abraham Bishop, *Connecticut Republicanism* (New Haven, 1800), preface. Bishop's remark (which he may not have used in his original oration) in this preface is "Intolerance with its hydra heads still roams about the State." But whether he refers to political intolerance or religious intolerance and whether, if the latter, he is simply talking about the attacks on deism and infidelity, is unclear. He refers often in his oration to the hoax of the Bavarian Illuminati concocted by the Federalists, but he does not refer to the oppression of the Baptists or of other dissenters, nor to the need for disestablishment. Like most Republican party leaders in 1800, Bishop did not think it expedient to make specific appeals to Baptist voters. In his appendix, however, he defends Jefferson against the unjust charge of atheism.

settled as a colony than they became unmindful of the goodness of God to them; and disregarding the natural inalienable rights of their fellow-men proceeded to exercise the same spirit of religious intolerance as that from which they fled by establishing an aristocratical hierarchy in religion." But, he noted happily, "the spirit of intolerance has greatly subsided, and the true principles of liberty and equal rights are better understood." He then gave thanks for the Revolutionary heroes — Franklin, Randolph, Hancock, Laurens, and Washington — and called the Revolution "one capital blow at the kingdom of the beast." Like all orators of the day he was eloquent about the rising glory of America. But he gave his vision an evangelical millennial flavor: "I may be deemed enthusiastic," he said, "but I believe God guided our victory" and "the divine conduct towards America is held up in providence to all nations as a specimen of the kind regard of the Lord to the liberty of man." For "the best way of destroying error in opinion is not to raise the civil sword, but to propagate the truth as it is in Jesus." "It is highly probable then that America is reserved in the mind of Jehovah to be the grand theatre on which he will accomplish the most glorious events." "America stands, in the earth, like the sun in the heavens, the center of light and the wonder of an admiring world who feel the influence of its rays." He noted with regret that there were still "unhappy divisions among us" and deplored "the rapid progress of infidelity, of licentiousness, of scepticism," but he also argued that only complete freedom for religion could curtail these and give the gospel the victory.

The two most direct political references in his oration concerned "The sacred rights of conscience" and the election of Jefferson. Concerning the first he stated that "It is much more to be desired that the constitution and statutes of every state [in the United States] were strictly conformable in all ecclesiastical affairs to the federal constitution" — by which he meant the disestablishment clause in the First Amendment. Concerning Jefferson, he said,

> Gentlemen, we have now a bright star in the presidential chair which arose in the time of British tyrannical darkness in our country, whose brilliant rays of republican light dawned over our land and illuminated the minds of our citizens and inspired them with the love of freedom and with ardor and zeal for our independence and liberty, of whose patriotism and love of liberty . . . of whose integrity and upright intentions we have had long experience . . . like the steady sun in the firmament [he] continues to shine and dispel the mists of error and smoking fogs of aristocracy, generated by the devotees and satellites of tyranny and despotism . . . Blessed be God that we have such a man at the helm of our national government.

That same year Elder Nehemiah Dodge also gave a Republican oration at a Fourth of July rally in which he was much more explicit about the

1007

need for disestablishment. He hoped that all civil magistrates would soon "be convinced that they have no right to assume the seat of God Almighty in making laws to regulate, dictate and control in matters of religion and act accordingly by withdrawing their aid from those who have nothing greater to lean upon and grant the petition of the oppressed, viz. to let us alone as to our religion." But what he meant by this "laissez-faire" doctrine was that God was the only true support for religion:

> Let us trust in God to secure and defend our churches . . . Let us trust in God to supply our churches with ministers, who calls them by his grace . . . Not like some who say if men have learning sufficient and have an inclination to the work, are licensed by the clergy and called by the major vote, they have a right and they only, to preach, and that pretending to an internal call from God as above mentioned is enthusiasm.[2]

After 1802 Republican newspapers gave considerable attention to the views of the Baptists and other dissenters. Several times they reprinted Madison's famous Remonstrance and Jefferson's Bill for Religious Freedom. They also printed the names of all those legislators who voted for and against the Baptist petitions since almost all of the Republicans voted in favor of them. The Federalists soon realized that they had lost the votes of the dissenters, but the only argument they could find to alter this was to proclaim themselves as the true defenders of Christianity. An editorial in the Connecticut *Gazette* in 1802 which reveals some of the alarm the Federalists felt is typical of their reaction:

> Among the various schemes which the enemies of our state government [the Jeffersonians] have adopted to promote their grand object, self aggrandizement, no one has been so successful as their attempt to enrol under their banners the minor sectaries of christians. Whether they be aggrieved or not the regards which the leading democrats profess for them are mere crocodile moanings. Such an association can answer no other end but to lessen the general influence of religion upon society and promote the work of confusion. Good may arise out of evil, but the wisdom of this world would say that the interest of Christianity cannot be promoted by advancing the power of its enemies.

The article stressed the point that Federalists were the true defenders of

2. Nehemiah Dodge, *A Sermon Delivered at West-Springfield, Massachusetts, July 5, 1802* (Hartford, 1802), pp. 19–22. Dodge had a long and colorful career in Connecticut. It started in the Baptist church in Hampton in 1788; from there he moved to Southington, to Berlin, and then to Middletown. In 1805 he became pastor of the Baptist church in Lebanon where he remained until 1814. In or about 1820 he became a Universalist. Thereafter he was pastor of the Universalist Church in New London. He early lent his support to the Republican Party and published many tracts and orations denouncing the established system. His position among the Baptists is discussed below.

Christianity against the infidel and deistic Republicans and that if "the minor sectaries" had the true interest of religion at heart they would stay with the Federalists and the Standing Order, for Christians must stick together.[3]

In April 1803 the *Connecticut Courant* took the same stand against dissenters and the anticlerical Congregationalists who sided with them. When a democrat is asked how he can support for office persons "openly opposed to the Christian religion," said the writer, he replies that "the civil magistrate as such has nothing to do with religion." He says "that the province of religion and that of politics are wholly distinct and ought never to interfere and that infidelity is no more inconsistent with the duties of the magistrate than those of a physician, a lawyer, a farmer or a mechanic." With this argument, said the writer, we vigorously disagree. "No Christian need be told that the end of all God's work is the happiness of his creatures" and since happiness depends on good order and morals in society, the magistrate had a duty to support Christianity. The Bible says that the magistrate is the minister of God for good to the people. For those who argue that the use of taxes to support religion is not for the best good of religion just let them compare Connecticut and Rhode Island. "Civil government is subservient to the great interests of religion." But the democrats are men "whose avowed object is to oppress the clergy, to deny them all support by law, and to break down the whole system of ecclesiastical polity." [4]

But the first article in which the Federalists appealed to the Baptists directly and by name appeared in the *Connecticut Courant* in April 1804. It merely repeated the earlier arguments, the ineffectiveness of which was sarcastically revealed in an answer written by "A Real Baptist and a True Republican." He began, "The piece appeared to me to be evidently designed for the purpose of electioneering; the writer however, will probably find the Baptists are too stubborn to be turned by flattery, hypocrisy, and misrepresentation." The writer in the *Courant* "compliments us on account of the orthodoxy and evangelical piety &c. of some of the champions of our faith. So Joab with his right hand took Amasa by the beard to kiss him and called him brother when his only intent was to murder him." What did the writer mean when he said "Most of the leaders in this country are the open and avowed enemies of the cross of Christ"? Certainly he could not mean "Tom Paine, for he holds no office, and can be considered as a leader only in opposing Christianity; for he supposes it will fall to the ground if it is not supported by the civil law; and every federalist who preaches that in order for religion to stand it must be supported by the civil law is one of his followers."

Doubtless the Federalist writer meant to attack "our President and

3. Connecticut *Gazette* (New London), June 9, 1802.
4. *Connecticut Courant,* April 6, 1803, p. 1.

heads of departments under his government." But "upon what ground did he assert that they are the open and avowed enemies of the cross of Christ? Surely not from any evidence, for had that been the case he could have stated it." And he gave none. His aspersions on the president are "unchristian, inhuman and wicked." The "real Baptist" then refuted the arguments that Jeffersonian democracy would lead "to the bloody scenes of France." The French people, he said, had been so badly oppressed and kept so ignorant that it was not surprising they went too far "under a false notion of liberty." He refuted the claims that "infidelity" and "democratical principles" were responsible for "the low state of religion in Virginia" by reminding the Federalists that "Within the four years past there has been a great revival of religion in many parts of Virginia and the States South and West of that." In addition

> the greatest part of the revivals of religion which have been within the past year in Vermont and many towns of New England have been principally among republicans . . . And that religion flourishes amongst those who are called democrats in Connecticut is evident from the late revival in the society of Chester in the town of Saybrook; and the present work of the Lord by his grace in the Baptist society of Stratfield.

The Federalist writer in the *Courant* had called the Virginians oppressive for "prohibiting Negroes whether bond or free from assembling in the night for worship;" but why do not the Federalists redress "the grievances of their brethren who are groaning under the galling yoke of ecclesiastical oppression at home"? And here he described a recent case of a Baptist distrained of a yoke of oxen for religious taxes and another Baptist who was "imprisoned in the gaol at Hartford in the cold season of the year where he lay for a long time while his family were suffering for his assistance at home."

> We presented a humble remonstrance and decent petition to the Assembly at their session at Hartford last May praying for redress of grievances; and notwithstanding some of the leading federal characters in both houses promised to use their influence to have our petition heard, and its merits tried, yet when it was brought forward, those very men were some of the first in opposing our being heard and the merits of our cause being tried . . . The alarm which federalists are continually sounding that *religion is in danger of being lost,* proves that they are not only destitute of real religion but are ignorant of what it is.

He concluded praising God for the "wise and good government and peaceable and mild administration" which Jefferson had provided the nation with for three years. This had in itself proven all of the Federalists' dire predictions in 1800 wrong.[5]

5. The Baptist's letter appeared first in the *Republican Farmer,* April 25, 1808, and was reprinted in the *American Mercury,* September 27, 1804, p. 1.

Although this letter was an effective bit of political banter, the most sustained and well-reasoned statement of the Baptists' position in Connecticut politics at this time appeared in a hundred-page tract entitled *The Age of Inquiry . . . A Clue to the Present Political Controversy in the United States.* It was published in Hartford in 1804 and signed "A True Baptist" by its anonymous author. From its content one assumes that the writer lived in New York State near Albany but had previously lived in Connecticut. Probably a good guess is that the author was Stephen S. Nelson, who left Connecticut and moved to Mt. Pleasant, New York, in 1801, after he had initiated the Petition Movement. The fact that the book contains an appendix which was a detailed reply to the report of the committee of the Connecticut General Assembly which rejected the petition in 1802 reinforces this identification.

The book had three purposes: the first was to prove that Thomas Paine's arguments against religion were wrong in assuming that the Bible supports monarchy and priestcraft. The second, that because the Bible really supports republicanism, it was the duty of all Christians to support republicanism. And the third was to arouse the New England Baptists (specifically Connecticut Baptists) to throw off the legal chains of ecclesiastical tyranny by voting for the Republican Party. Thus, the book was a campaign document to overcome those Federalist arguments which equated Republicanism with deism or infidelity and to overcome any Baptist doubts about the necessity of engaging in politics on behalf of their principles.

The author asserted that the Bible supported republicanism in church and state; that Popery and Episcopalianism tended toward monarchism; that Presbyterianism tended toward aristocracy; and that Pedobaptism in all churches would "ruin religious liberty . . . by laying a foundation to call in the aid of law to support religion." [6] In truth, "the Baptist constitution . . . [is] the source of religious liberty — the real friend of civil liberty." The Federalists tried to tell the Baptists "that we are acting in concert with infidels; and why should we not be, so far as infidels make use of right reason? I have attempted to make appear that so far they [the infidels who believe in separation of Church and State] are nearer to revelation than any kind of state religion." He also pointed out that "some Deists are federalists." Nevertheless, deism was wrong, whether it supported Republicans or Federalists, for only Christianity was in harmony with reason and with the Bible.

6. For a theological argument that the Bible supported republicanism written by one of the few Congregational ministers in Connecticut who was a Republican see Stanley Griswold, *Overcoming Evil with Good* (Hartford, 1801): "When Jesus Christ came every maxim and every precept he gave so far as an application can be made was purely republican . . . *Ye know,* says he, *that the princes of the nations exercise lordship over them and the great ones exercise authority upon them. But it shall not be so among you: but whosoever will be chiefest among you let him be servant of all.*" This was delivered in Wallingford at a celebration in honor of Jefferson's election.

To the Baptists of New England, he exhorted, "Why do you not arise . . . Arise and trim your lamps . . . display the glory of your principles and profession . . . You are the light of the world . . . Let your light shine." The Presbyterians (i.e., New England Congregationalists) are similar to Papists and to Episcopalians: "They likewise agree in the exclusion of the people and in the propriety of church and state combinations . . . it is an aristocracy . . . an aristocratic republic" which their polity and principles extolled. But "the Kingdom of Christ [is] a republic." Even the Methodist system tended toward monarchy with its hierarchical control.

The clearest proofs that the Federalists were antirepublican, said this author, were the Alien and Sedition acts which were "designed as an engine of party principles and to stop the mouth of free inquiry." Since "reason and revelation are perfectly consistent with each other," the Federalists must be wrong in claiming that revelation supports their conception of church-state unity. As for the Federalists' argument against Jefferson's religious views, "All their efforts for other proof that Mr. Jefferson is an infidel have failed them and indeed some of the principal things which they have quoted from his writings for that purpose are a part of one of the best pleas for religious liberty I ever met with." [7] And even if Jefferson were an infidel,

> Why so awful, pray? Which would be most conducive to the general good, to have an infidel at the head of public affairs who cares so little about religion that he would not disturb it, if he did it no good, but would leave every man to enjoy his own opinion; or to have an old bigotted professor of Christianity who would be continually interfering with men's opinions and disturbing the public peace by instigating and sanctioning laws to establish religion?

He quoted John Adams' *Defense of the Constitutions* to show that Federalists believed in a mixed form of government in which the principles of monarchy and aristocracy received equal weight with republicanism. And he quoted Jedidiah Morse's matter-of-fact claim in his *Geography* of 1791 referring to Connecticut: "The clergy, who are numerous and as a body very respectable, have hitherto preserved a kind of Aristocratical ballance in the Democratical government of the state which has happily operated as a check to the overbearing spirit of Republicanism."

He concluded the tract with a detailed attack on the certificate laws and all the other ecclesiastical laws of Connecticut. It was not a carefully organized work nor was it an original one in its arguments, but it explained clearly how the Baptists, and other dissenters, were able to reconcile their own pietistic view of society with the deistic views of Jefferson. The de-

---

7. Presumably this refers to Jefferson's preamble to his Bill for Religious Liberty in Virginia.

cision to join forces with the Republican Party was similar to that which the Baptists had had to make in 1775 between siding with the King or with the Standing Order — it meant choosing the lesser of two evils. In this case, better to side with a party which cared little about religion but much for liberty against a party which professed to be thoroughly orthodox in theology but which wanted a favored position for one denomination. In both cases the Baptists ultimately sided with the forces of individualism and change. Yet simultaneously, in both cases, their hesitancy — if not their downright reluctance — displayed their ambivalence, their uncertainty about whether their best interest lay in accepting mere toleration within the existing system or in siding with the forces seeking to overturn the system. Regarding siding with Jefferson this ambivalence sprang not only from a distrust of infidelity but also from a suspicion that deists like Jefferson cared so little for religion that although they would not disturb it, neither would they encourage it. The Federalists at least were firmly convinced that Christianity was essential to the well-being of the new nation.

Despite their great admiration of Jefferson as the spokesman for separation of church and state, the New England Baptists dissociated themselves from the deistic and anticlerical premises on which he based his stand. As lineal descendants of the Puritans they deplored Jefferson's theological position. No New England Baptist, for example, ever utilized Jefferson's phrase about "the wall of separation," though he had obviously coined this term with the Connecticut Baptists specifically in mind. The only incident which indicates that Jefferson's and Madison's radical views on this subject influenced any Connecticut Baptists (with the notable exception of John Leland) was the tract which Elder Henry Grew of Hartford wrote in 1810 attacking the New England custom of the governor's thanksgiving and fast day proclamations. These were formal traditions by 1800; the fast day proclamation was issued in April or May and the thanksgiving proclamation each November or December. Washington and Adams, as presidents, had proclaimed such days on a national basis, but national observance was voluntary. The governor's official proclamation in Connecticut made observance compulsory; according to Connecticut (and Massachusetts) law a fast or thanksgiving day, although usually a weekday, was a day of required worship and rest like the Sabbath; all of the prohibitions against travel, recreation, and labor which applied to the Sabbath were applied to these days. When Jefferson and Madison refused to authorize national days of fasting and prayer because they tended to break down the wall of separation, most New Englanders deplored their stand.[8] Elder

8. Some Separates, but no Baptists, had opposed these proclamations. Some Episcopalians had refused to observe public fasts and thanksgivings which conflicted with their own holy days and had been legally fined for this. As a result of the refusal of Bishop Seabury's church in New London to observe a national thanksgiving day proclaimed by President Washington on February 19, 1795 (because it fell within Lent) Governor Huntington proposed, and it became customary, that the annual

Grew's was the only known Baptist endorsement of their position in Connecticut.[9]

Grew's sermon was entitled *Christian Loyalty . . . Designed to Illustrate the Authority of C[a]esar and Jesus Christ.* He explained his views on church and state on page two:

> The author of the following pages has long been convinced that religious establishments by civil power are totally inconsistent with the rights of man and the nature of Christ's kingdom. He has lately more particularly considered whether the appointment of days for Fasting and Thanksgiving by any civil power is inconsistent or not with the prerogative of Jesus Christ. On mature reflection he is obliged to view it as inconsistent and he has acted accordingly.

Grew's argument was a pietistic one, though it brought him out on Jefferson's side. "A coalition between the true visible gospel church and the state is absolutely incompatible . . . the members of the state are generally unregenerate men of carnal minds who will act in matters pertaining to Christ's Kingdom according to their selfish principles." Hence, "no civil authority . . . under heaven may have any authority to enact any religious laws, to appoint any day or hour for religious worship or to dictate in any manner respecting our religious faith and practice." To do so was to usurp the authority of Christ which resided only in the church itself. "The appointment of national or state fasts &c. is wrong in itself whoever may appoint them." For fasts and thanksgivings "are direct acts of worship" and acts of worship cannot be required of the regenerate by the unregenerate. The civil magistrate could no more call upon all citizens to fast than he could say, "Let us pray." And "pretending to give thanks while the heart is still destitute of gratitude" would not only be forced worship but false worship.[10]

---

fast-day should fall on Good Friday. This satisfied the Episcopalians. M. Louise Greene, *The Development of Religious Liberty in Connecticut* (Boston, 1905), pp. 378, 406–407; also William DeLoss Love, Jr., *The Fasts and Thanksgiving Days of New England* (Boston, 1895).

9. Henry Grew (1781–1862) was born in England and came to Providence, Rhode Island at the turn of the century. In 1807 he became pastor of the Hartford Baptist Church, but his four years there were full of turmoil. In addition to opposing his congregation regarding observation of civilly ordained fasts and thanksgivings, and the incorporation of the church, he also seems to have advanced some doctrinal views which appeared to them to be Arian. He withdrew (or was dismissed) in 1811. During his long career he published some seventeen polemical tracts upon a wide variety of subjects. I am indebted to Professor L. E. Froom of Andrews University for information about Grew. See the photostatic copy of the records of the First Baptist Church of Hartford in the CSL. Eleazar Wheelock's protest against the proclamation of a fast day by the Continental Congress in 1775 is discussed in chapter 43. Isaac Backus, *History of New England,* ed. David Weston (Newton, 1871), II, 541.

10. Henry Grew, *Christian Loyalty* (Hartford, 1810). Since the Connecticut law requiring attendance by everyone at public worship at stated times was still on the

Grew's radical Christian pietism on this point may be seen as directly opposed to Jefferson's radical secularism (a kind of post-Christian pietism). Indication that Grew carried this view consistently in all of his church relations lies in his opposition to the movement within his church to petition the legislature for incorporation in 1811. The congregation and the church members voted on this jointly; Grew got into such a quarrel with his church about it that he resigned as pastor in June 1811. The council which was called to investigate the quarrel sided with the church. It said that Grew was wrong to argue that church and society must never unite in action because this would make the votes of the unregenerate non-members of equal or perhaps controlling force over the votes of the regenerate members. The council took the view that in petitioning the legislature the society was acting solely in a civil capacity. But to take this view was to yield much to the claims of the Congregationalists that a majority vote of a parish in choosing a teacher of morality was a purely civil affair. Grew's stand on this point resembles Elias Smith's protest in Boston against the Baptists' increasing conservatism and worldliness at this same time. Interestingly, Elder Thomas Baldwin of the Second Church of Boston, against whom Smith was most vehement, also sanctioned the action of Grew's congregation.[11]

Evidence after 1800 of growing conservatism among the Connecticut Baptists is not quite so strong as it is for the Baptists of eastern Massachusetts, but it does exist. For example, in 1801 one of the churches in the Danbury Association asked: "Is it the duty of a dissenter to acknowledge the right of civil government dictating in matters of religion so far as to give a certificate to the clerk of a Presbyterian [Congregational] society what religion they are of?" In the 1770's Isaac Backus and the Warren Association had no trouble answering this categorically. But the Danbury Association, even while it was petitioning for disestablishment, answered equivocally: "We are of opinion that it is oppression for one society to require certificates of another, but whether God requires us at this time to say as Shadrach, Mescheck and Abednego did in another case: 'Be it known to thee, O King, we will not,' we leave for the present for individuals to judge and determine for themselves as they can answer it to God." [12] In short, they were not willing to encourage civil disobedience.

In 1802 this association was asked "Is it agreeable with the Gospel and

---

lawbooks, it was even possible to fine or imprison a man who failed to attend a dissenting church to which he belonged on an official fast or thanksgiving day.

11. For this dispute see the photostatic copy of the records of the First Baptist Church of Hartford in the CSL. Deacon Luther Savage, one of the leaders in the Petition Movement, resigned with Grew over this issue, but Deacons John Bolles and Ephraim Robins did not. The Church wrote to Baldwin and to Elder Caleb Blood for their advice before petitioning the legislature. They desired incorporation in this instance only to empower the deacons to hold church property.

12. Minutes of the Danbury Baptist Association, 1801, p. 4.

consistent with the constitution of the Baptists to fellowship those Baptist Churches and to commune with those Baptist members who by the General Court are established and incorporated into Baptist religious societies and as such are known in civil law?" Again, where the Warren Association had been clear and forthright in opposing incorporation, the Danbury Association equivocated: "We would refer our Brethren to something like our answer to a query presented to this Association at our last session with regard to the certificate law." That is, the individual church should decide.

The question of freemasonry came before the Stonington Association several times before it elicited this irritated response in 1813:

> The Church at Exeter continued their repeated application for advice respecting the propriety of holding fellowship with Churches retaining as members men who are Free-Masons, and attend lodges and an answer being pressed not only by that Church but also by the neighbouring Church of South Kingston, some deliberation was had . . . we are of opinion that it is not proper to propose any query to the Association which cannot be answered directly without marring the union of Churches or infringing upon their independency. We think their query relative to masonry is of that sort and that they have no right to insist on a decisive answer — but if they do, we think . . . that every Church must decide for themselves . . .[13]

Denominational unity came before the pietistic perfectionism of the sectarian outlook.

This same conservatism is seen in the Connecticut Baptists' stand on the slavery question, though here they shared the views of Baptists elsewhere in New England in all periods. The most extensive statement on this issue, and apparently a representative one, was given by the newspaper writer who called himself "A real Baptist and a true Republican" in the Connecticut *Courant* in 1804. A Federalist writer had blamed Jefferson and the Virginia democrats for their failure to abolish slavery in the South as New England Federalists had in the North. The Baptist replied:

> The writer of the address in the next place compliments the Baptists with an account of the conduct of the 'democratic chieftain' of Virginia, as he calls them, to their slaves, and black brethren who are free; and quotes an act passed in that State prohibiting Negroes whether bond or free, from assembling in the night for worship. Upon which I will make a few animadversions.
>
> 1st. If the Negroes are as numerous as he has told us, that is nearly four hundred thousand slaves, beside those who are free, it must be supposed that the law which he mentions is an expedient to which the State is unavoidably driven. For I am informed by our own citizens who have

13. Minutes of the Stonington Baptist Association, 1813, p. 3.

often visited that country, as well as by those who have come from there here, that however well disposed some of them may be, yet there are many of them who under a pretence of going to public worship would take the opportunity to commit outrages and depredations.

2d. In the revolutionary war, Cornwallis with his british troops and tory followers, traversed a considerable part of that State, and sowed the seeds of insurrections among the Negroes which has been a great cause of their refractory conduct since and has rendered decisive measures (which may seem oppressive to us who are unacquainted with their conduct) absolutely necessary.

3d. I have found by my own observations, that some Connecticut Federalists have been zealously engaged in circulating negro stories just before freeman's meetings in this State. Once we were told by these pretended friends of order that the French had landed a large swarm of negroes, which was stated by some federalists to be a hundred thousand in number, upon the Carolina shores.[14]

This example of the pot calling the kettle black, though typical of political debate at the time, did not indicate a very strong feeling among Connecticut Baptists for the plight of the Negro slaves nor was it the best defense of Jefferson's position which could have been made.

One other tract of this period which attempted to persuade the Baptists that it was their duty to enter politics on the side of the Republican Party is interesting for its application of the old Separate-Baptist arguments against the covenant theology of the Puritans. Elder Nehemiah Dodge delivered it as an address "in honor of the Late Presidential Election of Thomas Jefferson" on March 4, 1805 in Lebanon. Dodge, a leading figure in the petition movement, was at that time pastor of the Baptist church in Middletown. His argument was that there was a direct relationship among the covenant theology, Jewish theocracy, Popery, British tyranny, and the Federalist Party: "Our federal Clergy tell us that the Jewish and Gospel church are all the same; that Abraham's Covenant was an everlasting Covenant of grace;" but to believe this is to submit to "This same old Judaizing, Popish, British yoke of bondage" which America threw off in 1776. To believe this is to forget that "the Apostles opposed Judaizing teachers . . . Britains separated from Popery . . . Presbyterians separated from Britains . . . their children separated from the British national church in '76 . . . Republicans separated from [John] Adams' administration . . . Baptists separate from law religion in Connecticut."

To my republican brethren [in the Congregational churches] who have been always taught and still incline to believe that the Jewish Covenant is still in force binding on you: Dear brethren, a line of consistency in

14. *American Mercury*, September 27, 1804, p. 3. The Baptist-Republican might also have pointed out that although the Federalists freed the slaves in Connecticut they denied them the right to vote.

> your religion and politics is the readiest way to convince the stubborn
> . . . see the corrupt fruit which has been always springing from a con-
> nection of Church and State . . . for you to continue your standing in
> Jewish churches and constantly pay your money to support those Judaizing
> teachers who are constantly trying to gull you out of your inalienable
> rights . . . is using your liberty as a stumbling block.

Infant baptism was the root of the problem, he said, and since this was
inculcated into all children in New England in their infancy, it was easy
to see how the priestcraft of New England kept itself powerful through
this corruption of gospel truth. The Congregational ministers told their
people that if they believed in infant baptism then "you must believe by
the same authority that Moses the king and Aaron the priest always went
hand in hand" and then "of course, we [the clergy] ought to be as intimate with Assembly men and civil rulers and give our counsel and receive their patronage and support and go hand in hand with them, as much
as ever Moses and Aaron did." And the clergy say "if you deny this
connection you must deny Abraham's Covenant" and "of course you must
deny infant baptism, for there is no other way to support that but by arguing from the old Jewish constitution and proving that we are in that same
Covenant." "In this way," Dodge concluded, "thousands and thousands of
men are led to support federal politics. Infant baptism is the middle link
between Church and State, the swivel they both play upon." [15]

To Baptist orators of this kind, Republican political rallies were simply
another kind of revival meeting, designed to convert Congregationalists not
only into Republicans but also into Baptists.

Dodge also charged that the Standing clergy claimed the right to be
intimate with legislators, that they "meet together in caucusses, called ministers' meetings, and consult what sort of representatives will be most
likely to promote rulers and laws favorable to their Jewish plan; then
with great pretension to piety like his holiness the Pope from the sacred
desk . . . extol, recommend and exalt heaven as near they can those
characters for rulers who are . . . most fond of making laws to support"
the Standing order. This charge had some substance in the election night
dinner given each year at the capital. All of the Standing ministers were
invited to this dinner, as were the newly elected legislators; there they
dined at public expense, a fitting symbol of the unity of church and state.
The election sermon was delivered on this occasion (always by a Congregational minister before 1818).[16] No dissenting ministers ever were
invited to attend these functions. The excuse for this was that only those

15. Nehemiah Dodge, *A Discourse Delivered at Lebanon, Connecticut* (Norwich,
1805); Dodge denounced the Standing Order as those who "acknowledge that Jewish
churches [which accept tax support] are nearer right than new Covenant, new-light
gospel churches," thereby assuming for the Baptists all the virtue of the New Lights.
16. In 1818 an Episcopal minister, Harry Croswell, gave the election sermon; the
first Baptist to have this honor was Elder Elisha Cushman in 1820.

ministers who served as civil officers by virtue of their election by a parish to be the teacher of the parish were entitled to do so.

It was inevitable that the dissenters would seize this symbol of Congregational privilege and establishment. The first mention of it occurred in 1801 in a letter to the Connecticut *Courant* protesting that the taxpayers had to pay for this dinner and stating (as Lyman Beecher was to say later in his autobiography) that after these dinners the clergy and laity met and decided whom to support for election the next year.[17] By 1803 the complaints had become so general that the *Courant* printed an answer to them explaining that many people had the mistaken notion that the clergy received pay and allowances for two days for their attendance at this function. All they received was their dinner at state expense and in 1803 this cost just $117.62.[18] For the dissenters this was $117.62 too much. Nothing official was ever done about these clerical dinners. After the Republicans became the majority party in the state many of the Congregational clergy ceased to attend them and the custom ended in the 1820's. But before this they provided vivid proof of the established church's favored status over the dissenters, and Republican orators made the most of it.

The clergy's exemption from militia duty and civil taxes was another touchy issue among Republican anticlericals. These exemptions applied equally to dissenting ministers in Connecticut, but since they had originally been designed for the Standing clergy they were interpreted as another example of privilege. No evidence exists that the Baptists opposed this ministerial prerogative, but a satirical letter signed "Soldier" appeared in the *American Mercury* in 1804 expressing the typical anticlerical attitude: "Soldier" resented the local parson who "spent four years of indolence at College with the muses buzzing into [his ears] . . . While I with the whizzing of balls and the groans of the dying for music was courting death in the field." Yet, he said, the clergy voted in town meetings even though they neither fought for their country nor paid taxes. When "Soldier" went to his friend, the local Justice of the Peace in his town, to ask whether he considered this privileged position fair, the Justice answered, "some privileges must be granted the Clergy. Government in these degenerate times has need of their assistance. Government alone is weak, but united with the Church it will stand forever." [19]

Apparently also many Baptists feared the Congregationalists and Presbyterians throughout the country were working for a national establishment of religion. One Republican article played on these fears, saying that al-

17. *Connecticut Courant*, February 9, 1801, p. 3.
18. *Ibid.*, June 20, 1803, p. 3.
19. *American Mercury*, March 29, 1804, p. 2. See also Nehemiah Dodge, *Discourse at Lebanon*, p. 27, where he attacks the learned ministry in these terms: ". . . does not an unhallowed, unconverted lover of filthy lucre go to college and learn the art of keeping the people in ignorance and then come forth A.M. after receiving the mark in the forehead and in the right hand tantamount to a Popish priest?"

though the Congregationalists posed as great patriots for their support of the Revolution, they favored the Revolution only because they hoped "that when separated from the English government we should have a church establishment of our own. Was it not supposed that Calvinism . . . would be omnipotent in the United states?" And "if a national presbyterian church was not contemplated by them during the revolution it is now advocated." [20] Another article written in 1801 asked, why did "Doct. Dwight write to Mr. Adams [when he was President] entreating him to use his influence to bring about an established religion?" The Presbyterians have always wanted "to have their standing order 'rendered by law the established religion of the country.' " [21] In 1802 the *American Mercury* stated it was now well-known that the Federalists "favor a national religious establishment" but that the Jeffersonians favored separation of church and state.[22] Since Federalists and Congregationalists obviously believed that an establishment like their own was good for Connecticut, it was difficult for them to deny that it would be good for the nation.

Despite the absence of any concrete political action by the Baptists as a denomination after 1804, their clear alliance with the aims of the Republican Party in overthrowing the old charter government is unquestionable. And except for the Episcopalians, the same applies to the other dissenting denominations, especially the Methodists.[23] Yet the combined weight of the anti-Federalist Congregationalists and dissenters had little effect on the state's political complexion before 1816. The nearest the Republicans came to victory was in the election of 1811 when they sided with a dissident faction of the Federalist Party to elect Roger Griswold instead of John Treadwell. The Republicans, and hence the dissenters, voted for Griswold because ostensibly he was a more moderate Federalist than his opponent both politically and religiously. Also, his running mate, Elijah Boardman, was an Episcopalian. This rejection of an incumbent governor for no reason other than that of party factionalism was a serious break with tradition in Connecticut. Lyman Beecher, among other conservatives, thought it gave a fatal blow to the stability of the Standing Order. "All the infidels in the state" voted for Griswold, Beecher declared, as did the

20. *American Mercury,* October 22, 1801, p. 1.
21. *Ibid.,* September 24, 1801, pp. 2–3.
22. *Ibid.,* May 6, 1802, p. 2.
23. For evidence of Methodists' complaints and oppression against the Standing Order in Connecticut see *American Mercury,* June 13, 1791, p. 2; *Farmer's Journal,* February 15, 1791, p. 4; April 26, 1791, p. 4; June 20, 1791, p. 4; *Connecticut Courant,* December 18, 1801; *Windham Herald,* October 4, 1804. George Richards, *Strictures on a Sermon Delivered by Mr. Nathan Williams* (Philadelphia, 1794); Abel Stevens, *Memorials of the Introduction of Methodism into the Eastern States* (Boston, 1848), pp. 56–57, 78, 292, 477, and the autobiographies of Billy Hibbard and Lorenzo Dow. In 1818 the Methodists petitioned for a law to protect their camp meetings from disturbance by mobs and ruffians; see *Connecticut Courant,* October 27, 1818, p. 3.

Episcopalians and "the minor sects" whose ranks had "swollen" rapidly in recent years and who had "complained of having to get a certificate to pay their tax where they liked." [24] But Griswold proved unfriendly to both the Republicans and to the Baptists, and his election was not a turning point in the state's political allegiance to the Federalist Party. When Griswold opposed the War of 1812, the Republicans turned to Elijah Boardman as their candidate, but Griswold was reelected in 1812 on the Federalist ticket. "Mr. Madison's War" gave a new lease on life to the Federalists and Boardman (who ardently supported the War) made a dismal showing as the Republican candidate for the next three years. The Federalists, however, proved to be their own worst enemies; their actions in these years brought about their downfall.

Life in Connecticut at the beginning of the nineteenth century seemed outwardly safe and secure in the hands of the Federalist oligarchy and their clerical allies in the Congregational churches. In reality the Standing Order was already in a state of rapid disintegration. The political fight between the Federalists and the Republicans, like the economic division between the merchant traders and the new industrial bankers and entrepreneurs, represents part of this reorientation. Beneath lay a breakdown in the social and intellectual structure — a breakdown accurately and vividly reflected in the rapidly intensifying quarrel over the respective roles of church and state. For in Connecticut, as elsewhere, the religious, social, political and even economic institutions by which men live are the product of their basic philosophical values, their way of evaluating themselves in terms of one another and of their divinities. In the Second Great Awakening, as in the First, two generations before, the sources of authority were shifting to meet new times, new needs, new hopes. Or, perhaps more accurately, given the inherent conservatism of New England, old hopes and ideals born in the 1740's and burgeoning in the Revolution were finally being realized.

The two poles, old and new, were represented by two different kinds of pietists (for New England was the most pietistic section of the pietistic nation). The theocratic (or corporate) pietists were represented by men like Jonathan Edwards, Jr., Nathaniel Emmons, Timothy Dwight, Lyman Beecher, Noah Webster, John Treadwell, Samuel Pitkin, and John Cotton Smith, who stood for the necessity of public maintenance of religion as the basis of the moral order and control of society. The voluntaristic (in-

---

24. Lyman Beecher, *The Autobiography of Lyman Beecher,* ed. Barbara Myers Cross (Cambridge, 1961), I, pp. 257–259. That some Republicans and dissenters interpreted the election in 1811 as the beginning of the end for the Federalists can be seen in a letter in the *American Mercury,* signed "Addison": "In 1811 the contest was between the clergy of the standing order and the Lawyers. In that case the republicans, benefiting by the circumstances, expressed their opinion of the candidates by coalescing with the lawyers . . . the *steady habits of Connecticut* received their vital wound, the dawn of religious liberty began to break" (March 26, 1816, p. 3).

dividualistic) pietists were represented by Baptists like David Bolles, Sr. and Jr., Asahel Morse, Amos Wells, Stephen S. Nelson, Daniel Wildman, Elisha Cushman and Asa Wilcox, who considered any establishment of religion a threat to Christian freedom and equality. Each claimed for its side Scriptural truth, the rights of conscience, inalienable natural rights, social contract, and constitutional law. Each believed in evangelical Calvinism as the basis of God's revealed will regarding the nature and destiny of man. Each was dedicated to the rising glory of American republican government and the coming of the millennium through the conversion of souls. Yet each could see only disaster, tyranny, anarchy, chaos — threats to all each held sacred — in the other's specific proposals for restructuring the old social order.

Left to the voluntaristic pietists — the Baptists and Separates alone — the breakdown of the Standing Order would have taken much longer. But there were four other groups situated socially and intellectually at different points between these pietistic poles who held the balance of power. And because each of these — in different ways and for different reasons — found itself more and more at odds with the Standing Order, all of them lent weight to the voluntarist cause.

Two of these four groups were rationalist liberals, two were Christian liberals. The most extreme group of rationalist liberals might be considered deists, although like their counterparts in the South, they were nominally members of the established church. These were men like Joel Barlow, Abraham Bishop, Joshua Stow, Pierpont Edwards, Gideon Granger, Oliver Wolcott, Christopher Manwaring, and John T. Peters. Their views corresponded to Jefferson's and Madison's in Virginia or to Joseph Hawley's in Massachusetts or to Ethan Allen's in Vermont. As exponents of republicanism, they were vehemently anticlerical, anti-institutional, anti-establishment; in theology they bordered on skepticism. They were at such odds with the Standing Order they were all Jeffersonian Democrats. If any such skeptical anticlericals existed among the Federalists they did not make their views known.

Less extreme than these, though shading off from them only in degree, were the latitudinarian or broad church Congregational liberals — men who in Massachusetts would have been Unitarians. These were generally good members of the established churches but too urbane, sophisticated, rationalistic or "enlightened" to accept the evangelical Calvinism and revivalistic fervor of the leading clergy of that church. Considering themselves men of candor, catholicity and tolerance they abhorred the heresy hunting, the experiential emotionalism, the polemical theological warfare among the clergy of all sects. The Puritan Counter-Reformation was anathema to them. They saw religion in utilitarian terms, not in evangelistic ones. Essentially conservative, usually well-educated and well-to-do, these men were apt to be lawyers and doctors who considered themselves emancipated

1022

from the narrow sectarianism of the New Divinity. To them the great virtue of religion was its inculcation of morality, self-discipline, virtue, honesty, and benevolence. Yet so essential did this group consider the moral teaching for the promotion of the general welfare and so unstable the voluntarism of the sectarians, that they can be characterized as among the most staunch supporters of a state-supported church. Their views differed little from those who favored the general assessment tax in Virginia (George Washington, Patrick Henry, Richard Henry Lee) or those who favored the general establishment in Massachusetts after 1780 (as did Robert Treat Paine and Theophilus Parsons).

Caught between the illiterate fervor of the Baptist voluntarists and the Counter-Reformation zeal of the Congregational theocrats, these men (like Zephaniah Swift, Hezekiah Ripley, James Hillhouse) were not comfortable with either the Federalists or the Republicans. Men in this group often switched sides (as did Roger Griswold, Oliver Wolcott, and George H. Richards). Those who, from the start sided with the Republicans (as did Joshua King, William Judd, Elisha Hyde, Gideon Tomlinson, and Ephraim Kirby — or in Massachusetts, James Sullivan, Ezekiel Bacon, and Levi Lincoln) tended to be restraining influences on the party, urging it to go slowly in yielding to the dissenters and in baiting the Standing clergy. So conservative did they keep the party in its early years that some of the Standing clergy who shared their views — Stanley Griswold in Connecticut and Thomas Allen in Massachusetts — were in advance of them. But because of the conservative influence of these men, the Republicans were able to win increased silent clerical support as time went by.

This moderate group of rationalist liberals had much in common with the first of the two groups whom I have called Christian liberals. In Connecticut these were the Episcopalians, a group which since before the First Great Awakening had attracted a large number of the educated and respectable among clergy and laity, a denomination which during and after the Awakening attracted those who disliked the rationalism of the deists but who equally disliked both the New Divinity of the Edwardseans and the evangelical piety of the Separates and Baptists. It has been said with some accuracy that in Connecticut the Episcopal Church was the equivalent of the Unitarian movement in Massachusetts; Unitarianism had been made ecclesiastically and socially untenable because of the effective crusade of the New Lights to remove the Old Light Arminians from the established churches. Generally, little distinguished Episcopalians like Jonathan Ingersoll, Elijah Boardman, William Samuel Johnson, Asa Chapman, and Isaac Beers from the rationalist liberals. Most Episcopalians were so socially conservative that they tended, until 1816, to be more comfortable with the Federalists than with the Republicans. They were too committed to Christianity (in its tolerant Anglican form) to sympathize with the anticlerical rationalism of Zephaniah Swift, Roger Griswold, or James Hillhouse, but they found themselves perfectly in accord with the latter's social, economic, and political views. It was the heedless and needless alienation of these Christian liberals by the Federalist Old Guard (despite the efforts of David Daggett) that finally swung the balance in favor of disestablishment after 1816, much as the Trinitarian Congregationalists were finally alienated from their party in Massachusetts by intransigence of the Unitarian Old Guard.

The second group of Christian liberals who stood between the pietistic poles of Dwight and Bolles were far less conservative and far less influential. These were the smaller sects like the Methodists, the Universalists, the Christ-ians, the Free Will Baptists, the Sandemanians, and a few of the eccentric liberal Baptists — notably John Leland and Nehemiah Dodge. Decidedly evangelical in temper, but far more liberal theologically than the average Baptist, many of these Christian liberals were in outright revolt against Calvinism; most were at least ambivalent toward it. Yet in social status, education, and wealth they were far closer to the Baptists than to the Episcopalians. Most of this group were from the beginning ardent Republicans — Whitfield Cowles, Thomas Barnes and Dr. Sylvester Wells among the Universalists; Dodge and Leland among the liberal Baptists; George Roberts and Daniel Burrows among the Methodists. Had they been more numerous, their efforts might have pushed the Republican Party toward disestablishment more rapidly. But their ranks were small and they were poor. Because of their departures from the predominant evangelical Calvinism of the vast majority of the inhabitants of New England they were considerably less respectable than the Baptists. Moreover, they were constantly quarreling among themselves. No love was lost between the heterodox Universalists and Christians and the more orthodox Methodists, Free Will Baptists and Sandemanians. These Christian liberals were considered heretics and non-conformists even by those with whom they had most in common.

The history of disestablishment in Connecticut after 1800 is the story of how each of these four groups of dissentients felt gradually more alienated from the narrow, partisan conservatism of the Federalists and the Beecherite clergy; how each in its own time and for its own reasons sided with the voluntaristic pietists to end the Standing Order which bent but which would not break its ties to the past. The result of this diversity of dissent was a far less clearcut victory for the Baptists than they achieved in Vermont and New Hampshire (more like that in Massachusetts). Neither did the Republican Party obtain a clearcut victory, for it too disappeared in the confusion.

For the Baptists the result was probably a satisfactory resolution of their own ambivalent stance between sectarian spiritual radicalism and middle-class social conservatism.

Chapter 52

The Rise of the Toleration Party,
1816–1817

Long have the congregational order held domination over the civil government of this State . . . An opportunity will present itself to the friends of equal rights on the 8th of April next to place all denominations of Christians on an equal footing.

Advertisement for the Toleration Party, *Columbian Register,* March 30, 1816

On February 21, 1816 a group of leading Republican Party politicians met in New Haven with a group of Episcopalians who had become disgruntled with the Federalist Party. Since the formation of the two-party system the Episcopalians had been the one dissenting denomination which firmly allied itself with the Federalists, but now they were ready to bolt their party.[1] As a result of this meeting the Republicans agreed to use their machinery to support Oliver Wolcott for governor and Jonathan Ingersoll for lieutenant governor in the next election and to call this ticket the American or Toleration Ticket. Neither Wolcott nor Ingersoll were Republicans. They had both been staunch Federalists for years. But Wolcott, who had lived in New York from 1805 to 1815, disliked the Federalists' opposition to the War of 1812 and deplored the Hartford Convention. He was a moderate liberal in religion, sympathizing generally with the Republican position on the need for political reform in Connecticut. Ingersoll, a Supreme Court Judge and member of the Council, was the leading Episcopal layman in the state. He joined the Republicans because he was convinced that the Standing Order was too bigoted ever to treat his denomination fairly.

1. *American Mercury,* February 27, 1816, p. 3. For general discussions of the role the Episcopalians played in disestablishment, see M. Louise Greene, *Development of Religious Liberty in Connecticut* (Boston, 1905), pp. 445–497, and Richard J. Purcell, *Connecticut in Transition, 1775–1818* (Washington, 1918), pp. 46–64, 332–419. See also William B. Sprague's *Annals of the American Pulpit* (New York, 1859), V, 35, where the Episcopal minister in Fairfield, the Rev. Philo Shelton, is credited with having arranged this meeting between the Republicans and the leading Episcopalians.

The Episcopalians had been Federalists for obvious reasons. As a denomination they had no objection to an established church system or to religious taxes, so they had never sympathized with the dissenting or anticlerical opposition to the Connecticut ecclesiastical laws. Moreover, their members were primarily educated and upperclass former Congregationalists who had left that denomination because they disliked the fanaticism and theological narrowness of the New Lights. In the absence of a significant Unitarian wing in the Congregational church of Connecticut the Episcopal Church grew rapidly in the post-Revolutionary years as the denomination for respectable latitudinarians. In addition, the Episcopal Church had always had a social tone which attracted the wealthy and excluded the common man. Only a wealthy aristocrat was able to bear the stigma of joining the denomination of the Tories without worrying about its effect on his social standing in the community. As wealthy aristocrats the Episcopal leaders who set the tone of the denomination had no use for the rabble-rousing democratic principles of the Republican Party and the unseemly behavior of ignorant pietistic enthusiasts like the Baptists and Methodists (they considered their denomination well rid of the latter zealots with their camp meetings and lay exhorters). Thus allied in religious, social, economic, and political temper with the ruling elite of the Standing Order, they were always accepted as a different kind of dissenter — treated with deference and respect, appointed to office, welcomed in marriage and business alliances, and generally accepted as members of the ruling elite.

Nevertheless an underlying antipathy existed between the Puritan and Anglican minds which was never quite forgotten in New England. Gradually the Episcopalians began to feel that they were not fully accepted as equals and that a kind of subtle discrimination was being maintained to keep them outside the inner circle of power and prestige. There were two specific complaints which emphasized the growing feeling after 1811 that their loyal support for the Federalists and the Standing Order was not sufficiently appreciated. First was that despite repeated petitions in 1804, 1810, 1812, and 1815, the General Assembly had refused to give their academy in Cheshire a charter to operate as Seabury College.[2] The lower house had approved the last two petitions but the Council had vetoed them on the grounds that Yale was sufficient to supply the educational needs of the state.

The second complaint concerned the Phenix Bank Bonus. In 1814 a group of wealthy Hartford men, many of whom were Episcopalians, petitioned for a charter for forming the Phenix Bank. As was customary in those days, the petitioners accompanied their petition with a promise to

---

2. *Connecticut Courant,* March 26, 1816, p. 3, and *Columbian Register,* January 27, 1816, p. 3. The *Courant* pointed out that the Democrats also voted against this petition. Episcopalians, unlike Baptists and Methodists, did send their sons to Yale in these years.

grant a bonus of $50,000 to the state which the legislature could dispose of when it granted the charter.[3] The petitioners took the liberty of suggesting that this bonus should be disposed by grants to the Yale Medical School and to the fund for the endowment of the Episcopal bishop's support, commonly known as the Bishop's Fund. The legislature granted the charter to the bank and its directors turned over $50,000 to the state. The legislature at once granted $20,000 of this to the Yale Medical School, but it refused to grant a penny to the Bishop's Fund. The remainder of the bonus was kept in the state treasury, ostensibly to pay war debts. The Episcopalians considered this action both dishonest and bigoted.[4]

In 1816 the Federalists were caught off guard by the formation of the new Toleration Party. They could hardly believe that the Episcopalians would desert them to side with what was really the Republican party. They were also worried that many lukewarm Federalist voters might have been alienated by the unpatriotic, secessionist actions of the Hartford Convention (and conversely thrilled by Jackson's victory over the British at New Orleans). Concerning disestablishment, the 1816 election was important for the revival of this dormant issue. The Episcopalian's disillusionment with the Standing Order made disestablishment, and even the attempt to overthrow the charter, seem far more respectable. The Republican party managers made the question of religious freedom the central one in the campaign. Typical of their oratory in spring 1816 was an advertisement inserted in the *Columbian Register* on March 30, 1816, announcing "A Meeting of the Friends of Equal Rights" to be held in Danbury on March 18. This advertisement like the Danbury meeting, was a political endorsement of the new party:

> Long have the congregational order held domination over the civil government of this State; long has every other denomination submitted to their domination. The Baptists have prayed and importuned; the Episcopalians have prayed and importuned and prayed again; while the Methodists and other denominations beholding the futility of importunities and prayers have quietly submitted to their fate. An opportunity will present itself to the friends of equal rights on the 8th of April next to place all denominations of Christians on an equal footing.

One of the salient butts of abuse in the campaign was "that Presbyterian manufactory — Yale College," which all inhabitants of the state were forced to pay taxes to support. "Do the sons of Episcopalians, of Baptists, or

3. The petition is quoted in Greene, *Development of Religious Liberty*, p. 441.
4. For a typical statement of Episcopal grievances at this time see *American Mercury*, March 12, 1816, p. 3; *Columbian Register*, January 27, 1816, p. 3. The latter article pointed out that the Episcopalians did not get their fair share of political offices; there was only one Episcopalian of nine men on the Supreme Court, only one of fourteen in the Council, none who were members of Congress, and none on the Yale Corporation. Other dissenters lacked even this token representation.

Methodists and others equally participate in the benefits and honors of that institution? Are clergymen of the various denominations invited to preach Election Sermons?" It was noted that Episcopal clergymen had occasionally been asked to give a prayer in the House of Representatives and *"once"* a Baptist was asked. But did this constitute a fair proportion? Was it fair that the Congregational clergy should feast at public expense at the annual election dinners? [5]

A writer for the Republican or Toleration Party put the disestablishment issue bluntly in March 1816:

> The ruling party insists that one particular denomination of christians ought, by the aid of human laws, to be endowed with peculiar rights and privileges; that other sects may be tolerated indeed, but that the adherents of the other sects shall pay taxes to the privileged order till they have, in a manner pointed out by law, made public declaration to what other denomination they choose to belong or have obtained permission that their taxes shall be appropriated to the support of their own denomination.
>
> Republicans contend that such laws have a strong tendency to produce an unnatural and adulterous connection between church and state; that religion is a subject not within the cognizance of a human legislature, except so far as it may have a tendency to effect the good order of society and to enforcing of legal contracts made in relation thereto; that no denomination ought to be particularly favoured by law.[6]

Clearly the new party was commited to more than the "Toleration" implied in its title. However, in spring 1816 the party did not specify how the privileged position of the Congregational church would be abolished.

At this time the Republicans were more interested in stirring up a general ferment among all discontented elements. For the purpose of arousing the dissenters, the party utilized the same kind of propaganda story about a religious conspiracy among the Congregationalists to subvert religious freedom and democracy which Republicans in New Hampshire were developing at this time from the Dartmouth College affair. The repeated attacks on

5. *Columbian Register*, March 30, 1816, p. 1. When the Federalist newspapers printed attacks on the Toleration Party as "ridiculers of all religion" and based on "infidelity" and "enmity to religion," the Republican newspapers answered that the new party consisted of "all the Baptists, all the Methodists, and a great many Episcopalians, Congregationalists, &c. &c." The writer of the article cited here claimed "The cause of toleration is the cause of God." The Connecticut *Courant*, speaking for the Federalists, argued that "the most of real Episcopalians are decidedly Federalist and generally are men of reputation and influence in society. Certificate episcopalians, who are such by certificate only [i.e., tax dodgers] are generally democrats." August 20, 1816, p. 2. When the Republicans were twitted for having formerly voted against the Episcopal petitions, they answered frankly, "Many of them did so on this distinct ground that the Episcopalians, while they were petitioning, were voting for the men who would assuredly negative their petitions [i.e., for the Federalists]. Since the Episcopalians take another course, republicans will support their just claims to a part of the Bonus." *Columbian Register*, March 30, 1816, p. 3.

6. *American Mercury*, March 5, 1816, p. 2.

Yale were part of this propaganda. But equally important was their effort to portray the burgeoning moral and religious reform societies spawned by Lyman Beecher and promoted through the fervor of the Second Great Awakening as dangerous new engines of ecclesiastical and political tyranny. Since these societies were formed by and led by Congregational laymen and ministers, it was easy to portray them as part of a Federalist political plot. The Charitable Society for the Education of Pious Young Men for the Ministry of the Gospel founded in 1814 was a Connecticut agency designed to raise money for Congregational ministerial candidates and its first President was that stout old Federalist, Judge Tapping Reeve of Litchfield. The American Bible Society founded in 1816 had as its President Governor John Cotton Smith. The Moral Reform Society founded in 1812 was presided over by former Governor John Treadwell. To devout Congregationalists these and other moral reform societies were purely and simply dedicated to the general spiritual uplift of the state and nation. But to the anticlericals and dissenters, the sight of these new forms of religious association led by the same ruling elite and the same Standing clergy who were so prominent in the Federalist Party conjured up new visions of oppressive clerical power. Party orators easily aroused the pietists' innate hostility to institutionalized religion. Doubtless, by some of their leaders, these societies *were* considered a means of reestablishing the prestige and influence of the Puritan system which had lost its thrust in the Revolutionary era.[7]

Unfortunately for the Federalists, Lyman Beecher played directly into the hands of the Republicans with two blundering speeches he delivered in 1814. One of these was *An Address to the Charitable Society*; the other, *A Sermon Delivered at Woolcot, September 21, 1814, at the Installation of the Rev. John Keyes* which was better known as "Building Up the Waste Places" from its text, Isaiah, 61:4. In them, Beecher not only displayed the Standing Order's usual snobbery and disdain for the dissenters, but he also boasted of the power and influence of the new moral and religious societies which, as he portrayed them, were designed to strengthen the ecclesiastical system of Connecticut and to stem the "very great declension of vital piety" which threatened it. Moreover, with his habitual penchant for grandiose plans, Beecher indicated clearly that these societies were to have a national, not just a local, thrust and purpose.

For example, he began his *Address to the Charitable Society* by pointing out that there was a population of eight million in the United States to be

---

7. For a general discussion of the "theocratic" implications of these societies which were led by Calvinistic Congregationalists and Presbyterians, see John R. Bodo, *The Protestant Clergy and Public Issues* (Princeton, 1954). For specific relationships between these societies and the defense of the Standing Order in Connecticut see Lyman Beecher's autobiography, *The Autobiography of Lyman Beecher*, ed. Barbara Myers Cross (Cambridge, 1961), and Sidney Mead, *Nathaniel W. Taylor* (Chicago, 1942).

properly cared for spiritually. To do this, the population should have one pastor to every one thousand souls or one pastor to every one hundred-fifty families. Thus the United States needed eight thousand ministers to meet its spiritual needs. Yet

> there are not . . . more than 3000 educated ministers of the Gospel in our land; leaving a deficienty of 5000 ministers and a population of five million destitute of proper religious instruction. There may be perhaps 1500 besides who are nominally ministers of the Gospel. But they are generally illiterate men, often not possessed even of a good English education [i.e., through eighth grade] and in some instances unable to read or write. By them as a body learning is despised. With a few exceptions they are utterly unacquainted with Theology . . . with the best intentions they are unable to exert that religious and moral and literary influence which it belongs to the Ministry to exert.[8]

This passage gave incalculable offense to the Baptists and Methodists, especially to the former who had believed that they were, half a century after the founding of Brown University, entitled to as much respect as the Congregationalists. Beecher particularly offended their pietistic voluntarism by adding, "It is not by preaching repentance and faith exclusively that the interests of religion are promoted. There is a state of society to be formed, and to be formed by an extended combination of institutions, religious, civil, literary, which never exist without the cooperation of an educated Ministry." It was the quintessence of Federalism to favor institutions over soul winning and political parties. When he said, "Illiterate men have never been the chosen instruments of God to build up his cause," he essentially dismissed the whole evangelistic temper of the Second Great Awakening, to say nothing of primitive Christianity.[9] Nor was it tactful when Beecher concluded, as he was expected to do by the Charitable Society, by an appeal for more funds to promote the education of Congregational ministers at Yale and Andover: "It is our duty then to engage deliberately in

8. Lyman Beecher, *An Address to the Charitable Society* (n.p., 1814). Beecher went on to explain why towns served by only uneducated ministers were to his mind "waste places": "Illiterate men, however pious, cannot command the attention of that class of the community whose education and mental culture is above their own." These cultivated people are very influential but "they will despise religion and neglect her institutions . . . when its chosen advocates are ignorant and unlettered men. Illiterate pastors cannot be the patrons of schools, academies and colleges. They cannot, and if they can they will not exalt society above their own level. Education, religion, and literature will be neglected in their hands; civilization will decline and immoralities multiply." Although students of the frontier will recognize here an accurate portrait of the anti-intellectual aspects of pietistic evangelicalism which the Baptists and Methodists justified in terms of "democracy" and the exaltation of the common (if converted) average man, it is also clear that Beecher's own brand of evangelicalism was as antidemocratic as theirs was anti-intellectual.

9. Beecher explained the illiterate apostles's success in the first century saying that they were guided by a special kind of divine inspiration not vouchsafed to illiterate ministers of later ages.

the enterprise of supplying our nation with qualified religious instructors. Religion is the last thing that should be committed to the hands of ignorant and incompetent men."

His sermon on building up the waste places was equally obtuse in its defense of the establishment at the expense of abusing the dissenters. Although Beecher regretted that the Puritans had once lapsed into "the halfway covenant" and Stoddardeanism, he had nothing but admiration for the ecclesiastical system of "our fathers" which "required every society by law to support the gospel and every family to contribute its proportion and [to] attend statedly upon its ministrations." He praised the Great Awakening for ending the halfway covenant and Stoddardeanism and for making "a credible profession of religion indispensable to church membership" but he deplored those separatists, Separates and Baptists, who became "the subject of enthusiasm which defied restraint and despised order" and who thus "laid the foundation and furnished the materials to build up the several denominations which now prevail in the State." As a result of these divisions "the covetous . . . soon learned to plead a tender conscience to save their money and joined themselves to some denomination which could help them on to heaven at the least expense." Beecher spoke with considerable feeling, and doubtless he represented accurately the anger, frustration, despair of those sincere supporters of the Standing Order who believed that sectarian self-aggrandizement, indifferent covetousness, and malicious political factionalism were heedlessly wrecking one of the most valuable, necessary, and honorable New England institutions.

> No plan has ever yet been adopted so effectual as legislative provisions which shut out individual discretion and require every man to pay for the support of the gospel according to his property. The experiment has been fairly made on our right hand [in Rhode Island] and on our left [New York] of what may be expected from voluntary associations [i.e., churches] and contributions for the support of divine institutions; and the result is that at least four times more religious instruction is secured by legal provision than have ever been provided to any considerable extent by voluntary discretions.[10]

Nothing could have been better contrived to give support to the Republican claim of a Congregational conspiracy against religious freedom than this advocacy of "legislative provisions which shut out individual discretion." Beecher apparently seemed determined to convince the Federalists to turn back the clock, though he was really advocating a new approach to the

10. Lyman Beecher, *A Sermon Delivered at Woolcot* (Andover, 1815), pp. 10–11. Beecher's quantitative approach to evangelism was more typical of his generation's approach to religion than it was to that of the early Puritans. He estimated 36 parishes of 218 were vacant at that time in Connecticut (p. 8). He included similar estimates of the need for education ministers in other states; e.g., New Jersey needed 100, North Carolina, 535, South Carolina, 379, etc.

problem with the moral reform societies, "a modified system of itinerancy or exchanges by settled ministers," and "the appointment of evangelists" to build up the waste places. But it was clear that the temper of Beecher's talks, like that of the Standing Order, was entirely out of sympathy both with the individualism and voluntarism of the dissenters and with the general optimism and faith in the common man and the democratic process of the Jeffersonians. The mood of Beecher and his party was epitomized in one sentence: "The heart of man is desperately wicked and freed from the restraints of religious instruction will go on indefinitely from bad to worse."

> From these waste places . . . sally forth the infidel . . . the universalist to quiet profligates in sin . . . the political empiric to augment his party, and the sectarian of every name to proselyte until a broad circumference around shall become as divided and weak and dissolute as Babel itself.

He had good reason to comprehend "the political empiric" of the Republicans since his own empiricism was so patent.

Beecher's addresses were published and distributed by his admirers throughout New England. And the attacks on them were loud and persistent. The Republicans found "Beecherism" an admirable means for launching the new Toleration Party, as this editorial in the *American Mercury* demonstrated:

> The Congregational order is dominant; it has control of our colleges, commencements, and general elections . . . The address of the Rev. Lyman Beecher [to the Charitable Society] exhibits in its spirituality and purity the present views of the Congregational order. Not content with an unprecedented degree of power, it claims to spread its wings over all the religious denominations to drive out of their desks all the uneducated clergy and to supply their places with the sons of Yale and Andover. This is the English translation of it; and this address got up under the patronage of Judge Reeve of the Charitable Society, of Governor Smith of the Bible Society, of Governor Treadwell of the Moral Society as promoters of Congregational schemes is to be considered as the great battering ram by which our walls are to be destroyed . . . If the present men and measures in Connecticut are to go on, we are to have no freedom of conscience and of worship . . . The episcopal, methodists, and baptist churches are to be kept down at any cost and all hazards.[11]

Particularly interesting for its expression of the new evangelical and pietistic individualism of the nineteenth century was a two-part attack on Beecher's address in the *Columbian Register* in February 1816. It took him to task for saying "Such then is the state of our nation; more deplorably destitute of religious instruction than any other Christian nation under heaven." [12]

11. *American Mercury*, March 19, 1816, p. 2.
12. Beecher, *An Address*, p. 11.

The anonymous writer said, "Strictly speaking the term 'Christian nation' in the present state of the world is a solecism. Jesus Christ redeems his people *out* of every nation. Rev. 5.9. The kingdoms of the world are not worthy of this holy character. Satan is the God of them. 2 Cor. 4.4." When Beecher used the term "Christian nation" it can only be supposed, said the writer, that he meant that in America "Christianity is generally professed, however, corrupted." [13] But this was not what Beecher meant at all. He used the term in the old sense of a Puritan Christian Commonwealth — a society permeated by religion and led by the clergy in state-supported churches. But the writer was correct in saying that in 1814 this term was no longer acceptable or meaningful. America not only had too many different religious views, but it also had too many self-doubts to be certain that it was worthy (yet) to be called "Christian." It had yet to purge itself of many Old World errors. To the pietistic mind of the nineteenth century, which this writer represented, only in the millennium could a nation truly call itself Christian. Yet in a slightly altered form the pietists shared the old Puritan concept that America was God's chosen nation and that it had a special mission "in the divine economy." That mission however was to be accomplished in the future — when all Americans were truly Christians. It was not something which had existed in the days of "our pious forefathers" as Beecher and the Standing Order claimed. It was not a lost era of primitive faith and Godly institutions — a Christian arcadia which had disappeared and to which, by means of legislation or moral reform societies, New England might yet return. What the Standing Order saw as a decline of hallowed institutions and an emerging era of barbarism, the pietistic dissenter saw as the breaking out from bondage of the children of God, the salutary and necessary destruction of corrupt institutions and ecclesiastical restraints. To the pietist it was precisely the evangelistic preaching of repentance and faith by pious, even if uneducated, preachers which was to bring on the millennium and make America, and ultimately the world, truly Christian — truly fit for Christ to rule over at his second coming. What Beecher foresaw as the advent of spiritual desolation — the sun setting upon the ruined institutions of Puritanism, the pietists saw as the sunrise of the latter days — the glory of the coming of the Lord in a land free from the shackles of an established church. Men were not saved or converted to Christianity by the institutions of church and state but by the direct personal confrontation of God and the individual.

The election in April 1816 did not oust the Federalists from power, but it gave them serious cause for alarm. Wolcott came very close to equaling the vote of John Cotton Smith for the governorship and Ingersoll actually defeated the Federalist candidate and became the Lt. Governor of the state under a Federalist governor. The Toleration party won eighty-five seats in

13. *Columbian Register,* February 17, 1861, p. 1.

the House. The city of Hartford voted for Wolcott and Ingersoll. In October, when representatives were again elected, the Toleration Party increased its total to eighty-seven seats, and for the first time a Republican won a seat in the upper house. The new party had good reason to expect both the governorship and a majority in the legislature in the election of April 1817.[14]

Recognizing their danger, the Federalists made a desperate attempt to mollify the dissenters and to weaken the new party's attacks on the establishment. The measure which it passed on October 31, 1816 for this purpose was "An Act for the Support of Religion and Literature." It proved to be the worst blunder the Federalists could possibly have made. It not only cost them the election of 1817, but it was the deathblow to the Federalist Party in Connecticut. Yet within the framework of the Federalist mentality, it had seemed like a generous and statesmanlike — if empirical — gesture. Under the terms of this act a large sum of money due to Connecticut from the federal government in payment for services rendered during the War of 1812, was to be divided among the leading denominations of the state in the following proportions (which were assumed to be numerically accurate): one-third of the money was to go to the Congregational societies (or parishes); one-seventh to the Bishop's Fund; one-eighth to the Baptist Societies, one-twelfth to the Methodist societies, one-seventh to Yale, and the remaining one-sixth was to remain in the treasury. The total sum to be thus divided was not yet known because the federal government had not yet settled the matter. But the state claimed a debt of $145,000. The Republicans said that the state would be lucky to get $25,000.[15]

14. For election results see *Connecticut Courant*, April 18, 1816, p. 3; *American Mercury*, October 27, 1816, p. 3. In this election the Republicans for the first time placed a man on the Council; he was David Tomlinson.

15. Ultimately the state received $50,000. Certain details of the act are important for an understanding of the furor it aroused. The bill reads, "one third part of what shall be received [from the federal government] . . . is appropriated for the use and benefit of the Presbyterian or Congregational denominations of Christians, to be by them applied for the support of the Gospel in their respective societies in proportion to the amount of their lists"; "one seventh part of what shall be received . . . is hereby appropriated for the use and benefit of the Episcopal denomination of Christians in this State; and the Trustees for receiving donations for the support of a Bishop are hereby authorized to receive and hold the same"; "one eighth part of what shall be received . . . is hereby appropriated for the use and benefit of the denomination of Christians called Baptists to be by them applied for the support of the Gospel in their several societies: and Samuel Beckwith, Elisha Cushman, Nathaniel S. Adams, James Treat, David Silliman, Josias Byles, Rufus Babcock, Ephraim Bound, Asahel Chapman, and Samuel Williams be and they hereby are constituted Trustees and made a body politic and corporate by the name of the Baptist's Trustees, with full power to fill all vacancies in their own body" and they shall receive it and apply it "for the use and benefit of said societies in proportion to their respective lists or any other way or manner they may judge just and reasonable"; "one 12th part . . . is hereby appropriated for the use and benefit of the denomination of Christians called Methodists . . . in their several societies": Metho-

Apart from the Federalists' interest in finding some means to continue state support for religion without hurting the consciences of the dissenters, this bill was thought to be a very clever device for splitting the new Toleration Party. The Federalists expected it to demonstrate that they were not "intolerant" and to indicate to the Episcopalians that they were now willing to help the Bishop's Fund. They expected it also to show the Baptists and Methodists that they too would be fairly treated and considered as denominational equals. And most important, knowing that the Republicans would vote against the bill, the Federalists hoped to show that the Republicans were not really interested in helping the dissenters but only in advancing their own political aims. The committee which recommended this bill as the best means of disposing of the money to be received from the federal government issued a report that they had considered many ways of applying the funds, including the school fund, the deaf and dumb asylum, and other charities. "But an appropriation to aid the Religious Institutions of this State is, in the estimation of the Committee, of much more importance than any other. By such a disposition of the balance in question every individual in the community will be directly or indirectly benefited."

> So far as funds are provided, the religions of all denominations will be relieved from burdens to which they are necessarily subjected. Even those Christians who do not acknowledge the right of the Civil Magistrate to enforce collections for these purposes, will find ample means for the disposition of the monies which they may receive to objects useful and necessary to the prosperity of their establishments.[16]
>
> It will be perceived by the bill which accompanies this Report that no preferences have been given to one denomination of Christians over another, but that in ascertaining the proportions which each are to receive, the Committee have been guided by a liberal policy towards those sectaries whose numbers are fewest. And it is confidently hoped that the religious of all classes will perceive in the measure . . . a disposition to foster and cherish them. As it may happen that for want of correct information some denomination may have been omitted, the Committee have deemed expedient that a part of the foregoing balance should be left unappropriated that the Legislature may have it in its power to supply any such omission when it shall be discovered.[17]

The dissenters were demanding disestablishment as an inalienable right

---

dists Trustees were to be Ralph Hurlburt, Jonathan Nichols, Jr., Alpheus Jewet, William Lyon, Elijah Sherman, Aron Hunt, and Samuel Frothingham. One seventh part went to Yale College for buildings and other purposes. The remainder was to stay in the state treasury for future disposal. *Connecticut Courant,* November 5, 1816, p. 3. Also in CEA, n.s. I, 17 a, b, c, d.

16. Perhaps the Federalists thought the Baptists would use the money to support foreign missions.

17. The report is printed in the *Connecticut Courant,* November 5, 1816, p. 3.

and they were given state aid as a form of charity. Clearly the Federalists had learned nothing from the great debate over the Western Lands Act of 1793.

Significantly, however, this report was signed by Jonathan Ingersoll, and the Federalist papers pointed out that while all of the Episcopalians in the legislature voted for the bill, all of the non-Episcopalian Republicans had voted against it. The bill passed by 103 votes to 90.[18] But though the Episcopalians voted for the bill and accepted their share of the money when it came, they did not return to the Federalist fold. The Republicans gauged correctly the public reaction to this act and had strengthened their position by opposing it. The bitter dispute which ensued during the next two years revealed in full detail the reasons for the downfall of the Federalists and of the Puritan traditions for which they stood. It also revealed the temper of the dissenters and the newly emergent attitude of Americans toward the role of religion in a democratic society.

The first of several arguments against the bill was that it was unfair both in the proportions it allotted and in its omission of several smaller denominations (Quakers, Universalists, Separates, Sandemanians). Another argument held that the money could be better used for other purposes. For the dissenters the important argument was that money allotted by the state for religious purposes was then, as always, a form of unity between church and state which was intrinsically unscriptural and potentially tyrannical. A subsidiary of this argument was that the state had no right, as the act did, to appoint trustees or officials for the Baptists and Methodists. Still another argument held that since the federal government had not yet paid the money to the state, it was foolish to start parcelling it out. And finally, it was said repeatedly that the bill's principal purpose was nothing but a form of partisan political bribery to win votes for the Federalist Party.[19]

The Baptist and Methodist representatives in the House ably stated their views of the bill in the debate preceding its passage. Speaking for the Baptists, Eden Burrows of Stonington observed, as the newspapers summarized his remarks,

> That we had not yet obtained this money which was to be given by the Act. It was moreover uncertain whether we should get it, and [he] inquired why Congress had not paid this, as well as other money that had been expended by this State? He did not know why the subject was brought forward at this time. The appropriation was he thought extremely liberal. The Baptists, to whose society he belonged, had not petitioned for it. He had doubts whether the passing of the bill would not involve the Legislature in the same difficulties which they had experienced in the

18. For a roll call list of the votes see *ibid.*, November 5, 1816, p. 3.
19. For a contemporary summary of the arguments see *ibid.*, November 12, 1816, p. 3.

Gore business [i.e., the Western Lands Act]. He was opposed to the bill.[20]

Speaking for the Methodists, Daniel Burrows from Hebron, opposed it because

> he doubted whether a divine was rendered more useful to his flock or his ecclesiastical diligence increased by an independent support . . . He then adverted to the English Clergy who had fat livings which were the principal causes of that depravity and corruption for which they were remarkable . . . The sect to which he belonged (the Methodists) would take a certain amount for their labour, and no more, provided the people were willing to give it. If, however, they could not pay, the pastor went without any remuneration. As to the appropriation for Yale College — some doubted whether a clergyman was any better for the advantages of a liberal education . . . Should the money be appropriated as the bill provides, the Baptists, who were divided into many sects, he feared would fall by the ears for a division of the spoils.[21]

The Federalists had answers to these arguments. They said that the bill "would reconcile men of all parties." "That the objects named in the Bill were worthy of and needed the patronage of the Legislature;" that the money had originally come from the people in the form of war taxes and should be returned to them; "that when money is appropriated to the support of religion and literature all classes and denominations must be equally interested in their object and ought to share equally in the distribution of the fund in question," and "that the provisions of this bill equally respected every denomination of Christians and as such ought to be supported by all." [22]

Once the act was passed the Episcopalians quietly accepted their share (which amounted finally to $8785.71) but the Baptists and Methodists fought strenuously for the repeal of the law. The Methodists were the more recently arrived and were still in a primitive stage of radical pietism; they were far more vehemently opposed than the more denominationally mature Baptists. Nevertheless spokesmen for both clearly made known their dislike for the act in numerous letters to the editor and in various resolutions passed at special meetings by churches all over the state. A letter signed "A Methodist" in the *Columbian Register,* November 9, 1816, called the bill "a bribe," a misuse of funds, and a gross unfairness in the proportion alloted to his denomination whom he estimated as twelve thousand adherents and whom he urged to "fly this delusive scheme to fetter your consciences." A

---

20. *Ibid.,* November 19, 1816, p. 3.
21. *Ibid.* This last remark revealed clearly why the Baptists and Methodists so seldom worked together even for disestablishment. No love was lost between them.
22. *Ibid.,* November 12, 1816, p. 3; November 19, 1816, p. 3.

letter signed "A Baptist" in the same issue of the same paper said the act should be called "An Act to secure the re-election to office of the present incumbents" and quoted one of its leading supporters admitting that the act was designed "to bring the Episcopalians, the Baptists and the Methodists over to them in a body."

The Methodist Society in Burlington, led by Elder Phineas Cook, met on December 25, 1816 and passed an acidulous set of resolutions against "such acts of bribery":

> *Resolved:* That we consider the act of the Legislature in appropriating the sum of $12,000 to the use of the Methodist Societies an insult on our virtue in representing to the world that in their opinion we could be bribed with that paltry sum.
>
> *Resolved:* That in our opinion the legislature of this State has no authority to take that money which the good people have paid for the defense of the country and appropriate it to the above use. In this act we deem the rights of man are infringed upon, individuals impoverished to support party politics, and in the end [it will lead some] to heap curses on the general government for refusing to give them money to make voters to support an expiring faction . . . the religion of Jesus Christ needs not the civil sword to support it . . . we cannot consistently nor shall we accept any part of said money . . . and we would caution all our friends not to do like Judas and sell their Master for 30 pieces of silver or less.[23]

A more extensive letter from "An Old Methodist" indicates how closely that denomination had come to adopting the same principles as the Baptists had on the church-state question (though before 1816 the Methodists had been generally silent upon the issue and had let the Baptists do most of the fighting in 1800–1807). This Methodist began by asserting that although the members of his denomination were

> republicans, it has been their wish to avoid political contention, but having to their sorrow seen the growing evils arising from the ambition of statesmen in union with the Congregational Clergy, claiming to themselves the sole right to teach men the way to heaven (see a publication by the Rev. Lyman Beecher), we feel it our duty and our privilege to lend our aid to remove the powers that be [because] . . . the past and present policy of the government of this state is calculated to endanger our civil and religious privileges. . . .
>
> We view the late appropriation of money for the support of Religion by the Legislature as a striking feature of the corrupt governments of the old world, and if not checked by the union of all republicans will eventuate in a union of church and state . . .
>
> Had the legislature repealed the certificate law and given us equal rights

23. *American Mercury*, January 7, 1817, p. 3.

with the congregational Churches, we should have believed they had done their duty; but instead of such an act of righteousness, they (that is the government party who are most of them congregationalists) have taken the people's money and give us a silver chain weighing 666 pounds, just the number of the Beast, Revelations 14 ch. 18 v.[24]

The following Methodist congregations were among those which passed and published notices of resolutions in which they refused to accept any of the money appropriated to them by the act: Greenwich, New Haven, Goshen, Burlington, Winsted, Granby, Glastonbury, Woodbridge, New Salem, Stratford, New Canaan, Andover and Humphreysville. Resolutions were passed which represented all of the congregations on the Methodists' circuits of Greenwich, Granville and Durham. The statement passed on November 29, 1816 by the society in Glastonbury may be considered typical. This act, they said, represented "a very bold and desperate effort to effectuate an union between Church and State" by those "who have hitherto delighted in reproaching and brow-beating us as a class of vulgar and illiterate set of enthusiasts regardless of all virtues and totally destitute of every good and moral principles, and also that our clergy are a set of worthless ramblers, unworthy the protection of the civil laws." We view this act with "pity and contempt — $12,000 given to 4000 Methodists! Three dollars per head! wonderful!!! Surely they must have supposed us less virtuous than Judas Iscariot." [25]

Many of the Baptists were equally vehemently opposed to the act. On December 5, 1816 the Baptist Church in Hartford met and voted to call a statewide convention of delegates to consider the act and to concert measures for effecting its repeal.[26] And on February 24, 1817, the Baptist church in Ashford, after passing a set of resolves denouncing the act for "forging chains to bind the consciences of posterity," voted to write to other Baptist churches in the state to ask them to consider sending a petition to the legislature asking for repeal of the act.[27] But neither of these plans were carried out, apparently because the Baptists were still opposed to any organizational unit which might threaten the autonomy of the individual churches. Several of the sets of resolutions passed by the Baptist churches referred to the fact that individual action by each church seemed more likely to be effective than action by a convention. Typical of the Baptist churches' resolutions was one voted on January 6, 1817 by the First and Second Baptist Churches of Groton:

Resolved as the sense of this meeting that it is not the province of any

24. *Ibid.*, January 7, 1817, p. 3. Presumably the amount alloted to the Methodists at that time was £666 in this Methodist's figuring.
25. *Columbian Register*, December 7, 1816, p. 2.
26. *Ibid.*, December 14, 1816, p. 2.
27. *Ibid.*, March 22, 1817, p. 4.

society of professing christians or a church of Christ in such capacity to interfere in legislative affairs so long as its oppressive power or fostering hand neglects to intermeddle with the affairs of Christ's Kingdom which is not of this world — Yet whenever the civil arm is stretched out to her for any other purpose than to guard their equal rights and privileges they ought in a dignified and a becoming temper of christians to express their views and sentiments upon the subject.

Resolved . . . that the legislative appropriation . . . ought to be deprecated.

. . . It is unjust to apply the monies of those who pretend to no religion and were paid by them for other purposes to the support of religion they do not believe in when it is known to be contrary to their desire: — also to oblige certain denominations of professing christians to help other denominations support their religion in addition to the expence of their own.

2d. It is unequal in its appropriation to the different denominations . . . comparing either the number of their societies, communicants, adherents or civil lists.

3d. It is evil in its effects: — it gives a precedence to future legislation . . . it is calculated to nerve that now palsying arm of civil and ecclesiastical power under which millions have groaned and died: — Also to tempt the unwary of the dissenting denominations to a departure from an important article in their dissention, viz. that civil authority never ought to meddle with the affairs of that Kingdom which is not of this world.

Resolved. That we . . . correspond with the Baptist Church in Hartford for the purposes suggested by them in some late resolves of theirs upon the subject of said appropriation, as the general sense of our denomination . . . may be ascertained better by their acting as individual societies.[28]

Similar resolutions were made by the Baptist churches in Andover, Hartford, Ashford, Windsor, New Canaan, and Stonington. It is noteworthy that in New Canaan the Baptists and Methodists united to make their protest, while in Andover the Baptists, Methodists, and Episcopalians united in their resolutions.[29] The three dissenting groups in Andover called for repeal of the act

Because we view it as designed to give a bias to the freedom of religious opinion by holding up to view a determination to advance the temporal interest of *one* favorite sect at the expence of every other, as designed to influence the freedom of elections by uniting Church and State under the same banner . . .

Resolved that in our opinion the aforesaid act is a counterpart to the certificate law and a like intolerant attempt to coerce and enslave the con-

28. *American Mercury,* January 21, 1817, p. 3.
29. For New Canaan see *Columbian Register,* December 23, 1816, p. 3.

science . . . *Resolved* . . . this appropriation is unjust in principle and distribution. Where is the Quaker, the Universalists, &c. Their certificates are lawful and they paid their share of this money. Their share is taken by legislative authority and given to others.[30]

In addition to the dissenters' protests, at least two towns, Preston and Danbury, passed resolutions at town meetings calling for the abolition of the act.[31]

But despite all of these protests and the general dissatisfaction with the act, it was never repealed. First because the Council was dominated by the Federalists until 1818 and they would not agree to a repeal. Second because once the Episcopalians and Congregationalists made application for their shares of the fund and these were granted to them, it became impossible to revoke the act. Finally, on February 10, 1818, the Methodist trustees appointed under the act held a meeting in Hartford and reluctantly voted to accept their share of the money. They regretted, they said, that the act had not been repealed, but they felt it was now too late to do so since some of the money had already been withdrawn. "Though a full proportion was not made in the act to the Methodist church, they do not think it right that what there is should remain useless seeing that the money is . . . the property of the people and that it is the voice of the majority that it should be received." [32] The trustees therefore applied to the state treasury and received $5125 for distribution to their societies.[33]

This action met with severe criticism from many Methodists, but "The simple truth is a federal [i.e. Federalist] Legislature appointed the board of Trustees, a majority of which were at that time and now are federalists and over whom the Methodists as a body can have no control. It is not surprising therefore that they, like true federalists, should have taken the bait." [34] How true this allegation was cannot be determined, but significantly none of those appointed as trustees were among the Methodists in the legislature who opposed the passage of the bill. After this, the only course left for Methodist churches which opposed the grants was to petition the legislature for permission to return the money given them by the trustees. This was actually done by several of their societies and the legislature accepted the money back.[35]

The Baptist trustees held out longer than the Methodists and at least one

30. *American Mercury,* April 1, 1817, p. 2. A letter in the *Connecticut Courant,* May 20, 1817, p. 2, stated that there were very few Methodists and Episcopalians in Andover and the so-called joint protest of the three groups was therefore a fraud to make the protest seem more important.
31. *American Mercury,* March 11, 1817, and March 25, 1817
32. *Ibid.,* February 17, 1818, p. 3.
33. *Columbian Register,* February 21, 1818, p. 2.
34. *American Mercury,* March 3, 1818, p. 3.
35. *Connecticut Courant,* October 20, 1818, p. 3; *Middlesex Gazette,* June 18, 1818, p. 1.

of them resigned rather than participate in accepting the money. But eventually, in June, 1820, they followed the Methodists' lead and accepted the $7687.50 appropriated to them.[36] By this time the new constitution had disestablished the Standing Order and the Baptists felt that the potential threats to religious liberty implicit in the act no longer applied.[37]

36. For the act incorporating the Connecticut Baptist Education Society to receive this fund see CEA, 2d ser., V, 51a. Also Purcell, *Connecticut,* p. 219; J. Hammond Trumbull, *Historical Notes of the Constitutions of Connecticut, 1639 to 1818* (Hartford, 1901), p. 36.

37. For a vote by a Baptist Society accepting the money in March 1820, see the ms. records of the Baptist Society in Wintonbury (under Hartford, Blue Hills Baptist Church), II, 15, in the CSL. Asa Wilcox in his tract, *A Plea for the Baptist Petition* (Hartford, 1818) has this interesting comment on the Appropriations Act: "Some money that was raised by the civil authority by taxation was given them [the dissenters] but because it came in that way and was to be used exclusively 'for the support of the gospel' it remains unaccepted. Had the legislature left it freely to the donees to appropriate it as they thought best, and if a method of dividing it could be found that would give general satisfaction perhaps it would have been accepted" (p. 16). The point of interest is that the Baptists seem to have objected more to the technical details of the state aid than to the principle.

The Toleration Party made the repeal of the Appropriations Act one of its primary campaign issues in spring 1817. For attacks on its religious injustices see *American Mercury,* March 11, 1817, and *Columbian Register,* March 29, 1817. For a tract by a liberal Congregational Republican favoring disestablishment at this time see [George H. Richard] *The Politics of Connecticut* (Hartford, 1817).

Chapter 53

Disestablishment in Connecticut,
1817–1818

It being the duty of all men to worship the Supreme Being, the Great Creator and Preserver of the Universe, and their right to render that worship in the mode most consistent with the dictates of their consciences; no person shall by law be compelled to join or support, nor be classed with, or associated to, any congregation, church or religious association.

Article VII of the Constitution of 1818

In April 1817, the Toleration Party in Connecticut won its first great victory over the Federalists. Oliver Wolcott was elected governor by a vote of 13,655 to John Cotton Smith's 13,119. Jonathan Ingersoll, unopposed by any Federalist candidate, was re-elected as lieutenant-governor. The Toleration Party had a slight majority of the lower house, roughly 103 to 98. Only in the Council did the Federalists still retain control. One of the new government's first acts in April was to appoint a committee to investigate the ecclesiastical laws with a view to modifying them consistent with the wishes of the dissenters who were so important in the victory. This was also in response to a surprising number of incidents concerning distraints for religious taxes early that year.

On January 4, 1817 the *Columbian Register* carried a letter signed by "A Countryman" which said,

> It is a lamentable fact that in this State and in this enlightened age, those persons who, to answer a good conscience, have left the Presbyterian (or established) order and attached themselves either to Episcopalian, Baptist, or Methodist churches are called on for taxes by the aforesaid established order and these taxes are rigidly exacted . . . Many of the writer's friends are in this predicament — and from observation I am induced to believe that a large number of our citizens are in the same situation.

A few months later, in March, a letter writer in New Haven noted,

Within a short time a poor man not far from this city had the misfortune to attend an Episcopal Church for three years without asking liberty of the congregational society's clerk; for this he . . . lost a cow [to the tax collector]. Within this last summer a number of individuals in the town of Southington (say about twenty) who were born and brought up in Episcopal and Baptist families have been taxed to pay the Congregational minister whom they do not hear. Is this Toleration? [1]

The incident in Southington aroused much attention in the next two months, partly because it concerned both Baptists and Episcopalians and partly because it was so clear-cut an example of the kind of injustice in the system which its opponents resented so deeply. It involved the members of one of the oldest Baptist churches in Connecticut and included direct descendants of that John Merriman who had aroused such a storm in the Great Awakening by asking the Rev. Philemon Robbins to speak in his church (then in Wallingford). A letter printed in the *Columbian Register* in April 5, 1817 summarized the story in the words of Anson Merriman:

Sir. — According to your request I now write you concerning the Tax laid by the Ecclesiastical Society against the Baptists and Episcopalians.

The Collector of the Presbyterian Society a few days since came to my house and demanded a Tax against me. I refused to pay it. My Father is a Baptist and always was. I have been a Baptist all my life — I have belonged to the Church for fifteen years and in full communion with the Brethren. I have three brothers of whom a tax is claimed, and [they] are all Baptists and always have been. Numbers more are in the like situation . . . It is expected they will collect these taxes in consequence of our not certificating off from the Presbyterian order.

It seems the Merriman boys, when they came of age, had failed to file certificates with the town clerk stating that they were members of the Baptist church. But the ecclesiastical society or parish had failed to tax them until 1816. Then the parish decided to be more strict in their enforcement. As a result they caught off guard a large number of dissenters who were technically in the wrong, though their religious dissent was well-known to those who levied the tax on them. A somewhat more detailed description of the situation appeared on April 26, 1817; it explained the problem of the Episcopalians in Southington:

I give you herewith the information respecting the situation of those persons who have been so unfortunate as to differ in religious sentiments from those of the Standing Order. And first the widow of Asher Dickinson: Her husband certificated off and joined the Episcopal Church about 20 years ago; since his death, say two years ago, the Congregationalists have laid a tax upon her and demanded it. Alpheus Brackett's parents belonged

1. *Columbian Register,* March 22, 1817, p. 2.

to the Episcopal Church and he has been educated in that way — Congregationalists have demanded a tax of him and in consequence of his refusal to pay it his property has been attached by their Collector.

Ebenezer Plant, Anson Merriman, Marcus Merriman, Leonard Merriman, and John Merriman all belong to the Baptist Congregation in this town, as did also their parents, and yet the Congregationalists have taxes against them.[2]

Legally all of these persons were liable because they had failed to file certificates. But the general laxity with which this law was enforced throughout Connecticut made the affair seem both arbitrary and an example of malicious harassment.

Another case of Baptist "persecution" for failure to pay religious taxes occurred in Windham about 1810. As Ellen Larned recounts it,

The death of Elder Benjamin Lathrop left the scattered Baptists without pastor or stated worship, so that they were again exposed to the exactions of the rate collector. Old Andrew Robinson when in Windham town one day had his horse taken from under him for a "priest rate." The old man shouldered his saddle and trudged manfully homeward, [mentally] revolving [plans for] relief from farther impost.

His means of avoiding further taxes was to organize a nondenominational dissenting society in his home to which he invited ministers of any denomination to preach; apparently he obtained enough regular preaching to qualify his group as a dissenting church.[3]

One of the most highly publicized cases of Federalist persecution of a Baptist minister occurred in 1812 when David Daggett the state's Attorney General indicted Joshua Bradley as "a person of an evil disposition" who tried "to impose himself upon many of the citizens of . . . Wallingford . . . North-Haven, East-Haven and Branford . . . as a preacher of the gospel . . . and thereby to seduce and draw away from their respective pastors and ecclesiastical societies to which they belong many of the aforesaid citizens." Bradley's alleged crime was not itinerating but displaying "a certain false forged and counterfeited paper, certificate or letter purporting to be a letter of recommendation" signed by the Rev. Moses C. Welch, Standing minister of Mansfield. Bradley had indeed preached in all of these, and other towns, from 1807 to 1811, and he had helped to form Baptist churches in some of them. But he denied ever having shown anyone a false letter of recommendation from Moses Welch. He was astounded that anyone would think he would try such a trick since during the six months or so that he preached in Mansfield in 1807, Welch had bitterly opposed him.

2. *Ibid.,* April 26, 1817.
3. Ellen Larned, *History of Windham County, Connecticut* (Worcester, 1880), II, 411.

Arrested in Wallingford (where he had founded a school in 1809) Bradley was tried in August 1812 and declared not guilty by the jury. It does not appear that Daggett even had a copy of the letter which Bradley was purported to have forged. The whole incident seemed spitefully produced by Welch who had convinced Daggett of Bradley's bad character and influence. That Bradley came to Connecticut from Rhode Island in 1807 probably contributed to his being mistrusted.[4]

Few Baptists in Connecticut succeeded in obtaining any important governmental posts, but occasionally one was appointed justice of the peace. The appointment was a matter of political patronage, however, and woe to the justice who failed to support those who had rewarded him. Such appears to have been the fate of Agur Judson of Stratfield, who, although he was a Baptist, had been appointed as a justice of the peace. In 1804 he was deprived of his post as punishment for attending the Republican convention in New Haven in August 1804 which demanded the replacement of the royal charter by a constitution. Judson was one of five justices relieved of office for this action; that he was a Baptist was not directly involved in his participation in the convention. Nevertheless, from the Baptist (and Republican) viewpoint, it was one more example of persecution by the Standing Order. The Federalists maintained in defense of their action that any judge who thought the charter was not a proper form of government had no right to administer the laws under it.[5]

The continued appearance of cases like these gradually convinced even those willing to tolerate some form of public support for religion that under the Federalist Party no fair system could ever be devised. But unhappily for the Baptists, the victory of the Toleration Party did not immediately produce much in the way of reform.

The committee appointed by the legislature to scrutinize the ecclesiastical laws in May 1817 produced a bill which offered only two minor changes. Instead of requiring that certificates should be filed with the parish or society clerk, they were to be filed with the town clerk. The other change permitted persons who shifted from one church to another within the same denomination to be exempt from taxes or voluntary agreements in the society he had left. It also permitted all societies to levy taxes for the support of their worship if they wished (thereby in effect incorporating all dissenting societies).[6]

Published debates on the bill to introduce these changes reveal that neither party was pleased with it. The Federalists objected that it would

4. *Trial of Joshua Bradley Upon An Indictment for Forgery* . . . (Middletown, 1812). Author unknown.

5. M. Louise Greene, *The Development of Religious Liberty in Connecticut* (Boston, 1905), pp. 433–435. R. J. Purcell, *Connecticut in Transition* (Washington, 1918), pp. 259–260.

6. *Connecticut Courant,* June 3, 1817, p. 2. J. Hammand Trumbull, *Historical Notes of Constitutions of Connecticut, 1639 to 1818* (Hartford, 1901), p. 38.

wreck the located societies (i.e. territorial parishes). They succeeded in having that section of the bill removed which allowed a man to shift to another church within the same denomination. The dissenters, like Daniel Burrows of Hebron,

> said we were endeavoring to erect a fabrick without a foundation. To legislate at all upon the subject of christianity was in his mind the highest absurdity. The church of Christ is built upon a foundation not to be strengthened — nor even to be shaken by the feeble powers of man . . . Why should every denomination of christians be compelled to bow to the standing order in Connecticut? They have a mortgage on every foot of land in the state. . . . He thought all the laws upon the subject but rubbish and heartily wished to see them swept away.

Samuel Robinson of Guilford said, "if we attempt to improve the present abominable system we jumpt out of the frying pan into the fire." [7] The bill passed as amended by the Federalists, but it offered no help for those, who like the Baptists and Episcopalians of Southington, simply did not want to turn in certificates.

This feeble attempt at reform (the Republicans claimed that anything more basic would have been vetoed by the Federalist Council) aroused the Baptists to the point of circulating a new petition which they submitted to the General Assembly on May 3, 1818. It was argued before both houses by David Bolles, Jr. who had been closely associated with the earlier petition movement. This petition traversed the usual grounds of complaint: "That the laws of this State establishing the denomination of christians who are called the presbyterian, congregational or consociated churches are injurious to your petitioners and the dissenters generally throughout the state." These laws were "unscriptural, unequal, and contrary to the true principles of religious liberty." It was wrong for "any person to be considered as belonging to any religious body [i.e., the territorial parish] until he has by his own act by their consent made himself a member of it." The tax exemption system by means of certificates was "liable to be traversed in a court of law as often as the standing order choose to dispute it" and "a majority of the courts and juries usually belong to the favored sect" so that favoritism was inevitable.

The petition differed in a few points from the petition of 1801. It took a somewhat more complaisant tone: "It is not pleasant to say these things; but more unpleasant to bear them." It used the pragmatic argument that "It is impolitick in a free state to pass laws which favor one class of citizens more than others." It pointed out that "aspiring and ambitious men in the state are tempted to profess a religion which they disbelieve" because "those who make laws to favor a religious denomination of people have been

7. *Columbian Register,* June 14, 1817, p. 1.

usually careful to select their officers from the favored sect or at least to promote those who approved their conduct." (This was not only the basis for comparing the New England system to the Anglican establishment in England but also a recognition of the Federalists' failure to make room for dissenters in their party or in the government.) The influence of John Leland's liberal views is evident in the petition's admission that "The dissenters are under necessity to defend by argument the rights of infidels to save their own from injury by means of the laws in question, because the friends of these laws maintain that they are necessary for the purpose of getting the money of infidels to support the gospel." The admission was grudging and reluctantly wrung from them, but at last the Baptists had reached the position Roger Williams had advocated so long ago. "A Christian has no better right to take the property or person of an infidel than the infidel has to enslave the Christian." Circumstance, not conviction or principle, had brought the Baptists to concede that total religious freedom included infidels and nonbelievers. But that they had still not reached the point of complete separation became evident in that part of the petition which dealt with the act of 1816 for the support of religion. Here the Baptists said they had refused to accept this money because it "was to be used exclusively 'for the support of the gospel.' " But then they went on to add, "Had the legislature left it freely to the donees to appropriate it as they thought best and if a method of dividing it could be found that would give general satisfaction, perhaps it would have been accepted." Thus, if the money could have been used for missionary work or for education, then the dissenters would have had no objection to receiving aid from the state. This lingering belief that the state could encourage religion led the Baptists in subsequent years not only to accept their share of the money but on at least one occasion to request Congress to give federal aid to missions. Williams' and Leland's message never quite registered with the Baptists.

Finally, the petition added the new argument that "they confidently believe many dissenters have left this state and gone to inhabit the wilderness rather than dwell in their native land under the aforesaid laws and the treatment they received and expected to receive from the established order by reason of them." This was the closest the Baptists had ever come to using an economic argument on behalf of religious liberty. The petition concluded on the old note of individualism and voluntarism, however, phrased in terms with which both Jeffersonian liberals and pietists could agree: "Truth is great and will prevail if left to herself." [8]

What the petition asked the legislature to do was to "enact that no man shall be compelled to support any religious worship, place or ministry what-

8. *American Mercury*, August 18, 1818, p. 2. The petition was signed by Asa Wilcox, Asahel Morse, Augustus Bolles, and Elisha Cushman, the foremost Baptist leaders in Connecticut. See also Asa Wilcox, *A Plea for the Baptist Petition* (Hartford, 1818).

soever unless by express personal contract, nor shall be enforced, restrained, molested or burthened in his body or goods nor shall otherwise suffer on account of his religious opinions or belief." To implement the petition James Stevens, the representative from Stamford, submitted a bill for a new certificate law which would require the clerk of each society (standing or dissenting) to list all the persons now taxed in his society (i.e., territorial parish, voluntary congregation, or incorporated poll parish) and thereafter to add only such persons to the list who asked to have their names added.

> Be it enacted &c. that the clerk of each ecclesiastical society in this State, which supports its ministry by taxing shall enrol in a book . . . the name of each person as a member of such society who was lawfully taxed by it as a member thereof within the year preceding the passage of this act, also the name of each person who shall in a writing by him subscribed hereafter request such Clerk to enrol him as a member of such society and none but such as become enroled as aforesaid and the land of non-residents of the same sect shall be liable to be taxed for religious purposes.[9]

(Nonresidents were of course to be allowed to sign off by certificate at any time as were residents.) This bill was in effect a gradual disestablishing act, for eventually all societies would be made up entirely of voluntary members. For the present, however, territorial parishes would be allowed to continue to tax all those inhabitants who had not signed off but they could not add new inhabitants (either as children came of age or outsiders moved in to live) to their tax list without written consent from the new inhabitants. This bill would have prevented such difficulties as those in Southington and have done away with almost all the certificate problems.

The legislature, despite its Republican majority, postponed action on both the Baptist petition and on Stevens's new certificate bill until the next session, and by that time the new constitution was in effect.[10]

The call for a constitutional convention was officially pronounced on November 4, 1817 by Moses Warren, chairman of the Republican Party in the state and a Baptist.[11] For the Republicans a reform in the religious laws of Connecticut was only one aspect of a much larger program of political reform. This political reformation was to be accomplished not by piecemeal measures like the new certificate bill, but by a scrapping of the old charter under which Connecticut had been governed since 1662 and the inauguration of a new constitution made by the people. This had been the Republican goal since 1800. Now at last they were in a position

---

9. *Middlesex Gazette,* June 11, 1818, p. 2.
10. For a complicated instance of religious taxation at this time in New Haven which was considered oppressive by some but accepted by the man concerned, see *Columbian Register,* June 20, 1818, and July 4, 1818.
11. *American Mercury,* November 4, 1817.

to achieve it. Following the official party call for a convention, under Republican leadership, resolutions endorsing the idea were adopted in town meetings all over the state. In the election of March 1818, the Toleration Party finally won control of both houses of the legislature and the decision to call a convention was taken by vote of the General Assembly on June 2. The election of delegates took place on July 4 — doubtless to encourage the election of Jeffersonians. Of the delegates chosen, 105 were of the Toleration Party and 96 were considered Federalists. Among the delegates there were at least seven Baptists: Moses Warren, George Leonard, Edmund Freeman, Asahel Morse, John Daboll, Amos Gallup, and Eliakim Marshall. There was one Methodist, Daniel Burrows; one Universalist, Sylvester Wells; and one Separate, Zacheous Waldo. There may well have been others who were dissenters or who attended dissenters' churches.

Before the convention met on August 26, 1818 the Baptists and Methodists throughout the state met to adopt resolutions concerning the principles which they wished to have embodied in the constitution. A Federalist declared of these meetings:

> The course which the Baptists and Methodists are pursuing is indeed extraordinary . . . It appears that meetings have been separately held by these two denominations in various towns and one uniform preamble and resolve has been adopted by them all: who was the author or from whence they originated is not generally known; but that these resolves have been circulated far and wide is very apparent — and that those who have so readily adopted them have discovered no great share or understanding or opinion of their own, but are disposed to do as they are bid by others. In the preamble to these resolutions these sectarians all declare their cordial approbation of the measure calling a convention and then pass a resolve in the words following, viz. "Resolved that no constitution of civil government shall receive our approbation or support unless it contains a provision for securing the full and complete enjoyment of religious liberty." . . . The ground taken by these sectaries seems to preclude every argument that might be adduced in support of the principle on which our laws are founded.[12]

The Federalists never did understand the practice of pressure politics by interest groups.

It is unclear that the Baptist and Methodist meetings were so well-organized and uniform in their proceedings as this writer assumed, but it is clear that the dissenters were firm in their resolve that this constitution must embody their principle of disestablishment. The most forceful set of resolves adopted were those of the Hartford Baptists, signed by Benjamin Fowler and Jeremiah Brown:

12. *Connecticut Courant,* August 25, 1818, p. 1.

The people of this state having derived from their ancestors the principles of civil liberty, and as a self-evident truth resulting from the fitness of things, it follows that in the exercise of their religious freedom, human laws should not interfere.

To cherish with solicitude and maintain with firmness their inestimable rights are among the first duties of *freemen*. And having recently elected delegates to meet in convention for the purpose of forming a constitution of civil government, it is peculiarly proper for the people as individuals or particular communities to examine and point out such defects or evils as shall be found to exist in our present form of government or laws in force. In the hope that the proposed written constitution will be founded on such principles and the powers of government so organized as to provide new guards for their own and the safety and happiness of posterity.

All candid men who examine the subject, it is believed, will agree that in this state Religion is established and supported by law; and however mild and just may be the general deportment of individuals whose religious views are in accordance with that establishment, still it is not merely as series of oppressive acts or instances of individual suffering multiplied as they have been, but the nature and tendency of all ecclesiastical systems that are the subject of iniquity — That it has authorized in this state and still allows a species of tyranny oppressive to individuals and subversive of the general welfare we think cannot be denied.

It is not intended to examine the history of judicial proceedings in Connecticut arising under ecclesiastical laws which authorize one sect of professing christians to build houses of public worship and to support their religious teachers by taxing other sects who conscientiously disapprove the sentiments and instructions of those teachers they are so compelled to support.

A bare reference to cases of this nature would far exceed the limits prescribed to these remarks, and notwithstanding repeated applications have been made for the repeal of laws so palpably unjust — still those applications even down to the session in May, 1818, have been either rejected or disposed of in a manner far differently in our view from that liberal and just policy which it was reasonable to expect would have characterized the proceedings of an enlightened legislature. And as the period is approaching when we may in common with our fellow citizens be called to exercise the high duty of examining and approving or rejecting the new form of civil government. Therefore,

Resolved as the sense of this meeting that Religion, or the duty men owe their Creator, and the manner of discharging it, ought to be left to the reason, conviction, and conscience of every man — That these rights are inalienable — that all acts of the civil magistrate, either in the form of constitutional provisions or the ordinary acts of the legislature which in any manner restrain the free exercise of religion or compel any man to contribute to the support of any religious worship or to the public teachers thereof are oppressive, and regarding our duty as faithful members of a free state, no considerations shall induce us to give our support to a written constitution delegating powers to civil government inconsistent with the views expressed in the preceding preamble and this resolution.

Resolved, That the doings of this meeting be signed . . . [and published].[13]

The Federalists' reaction to this and to similar resolutions demonstrated the mood and temper of the convention. Even with the best will in the world the Federalists could not bring themselves to see the issues as those of inalienable or minority rights. They argued as though the dissenters and the Republicans were denying the rights of the majority and claimed that the Standing Order represented the will of the people. I am astounded, wrote one Federalist, by

> the character of the claim set up by the Baptists and Methodists that the ecclesiastical laws shall all be repealed and the community at large *be placed on the footing that pleases them.* These denominations are a small minority compared with the Presbyterians and Episcopalians; or indeed with the Presbyterians alone. With what face can they claim of the majority that the laws of the State shall be rendered inconvenient and injurious to the interests of *the many,* and made to suit the views or the feelings of *the few.* The fundamental principal of a republican government is that *the majority shall govern* . . . Every privilege which in reason justice, or decency they can demand is afforded to them already; and if they are not satisfied with such a state of things there is no good reason to conclude that they will be satisfied with anything short of the absolute control of the reins of government. To them they will be entitled *when they become a majority, and not till* then.[14]

The writer not only failed to see the revolution which the Toleration Party and the constitutional convention itself symbolized but he also failed to see how many nominal Congregationalists agreed with the dissenters on this point. (There was no religious census available to determine accurately the numbers in each denomination.)

The day after the convention met it chose a committee of three members from each county to prepare a draft of the constitution. Although this committee contained two Baptists who were graduates of Brown — George Leonard (Learned or Larned) and Edmund Freeman — neither of these drafted the article on religion. That was done by two ardent Republicans — Joshua Stow, a freethinker from Middletown, and Gideon Tomlinson, a Congregational liberal from Fairfield.[15] Its wording therefore bears the liberal and not the pietistic Christian stamp, mute evidence that the New

13. *Ibid.,* August 11, 1818, p. 3.
14. *Ibid.,* August 18, 1818, p. 2. This letter was signed "Another Freeman." He claimed that the Episcopalians were not in favor of "the revolutionary system" advocated by the Baptists and Methodists. But, although the Episcopalians did not submit petitions and resolutions for disestablishment, neither did they oppose it. Generally they were ready to accept it as inevitable.
15. Purcell, *Connecticut,* pp. 384, 400; Trumbull, *Constitutions of Connecticut,* p. 57, no. 5.

England dissenters, like those in Virginia, could never have attained their goal without the support of those who, in religious terms, they considered their and society's worst enemies.

The draft of the constitution contained three particular references to religion. These were Sections Three and Four of the Declaration of Rights and Article Seven entitled "Religion." Section 3 of the Bill of Rights passed without amendment or debate:

> The exercise and enjoyment of religious profession and worship, without discrimination, shall forever be free to all persons in this State, provided that the right hereby declared and established, shall not be so construed as to excuse acts of licentiousness, or to justify practices inconsistent with the peace and safety of the State.

But Section Four aroused both debate and amendment. As originally drafted it read, "No preference shall be given by law to any religious sect or mode of worship." When this section appeared for discussion, former Governor John Treadwell moved to substitute the word "Christian" for the word "religious." This amendment provoked considerable debate because it was not clear whether Treadwell was simply preparing the way for a religious test to exclude non-Christians from officeholding or whether he had some broader purpose in defense of the established order. Many of the delegates assumed that the adoption of this amendment would give the state the right to define who was and who was not a Christian, and by implication the state might then also have the right to pass laws to support or maintain the Christian religion in preference to others. Hence the question of Treadwell's amendment raised at the outset the whole question of the stand the convention would take on religious taxation and certification.

In addition to Treadwell's amendment, Elder Asahel Morse, put forward the following amendment:

> That rights of conscience are inalienable; that all persons have a natural and indefeasible right to worship Almighty God according to their own consciences; and no person shall be compelled to attend any place of worship or contribute to the support of any minister, contrary to his own choice.[16]

Nathan Smith of New Haven, a conservative Episcopalian, said that he thought Section 4 was all right as it was originally drafted and that he wanted neither changes nor additions:

> He was willing for one to vest in the Legislature supreme power on this subject; it [Section 4] was consistent with the idea that one Christian denomination should not be built up at the expense of another; it was not

16. Trumbull, p. 56.

inconsistent for a society to pay *no* tax but if he wished to join a society which was disposed to pay taxes *he* ought to have the privilege and the legislature ought to have the power of regulating this subject.

In other words, Smith did not want total separation of church and state written into the constitution regarding religious taxes, and he had no objection to special ecclesiastical legislation enabling those religious groups which wished to use the power of the state in levying and collecting taxes for their support to do so. This turned out to be the crucial issue in the debate over disestablishment.

The Methodist, Daniel Burrows, took a view more typical of the pietistic dissenters.

> He would not agree that the legislature have a right to make laws on this subject — if they had, *he* had always been in error concerning it. In the first place he doubted the power altogether — if they had power to legis- late on the subject they had power to legislate on matters of *conscience* — he was altogether opposed; but *he* was not opposed to the question of the 4th section if it amounted to a religious test, that no man should hold office who did not embrace the Christian religion; if that was the idea [behind Treadwell's amendment] he had no objection — but if it was de- signed to give a right to *legislate* on religious concerns, he was still more opposed.

It is a mark of the still indistinct conception of separationism among dis- senters that Burrows could accept religious discrimination for officeholding and yet be so vehement against ecclesiastical legislation to permit religious taxes by those who wanted to tax themselves.

Joshua Stow, whose Jeffersonian deism typified the mood of the non- dissenting (i.e. liberal or anticlerical Congregational) Republicans,

> remarked that this question [concerning ecclesiastical legislation] had been agitated ever since his memory, and he conceived it to be the only true ground that the legislature have a right to legislate on all subjects relating to this world [only] — if they step off the ground at all and presume to legislate on the subject of religion they carry the matter too far. Christ's kingdom was not of this world, and all had a right to worship in their own way . . . Look at the neighboring state of N. York, New-Jersey and others — their government is founded on religion as well as ours — *there* the legislature has interfered and you find nothing but constant *petitioning:* — the same is the case in England where they have an estab- lished religion — it would be a radical error if this subject should not be put at rest — he doubted whether this Constitution could be carried into effect until this subject should be entirely put to rest.

The delegates then voted on Morse's amendment. They did not pass it. Someone then moved to add just the last clause of Morse's amendment beginning "Nor shall any person be compelled to attend any place of worship or contribute to the support of any minister . . ." but this also did not pass. The delegates then voted on Treadwell's amendment and it passed.[17] Obviously the total disestablishment the pietists and anti-clericals desired would not prevail.

Article Seven, drafted by Stow and Tomlinson, was divided into two sections and contained the heart of the disestablishment proceedings. The two most important aspects were that no one should be automatically classed or associated with any church or society or parish, and that anyone might sign off or separate from any religious society without stating that he was going to attend or join any other society. The article did, however, state expressly that those societies or parishes which wished to levy on and collect taxes from their members should have the right to do so.[18] But it made membership dependent in the future on voluntary action by those who wanted to join a society or parish.

> 1. It being the right and duty of all men to worship the Supreme Being, the great Creator and Preserver of the universe, in the mode most consistent with the dictates of their consciences; no person shall be compelled to join or support, nor by law be classed with or associated to any congregation, church, or religious association. And each and every society or denomination of christians in this state, shall have, and enjoy the same and equal powers, rights, and privileges; and shall have power and authority to support and maintain the Ministers or Teachers of their respective denominations, and to build and repair houses for public worship by a tax on the members of their respective societies only, or in any other manner.
> 2. If any person shall choose to separate himself from the society or denomination of christians to which he may belong, and shall leave a written notice thereof with the Clerk of such society, he shall thereupon be no longer liable for any future expences, which may be incurred by said society.

Insofar as this article still permitted the collection of taxes by civil authority and still required certificates for those who wished, at least in the first instance, to separate from any society, it was distinctly a conservative measure. Yet essentially it removed the core from the established or privileged position given to the Congregational parish system and was therefore bitterly contested by the Federalist delegates. Former Governor Treadwell put his objections this way:

17. *Connecticut Courant,* September 8, 1818, pp. 2–3.
18. If this appears inconsistent with Stow's remark on Treadwell's amendment, quoted above, the difference seems to be that Stow feared that Trumbull's amendment would have left future ecclesiastical laws up to the legislature, and he wanted the matter embodied in the constitution in such a way that the legislature could not move beyond its limits.

If I understand [Article Seven] it goes to dissolve all ecclesiastical societies in the State . . . This, Sir, takes away their rights and privileges, it recognizes no ecclesiastical association, but leaves all as it were in a state of nature. Sir, I have no idea of making distinctions between denominations . . . when a particular denomination prevails, I would make it the standing denomination of the place and others should enjoy the privilege of separating from it . . . this [article] is to dissolve the whole union. Sir, I am unwilling that these associations should be thus dissolved; they have certain rights and privileges as corporate bodies and unless they have forfeited those rights they cannot justly be taken from them.[19]

Treadwell's concern for the corporate rights and privileges of the established societies or parishes was similar to the claim answered by Zephaniah Swift in the 1790's. It was also being raised at this time in New Hampshire. That is, that disestablishment was contrary to the federal constitution since it abrogated contractual rights (between minister and parish) guaranteed by the state.[20] Asa Wilcox gave the most succinct answer to this argument in Connecticut in 1818 when he denied that any question of impairment of contract was involved:

These [religious] societies are corporations by force of the civil law; and it would be absurd to say that the authorities which consituted them could not vary nor regulate them. It has been declared who may vote in such societies, and who shall and who shall not be liable to taxation by them. It [the state] has from time to time altered this liability and may now as well say that no one shall be holden to pay it as to say that such shall be exempt as have given certificates and joined another society. The ministers of these societies were settled knowing that the legislature possessed this power and cannot say it is unprecedented to use it.[21]

Equally significant was Treadwell's claim that the destruction of the standing parishes would reduce Connecticut to "a state of nature." It was inconceivable to the Federalist conception of a corporate Christian commonwealth that society could exist for long without a civil recognition of and support for religion — specifically the Christian religion. Treadwell and the Federalists of the Standing Order were in this sense the men of little faith in the American experiment; they did not believe that a voluntaristic Christian commonwealth could maintain itself in peace and order; that was not what they had bargained for when they favored ratification of the federal constitution.

Joshua Stow rose to defend Article Seven against Treadwell. In earlier days, he said, religion was established by law in Connecticut, "in a time

19. *Connecticut Courant*, September 22, 1818, pp. 2–3.
20. See chapter 44.
21. Wilcox, *Baptist Petition*, p. 15. Wilcox made good use of Backus's history of the Baptists to prove the past oppressions of dissenters in Connecticut.

when men were not as liberally disposed" as now, "or at least when there were not as many denominations as there now are." The purpose of Section Seven is so that in future

> a person shall consent to support [religion] but with his voluntary consent. If an individual enters a town now he must enter his name as belonging to some denomination of Christians. This law [Article Seven] was made so broad as to compel no such thing; but it [also] designs that all who have been caught in these bands may be let out. If any man says he has been imprisoned unlawfully, this will let him out and he may go free; hereafter we will have no such restraint. As to the present section [Section Two of Article Seven] if it is altered in any way it will curtail the great principles for which we contend and society will be disturbed as here to-fore.

Stow also pointed out that even the Congregationalists were no longer agreed on the use of religious taxes; some of them "say that if their preachers continue to preach certain doctrines they shall be dissatisfied; they will not pay for preaching they don't believe, — and, Sir, on this principle of liberality [Article Seven] they will not need to." In short, it would save many disputes within the Standing Order over the choice of ministers with Hopkinsian or Unitarian, Calvinist or Arminian, views and it would save dissatisfied Congregationalists from signing off hypocritically and pretending to be Baptists or Episcopalians to avoid such forced support.

The article, said Stow, did not require Congregational societies to stop laying taxes; it did give them the force of law to collect such taxes.

> Some societies will tax themselves and some will not . . . Some societies will sell pews and others will rent them . . . The gentleman from Farmington [Treadwell] would make the congregationalists the predominant order, but, Sir, this is not agreeable to the spirit of the times. It is well known that certain orders don't want this privilege [i.e., the Baptists would not want to be the Standing Order in any parish just because they were a majority] and it would be idle to grant them what they don't want.

In short, said Stow, the Puritan conception of a Christian commonwealth supported by law was a dead issue already — dead among the Congregationalists as well as among the dissenters.

Nathaniel Terry of Hartford, a staunch Federalist, supported Treadwell's opposition to Article Seven by arguing that it mistook a civil matter for a matter of conscience:

> The principle on which our [present ecclesiastical] law is founded is here cut up by the roots; our law does compel a person to belong somewhere, though he has the liberty to belong where he pleases; but here it is declared

that it shall be at the option of the person whether he belongs to any denomination [or not] . . . the question is whether religion shall be supported *somewhere;* does this interfere with the rights of conscience? no more, Sir, I beg leave to say, than it does to be taxed for the support of a war which I don't approve of [as in 1812]

or for the support of schools to which I do not send any children.

To this Stow gave a more pietistic answer, relying not on the spirit of the times but on the Baptist argument that forced support of religion could lead to idolatry:

> I deny that the Legislature have a right to compel a man to support public worship: if they have that right they have a right to say what is public worship and where and in what manner he shall support it: this is impolitic . . . If a power has a right to say what public worship is, it may go to support idolatry. The Bill of Rights says that it shall be free for all men to worship God according to the dictates of their own conscience: now if you make a law that a man shall worship somewhere and that man should think it his duty to worship the devil, you would *compel* him to worship the devil.

The state might, for example (though Stow did not say this) have to use its power to collect taxes to support a heretical Universalist or Unitarian Church or even a "heathen" Mohammedan or an "infidel" deist congregation. The old Puritan argument for an exclusive state church had come full circle and was being used by voluntarists to abolish what in the seventeenth century it had been used to establish.

After Treadwell rose again to demand amendments to Article Seven to retain the old system, a Separate-Baptist delegate from Windham, Zacheus Waldo, expressed the deep-seated animus behind the dissenters' support of voluntarism:

> In old times we are told that Pharoah would not let the people go . . . Much is said, Mr. President, about religion. "Love the Lord thy God &c." Those who do not [do] this must take the consequences. I would not compel them to do it. The worst thing that ever was is an established religion. This has been the case with the Mahomedan and Roman Catholic. When I was a little boy it caused more bloody noses than anything else: "ah, you *separate,* you *separate,*" the other boys would cry [at me]. I'm sorry I ever took so much notice of them [as to hit them in the nose], but now thank God for the privilege of expressing my opinion and giving my vote against it.

Samuel Hart, a Republican from Berlin, said that the argument of Treadwell and Terry, looks a little like this — one man says to another, you help me support my truth and I will help you support your falsehood. I have no idea of supporting error. I don't like it — and I shall make use of all my weapons to destroy it. There are two kinds of religion brought in here, one of the heart and the other of the head. It seems we can do nothing about supporting the religion of the heart — but you can compel a man to pay money [to support a religion of the head] — and will this promote the good morals, happiness, and peace of society? According to [the] reasoning of the gentlemen [from Hartford and Farmington] the more money you spend the more religion you have.

The first test of the Article came on a motion to adopt the first section. This passed 103 to 86. The Federalists later moved to omit the second section completely, but this failed by almost the same majority, 105 to 84. The Federalists' only success on this issue came in the addition of two sentences (and some slight rewording) to Section One which were proposed by Nathaniel Terry. These sentences made explicit the assumption that the existing religious societies might continue to exist as corporate bodies made up of their present members and that these members had a right to levy and collect taxes by majority vote to build and repair meeting-houses. These concessions were passed without a record of individual votes. They doubtless clarified the legal status of the societies, but they did not alter their disestablishment. The final wording of Article Seven as it was incorporated into the constitution (with the two Federalist amendments in italics) read:

ARTICLE VII

Of Religion

Sect. 1. It being the duty of all men to worship the Supreme Being, the Great Creator and Preserver of the Universe, and their right to render that worship in the mode most consistent with the dictates of their consciences; no person shall by law be compelled to join or support, nor be classed with, or associated to, any congregation, church, or religious association. *But every person now belonging to such congregation, church, or religious association, shall remain a member thereof, until he shall have separated himself therefrom, in the manner hereinafter provided.* And each and every society or denomination of Christians in this state, shall have and enjoy the same equal powers, rights and privileges; and shall have power and authority to support and maintain the ministers or teachers of their respective denominations, and to build and repair houses for public worship, by a tax on the members of any such society only, *to be laid by a major vote of the legal voters assembled at any society meeting, warned and held according to law,* or in any other manner.

Sect. 2. If any person shall choose to separate himself from the society or denomination of Christian to which he may belong and shall leave

1059

written notice thereof with the clerk of such society, he shall there upon be no longer liable for any future expenses which may be incurred by said society.

On September 15 the convention accepted the new constitution by a vote of 134 to 61, which indicates that about thirty Federalists had become reconciled to the new religious principle of voluntarism. On September 29, a writer in the *American Mercury* urged the people to ratify the constitution; he had this to say of Article Seven: "This article does indeed exempt those persons who do not choose to belong to the located societies from being taxed — but it on the other hand confirms the right of the located societies to tax *themselves;* and what more than this can any candid man require? All denominations are placed upon an equal footing, and dare any man of sense say this is wrong?" [22]

At the next election the towns ratified the constitution, 13,918 to 12,364. Had the convention or the legislature required a majority of two-thirds for ratification, the constitution would not have succeeded. To what extent the religious issue narrowed the majority is difficult to say. Very little controversy concerning the constitution appeared in the newspapers, nor were any tracts dealing with the religious clauses of the constitution printed. However, there were less than three weeks between the time the convention adjourned and the election on October 5, so this lack of discussion is not strange. The issue had been thoroughly aired in the newspapers during the convention.

Attempts to correlate the vote for ratification with the location of dissenting congregations do indicate that in towns where there were one or more dissenting congregations the vote for ratification was heavy. But since the vote for ratification was also heavy in some towns where there were no dissenting churches and few dissenters, it seems clear that the issues were far more broad than disestablishment.[23] Connecticut had undergone a social and intellectual revolution, and disestablishment was one important phase of that revolution. "The die is cast," said the *Connecticut Courant* on October 20, 1818; "The freedom of Connecticut, reared at the expense of the blood and treasure of our venerable forefathers is prostrated in the dust." But any attempt to interpret Connecticut's second revolution primarily in religious terms would be a distortion. A broad cultural reorientation had taken place, not merely an ecclesiastical one.

Surprisingly the Baptists did not make much of their victory. Doubtless there were many sermons and prayers of thanksgiving in their churches throughout the state, but the only permanent records of the event are con-

22. *American Mercury,* September 29, 1818, p. 3.
23. The towns were asked to vote only yes or no on the whole constitution so there is no way of discovering what particular clauses were more or less popular. Purcell, *Connecticut,* pp. 408–416.

tained in the minutes of the Baptist Associations. The New London Baptist Association (newly formed in 1818 when the Groton Union Conference dissolved and its churches either merged with the Stonington Association or joined the new Association) made a brief statement in its circular letter of 1818:

> We congratulate you on the kind interference of Divine Providence in favor of *Religious Liberty* in this State in removal of those impediments which have so long lay in our way; but God forbid that this liberty should ever be perverted to licentious purposes. Let us therefore labour to cultivate friendship and harmony with our brethren of different sentiments.[24]

The Danbury Baptist Association waited until 1819 to note in its Circular Letter, "Our fathers suffered persecution and we have felt the evil of an ecclesiastical establishment; but the difficulty is removed and our religious liberty [is] secured by the supreme Law of the State. Brethren we live in an auspicious day. A *day* for which our fathers prayed and which they desired to see. A *day* for which *we* have prayed and which *we,* by the blessing of our God, have obtained." [25]

Lyman Beecher spoke for the despondent Congregationalists: "I remember," said his daughter, "seeing father the day after the election, sitting on one of the old-fashioned rush-bottomed kitchen chairs, his head drooping on his breast, and his arms hanging down. 'Father,' said I, 'what are you thinking of?' He answered, solemnly, 'The Church of God.' " Looking back on it later, Beecher said in his autobiography, "It was a time of great depression and suffering. It was the worst attack I ever met in my life" (excepting his trial for heresy in 1835). "It was as dark a day as ever I saw . . . The injury done to the cause of Christ, as we then supposed, was irreparable. For several days I suffered what no tongue can tell for the best thing that ever happened to the State of Connecticut." Beecher, looking back and reconciling himself to the revolution that had occurred, declared himself pleased with it: "It cut the churches loose from dependence on state support. It threw them wholly on their own resources and on God." [26]

The Rev. Thomas Robbins of Windsor was never so reconciled. But like Beecher he shared the despondency of the moment. In June 1818, he wrote in his diary, "The Assembly have risen and concluded the first Democratic, and probably the most disgraceful session ever held in this State." A few weeks later he noted, "The universal suffrage law is horrible." And on September 16, "The Convention rose and left us a constitution

24. New London Baptist Association Minutes, 1818, p. 7
25. Danbury Baptist Association Minutes, 1819, p. 13. The election sermon of Elder Elisha Cushman in 1820 made no reference to the entire issue.
26. Lyman Beecher, *The Autobiography of Lyman Beecher,* ed. Barbara Myers Cross (Cambridge, 1961), I, 252–253.

which, as a State paper, I consider contemptible." [27] Yet in Robbins' east parish in Windsor nothing much changed for him and his church. His congregation still met as a society, still levied taxes on their members by majority vote, and still sent out a collector to collect it and pay it over to Robbins, just as had always been done. Robbins's diary contains periodic references to "my collector" who came to his study regularly to pay him the tax money which was his salary. No disputes arose. The church did not decline. The old system continued its function here, as elsewhere in the state, in the same way for many years to come.

But neither Baptist nor any other dissenter in Connecticut was ever again taxed against his will or against his conscience.[28]

27. Chandler Robbins, *Diary,* ed. I. N. Tarbox (Boston, 1887), I, 744, 748, 757.

28. One of the issues which was not settled in 1818 was the Universalists' right to testify in court. For a discussion of the famous "Litchfield Decision" in 1828 and the "Religious Freedom Bill" of 1830 which rectified it, see the *Universalist Trumpet,* June 5, 1830, p. 195; June 12, 1830, p. 198, June 19, 1830, p. 202.

PART XII

The Dissenters and the Jeffersonian Republicans in Massachusetts,

1800–1820

"It afforded peculiar relief to the Baptists and other dissenters."
Elder David Benedict on the Religious Liberty Act of 1811

Chapter 54

James Sullivan and the Republican Party, 1800–1808

The Baptists, by attaching themselves to the present administration [i.e., Jefferson's Republican Party] have gained great success in the United States and greater in New England than any sect since the settlement even beyond comparison. This seems to be a warning to the Churches of other denominations.

The Rev. William Bentley, in his diary, January 1802

The dissenters' long fight for separation of church and state in New England came to a successful climax in the years between 1800 and 1833. The victory was only one element in the social revolution which transformed the old Bay Colony from an aristocratic, Calvinistic, corporate Christian commonwealth into an egalitarian, Evangelical, laissez faire democracy. It was a victory of the common man on the rise over an old elite which yielded only reluctantly to the pressure of majority rule. The Federalist Party and the Unitarian Clergy waged a determined fight every inch of the way to "hold fast to the time-honoured ways of our pious forefathers." That the Eleventh Amendment to the Massachusetts constitution, which put an end to compulsory religious taxes, was ratified overwhelmingly by those who made the effort to vote in an apathetic popular referendum in November 1833 indicated how effectively the Standing Order had stood in the gap beyond its time — a thin red line against the barbarian horde whose sheer weight of numbers finally overwhelmed it. Except for "The Religious Freedom Act" of 1811, passed in a great outburst of popular protest against a reactionary decision of the state Supreme Judicial Court, the Standing Order effectively blocked, ignored, side-stepped or compromised every serious threat to the favored position of the established church throughout the entire Jeffersonian Era. Had the Congregational churches been willing to compromise over the Unitarian movement within the Standing Order the practice of compulsory religious taxes might have survived even longer. The people of Massachusetts never really accepted

Jacksonian democracy and even many of the dissenters had apostatized from Jeffersonianism to become Whigs by 1833. Nevertheless after 1800 the Standing Order was constantly on the defensive.

In this last round of the battle for disestablishment the Baptists were materially assisted by new dissenting groups. In some respects, after 1811, the Methodists and Universalists played more dynamic roles than the Baptists did. The Baptists in this generation completed their development from a sect to a denomination in New England and the torch of pietistic protest passed to the younger sects. The Baptists had not abandoned their disestablishmentarian principles or goals. They simply preferred to devote more effort to other pietistic activities — revivalism, home and foreign missions, Sabbath schools, seminaries, temperance, Sabbatarian legislation, and the host of other benevolent and philanthropic evangelical reforms of the period. They also suffered from the growing pains of respectability and institutionalization. For many Baptists the Religious Freedom Act of 1811 gave them sufficient freedom to constitute victory. Failure of the constitutional convention of 1820 to enlarge on this act seemed evidence that complete separation — i.e., the abolition of compulsory religious taxes — would not happen soon. Busy reaping a rich harvest of souls in the Second Great Awakening, fighting off schisms within their ranks, competing with new pietistic sects, seeking rapprochement with "the Orthodox" or Trinitarian wing of Congregationalism, attacking deism and Unitarianism, and above all turning their attention to new horizons of national and international Evangelical activity, the Baptists relaxed their efforts to wipe out the last vestiges of church-state unity in Massachusetts and left the initiative to those younger and still radical pietists who felt its restrictions more keenly.

Although the Baptists in Massachusetts, as in Connecticut, were almost wholly committed to Jefferson's Democratic-Republican Party in the early 1800's, that party proved not to be as helpful to them in Massachusetts as it was in Connecticut. The Massachusetts Republican Party was led by a combination of Trinitarian-Congregationalists and Unitarians who had no real desire to end the church-state system; nor did the Massachusetts party have such an effective political issue as the lack of a state constitution to use as a weapon in their quest for power. Moreover, unlike Connecticut, there were sufficient respectable and liberal Congregationalists in Massachusetts to lead the new party without including dissenters and radical deists. Baptist and other dissenters were important as voters, and religious concessions were made or promised to them during the few terms the Republicans were in office in this period (1807–1808, 1810–1811) but the dissenters were so solidly and irrevocably opposed to the Federalists that it was unnecessary to do much to keep them in the Republican ranks. Even more than in Connecticut, Republican politics was an internal conflict within the Standing Order.

Although the Republicans frequently used the phrase "religious liberty" as a political war cry in Massachusetts, they did not mean by it what the dissenters did. For Republican politicians it meant primarily liberty from clerical support of Federalist policies. They wanted the Standing ministers to stop using their pulpits, pens, and prestige to attack the new Jeffersonian movement. Good Jeffersonian doctrine denounced the interference of an established priestcraft in the affairs of running a democratic society, but the New England Jeffersonians did not share Jefferson's antipathy to the concept of a Christian nation or to the public support of religion by compulsory religious taxes. The Republican Party was born, flourished and died in Massachusetts without ever advocating Jefferson's position on disestablishment. Many historians have been deceived (though probably few contemporary dissenters were) into thinking that Republican leaders like James Sullivan, Benjamin Austin, Elbridge Gerry, Levi Lincoln, Joseph Story, or William Bentley were committed to the same view of separation of church and state as were Backus and the Baptists. But a careful reading of their works reveals that none of them ever had any serious intention of trying to abolish Article Three of the Bill of Rights to create a completely voluntary system of church support in Massachusetts. And most Republican leaders scarcely concealed their dislike for the Baptists and other dissenters both socially and theologically.

Although Paul Goodman is undoubtedly correct in saying that the Democratic-Republican Party was "the party of opportunity" and opportunism, seeking to aid "outsiders" to break into the monopoly of economic power and social prestige held by the Federalists, and although this party of dissidents and arrivistes thereby became the logical party for the dissenters and received their almost unanimous support, it does not follow that the party was willing to court dissenters at the expense of the more numerous and more important Congregational and Unitarian elements of the community. The Republican Party included so many different and shifting factions that it could not afford to favor any one of them — least of all that minority least important socially and economically. There was nothing radical about the Republicans. They sought no fundamental changes in the structure of New England society. As Goodman points out, by 1815 the party had achieved its limited goals; but the Baptists were still far from attaining theirs. Goodman states that "By 1815 those who had formerly been alienated from established authority were no longer outsiders . . . newcomers enjoyed public office and civic esteem, presided over prosperous banks and bustling counting houses, worshipped in greater equality and farmed lands of their own . . . Success thus deprived the Republican Party of its reason for being." [1] But there were few Baptists in public office and fewer who presided over prosperous banks and

1. Paul Goodman, *The Democratic-Republicans of Massachusetts* (Cambridge, 1964), p. 204.

bustling counting houses. They enjoyed equality in worship, but they were still "certificate men" and were still far from enjoying "civic esteem."

There were a few anticlericals in the party who enjoyed baiting the establishment. They worked as hard as the Baptists did for its abolition, but they were always the radical wing of the party. The influential leaders and spokesmen were generally rather patronizing toward dissenters. Social prejudice produced levels of discrimination even within a party of outsiders. To most Republicans the Baptists were still stereotyped as "illiterate," "illiberal," and "ignorant." [2] Their Calvinism was "dogmatic" and their system of closed communion "bigoted" and "uncharitable." Their insistence upon adult immersion (in public ceremonies) was both "superstitious" and "ostentatious." Their evangelical preaching was considered "enthusiastic" and their revivalism and proselyting "fanatical" and "tasteless." True, under the leadership of men of learning and refinement like Stillman, Manning, (Hezekiah) Smith, and Baldwin the Baptists achieved a certain degree of respectability before 1810 — especially around Boston. Stillman become so refined, so eager to adapt himself to the ways of Boston's ruling elite that he preferred the Federalist to the Republican party.

The legislature was willing to flatter such men by occasionally asking them to deliver election sermons, to serve as legislative chaplains, and to give the Artillery Sermons. But all acknowledged that most Baptist ministers were "unlettered mechanics and farmers" and their congregations were composed of "the lower classes" who "warped off" from the solid teaching of the parish ministers as much out of the desire to "dodge taxes" as out of ignorant zeal for "false doctrine" or "hair-splitting" quibbling over "nonessential" aspects of polity and ritual.[3]

The Rev. William Bentley of Salem, though an ardent Jeffersonian and an exceptionally liberal Unitarian, reflected clearly the general disdain — if not contempt — with which many Republican leaders looked on even the most distinguished Baptists of the day. Referring to the town of Middleborough in 1812, he remarked, "This is the region in [which] the Historian of the Baptists, Mr. Bacchus, had his scene of glory & from whence we had his irradiations." [4] At the death of Hezekiah Smith of Haverhill in 1805, Bentley characterized him as "a man of strong zeal, of strong lungs, and fond of proselytes. But a man of little learning, small pulpit talents, & no dawn of genius. He had become more moderate in his last years,

2. The characterizations of the Baptists quoted in this paragraph are from William Bentley, *The Diary of William Bentley,* 4 vols. (Salem, 1904–1914). Bentley's relationship to the Baptists is discussed more specifically in Chapter 59. The relationship between the party and the Baptists differed considerably in the District of Maine. I speak here of the Baptists in Massachusetts.
3. See Noah Worcester, *Impartial Inquiries Respecting the Progress of the Baptist Denomination* (Worcester, 1794) for a statement by a Federalist, Unitarian minister which reflects an attitude toward the Baptists which differs little from Bentley's.
4. Bentley, *Diary,* IV, 102.

but to me he was always a tedious, unmeaning and disgustful creature." [5]
Bentley had little better to say of Samuel Stillman: "the Bishop of the
Sect & the only [Baptist] man of respectable pulpit talents in New England.
He is a man of little science or theological skills as his printed sermons
prove, but he is agreeable, lively, & successful in the pulpit." [6] Bentley
always referred to Thomas Baldwin as "an illiterate preacher" and pointed
out that he had been a blacksmith by trade.[7] He reported that Baldwin
replaced Stillman as the leader of the Baptists after 1807, but professed
himself unable to understand the source of his popularity. He dismissed
Baldwin's theological tracts in defense of Calvinism and antipedobaptism
as erroneous in theology and devoid of originality or wit.[8] When the inevitable happened and a Baptist church was formed in Salem in 1805,
Bentley described this as "a dark day because we were afraid of the un-
charitableness of this Sect which has been the most illiterate in New
England." [9] Though he was invited to the ordination of Lucius Bolles, a
Brown graduate, as elder of this church (performed by Stillman and
Smith) Bentley did not attend. He gave as his excuse that Baldwin had
recently written that in Salem "there were no Christian Churches. This was
a declaration of war against our associations," said Bentley.[10] The only
Baptist about whom Bentley ever spoke kind words was James Manning
of Rhode Island, whom he apparently knew only by reputation: at
Manning's death in 1791 he spoke of him as "a fine person" who "was
entitled to the public esteem" in which he was held.[11]

Bentley's animosity toward the Baptists competely overrode any claims
they might have had on him as a party leader for the support they gave
to the Republicans, and it demonstrates the uneasy relationship of the
Baptists and Unitarian-Congregationalists within the party. The Republicans were often hard-pressed to win votes in Essex County and in Salem,
and one might think that Bentley, as the leading figure of the party and
part-time editor of the *Essex Register* would have welcomed them, or at
least have shown them some civility. But on the contrary, he seems to have
felt that the Baptists gained more from their association with the party
than the party gained from their votes: "The Baptists," he wrote in
January, 1802, "by attaching themselves to the present administration

5. *Ibid.*, III, 137.
6. *Ibid.*, III, 137, 143. See also II, 25, 37; III, 313, for other disparaging remarks.
7. *Ibid.*, I, 212; III, 157, 313. Fortunately he had not heard the charge that
Baldwin was born "out of wedlock." See letter of Elihu Hyde to Isaac Backus, November 15, 1783, in BP(AN).
8. *Ibid.*, II, 260.
9. *Ibid.*, III, 133.
10. *Ibid.*, III, 133. It is amusing that Baldwin and the Baptists took the view that
parishes which had only a Unitarian minister preaching in them were destitute of
the gospel, and yet they highly resented Lyman Beecher's view that places which had
no ordained, learned minister were destitute of the gospel.
11. *Ibid.*, I, 282.

[i.e., Jefferson] have gained great success in the United States and greater in New England than any sect since the settlement, even beyond comparison. This seems to be a warning to the Churches of the other denominations." [12] He meant it as a warning to the Congregational churches — that if they continued to support the backward-looking Federalists many of their liberal or republican members would join the Baptists.

To Bentley, the Baptists' growth was not because of their doctrines, their piety, or their evangelism, nor even because of their advocacy of religious liberty. Instead, it was because of the popular distaste of Hopkinsianism in the Standing churches, the overbearing tyranny of the Federalist clergy, and the facility of the laws exempting Baptists from religious taxes. He saw the growth of the Baptists and of the other "outrageous sects" (Universalists, Methodists, Christ-ians) as a negative movement, a reaction or protest among the churchgoers of Massachusetts against the theological and political rigidity of the Standing Order. It is not far-fetched to suggest that Bentley and most of the supporters of the Republican Party (lay and clerical) who were members of the Standing churches believed that it was necessary to elect the Republican Party to power in Massachusetts to preserve the established system.

Bentley and his party colleagues believed that once the Republicans were in power and once their liberal Unitarian views pervaded the theological preaching of the clergy, the sects would gradually disappear, the common man would return once more to the parish churches and support them gladly. They looked forward to the day when parish ministers would be democrats rather than aristocrats, when the theology preached from the parish pulpits would be rational enlightened Unitarianism rather than the tortured, emotional, Calvinism and Hopkinsianism of the past. "The Congregationalists begin to be alarmed at the great progress of the Anabaptists," he wrote in 1802, "but the progress is not from their [the Baptists, religious] opinions, but from their political situation of opposing the busy Clergymen who are tools of the Anti-Jefferson party . . . oppression will make more friends for the Anabaptists among those who despise their opinions & their sect." [13] The following year he noted,

> The active part the regular clergy have taken with the opposition of the present administration has thrown all the discontented into the sect of the Baptists who have been by law exempted from taxes. The introduction of laymen, as they are called, or zealous persons without a public or regular education [into the ministry], has much contributed to inflame the zeal and everywhere we find convulsions, separations, zeal and spiritual gifts celebrated.[14]

12. *Ibid.,* III, 409. See also III, 419.
13. *Ibid.,* III, 419.
14. *Ibid.,* III, 65.

Wherever a new Baptist church was formed Bentley looked for, and usually found, evidence that a Hopkinsian or some other crabbed, "bigoted," Federalist clergyman had antagonized the Jeffersonians, the republicans of the parish and that these good men, honest farmers and tradesmen, had consequently signed off from the parish by certificate to form a Baptist church (even though they did not really agree with the Baptist teachings) rather than support such a minister: "The Congregational churches are infested with a sett of men called Hopkintonians & who create contentions wherever they come . . . While the anabaptists without education & reputation profit by the dissensions." [15]

Like Ezra Stiles, Bentley longed for the days of Jeremiah Condy and the "catholic," "educated," and broad-minded spirit of "the Old Baptists." [16] But the continual activity of illiterate Baptist evangelists merely fomented discord. "This day the Baptist meeting was an ordination of an Evangelist," he wrote in 1811. "The Candidate was Harry Clarke, a young seaman who lately, in a mad fit, went barefoot [from Salem] to Providence & has since become a fanatic of the first chop. Baldwin, Bowen, & Chaplin had a hand in the solemn farce. Thus we see the old fanaticism [of the First Great Awakening] returning." [17]

A considerable part of Bentley's (and other Unitarians') opposition to the Baptists was their insistence on immersion — "immersing their disciples in water and ignorance," as Bentley put it.[18] Bentley, who habitually called Baptists "Anabaptists," considered it mere "superstition" that Baptists insisted on dipping persons who had already been baptized (usually in infancy) by sprinkling.[19] He interpreted this to mean that Baptists believed no one could enter heaven who had not been dipped. And he

15. *Ibid.,* I, 196; see also, III, 30, and III, 36.
16. *Ibid.,* I, 161.
17. *Ibid.,* IV, 54. Bentley claimed that it was from such mad preachers that new sects arose often through the schisms they fomented among the Baptists. After Elders Elias Smith and Abner Jones left the Baptists to form the new sect of "Christ-ians" they came to Salem in 1807 to try to draw off some of Elder Lucius Bolles's new members. Bently noted, "It is necessary to check this uncharitable and ignorant sect which multiplies its lay preachers among us . . . It is from the infamy of the sect [the Baptists] and its blind guides, that the greatest evils are apprehended, not from what they know, but because they know nothing at all." III, 272–273. Bentley also noted with astonishment that "the Baptists & their black and white preachers" seemed to thrive on ignorant preaching. III, 76. And when "the Negro Minister [Thomas] Paul" preached in Elder Bolles's church, "one family only disclosed displeasure." III, 490. At one point Bentley came to the conclusion in comparing the Baptists with the Methodists that "the Baptists exceed them in zeal & are more distinguished by the ignorance of their preachers." III, 86. Even Elder Baldwin in Boston, he noted, had tried "the Methodistic method of conversion" by "preaching in the isles of the Church." I, 280. This was in 1791. Baldwin, finding this practice was not considered respectable in Boston, soon gave it up.
18. *Ibid.,* I, 363.
19. *Ibid.,* II, 151.

delighted in pointing out certain ludicrous episodes concerning the ritual. For example, he noted that Elder Lucius Bolles of Salem had caught cold while "dipping" in winter and had thenceforth declined to perform the ceremony except in warm weather "as it too much endangers the health of the Spectators." [20] He ridiculed the case of a Baptist woman who complained that her elder, in his haste to perform the rite, had only "half-dipped" her (she had not been completely immersed) and the church was thrown into a theological quandary over the efficacy of this botched performance.[21] Apparently it was the custom in some Baptist churches for the officiating minister to carry the female candidates for immersion from the shore into the river and out again. This could become embarrassing as Bentley reported: "Last Sunday Dr. Stillman [a small, frail man] carrying a corpulent woman into the water was thrown down by her and was obliged to receive help from the Bystanders. Several incidents have tended to make this mode ridiculous." [22]

In sum, Bentley — though a Republican of the most ardent stripe — considered himself a member of the intellectual and social elite of Massachusetts — which he was. That he was a Jeffersonian did not make him a democrat, nor did it make him tolerant of fools and fanatics. If he read novels he doubtless relished H. H. Brackridge's *Modern Chivalry,* a satire on Jeffersonian democracy. His stance on religious taxes seems to have been as conservative as that of most Federalist Unitarians. Nothing in his voluminous diary and writings indicates that he ever doubted the virtue and necessity of having a tax-supported established church — though he willingly granted all possible toleration to dissenters. In Salem, as in Boston, Newburyport, Worcester and other large cities in these years, no religious taxes were levied and the problem of oppression and tax-dodging therefore did not register fully with Bentley. It had not been a factor in the rise of the Baptists in Salem. His own church supported him by subscription and pew rents and his only worry was that the dissenters would draw off so many of his congregation that the remainder would find the burden of his voluntary support too great.[23] He sadly noted cases among his colleagues where this had occurred. But in Salem he found that the dissenters attracted only the lower and lower-middle classes so that he never faced any defections by his wealthy parishioners.

Of course the Baptists and other dissenters responded in kind to men like Bentley. They saw them as intellectual snobs and enemies of "gospel

20. *Ibid.,* III, 143.
21. *Ibid.,* III, 145.
22. *Ibid.,* III, 85.
23. Or perhaps it would be more accurate to say that he felt generally that this was the result of the Baptists' advent in a town. His own church was well-stocked with some of the wealthiest and most cosmopolitan sea captains and merchants in New England; they were not likely to become Baptists.

religion" (hence their habitual use of the term "infidel" to describe Unitarians). They never saw Bentley as a wise or respected leader of their political Party. The Republican Party granted concessions to the dissenters less out of a common feeling of unity or sympathy than out of an abstract commitment to certain liberal and republican principles. The Baptists and the Party leaders were united in their negative hatred of the Federalists and the Standing Order as reactionary impediments to republican liberalism, but they were not themselves agreed as to what liberalism meant. It certainly did not mean including ignorant fanatics in the power structure of the Republican Party, and this marks one of the significant differences between Jeffersonian and Jacksonian liberalism. The Congregationalist Yankees (Trinitarian or Unitarian) were no more willing to accept the lower class Baptist or Methodist as one of themselves than were the Anglican Southern gentlemen (deistic or orthodox). Even though the Puritan theological rationale for an establishment was gone by 1800, the Puritan social rationale for an aristocracy — a rule by the wise and well-born — remained.

This attitude was not limited simply to clerical Jeffersonians like Bentley. It pervaded the Republican party. Republican politicians saw no need to yield to the dissenters' demands for the abolition of compulsory religious taxes. On the contrary, they agreed with Bentley that religion was essential to social order, that no state could survive without it, and therefore that the state was obliged to lend its support to the church. As politicians they did not express this view openly. They developed a fine sense of ambiguity regarding the term "religious liberty" so that they could employ it without offending Unitarians, Congregational Trinitarians, or dissenters. They exalted both religion and liberty, and with one or two notable and unrepresentative exceptions, none of them ever indulged in Thomas Paine's crude assaults on clericalism, religious creedalism, or ecclesiastical institutionalism.[24] They thought Paine was absolutely wrong-headed in attacking organized religion, and they took the same stand on the French Revolution, deploring its attacks on Christianity and its wild terrorism, but glorifying its overthrow of Monarchy and the Papacy. They devoted considerable effort to proving that Jefferson was not an atheist or an infidel or a deist, but even more effort to proving that he was the friend of the farmer, the mechanic, the debtor, the dissenters, and the rights of local self-government. They attacked Federalist clergymen (Unitarian and Trini-

24. For a discussion of the Republican Party's attacks on clergymen who meddled in politics (on behalf of the Federalists) see below. The most notorious examples of anticlerical, deistic Republicans in New England were in Connecticut — Abraham Bishop, Pierpont Edwards, and Joel Barlow. The most notable examples in Massachusetts were Joseph Hawley, James Sullivan, and Joseph B. Varnum. For an interesting defense of the anticlerical Republican, Joel Barlow, by a Boston Republican, see the *Independent Chronicle* (Boston), November 25, 1805.

tarian) not for their religious views, which were permissible in their place, but for using their special monopoly of parish privilege to enter blatantly into partisan politics on behalf of one faction against another — or more accurately on behalf of a group of monarchist, aristocratic, wealthy, well-born, bigoted, selfish men in opposition to the democratic, average, liberty-loving, patriotic supporters of the general good.

On the difficult question of disestablishment, however, the Republican political leaders said nothing. They were ready to aid persecuted dissenters in specific instances when they had to (as in 1811). And they made glowing speeches against instances of clerical oppression and bigotry. But they never advocated separation of church and state. This stand was inevitable if the party wanted to wean nominal Congregational voters from the Federalists to gain support for the political and economic objectives which it considered of primary importance.

Paul Goodman points out that a group of Congregational ministers supported the Republicans and favored the extension of religious liberty to dissenters. But men like Thomas Allen, Joseph Barker, Ephraim Judson, David Sanford, Solomon Aiken, and Samuel Niles were a tiny fraction of the Standing ministry. At no time before 1825 could the Republicans boast of support from more than half a dozen of the 200 to 250 Standing ministers in Massachusetts. Few of these ministers published anything on behalf of the party and none of them called for total disestablishment. Like John and Ezekiel Bacon, two of the party's leading lay Congregational liberals, they favored the most complete religious freedom for dissenters short of disestablishment. And for every Republican who sided with the dissenters, there were half a dozen, like George Blake, and William Bentley, who sided with the Standing Order on the importance of public support for religion. The Republican Party was throughout its lifetime unable to resolve within its ranks these conflicting opinions on disestablishment. The question of religious liberty was often a divisive and embarrassing one as well as a useful rallying cry.

The career of James Sullivan, the first Republican to be elected Governor of Massachusetts (in 1807 and 1808) is as perfect an exemplification of the politician's attitude on the establishment as Bentley's career is of that of the liberal clergy. Sullivan's father was born in Ireland, a Roman Catholic, but when he came to Maine in 1723 he adopted Congregationalism. James Sullivan, born in Berwick in 1744, was brought up a moderate or Old Calvinist within the parish church. He entered the law and during the Revolution was elected to the Provincial Congress and to the legislature many times. From 1776 to 1782 he was a member of the Massachusetts Supreme Court, and he helped to reorganize the laws of the state after the adoption of the constitution in 1780. He moved to Boston in 1783, joined the liberal Brattle Street Church and served several terms in Congress after resigning from the Supreme Court. In 1790 he became Attorney General of the state and in 1797 became the Jeffersonians' candidate for Governor. He played a leading role in Republican political affairs thereafter and died in 1808 at the end of his second term as Governor.[25]

When he joined the Brattle Street Church the Rev. Samuel Cooper was its pastor; among its members were John Hancock, James Bowdoin, and Samuel Adams, all of whom were, like Sullivan, moderate Calvinists and defenders of the establishment. Sullivan was said by some to have helped to write Article Three of the Massachusetts constitution, but this seems dubious since he was not on the committee which drew it up. He was, however, a frequent contributor of pseudonymous letters to the newspapers, and it is entirely possible that he wrote some of the letters defending Article Three against Backus and the Baptists.[26] A few years later he developed some qualms about the ecclesiastical pretensions of some of the clergy and in 1784 wrote a prophetic tract defending that aspect of Article Three which gave the town or parish the sole right to hire the minister regardless of the wishes of the members of the church. He wrote this in answer to a tract by the Rev. Peter Thacher of Malden entitled *Observations upon the Present State of the Clergy of New England* (Boston, 1783), in which Thacher deplored the decline of religion, the failure of the people to give liberal support to their ministers, and the tendency of some towns and parishes to interpret Article Three to mean that a minister could be fired as well as hired at the sole discretion of the voters in the parish. Thacher argued that a parish could break its contract with a minister only on the advice and consent of a council of Standing Ministers.

Sullivan came to the defense of majority rule in the parishes in his *Strictures on the Rev. Mr. Thacher's Pamphlet* published in 1784. He denied Thacher's claim that religion had declined and said that ministers were better paid by thirty per cent than before the Revolution. He said that he knew of only three instances in which Standing ministers had been dismissed by a vote of the parish which had not first consulted a Council. But the heart of his pamphlet was a defense of the parish as a civil institution which should be governed by majority rule. Thacher seemed to him to be trying to return church-state relations to the pattern of the seventeenth century when the church members' wishes were superior to the parish's in the choice of the minister. Sullivan called this practice, embodied in the ecclesiastical laws of 1693 and 1695, a "glaring piece of

25. For a general discussion of Sullivan's attitude toward religious liberty see Thomas C. Amory, *Life of James Sullivan* (Boston, 1859), esp. I, 182–185. If his theological views followed those of the pastors of the Brattle Street Church, he became steadily more Arminian and Unitarian after 1783.

26. An anonymous tract, *A Blow at the Root of Aristocracy* (Boston, 1812), claimed that Sullivan "said in open court that he assisted in forming the Bill of rights." This was in the case of Pickering *vs.* Harvard.

religious tyranny" which was "the never failing source of dissension and had its effect in producing Quakers and Baptists in abundance" [27] (evidently a deplorable fact in his eyes). Sullivan then went on to defend the innovations in the ecclesiastical practice embodied in Article Three:

> But our declaration of rights, the happy basis of our constitution, provides not only that there shall be no subordination of one sect to another but that the several towns and parishes shall at all times have the exclusive right of electing their own teachers of religion and morality; not that the church members of each town and parish shall, but the town or parish as a civil corporation shall have this right, which is all that could be done in the nature of free exercise of conscience in religious matters. For if the people as a body have authority to dispose of the church, Christ is not the head of it . . . If the church do not agree that the teacher chosen by the parish where they are inhabitants shall be their pastor, they may choose another, but they cannot expect the parish to maintain them [and their new choice]. The first principle in a civil corporation is that a majority shall govern.[28]

Three points evident in this tract not only defined Sullivan's personal attitude toward the establishment, but also characterized the prevailing view of the Republican Party of which he became the standard bearer. First, it was evident that he did not advocate separation of church and state; second, that he interpreted Article Three broadly so as to favor the parish over the church and thus to foreshadow the decision of Judge Isaac Parker in the famous Dedham Case in 1821; and third, that he shared the general anticlericalism of the Jeffersonians while at the same time maintaining the conservative New England belief that a Christian society required a state-supported establishment of some kind. In addition, there is a clear tone of condescension toward the dissenting sects and an obvious plea to the Standing Order for a tolerant latitudinarianism and a democratically run parish system as the only fair and practical basis for sustaining the important function and traditional status of the Congregational church.

Sullivan was to advocate these same views throughout the rest of his career; he never went beyond them. In 1795 he argued a case in the Su-

27. James Sullivan, *Strictures on the Rev. Mr. Thacher's Pamphlet* (Boston, 1784), p. 22. The gist of this sentence seems to be that if Thacher's ecclesiastical clericalism were to prevail the Congregational churches would lose even more members to the dissenting sects. Sullivan here reveals the prevailing liberal or latitudinarian view which we have noted in Jeremiah Smith of New Hampshire and Zephaniah Swift in Connecticut: the view that the Standing Order must strive for an all-inclusive or comprehensive unity by avoiding both doctrinal rigidity and clerical domination; a broad church establishment would offend none and thus there would be no quarrels over religious taxation.

28. *Ibid.*, p. 27. On this same page, Sullivan stated that Quakers and Baptists were not permitted to sit on juries deciding cases between a parish and its minister, presumably because they were legally excluded from parish affairs and were not apt to be impartial about them.

preme Judicial Court in which he used precisely the same arguments to prove that a minister who was dismissed over his objections had no right to claim the power to veto the actions of his church members when they acted in accord with the decision of an *ex parte* council (after the minister had refused to join in calling a mutual council).[29] Sullivan was active in many lawsuits concerning the ecclesiastical laws. He usually, but not always, defended dissenters. We have noted his defenses of Gershom Cutter (a Baptist) and John Murray (a Universalist) in the 1780's. As State Attorney General in 1804 he prosecuted a Baptist who allegedly signed false certificates for some persons claiming to belong to his church.[30] This case for the state he lost, but two other cases in which he defended the right of Baptist ministers to recover the religious taxes of their parishioners he won, Pickering *vs.* Harvard (c. 1804) and Smith *vs.* Dalton (1805).[31] We have already noted the famous cases in which he tried to clarify the position of Roman Catholic priests and the case he lost in 1804 on behalf of a Methodist circuit rider.[32]

Insofar as Sullivan argued such cases on the side of the dissenters he won their gratitude and earned the enmity of the more conservative defenders of the establishment. But to argue from this, as his biographer did, that the Murray case changed him from a defender of Article Three to an opponent of it and that after this Sullivan was "opposed by every conviction to any connection between Church and State" is to misunderstand his position.[33] That position lay squarely between that of the ardent Federalist defenders of the establishment (lay and clerical) and the ardent opponents of the system, the dissenters. To the extent that he took a middle stand on an issue which for the dissenters brooked no compromise, he was a conservative defender of the establishment. Insofar as he opposed the rigid maintenance of the system advocated by the Federalist politicians and insofar as he worked his way theologically toward Unitarianism and was cool toward the Puritan Counter-Reformation of Jedediah Morse and Lyman Beecher, and insofar as he supported Jeffersonian reform, he was a liberal. Sullivan was a Republican and a supporter of Jefferson for many reasons, but disestablishment was not one of them. Not only did he never make a speech or write a tract advocating it, but also in his first address

29. See the account of Hawes *vs.* Mann in MHS *Collections,* 1st ser. V (1795), 49. This was apparently written by Sullivan.
30. See Commonwealth *vs.* Ebenezer Stow (1804) in *Reports in Cases Argued and Determined in the Supreme Judicial Court of the State of Massachusetts,* ed. Ephraim Williams, *et al.* (Northampton, 1805), I, 54. Hereafter referred to as *Massachusetts Term Reports.* Sullivan lost the case when the jury decided for the Baptist.
31. For Pickering *vs.* Harvard, see *Blow at the Root,* p. 4; for Smith *vs.* Dalton, see the *Independent Chronicle,* October 24, 1805. These are also referred to in Amory, *Sullivan,* II, 16, and in Nathan Dane, *A General Abridgment and Digest of American Law,* 9 vols. (Boston, 1823–1829), II, 329 ff.
32. Chapter 34, pp. 658–659.
33. Amory, *Sullivan,* I, 186, 358.

to the first Republican legislature in Massachusetts when he became governor in 1807, he said that the constitution of Massachusetts as it then existed "excludes all persecution and intolerance on principles of religion and modes of worship." He put forward no proposals to alter the ecclesiastical system.[34]

According to his biographer, Sullivan often wrote under the pseudonym of "Farmer" for the newspapers. On September 2, 1802, a letter signed "Farmer" appeared in the *Independent Chronicle* which stated, "The writer has been represented as opposed to Religion, to the Clergy . . . No, the writer is a friend to Ministers and an enemy to their faults and their crimes and their follies and will ever combat them [i.e., their faults]. As 'teachers of religion, piety, and morality' they will and ought to be supported; as the 'propagators of sedition, slanders, libels and modern federalism' they ought to be opposed." [35] If Sullivan did not write this, it certainly expresses his view. Since it did not say specifically that ministers who stayed out of politics should be supported "by religious taxes," the Baptists were left to assume that the writer meant only that no one begrudged financial support to a good minister.

The success of Sullivan's studied ambiguity on the question of religious taxes was demonstrated by a dispute after his death on precisely what his stand would have been on the Religious Freedom Act adopted in 1811. A writer who signed himself "A Washingtonian" in the Boston *Gazette* (implying that he was a member of the ultra-conservative Federalist Washingtonian societies which arose at this time) stated that Sullivan never approved of the idea of disestablishing the church and offered as proof that in one of his thanksgiving proclamations as governor Sullivan had thanked God "for marking out the place of our habitation where the gospel is enjoyed in the most perfect freedom of conscience without persecution or restraint, every one having equal right to worship God according to the dictates of his reason." [36] This was answered by "Gallio" in the *Independent Chronicle* who insisted that Sullivan opposed ecclesiastical taxes because he often argued cases for dissenters in the courts and because he wrote a letter to a man on March 24, 1806, in which he said,

34. Sullivan, like all Republicans, was always ready to attack Federalist clergymen who injected partisan politics into their sermons. See, for example, his attack on Jeremy Belknap and Prof. David Tappan, Amory, *Sullivan*, II, 57. Also his tract, *The Altar of Baal Thrown Down* (Boston, 1795).

35. See Benjamin Austin's defense of "Farmer" in the *Independent Chronicle*, February 1, 1802, in which Austin said that if ministers would keep out of politics then parishioners would not begrudge them financial support. From all available evidence, by 1804 the ministers of the Standing Order did come to recognize that they must refrain from any actions which could be interpreted as favoring any political party if they were to avoid splitting their parish. But their private views were usually well-known.

36. Boston *Gazette*, June 17, 1811.

In regard to the rights of conscience as established by our Constitution, my opinion was fully heard when I was a member of the Convention [of 1780] that formed that instrument — and has been publicly uniform ever since and openly expressed in a great number of trials where the rights of Baptists, Methodists, Universalists, Episcopalians, and Quakers have been brought into question. I am under no prejudice in favor of those denominations or either of them. I was educated a dissenting Congregationalist and have for near thirty years been a member of a church of that order . . . This is and always has been the predominant sect in New England — and having too much connexion with the civil power there has been a degree of persecution. In all countries where the ecclesiastical power has been able to grasp the civil sword there have been persecutions . . . All attempts to worship in compliance with the compulsory establishments of civil power because it is directed by such power can be but a species of idolatry, or worshipping of the creature instead of the Creator.[37]

If this was the best evidence that he favored the abolition of compulsory religious taxes that could be produced from Sullivan's long career, it tends to support "A Washingtonian" rather than "Gallio." Even the most ardent Federalist clergyman would admit that the establishments of other countries went too far, and that even the Puritans went too far, in mixing religious and civil power. But Sullivan's letter does not contend that such power existed in 1806. He implies that the constitution of 1780 effectively curtailed that power and provided that separation of church and state which was desirable. The only forthright statement in the letter is Sullivan's claim that he stood on this question in 1806 precisely where he stood in 1780. This would mean that he supported Article Three, believing that compulsory religious taxes did not constitute an establishment or any favoritism toward the Congregational church so long as the law was equitably executed to exempt bona fide dissenters from such taxes. And this was precisely the position of the Republican Party in Massachusetts.

On this question, the crucial test of Sullivan's position, and of the Republican Party's, came when they finally assumed power in 1807. In that year they not only elected Sullivan governor but won control of both houses, and although they lost a number of seats in the succeeding election, they retained control in 1808. The party in those years took no official position and put forward no bills on behalf of the dissenters. When a bill was introduced in 1807 to liberalize the system of exemption from religious taxes the Party gave it no official support and despite their majority in both houses it failed to pass.

It is not clear who introduced this new certificate bill in 1807, but its chief support came from a few liberal Congregationalists in the Republican Party like Ezekiel Bacon of Pittsfield (Stockbridge) and from Baptist lead-

37. *Independent Chronicle*, July 4, 1811.

ers like David Goodwin of Charlestown.[38] The bill was introduced on June 17, 1807, and as its text indicates, it was concerned more with the question of incorporation than with disestablishment. It was a forerunner of the Religious Liberty Act of 1811 rather than of the amendment abolishing religious taxes in 1833.

Section one of the bill specified that the tax assessors in each parish or town "shall omit the taxes" for the support of ministers and maintenance of meetinghouses on "all such persons living within the limits of the same as belong to and usually attend public worship with any other religious society than that for whose use such tax may be voted and assessed whether incorporated or unincorporated." This clause not only would have clarified the problem of incorporation (and thus forestalled the famous decision in the Barnes case in 1810 which took the opposite view) but it also got around the old problem of how such taxes were to be returned to dissenters once they had been paid. Although in most towns bona fide dissenters were being omitted from the tax lists, according to the strict interpretation of the law dissenters were still required to pay their taxes and then their minister was supposed to apply to the parish or town treasurer to have these sums turned over to him (or to sue for it if the treasurer questioned his right to all or any portion of it).[39] The bill also provided a model for certificates for those claiming exemption from religious taxes:

> We the subscribers, _____ Public Teacher and Committee of the religious society of Christians called _____ do hereby certify that _____ of the Town, District or Plantation of _____ doth belong to said society of Christians in the _____ and that he or she (as the case may be) frequently and usually when able attends with us in our stated meetings for religious worship and hath complied with all the terms required by said society to constitute him a regular member thereof.

38. Bacon, a Yale graduate (1794), practiced law in Stockbridge, was elected to the legislature in 1806 and 1807; served in Congress 1808 to 1813; became chief justice of the court of common pleas in 1813; and moved to Utica, New York in 1815. See his autobiography, *Recollections of Fifty Years Since* (Utica, 1843). For Goodwin (1744–1825) who was a member of Stillman's church before he moved to Charlestown in 1801, see the obituary in the *Massachusetts Baptist Missionary Magazine*, I, n.s. (1825–1826), 97. Paul Goodman states that Judge John Bacon, Ezekiel Bacon's father, "introduced" this bill. But the bill was introduced in the house and Judge John Bacon served in the Senate. Moreover, Judge Bacon had served his last session in the Senate in February 1807 and the bill was not introduced until June 1807. Goodman's error is based on William Bentley's error in his *Diary* (III, 345) in which he states that Judge Bacon, President of the Senate, supported the bill. This in turn is based on a statement in the *Independent Chronicle,* February 18, 1808, p. 3, which states that Judge Bacon was among those who "advocated" the bill. Evidently the *Chronicle* confused Ezekiel Bacon with his father. But there is no other indication in any source as to who *introduced* the bill or what other Republicans supported it.

39. The manuscript copy of the act is filed in the MEA under the date of the act. It is unclear when the alterations noted below were inserted.

This certificate was to be signed by a pastor ("Public Teacher") of the dissenting church and "two other persons" of that congregation.

One of the most interesting aspects of this bill was that as originally written it was concerned with dissenters "of a different denomination," but at some point in its consideration it was altered to apply to persons of any other "religious society" or congregation. This probably indicates that its proponents were seeking to win the support of Trinitarian or Unitarian Congregationalists who were dissatisfied with their parish minister but who did not want to join a dissenting sect. By the terms of this bill such "Separates" or schismatics could form Congregational or Unitarian congregations and obtain exemption from supporting the parish even though, legally speaking, they did not belong to a different denomination from that officially established. That is to say, a group of Trinitarians who thought their parish minister was too Unitarian could break off and by signing certificates form a second Congregational church in the parish; and the same held for proto-Unitarians who disliked the Calvinism or Hopkinsianism of a Trinitarian parish minister. The bill, in short, recognized the cleavage within the established system and anticipated the creation of the new Unitarian denomination (which finally emerged officially in 1825).[40]

If this bill was too conservative for the Baptists it was still far too radical for the Federalists and for many Republicans. Apart from encouraging schisms within parish churches, it would have broken down the still operative (though legally unclear) principle which prevailed in many towns that only incorporated dissenting congregations were entitled to exemption; more important it would have sanctioned any and all kinds of schisms from the parish churches regardless of their basis in conscience. The Federalists quickly labeled it "The Infidel Bill," and the Republican majority postponed consideration of it to the next session. The bill was read for the first time on January 20, 1808, and on February 4, after a second reading, it was rejected by a vote of 127 to 102. As of June 1807, when the bill was first introduced, the Republicans claimed to have 259 representatives to the Federalists' 124, and although the succeeding election had reduced their majority, they were still in control when the bill failed.[41] Shortly after its defeat, an editorial in the *Independent Chronicle,* the leading Republican newspaper, discussed the bill's fate in evasive if not defensive terms:

> A bill was before the present legislature to give every man a right to worship God agreeably to his conscience without being robbed of his money to pay those whom he could not attend. This bill was called in the

40. Unfortunately it is unclear whether this was a serious and well-intentioned effort to cope with the growing division within Congregationalism or whether it was a subtle effort by opponents of the system to subvert it. From the supporters of the bill the former seems more likely, but from the opposition of the more rigid Federalists, they seemed to think it was to subvert the system.
41. *Independent Chronicle,* May 12, 1808.

federal papers an act for the support of *infidelity*. To show the absurdity of this appellation we will only mention the members of the legislature who advocated the bill, viz. Judge Bacon and Deacon Goodwin and the opposers, Mr. Wheaton and the pious Mr. Benjamin Whitman! Is it possible that Judge Bacon and Deacon Goodwin should be the advocates of infidelity against Lawyer Wheaton and Lawyer Whitman? This is quite a phenomenon! These two lawyers may have an extraodinary zeal in the *cause of Religion* but we cannot conceive that Judge Bacon and Deacon Goodwin should become their antagonists provided *real Christianity* was to be promoted by the measure. The fact is, the same deception takes place in religion as in the judiciary; and provided one class of men are supported under false colors, the temple of Diana will be filled with teachers to suit the purposes of their party. And the judiciary is equally an object for certain individuals if they can hold men in office who will go all lengths to support their measures.

In short, we live in an age of deception.[42]

From this it appears that the Republicans were more interested in blaming the Federalist lawyers for the bill's defeat and in clouding the issue by references to the judiciary than in explaining the failure of their own majority to support the bill. No editorials or article supporting the bill had appeared in any of the Republican Papers at any time and Governor Sullivan took no public stand on it though he appears to have supported it privately. William Bentley's diary contains the only contemporary comment on the bill, and he was as noncommittal as the *Independent Chronicle:*

> The first object of the worship Bill is to remove all legal impediments to any voluntary religious association, or in other words to destroy parish lines so far as regards the payment of teachers of religion. The Bill was negatived upon 4 Feb. by 127 to 102 & I do not think that the numbers are far from the relative progress of opinion on the subject. The friends of the Bill were those who are opposed to all religious establishments upon the principles of civil liberty, & from an aversion to the Clergy, who appear freely in all controversies in the Commonwealth on the side of power . . . The increase of the sects must eventually make this law necessary . . . all the parishes formed by law do not number more than double the number of Baptists. And we are to remember that the Congregational Churches agree only in one point, that is, they rest upon the establishment of Parish Laws.[43]

Bentley obviously felt that the radical anticlerical wing of his party was responsible for the bill, and his failure to note any particular actions by the dissenters themselves in its favor is significant. His own reluctance to sympathize with the measure (though he saw it coming) and his statement that the Unitarians, the Old Calvinists, and the Hopkinsians in the establishment

42. *Ibid.,* February 18, 1808, p. 3.
43. Bentley, *Diary*, III, 345–346. The obvious abstention of many legislators is probably significant too.

all agreed at least in favoring a tax-supported religious system indicated clearly enough why the Republican Party was not willing to support the bill even though it had the votes to pass it.[44]

James Sullivan died in December 1808. His contribution to the cause of separation was twofold. First, as a lawyer and as Attorney General he can be credited with pushing the limits of toleration to their extreme within the system, particularly by insisting in the courts on the most liberal and democratic interpretation of Article Three as in the Murray case. Second, as a Republican, his efforts to keep the established clergy out of politics and to whittle down the control of the Federalist elite by expanding the electorate seriously weakened the conception of the aristocratic Christian corporate state on which the establishment rested. Together these two contributions represent the main thrust of the Jeffersonian Revolution in New England. The Republicans undermined the ecclesiastical side of the Standing Order indirectly rather than with a frontal assault.

44. There is no indication in any of the Baptist materials of this date, published or unpublished, to indicate that the denomination was active in support of the bill. The Massachusetts Archives contain no petitions in its support from any group. The Baptist Association Minutes are silent on the bill. The conclusion seems to be that it was a trial measure, advanced independently by a small group of the more radical anti-clericals in Republican Party.

Chapter 55

The Barnes Case and the Religious Liberty Act, 1810–1817

It remains for the objector [to religious taxes] to prove that the patronage of Christianity by the civil magistrate, induced by the tendency of its precepts to form good citizens, is not one of the means by which the knowledge of its doctrine was intended to be disseminated and preserved among the human race.

Chief Justice Theophilus Parsons, Barnes *vs.* First Parish, 1810

The defeat of "the worship bill" of 1807–1808 (as Bentley called it) by a Republican administration seemed to leave the dissenters no hope for any alteration in the ecclesiastical system. The Republican Party in Massachusetts was not going to follow the pattern of the party in Connecticut by making disestablishment a party issue. Probably the whole matter would have lain dormant for another decade or so had not the Supreme Judicial Court aroused concern by its decision in the case of Barnes *vs.* Falmouth in October, 1810, and then followed it up within a year by similar decisions in Turner *vs.* Brookfield and Lovell *vs.* Byfield.[1] In each of these cases the court declared emphatically that only incorporated dissenting societies could recover religious taxes paid to the established parishes; all other congregations were not recognized by law and therefore their members' taxes belonged to the parish in which they lived. This issue had long been in an equivocal state, but these decisions attempting to clarify it, although laudable in their clarity, were deplorable in their construction. Dominated by Federalist-Unitarians, the Supreme Court had given the most conservative, if not reactionary, interpretation possible to Article Three of the Declaration of Rights.

As Nathan Dane pointed out a few years later in his *General Abridge-*

---

1. These cases are discussed below. Also *Reports in Cases Argued and Determined in the Supreme Judical Court of the State of Massachusetts*, ed. Ephraim Williams *et al.* (Northampton, 1805), VI, 401; VII, 60, 230; hereafter referred to as *Massachusetts Term Reports;* Mark De Wolfe Howe, *Cases on Church and State in the United States* (Cambridge, 1952), pp. 27 ff.

ment and Digest of American Law, there had been six "solemn decision[s]" by the Supreme Court of Massachusetts between 1783 and 1804 which declared that dissenting congregations did not have to be incorporated to recover their religious taxes. He added, however, that "there were always respectable opinions to the contrary." [2]

Typical of the cases to the contrary was that of Kendall *vs.* Kingston which was decided in October 1809. Ezra Kendall had been ordained as an evangelist and in the fall of 1804 he was hired by the First Baptist Church in Middleborough to assist the aging Isaac Backus by preaching half time. Kendall gave the other half of his time (two Sundays each month) to the Baptist church in Kingston, Massachusetts about twenty miles away. In Middleborough Kendall received his pay from voluntary contributions, but in Kingston his congregation was taxed for the support of the Standing Church and so he brought suit against the selectmen (it turned out he should have brought it against the treasurer, but this proved irrelevant) in that town to have the religious taxes of his hearers paid over to him.

In making its decision, the Supreme Judicial Court ruled that Kendall failed in his action "as not being a public teacher authorized to sue for the ministerial taxes paid by his hearers" in Kingston. First, the Baptists in Kingston were not incorporated. Second, Kendall was only an evangelist and not the ordained or settled minister there. Third, the certificates he gave to his hearers asserted that they "usually attend" public worship under him and attending two Sundays out of four was not "usually." And finally, if Kendall were to receive the whole of his hearers's religious taxes he would be obtaining a whole year's salary for a half year's work. "If half the year is sufficient," said the court, to enable a dissenting minister to obtain the religious taxes of his hearers, "so may a quarter or less portion of a year be sufficient. The mischiefs from such a construction would be extreme. And if a minister, so retained, for any portion of a year, may take from the regular pastor of the parish his support, it will soon be seen that our regular parishes will be broken up for the benefit of disorganizing sectarians." [3]

Obviously the Supreme Judicial Court was determined to aid the "regular" or established parish minister against such sectarian mischief-makers

---

2. Nathan Dane, *A General Abridgement and Digest of American Law,* 9 vols. (Boston, 1823–1829), II, 337. What six decisions Dane referred to is only a matter of conjecture since no official printed records of the decisions of the Court existed before 1804 and the manuscript files are incomplete. But the following cases might be cited: the case of the Baptists in West Cambridge; the Balkcom Case; John Murray's case; Briggs *vs.* Stoughton; Pickering *vs.* Harvard or Boxborough; and Smith *vs.* Dalton, 1804. Also Montague *vs.* Dedham, 1808; and the case of Abishai Crossman of Chelmsford, c. 1789 mentioned in Dane, II, 329. The decisions which seemed to indicate that dissenters must be incorporated to recover religious taxes are even harder to identify beyond the West Cambridge case of 1783–1785. See also *Independent Chronicle,* June 13, 1811, p. 1, which contains an able summary of the legal position at that time and mentions most of these cases.

3. *5 Massachusetts Term Reports,* 524–525.

whenever it could. Ironically, less than a decade later, the same court was forced to uphold a sectarian minister's right to his hearers' taxes even though he preached to them only one-quarter time.

The case of Barnes *vs.* Falmouth involved a Universalist Congregation; those of Turner *vs.* Brookfield and Lovell *vs.* Byfield involved Baptists. But the ramifications of these cases concerned Episcopalians, Methodists, Quakers, Shakers, and Separates as well. The Barnes case arose from a request by the minister of a Universalist congregation in the First Parish in Falmouth (District of Maine) that the religious taxes paid by two of his members (James Buxton and Amos Knight) for 1798 to 1805 be paid over to him by the parish. There was no question that Thomas Barnes (Barns) was a duly ordained Universalist minister and that Buxton and Knight were members of his church, but the Court of Common Pleas had sustained the claim of the parish that Barnes was not entitled to recover their religious taxes because his congregation was not incorporated and the constitution entitled only public teachers of incorporated religious societies to recover such taxes.

In his decision, Chief Justice Theophilus Parsons sustained the opinion of the lower court and answered four objections raised by the Universalists' counsel.[4] To the objection that if the lower court's interpretation of Article Three were correct then "the constitution sanctions persecution," Parsons replied that "The great error lies in not distinguishing between liberty of conscience in religious opinions and worship and the right of appropriating money by the state" for purposes of the general welfare. "The former is an unalienable right; the latter is surrendered to the state, as the price of protection." The plaintiffs had full freedom of conscience and of worship. But they could rightly be taxed to support the Protestant religion because this was "the price of this protection" which religion renders to the state, and it was properly written into the constitution by duly elected delegates and ratified by the required proportion of the citizens.

To the objection that it is "intolerant to compel a man to pay for religious instruction from which, as he does not hear it, he can derive no benefit," Parsons answered that "The like objection may be made by any man to the support of public schools, if he have no family who attend; and any man, who has no lawsuit may object to the support of judges and jurors on the same ground." Religious instruction supports "correct morals among the people" and cultivates "just habits and manners, by which every man's

---

4. The decision is printed in Howe, *Cases on Church and State*, pp. 29 ff. 6 *Massachusetts Term Reports*, 401. See also Richard Eddy, *Universalism in America* (Boston, 1886), II, 378, who notes, "The counsel for the defendent also made the argument which, as we have seen before, was the basis of the decision in the New Hampshire cases that denominational differences were not to be determined by doctrines but by ecclesiastical government; and as the Universalists were congregational in their mode of government, they were not a different sect from the Congregationalists" (*ibid.*, II, 20–30).

person and property are protected from outrage and his personal and social enjoyments promoted" and thus all persons derived benefits whether they attended church or not. "It remains for the objector to prove that the patronage of Christianity by the civil magistrate, induced by the tendency of its precepts to form good citizens, is not one of the means by which the knowledge of its doctrine was intended to be disseminated and preserved among the human race."

To the objection that "the faith and precepts of the Christian religion are so interwoven that they must be taught together," he admitted that this was true, but he denied that it in any way interfered with the rights and doctrines of the churches. "If the state claimed the absurd power of directing or controlling the faith of its citizens, there might be some grounds of objection. But no such power is claimed." If persons who attended church had their souls saved as well as their morals improved, that was an additional benefit to them, but it was not part of the state's plan for patronizing Christian churches and was, in effect, irrelevant to it.

And finally, to the objection that Article Three was designed to exempt members of unincorporated as well as incorporated Christian societies from paying to the support of the parish church of the majority on their fulfilling certain requirements (via certification), Parsons replied, "We are all of opinion that the constitution has not authorized any teacher to recover, by action at law, any money assessed pursuant to the third article of the declaration of rights but a public Protestant teacher of some legally incorporated society." Article Three enjoins on "towns, parishes, precincts or other bodies politic, or religious societies" the duty of levying taxes to support public Protestant teachers. Since a voluntary religious society could not enjoin by law the support of its teacher, the article must have meant that only incorporated religious societies were exempt from supporting the parish church. Moreover, "what society must be deemed a public society is certainly a question of law." And

> If the society be not incorporated, what rules are prescribed by law by which its character may be defined? Does it depend on the number of the associates, or on the notoriety of the association? . . . A public society is a society known in law, formed by the public authority of the state; and a private society is formed by the voluntary association of private persons, the powers of which are derived from the individual consent of each member.

Simply that a congregation had public meetings did not make it public. As for the claim that the last paragraph of Article Three allowed "no subordination of one sect or denomination to another," that "has no relation to the subject before us. Its object was to prevent any hierarchy or ecclesiastical jurisdiction of one sect of Christians over any other sect . . . It was also intended to prevent any religious test as a qualification for office."

Thus, Parsons and the other judges on the court were convinced that those who drafted, approved, and ratified Article Three actually meant to exclude all unincorporated dissenting congregations from the right to exemption from religious taxes. That is, they meant to leave it entirely to the legislature to define in each case where a dissenting congregation sought recognition, whether or not it was a bona fide Protestant church engaged in proper worship of those Christian principles designed to sustain the peace, order, and moral fibre of the commonwealth. In the subsequent court decisions regarding Turner and Byfield the judges sustained this opinion for Baptist as well as for Universalist societies.

If the policy laid down by the court in these cases was rigidly adhered to, each of the dissenting congregations in the state had no choice but to petition the legislature immediately for an act of incorporation or else to submit to religious taxes without any hope of recovering them. The legislature in turn faced the difficult task of either granting all of these petitions without investigation of their merits or else of trying to sift out the deserving from the undeserving.

Of the ninety-one Baptist societies or congregations in Massachusetts in 1810, less than half were incorporated.[5] Even fewer of the societies of other dissenters were incorporated. Many dissenters, especially among the Baptists, had conscientious scruples against seeking incorporation by the state since it seemed to acknowledge the power of the civil authority to regulate the church of Christ. For those who had no such scruples and who had the money and energy to undertake petitions, the problem was not serious. Many of these at once made application to the legislature. But for the vast majority of dissenters, the court's decisions raised an issue of freedom of conscience.

Caught in this dilemma, some of the Baptist churches tried to assuage their consciences by special votes imposing restraints on their use of the taxing power inherent in their act of incorporation. The resolution passed by the Baptist congregation (society) of Chester immediately after it was granted incorporation in May 1811 was typical:

> we disavow the exercise of all power and authority by virtue of the act of incorporation to tax our members for the support of social and religious worship or the institutions of the Gospel; . . . all the benefit or advantage we intend or wish to derive from the Act of incorporation is merely defensive in order to guard and defend our persons and property against the unjust claims and demands of the town or other religious society to oblige us to pay for the support of their religious tenets.[6]

5. According to my count of the incorporation acts in the *Private and Special Statutes of the Commonwealth of Massachusetts* there were forty-one Baptist congregations or societies incorporated by the legislature between 1791 and 1811.

6. Appendix to Martin Phelps, *Scripture Reasons for Renouncing the Principles of Pedobaptism* (Northampton, 1811), pp. 30–31.

The Republicans had lost the election of 1809 but had returned to power under the leadership of Elbridge Gerry in the spring election of 1810. Gerry made no mention of religious problems in his first message to the legislature in June of that year. His only remark on the subject of religion was an endorsement of the status quo: "The provisions made by the Constitution and laws for the establishment and promotion of literature, religion, and morality and the social virtues, supported as they have been and assuredly will be by Government, cannot fail to attain their desirable objects." [7] And even after the Barnes decision was announced in October, there was no legislative reaction in the winter session of the legislature during January–February 1811, though someone took the trouble to have copies of the decision printed and laid on the desk of each legislator at the start of the session.[8] It took several months for the momentum of dissenting excitement to build up.

In the winter session a number of dissenting societies, attempting to comply with the Supreme Court's ruling, presented petitions for incorporation. These were the first indication that a major political issue was building, for according to the Republican newspapers, the Federalists opposed these efforts. An editorial in the *Eastern Argus* (Portland) on May 2, 1811, said:

> It is a fact that the Federalists in the Legislature last winter did attempt to support the Judiciary against the Baptists, Methodists, and Sectarians generally; in one branch every federal vote was repeatedly given against incorporating those societies, with the privilege of admitting members; notwithstanding the constitution expressly provides "that all monies paid by the subject . . . shall, if he require it, be uniformly applied to the support of the public teacher or teachers of his own religious sect or denomination . . ." *The object of the federalists was to strike out of the acts what is generally called the vibrating principle;* and in future instead of the people's worshipping where they were disposed, they would worship at such places as they [the Federalists] were disposed to permit them.[9]

"The vibrating principle" was the section, or sections, written into the incorporation acts of dissenting societies which spelled out how a person was to sign off of a parish and on to his dissenting society and how he might also sign off of the dissenting society and back into the parish again. The following paragraphs from the incorporation of the Baptist Society of Haverhill in 1793 indicate what "the vibrating principle" entailed:

> Any and every person in the town of Haverhill and in the neighbouring towns in said County of Essex who may at any time hereafter actually become a member of and unite in religious worship with said [Baptist]

7. *Independent Chronicle*, June 11, 1810, p. 1.
8. *Ibid.*, May 13, 1811, p. 1.
9. *Eastern Argus* (Portland), May 2, 1811, p. 2. The italics are mine.

Society in Haverhill, and give in his or her name to the clerk of the parish to which he or she belongs, with a certificate signed by the minister or clerk of said Society that he or she hath actually become a member of and united in religious worship with said Baptist Religious Society in Haverhill, fourteen days previous to the parish meeting therein to be held in the month of March or April annually, shall, from and after giving such certificate with his or her polls and estates be considered as a member of said Society. *Provided however,* That such person shall be held to pay his or her proportion of all monies assessed or voted in the parish to which he or she belonged previous to that time.

And be it further enacted by the authority aforesaid That when any member of said Society shall see cause to leave the same and unite in religious worship with any other relogous Society in the town or parish in which he or she may live and shall give in his or her name to the Clerk of said Baptist Religious Society with a certificate signed by the minister or clerk of the parish or other incorporate religious Society with which he may unite that he hath actually become a member of and united in religious worship with such other parish or other incorporate religious Society fourteen days previous to their annual meeting in March or April and shall pay his or her proportion of all monies voted in said Society to be raised previous thereto, shall from and after giving such certificate with his or her polls and estates be considered a member of the Society to which he or she hath so united.[10]

It is easy to see why the Federalists, as defenders of the Standing Order, might object to this system of permitting people to sign on and off of the parish virtually at will. It encouraged "church hopping" for inconsequential reasons — not liking a minister's personality or objecting to church discipline or resentment over a minor difference of doctrine or simply a dislike for religious taxes. However, when the dissenters and the Republicans found the Federalists trying to tighten up the vibrating principle in 1811, they immediately interpreted it as an attempt to use Judge Parsons' decision in the Barnes case as a springboard for a campaign against religious toleration.[11] In 1811 the Republicans needed a good campaign issue.

While the *Eastern Argus* and the Republican political orators probably exaggerated the danger to religious liberty involved, it was true that of the three incorporation acts granted by the legislature in this winter session, none contained the vibrating principle. One should compare the sign-off clause in the incorporation act voted for the Baptist Society of Amesbury on February 25, 1811 with the clauses in the Haverhill incorporation act.

10. *Private and Special Statutes of the Commonwealth of Massachusetts,* 3 vols. (Boston, 1805), I, 403. Most of the incorporation acts granted to dissenting societies from 1791 to 1810 included such clauses, though they varied somewhat in minor details.
11. Probably at the time many Federalists were led to oppose the vibrating principle less from dislike for the dissenters than from fear of the threatening parish schisms between Unitarians and Trinitarians.

The Amesbury act omitted entirely the section permitting persons who signed off to vibrate back to the parish (or off to a third society) and it considerably tightened up the procedures for signing off the parish in the first instance:

> Be it also enacted That any person in said town of Amesbury [note the omission of reference to persons in adjoining towns] who may at any time hereafter actually become a member of and united in religious worship with the said Baptist Society and give in his or her name to the Clerk of the town and also to the Clerk of the parish to which he or she did formerly belong and receive a certificate of admission signed by the Minister or Clerk of the said Baptist Society fifteen days previous to the annual meeting of the said society which certificate shall set forth that he or she has constantly attended public worship with said Baptist Society *for at least one year previous to his receiving such certificate* such person shall from and after the giving of such certificate with his or her polls and estates be considered as a member of the said society.[12]

In short, in addition to obtaining a certificate of admission from the dissenting society he wished to join, a dissenter had to support both the parish church as well as his dissenting church for at least one year. If this were the direction in which the Federalists wished to move, the dissenters were well advised to take the actions they did.

Apart from this indirect result of the Barnes case (if indeed there was any connection at all), the earliest public attention to the issue came in a series of eight letters in the *Independent Chronicle* which began on March 18, 1811, signed "Berean." Their author appears to have been a Baptist, a defender of "evangelical truth," an opponent of "the blending of Church and State," and a man familiar with Isaac Backus's arguments.[13] His arguments were not only a direct rebuttal to those of Judge Parsons in the Barnes case, but also a cogent statement of the Baptist position on church and state at this time.

---

12. *Private and Special Statutes*, VI, 315; my italics.

13. *Independent Chronicle*, May 11, 1811 to June 10, 1811. It would be interesting to know who "Berean" was. It was apparently not Thomas Baldwin, for "Berean" opposed incorporation under any circumstances, but Baldwin favored it for some purposes. The letters lack Leland's pungent stylistic flavor. Some evidence indicates it may have been a Freewill Baptist since Berean attacks "the Calvinistic Baptists in a town in the District of Maine [who] lately taxed the Freewill Baptists in the same town for ministerial support and because one of the latter did not pay, attached and sold his horse." *Ibid.*, March 18, 1811, p. 1. The letters bear many resemblances to the views and style of Elias Smith, especially to the pamphlet he published anonymously that year entitled *Madison and Religion* (Philadelphia, 1811); but it seems unlikely that Smith would have referred to Samuel Stillman as "the venerable Stillman" the way Berean did. It might have been Ebenezer Nelson, Sr., of South Reading; Joseph Grafton of Newton; Nathan Williams of Beverly; or Lucius Bolles of Salem. Whoever it was was well read in the works of Isaac Backus; he considered himself a defender of "evangelical truth" as well as an opponent of an established church.

"Berean" began by contrasting Parsons' position to James Madison's. Madison had not only refused to issue the usual presidential requests for national days of thanksgiving and fasting, but he had also twice vetoed acts of Congress which he felt infringed upon the principle of separation: one of these had incorporated an Episcopal church in Georgetown and the other had granted land in the Mississippi territory to a Baptist congregation.[14] In his veto messages Madison recognized, said Berean, the truth of Christ's statement "My kingdom is not of this world." But Chief Justice Parsons had in his decision provided "a 'yoke of bondage' which the people cannot easily bear, and to which it is hoped they will not submit until every proper exertion has been made to free themselves . . ." Parsons had forgotten that "If a Church or 'religious society' can be 'formed by the authority of the State' the same authority can destroy it; for it is a well established principle that the power which can create can also destroy." Many people in Massachusetts seemed to think that the state had no established church, he said, but the

> third article of the Constitution as effectually enacts a civil establishment of religion as any political constitution in existence . . . It delegates to the majority in any parish the power of erecting such a kind of public worship as may please them provided it bears the name of "Protestant." . . . In one parish the Arian religion may be established, in another the Calvinistic, in a third that of the Universalists, &c., &c.

To be consistent there should be "an appendix to our Constitution in which should be defined beyond all doubt what is the specific nature of 'the Protestant religion.' " As matters now stood, it was up to the court or the legislature (when granting incorporation) to define this term.

"Berean" here put his finger on a central factor in the changing church-state situation in Massachusetts: the increasing tendency toward an Erastian policy in Parsons's decision — an effort to emphasize the utilitarian aspect of Christianity at the expense of its pietism. Judge Parsons had virtually declared the spiritual content of Christianity irrelevant — certainly secondary — to its assistance to the state in the protection of property and propriety in instances where there were no laws applicable or constables handy. "There are many precepts of Christianity of which the violation cannot be punished by human laws," Parsons declared, "and as obedience to them is beneficial to civil society, the state has wisely taken care that they should be taught." If the moral teaching taken care of by the state also helped some people to get to heaven, that was an extra benefit but one irrelevant to the state:

> As Christianity has the promise not only of this but of a future life, it cannot be denied that public instruction in piety, religion, and morality

14. Anson Phelps Stokes, *Church and State in the United States* (New York, 1950), I, 347; Elias Smith, *Madison and Religion* (Philadelphia, 1811).

by Protestant teachers, may have a beneficial effect beyond the present state of existence. And the people are to be applauded, as well for their benevolence as for their wisdom in selecting a religion whose precepts and sanctions might supply the defects in civil government . . . they adopted a religion founded in truth; which in its tendency will protect our property here and may secure to us an inheritance in another and better country.[15]

Such a concept of religion ran counter to the whole emotional thrust of the Second Great Awakening then shaking the nation. For while this Awakening did produce a new theological consensus and sense of fellowship among evangelical Christians, it also greatly heightened sectarian rivalry and denominational particularity. The Unitarians' broad-church plan of public establishment was rapidly becoming as dated as deism.

While "Berean" made no effort to identify Parsons' decision as a Unitarian or Federalist plot, he did stress its special pleading. "It is seriously believed that an improper partiality to a religious establishment has beguiled the Chief Justice into an unconstitutional and illegal decision respecting unincorporated religious societies." [16] It was inconceivable, he said, that either the dissenters or the majority of the delegates at the constitutional convention of 1780, or the majority of voters who ratified Article Three, understood the words of that article to mean what Parsons said they meant. As a matter of historical fact, said Berean, not one of all the dissenting religious societies in the state was incorporated in 1780. Did those who formed and ratified the constitution seriously mean that these congregations should either not be exempted from religious taxes or else that they should all apply at once to be incorporated? "The Rev. Mr. [Jonas] Clark of Lexington and Dr. Stillman were warm advocates for religious liberty, but these venerable christians would have spurned at the idea of losing the support of their parishes if they were not enlisted under the secular banner of incorporation." [17] He argued further that the marriage act of 1786 recognized in law the right of ministers of unincorporated dissenting congregations to perform marriages and thus assumed the legal existence of their churches: "If no religious society, with its minister, can be recognized in law unless incorporated, how numerous are the adulterers in Massachusetts?" Judge Parsons was clearly pushing the ecclesiastical interpretation of Article Three in a direction unanticipated at the time it was written.

"Berean's" argument on this point was given a better legal and constitutional exposition in an important but unsigned letter printed in the *Independent Chronicle* on June 13, 1811. The writer was apparently a lawyer (perhaps Joseph B. Varnum or Judge Ezekiel Bacon) whose sympathies

15. Howe, *Cases on Church and State*, pp. 32–33.
16. *Independent Chronicle*, May 27, 1811.
17. *Ibid.*, May 13, and May 23, 1811. There is no evidence that Jonas Clarke ever opposed Article Three as written.

were wholly with the dissenters. They were, he said, rightly indignant at Parsons's decision in Barnes *vs.* Falmouth: "This was an action of assumpsit brought to recover a sum of money" assessed and collected from James Buxton and Amos Knight for religious taxes. "This action was brought in the usual way and attempted to be sustained upon the same principals that actions of a similar nature had been for the term of thirty years last past, viz. upon the received construction of the 3d article in the Declaration of Rights in the Constitution." Parsons' decision "is a departure from the opinion of all former Judges who have decided on similar cases as well as from the opinion of the community at large." If the judges interpret the constitution differently

> from time to time, how are the citizens ever to know what rights the Constitution secures them? If it ever could have been thought doubtful whether a minister of an unincorporated religious society were to be considered as a "public protestant teacher of piety, religion and morality" within the meaning of the Constitution, we should suppose that the known and settled usages of the Supreme Court from the establishment of the Constitution to the year 1810, a space of thirty years, had fully settled the principle.
> It is said, however, that the present Chief Justice draughted the 3d article in the Declaration of Rights and hence that he must know what its true meaning is; but if other Justices "learned in the law" have not been able to ascertain its meaning during the above space we think it high time that the article itself was amended and rendered so plain that not only ordinary Judges but common people might be able to understand it.

It was inconceivable that the delegates who adopted Article Three thought it applied only to incorporated dissenting bodies:

> Would the venerable [Noah] Alden who was himself the minister of an unincorporated society and who was one of the Committee to whom this article was referred ever have given his consent to it had he understood it as now explained? It cannot be admitted. . . . The community at large understood this article as embracing all unincorporated societies which made voluntary provision at their own expense for the public worship of God. Accordingly in many instances monies thus assessed and collected have been refunded to the teachers of his "own sect," on whose instructions he attended. And in cases where this has been refused, actions have been instituted and maintained on the simple grounds of the Constitution. These cases are too well known as well as too numerous to be detailed on this occasion. It may be proper however just to notice two or three as being full to our purpose.
> About twelve years ago an action was instituted by the Rev. Joel Briggs, the minister of an unincorporated society in Randolph, Stoughton, &c. against the inhabitants of Stoughton. The case was argued and decided at Dedham in the County of Norfolk, August term A.D. 1799 in the Supreme Judicial Court, before the Hon. Francis Dana, Chief

Justice; Nathan Cushing, Thomas Dawes jun Esq'rs Justices, and judgment rendered for the plaintiff as will fully appear by reference to the records of said court. This action was brought by Mr. Briggs to recover certain monies which had been assessed and collected for religious purposes of several of his hearers who were inhabitants of Stoughton.

In 1805 at the September term at Lenox in the County of Berkshire another important case was argued and decided before the Supreme Judicial Court. This action was originally brought by the Rev. Ebenezer Smith against the inhabitants of Dalton. This action was commenced before Joshua Danforh Esq. a j.p., by Elder Smith, the teacher of an unincorporated Baptist Society, for the money collected from Samuel Whipple, one of his hearers, by virtue of a tax levied by the Congregational Parish in Dalton for the settlement and salary of their clergyman, the Rev. Mr. Jennings. At this court judgment was given in favour of the plaintiff. The defendant appealed to the Common Pleas. This court also gave the case in favour of the plaintiff. The defendant then filed a bill of Exceptions and brought a writ of error thereon to the Superior Court. The case was argued for the plaintiff in error by Messrs. Dewey and Gold and for the defendant in error by Messrs. Sullivan and Bidwell.

The merits of the case were considered to rest upon two questions. 1st, whether the teacher of an unincorporated society of Baptists is entitled to the money collected of his hearers by virtue of a Congregational parish tax? 2d, whether a general *Indebitatus Assumpsit* is a proper form of action to recover the money thus collected. These points were argued with great ability and at great length. The Court, composed of Judges Strong, Sedgwick, and Sewell, having taken time to consider the case, unanimously decided both points in favour of the defendants in error and gave their reasons at large for affirming the judgment of the Court of Common Pleas.

Here the principle was admitted by the supreme bench which has lately been denied in the case of Barnes vs. Falmouth and a decision given directly contrary! What still renders it more remarkable is, one of the same Judges was active in both discussions [i.e., Judge Sewell]. Hence according to His Honour's opinion what was constitutional in 1805 was unconstitutional in 1810! [18]

He then considered the case of Montague *vs.* First Parish of Dedham in which Justice Parsons presided. "This was an action in *indebitatus assumpsit* for money paid and received pending in the County of Norfolk. It came before the court upon an agreement of facts and was submitted without argument." Parsons said in this case, "It appears that the defendants are a regular Congregational society of Christians and that within the limits of the parish there is a regular Episcopal society of christians of which the plaintiff is the rector and incumbent." This case was decided at the March term, 1808.

But what is there in all this to prove that the Chief Justice had not been uniform in his decisions? We answer; the foregoing society is acknowl-

18. For another account of this case and others like it see *Independent Chronicle,* October 24, 1805.

edged by the Judge to be a "regular" society; by which it is understood
to be a religious society within the meaning of the Constitution and not a
voluntary society which is under no legal obligation to elect or support
a teacher. But is the episcopal society of Dedham a regular incorporated
'religious society'? We certainly think not. That the Rev. William Montague and several other are incorporated for a particular purpose is readily
admitted. But does this act of incorporation convey to them the powers
of a religious society? Would it be possible in consequence of this act
(which only incorporates them with power to take care of certain land)
to oblige them to 'elect or support a teacher'? We can perceive nothing
in the act which would lead to such a conclusion. By a recurrence to this
we presume that every candid man must be satisfied that there is nothing
in it which would oblige this incorporation to support a 'public protestant
teacher of piety, religion, and morality' any more than an incorporation
for the purpose of making a turnpike or for laying an aqueduct!

The lawyer for the dissenters concluded,

The object of the foregoing is not to charge the Judge with intentional
wrong; but to show the necessity of legislative interference in order to
render the laws more plain and simple and the decisions in future cases
more uniform. It must be evident that the laws as they now exist operate
very unequally. That while thousands in the metropolis are exempted by
law from paying a cent towards the support of 'public worship or public
teachers' many in other parts of the state are obliged to pay a double
ministerial tax. And notwithstanding 'the inconvenience' is said by the
honorable Judges to be 'merely pecuniary and of no great magnitude' we
think it sufficiently so to entitle the aggrieved party to legislative attention
and redress.

This plea for legislative reform on June 13 merely echoed the plea made
by "Berean" at the conclusion of his eight articles three days earlier:

If by a Judicial decision as to the meaning of a part of the Constitution
the religious rights of the Citizens of Massachusetts may be invaded and
destroyed, is it not time for the people by their representatives to examine
whether their civil rights are not endangered also? The plan for an introduction of aristocracy in America may be very gradually developed but in
the case under consideration the question is seriously asked, Does there
not appear to be such a bold 'experiment on our liberties' as to cause just
ground of fear?

"Berean" claimed that Parsons' requirement that dissenters be incorporated to attain religious liberty was "the doctrine of exclusive patronage" to
a special group, those already incorporated as parishes. This made it necessary to ask "whether the facility with which various kinds of incorporations
have been obtained has not had a tendency to create something of the
nature of the 'privileged orders' among the European nations?" The Jack-

sonians' dislike for corporate privilege and monopoly finds here a pietistic antecedent. Where, concluded "Berean," is "that liberty where with Christ has made us free" if all religious societies "are dependent on the discretion and will of the legislature" for incorporation? "Let the friends of Jesus stand aloof from all these civil incorporations of religious societies" and remember Christ's words, "Call no man your father upon the earth." [19]

But the dissenters' action did not wait on these two pleas. On April 17, 1811, after only two of "Berean's" letters had appeared, they held "a large and respectable meeting" in Reading where they voted a set of resolutions, after giveng special thanks to the "berean" for his "defence of Religious Liberty." One resolve "Voted to petition the Legislature of this Commonwealth for an exempting law where by the person and property of all denominations shall be exempt from taxation for the support of Religious Teachers on whose instructions they do not attend." Another deplored the decision in the Barnes case; a third stated "That we view with detestation all connexion between Church and State"; and a fourth praised President Madison for "recognizing the distinction between Civil and Religious Functions." These resolves were ordered printed in three newspapers and were signed by Noah Smith and Lilley Eaton, Jr. Though no report of the meetings or resolutions said so, Smith and Eaton were both members of Elder Ebenezer Nelson, Sr.'s Baptist Church in Reading and the meeting was apparently primarily a Baptist affair.[20]

Three weeks later the *Independent Chronicle* printed a letter addressed "To the Berean" asking him "whether it would be advisable to alter the Constitution . . . Or whether the Constitution as it now stands is to be disregarded? and what department of government is competent at present to afford the relief he wishes for?" Berean answered this inquiry by saying that the most effectual way to solve the problem would be to call a constitutional convention "to reconsider and repeal the third article of the Constitution and to conform it to that part of the Federal Constitution which provides that no law enacting a religious establishment shall ever be made." But, he added,

> as a revision of the Constitution may be considered as too great work at the present time, it appears to the writer that as the Constitution is contradictory, it leaves room for the Legislature to interpose its authority by revising and amending the several statutes respecting public worship and passing a law that all sects shall have equal privileges and that no man shall be taxed for the payment of any teacher of morality whom he does not choose to hear.[21]

Shortly after this the Baptists began a petition movement. Thomas Bald-

19. *Ibid.*, June 10, 1811, p. 3.
20. *Ibid.*, April 25, 1811, p. 1.
21. *Ibid.*, May 13, 1811, p. 1.

win, Nathan Williams (of Beverly), and Lucius Bolles (of Salem) wrote a circular letter to all the Baptists of the state; with it they sent a printed petition for which the letter requested them to obtain signatures to send to the June session of the legislature.[22] The petition stated that despite the fact the Constitution guaranteed religious freedom and equality to all denominations of Christians (in Article Two and in the last clause of Article Three) "the late decisions of the Supreme Bench" have put "a new construction" on Article Three. By permitting only incorporated societies to recover religious taxes from established parishes, "a great proportion of persons who regularly worship in unincorporated societies will be obliged to pay to the support of teachers with whom they disagree in principle, and from whose instructions they conscientiously dissent; and without any legal remedy whatever." This, the petition went on, was subjecting dissenters "to a double proportion of ministerial taxes." Furthermore, the new court decisions were responsible for "the unusual and increasing number of petitions to the General Court for acts of incorporation;" but while these might aid some, "many have conscientious scruples" against incorporation. Therefore, to remedy these evils "and place your petitioners upon an equal footing of privileges with their fellow citizens, we pray your Honors to . . . cause the several laws respecting the worship of God to be so revised and amended that all denominations of christians may be exempt from being taxed to the support of religious teachers, excepting those on whose ministrations they voluntarily attend."

These petitions, signed by thousands (one estimate said fifteen thousand) of persons of all denominations, were presented to the legislature at its next session. The atmosphere of crisis gradually mounted, until a few days before the session opened some letters to the newspapers were calling for the impeachment or dismissal of the judges of the Supreme Judicial Court.[23] At the election that May the Republicans obtained a clear majority in both houses, 332 to 302 in the House and 21 to 19 in the Senate. Governor Gerry was forced to take some account of the religious issue in his speech to the legislature and noted,

> A late solemn decision of our supreme judicial court has limited the right of protestant teachers of piety, religion, and morality to demand the Taxes paid by their respective hearers for the support of public worship to those incorporated societies and has produced a great excitement. This may render indispensable an attention to the subject and further provisions to encourage by every possible means the liberty of conscience in relating to religious opinion and worship.[24]

22. This petition is printed in David Benedict, *A General History of the Baptist Denomination in America*, 2 vols. (Boston, 1813), I, 447–449.

23. See, for example, the letter signed "Harvard" in the *Independent Chronicle*, May 23, 1811.

24. *Ibid.*, June 10, 1811, p. 2. For the Senate's answer to Governor Gerry, pledg-

As soon as the session opened on June 6, the dissenters, led by Estes Howe of Sutton, presented a bill on the subject. (The House ordered that six hundred copies of the decision in Barnes *vs.* Falmouth be printed and given to the legislators.[25] Elder Josiah W. Cannon, a Methodist who represented Nantucket, "moved that 1000 copies of Mr. Madison's memorial against a 'General Assessment' to the Viriginia Legislature in 1785 be printed for the use of the members" but it was voted down.[26] At the second reading of the bill on June 8 it "underwent considerable debate." [27] Among those who spoke in its support were Elder John Leland, representing the town of Cheshire, who had consented to run solely for this purpose. From Leland's speech it appeared that the bill, as originally drawn, contained a section which would have granted automatic incorporation to all existing dissenting societies. To this Leland objected:

> The second section of the bill before the House, I object to. It recognizes principles which are inadmissable — invests all non-corporate societies with corporate power — puts the mischievous dagger [of civil power] into their hands, which has done so much mischief in the world, and presents no balm for the wounds of those who cry for help.
>
> The petitioners do not ask to be known in law as corporate bodies, but to be so covered that religious corporate bodies shall not know, and fleece them; but this action puts the knife into their hands against their wills; a knife, sir, which is more pestiferous than Pandora's box. The interference of legislatures and magistrates in the faith, worship, or support of religious worship is the first step in the case which leads in regular progression to inquisition; the principle is the same, the only difference is in the degree of usurpation.[28]

Leland also disliked the fact that the bill still required certificates, and he made clear that he hoped the whole principle of tax support for religion would be abandoned. "Yes, Mr. Speaker, if there was no money to be got, we should never hear of these corporations. How strange it is, sir, that men who make such noise about Christianity, should be afraid to trust the promise of God, unless they can have legal bondmen, bound by incorporation." The more interesting part of Leland's speech was a paraphrase he offered — "a good translation" he put it — of Articles Two and Three as they were understood by those who wrote and ratified them:

> Let those towns, parishes, precincts and other religious societies possessed of corporate powers, support their religion by force of law, but if there

ing their assistance, see *ibid.,* June 20, 1811, p. 1. The House's answer ignored the issue, *ibid.,* June 17, 1811, p. 2.

25. *Columbian Centinel,* June 8, 1811, p. 2.

26. *Ibid.,* p. 2.

27. *Independent Chronicle,* June 10, 1811, p. 2.

28. Pittsfield *Sun,* June 6, 1811, pp. 1–2, and John Leland. *The Writings of Elder John Leland,* ed. L. F. Greene (New York, 1845), pp. 353–358.

be any one residing within the limits of those corporate bodies who attends other worship and yet has no scruples of conscience in being legally taxed, his money when paid, if he requests it, shall be paid over by the collector, to the minister of his choice. And whereas there are many religious societies who have scruples of conscience about availing themselves of corporate powers; if such societies voluntarily, in their own mode, make suitable provision for the maintenance of their ministers, all such societies of Protestant Christians, properly demeaning themselves as peaceable citizens shall not be forced by any law to support the teachers of worship of any other society. But as we cannot well know how these principles will operate on experiment, we lay down one fundamental maxim, as a polar star, for the legislature — no subordination of one religious sect to another should be established by law.

Regarding Parsons' decision he minced no words:

According to a late decision of the bench . . . nonincorporated societies are nobody — can do nothing and are never to be known except in shearing time, when their money is wanted to support teachers that they may never hear. And all this must be done for the *good of the state.*

Leland pointed out that all of the states outside New England had separated church and state without any disastrous results, and he poked fun at those Congregational missionary magazines in Massachusetts which on one page "plead for law-regulated religion" lest the commonwealth become irreligious and on "the next page they will narrate the wonderful works of God in those states wherein there are no religious laws." To him it looked like "the old firm of Moses and Aaron — ruler and priest — where the language is 'you comb my head and I'll scratch your elbows — you make laws to support me, and I'll persuade the people to obey you.' "

Elder Cannon, speaking for the bill, took a similar stance on behalf of the Methodists. He quoted George Washington and James Madison against religious establishments; he said he had traveled in the Southern states and found no irreligion there; he complained of "a double portion of ministerial tax" being levied on dissenters; he asked why the city of Boston should have special privileges which other towns were denied, and he demanded that some supporter of religious taxes "point out one single passage [in the Bible] where the Saviour or his Apostles called on the rulers of the state to make laws to compel people to build meeting houses or to pay ministers." To him the established system of Massachusetts was "an eternal disgrace to the state." "The American people have fought, bled, tasted and enjoyed the sweets of civil liberty and this state now calls aloud for the enjoyment of religious liberty. Not, sir, a liberty to turn deists and destroy the fair foundation of Christianity, but a liberty to worship the Supreme Being according to the dictates of conscience." Cannon predicted that if the bill were not passed the fifteen thousand petitioners would be heard from again. (Leland had claimed that thirty thousand persons favored the bill.) [29]

As a result of these and other impassioned pleas, the bill was revised and amended to omit the section granting general corporate powers to all religious societies and granting instead the right of any society, "corporate or unincorporate," to recover the religious taxes of its adherents. When the vote came as to whether the bill should have a third reading or not, the House voted 159 to 157 against it. But when a role call vote of the yeas and nays were demanded on a motion to reconsider this voice vote, the motion to reconsider passed 229 to 107. The bill then went to a committee of Cannon, Eleazar W. Ripley and Christopher Webb. Three days later in its revised form the bill again came to the floor where

> Mr. Mills, to test the principle of the bill, moved to strike out a leading section which was advocated by the mover and Mr. Hooper; and opposed by Messrs. Cushman and Cannon, and negatived 212 to 184. The passage of the bill was then advocated by Messrs. Cannon, Ripley, and others and opposed by Messrs. Green (of B.), Townsend, Foster (of L.), Bigelow, and Whitman and in the evening the question "Shall the bill pass?" was decided in the affirmative; but the House being thin a reconsideration of the vote [was voted to be taken the next day].[30]

The next morning, June 11, the bill passed the House by a majority of forty-three. "The arguments on both sides were very animated." [31] It passed the Senate on June 14. Significantly, neither the Republican nor the Federalist newspapers gave more than a few lines to discussing the bill editorially. Obviously for both parties it was a touchy political issue which was bound to alienate many voters in both parties no matter how it was resolved. The Federalists thoroughly disliked the idea of a legislative majority subverting decisions of the judiciary. But probably the Republicans were just as uneasy about the act, for their party bore the main responsibility for it and they were far from enthusiastic about it. William

29. Cannon's speech is in the anonymous tract, *A Blow at the Root of Aristocracy,* (Boston, 1812), pp. 14–18.

30. *Columbian Centinel,* June 12, 1811, p. 2. Neither Eleazar Wheelock Ripley nor the Rev. Joshua Cushman, two representatives from Maine who supported this act, was a dissenter; but both were liberal Republicans. Ripley, of Waterville, a Dartmouth graduate (1800) and a lawyer who entered the army in 1812, rose to Major General and moved to Louisiana. Cushman, of Winslow, was a Standing minister, Harvard 1788, but evidently like William Bentley, he was both a liberal Unitarian and a Republican. Clearly the representatives from Maine were sympathetic to the dissenters in these years, but it is unclear that either Ripley or Cushman favored disestablishment. Cushman was supported by religious taxes during his ministry. See Edwin C. Whittemore, *History of Waterville, Maine* (Waterville, 1902), pp. 58, 150, 564, 440–441.

31. Pittsfield *Sun,* June 2, 1811, p. 2.

Bentley made no mention of the bill (either before, during, or after its passage) in his otherwise detailed diary. The *Independent Chronicle,* the chief Republican organ, gave it only the barest mention as a news item and no editorial comment whatsoever.

On the whole the dissenters considered they had done very well for themselves. David Benedict in his *History* published two years later summed up the prevailing view of the Religious Freedom Act for his denomination:

> It afforded peculiar relief to the Baptists and other dissenters, but still neither party is altogether satisfied with it. The Congregationalists are afraid that they have given up too much, but the dissenters suppose they have not yet obtained what they claim as their just and indisputable right, viz. a free exemption from all taxes and all certificates. They think it best, however, for the present, to shift along with what they have got and obtain the rest when Providence shall open a door.[32]

The act finally passed was relatively simple. In its first section it stated that all religious taxes should be paid to the public teacher of religion of each taxpayer's own religious sect "and it shall be sufficient to entitle any such teacher or teachers of a corporate or unincorporate religious society to receive the same monies of the town, district, parish or religious corporation which shall assess, collect or receive the same, that he be ordained and established according to the forms and usages of his own religious sect and denomination." The second section defined the certificate which a dissenter must file with the Clerk of the town where he lived so his pastor might collect his taxes. The third section gave to unincorporated religious societies the power to manage and to improve any gifts or donations they might receive through trustees appointed by themselves. The fourth section stated that ministers of all sects ordained over societies corporate or unincorporate were entitled to exemption from civil taxes in the towns where they lived.[33]

For a time after the passage of the act, considerable uneasiness existed among the dissenters on two counts. First, because they thought the Federalists would repeal the act as soon as they regained control; second, because they thought that the Supreme Judicial Court would at the first opportunity either rule it unconstitutional or vitiate its force. The Federalists had attacked the bill even before it was enacted. A writer in one Federalist paper attacked Governor Gerry for even suggesting that such a bill was needed. The governor's speech, he said, was an attack on the clergy, trying to "plunge a dagger into their bosoms." Moreover,

32. Benedict, *History,* I, 449.
33. Mass. State AR, V, 387. For some reason the Massachusetts Archives contain none of the petitions submitted to bring pressure in support of this act.

This part of your Speech amounts to a recommendation to the Legislature to control the Judiciary. The object of your Excellency and your party is well known. Under the pretence of a tender regard to conscience you mean to break up all the present parishes and by enlisting the cupidity and avarice of men on your side to hold yourself up as having delivered men from the tyranny of priests and from the gripe of taxes for the support of religious worship.[34]

After the act passed a Federalist wrote in the Boston *Gazette,* "the General Court have dissolved all legal connection between pastor and parish. And five or three men can now form a religious society, choose one of their number for a teacher, ordain him in their own way, by pouring a bottle of wine over his head or otherwise, and spend Sunday in playing cards" and they will be able to certify themselves and anyone else who joins them so as to free them from religious taxes.[35] Another antidemocrat wrote that he saw in the act "a concentration of the civil and religious democracy of our country which by a joint effort will level with the dust and trample under foot the noblest monuments of religion and literature of which our nation can boast." [36]

But these and other fulminations were not so fearful as the bill which the Federalists introduced at the winter session in 1811–1812. One of the sections in this bill read:

And be it further enacted That any citizen of the Commonwealth who shall not specially unite himself to any particular religious society shall be deemed and considered a member of the congregational society in the town where he or she may reside.[37]

This bill produced a series of letters by "The Inspector" in the *Independent Chronicle* and a powerful anonymous pamphlet entitled *A Blow at the Root of Aristocracy* to alert the dissenters against it.[38] "Friends to Religious Liberty, Look to your Rights" said the Inspector. This bill is "a stepstone to hierarchical aristocracy if not to absolute monarchy . . . a bold and daring attempt on our civil and religious liberty . . . Are you willing to have a law passed that shall compel you to specially join some religious society or else be dragged headlong against your consent into the Congre-

34. *Independent Chronicle,* June 24, 1811, p. 1.
35. *Ibid.,* June 27, 1811, p. 2.
36. *Ibid.,* July 4, 1811, p. 1. This same writer claimed here that Governor Sullivan had never favored either the abolition of compulsory religious taxes or disestablishment.
37. *Ibid.,* March 12, 1812, p. 1.
38. These writings resemble the work of Elder Josiah W. Cannon, but there is no way of knowing whether he wrote them. This tract is not to be confused with John Leland's tract with a similar title published in 1801

gational Society?" [39] The anonymous writer of *A Blow at the Root* made it clear why some dissenters considered the bill worse than the old certificate laws of the eighteenth century; they were fearful that its intent was to limit tax exemption only to dissenting *church members* and not to adherents or *regular attenders:*

> Can any *specially* belong to a religious society who are not church members? If this bill passes we must be contended with our church members and give them [the parish churches] all the members of our congregation.[40]

Since the Revolution there had never been any serious question that a dissenter was exempt if he regularly attended and contributed to a church of another denomination. It is doubtful that the Federalists really intended to overturn this principle. But some anxious dissenters interpreted the word "specially" in the new bill to mean that only full members could claim exemption from the Congregational taxes: "the congregationalists wish to be authorized by the legislature to claim all the sheep which are not marked." [41] If this interpretation were correct, the Congregationalists were trying to deplete the ranks of the dissenters by two-thirds or more.

Because the legislature was still dominated by the Republicans at the time this bill was introduced, "The Inspector" felt called upon to explain that the bill was by no means a Republican-sponsored measure but that it had been introduced by a committee made up of "one federalist, one nominal and one real republican." The "nominal republican" was "a congregational minister and having an interest in obtaining such a law he joined the federal member in that antiscriptural oppressive and unconstitutional thing." [42] This explanation only revealed again how divided the Republicans were on the issue.

In any event, this bill, though it was referred to the next session of the legislature — which was dominated by the Federalists — did not pass. Nor did any bill pass which weakened the act of 1811. And in 1817, Chief Justice Isaac Parker reluctantly upheld the constitutionality of the act, thus ending the judicial threat to its enforcement.[43] Meanwhile, many dissenting

39. *Independent Chronicle*, March 12, 1812, p. 1.
40. *Blow at the Root*, p. 19.
41. *Ibid.*
42. *Independent Chronicle,* April 12, 1812. The writer of this article claimed that "except for a double-minded few" all of the Republican members of the legislature had voted for the Religious Freedom Act while "on the federalist side it had not a single advocate or vote. A few of that party left the house because they were ashamed to oppose" it.
43. 14 *Massachusetts Term Reports,* 340; Howe, *Cases on Church and State,* p. 36. Parker's decision is that of a typical Federalist-Unitarian statement on the danger of tampering with the Standing Order. For a good, but brief, discussion of

societies had taken the trouble to get incorporated, just in case.[44] Not until 1820 did the Baptists find that "Providence" had opened an opportunity for them to push again toward the separation of church and state in Massachusetts.

Yet they could hardly claim that they were suffering anything like persecution after 1811. The extent to which the Religious Liberty Act had limited the power of the Standing Order to restrict dissent is evident from the test case which upheld the constitutionality of that law. It was brought by a Baptist, Daniel Adams, who belonged to the Baptist church in Barre. Adams lived in the neighboring town of Rutland and in 1813 the assessors taxed him $5.50 for the support of the Standing church in Rutland on the ground that he did not regularly attend a duly constituted Baptist church. The assessors based their claim on the fact that the church in Barre had no regular pastor or preaching but was served once a month by Elder Zenas Leonard, pastor of the Baptist church in Sturbridge, eighteen miles away. Adams claimed that this was nevertheless a legal dissenting congregation under the terms of the Religious Liberty Act, and, having submitted a certificate of his membership in that church, he refused to pay his tax. The constable of Rutland, Howe, distrained a heifer belonging to Adams and sold it to pay Adams' tax. Adams brought suit against Howe for trespass.

Howe lost the first trial in September 1816, but he won an appeal in March 1817. The case came before the Supreme Judicial Court in September 1817. Howe's attorney relied upon the decisions of the Court in Barnes *vs.* Falmouth and Turner *vs.* Brookfield, arguing that the Religious Liberty Act was unconstitutional because it contradicted Article Three as it was interpreted by these decisions. If the congregation in Barre were a legally recognized ecclesiastical society, said the attorney, than any number of people in any kind of sect, even Mahometan, could form a congregation and claim exemption from religious taxes. Judge Parker admitted that the Barre church was not incorporated, that it had no minister duly settled over it, and that it did not meet regularly, nevertheless he ruled that under the terms of the Religious Liberty Act a certificate from that church was legal because the Act was within the scope of legislative prerogative under the Constitution. Parker acknowledged "the great inconvenience, and the injury to public morals and religion, and the tendency to destroy all decency and regularity of public worship" which had resulted from the excessive "indulgence granted by the legislature," but he could not honestly say that they did not have the right to wreck the system of their forefathers if they wished to

---

the Religious Freedom Act of 1811 and of Adams *vs.* Howe see John D. Cushing, "Notes on Disestablishment in Massachusetts, 1780–1833," *William and Mary Quarterly,* XXVI (April 1969), pp. 185–188.

44. Between 1811 and 1816 seventy dissenting societies were incorporated. Edward Buck, *Massachusetts Ecclesiastical Law* (Boston, 1865), p. 43.

do so. He may have hoped, as he implied, that "subsequent legislatures may correct" the "evil tendency or inexpediency" of such "pernicious" laws, but there was nothing the court could do about such negligence or dereliction of duty.[45]

Parker's disgust was shared by most of the Unitarians and Trinitarians, but they were not yet ready to give up, as they demonstrated at the constitutional convention of 1820.

45. 14 *Massachusetts Term Reports,* 340–351.

Chapter 56

The Baptists Seek Respectability, 1800–1830

The Baptists are desirous of becoming *"popular* and respectable," to use their own words.

The Universalist Trumpet, March 28, 1829, p. 155

Except for the brief flare-up of excitement following the Barnes case, in the early decades of the nineteenth century the Baptists did not take a great deal of interest in political affairs in Massachusetts. As individuals they supported the Republican Party solidly on election days and agreed generally with its political, economic, and diplomatic policies, but as a denomination the Baptists in Massachusetts, as in Connecticut, preferred to be apolitical. This policy received official endorsement in the circular letter of the Boston Baptist Association in 1812:

> For several months past political subjects have in an unusual degree arrested the public mind. Men of all ranks seem busily employed in canvassing measures of government, and in expressing each one his opinion concerning them. We mean not to condemn this in an unqualified manner. In all free governments the people are bound to watch over their liberties with a jealous eye; and they have an undoubted right to declare their minds freely, though respectfully, concerning the conduct of men in power.
>
> But brethren, take heed lest you enter too largely into disscussions of this nature. If you do, they will cerainly prove the bane of your souls, and eventually pierce you through with many sorrows. We will venture to say you cannot feel the ardour of a political partizan and that of a humble spiritual christian at the same time. While you are warmly engaged in ruminating on affairs of state and in searching for arguments to puzzle and confound a political opponent, you cannot be meditating on the precious 'word of life' nor furnishing yourselves with the means of resisting your spiritual foes. The spirit of this present evil world is directly opposed to the spirit of Christ, and cannot be habitually indulged without destroying the exercise of religion in the soul.[1]

1. Boston Baptist Association Minutes, 1812, p. 10.

This distaste for the corruption of politics was no doubt emphasized in 1812 because "Mr. Madison's War" made life difficult for the Republicans (and doubly so for dissenting Republicans) in Massachusetts. But it was not new. The *Massachusetts Baptist Missionary Magazine* at its founding in 1803 took pains to point out to its readers in an introductory address "To the Public" that "neither party politics nor party religion called forth our exertions" in founding the magazine. The Standing Clergy had for several years been roundly denounced by Republicans for mixing politics and religion to attack Thomas Jefferson, and the Baptists could not consistently take to the hustings against Federalism. It was accepted doctrine among dissenters that the fundamental failing of an establishment was that it mixed Christianity and politics.

Nevertheless there was a new element in the otherworldly orientation of the nineteenth-century Baptists which made their approach to politics quite different from that of their colonial predecessors. Where the Revolutionary Separate-Baptists had strenuously engaged in tough-minded lobbying and power politics through their Grievance Committee, the nineteenth century Baptists preferred to reform the world by saving souls and improving morals. Why spend valuable time, talent and money lobbying to change a few legislative votes when by Christian evangelism and revival meetings hundreds — thousands — of souls could be converted to Baptist views? "This present evil world" was rapidly changing, improving, progressing; the birth of the American republic had ushered in a new era for mankind. Now God's grace and human benevolence were on the verge of bringing in the millennium. Party politics seemed insignificant to those anticipating the imminent Second Coming of the Lord.

At the same time the Baptists were conscious that their hitherto small and despised sect was now a large and respectable denomination in America; it was destined to play a large role in advancing the coming Kingdom of God on earth. Now in its third generation since the Separate-Baptists reformation of the 1740's, it was at last beginning to be influential in New England and it wished to be worthy of its position and responsibilities. Home and foreign missions, moral reform societies, and an educated ministry were the new paths to religious honor. The Baptists trod them with jubilant feet in the opening years of the century.

Therefore, that Baptist missionaries to the "destitute" parts of New England were instructed to avoid politics as "irrelevant" to their work and "subversive" of success is not surprising. Elder Joshua Bradley of Mansfield, Connecticut wrote to the Boston-edited missionary magazine in 1808 describing a revival just before the annual election in May and noted, "I have not heard any one among us express the least desire for political sermons; but vastly to the contrary." [2]

2. *Massachusetts Baptist Missionary Magazine* (Boston), I, 8; *ibid.*, I, 85.

This same attitude was consistently maintained in local and national politics by the *Christian Watchman,* the Baptist newspaper founded in Boston in 1819. "We have ever stood," said the editor in 1825, "entirely aloof from party politics . . . political zeal in Christians and especially in christian ministers is little better than spiritual disloyalty. As members of the civil community their duty is not fulfilled but by subjection to the powers that be and by leading quiet and peaceable lives in all godliness and honesty." [3] A Baptist sermon on the almost simultaneous deaths of Thomas Jefferson and John Adams in 1826 summarized the pietistic attitude toward politics and politicians which has dominated American evangelical thought since then:

> It seems now almost taken for granted, that a man who takes any share in political arrangements must, under all circumstances, act with his party, let them act right or wrong . . . Now whether a christian may or may not be a politician, I have no question whatever to raise. It must be left to his own conscience . . . But . . . we beg leave to say that a christian has no right any where or under any circumstances to be any thing else than a christian. He must ask about a political as well as any other act, the question, Is it right or wrong — and by the answer to that question must he be guided. It is just as wicked to lie about politics as to lie about merchandise. It is just as immoral to act without reference to the law of God at a caucus as any where else . . . no man can more surely be putting an end to his religion, than by frequenting any circle which he must enter without his religion.[4]

In their own way the Baptists disliked democratic politics as much as did the aristocrats of the Standing Order. "Politics" was fast becoming a dirty word in America, "politician" a synonym for scoundrel. Neither the pietistic evangelical in his individualistic search for perfect moral freedom nor the pietistic theocrat in his paternalistic quest for perfect moral order could stomach the pragmatic expediency of party politics. A man endangered his spiritual welfare as surely in a party caucus as in a gambling den.

John Leland's dedication to the political reforms of the Jeffersonian and Jacksonian parties was one of the principle reasons why his colleagues distrusted him. "That which probably interfered more than any thing else with his usefulness as a minister," wrote one of them "was his almost mad devotion to politics. He was a very prince among the democrats of his day; and some would doubtless say that he magnified his office as a politician at the expense of lowering it as a Christian minister." [5] Disliking so many aspects of the democratic, laissez-faire, catch-as-catch-can world they had done so much to create, the Baptists worked on the hope that another world would

3. *Christian Watchman* (Boston), December 9, 1825, p. 3.
4. *Massachusetts Baptist Missionary Magazine,* VI, 259.
5. William B. Sprague, *Annals of the American Pulpit* (New York, 1860), VI, 185–186.

soon replace it — a utopia of supernatural goodness and righteousness where no one would have to compromise any of his christian ideals because all would be perfect and Christ the only lawgiver.[6]

The Baptists' loss of interest in direct political action was also connected with their increasing concern for institutional growth as a denomination. Generally the Baptists believed that they were sufficiently free and well-organized by 1800 to direct their attention to other goals. There were many statements, both official and unofficial, by Baptists in this period congratulating themselves upon the extent of their freedom in Massachusetts — especially after 1811. In September of that year the Warren Association published a circular Letter to its members pointing out the historical shifts in their favor over the years:

> Our fathers for several years laboured under various trials. In many sections of our country the principles of religious liberty were but imperfectly understood and very partially enjoyed. The smiles of Heaven, however, were propitious in their exertions . . . We meet [today] under external circumstances far different from our fathers. Unmolested in the enjoyment of our religious privileges, we sit quietly under our vine and under our fig-tree. By a late provision of the civil government of this Commonwealth, those embarrassments which have heretofore existed are removed, and we are under increased obligations for gratitude to our heavenly Parent for his bountiful provision.[7]

Three years later a published address of the Boston Baptist Association stated:

> If we compare the present state of our denomination in this land with the state it was in 50 years since, we shall see great cause of encouragement and thankfulness. We were then oppressed; we have now full liberty to worship God according to the dictates of our own consciences. We were then few in number; we have now increased to a multitude. The Lord has indeed done great things for us whereof we have reason to be glad.[8]

Astounded by their success and giving all the credit to God rather than to the Grievance Committee or to the Republican Party, the Baptists could hardly do other than devote themselves to His service. "Many are asking when will the Millennium commence?" said the Baptist *Christian Watchman* in 1833; "The reply to this may be couched in very few words — It will be ushered in with full glory when the world shall be converted to the Protestant

6. For Baptist predictions of the millennium's arrival in 1830 and 1847, see *Christian Watchman,* November 25, 1829, and April 2, 1833. For an excellent description of the perfectionist mind in America after 1800, see John L. Thomas, *The Liberator* (Boston, 1963).

7. Warren Baptist Association Minutes, 1811.

8. Boston Baptist Association Minutes, 1814, p. 14. See also *Massachusetts Baptist Missionary Magazine,* IV, 120.

principle of practically yielding their hearts and lives to the precepts and doctrines of the gospel." [9]

Searching for the best means to implement their ideals of evangelism and Christian philanthropy, they turned to the Mother country. To the models which their evangelical brethren in England provided, the Americans added their own well-developed practice of itinerant mass evangelism, the New Divinity doctrine of "disinterested benevolence," and their inherent genius for voluntary association. The result was a century or more of the most intense activity for Christian benevolence that the world has ever seen. Looking back on it now we see this movement in terms of the multifarious organizations designed to promote home and foreign missions, Sunday schools, Sabbatarian legislation, Bible and tract societies, moral reform societies, temperance organizations, evangelical journals and newspapers, religious colleges and seminaries, and the manifold attempts to regulate the moral content of novels, plays, art, and poetry. But at the time, all of these activities were only secondary techniques or tools for converting (and keeping converted) the world to Christ. The central theme of all the evangelical thought and action in this movement was the conversion of souls — every activity was geared to this end.

None of these Christian activities directly concerned politics but for the Baptists, as for other evangelicals in America, Christianity became identified with republican government, and republican government became identified with the manifest destiny of the United States or of the Anglo-Saxon race. Thus the establishment of Christian civilization, government, and morality throughout the world became the ideational center of Baptist theology and activity. The greatest Baptist spokesman of the nineteenth century, Francis Wayland (who became pastor of the First Baptist Church in Boston in 1821), eventually put into classic form the evangelical world view in his works on moral science and political economy. In the latter, written in 1837, he said,

> the surest means of promoting the welfare of a country is to cultivate its intellectual but especially its moral character . . . the wealth and happiness and power of every nation are in exact proportion to its intellectual and moral character . . . Can any one doubt that Great Britain and France reap incomparably greater advantages from each other in their present condition of advanced civilization than either of them should if the other were in the condition in which it was found by Julius Caesar? . . . How much greater benefits does North America confer upon the world than it would if it were peopled by its aboriginal inhabitants? . . . how greatly would the comforts and luxuries of men be increased if Africa were peopled by civilized and christianized men?

This was the spirit that underlay evangelical philanthropy and missions in

9. *Christian Watchman,* April 12, 1833, p. 58.

the nineteenth century — enlightened self-interest for the glory of God and the prosperity of man:

> Now if these things be so, and that they are so I see not that any one can dispute, it seems to me that civilized nations could in no way so successfully promote their own interests as by the universal dissemination of education and the principles of religion.[10]

The Baptists modestly assumed that their polity and principles of religion were both the most truly American and most in harmony with scriptural truth. In the early years of national myth-making the Baptists published the "fact" that Thomas Jefferson was influenced in writing the Declaration of Independence by Baptist principles. It appears that Jefferson had visited the Baptist church of Elder Andrew Tribble (or Trebble) in Albemarle, Virginia just before July 4, 1776 and had remarked, after conversing with Tribble, that he found the congregational polity of the Baptists to embody the most important features of democracy.[11] Similar myths were told for most other evangelical denominations, but it is not inaccurate to state that the Baptist view of life *was* very close to the American view of life in the nineteenth century.

But the contradictions in the Baptist (or evangelical) concept of the Christian-democratic society are, to the twentieth century mind, of such astounding proportions that it is difficult to see it as much more than pious cant or delusive hypocrisy. In addition to outrageously naïve Christian imperialism abroad, the Baptists clearly espoused the tyranny of the evangelical majority at home. To civilize and Christianize America it was necessary to enforce moral uniformity and conformity by law on non-evangelical minorities for their own and the nation's good. To eschew party or partisan politics was not to deny the claims of Christian politics to promote and enforce the moral purity of the nation. One of the earliest such efforts occurred in the 1820's when the Baptists threw themselves headlong into the campaign to prohibit the delivery of the United States mails on Sunday. The leaders of the movement could not understand why John Leland and a few other Baptist stalwarts thought this effort inconsistent with the Baptist position on separation of church and state. Not long afterward the Mormons and Roman Catholics were told to conform or leave. It is difficult, now that we have lived through the Fundamentalist movement and the Scopes trial, to look back on the beginnings of evangelical moral reform and comprehend the profound humanitarian impulses of Christian love, self-sacrifice, and

10. Francis Wayland, *The Elements of Political Economy* (New York, 1837), pp. 139–140. Wayland was the President of Brown University from 1827 to 1855. For a similar statement by the pastor of the Third Baptist Church of Boston in 1824 see the election sermon of Daniel Sharp, *Discourse Before William Eustis, Governor of Massachusetts* (Boston, 1824).

11. The story is printed in the *Christian Watchman*, July 14, 1826, p. 130.

unselfish devotion to a higher cause which underlay it. We tend today to sympathize more with those anticlerical Jacksonians who turned upon the religious reformers as a new kind of antirepublican subversives — Jesuitical priests trying to create "a christian party in politics," bigoted fanatics ready to persecute any who did not worship at their altars.

A good measure of the shift which took place among the status-seeking Baptists of New England in these years is that the denomination found itself sadly split on the suitability of Andrew Jackson for the Presidency of the United States, even though Jackson had much better claim to theological orthodoxy and practice than did Thomas Jefferson. To the old-fashioned (some said "backward") rural Baptists for whom John Leland was spokesman, Jackson was the true inheritor of the Jeffersonian mantle; but to the respectable eastern and urban Baptists who were the real leaders of the denomination, Jackson did not conform nearly so well to their ideal of a righteous ruler as John Quincy Adams (the son of their old archenemy).

The Baptists' rapid growth in these years was one of the most important factors in this shift of opinion. From a total of 90 Baptist churches with 7000 members in 1800, the denomination in New England grew to 166 churches with 12,743 members in 1824 and to 174 churches with 17,000 members by 1830. The number of adherents or nominal Baptists was more than double the number of members. If one subtracts the Unitarians, there may well have been more dissenting churches than Congregational churches in Massachusetts by 1820.[12] As the number of churches grew the old associations became too large and new associations formed from them. Most important of the new associations was the Boston Baptist Association formed in 1812 by an amicable division of the Warren Association. This was a logical step since the center of Baptist influence had by this time shifted to the Boston area. The leading figures in the denomination since the deaths of Backus and Manning were in Boston and its vicinity, and generally they continued to be. In evangelicalism, as in all other things, Boston became the hub of New England even though socially and politically the city was dominated by the Unitarians.

The new crop of religious leaders who replaced Backus, Manning, Stillman and Hezekiah Smith lacked the heroic lustre of these primitive champions of the faith. Moreover, as the orthodox Trinitarian Congregationalists turned their attention to the same evangelical goals, their more able and wealthy leaders outshone the Baptists's religious efforts. Historians have rightly given most of their attention to evangelical Congregationalists like Jedidiah Morse, Lyman Beecher, Timothy Dwight, Jeremiah Evarts, and

---

12. According to figures Enoch Mudge offered in the constitutional convention of 1820, there were at that time in Massachusetts 373 Congregational societies and 325 dissenting societies. Mudge included the Unitarians among the Congregationalists and underestimated the number of Baptist congregations. See *Journal of Debates and Proceedings* (Boston, 1853), p. 558.

Leonard Woods rather than to the less effective and less influential Baptists who were doing the same things during this time. Except for Luther Rice and Adoniram Judson, two Congregational missionaries who became Baptists in 1812 after embarking for India, the Baptists produced no popular figures before Wayland to compare with the Congregational leaders. Lack of education, lack of money, lack of prestige, and above all lack of self-confidence seriously handicapped the Baptists in their benevolent reform activities in New England. But despite these handicaps, they made a significant contribution to the religious movements of their day.

The leading Baptists of Massachusetts in this period (apart from the eccentric John Leland) were Thomas Baldwin, Nathan Williams of Beverly, Lucius Bolles of Salem, Caleb Blood, Joseph Grafton, Elisha Andrews, Ebenezer Nelson, William Batchelder, Zenas Leonard, Charles Train, Daniel Sharp, J. M. Winchell, James D. Knowles.[13] All of these were clergymen; only one of them (Bolles) had a college education; and despite their unquestioned devotion to their cause, none of them left any distinctive or lasting mark behind them.

Thomas Baldwin of the Second Baptist Church of Boston, towered above them all in prestige and in reputed learning until his death in 1826. But none of his many published tracts and sermons are worth remembering today. His polemical defenses of immersion and adult baptism merely repeated old arguments. His fast day, thanksgiving, and elections sermons were routine performances, lacking in originality of thought or style. He concentrated what ability he had upon making himself a respected and respectable image for his denomination; his chief roles were those of publicist for Baptist activities, peacemaker within his denomination, and liaison officer with the leaders of the other evangelical denominations.

Baldwin was born in 1753 in Bozrah, Connecticut, of Congregational parents.[14] His family moved to Canaan, New Hampshire in 1769. From 1775 to 1780 he served as a deputy to the legislature from the town of Canaan. Converted to Baptist views in 1781, he felt a call to the ministry and became an itinerant evangelist throughout Vermont and New Hampshire for the next eight years. In 1790 he accepted the call of the Second Baptist Church of Boston where he immediately assumed a position of leadership in the denomination. Though he had only a common school education, he received an M.A. from Rhode Island College in 1794 and a D.D. from Union College in 1803. In 1802 he was chosen to deliver the election sermon before the Massachusetts legislature, and he served several times as chaplain to the House of Representatives. In 1802 he

13. See Sprague, *Annals,* VI, for biographical sketches of these men. The leading lay figures among the Massachusetts Baptists in these years were Heman Lincoln, John Sullivan, James Loring, Ensign Lincoln, and Joseph B. Varnum.

14. See Elder Elihu Hyde's letter to Isaac Backus, November 15, 1783, in BP (AN), in which Hyde claims that it was common knowledge in New Hampshire that Baldwin was born out of wedlock.

was instrumental in founding the Massachusetts Baptist Missionary Society and the next year he was appointed by the society to edit the *Massachusetts Baptist Missionary Magazine,* the first regular Baptist publication in New England. Thereafter no Baptist activity was complete without his endorsement and participation, and he served as president or trustee of most of them. He helped found the Baptist Triennial Convention for foreign missions in 1814 and the Massachusetts Baptist Convention in 1824. In 1820 he was chosen as one of the delegation from Boston to the Constitutional Convention. He took a great interest in promoting denominational unity not only in New England but throughout the nation. He served in his last years as president of the national board of foreign missions. His most famous and popular work was a series of letters published in 1810 in which he disputed with the Rev. Samuel Worcester, a Trinitarian Congregationalist, over the principle of adult immersion. He published over thirty-five tracts and sermons before his death in 1826, none of which dealt with the separation of church and state.[15]

Among the organizations and activities in which the Massachusetts Baptists took most pride and interest during these years the Missionary Society was of prime importance. Originally designed to promote and foster home missionary activities in New England, this society also contributed to the support of the British Baptist Foreign Missionary Society; its magazine devoted much space to the work of William Carey and David Marshman in Serampore, India. After 1812 when Luther Rice and Adoniram Judson turned Baptist on their way to India, the society divided its interest between supporting home and foreign missions. The *Baptist Missionary Magazine* was devoted almost exclusively to reports of revivals and conversions written in letters and published in other journals by the various home and foreign missionary agents as well as by settled Baptist pastors reporting showers of blessings in their own congregations. The annual minutes of the various Baptist associations were filled with the same kinds of reports along with constant exhortations to increase the donations for support of evangelical activities and to multiply the prayers for the success of the evangelists involved. Some of these exhortations indicate the emergence of the doctrines of Christian imperialism among these Baptists who were determined to convert the world to gospel truth as they saw it.

An article in the *Baptist Missionary Magazine* in 1820 entitled "Christian Action" and probably written by Thomas Baldwin, epitomized the "practical" side of pietistic activism:

> The Christian religion is in its nature *practical.* Its design is not to afford matter for curious speculation, not to give scope to the reveries of a vacant hour, but to influence the conduct. It operates on the affections

15. See Sprague, *Annals,* VI, 209, for a biographical sketch and bibliography of his writings.

as well as on the understanding . . . Its object is such as should produce the highest degree of activity in its votaries. This is no less than to emancipate the world. But to emancipate it from what? From temporal servitude? from civil tyranny? That indeed would be an object worthy of an American. But what is that compared with deliverance from perpetual servitude? from the slavery of the mind? the slavery of sin? The object rises above all estimation and should inspire every Christian . . . Another reason why Christians should be active is that *the present is an auspicious period.* Had we lived thirty years ago, few of those opportunities which we now enjoy . . . would have been afforded us. The Christian world had not then learned to do good by united and systematic efforts. The present is auspicious not only because many are combined for the advancement of benevolent objects, but because God blesses their exertions and gives us reason to believe that he will still more abundantly bless them.[16]

And of all the objects of Christian action, Baldwin said in 1811, foreign missions was the most important. To convert heathen to American Baptist Christianity would save them from the sin of idolatry and advance them on the road to civilization;

> That Christianity is a doctrine of benevolence none but its decided enemies will deny. But in nothing is this lovely disposition more clearly and advantageously displayed than in missionary exertions. Here the benevolent heart finds an object worthy of its boldest efforts. Here it enjoys the pure and unalloyed pleasure of endeavouring to advance the glory of God and the happiness of immortal beings, without being conscious of any selfish motives. This is that heavenly charity that seeketh not her own . . . The Baptist mission to India leads the van of this glorious army. It not only stands foremost in point of time, but in extent of usefulness to the Christian cause.[17]

To engage in an absolutely pure Christian act "without being conscious of any selfish motives" was the height of an activistic pietist's dreams:

> When young men are engaged in the closing years of study in our public institutions, and sometimes earlier, the question usually comes up — 'Where shall I spend my life? Is it my duty to go to the heathen — or to the Western Valley [The Mississippi — as an evangelist] — or sit down among the endearments and refinements of my own native circle?' . . . The heathen world, every such young man will allow, has the greatest claim upon his services.[18]

And so the pious young men of the nineteenth century, imbued with a

16. *Massachusetts Baptist Missionary Magazine,* n.s., II, 320. Although the title of the magazine changed to *The American Baptist Magazine* in 1812, I have retained the original title throughout for convenience.
17. *Ibid.,* n.s., III, iv.
18. *Ibid.,* n.s., XIII, 131.

desire to serve mankind and to do the will of God, "literally left all to follow Christ," to "seek the emancipation of thousands from gross darkness and superstition," "to rescue miserable victims from perishing beneath the wheels of Juggernaut," "to seek to preserve to helpless and friendless children [of India], their mothers, who are accustomed in vast numbers annually to burn with their husbands upon the funeral pire," to "seek to demolish idols and close the doors of heathen temples, while they declare the true God, and throw open to perishing souls the gates of salvation and eternal glory. This labour of love we owe to idolators." [19]

The Baptists were not averse to mixing American and Baptist chauvinism with their appeals for foreign missionaries: "Shall not America furnish her proportion of these missionaries? And shall not churches of our denomination manifest as much ardour in this holy enterprise as those of any other?" [20] The merging of Christianity and patriotism was inevitable:

> There is undoubtedly no one circumstance more favourable to the best interests of our beloved country than revivals of genuine religion . . . That surprising operation of the Spirit of God by which he enlightens the understanding and regenerates the soul produces an influential principle of belief and action which can never be destroyed . . . Do we lament the dissipation of the age, the foul profaneness of the blasphemer, a contempt of the Sabbath, of the ordinances of the gospel and of its holy precepts? This work of God in the renovation of the heart . . . [implants] in the soul a supreme and holy affection to God and his law. As therefore Christians love their country; as they regard the interests of civil society; as they desire the best and endless good of immortal souls [let them pray for and work for revivals of religion].[21]

Truly to love one's country was to try to convert it to Christianity or to carry its Christian civilization abroad. When John Quincy Adams was elected to the Presidency in 1824 the *Christian Watchman* praised his acknowledgment of "the divine superintendence" over America in his message to Congress by noting, "In our happy country we have reason to rejoice that the basis of all our political institutions is the Christian faith and that the perpetuity of our splendid republican fabrick is known to rest on no other basis. When the righteous are in authority, then well may the people rejoice." [22]

In addition to the Massachusetts Missionary Society, the Baptists organized the Baptist Evangelical Tract Society in 1812 [23] and the Lord's Day Schools Association in 1817.[24] In 1819 the Baptists launched their first

19. Boston Baptist Association Minutes, 1813, p. 10.
20. *Ibid.*, 1816, p. 12.
21. *Christian Watchman*, April 14, 1821, p. 71.
22. *Ibid.*, December 16, 1825, p. 7.
23. *Massachusetts Baptist Missionary Magazine*, n.s., III, 217.
24. Boston Baptist Association Minutes, 1817, p. 11. Elder Lucius Bolles had

weekly magazine, the Boston *Christian Watchman,* edited by John E. Weston and a man named True (probably also with the assistance of James Loring who later succeeded Watson as editor and who controlled the publishing firm of Manning and Loring in Boston).[25] In 1828 they founded the *Baptist Repository and Christian Review* in Boston. This was a monthly journal of articles on theology and of literary interest to the Baptists, comparable to *The Spirit of the Pilgrims* which Lyman Beecher founded in Boston that same year for "the Orthodox" or Trinitarian Congregationalists.[26]

Next to missions and revivals education was the subject which interested Baptists most during this period. It provides one of the best clues to the changing character of the denomination. The Baptist leaders, especially in the Boston area, were insistent on the need for more and better-educated ministers. But they found it difficult to convince their rural brethren of this. In their attempts to do so they became rather equivocal about the relative merits of the internal gift to preach (for which Backus and the Separates had fought so hard in the First Great Awakening) and about the necessity for a learned ministry to cope with the demands of denominational respectability. In addition, the advocates of denominational colleges could not at this time make up their minds concerning the extent to which state aid to colleges in money or land grants was their due, and if it were, what claims, if any, this gave the state over the administration of the college. The Baptists fully supported public schools on the assumption that they inculcated the fundamental moral and scriptural truths of the Christian Protestant religion through natural theology and the Bible taught without denominational emphasis. But they also felt the necessity for Sunday Schools as a denominational supplement to the public schools; these trained the young in the specific doctrines of the denomination and led them to expect (and be carefully prepared for) a conversion experience followed by immersion and church membership at some time in puberty.

In their entire treatment of education the Baptists demonstrated clearly their desire to create a Christian society in which the state and the churches would coordinate the task of training the young to produce upright Christian citizens and yet to leave the parent free to see that his offspring were guided

---

persuaded them not to use the term "Sunday Schools" because Sunday was a heathen name.

25. The *Christian Watchman* was not founded as the result of any official denominational action but from the private interest of two young printers, one of whom (Weston) was not at the time a Baptist. However, it quickly won denominational support and endorsement. When Weston turned Baptist and became pastor of the East Cambridge Church, James Loring, deacon and clerk of the First Baptist Church of Boston, succeeded him as editor. Although the editing was hardly exciting, the paper provided one of the most effective means of denominational unity and propaganda that the Baptists had ever had. But generally it eschewed politics; it gave scant attention to the fight for disestablishment. For further information about Weston see Sprague, *Annals,* VI, 713–714.

26. *Christian Watchman,* March 7, 1828, p. 39.

by and into his own particular Protestant denomination. The concept of inevitable adolescent conversion, the institutionalization of mass revivalism, the promotion of Sunday schools and family prayer, all constituted devices to ensure a steady flow of new members into the churches within the sphere of voluntarism and separationism. But just as the Puritans had based their religious and educational system on the overwhelming predominance of one denomination backed by laws of conformity and uniformity, so the Baptists based their conception of a Christian America on the overwhelming predominance of evangelical Protestantism. After 1830, when an increasing number of Roman Catholics began to complain about paying taxes to support Protestant-oriented schools, the Baptists saw no analogy between this and their former complaints against parochial taxes to support the Standing Order.

To overcome the objections of those rural pietists who still opposed an educated ministry, the Baptist leaders offered several lines of argument which demonstrated their effort to pattern their denomination on the model of the Congregationalists. Starting with the claim that since God gave man a mind He must have meant him to use it, these leaders went on to more sophisticated and pragmatic reasons for an educated ministry. Although the gift of the Holy Ghost was of course essential and helpful (the Baptists by no means gave up their insistence upon a converted ministry), it was no longer sufficient to meet the needs of the times and of the denomination. First, church members demanded better (meaning more learned) edification from the pulpit than they had before; second, there were more erroneous theological views to be combatted than before and only a learned man could combat them forcefully and accurately; and third, it was necessary for the Baptists to reach the educated and cultivated people in society as well as the common people, and the educated would not come to hear un-learned ministers, no matter how filled with the Spirit the preachers were. An educated man was better able to express his ideas clearly and forcefully, and although the apostles were not learned men, they were given special miraculous gifts which were not available to ministers today. Above all, the Baptist leaders sought to combat an inherent anti-intellectual quality in pietism by stressing that knowledge and learning were not necessarily op-posed to piety and religion, that they could help men to understand Scrip-ture, divine law, and natural philosophy better when they were used prop-erly.

Underlying these arguments was the obvious desire of the Baptists (or at least of their urban leaders in the vicinity of Boston) to be respected and respectable. Having won religions freedom and equality, they now wanted leadership and distinction. And they were willing to accept the standards set by the older denomination and the ruling elite as the measure-ments of it. "The want of qualification in their ministers," said one Baptist of his denomination in 1833, "has prevented men of intelligence from attending their places of worship . . . It has disqualified their ministers to meet those of other denominations on terms of equality and has to a great extent kept them in the background . . . They have been humbled by a conviction of inferiority and have necessarily yielded the precedence to those who were nothing loth to accept it." [27]

Despite these explicit inferiority feelings, even though they felt unable to meet them as equals, the Baptist clergy were at last beginning to mingle with the college-educated Unitarian and Trinitarian Congregationalists. Members of the Baptist laity also began to feel concerned for their own upward mobility (both socially and spiritually). They began to want their ministers to meet the external standards of the Congregationalists (instead of to repudiate them), and they began to expect their ministers to speak to them in a more cultivated manner. "It was a fact too well known to be denied," said one advocate of the Baptist Education Society, "that there was a powerful prejudice operating in the community against hearing the sermons of men who were unacquainted with the classics or who had not been favoured with a regular course of Biblical information and study . . . a prepossession prevails against the uneducated man and his message which it is almost impossible to counteract." [28] This writer was referring not to the Congregational community but to the Baptists themselves.

But there was also an evangelistic impulse to reach the upper classes, to convert them to Baptist truth, and thus win new laurels for the denomination.

> There are some men in the higher circles of society who can be prevailed to attend only a ministry where evangelic truth is united with classic learning; but their souls are as precious as are the souls of the poor. It ought to be recollected that other christian societies [notably the Trinitarian-Congregationalists] are providing for the education of candidates for the ministry with a zeal exceeding every past effort. Let us not permit their activity to hurl reproaches on our supineness and delay.[29]

Obviously the old resentment and distrust of the rich and educated had waned; the evangelical zeal of the Trinitarian Congregationalists in founding

27. *Ibid.,* January 11, 1833, p. 5.
28. *Ibid.,* September 18, 1829.
29. *Massachusetts Baptist Missionary Magazine,* n.s., III, 212. At the same time the Baptists were beginning to emphasize the importance of education and to seek to reach the well-to-do, the New England Methodists were explaining to their followers that education was far less important than was the gift of the Holy Spirit and that rich supporters might be a burden to the church rather than a help. For these Methodist arguments which virtually duplicate those used by the Separate-Baptists in the 1740's and 1750's, see George C. Baker, Jr., *An Introduction to the History of Early New England Methodism* (Durham, 1941), pp. 12–20. The continuity of American pietism remained unbroken though its exponents took a new name.

Andover and other seminaries was a powerful competitive stimulus to do likewise.

The executive committee of the Education Society reported in 1827 that there were fifty-five Baptist churches destitute of pastors in Massachusetts,

> But these destitute churches and villages not only want ministers but it is required that they should be men of education. Many of our churches insist on the highest and best qualifications in the sciences and in Biblical Literature and Theology; and almost all while they look on the improved and rapidly improving state of society expect some intellectual culture in those men who are to be associated with them as their spiritual guides.[30]

This desire for a learned ministry was not new in 1827. Eleven years before the Boston Baptist Association had urged the same need:

> It is a mistaken [i.e., provincial and old-fashioned] idea that nothing more is requisite to fit a pious man for discharging the great duties of the Gospel ministry than the possession of natural gifts . . . natural gifts . . . never appear to the best advantage unless cultivated and matured by a good education . . . No position is more groundless than that which represents knowledge as unfriendly to religion. Ignorance has always been the prolific source of enthusiasm, superstition and vice . . . It is indispensably necessary that every preacher have more knowledge of divine truth than the people whom he undertakes to instruct . . . he must be acquainted with those languages in which the Bible was originally written . . . an extensive acquaintance with history is highly important [to demonstrate the fulfillment of prophecy] . . . a knowledge of the customs which anciently prevailed . . . Geography . . . Rhetoric . . . Logic and Mathematics assist his reasoning power; while Philosophy and Astronomy enlarge his mind and fill him with admiring thoughts of the wisdom, goodness, and majesty of God. Extensive erudition not only assists a preacher greatly in the ways above enumerated, but invest him with a commanding influence over the minds of others — an influence which men grossly illiterate very seldom acquire.[31]

The Address of the Boston Baptist Association in 1814 endorsing the formation of the Baptist Education Society and recommending it to their brethren pointed out "That an early acquaintance with some of the liberal arts and sciences and especially with sacred literature must be very beneficial to a gospel minister by enlarging his mind, facilitating the communication of his ideas and assisting him to maintain the truth against the assaults of acute and learned adversaries." [32]

The Baptists' new interest in education, however, had a specific philoso-

30. Boston Baptist Association Minutes, 1827.
31. *Ibid.*, 1816, pp. 13–14.
32. *Ibid.*, 1814. See also *Massachusetts Baptist Missionary Magazine*, n.s., II, 423–432, for a series of letters answering objections to a learned ministry.

phy underlying it. They were not interested in knowledge for its own sake, but for the sake of the assistance and efficiency which it would provide in the furtherance of evangelical progress. Consequently they understood clearly that the institutions which they would found and support were to be denominational in their sponsorship and control, even though they were not necessarily so in their requirements for entrance. The Baptists consistently recommended only such institutions (particularly Brown, Hamilton, and Waterville) to their members. In addition, the education offered at these institutions was designed primarily to inculcate religion and to build Christian character, not to furnish the mind; the training in the liberal arts and sciences was definitely secondary and subsidiary to the moral training of the student and to his spiritual development. Thus the most important college function each year in the Baptists' colleges (as in other evangelical colleges in the nineteenth century) was the annual revival meeting and prayer meeting each spring which was designed to convert the souls of any students still lacking this prime spiritual requisite for Christian service. Getting converted was as much a *rite de passage* for a Christian gentleman as getting a degree. Whenever there seemed to be signs that an awakening of spiritual interest was stirring at a Baptist college, the President and faculty (almost all of whom were ordained ministers) immediately suspended all classes and the student body assembled daily in the college chapel to promote the work of the Lord.[33] Since the most desirable use to which any young man could put his talents and education was the saving of souls (as a pastor, an evangelist, or a missionary) the training of young men in college was geared primarily toward this end. For this purpose the Baptists also created seminaries where those who felt the call to preach might separate themselves from those who chose to follow the lesser pursuits.

The Baptists began, in 1816, to make plans for the founding of a seminary at Newton, Massachusetts, and the minutes of the Boston Baptist Association for that year explained succinctly the necessity for such an institution. One of the primary causes was the increasing secularization at Brown University:

> In order to carry our design [for a learned ministry] into complete execution, a few seminaries must be erected and endowed. We have it is true a University which holds a respectable rank among the literary institutions of our country . . . But it is not well adapted, in all respects, to the object which we have now in view . . . it affords but few advantages to those who are immediately engaged in the study of divinity.
> Besides, in this, as in almost every other literary institution, a large proportion of the students are destitute of the grace of God. Some of them are immoral, and of course very unfit to be the constant and intimate associates of pious youth, especially such as are intended for the

33. For an example of this at Brown see *Christian Watchman,* April 22, 1820, p. 3.

Gospel ministry . . . A pious young man residing in any of our Colleges is surrounded by temptations of every kind, and is in danger of suffering much both in his principles and morals . . . How many have we known who, on leaving College, appeared to have lost that devotional spirit and that holy ardour in the service of God which characterized them at the time of their admission! . . . To prevent these evils in future, it is, we apprehend, incumbent on us to erect a few seminaries . . . which shall admit no students but those who, in a judgment of charity, are real Christians.[34]

Thus, a Christian education was needed to promote a Christian society, and only converted Christians were entitled to be educated for its spiritual leadership.

In the interest of promoting such an educational system of higher learning, the Baptists initially saw no reason why the state should not grant some form of financial aid. If Harvard, Williams, Bowdoin, and Amherst could receive grants of land and money from the Massachusetts legislature, why should not Waterville College from the Maine legislature?[35] It was not immediately evident to the Baptists that there was any similarity between this form of state aid to the promotion of teachers of piety, religion and morality and the parochial taxes for Congregational ministers. The *Christian Watchman* in 1819 praised the Virginia legislature for its financial aid to the new University of Virginia: "Virginia has here set a noble example" to other states by the rich endowment it had bestowed upon the college. However, the writer went on to say,

It was not without regret and surprize, however, [that we] understood that no provision had been made in this splendid Institution for theological science. A science we will call it for theology unquestionably possesses both a scientific and literary character . . . we confess our astonishment that the department of Divinity should be entirely passed over by gentlemen of such liberality as were primarily consulted . . . May we not fear the omission will be regarded abroad, where, we conceive, it is unparalleled, as discreditable to our country.[36]

This was not only another strike against Thomas Jefferson, but also, more important, it seemed to imply that state legislatures might and perhaps

34. Boston Baptist Association Minutes, 1816, p. 15. Newton Theological Institution was founded in 1825 in Newton Centre, Massachusetts.

35. After 1805, the Baptists shared the Trinitarian-Congregationalists' dislike for Harvard, not only because it was the center of Unitarianism, but also because it was the center of Federalism. See *Christian Watchman*, November 25, 1820, and June 11, 1830. They also shared in the belief that it was the Harvard-Unitarian clique who were opposing the charter of Amherst in 1819–1820. The Baptists lent some support to the movement to charter Amherst on the ground that an orthodox, Trinitarian college based upon "experimental religion" was needed in the western part of the state. *Ibid.*, February 21, 1824, p. 42; April 24, 1824, p. 3.

36. *Ibid.*, December 4, 1819, p. 3.

should require all public institutions to include religious training in their curriculum.

When Waterville College (later Colby) was chartered by the Massachusetts legislature as the Maine Literary and Theological Institution in 1813, it asked for and received the grant of a whole township of land in the center of Maine to endow it, though it was well-known to be a Baptist institution and was referred to in the legislature as "the Baptist College" in Maine.[37] A year later the trustees of the institution requested permission from the legislature to move their college to Waterville; this was granted, though some legislators feared it would compete too much with Bowdoin College in this new location. Then in June 1818, the trustees again petitioned the legislature, this time for a grant of four townships of land in the interior and a grant of $3000 a year to be paid to the institution by the state out of the Bank Tax. The Federalists opposed the bill and were able to block it until after Maine became a separate state. But the debate over the issue at the legislature's winter session of 1818–1819 reveals the Baptists' attitude on this issue. The report of the Committee set up by the legislature to examine the request of the trustees read:

> Your committee have given to this subject all that consideration which its importance demands and which the interest and just expectations of so large a number of our fellow citizens entitles it to, and they are of the opinion that the passage of the bill reported in the last June session of the Legislature is a correct and proper measure for the reasons given by the petitioners themselves, viz.: "That the petitioners and others associated with them are about one third of the whole population of this Commonwealth — that they contribute nearly in that proportion to the general expenditure of the State — that not a Baptist nor a Methodist is now employed as an instructor either at Harvard, Williams, or Bowdoin Colleges. That the expense of education at these colleges is such that persons cannot avail themselves of the advantages who are in moderate circumstances. That the petitioners are desirous of having their children educated under the direction of persons whose religious opinions accord with their own and where the expense will be within the means of all the prudent and industrious portion of the community." [38]

The legislature, however, refused to accept the report. At this the *Eastern Argus,* a Republican paper in Portland, voiced the general indignation of the people of Maine:

> This Institution has excited great interest in all parts of this Commonwealth in consequence of the opposition which it has experienced from the fed-

37. A. H. Newman, *A History of the Baptist Churches in the United States* (New York, 1894), p. 406. Instruction began in 1818 under Jeremiah Chaplin, but the school did not open officially as a college until 1820. In 1826, because of a large donation from Gardner Colby, its name was changed to Colby University.

38. *Independent Chronicle,* March 27, 1819, p. 2.

eral party. It will be recollected the Trustees petitioned the Legislature the last June session for such aid as had been granted to similar Institutions [Bowdoin and Williams]; a report was made in favor of the Petition and a Bill passed to a *second* reading in the Senate giving to the College four townships of the government's wild land in the District of Maine and 3000 dollars a year from the Bank Tax. As this was much less than had been previously given to Williams and Bowdoin Colleges opposition was not to have been expected. Contrary to the reasonable expectations of the Trustees, the Bill was referred to the next session of the General Court.

The Baptists being generally alarmed at what they considered a system of favoritism and partiality petitioned from all parts of the District of Maine, requesting that the Bill which had been reported at the June session might be passed, believing that a fair distribution of privileges among the different orders of the people required this measure.

Petitions were accordingly presented from all parts of the District of Maine. No less than 120 signatures were affixed to the one from the town of Brunswick alone, the place where Bowdoin College is situated, and these signers undoubtedly possess more than three-fourths of the property of the place.

Notwithstanding the reasonableness of the request of these numerous petitioners and the report in their favor, every Federal Senator voted against the passage of the Bill while every Republican Senator voted in favor.[39]

Samuel Fessenden, a Senator from Cumberland, Maine stated the reasons for the Federalists' opposition to the bill in his speech against it:

> Mr. President, when the Baptist College was incorporated, it was no doubt the intention of this Legislature that it should not interfere with the other Colleges of the State; it was therefor, Mr. President, to have been located in the township of land in the interior of Maine granted to the Institution by the Government. As soon as the act of incorporation was obtained, we find, Mr. President, the Trustees petitioning the Legislature for permission to locate the College in the County of Kennebec or Somerset; this liberty was granted them and they have located their College at Waterville; and are they now satisfied? No, Mr. President, they now request to be placed on the same footing that Williams and Bowdoin Colleges are; this, Mr. President, I will never consent to; one College is all that is necessary to the District of Maine, and I have no idea of conveying or giving any aid to any College whatever, that is to be in the way of a rival to Brunswick College [Bowdoin]. If the Baptists want a College let them put it in operation in the interiour where it was first contemplated to have been, and I have no objections, Mr. President, to their College provided they can support it. Sir, situated as it now is there appears to be a disposition to bring it forward not only as a rival, but as an Institution calculated to destroy Bowdoin College.
>
> The Baptists in their petition say they have a claim to the four townships of land and 3000 dollars a year because so much has been given to Bowdoin and Williams Colleges. If we give to these Baptists what they

39. *Eastern Argus,* March 16, 1819, p. 2.

now ask, how long will it be, Mr. President, before the Shakers and the Cochranites will make a similar request.

I am prepared, Mr. President, to say that they shall not have a dollar. We have an application from Bowdoin College for aid; they want it; and if the Baptists want their children educated, let them send them there; and as to its being more expensive, I do not believe that it will be so.

They talk about the different orders of the people being accommodated; they are all accommodated at the present Colleges at least as far as it is necessary they should be. And I hope to hear no more of Baptist and Methodist Petitions for the endowment of Colleges; and, Mr. President, we shall hear no more on this subject if we say to the petitioners that we have not any thing for them, which I am prepared to do.[40]

When Maine became a state, the Baptists had their way; they were given a generous grant by the Maine legislature for Waterville College which they readily accepted.

But a dozen years later the Baptists had changed their minds about state aid to denominational colleges and seminaries. In an editorial entitled "Government Patronage of Religion" in the *Christian Watchman* on April 13, 1832, the editor urged that all religious colleges, which in effect meant in his opinion all colleges, should give up any support from the state. He pointed to Harvard, Amherst, and Bowdoin as places where state aid had led to legislative interference in the government of the college: "when the government bestows its patronage, it demands the homage of a submission and the right to dictate." Since all colleges have some theological and denominational leanings, said the editor, we "doubt the [validity of the] policy of supporting with public money high literary institutions." Instead let "each religious denomination [remain] unshackled by civil patronage." The government should limit its support to the common schools where nonsectarian teaching was provided free to all.[41]

As a result of their growing interest in the various educational and benevolent activities of the day, the Baptists found themselves in a new and ambivalent position regarding the Trinitarian or Orthodox wing of the Standing Church. On the one hand their growing respectability, their similarity in theology, and their complementary efforts to save the world for evangelicalism produced a more friendly relationship between them. But on the other, the more the Baptists and the Congregationalists came to resemble each other, the more they threatened one another. This was a problem all of the evangelical denominations shared at the beginning of the nineteenth century. Growing similarity bred increasing antagonism. The less they differed in the essentials or fundamentals of evangelicalism the more each denomination stressed its distinctiveness in nonessentials. More than a century passed before the multifarious evangelical groups in

40. *Ibid.*, Also March 23, 1819, p. 2.
41. *Christian Watchman*, April 13, 1832, p. 58.

America were able to overcome their rivalries to consider the formation of an ecumenical federation of denominations.

The Methodists, who were just beginning to get a foothold in New England from 1800 to 1820, did not have so great a problem in this regard. At that time their popularity and success rested on their appeal to those among the poor and unsophisticated who found even the Baptists too formal and respectable. For the Massachusetts Baptists the problem was particularly acute at this time because it was the Trinitarian-Congregationalists who held the key to the final stage of disestablishment. What the Baptists referred to in 1820 as "the natural shyness of our denominations" was compounded by many factors extending over two centuries. But in the early nineteenth century it came down to whether their political differences (Republican *vs.* Federalist) were more important than their social and religious similarities (middle-class evangelical Calvinism)? The shifting political alignment in the 1820's (and the Dedham Case) helped considerably to resolve this.

Chapter 57

The Baptists and the Trinitarian-Congregationalists, 1812–1828

To go down into a river to be publicly baptized is considered by many a mean and degrading thing . . . It is but just to observe that the Baptists as a body do not lay stress upon going down into a river.

Letter in the *American Baptist Magazine,* 1820

The Baptists saw the first real glimmer of hope for the end of compulsory religious taxation and the certificate system in the growing antagonism between the Trinitarian (Calvinist) Congregationalists and the Unitarian (anti-Calvinist) Congregationalists in the opening decades of the nineteenth century. Despite the rapid growth in their ranks, the Baptists and other dissenters were still far from having enough votes to overthrow the establishment in Massachusetts. But if the Trinitarian-Congregationalists could be persuaded to see the dangers of a system of religious taxation which gave aid and comfort to Unitarian infidelity, then the amendment of the state constitution was a distinct possibility.

That the Baptists were keenly alert to all of the implications of this situation and eager to exploit it is evident from their actions and writings in these years. Stressing their own Calvinist orthodoxy, their congregational polity, their descent from and veneration of the piety and experimental religion of the New England founding fathers from whom they derived, the Baptists joined the Trinitarians in denouncing all aspects of infidelity and rationalism and promoting all of the revivalistic activities of the Second Great Awakening. Like the Trinitarian-Congregationalists, they lamented the rise of all those new sects — from the fanatical Methodists to the deistical Christians and Universalists — which catered to the thoughtless, the ignorant, and the unwholesome elements in the population. Above all, the Baptists took every opportunity to stress their own dedication to benevolence, moral reform, Christian evangelism and an educated ministry; clearly they consciously imitated the Congregationalists to seek the Congregationalists' approval.

Their efforts were noticed and rewarded. Tentative gestures of friendship and fellowship came from both sides and certain individual leaders managed to establish significant bonds of respect. But unfortunately the old springs of disdain and distrust still flowed too deeply. The Baptists were morbidly sensitive to the slightest hint of prejudice or patronization. The Congregationalists were unable to forget their traditional social and intellectual superiority and the many abusive taunts they had received over the years from those who had stolen their followers and attacked their system. It is painful to record how the groping, well-intentioned efforts of the two groups ended in bitterness and humiliation. So long as the Congregationalists were committed to their privileged position and the Baptists felt inferior, all efforts at total reconciliation were bound to fail.

Two articles which appeared side by side in the columns of the *Christian Watchman* on July 13, 1822 epitomized the heart of the matter. The first was an editorial applauding the "highly successful" movement to bring the evangelical denominations together by means of joint efforts in Christian endeavor: "An experiment is now making in the Christian world upon a more extensive plan than was ever before adopted of uniting different denominations of Christians in objects for the general interest of the Church." But in the next column appeared a notice urging the Baptists to be extremely cautious about uniting with other denominations in Christian worship or prayer meetings.[1] A movement toward interdenominational union among some Baptists and Pedobaptists in Worcester led the writer of this warning to fear that the Baptists might give up their distinctive tenets and practices for which they had suffered greatly over the centuries.

For the Baptists the question of infant baptism remained important, and with it went the policy of closed (or close) communion which had been adopted in the 1750's after the failure of the open communion policy between Separates and Separate-Baptists. In the opening decades of the nineteenth century a few Baptists began to advocate a return to a policy of open-communion with Calvinistic (Trinitarian) Congregationalists. In the 1820's there was a particularly strong movement for this in northwestern Vermont where relations between the two groups had always been friendly and where sparse settlement and lack of wealth made the maintenance of two churches unfeasible. A similar movement began in certain areas of New Hampshire and in western Massachusetts (like Worcester), where religious taxation had ceased to be a source of argument. The college-educated Baptist ministers who came to New England from the Middle Colonies (Manning, Stillman, Hezekiah Smith) had tried to maintain the practice of interdenominational fellowship they had known there. James Loring, who knew Stillman well, later wrote, "The Doctor was a man of most catholic spirit; and he always felt so ardent an attachment to, and

1. *Christian Watchman,* July 13, 1822, p. 123.

such an intimate union with, all whom he believed to be real Christians that I think had he consulted his *feelings* only, he would have avowed himself an open communionist. But from all that I ever heard him say on the subject, I believe he did not consider the practice correct." Thomas Baldwin stated that

> When Dr. Stillman first came to Boston his evangelical brethren in the ministry of the Pedobaptist denomination expected that he would commune with them, and . . . their opinion was founded on some remarks made by Dr. Stillman which were understood by them to be favorable to such communion. The Doctor, however, found the brethren of his church and other Baptists unfavorable to the intercourse, and he gave it up.[2]

Although circumstances in Rhode Island made it difficult for President Manning to be friendly with the Congregationalists (especially after the dispute with Ezra Stiles over the college charter), initially he had hoped to be on friendly terms with all denominations, and he always sought to fulfill the charter obligations by having Congregationalists on his board of trustees. Hezekiah Smith had established friendly relations with the Congregationalists around Haverhill and preached to members of their churches until they discovered he was an antipedobaptist.[3] But the most that these early ecumenical efforts could have hoped for was friendly Christian fellowship between the clergy of the two denominations. Open communion in terms of free interchange of communicants and members was out of the question. Legal definition as much as religious doctrine had created denominational barriers; social animosity rigidified them.

Not until after 1810 was a policy for open communion tentatively

2. *Massachusetts Baptist Missionary Magazine,* n.s., IX, 311n. It is significant that, although three Congregational ministers (and a Methodist) acted as Stillman's pallbearers in 1807, the custom of asking Congregational ministers to participate in the ordination of ministers of the First Baptist Church of Boston (which had begun with the Mathers in 1718) ended with Stillman. No Congregationalist participated in the ordination ceremonies of Stillman's two successors and those who were asked to be present at Wayland's ordination in 1821 were not asked to participate in the ceremonies. Nathan E. Wood, *History of the First Baptist Church of Boston* (Philadelphia, 1899), pp. 299–313. William B. Sprague, *Annals of the American Pulpit* (New York, 1860). VI, 211. For Hezekiah Smith and Manning see their biographies by Reuben Guild. See also Edward Dorr Griffin, *A Letter on Communion at the Lord's Table* (Boston, 1829), in which he said that Stillman was an advocate of open-communion.

3. Thomas Baldwin, representing (in his pre-Boston days) the more narrow views of the late eighteenth-century rural Baptists, published a tract, *Open Communion Examined* (Windsor, 1789), while he was pastor in Canaan, New Hampshire, in which he asserted the unscriptural practice of "free communion" with pedobaptists: "what Paedobaptists believe and practice for baptism is so *essentially* different from Christ's appointment that in our opinion it cannot be baptism." However, he said he was willing to join with Congregationalists in prayer and occasional worship. And after he came to Boston he enjoyed very close relations with the Trinitarian-Congregationalists. But no pedobaptists participated in his ordination over the Second Baptist Church of Boston in 1790.

broached by any of the more prominent Baptists in New England. But neither of the two who took the initiative lived in Massachusetts: one was Elder Charles Brooks of New Hampshire and the other Elder David Benedict of Pawtucket, Rhode Island. Brooks wrote a tract on the subject, *An Essay on Terms of Communion,* in 1822. And in England, the prominent Baptist minister, Robert Hall, constantly urged this policy on his brethren in these years.

The most clear and forthright discussion of the Massachusetts Baptists' position on open communion appeared in *The American Baptist Magazine* (successor to the *Massachusetts Baptist Missionary Magazine*) in September 1829, in an anonymous review of Edward Dorr Griffin's *A Letter on Communion at the Lord's Table Addressed to a Member of a Baptist Church.* Griffin, formerly pastor of the Park Street Church in Boston and at this time President of Williams College, was, with Jedidiah Morse and Lyman Beecher, one of the leading figures in the Trinitarians' fight against Unitarianism. All three of these men had at one time or another made efforts to be friendly to the Massachusetts Baptists and to welcome them as allies in the fight against infidelity. In this *Letter* Griffin professed himself an advocate of open communion between the two denominations (both of whom had good reasons for making common cause against the Unitarians). Griffin threw the blame for the lack of communion between the two denominations on the Baptists' narrowness. He maintained that "The separating point is not about the subjects of baptism but merely the mode. If we could be considered as fairly baptized, our Baptist brethren certainly would not exclude us merely because we apply the seal to infants." He was willing to assume for the sake of argument "that immersion is the better form of baptism" but of course Congregationalists since the days of Charles Chauncy and John Cotton had accepted the validity of immersion. However Griffin listed eight reasons why he did not think the practice of sprinkling was "so radical as to destroy the validity of the ordinance." He stressed among these "If the exact form of baptism were essential to its validity the form would have been so clearly defined that no honest mind could mistake it" in the New Testament, and "If nothing but immersion is baptism, there is no visible church except among the Baptists."

Although this appeared to be merely a repetition of Thomas Cobbett's seventeenth century argument that the Anabaptists "make our churches a nullity," Griffin argued in a different context. Implicit in his argument was that if infant baptism by sprinkling were contrary to God's will, then why did He bless those who practiced it with so many conversions in revival meetings? The Baptists in the seventeenth and eighteenth centuries had objected that infant baptism was a symbol of the corruption of the Puritan churches because it represented the fatal link between the territorial parish (created by the state) and membership in the church (which could come only through the supernatural power of Jesus Christ). They felt also that the ritual symbolized the decadence of the Puritan churches, especially after the Halfway Covenant and Stoddardeanism led to the easy accession from infant baptism into full church membership without any conversion experience. Both of these elements had disappeared by 1829. The Trinitarians were no longer so concerned with the connection between church and state and were about to join the Baptists in seeking its abolition; the New Light Congregationalists had abandoned the Halfway Covenant and Stoddardeanism long ago; and all Trinitarians now accepted the pietistic position that only born-again Christians were entitled to full church membership. Thus in 1829 the Congregationalists' claim that baptism was a "non-essential," whatever the theological rationale, came from a context different from that of 1668. Griffin admitted, however, that some mode of the rite of baptism was essential to a visible church, if not to salvation, and that he would never admit a Quaker or any other unbaptized person to communion in his church.[4]

The Baptist reviewer was pleased, he said, to see that Dr. Griffin considered baptism of vital importance. And he began by denying that Baptists held that "where there is no baptism [by immersion] there are no visible churches." Baptists had never believed in the popular phrase so often used against them, "Be dipped or be damned." They did, however, hold that "those communities of Christians who have abandoned the primitive practice in respect to baptism are churches not in a state of order." What annoyed the reviewer most was Griffin's assumption that "nothing separates the Baptists from Pedobaptists but a little water." It was not, as Griffin said, a question only of the mode, but of the subjects to be baptized. Griffin's phrasing of the problem contributed to the widespread "opinion that members of the Baptist churches are most unreasonable in their practice." Baptists were as much concerned with adult baptism as they were with total immersion. "Unconscious babes" could not be "considered suitable candidates for an ordinance" designed to admit men to full communion in the Church of Christ. "We cannot regard that as valid baptism which is administered without a profession of faith in Christ made by the candidate himself." That, and not immersion, was the real crux of the closed-communion policy. Baptists believed it "a lamentable error" to hold that baptism was "merely an outward ceremony" rather than "a most solemn act of worship": "the profession of personal faith in the Saviour" following "a great moral change" in which "intelligence and moral goodness are requisite." It did not matter to the reviewer that the Trinitarian-Congregationalists now required the same profession of faith following conversion before granting full membership.

Open communion was not possible because, said the reviewer, "we cannot regard as baptized those who have not been immersed." And if they

4. For the review of Griffin's tract see the *American Baptist Magazine*, n.s., IX (1829), 292.

were not immersed, the Baptists took the same view of admitting them to communion that Griffin took of the Quakers.[5] As for the demonstrable fact that God blessed pedobaptist revivals, this was because they preached the fundamental doctrines of the gospel accurately. Yet "if they should receive the whole truth of God . . . a still greater blessing" would "rest upon them both at home and abroad." (This explained why the Baptist denomination was growing more rapidly than was either the Congregational or Presbyterian, but it did not explain why the Methodists grew faster than the Baptists.) Consequently the reviewer concluded by rejecting Griffin's accusation "that the refusing to mingle ourselves with out Pedobaptist brethren in celebrating the Lord's supper is a violation of the spirit of Christian love and union." The reviewer was sorry to see that Griffin resorted to this "hackneyed commonplace in which many people indulge" against the Baptists. "Our hearts were pained by the unkind remarks." "Our practice does not imply want of love for the disciples of our Lord; it implies conscientious adherence to principles which we think our Lord has established in his church." It was all very well for the Pedobaptists to profess liberality since all forms of baptism were valid to them, but "since it is the Pedobaptists who have departed from the command, we confidently and solemnly ask, who are to be blamed for the want of union between them and us?"[6]

But although the Baptists would not yet unite in communion with the Trinitarians, they could and did unite with them in opposition to Unitarianism. They were as loud as Morse and Beecher in denouncing Harvard's infidelity. They defended the revivalism of the Second Great Awakening and its "new measures" against Unitarian attacks, and they proclaimed their continued adherence to Calvinism despite the Unitarian, Universalist, and Methodist departures from it. The *Christian Watchman* gave much space (and explicit approval) to Lyman Beecher's various diatribes against Unitarianism and the other infidelities and evils of the times. Like the Congregationalists, the Baptists adopted all of the moral reform movements of the day, and since Beecher was the spearhead of these efforts his phillipics against gambling, theatre-going, dancing, and other evangelical vices, were freely quoted and praised. The *Christian Watchman* particularly praised Beecher's lectures on "Political Atheism," thereby revealing unconsciously its own shift from Jeffersonianism.[7] And when the Unitarians

5. The Biblical text used to prove that immersion was an essential teaching of Christ was Colossians 2:12: "Buried with him in baptism wherein also ye are risen with him through the faith of the operation of God who hath raised him from the dead"; or, as the reviewer phrased it, "Therefore we are buried with him by baptism into death; that like as Christ was raised up from the dead by the glory of the Father even so we also should walk in the newness of life."

6. The reviewer did not ignore the issue of church and state, but he gave it a minor part in his argument.

7. *Christian Watchman*, November 26, 1830, p. 188. Beecher said publicly to

made much of Beecher's dispute with Charles Grandison Finney over the "new measures" and "protracted meetings" of western revivalism in the 1820's, the Baptists came to Beecher's rescue and portrayed his famous New Lebanon Conference with Finney as merely a friendly effort to promote the best kind of revivalism.[8] Finney's revivals in New York state received sympathetic coverage in the *Christian Watchman* as did Finney himself.

Where Unitarianism was concerned, the Baptists felt that a unity among evangelicals was essential in fighting this dangerous threat to orthodoxy. Nor would the Baptists countenance any of the charges against Beecher and Nathaniel W. Taylor that the New Haven Theology (which eventually split the Calvinist camp in the 1830's) was in any way heretical. Like Beecher, the Baptists were more interested in revivalism and benevolent reform activities than they were in theological hair-splitting. Also, like Beecher, by 1828 they began to modify their strict apolitical stance and to anticipate before too long that orthodox, evangelical Christians would control the political actions of the nation. That year the *Universalist Trumpet* noted this tendency with alarm when it reported a Fourth of July Oration by Elder James Davis Knowles, the fiery successor of Thomas Baldwin as pastor of the Second Baptist Church in Boston. Knowles entitled his speech "The Perils and Safeguards of American Liberty." In words which might have been cut from any of Beecher's political sermons, he declared,

> Another way in which Christianity is, I doubt not, destined to operate for the salvation of this country, is that Christians will combine their influence more than they have ever yet done for the support of pure political principles . . . If they were united in their suffrages, they might even now decide almost any great and general question. . . . This union of Christians will hereafter regulate political power in this and every other country.[9]

But despite all these forces pulling the Baptists and Congregationalists together, the traditional animosities and distrust were still too deep to be easily overcome. The Baptists opposition to open communion, despite their arguments from theological principle, was really prompted by fear of being dominated or swallowed up by their intellectual and social superiors, thus losing their own identity. Their unique Baptist practices gave them a

---

the Baptists in 1829, "Your light was kept burning and shining [in Boston] when ours [Congregational Calvinism] had gone out." Wood, *First Baptist Church of Boston*, p. 328.

8. *Christian Watchman*, August 10, 1827, p. 147. For the New Lebanon Conference and the "new measures" which Finney introduced into revivalism, see W. G. McLoughlin, *Modern Revivalism* (New York, 1959), chaps. 1 and 2.

9. *The Universalist Trumpet*, August 23, 1828, p. 30. For discussion of the Baptists changing stance on politics and moral reform after 1828, see Chapter 58.

sense of security and distinctiveness which was self-justifying. Baptist champions frequently argued that the Congregationalists sought Christian union with them because they were afraid that the Baptists were winning away all of their members or because they were unable, by themselves, to defeat the Unitarians. David Benedict, though favorable toward open communion, was aware of the defensive attitude in both camps: It was true, he said in 1820, "I am considered half a Pedobaptist by many of my brethren on account of the rumors of my liberality" in regard to open communion. But "in too many cases *close communion* is used as a convenient pretext against the Baptists" to prove them bigoted, while "the Baptists are afraid that open communion would depopulate their churches and the Pedobaptists have the same fears of immersion with respect to theirs; and while this spirit prevails there can be but little prospect of their uniting together in any great degree." [10]

That the Baptists suffered from their inferior social position is evident in almost any discussion regarding the denominations' problems. In 1820 a letter appeared in the *American Baptist Magazine* which discussed frankly the "Objection against joining a Baptist church" as voiced by an imaginary correspondent. The objector remarked, "There are obstacles in the way of a person of taste and refinement joining a Baptist church." And the writer answered, "To go down into a river to be publicly baptized is considered by many a mean and degrading thing . . . It is but just to observe that the Baptists as a body do not lay stress upon going down into a river. In Europe they almost universally have baptistries in their meeting-houses . . . But this is a mere circumstance." After discussing the importance of the ritual the defender continued, "The Baptists, Sir, though despised, are happy in being supported by Scripture." And those "gentlemen of taste and refinement" who opposed the Baptists, you will find usually to be "gentlemen who can sing a jovial song at a tavern, and the praises of God in his house, can attend the ball-room, card-table and theatre, and the table of the Lord, without remorse of conscience or any sense of discrepancy, or even once recollecting that friendship of the world is enmity with God." In short, a true Christian was despised by "men of the world," but that was his mark of his dedication to true religion.[11]

Nothing revealed more clearly the inferior status of the Baptists in New England than the letter which Adoniram Judson's wife wrote from India in September 1812, after her husband had been converted from a Congregationalist to a Baptist while on his way to take up missionary duty:

10. *Christian Watchman*, September 9, 1820, p. 4.
11. *Massachusetts Baptist Missionary Magazine*, n.s., II, 429–431. The defensive bravado was also evident in the favorite Baptist hymn of the period sung by those who marched to the river to be immersed while crowds of curious Congregationalists stared at the bizarre spectacle. Its first line began, "I am not ashamed to own my Lord."

"Can you, my dear Nancy, still love me, still desire to hear from me, when I tell you I have become a Baptist?" [12]

The humiliating social rebuff which could be inflicted on any Baptist who presumed to carry his desire for friendship or equality too far was dramatically publicized in the pages of the *Christian Watchman* in the summer of 1820. It concerned Elder David Benedict, the Baptist historian, a graduate of Brown and one of the most esteemed members of his denomination at that time. He had endeavored unsuccessfully to encourage his brethren to support all of the benevolent societies which the other evangelical denominations founded rather than to organize duplicate denominational societies of their own. One of the societies which he supported was the American Education Society. Founded in 1816, dominated by Congregationalists and Presbyterians, it claimed to be nonsectarian and to grant scholarships to pious youths of any evangelical denomination who wished to study for the ministry. Benedict had helped to raise eighty dollars among the Baptists of Pawtucket, Rhode Island for the support of this society. And when two young men who were studying under his supervision to prepare to enter a seminary had reached the appropriate point in their studies, he applied to the society for scholarship aid for them. His friends pointed out that his students would have no chance of success since the society was dominated by Congregationalists, but he refused to think so little as this of the society and its administrators.

In March 1820, he took his two students, sixteen and eighteen years old, to Andover, Massachusetts, where the examining board interviewed all applicants for scholarships. To his surprise he found that it was a prerequisite for all applicants that they "have studied the Latin language at least three months." So he took his students back to Rhode Island without submitting them to the examination and during the next three months he tutored them in Latin. On July 1st he went to Andover again for the next scheduled examination. His students failed to pass and the editor of the *Christian Watchman* was so angered by the story Benedict told him of the examination that he wrote an editorial citing the affair as a typical example of Congregational prejudice against the Baptists. To this editorial the Board of Directors of the American Education Society, of which Sereno E. Dwight was the President, wrote a sharp reply in which they said that they were not at all prejudiced against Baptists or other sects and that in fact "several Baptists and numerous Episcopalians" had been given scholarships over the years. The only reason that these two applicants were turned down was that they did not know sufficient Latin and this could be attributed to their choice of "a very incompetent instructor" to prepare them.[13]

12. *Ibid.*, n.s., III, 294.
13. *Christian Watchman*, July 15, 1820, p. 3; July 22, 1820, p. 3; August 5, 1820, p. 3; August 26, p. 4; September 9, 1820, p. 4. Benedict's students wanted to enter Phillips Academy and presumably from there go to Andover Seminary. Sereno

Benedict could not let this affront to his scholarship go unchallenged, so he published a detailed letter describing the whole proceedings of the incident. This confrontation of the leading Congregationalists of New England with one of the leading and most sympathetic Baptist leaders reveals volumes about the relationship between the two groups.

Benedict said he had applied to the American Education Society for aid though he "knew it was under Congregational sway" because "I had every reason to expect I should be kindly and cordially received and that no party feelings would be displayed" and "that no injurious reflections would be made on the denomination to which I belong." He pointed out that he had helped to collect money for the Society and saw no impropriety in expecting students from the Pawtucket area to apply for some of it. "Being willing to make a greater advance towards the Pedobaptists than some of my brethren, I resolved to make the application which has involved me in so much mortification and trouble. The result has verified all the predictions of the Baptists and frustrated all those of the other side."

> [When I went to Andover,] the morning before the examination I called on Mr. Dwight, one of the Board of Directors and one of the examining Committee, for a friendly interview on the subject and stated to him the object of my visit. He answered me with coldness and reserve. Mr. Emerson of Salem, another gentleman of the Committee was present; very soon they both retired and shortly after Mr. Dwight returned alone and began to enquire the state of the Baptist [Education] Funds &c. I answered him according to fact. When he immediately observed, 'I do not think there is comeliness in the application.' Astonished and almost confounded, I asked him why? why? Said he with emphasis, 'The Baptists have refused to cooperate with us, have opposed us &c.' With perfect amazement I replied, 'This, Sir, is a kind of repulsive language I did not expect to hear after all your professions of liberality and impartiality [as a Society].'
>
> I next questioned the fact of the Baptists having opposed them [in forming their Society]: 'Yes,' said he, 'they have; Dr. B[aldwin] and the Baptists in Boston opposed our plan and refused to cooperate with us.' I then observed that if this were a fact, which was all new to me, that I could not be accountable for all the Baptists had said and done . . . I also observed that I had not opposed them — that I acted for myself and was taking a step which I doubted whether any Baptist minister of my acquaintance would take — that I did not consider that I was acting the part of a beggar of the charity of others but was putting in a righteous claim for a part of the funds to which we, with other Baptists, had contributed. I further observed . . . that they need not fear being overrun with Baptist students for the natural shyness of the two denominations would hinder our people from applying.

Dwight later replied to Benedict's version of the incident and denied its accuracy. Benedict closed the controversy by again avowing his willingness to endorse open communism but fearing that "we have not arrived at that golden age of charity in which different denominations will repose an unsuspicious and unprejudiced confidence in each other."

Dwight then said that the applicants should take the examination since they were there. After they were examined the students told Benedict that the examination had been "very hasty and partial" and that they were sure they had failed it. When Benedict went to the Board the next day to learn its decision, Dr. Dwight told him his students had failed. Benedict discovered that no more than twenty of the two hundred to three hundred students who had received aid from the Society were non-Congregationalists. As for the insult to his scholarship, said Benedict, I "shall console myself with the belief that my literary reputation will not be graduated by the *ipse dixit* or petulant sneers of a bad tempered or prejudiced opponent." But it was apparent that Benedict would not soon again attempt to presume on the friendship of Trinitarians or encourage his brethren toward open communion.

The Baptists had other more clearcut examples of Congregational prejudice against them. In 1814 the *American Baptist Magazine* took notice of Lyman Beecher's unkind remarks toward "illiterate" ministers in his *Address to the Charitable Society* and sought to refute his slur with evidence of the great evangelistic success of Baptist itinerants in the southern and western states in building up waste places.[14] When the Rev. Eliphalet Pearson repeated Beecher's charges in a sermon in Boston before the American Education Society, Thomas Baldwin pointed out that it ill-behooved a denomination rent by Arianism and Socinianism to jibe at the inability of the Baptists and Methodists to spread the true gospel in America.[15]

The Baptists were also subject to occasional abuse from Congregationalists on the grounds that by insisting on the ritual of baptism by immersion, they frequently injured the progress of revival meetings. Nothing more annoyed an evangelical in this period than to be told that he in any way hindered God's work in revivals; the Baptists found this the cruelest blow of all from "their Congregational brethren." When the *Boston Recorder* (a Trinitarian-Congregational newspaper) in 1828 asked its readers to send them all information of revivals which had been hindered or halted because some Baptist had injected a controversy over immersion, the *Christian Watchman* replied bitterly; this was "a wanton attack on the feelings and character of their Baptist brethren" and an appeal "to the bad feelings of good men." "It can have no other object than to produce disaffection, jealousy, and recrimination." [16] But the *Watchman* did not deny that there might have been some cases where it had occurred.

However, the Baptists were a long way from the days when such attacks would have intimidated them. They felt themselves sufficiently secure in the eyes of the world, if not in the eyes of gentlemen of taste, education,

14. *Massachusetts Baptist Missionary Magazine,* n.s., IV, 238, 405.
15. *Ibid.,* IV, 413.
16. *Christian Watchman,* July 4, 1828.

and refinement, to take positive action to assert their equal status. By the 1820's they were noting with pride that their churches were no longer being organized on the outskirts of towns and villages or in the wastelands between settled places where they had been content to serve only the off-scourings or the neglected members of Congregational parishes and where, to avoid strife, they had humbly maintained themselves at a discreet distance from the center of community life. Instead the Baptists were now building their meetinghouses in the center of towns, often right next door to or across the village green from the meetinghouse of the Standing Order.[17] In the eighteenth century this had happened so seldom that Isaac Backus thought it worthy of remark in his history of the Baptists that in 1765 Hezekiah Smith had actually gathered his new church in Haverhill "in the heart of the town." But in 1831, a writer in the *American Baptist Magazine* asked rhetorically, "And where, we would ask, is a more suitable place for a church to be gathered than in the heart of the town?" True, "in former times . . . our brethren did not presume in ordinary cases to enter these fortified places. The towns, it will be recollected, were circumstanced by parish lines in those days and whoever entered the sacred enclosure of a parish besides their own chosen pastor, was regarded as a sacrilegious depredator of the church of Christ . . . This state of things . . . compelled our brethren" to build on the outskirts of the towns. "Almost every ancient Baptist meeting-house in New-England is located in some retired and uninhabited spot where the traveler would sooner expect to find a hospital for the accommodation of persons afflicted with an infectious disease than a house of worship for the frequent assemblies of a Christian people." But now, "times are changed." [18]

While the Baptists were irked and affronted by the Congregationalists' unwillingness to accept them as equals in the fight against Unitarianism and Nothingarianism, they were themselves unwilling to accept the Methodists as allies in their activities. In the first place, the Methodists were heretical because they were Arminians,[19] men who denied the doctrines of election, moral depravity, and perseverance; and in the second place they were un-American (or at least un-republican) because their church government was based on episcopacy: "The best regulated and most influential and oppressive aristocracy in the United States is the government of the Methodist Church. It is entirely repugnant to the principles of republicanism and religious liberty." [20] When Methodists like Josiah Cannon were fighting

17. See, for example, *ibid.*, October 16, 1829, p. 168, where a dispute on this issue occurred in Westminster.

18. *Massachusetts Baptist Missionary Magazine*, n.s., XI, 85–86.

19. *Christian Watchman*, December 7, 1832, p. 193, and December 4, 1830, p. 191. For Methodist attacks on the Baptists in these years, see George C. Baker, Jr., *An Introduction to the History of Early New England Methodism* (Durham, 1941); and Billy Hibbard, *Memoirs* (New York, 1843).

20. *Christian Watchman*, March 26, 1825, p. 60.

for separation of church and state the Baptists did not repudiate their assistance, but having themselves just risen from the ranks of despised exhorters and fanatics, the Baptists felt it necessary to maintain their dignity by refusing to associate with or publicly to endorse the Methodists. It is a measure of how far the Baptists had come since the 1740's that they felt ill at ease with this new wave of pietism and thought it crude and erroneous both in its principles and its practices. They welcomed the various schisms among the Methodists in these years just as the Standing Order had welcomed the schisms among the Separates and Baptists in the First Great Awakening.[21]

Nevertheless, if it came to defending the Methodists or acquiescing to the Unitarians' criticism of them, the Baptists recognized kinship with the Methodists clearly enough. Whatever else might be said against the Methodists, they did believe in "experimental" religion. They demanded a conversion experience for members, and they were not afraid of appealing to the religious affections of their hearers in presenting the gospel message. When Robert Southey's critical *Life of Wesley* appeared in 1821, the *Christian Examiner* came to Wesley's rescue. Noting that Southey was a Unitarian, the Baptist editor commented, "This work appears to have been compiled for the purpose of bringing into disrepute the cause of experimental religion. There is a decided hostility in the hearts of all unregenerate men to vital piety and with many it seems to be a very important object to deride and ridicule those exercises and principles which they do not understand." [22]

Although the Methodists were undoubtedly one of their chief rivals among the dissenting sects, the Baptists found them less obnoxious than several of the others, notably the Freewill Baptists, the Christian, and the Universalists. The Universalists were important rivals because they provided the logical choice for those among the lower classes who developed a growing distaste both for Calvinism and for revivalism. Deism was never an organized church, but it constituted a significant movement against the Calvinism of the Revolutionary era. Upperclass deists in Connecticut tended to enter the Episcopalian church; in Massachusetts they became Unitarians. But the lower class anti-Calvinists turned to Methodism, to Universalism, to the Freewill Baptists, or to the Christians, depending on which of these alternatives reached them first or on how radical was their rejection of Calvinism or their anticlericalism. The least radical rejection of Calvinism was probably Methodism, and probably many anti-Calvinists chose the Methodists or the Freewill Baptists less from any differences inherent in these sects than from personal or coincidental factors. The Methodists had the advantage of their highly organized circuit riding system and lay-

---

21. See for example *ibid.*, January 2, 1829, p. 2.
22. *Ibid.*, April 7, 1821, p. 67; April 14, 1821, p. 72.

directed "classes" in reaching outlying or unsettled areas. The Freewill Baptists had the advantage of a congregational polity and an uneducated ministry chosen by and from the converts themselves. The Methodists suffered from their former association with Episcopalianism, their Toryism in the Revolution, and their episcopal government. The Freewill Baptists suffered from their association with the ancient social prejudice in New England against Anabaptists and immersion. The Universalists and Christians appealed only to the more radical in theology, to persons sufficiently rationalistic to reject much of evangelical orthodoxy; among the poor and provincial this group was always small.

The editor of the *Christian Watchman* said that he saw little theological difference between the Universalists and the Unitarians (a conscious jibe at the latter who considered themselves far more orthodox). And he agreed with those judges who refused to accept Universalists as credible witnesses in court on the grounds that no one who doubted the belief in rewards and punishments after death could be relied on to tell the truth. In addition, the Baptists contended that such a contemptible religious view could only be held by persons of very low standing in any community: "Universalism is believed and advocated by too many abandoned wretches" to be given serious consideration by a respectable person.[23] As in the case of the Methodists, the efforts of the Universalists toward disestablishment were not repudiated. But neither were they praised or cooperated with.

Since the Freewill Baptists and the Christians both originated as pietistic schisms from the Baptists, it is not surprising to find in their criticisms of the denomination a reaction against the growing respectability and institutionalism of those sophisticated leaders who had "lost the Spirit." The unsophisticated pietists viewed efforts by urban Baptists and Congregationalists to raise money to promote foreign missions and the other religious and philanthropic reforms of the day (including education) as an indication of worldliness, an attempt to rely more on the machinery of men than on the Spirit of God.[24] After 1800 they were joined in this protest by many Calvinistic Baptists in the rural areas — the so-called "hardshell" or "anti-mission" Baptists. John Leland was well-known for his distaste for this aspect of denominational activity, and the Baptists felt it necessary to apologize for "his peculiarities and erratic" attitudes: "Some of his views are eccentric" said the editor of the *Christian Watchman* in 1832.[25] Leland, for example, believed that Sunday schools were unnecessary because they

23. *Ibid.,* January 19, 1827, p. 26; March 16, 1822, March 26, 1825, p. 60.
24. For examples of opposition by Freewill Baptists and Christians to Baptist philanthropy, see *ibid.,* September 22, 1821, p. 101; June 20, 1822, p. 115; *Boston Recorder,* September 25, 1833, p. 154, and *Universalist Trumpet,* August 9, 1828, p. 21. See also Elias Smith's publications described in Chapter 38; B. C. Lambert, "The Rise of the Anti-Mission Baptists," unpublished doctoral dissertation, University of Chicago, 1957.
25. *Christian Watchman,* February 24, 1832, p. 29.

could not produce conversions and they might lead young people to simulate it. He also opposed asking the state to make laws to enforce the Sabbath observance, to end dueling and lotteries, and to prohibit the sale and consumption of alcoholic beverages, because these were matters for individual reformation. Anti-institutionalism of this sort often led Baptists to join one of the new and more radically pietistic sects. After 1835, when the regular Baptists modified their rigid Calvinism along the lines of the New Haven theology, many rural Baptists repudiated their leaders as Arminians.

One of the urban Baptists' more revealing attempts to counter the rural Baptists' tendency to oppose the creation of large benevolent societies was a circular letter, "Christian Liberality," published in 1821 by the Worcester Baptist Association. Partly it was an attack on the snobbery of the Trinitarians and on the heterodoxy of the Unitarians, who called themselves "liberal Christians" and who received considerable praise for their liberality in philanthropic activity. But few Baptists ever turned Unitarian, and the circular letter was more directly concerned with countering those rural pietists to whom the Universalists and the Christians appealed, those who adhered to John Leland's anti-mission and anti-benevolent society attitudes. The Worcester Association's letter sums up very accurately the social and religious outlook which, by 1820, characterized the dominant wing of the denomination.[26]

The term "liberal," said the Worcester Association, has become "hackneyed" and "one party [the Unitarian] in religion have arrogated it exclusively to themselves." Moreover, "It had been so long and confidently asserted that the Baptists are bigoted and illiberal that many persons who judge and condemn them before they hear and examine" them have come to dislike them. "It is true, our sentiments necessarily subject us to a greater restriction in our intercourse with the Christian world than the sentiments of other Christians by compelling us to adhere more strictly to the ordinances of the gospel [believer's baptism by immerson]. But before the charge of illiberality will fix on us upon this account, it must be proved that these sentiments are unscriptural." For the Unitarians to claim to be liberals because they placed philanthropy above orthodoxy was a grave distortion of the gospel meaning of benevolence. And for the Trinitarian-Congregationalists to denigrate the Baptists was equally unbenevolent.

> True benevolence consists in the love of being in general without respect to the comparative good or bad qualities of individuals. Jesus Christ teaches us that the love of our neighbour . . . extends not only to our brethren and fellow citizens, but to foreigners, to the baser classes of men, and even to apostates from true religion. . . . Liberality of feeling con-

26. *Ibid.*, September 22, 1821, p. 101.

sists in exemption from the narrow prejudices accruing from education, from early associations, from pride of piety, and from interest. Truly liberal Christians of different denominations view each other not as enemies, having nothing in common except that they both belong to the church militant, but as members of the same family, as belonging to different regiments of the same loyal army though they are so unfortunate as not to understand a certain part of the discipline alike . . . The term liberality primarily means generosity or munificence . . .Where true liberality exists, it will manifest itself in a general concern for the advancement of human happiness.

For the Trinitarians to refuse to cooperate with the Baptists in benevolent societies was as illiberal as for the Unitarians "to be feelingly alive to the temporal miseries of men" but "totally indifferent to their moral wretchedness."

As for those Baptists who opposed a salaried ministry or salaried evangelists and missionaries. "To imagine that because the grace of an all-sufficient God in the pardon of sin is free, that therefore no obligation rests on men to support those who conscientiously devote their time to the advancement of religion is absurd and contradicts the plainest intimations of God's will." "The great charitable objects which are now before the Christian publick constitute the distinguishing characteristick of the present age . . . three of the more important of these objects are embraced by the Charitable Society . . . Foreign and Domestick Missions, and the Education of indigent Young Men designed for the Ministry." "A liberal man discovers a most glaring inconsistency in the conduct of those who pray that the kingdom of God may come and yet do nothing to promote it."

The Baptist leaders saw in this pietistic anti-institutionalism a rejection of the Christian duty to bring about the Kingdom of God on earth, a tendency to ask God to do what He meant men to do for themselves. Thus the new liberalism of the denomination ran directly counter to the anti-institutionalism of the pietistic old-fashioned Baptists. The Calvinistic Baptists had always embodied the activistic elements of the Puritanism from which they derived, and although in the colonial period this had taken the negative form of attacking the Standing Order, the dawn of the nineteenth century saw them beginning a new career of positive, benevolent reform activity. Of what use was religious freedom and republican government if men would not help themselves? Baptist leaders therefore saw in the anti-mission and anti-institutional pietism of the rural Baptists, Christians, and Freewillers, not the upholding of their own colonial outlook but its rejection. They had fought hard to break down a state church which Satan had constructed to restrict the free propagation of the gospel. Now that the establishment was tumbling down and the path to the reformation of the world lay open, the more liberal Baptists could not comprehend those

1143

who held back from the task. They had seen the institutional failings of their Puritan opponents very clearly, but now they failed to see the potential dangers in their own institutionalized forms of Christian endeavor.

They failed to see that the power of voluntary ecclesiastical and benevolent societies could be just as corrupting, as overbearing, as soulless as the corporate societies of the Puritan Commonwealth which they had helped to destroy. They failed to see in their advocacy of mass evangelism for the speedy conversion of the world, the potential dangers of pragmatic or expedient "new measures" for inducing regeneration, the calculated professionalization of evangelism, the use of arithmetical and statistical measurements for Christian success. And they failed to see in their advocacy of state enforcement of personal and social morality in the years after 1828 the possibility that "the Christian Party in politics" might become simply the tyranny of the evangelical majority.[27]

Slowly but surely, as the 1820's ended, the Baptists moved into the mainstream of the new American evangelical consensus and became part of the establishment, the dominant structure. But before the Trinitarian-Congregationalists' decision in 1829 to abandon the system of compulsory religious taxes in Massachusetts, the relations of these two major evangelical denominations in New England remained in such tension and mutual suspicion that true Christian fellowship, open communion, and meaningful philanthropic cooperation were impossible between them. Only a resolution of their differences over church and state could resolve the dilemma. Because of forces beyond them both this resolution evolved rapidly between 1820 and 1828.

27. For further discussion of the Baptist endorsement of Ezra Stiles Ely's and Lyman Beecher's views of a Christian party in politics, see Chapter 61.

Chapter 58

Political and Sectarian Viewpoints
on Disestablishment,
1820

God forbid that we compel a conscientious Baptist or Methodist or Friend to support Episcopacy or Presbyterianism and vice versa; but the question is whether Infidels and Nothingarians shall enjoy the blessings of a government that derives all its stability and equity from Christianity without doing any thing to support this essential pillar of State prosperity?

The Boston Recorder, September 16, 1820

The last time the Baptists led the fight for disestablishment in Massachusetts was in 1820. When the District of Maine was separated from Massachusetts by referendum in June 1819, the Republican Party began to call for a constitutional convention to adjust the political aspects of the constitution to this new state of affairs. The Baptists saw in the convention a chance to amend Article Three and thus to alter the religious aspects of the Constitution. In January 1820 the *Independent Chronicle* began to refer to the need for a convention as a means of reforming Harvard College.[1] By March the Republicans were talking of the necessity for a convention to reform the number of state Senators and to redistrict the state. Soon a whole host of important reforms requiring a convention were discovered — including new suffrage regulations, new methods of electing the council, limiting the sessions of the legislature to one a year, reforming the judiciary, and changing the militia laws. On all of these questions the Republicans had definite views concerning increasing direct democracy and making the judiciary and the legislature more responsive to the will of the majority.

The religious issue entered the picture in May when letters began to appear in the newspapers urging abolishing the religious test oath for officeholders and the amending or abolishing of Article Three of the Declaration of Rights. On May 27, 1820, the *Christian Watchman* began

1. *Independent Chronicle,* January 26, 1820, pp. 2, 4.

a vigorous campaign urging abolition of Article Three and promoting disestablishment through a series of letters signed "Philologus"; these continued for several months and touched on every aspect of the problem. The Federalists, who saw little to gain for their side, were reluctant to call a convention. However, on June 16, the legislature voted to hold a referendum to see whether the voters wanted a convention, and on August 21, a majority of the voters expressed their desire for it. The delegates were chosen on October 26 and the convention took place in Boston between November 15, 1820 and January 9, 1821.

The religious issue assumed major proportions after it became certain that a convention would be called. The dissenters, after nine years of lethargy over disestablishment, came to life when they saw a chance to abolish completely compulsory religious taxes. The Republicans pushed for all of those reforms which were to be associated with the rise of Jacksonian democracy. And a number of the Trinitarian-Congregationalists, watching the progress of the Dedham case through the courts at that time, broached the possibility that some changes were needed to protect the church members' ancient right against the majority rule by the parishes.

When the convention began, there were four different points of view on the question of Article Three. Generally the dissenters, led by the Baptists, the Universalists, the Methodists (and supported by a few liberal Unitarians and one or two Trinitarians) argued, as they always had, for its complete abolition in order to put an end to the established or privileged position of the Congregational-Unitarian churches or the union of church and state. At the opposite extreme, the Federalist-Unitarians were united in opposing any alteration in the status quo — though some of them wanted to curtail some aspects of the Religious Freedom Act of 1811. In between were the Trinitarian-Federalists and the Republican Party leaders, neither of which was precisely certain where it stood on the religious issue. The Republicans, though they still contained the bulk of the dissenters and though the mass of their supporters were nominally Trinitarian-Congregationalists, were led — as always — by the Unitarians and anticlerical Congregationalists. As a party, the Republicans felt that they could not take a clear stand on this issue without dividing their ranks; they therefore officially kept a discreet silence. The Trinitarians, rankling from the Unitarians' control of the Federalist Party (and of Harvard) and aware that a series of court decisions (by Unitarian judges) was gradually subverting or eroding the ancient customs and usages of church and parish government, were as divided as the Republican Party. They had no desire for disestablishment, but neither could they stand by and let the Standing Order be perverted to Unitarian uses and control. Like the Republican Party press, the Trinitarian press remained either silent or ambiguous on the issue.

The Boston *Recorder,* chief organ of the Trinitarian-Congregationalists in Boston, devoted most of its comment on the convention to demands that

1146

the religious test oath for office holding be preserved. To abolish the test oath so that anyone could hold office "no matter whether he be an Infidel, an Atheist or a Mahometan" would be "an insult to Jehovah" and show "contempt for the piety of our ancestors." "The machinations of the Deists" to take this step and "their nefarious designs on our religious privileges" must be fought.[2] No man deserves to hold office "who does not admit the existence of God and the retributions of the judgment day," wrote the editor with obvious reference to the Universalists.[3] But the *Recorder* went so far in denouncing the enemies of the test oath as "infidels" and "atheists" that the Baptists and Methodists protested. They did not care for the test oath and they were not infidels or atheists. To their protests the *Recorder* answered with the habitual disdain of Congregationalists for dissenters: "Some professing Christians complain because they are classed with Infidels when they publicly call for a State Constitution which shall make no recognition of Christianity and open the door . . . for . . . Infidels and Atheists to all places of trust and honor. . . . Now for ourselves we see no injustice in giving them this classification. . . [for] many of them . . . act with every infidel and every disorganizer in the land; they adopt the same reasonings . . . [and] act together: in this and though they claim to be arguing for "civil liberty" and "conscience" they are "uniting with the enemies of Christ."[4] "Is that a conscience worth regarding, or is it a conscience in any sense, that tramples the authority of God under foot and discards the sanctions of religion throughout as unwholesome restraints?" Like the seventeenth century Puritans, the Trinitarians also feared that God would punish the nation if it insulted Him by omitting any reference to Him in the constitution: "With us it is a maxim that God treats nations according to their visible character and confirms or removes their privileges according to their conduct toward him in their collective capacity; and for this reason, as patriots no less than Christians" the test oath must stand.[5]

However, the *Recorder*'s statements on religious taxation were much less forthright. "Our readers ought to be aware," said the editor in May 1820, "that a strenuous effort will be made when our State Constitution shall be revised, to exclude from it every recognition of Christianity and to prostrate all the bulwarks of religious order."[6] But "With regard to the best method of supporting the institutions of the gospel," said an article in September, "we have never said that the mode of taxation hitherto adopted is preferable to some other modes." The editor was willing to leave the mode of supporting religion to the members of the convention: "God forbid that we

2. Boston *Recorder*, May 13, 1820, p. 79.
3. *Ibid.*, May 27, 1820, p. 87.
4. *Ibid.*, September 16, 1820, p. 151.
5. *Ibid.*, September 30, 1820, p. 159. This equating of Orthodox Christianity with American patriotism was beginning to infuse all evangelical thought.
6. *Ibid.*, May 13, 1820, p. 79; September 16, 1820, 151.

compel a conscientious Baptist or Methodist or Friend to support Episcopacy or Presbyterianism and vice versa; but the question is whether Infidels and Nothingarians shall enjoy the blessings of a government that derives all its stability and equity from Christianity without doing any thing to support this essential pillar of State prosperity?" Admitting, however, that the state was aided by the existence of Christian churches, surely "then all classes of [the] community ought to submit cheerfully to the burden of maintaining them." With their usual obtuseness the Trinitarians still maintained that "The hue and cry raised against taxation for the support of religion is primarily from those who worship no god but mammon or lust." As for those Trinitarians "whom we 'love as brethren' " who, doubting the usefulness of religious taxes, unite with infidels and tax dodgers in opposing Article Three, we wish they would cease this "and be separate nor touch the unclean thing. If irreligion is to triumph, let it not boast of the aid it has received from Christians." [7]

The gist of this editorial was clear: the Trinitarians wanted some kind of state support for religion. But this was their only editorial on the subject during the entire convention, and at least on behalf of conscientious objectors, it left the door open to serious revisions of Article Three. When he was challenged to provide direct evidence from the New Testament for "a legal establishment of Christianity," the editor of the *Recorder* demurred: "The New Testament establishes certain principles," one of which was respect for God by the magistrates; one may deduce from this an establishment if the rulers find that the best mode of showing respect. But that is all he would say.[8] In this respect the Trinitarians had come far from their pious ancestors who had no trouble finding Biblical proofs for tax support, in the New as well as in the Old Testament.

An anonymous letter, which the editor called to his readers' attention a few days before the convention assembled, was the only indication in the *Recorder* that the Dedham case (on which a final decision was not announced until after the convention had adjourned) would, if decided in favor of the parish, make the established system lose its appeal for the Trinitarians. This letter noted that some opponents of religion were trying, with the aid of court decisions, to subvert the intent of Article Three, by asserting that it was right "to take from churches all voice in the settlement of ministers and throw that solemn business wholly into the hands of the territorial corporation." By this means the parish might, "against the voice of the church," dictate who should be the minister and "shall carry with them the property vested in the church for pious and charitable uses." If these views prevailed, said the writer, he would rather see Article Three dropped altogether and have it replaced by "voluntary associations under

7. *Ibid.,* September 16, 1820, p. 151.
8. *Ibid.,* September, 30 1820, p. 159.

special acts of incorporation which would supply the place of the present order of things and perhaps in the present state of society be a real improvement." However, the writer hoped that rather than this the convention would "insert an explanatory clause" into Article Three which would make clear that the church, not the parish, had the ultimate choice of its minister and could control its own property regardless of the parish's vote.[9] In commending this proposal to his readers, the editor indicated that the established system might yet be made serviceable to orthodoxy.

Beyond these vague remarks the *Recorder* never ventured any opinions, not even after the convention had adjourned. It neither approved nor disapproved of the convention's work, except to print a letter protesting against the proposed amendment to open the Harvard Corporation and Board of Overseers to members of all denominations of Christians.[10] In May 1821 it printed without comment the results of the voting on the proposed constitutional amendments. The Trinitarian delegates made some efforts to obtain constitutional changes in Article Three that would have been more favorable to them. But officially the *Recorder* and other organs of the denomination let the Unitarians and the sectarians fight out the issue. In the convention most Trinitarian clergymen who were delegates voted consistently with the Unitarians against all measures aimed at disestablishment.

The Republican Party's equivocal stand can be measured in the *Independent Chronicle,* its chief organ in Boston. This paper carried thousands of words advocating all kinds of political alterations in the constitution, but only once did it touch editorially on the question of altering Article Three; then it did so merely in passing. It simply raised a rhetorical question — or rather, two questions: "If it is necessary to the support of good order in society and to the security of property that Religious establishments should be maintained at the public charge, which for the purpose of the present enquiry we need not either admit or deny" then how was it that cities like Boston and Salem were permitted to be exempt from all religious taxes? [11] It offered no answer regarding either the necessity for an establishment or the fairness of exempting cities from the system. True, the newspaper printed several letters favoring the alteration of Article Three, though one might easily say of such letters that the editor was merely permitting various elements in his party the right to express themselves.[12] A writer who

---

9. *Ibid.,* November 11, 1820, p. 182. The writer did not mention the Dedham case or any of its predecessors, but he was obviously aware of their portent and his view was a forecast of the stand the Trinitarians would take by 1830.

10. *Ibid.,* April 7, 1821, p. 59.

11. *Independent Chronicle,* November 18, 1820, p. 2.

12. For example, in May 1820, a letter to the *Independent Chronicle* signed "Shethar" attacked a letter in the Boston *Recorder* for criticizing opponents of the test oath and advocates of disestablishment. Shethar found it "highly reasonable and founded on the nature and fitness of things" that the Constitution should provide "a guarantee that no man should be compelled to pay his money for the support of any religious teacher whose conduct and doctrine he disapproves and on whose

called himself "Gracchus," whose series of letters on the coming of the convention bore the stamp of an official party comment, mentioned the religious issue only once, and his comment was as equivocal as was the editor's: "the toleration question will come up, so interesting to a numerous, respectable and pious portion of our people; whether the clergy shall, like all other citizens of a Republic depend for their support and consequence upon their talents, virtues, usefulness and the confidence of the people." [13] But he posed no alternative and left the issue unresolved.

Throughout the debates in the convention, which were printed daily in the *Independent Chronicle,* the Republicans offered no comment on what was, with the possible exception of the property qualification for voting, obviously the most hotly debated issue on the floor. And when the convention ended with the Federalists victorious against every effort for reform, the editor, while commenting on the general ineffectiveness of the convention (from the Republican viewpoint) said that the proposed amendments, feeble though they were, should probably be endorsed.[14] He made no specific mention of disappointment that Article Three was not abolished or that the dissenters had failed to wring any concessions to their religious principles. He mentioned only the party's political disappointments. The nearest the *Chronicle* came to expressing itself on the convention's treatment of religion was in a semiofficial series of letters commenting on the convention signed "Leo." In his eighth letter Leo stated that Article Three was "a vestige of the strong sectarian principles of the puritans." "It was not a little surprising that gentlemen of the law were the chief advocates of" maintaining the present system. "What an age we live in," that ministers of the gospel who voted with the lawyers "mistook what would best promote their interests and serve the cause of religion." As to what the best interests of religion were, Leo said only, "As the natural tendency of Religion is to do good, it does not require legislative authority to enforce it. In all free governments it should be left to its own powerful influences." [15] A dissenter might very well have interpreted this letter as expressing regret that the convention did not favor disestablishment, but Leo did not specifically say that that is what it should have done. And any dissenter who read the debates as printed regularly in the *Chronicle* could see for himself that most of the leading spokesmen of the Republican Party at the convention, men like Levi Lincoln and Joseph Story, had opposed any attempt at complete disestablishment. Only two or three of the Republican leaders,

---

instructions he does not attend." May 20, 1820, p. 2. However, no letters appeared in the *Independent Chronicle* defending Article Three vigorously; on the whole, therefore, the Party leaned toward its revision.

13. *Ibid.,* September 6, 1820, p. 2.
14. *Ibid.,* January 6, 1821, p. 1; February 28, 1821, p. 3.
15. *Ibid.,* February 28, 1821, p. 3.

among them Joseph B. Varnum, one of the few Baptists among the party leaders, aggressively backed the dissenters' position.[16]

The dissenters' views had a clear and strong voice in the Baptist *Christian Watchman,* founded only a year before the convention. On May 13, 1820, a strong letter from "A Friend to Religious Liberty" urged that the coming convention abolish Article Three and end all religious taxes. "I am not able to see any good reason why the Constitution of Massachusetts should regulate religion any more than the Constitution of the United States." Reflecting the usual Republican sympathy for the small rural towns, this writer raised an issue which was a central theme of the debate in the convention: "There is certainly no good reason why our christian brethren in the country towns should not have as large a portion of religious freedom as the inhabitants of Boston." He even pointed out to pedobaptist brethren that it was now not uncommon for Trinitarians to be forced to pay taxes to support Unitarian ministers.[17]

Another pseudonymous letter writer in the *Christian Watchman* produced a series of six letters which ran from May through August 1820. These touched on all the relevant points which, from the dissenters' viewpoint, should be raised at the convention. This writer, "Philologus," said "The present is an important crisis" which could be compared to the Constitutional ratifying convention of 1788.[18] Although the Religious Freedom Act of 1811 had been some assistance, he wrote, "Many people have desired a repeal of this law." Since party feeling was at a low ebb now, this was a good time to reconsider the state's entire position on this question. He urged the Baptists to elect to the convention any men, regardless of party, who would vote to end the establishment under which they had suffered for two centuries. "Let a religious test and religious taxation be expunged and a provision inserted that the Legislature shall make no law respecting a religious establishment or abridging the free exercise of religion." [19]

These and other letters were fully endorsed by the journal's editor who demanded "obliterating" from the constitution "the unnatural alliance which it comprises of Church and State." [20] The editor was particularly incensed when a writer in the *Columbian Centinel,* the organ of Federalism, argued with the usual paternalistic disdain for the masses that the state must support religion because "the mass of the people is not yet, nor is it easy to believe it should soon become, sufficiently enlightened to be safely

16. Varnum did not become a Baptist until 1819. His position in the party was not related to his representation of the dissenters.
17. *Christian Watchman,* May 13, 1820, p. 3.
18. *Ibid.,* May 27, 1820, p. 3.
19. *Ibid.,* August 12, 1820, p. 3. "Philologus" wanted Massachusetts to copy the wording of the First Amendment to the Federal Constitution.
20. *Ibid.,* August 19, 1820, p. 3.

left to choose its own opinions in politics, religion, or literature; if they were so left, to say that they would be guided by chance is little; the case would be much worse; they would be guided by their own perverse and depraved appetites." To this the horrified Baptist editor answered:

> We confess we cannot apprehend how this doctrine essentially differs from the opinion avowed by the Romish church that 'ignorance is the mother of devotion.' If the people are thus incompetent to judge for themselves, another Popish theory will be established, that 'the laity ought not to be trusted with the reading of holy scriptures, lest they should pervert them.' These principles extend to the annihilation of all religion, for the scriptures represent it as the effect of man's own convictions of the nature of truth and duty and not as the belief of any sentiment which another chooses for him without those convictions. But we are not willing to believe that our fellow citizens are so deplorably sunk in the darkness of ignorance and mental imbecility. If they are really thus degraded, it will prove them unworthy of an elective republican government, for we are told 'they are not fit to choose their own opinions in politics;' of course it is [then] unsafe to trust them with the choice of their own rulers.[21]

Just before the convention began the editor warned the delegates "to be on their guard against a plan to frustrate all their hopes of a salutary reform" of the constitution. This was a Federalist plan, or plot, to propose, as soon as the convention assembled, "that no alteration be permitted in the Constitution excepting what may be unavoidable in consequence of the separation of Maine from Massachusetts." [22] This, if it were adopted, would end any hope of altering Article Three. For the Baptists this convention seemed their golden opportunity at last, perhaps their only opportunity for another generation, to end the establishment in Massachusetts as it had recently been ended in Connecticut and New Hampshire.

The *Columbian Centinel,* speaking for the Federalist-Unitarians, was as vehement in demanding that the constitution remain unchanged in all respects as the *Watchman* and the *Chronicle* were for changing it in all respects. Of all the defenses the Standing Order made of the status quo at this time, none better suited the *Centinel* than that of Chief Justice Isaac Parker (the judge who would shortly deliver the fateful decision in the Dedham case). Parker was both a staunch Federalist and a staunch Unitarian. He was also a highly respected jurist. But his opponents in this matter considered it highly unethical that he should have chosen to defend his political and religious principles in a charge to the grand jury of Hampshire County, delivered from the bench on the eve of the convention.[23]

21. *Ibid.,* August 5, 1820, p. 3.
22. *Ibid.,* November 4, 1820, p. 3. That is, the Baptists and Republicans feared a plot to limit the area of discussion at the convention.
23. The charge to the grand jury appeared in the *Columbian Centinel,* October 11, 1820, pp. 1–2. For bitter attacks upon it see the *Christian Watchman,* October 14,

Actually, however, Parker's charge to the grand jury in 1820 was not much different from those which Robert Treat Paine delivered as Attorney General in the 1780's or from those of any other state judges on similar occasions.[24] It constitutes a classic statement of the Federalist position on church and state, and it is especially important since Parker was elected a delegate to the convention and was then chosen its president. As president he played a major role in its debates on the religious issues.

The *Centinel* devoted its entire first page and half of its second page to the address, heading it "Amendments of the Constitution." Clearly Parker spoke for his party in expressing to the grand jury his hope that the convention would make no alterations in the religious establishment. He began by pointing out that the towns from which the grand jurors came would soon be electing delegates to the convention and it behove towns to choose wisely. That many persons had not voted either for or against holding a convention probably indicated that "apprehensions of unnecessary change withheld a great majority" from voting on "a measure which they thought might by possibility put in jeopardy the civil and political blessings they so highly value." After all, Massachusetts had for forty years enjoyed a tranquil and prosperous government and its people "have enjoyed all the privileges and blessings which civil government is designed to secure with so little restraint of personal freedom, so entire a liberty of conscience and opinion in matters of religion and politics, with the uncontrolled right of making their own laws," that who could blame those who feared that any change might be for the worse — might "bring into danger that Constitution by which their singular prosperity has been maintained?" Consequently "care and discretion should be used in the choice of" delegates "lest a spirit of innovation should prevail" at the convention. (Nothing caused the Federalists more anxiety than "a spirit of innovation.")

Parker then made a statement which many Republicans and dissenters feared was prophetic of the Federalist strategy for preventing the spirit of innovation from making itself felt. "Probably it will be a question with the Convention whether any alteration shall be proposed except what may be founded on the exigency which called the convention into being;" all else was to remain outside the sphere of the convention. Parker suggested that the grand jurors ask the town voters to consider this possibility in instructing their delegates. However, he did not wish to influence them; he had no "desire to impose my opinion upon others" he said to his captive audience. He merely wished to acquaint them with some of the (dangerous)

1820, p. 3; October 21, 1820, pp. 2, 3; *Independent Chronicle,* October 18, 1820, p. 2. The charge was really less polemical than Parker's defense of the establishment from the bench in 1817 in his decision for Adams *vs.* Howe.

24. See, for example, the charge to the grand jury by Chief Jutice Theophilus Parsons in 1806 quoted in Theophilus Parsons, Jr., *Sketch of the Character of the Late Chief Justice Parsons* (Boston, 1813), pp. 201–204.

innovations which might be proposed so that they would be aware of them.

He began with Article Three. After he quoted it, he remarked that "this article was evidently drawn up with great deliberation and care." He noted that "the Protestant christian religion being that which alone has been professed by the people from the first establishment of the colony might be considered as the established religion of the country." Article Three was designed to support that establishment. But there were some who were arguing that Article Three "ought to be expunged" because government has no right to legislate in "matters of opinion and conscience." How erroneous this was could be seen by examining the preamble of Article Three which clearly showed that it was not written to control consciences but for "the happiness of the people . . . and the good order and preservation of civil government" which "essentially depend upon piety, religion and morality." Since these require "institutions of the public worship of God" and "public instructions in piety, religion, and morality," naturally the people, through their government, have a right and a duty to see that protestant churches and teachers of piety, religion, and morality were supported. Without them there could only be "barbarism" or "despotism." The public support of religion was especially important in a republic for "in free government, if the people themselves are not intelligent and virtuous" the result would be "anarchy and misrule."

Now some persons who granted the state's right to support religion nevertheless opposed Article Three because, he said, though it was proper in principle, it had not worked well in practice. However, careful examination would show any honest man "that the restraints imposed upon the Legislature and the rights secured to the citizen render it impossible that there should be any exercise of this power in a manner which would have the slightest tendency to infringe the rights of conscience." The constitution prevented any law compelling attendance at a particular church; it allowed everyone's religious taxes to be paid to the church of his choice; it allowed no protestant denomination to be subordinate to any other. "Where then is the religious restraint or the violation of rights which some [dissenters and Republicans] have complained of? Surely there is not a man in the Commonwealth who has felt them. What freedom can be more perfect" than ours?

Some people, he noted, did say that they wished to attend no church at all or that they could not find one of their own persuasion conveniently near. Of such persons Parker was sure "the number must be small . . . But small or large, it is clear to my mind that no wrong is done by obliging them to contribute to the support of the regular ministry in the parish in which they dwell." Whether they attended a church or not, they certainly benefited from the inculcation of piety, religion, and morality. Even "a Mohametan, a Jew, an Atheist or a Diest" would admit that and would find the expense well worth it. (Thus the Federalists and Republican anti-

1154

clericals combined to force the dissenters to the limit in their redefinition of liberty of conscience. Against their own better judgment the dissenters were compelled to argue at last that even the irreligious, the infidel, the non-Christian had the right *not* to attend or to support Christian churches in a Christian nation. This was difficult for them to acknowledge, and at the convention many of the dissenting delegates, including some Baptist ministers, admitted that they agreed with Parker on this point.)

Parker also reasserted the standard Erastian and utilitarian view of an establishment which the pietistic dissenters found wrong-headed and un-scriptural. "It should be remembered that our religious institutions partake largely of a civil character and are most essential props of the government and social order," for "who can tell how many children are kept in the paths of honesty and virtue by the pious lessons taught from the pulpit instead of being allowed to run loose preying upon the community, or how many crimes have been prevented by the constant and zealous instructions which the young are receiving from their revered pastors." (To the dis-senters the principle result of preaching by those "revered" parish pastors who were Unitarians was to lead their hearers straight to hell, and of those who were Trinitarians, to cast asperions on dissenters.) Parker's upper-class and rationalist-Unitarian bias became evident when he said, "I scruple not to say that the security of property and possessions, the personal safety of our fellow citizens . . . results more from the silent influence of religious and moral habits required and strengthened by religious education than from the severity of the laws." (It was some advance in penology to prefer preventive measures rather than harsh repressive ones, but no pietist would claim that a man could overcome his innate moral depravity merely by training, education, and self-discipline. A change of heart, not a change of habits, was the best guarantee for security, safety and pros-perity.)

Parker then discussed other aspects of the constitution which might be considered at the convention, the reapportionment of representation, the frequency of elections, and the test oath. On the last he sided with the Trinitarians: "There is certainly no very obvious impropriety in a christian people requiring that those who make the laws and execute those laws should be Christians, nor is it very desirable that Jews or Mahometans should be permitted to exercise those powers, for it would be among the first duties of their faith to do everything in their power to destroy the christian religion. It is enough for them to be tolerated." (Did Parker imply the converse of his theory, that Christians were committed to destroying the faiths of minorities?) "And as to *Deists,* I cannot but think that those who are able to resist the testimony in favor of revealed truth have such perverted understandings that the community will suffer no loss by their exclusion."

This note of intolerance and smugness was what aroused the writer of the only letter which the *Centinel* printed in response to Parker's charge. Signed "Conscience" it appeared in the next issue on page one. "Conscience" said that while the Unitarians claimed to be "liberals" Parker was anything but liberal; Parker's statement may be summed up to read that "all who did not believe with him must be either ignorant, negligent, or vicious characters and consequently unfit to discharge the duties of official station." But "Conscience" was not a dissenter, and the *Centinel* demonstrated political astuteness in giving prominence to this letter, for it was written by a deist: he had traveled around the world, he said, and "have not yet been able to discover that the scale of virtue is in favor of professors of Christianity." "The reverse," he said, "is true." He had found that Mohametans and Pagans were "unchanging" in their beliefs "while Christians change their varying creed from one God to three or from three to one as whim, fashion or superstition may dictate." Then paraphrasing Thomas Paine, he concluded, "I believe in one God only, in the Saviour so called, but as a good man" who "pretended to nothing more." As for our pious Puritan ancestors, they not only persecuted dissenters but also were so superstitious as to hang witches.

Readers of the *Centinel* were to believe that only deists, infidels, men who thought paganism or Mohametanism superior to Christianity, and those who vilified the glorious founders of New England would disagree with Judge Parker's charge. Parker's decision in the Dedham case six months later should not have been a surprise to those who read this charge carefully, just as no one doubted where he would stand on Article Three in the convention.[25]

The convention itself, although it threw a brilliant light on the contradictions and confusions into which the ecclesiastical system had fallen over the years through constant erosions in law and in practice, also revealed clearly that the time had not yet come when these conflicting opinions could be satisfactorily resolved. The three central religious issues of the convention centered on the requirement of an oath for all officeholders, the Unitarian control of Harvard, and the necessity for public support of religion. Phrased as questions, these issues were argued in the following terms: Is Harvard College a private institution to be controlled by a self-perpetuating body of Unitarian trustees for the benefit of their particular views or is it a public institution subject to control by the state for the benefit of citizens of all faiths? Is an oath of office requiring belief in Christianity essential to the preservation of a Christian state or does civil liberty require that citizens of any faith or none be eligible for any office? Is the present system of religious taxes with exemption for Protestant dissenters and certification to identify membership in bona fide Protestant

25. The editor of the *Chritisan Watchman* frankly stated after denouncing Parker's charge that he hoped Parker would not be elected as a delegate to the convention.

churches essential to the peace and safety of a Christian commonwealth or a hindrance to it? The convention (and the subsequent Dedham decision) proved to be more educational than it was rectifying.

Everyone was aware of some of the difficulties and most delegates were prepared to go to great lengths to conciliate and compromise even further with those who were dissatisfied. Yet regarding religious taxes it turned out that no solution, no compromise, could command a majority of sufficient size to effect a workable reform in the system. Nor could the opponents of the system muster a majority for its total abolition. When the crucial votes were taken, the delegates were split into almost equal camps, and none of the many devices for compromise could transform this equal division into a politically viable majority. As a result the convention left the ecclesiastical structure unchanged. The voters rejected the few feeble alterations proposed. Experience and the passage of time were left to work out the final resolution.

But this the convention did reveal, that drastic change, probably amounting to disestablishment, would someday have to come. The basic question which the convention really met to answer in 1820 was "Is this the time to abandon the old system?" In some respects the comparative apathy and acquiescence of the dissenters between 1811 and 1820 helped to persuade the delegates that they were not sufficiently upset to warrant abandoning a system to which so many still clung so fervently. The convention therefore decided that there would be less confusion for the commonwealth to retain the system at that time rather than to change it. The decision was probably overcautious, but in the end it may have saved the state from some sharp and bitter animosities.

Still one cannot say that any of the major viewpoints lacked able and forceful proponents in the convention. It was an extremely capable and experienced body of men, and the convention votes probably represented accurately the general feelings at the time. During the two months of debate the dissenters among the delegates, seeking different methods of reform, made four or five distinct assaults on the establishment. No one could accuse them of not having done their best. The leading figures in these assaults were Baptist clergymen, notably Thomas Baldwin of Boston, Nathan Williams of Beverly, and Ebenezer Nelson, Sr., of Malden.[26] They were aided greatly by a Congregational anticlerical layman from Pittsfield, Henry H. Childs, and three Baptist laymen, Joseph B. Varnum of Dracut,

---

26. Ebenezer Nelson, Sr. (1753–1825) is not to be confused with his son, Ebenezer Nelson, Jr. (1787–1852) who was pastor of the Baptist Church in Lynn from 1820 to 1827. Nelson, Sr., who may well have written the articles signed "Berean," had been ordained in Taunton and was pastor of the Baptist church there before moving to South Reading. His pastorship in South Reading lasted from 1804 to 1815. He then accepted the Malden pastorate in 1815 and remained there until 1823 when he resigned because of ill health. William B. Sprague, *Annals of the American Pulpit* (New York, 1860), VI, 677–678.

Martin Phelps of Chester, and Heman Lincoln of Boston. All three of these were prominent in the Republican Party. They were also assisted by Elder Zenas L. Leonard, a Baptist minister from Sturbridge; Elder Abisha Samson, a Baptist minister from Harvard; Elder Enoch Mudge, Jr., a Methodist from Lynn; the Rev. Paul Dean, a Universalist from Boston; the Honorable Holder Slocum, a Quaker from Dartmouth; Jonah Hussey, a Quaker from Nantucket; and the Rev. Thomas Whittemore, a Universalist from West Cambridge.[27]

These men's efforts to expunge or revise Article Three were beaten down primarily by the vigorous opposition of the Federalist-Unitarians led by Daniel Webster, Samuel Hoar of Concord, Leverett Saltonstall of Salem, Thomas Dawes of Boston, Samuel Hubbard of Boston, James Savage of Boston. Significantly, these Boston Federalists were joined in defense of Article Three by a leading Republican-Unitarian, George Blake of Boston. Strangely enough, Isaac Parker and his colleague on the Supreme Judicial Court, Samuel S. Wilde of Newburyport, who had fought as vigorously as any against total disestablishment, were ultimately willing to make a serious attempt to meet in a compromise measure the major objections by the dissenters and anticlericals. These Federalist compromisers were joined by three leading Republican compromisers — Levi Lincoln, Joseph Story, and Robert Rantoul, Sr. — none of whom favored complete disestablishment but all of whom wished to grant the dissenters as much else short of that as they could. Unitarian clergymen like Joseph Tuckerman of Chelsea, and Henry Ware of Boston, tended generally to take the position of the compromisers. Trinitarian-Congregationalist clergymen, like Edmund Foster of Littleton and Rev. Joseph Richardson of Hingham, generally sided with the Federalist intransigents, as did two leading Episcopalians, the Rev. James Freeman of King's Chapel, Boston and Judge Samuel P. P. Fay of Cambridge.

The debates in the convention not only reveal clearly the prevailing outlooks on the question of religious liberty in Massachusetts in 1820, but they also throw considerable light on the shifting social and intellectual thought in New England during this period of transition from the Federalist to the Whig Era. At the convention men holding all points of view were

27. Because it has been impossible to determine the religious affiliations of all of the delegates, it is not clear precisely how many among them were dissenters. However, the dissenters seem to have been fairly represented, with prominent and articulate members from all of the significant denominations present. Although statistics (presented in Chapter 59) were offered at the convention to indicate that in 1820 there were in Massachusetts almost as many dissenting churches as there were Congregational churches, the Congregationalists were a majority of the population (probably two-thirds or more). Nevertheless, as the voting on key issues disclosed, support by anticlerical Republican Congregationalists and, in some cases by Trinitarian-Federalist Congregationalists who were ready to abandon an establishment controlled by Unitarians, gave the anti-establishment forces nearly half of the votes in the convention.

required to express and defend some of their basic and usually unspoken assumptions about political and social theory, and particularly about that most vital of all New England (and American) issues, the relationship between a man's religious conscience and his political convictions. As one would expect, in this crucial turning point in American life and thought between the colonial concept of the Calvinistic, corporate state and the new nineteenth-century concept of the individualistic, voluntaristic, evangelical state, the delegates' views reflected partly history and partly the future. Few, if any, of them were entirely consistent; most said frankly that they were "of two minds" about the critical issues. The convention thus revealed how slow the evolution of republicanism in New England was and how reluctantly the old order yielded its elitist and paternalistic view of political theory.

Chapter 59

The Debate over Article Three
in the Constitutional Convention of 1820

The time is rapidly approaching when men professing to be Christians will be so opposed [to each other] that if this part of the Constitution [requiring public support of Christianity] is retained the Commonwealth will be in a state of greater dissension from theological differences than they have ever been from political controversies.

Henry H. Childs of Pittsfield in the Constitutional Convention of 1820

At the beginning the convention turned over to various select committees the problem of recommending alterations in the Constitution of 1780. The committee which considered the Declaration of Rights reported on December 6 a set of resolutions which were the framework on which the debates over Article Three developed.[1] These resolutions altered the prevailing ecclesiastical system only in a few details. The first of these resolutions added the words "Incorporated or unincorporated" to the first paragraph of Article Three, thereby making the central feature of the Religious Freedom Act of 1811 a basic part of the constitution. The second resolution concerning Article Three substituted the word "Christian" for "Protestant" to recognize Roman Catholic churches and their ministers among legitimate dissenters. The third annulled the paragraph requiring every citizen to attend public worship. The fourth advocated retention of the paragraphs investing the legislature with the right to require the towns and parishes to levy taxes for the support of religion and providing that every town, parish and religious society had the exclusive right to elect its own religious teachers. The fifth provided the following complicated substitute for the paragraph dealing with the method by which dissenters were to recover their religious taxes for the use of their own sects:

1. *Journal of Debates and Proceedings of the Convention of Delegates Chosen to Revise the Constitution of Massachusetts* (Boston, 1853), pp. 199–200. Hereafter referred to as *Journal of Debates*.

And all moneys paid by the citizen to the support of public worship and of the public teachers aforesaid, shall, if he require it, be applied to the support of public worship where he shall attend, or the public teacher or teachers on whose instruction he attends whether of a society incorporated or unincorporate; provided there be any one whose instructions he attends, otherwise it shall be paid towards the support of public worship and teacher or teachers of the parish or precinct in which the said moneys are raised. *Provided however,* That any inhabitant of any parish or members of any religious society whether incorporated or not, may at all times unite himself to any society within this Commonwealth, incorporated for the support of public worship, and having first obtained the consent of such society with which he shall so unite himself — and having produced a certificate signed by the clerk of such society to which he hath so united himself that he hath become a member thereof, and filed the same in the office of the clerk of such parish or society to which he hath belonged and in which said moneys are raised, he shall not, while he shall remain a member thereof, be liable to be taxed for any moneys raised after the filing of such certificate for the support of public worship or of any such public teacher except in the society with which he so united himself until he shall cease to be a member thereof. *Provided* also, that whenever any number of persons not less than twenty, shall have associated themselves together for the purpose of maintaining public worship and public religious instruction and shall have caused a copy of such agreement to be filed in the office of the clerk of the town or towns to which they shall respectively belong, — they shall in regard to the support of public worship and the maintenance of public teachers, have all the powers and be subject to all the duties of parishes within this Commonwealth — and all persons so associated while they continue members of such society, shall not be liable to be taxed elsewhere for the support of public worship or of any public teacher of piety, religion and morality. And any person may become a member of such society so united and certified as aforesaid, if such society shall consent thereto, and shall not, after he shall have procured and filed in the office of the clerk of the town to which he shall have belonged, a certificate signed by a committee or the clerk of such society of which he shall so have become a member, that he has become a member of such society, and attends public worship with them, shall not be liable to be taxed elsewhere, for any money raised after he shall have filed such a certificate, so long as he continues a member thereof, and shall attend public worship with such society, and shall while he is a member thereof be holden to contribute to the support of public worship and of the public teacher or teachers in said society.

The complexity of this revision indicated how unwieldy the system had become. The sixth resolution recommended retention of the final paragraph of Article Three granting equal protection by law to all peaceable denominations and permitting no subordination of one sect to another be retained.

These recommendations of the select committee amounted to a clarification of certain legal details regarding religious societies and religious taxes and the incorporation into the constitution of certain important aspects of the Religious Freedom Act of 1811. The most important innovation for the dissenters would have been to exempt all persons who joined any religious society — corporate or unincorporate, as defined in the new or revised third article — from paying any religious taxes to the parish in which he lived. As it was originally written, Article Three required everyone to pay a religious tax which would then be returned to his denomination via the minister of the church which the dissenter attended. But perhaps more important, the revision also granted Unitarians and Trinitarians the right to sign off from a parish and to form their own separate churches.

However, these revisions were not satisfactory to the dissenters. They already had obtained most of these new privileges through the Religious Freedom Act. The principle of compulsory taxation and the system of certification for dissenters still remained under this revision. Some dissenters, acknowledging that there was some virtue in having the principles of the Religious Freedom Act imbedded in the constitution where the legislature could not repeal them, argued that the proposed revision of Article Three made it both less clear and less full in its privileges than the system which currently prevailed.

This select committee's report was later condensed from six into three articles, and on December 20 the convention went into a committee of the whole to discuss them. At the beginning the proponents of disestablishment offered two substitutes of their own for Article Three which would replace the articles of revision the committee proposed. The proposal offered by Martin Phelps of Chester need not concern us since he later withdrew it in favor of the second proposal offered by the noted physician and Republican legislator, Dr. Henry H. Childs of Pittsfield.[2] Childs's proposal, which he

2. *Ibid.*, p. 346. Childs was the son of the Revolutionary army surgeon, Timothy Childs. A graduate of Williams College, he served in the legislature in 1816 and again in 1827 and 1837, founded the Berkshire Medical Institute, taught medicine at Williams, and became Lt. Governor in 1843. He was a Congregationalist but an anticlerical, antiestablishment Republican. Phelps was also a physician. Born and raised a Congregationalist in Haverhill, New Hampshire, he moved to Belcher, Massachusetts, in 1796. After he joined the Congregational church there he engaged in some polemical tracts with Federalists and Hopkinsian pedobaptist clergymen and in 1810 adopted antipedobaptism. See particularly his tract *Scripture Reasons for Renouncing the Principles of Pedobaptism* (Northampton, 1811), with an appendix by Elder Abraham Jackson defending Phelps from Federalist aspersions. His career is typical of the path many Congregationalists followed in their revolt against the Standing Order during these years. Phelps's proposal was short and simple in its sweep: "No man ought to be compelled to attend any religious worship, or to the erection or support of any place of worship, or to the maintenance of any ministry against his own free will and consent. And no power shall or ought to be vested in, or assumed by, any civil authority or magistrate that shall in any case interfere with or control the rights of conscience in the free exercise of religious worship or discharge of religious duties." Phelps added a proviso which permitted those societies which currently supported their worship and teachers by

offered on behalf of Thomas Baldwin who was temporarily absent, was modeled on the one the Connecticut constitutional convention had adopted two years before:

> . . . no person shall by law be compelled to join, or support, nor be classed with or associated to any congregation or religious society whatever. But every person now belonging to any religious society whether incorporated or unincorporated shall be considered a member thereof until he shall have separated himself therefrom in the manner hereinafter provided.
>
> And each and every society or denomination of Christians in this State shall have and enjoy the same and equal powers, rights and privileges; and shall have power and authority to raise money for the support and maintenance of religious teachers of their respective denominations, and to build and repair houses of public worship by a tax on the members of any such society only, to be laid by a major vote of the legal voters assembled at any society meeting warned and held according to law.
>
> *Provided nevertheless,* That if any person shall choose to separate himself from the society or denomination to which he may belong and shall join himself to another society of the same or different denomination, he shall leave a written notice thereof with the clerk of such society, and shall thereupon be no longer liable for any further expenses which may be incurred by said society.
>
> And every denomination of Christians demeaning themselves peaceably and as good citizens of the Commonwealth, shall be equally under the protection of the law. And no subordination of any one sect or denomination to another shall ever be established by law.[3]

Once this substitute was on the floor the alternatives of minor revision of the system or complete disestablishment were fairly before the delegates. Childs's (or Baldwin's) proposal was referred to the committee of the whole and came up for discussion after the select committee's report on the Declaration of Rights was brought forward.

Since George Bliss, the chairman of the select committee, was ill, its resolutions were presented and defended by George Blake who, though a Republican in politics, sided with the Federalist-Unitarian position in religion.[4] Blake said that those who wanted to expunge Article Three

---

taxation to continue to do so, but that permitted anyone to sign off these societies at his own will and permitted no person to be classed with any society without his express consent. *Journal of Debates,* p. 357.

3. *Ibid.,* p. 347.

4. For Blake's Republicanism see Paul Goodman, *The Democratic-Republicans of Massachusetts* (Cambridge, 1964), pp. 100, 146, 183. The committee had now condensed its original six resolutions on Article Three into three resolutions expressing the same alterations and these were referred to throughout the debate as the second, third, and fourth resolutions in revision of the Bill of Rights: the second concerned the annulment of compulsory church attendance; the third contained the changes on incorporation and the substitution of "Christian" for "Protestant"; and the fourth dealt with the subject of religious taxation.

seemed not to realize that this part of the Constitution was designed to "restrain the power of the Legislature in relation to religious subjects" and not to grant it extra powers. The legislature had all the power it needed to enact religious laws under the article granting it the right to make all wholesome and reasonable laws for the good of the Commonwealth. Everyone recognized that some restraints were necessary to protect the rights of conscience and that was what Article Three of the Declaration of Rights was designed to do. This article rightly assumed, however (and the majority of the select committee agreed with the assumption) that the happiness, good order, and preservation of civil government essentially depended on piety, religion, and morality and that these could not generally be diffused through the community except by the institution of public worship of God and public instructions in piety, religion and morality. Therefore, the majority of the committee, and of the commonwealth, said Blake, believed it was proper to retain the principle of compulsory religious taxation. However, there were some dissenters on the committee, he continued, who, although they agreed with the first two propositions, disagreed with the third: "They argued that religion would take care of itself and therefore everything might be safely left to each individual to give it that support which he might see fit." The issue of corporate *vs.* individual responsibility was clearly the crux of the argument. He admitted that the proposal to retain religious taxation had been adopted by only a small majority of the select committee, that it was essentially a compromise between maintaining the old article and abolishing it.

Blake also noted that on one crucial aspect of tax exemption the committee had decided to leave the formulation of the procedure to the legislature. And this involved, though he did not use these terms, the delicate question of exempting Unitarians and Trinitarians from paying to support a Congregational minister with whom they differed. As Blake put it, this question was how to grant exemption to a person who wished to join another religious society or parish of the same sect or denomination to which he already belonged. However, Trinitarians and Unitarians were granted the right to sign off under the select committee's compromise proposal.

When the convention delegates as a committee of the whole were asked to vote on the proposal to revoke the requirement of compulsory church attendance for all citizens of the Commonweath, the motion passed overwhelmingly, 296 to 29. But when the debate proceeded to the other proposed revisions there was no such meeting of minds. Leverett Saltonstall, a leading Federalist-Unitarian, moved to strike the other revisions proposed by the select committee and to leave Article Three unchanged except to change "Protestant" to "Christian" and to add a clause providing "that real estate shall be taxed for the support of public worship in the town, parish, or precinct in which it shall be situated." [5] The latter was a means of strengthening the parish system's shaky financial position; it was supported by Samuel Hoar of Concord, another of the Federalist-Unitarian stalwarts. Hoar said that he found the select committee's proposed revisions not only cumbersome and unwieldy but "to be in substance pernicious. They were going to change one of the fundamental principles of our government."

Hoar said he could not find that the experience of forty years under Article Three had in any way been "prejudicial to this country" [i.e., Massachusetts]. "No evil could be pointed out from suffering it to remain, to be compared with those which would arise from abolishing it." [6] He particularly objected that the proposed revisions

> extend to all Christians the rights which were peculiar [under the law of 1811] to persons of a different denomination from Congregationalists. It gives power to a Congregationalist, for any reason, to change his religious instructor and prevents his being taxed in any place except where he attends public worship; the consequence will be that all lands of non-resident proprietors will be exempted from taxation for the support of religious worship in any place. Was not this a great evil? He could name towns in which one-third part of the land was owned by citizens of different towns and was assessed for the support of public worship in towns where it was situated. Deduct this portion of the taxes and in many towns it would in a great degree derange their system of supporting public worship.

In short, the select committee's compromise went too far; if Trinitarians and Unitarians were permitted to sign off in any parish and to take with them their religious tax money on their polls and estates, there would not be enough taxable property in many places to maintain the parish system. (This was similar to the dilemma in the 1740's when the Separates or Strict Congregationalists throughout the colony wanted tax exemption.)

Hoar spoke also against the revision which attempted to define a "religious society" in terms of a minimal membership of twenty persons. He found this laughable. Any group of persons who opposed religious taxes could form such a group. Hoar, like all the conservatives, was convinced that the fundamental issue was a dislike for paying taxes, and he wanted no loopholes for tax dodgers. He had no faith, he said, "that religion would be supported voluntarily" (the Calvinistic Baptists had more faith than the Unitarians in the benevolence of man and of God in this respect). "He be-

5. *Journal of Debates,* p. 352. Saltonstall referred to this latter clause several times. It was designed to give greater security to the parish system which, according to the current laws and court decisions, had its taxes drained away by every dissenter or Congregationalist who lived outside the parish.

6. *Ibid.,* p. 352. Hoar argued that "religious instruction, in a political point of view" was "as necessary as literary [public school] instruction."

lieved the only alternative" for Massachusetts was to support religion and morality by compulsory religious taxes "or by a standing army." He went on to say specifically, what many dissenters had always feared, that he did not want to incorporate the Religious Freedom Act of 1811 into the constitution because it was "a bad law" and might be abused; to put it into the constitution would take its repeal or revision out of the hands of the legislature, "tying up their hands for all future time."

At this point, Elder Enoch Mudge, a Methodist minister from Lynn, rose to defend the dissenters' position and to oppose Saltonstall's and Hoar's amendment. He did so

> because it would tend to introduce great confusion and evil . . . The arguments which [Hoar] had used were precisely those which he would have used to show that the provisions of the constitution ought *not* to be retained. He could show in every part of the Commonwealth instances in which great injustice and oppression had been suffered by individuals; he could point to an individual on the floor [of the convention] who had had his property taken from him to the amount of 300 dollars for the support of public worship in a form which he did not approve.

The compulsory tax system was in itself discriminatory because in practice it granted "an exclusive right" to one sect. "The Episcopalians, the Baptists, the Friends have never exercised the right" of taxation. They did not believe in it. "He wished to strike from the constitution a provision that was not necessary for the support of religion and which tended to produce strife and jealousy." The abolition of Article Three "would reduce all the religious communities to a level and would introduce a spirit of harmony and emulation for the support of religion." [7] This was the Jacksonian leveling of the future, the competitive system of laissez faire. It was, to parody the First Amendment, an expression of the dissenters' belief that "the state shall make no law respecting an establishment of religion or prohibiting the *free enterprise* thereof."

The next day the convention voted to pass over Saltonstall's amendment temporarily. It then took up Henry Childs's substitute for the select committee's proposals. Childs said that he and the dissenters agreed fully with Hoar and Saltonstall that "the support of institutions for religious instruction and worship were essential to the happiness of the people and the good order of society." But he insisted that these ends could only be attained by "the free support of every individual according to the dictates of conscience." Actually, he continued, that was about what the practical situation had been in Massachusetts since 1811: "The principles of the third article . . . had been abandoned in practice and the resolutions before the committee [the convention sitting as a committee of the whole] did not

7. *Ibid.*, pp. 355–356. On December 21, the convention voted as a committee of the whole temporarily to pass over Saltonstall's amendment.

deviate from what had been the practice for many years in the Common-wealth — what had been recognized by the Legislature — and from the general sentiment of the people." Hoar and Saltonstall, he said, were sup-porting a dead law, a system which had ceased to exist as soon as dissenters had been given liberal provisions for exemption from paying to support the parish. Supporters of the establishment were mistaken in attributing the high level of morality and virtue of Massachusetts to its "inefficient and inoperative" religious system. "It was to be attributed to the general support of the common schools — they were the *primum mobile* of improvement in the Commonwealth." Here was another harbinger of the future, the Amer-icans' faith in education as the most important vehicle for progress, moral-ity, and virtue. Not surprisingly, the rise of interest in the public school system and the decline of religious parochialism went hand in hand in New England. Though Childs did not say it, the evangelical dissenters who agreed with his position and who also supported improved public schools, were not necessarily favoring a more secular culture. They were merely transferring to the role of evangelistic religion (through the institutions of the Sunday School and the religious revival) the functions which previously had been incorporated within the parish system. In the interest of freedom of conscience, the dissenters divided the old corporate functions: the school teacher replaced the minister as the inculcator of morality (what the pietists called "mere morality"), virtue, and partiotism; the minister (or the profes-sional evangelist) became the saver of souls.

By stressing the role of public education Childs and the dissenters were able to overcome the Congregationalists' and the Puritans' old argument that voluntarism was incapable of producing a moral and upright com-munity, as the example of Rhode Island clearly demonstrated. As Childs said,

> The example of Rhode Island has been appealed to as a case to show the necessity of some constitutional provision for the support of religion . . . But the low state of morals and improvement in that state could not be attributed to the want of a compulsory provision for the support of religion, but to their want of common schools . . . The example of New York, he said, had been appealed to, but there was there the same want of schools as in Rhode Island." [8]

It was understood that the public schools had an obligation to inculcate respect for and understanding of the Christian principles of religion and ethics, but it was no longer necessary to require the parish minister to certify to the Christian orthodoxy of the school teacher or to come into the class-room periodically to put the children through the shorter catechism of the Westminster Confession (which was still being printed in most New Eng-

8. *Ibid.*, pp. 358–359.

land primers). The pietistic view of religion as essentially an experiential and individualistic matter was about to triumph. "The general diffusion of education by common schools and not . . . the provision [by law] for the support of religion," said Childs, was the true basis for the general welfare and safety of the state. It also marked a new way of life for America.

Childs also emphasized the new direction of American life when he objected that even the substitution of the word "Christian" for "Protestant" in Article Three was an ineffective way of trying to consider the religious diversity in the state. The purpose of this was laudable enough: to expand the definition of legitimate dissent so that Roman Catholics might claim for their teachers exemption from religious taxes. But was "Christian" any longer a meaningful definition? Many thought Universalism and Unitarianism were not Christian. Who could "define Christian" any more?

> Clergymen differed on the subject. What would be called Christianity by one would be called infidelity by another . . . The time was rapidly approaching when men professing to be Christians will be so opposed that if this part of the Constitution is retained the Commonwealth will be in a state of greater dissension from theological differences than they have ever been from political controversies.[9]

Unlike Hoar, Childs implied that a standing army would be more necessary for the maintenance of safety under an established system than under a voluntaristic one. Childs thought that the division between church and state was perfectly easy to define: "So far as the laws can take cognizance of offences against good morals, government has a right to interfere; but the principle which leads us to worship God is beyond the control of government."

At this point in the debate the Rev. Joseph Tuckerman, a Unitarian from Chelsea, took issue with Childs. He was convinced that religion, not public education, was the bulwark of the Commonwealth: "For our very knowledge of the principles of pure republicanism we are indebted peculiarly to christianity." How could Childs argue that the establishment was both "a usurpation of inalienable rights" and also that Article Three was "inoperative"? In fact, it has been "the direct influence of this article [which] has secured them from the necessity of using this power." But annul the power given in the article and religion, morality, and republicanism would all decay. While Tuckerman agreed that "our schools are nurseries of morality," he denied that Rhode Island or New York, with or without schools, could match Massachusetts' elevated moral character. Public schools began as the result of an established religious system and without it, they could not be sustained, at least with any moral vigor. Tuckerman, with the typical conservative upperclass lack of faith in the common man,

9. *Ibid.,* p. 359.

maintained that a secularized system of public education could not possibly inculcate the Christian ethic on which the safety of republican government depended. And as a Unitarian he had no faith in the efficacy of religious revivals. Effective social control required a state church.

As for the problem of defining Christianity, Tuckerman had no difficulty with that: "It consists essentially in the great and essential principles in which its believers agree; in a conviction of the divine authority of its author, and of the obligations of the duties of his religion. Fenelon was a true Christian; and so was Wm. Penn; and so was Watts; and at least equally so was Lardner." Then perhaps seeing a frown upon the faces of the Trinitarians, he added, "This definition of christianity may not be satisfactory to all" but "It comprises however the christianity recognized in this article, and for which the advocates of the article contend" — a confession that Article Three was perfectly satisfactory to the Unitarians. He recognized, he said, that through some judicial decisions "the article had received a construction which had occasioned some evil" in its treatment of Trinitarians and Unitarians. He therefore differed with Hoar and Saltonstall: "He thought a Trinitarian ought not to be obliged to pay his tax for the support of Unitarian worship" and vice versa. But "as no state ever did or can flourish without religion any more than without a judiciary, it was quite as reasonable that every individual should be obliged to support religion in some form as that he should contribute to the support of established courts of law." [10]

Ebenezer Nelson, the Baptist elder from Malden, could not let this stand. He rose to assert the evangelical pietist's view that "The Lord Jesus Christ declared that his kingdom was not of this world . . . and he asked whether the Legislature of this Commonwealth had a right to make laws for this kingdom." He doubted that "the Christian religion would go down if not supported by the civil arm," and as proof he brought forward a new but powerful argument in the arsenal of disestablishmentarianism: "He referred to great exertions which had been made and are now making for its support and extension by the British Foreign Bible Society and other institutions of the kind which would despise calling in aid from the civil arm." Next to the Awakening itself, the great outburst of Christian philanthropy on behalf of missions and benevolent reforms since the turn of the century provided the dissenters the most powerful argument they could have that voluntarism could succeed. Nelson said that he would not expunge Article Three en-

---

10. *Ibid.*, p. 362. Tuckerman, in a later speech, made one of the few remarks which touched on the Negro's position in Massachusetts at this time. He was commenting on the need to retain the religious test oath to exclude non-Christians from office, and added, "if there was any probability that any people of color would be elected to fill either of these offices [governor or lieutenant governor] he presumed that no doubt would be felt, either as to the right, or the propriety, of their exclusion." *Ibid.*, p. 169.

tirely, for that would appear to leave religious support entirely up to the legislature. He would replace the current article with "a provision to restrain them [the legislature] from making any laws on the subject and one other provision to prevent subordination of one denomination to another." [11]

The defenders of Article Three found several chinks in the Baptist argument. Cyrus Stowell, a Federalist of Peru, pointed out that "For the past twenty years the Legislature had been constantly petitioned to incorporate religious societies; and why? because societies could not enjoy their rights without being incorporated. These petitions are granted of course. They have their rights secured — religion flourishes." What is the complaint? The Rev. Edmund Foster, a Trinitarian-Congregationalist from Littleton, pointed out "that between the years 1809 and 1814 there were seventy religious societies made application to be incorporated; and of these there was but one of the denomination of Congregationalists. Why make these applications if the civil government is of no use to religion?" George Blake, the Federalist leader, said he still did not see the distinction which Childs and Nelson made between the things of this world and those of the next. Was not morality a subject of civil law as well as a fundamental aspect of religion? Their argument, taken literally, "would prevent our enacting laws against blasphemy, breach of the Sabbath, murder, theft, and other things forbidden in the ten commandments." The Rev. James Freeman of King's Chapel pointed out that the Baptists (like Nelson and Baldwin) did not speak for all dissenters. He too represented "a minority" — the Episcopalians (in fact his church was closer to the Unitarian than to the Episcopalian position, but it retained its colonial affiliation). "He could say for himself and his friends of his religious sentiments that they had never found any inconvenience from the operation of the third article. From the year 1730 they had always enjoyed and expressed their sentiments freely." Warren Dutton, delegate from Boston, said the argument of those favoring disestablishment "proceeds wholly on a mistake; for it supposes that men will always do what is for their permanent welfare to do." But "This is not true. Reason is against it; all experience is against it." Society could not depend for security on the willingness of men to do their duty. And he could rightly point to the failure of many voluntary religious societies to fulfill their obligations to their pastors. Disestablishment would ruin the ministerial profession. It would "operate as a discouragement to young men of education and virtue from entering into a profession where the means of support were so uncertain and precarious." [12]

On all of these counts the Baptists were vulnerable. They had utilized the power of the state to incorporate their societies. They had insisted that the state must enforce the revealed laws of the ten commandments. They had

11. *Ibid.*, p. 363. In short, Nelson supported the resolution of Martin Phelps of Chester.
12. *Ibid.*, pp. 364, 383, 364, 367, 371.

failed to receive any strong support from Episcopalian, Shaker, or Quaker minorities in their fight for disestablishment — these sects showed no signs of discontent with the system and claimed no oppression from it. And the Baptists, like the Separates, had often and publicly bewailed the failure of even their own members to live up to their Christian obligations to support their pastors.

On December 23, Childs reworded the opening sentence of his resolution on Article Three to make clear that it was not designed to promote irreligion but to provide the best method of promoting worship:

> As the happiness of a people and the good order and preservation of civil government essentially depend upon piety, religion and morality; and as these cannot be generally diffused through a community but by the public worship of God; and as the public worship of God will be best promoted by recognizing the inalienable right of every man to render that worship in the mode most consistent with the dictates of his own conscience; therefore no person shall by law &c.[13]

Elder Nathan Williams of Beverly next tried to show that the proponents of disestablishment were not "in favor of removing all religion from the State" but were simply trying to provide the best system in which religion could flourish. He was convinced that Article Three as it was enforced in many towns was "unequal" and "favored one religious denomination." And there was no way to enforce Article Three without favoritism and oppression, for in effect it "had established one particular denomination."

In the course of this statement, Williams said he "agreed that contracts between the teachers and societies ought to be enforced" though some Baptists disagreed with him. Edmund Foster picked up this point and said that "in admitting this," Williams "gave up his argument." For if the government could and should enforce the support of voluntary contracts with ministers, what was wrong with its enforcing the contracts voluntarily made by towns and parishes? How could Baptists argue that the government ought not to interfere in the support of religion and then argue that they should do so in this instance? Foster also turned the Baptists against each other by saying, "If religion could take care of itself, why does it not go to India of its own accord without the aid of numerous societies for propagating the gospel?" The anti-mission Baptists, like Leland, would have agreed that the Baptists were inconsistent here and should abandon missions. But Foster said, "No; God requires that means should be used for the support of religion." [14]

Many other arguments, pro and con, were put forward concerning Childs's resolution, including Saltonstall's stirring peroration appealing to

13. *Ibid.*, p. 381.
14. *Ibid.*, p. 382.

the traditions of their fathers and his fears that "Our temples will decay and fall around us. Those beautiful spires that now ornament our towns and villages will fall to the ground . . . Let us not in one hour destroy the venerable work of two centuries!" [15] When the vote was taken, the resolution failed 221 to 161; the dissenters had lost their first effort to end the establishment. When the debate resumed on the original resolutions of the select committee, they tried a new line of attack.

Thomas Baldwin "moved to strike out 'shall' and insert 'may' — so as to read that the Legislature *may* from time to time require towns, &c, to make suitable provision, at their own expense, for the support of public worship." But the Rev. Mr. Foster of Littleton saw through this at once: "If they substituted 'may' the Legislature might make it an apology in all cases for neglecting their duty." Judge Isaac Parker (having turned the chair over to Joseph B. Varnum) said that in his opinion "if the word 'shall' should be struck out, the next Legislature would have their feelings, and would repeal all the laws for the support of public worship." [16] This was obviously Baldwin's hope. But the convention voted against this amendment, 203 to 151.

The convention then passed by a vote of 185 to 113 the motion Leverett Saltonstall originally made to amend the resolutions of the select committee by substituting for them "a resolution that it is not expedient further to amend" Article Three than by providing "that the taxes raised upon the real estate of non-resident proprietors shall be applied towards the support of public worship in the town, precinct or parish in which such real estate shall be situated and also to provide that the word 'Christian' shall be substituted for 'Protestant.' " In the debate which followed on this amended resolution to revise Article Three, Governor Levi Lincoln opposed its adoption. He stated that "he was in favor of supporting religion [by taxation], and as the father of a family, if he were reduced to the alternative, he would prefer that his children should have the moral and religious instructions of Sunday rather than the literary instruction [of the public schools] of the other six days of the week." But he could not approve of Saltonstall's resolution because by it "Persons would be taxed . . . for the support of a religion which they disapproved," and "This was a tyranny which no freeman ought to endure." He pointed out that by taxing the land of nonresident proprietors in a town for the minister's support, the minority of a town's inhabitants could keep in office a minister whose views were "contrary to the wishes of a majority of the corporators of such town." And he described "a town near to Worcester" where "the teacher was half supported by these taxes, while his religious principles were totally abhorrent to those of the majority" in the town. This was a "monstrous impropriety and absurdity." [17] The vote was then taken on adopting Saltonstall's resolution as the recom-

15. *Ibid.,* pp. 389–390, p. 396.
16. *Ibid.,* pp. 396, 398.
17. *Ibid.,* p. 417.

mendation of the committee of the whole to the convention; it was defeated 226 to 15.

Next the convention took up Samuel Hoar's motion which stated it was not necessary to make any further alterations in Article Three other than to abolish compulsory Sabbath attendance and to substitute the word "Christian" for "Protestant." [18] The chair ruled that if Hoar's resolutions were adopted "it would do away [with] all further questions on the third article" so far as the convention was concerned. Hoar stated it as his opinion that "nothing better than the third article can be obtained," and he therefore proposed to maintain the status quo.

Deacon Heman Lincoln of the Second Baptist Church of Boston, a leading Republican, opposed this view. He pointed out that if the constitution remained unchanged this would leave the legislature free to repeal the Religious Freedom Act of 1811 (under some Federalist majority) and thus to end religious liberty. He was convinced that "the time would come when this system of the constitution would be repealed," that the law of 1811 had in effect already repealed it, and that therefore the constitutional convention should make this repeal part of the constitution. Significantly, the even division of opinion in the convention meant both sides felt that to leave the matter of religion to the legislature would be to leave the question of religious liberty in the hands of their opponents. The Federalists, therefore, wanted guarantees for the system written into the constitution, while the dissenters wanted the law of 1811 written into it. William Prescott, a leading Federalist-Unitarian from Boston told Heman Lincoln he saw no reason why the law of 1811 should not remain simply a statutory enactment which the legislature might alter as it saw fit: "Why was the Legislature not to be trusted?" [19] Prescott forgot that a few days earlier when Baldwin's motion that the legislature "may" require religious taxes was being considered, those in his party opposing it had been the ones who feared that the legislature would neglect its duty.

George Blake of Boston said in support of Hoar's motion, "It would be better for them to have a millstone hung round their necks and be cast into the deep than to give up the third article." Elder Zenas Leonard of Worcester answered that he did not consider liberty of conscience safe under Article Three even with the law of 1811. If the language of Article Three was not "Machiavelian," at least it was "ambiguous and he wanted it made intelligible." To Leonard the system of religious taxation too often meant a man was compelled to support what was to him a heresy.[20] Abraham

18. *Ibid.,* p. 419. Hoar said specifically that the purpose of the second change was "to let in Roman Catholics to all the privileges enjoyed by other denominations." This action of friendliness to Roman Catholics preceded the Catholic Emancipation Act in England by eight years, but it failed of ratification along with the other proposed revisions of Article Three.

19. *Ibid.,* p. 420.

20. *Ibid.,* p. 421.

Holmes of Rochester feared that the Federalists would repeal the law of 1811 and doubted whether "we were safe in the hands of the Legislature" on such a question. If Prescott's faith in the legislature were justified "no constitution was necessary." But clearly the dissenters did not trust the legislature either because as a minority they feared majority rule or else because they suspected that the power of the Federalist ruling elite would manage the legislature for its own ends.

Compromise was impossible so long as the Federalists feared that the legislature might neglect its duty to support religion and the dissenters feared that it might neglect its obligation to support religious liberty. It is noteworthy that the Federalist-Unitarian descendants of the Puritans seemed to be taking the more pragmatic stand, at least to the extent of arguing that church-state relations were a matter for continual adjustment and reformulation by the legislature, while the disestablishmentarians were intransigent that the legislature must be bound by the constitution. This was especially important because the dissenters were primarily Republicans seeking throughout this period to reform the constitution to bring the government more directly under the will of the majority. Obviously both sides saw the issue as a matter of principle to be enshrined in fundamental law. On the other hand, the Federalist-Unitarians were intransigent at least on the point that some form of state sanction was necessary to maintain Christianity. Significantly too, no one spoke for secularism as a solution to the dilemma, though both sides hurled the accusation that their opponents' position led directly to secularism. If deism had ever been a serious threat to religion in Massachusetts that threat was clearly gone by 1820.

As Elder Thomas Baldwin said, "Everybody agreed . . . in respect to the value and importance of religion. The question was how religion could be best supported" while at the same time every man was guaranteed the right "to worship where he pleased and not to pay where he did not worship." Baldwin and the majority of the Baptists at least agreed with the supporters of compulsory taxation in their willingness to let deists, agnostics, atheists, and Nothingarians pay for the support of the established church in each parish. "He was willing," he said, "that parishes should have power to tax all persons within their limits who are not enrolled in any other society." Rights of conscience did not extend to infidels and atheists. Only bona fide Christian dissenters whose inalienable rights of conscience were infringed on in the prevailing system were entitled to them. How could a nonbeliever plead conscience? Baldwin said flatly, "He was willing that all who do not belong to other [religious] societies should be taxed in the regular parish. But he wished to be on the same level with his fellow Christians." [21] He even admitted, and here he went further than the rural pietists in his denomi-

21. *Ibid.*, pp. 422, 423.

nation, that "the law of 1811 furnished a security for all that he wanted." He feared only that it might be repealed: "He knew that attempts had been made to repeal it." He even went so far as to say that this act "gave general relief" to dissenting claims to oppression and "He did not know of any instance of injustice [to a dissenter] since" it had been enacted.[22]

Heman Lincoln who followed Baldwin, disagreed with his view that the act of 1811 had ended all oppression: "If gentlemen would appeal to the records of the courts of justice and of the Legislature, it would be found that great inconveniences had arisen" since 1811.[23] However, Lincoln agreed with Baldwin in his "contempt" for persons who were unwilling to support religion by being members of some Christian congregation. And as far as he was concerned, he said, the ministers were "the most important class of men" in the Commonwealth. "The prosperity of the Commonwealth [was] inseparably connected" with their support and the support of religion in general. "He preferred calling on the better feelings of men" rather than "resorting to the aid of law" for the support of religion," and here he expressed the dissenters' and the Republicans' generally more optimistic attitude in this era. But for the sake of arriving at some compromise he was ready to join in a conciliatory proposal which Elder Nathan Williams introduced on December 27 — a proposal in which the believers in a Christian commonwealth — Unitarian, Trinitarian, and dissenters — all joined forces against the unbelievers, the tax dodgers, the Nothingarians.

The dissenters' put this second major assault on Article Three so adroitly that it badly split the Article's defenders and very nearly produced a drastic revision in its principles. To bring these proposals to the floor the convention had to vote that consideration of Hoar's resolutions be temporarily withdrawn; this was done as a concession to the dissenters. Williams then

---

22. Baldwin and the other dissenters argued among themselves as to how much oppression had taken place since the Religious Freedom Act of 1811. Elder Nathan Williams claimed that he could produce a list of grievances which would "take days to relate" but he believed "it would do no good" (p. 427). Saltonstall argued that only "Ten or fifteen cases [of oppression] had been named for the last forty years; none of them . . . within the last ten years" (p. 424). No one provided the statistical evidence of oppression to refute him. It was not an era when statistical evidence was popular in political debate. Both sides saw the issue primarily in terms of theory and principle.

However, one interesting statistical quarrel was introduced incidentally into the debate, comparing the number of Congregational churches and dissenting churches. Defending support of the prevailing system, the Federalists on several occasions claimed the right of the majority to prevail and at one point stated that there were 450 Congregational churches in the state compared to 150 dissenting churches (p. 453). To this Enoch Mudge offered counterstatistics that there were only 373 Congregational churches in the state and 325 dissenting churches (p. 538). Mudge's figures were doubtless more nearly correct, but no one thought the matter worth pursuing at this mundane sociological level.

23. *Ibid.*, p. 423.

said that he was ready to approve of the third resolution offered by the select committee (changing "Protestant" to "Christian" and including the act of 1811 in it) though he would have preferred to change a few words in the way it was stated. He continued: "He agreed with [the] gentlemen who were for retaining the article in all their zeal for the support of religious worship . . . He approved of the injunction contained in the article for the support of public worship" by the legislature's requiring the towns and parishes to undertake this. Before he went on to discuss the select committee's fourth proposal regarding the new method of exempting dissenters, he asked that the convention vote on their third one. This it did and the dissenters, following Williams' lead, voted for it and it passed 200 to 54.[24]

Then Williams proposed to strike out the fourth resolution as presented by the select committee and to substitute the following clauses to protect dissenters:

> Resolved, That every religious society, incorporated or not incorporated, shall have power to raise moneys for the support of their respective teachers, and incidental expenses, in such manner as they shall determine by the vote of a majority of the legal voters assembled at any meeting, warned and held according to law.
>
> And every person shall have and enjoy the full liberty of uniting with and paying to the support of whatever religious society he may choose, within the limits of this Commonwealth, whether incorporated or not. *And every person neglecting to unite himself with some religious society for the purpose aforesaid, shall be classed with the parish or precinct in which he may reside, and shall be liable to be taxed by the same.*
>
> And every denomination of Christians demeaning themselves peaceably, and as good subjects of the Commonwealth, shall be equally under the protection of the law; and no subordination of any sect or denomination to another shall ever be established by law.[25]

While this was obviously a strategic retreat from the dissenters' earlier stand for complete disestablishment, it ended taxation levied by the town or parish on all inhabitants and placed the power of voting religious taxes solely within each religious society or congregation, established or dissenting, incorporated or unincorporated. Thereby it granted corporate power to all existing religious societies to levy taxes, a measure which the legislature had turned down in 1811 and against which Leland had spoken at that time.[26] Religious societies which did not wish to utilize this power would not do so and would never again be subject to such taxes. On the other hand, those Congregationalists who felt that religious taxes were a sacred right and duty,

24. *Ibid.*, p. 426.
25. *Ibid.*, p. 426. Italics are mine.
26. Isaac Parker said that Williams' resolution would incorporate "by a single act four or five hundred parishes" p. 429.

could continue to levy them on their own members so long as they chose. The resolution also granted every individual the right to join any society he chose and even to shift to another society of the same denomination — a point which the dissenters thought would attract (and did attract) support from many Unitarians and Trinitarians who disliked paying taxes to one another's ministers. But most important, the resolution overcame the fear of the supporters of Article Three that tax dodgers might somehow find it easy to escape supporting religion and thereby destroy the principle that all citizens had an obligation to society to support religion somewhere. Williams, like Baldwin and Heman Lincoln, was perfectly willing to agree that "He had no favor, no fellowship or affection for the man who would screen himself from just taxation by joining a society where taxes are not imposed by law." [27]

This resolution cut so neatly to the heart of one of the central problems that for a time the dissenters had the happy spectacle of seeing such stalwart opponents of disestablishment as Judge Parker, Thomas Dawes (who had been a member of the convention of 1780 and a defender of Article Three) and Samuel S. Wilde arguing vehemently in support of it against the equally vehement objections of such other stalwart opponents of disestablishment as Samuel Hoar, George Blake and Daniel Webster.[28] Parker proposed, and Williams accepted a minor amendment to the resolution, but he said "he was willing to do anything to accommodate [Article Three] to the views of every class of persons as far as it could be done consistently with preserving the essential principle itself." He considered the "essential principle" to be that "a legal provision for the support of public worship" should be imbedded into the constitution. And he felt that Williams' resolution accepted this principle, and was therefore a fair "compromise" between the defenders and opposers of Article Three.

Parker's minor amendment to Williams' resolution was designed, he said, to avoid the kind of fraud which had been at issue in the recent case of Adams *vs.* Howe where "a minister had been employed . . . to administer to them only one week in four." Under the law of 1811 the court had had to uphold the right of the members of this group to tax exemption. He therefore asked Williams to amend his second paragraph to provide "that a per-

---

27. *Ibid.,* p. 427.
28. For Dawes see *ibid.,* p. 430. This measure seems also to have pleased the Baptist Republican leader Joseph B. Varnum of Dracut who said that he thought Henry Childs's original resolution to abolish Article Three went too far (p. 536). Joseph B. Varnum (1749/50–1821) was the younger brother of James Mitchell Varnum (1748–1789) of Rhode Island. Elected to Congress in 1795–1796 and the U.S. Senate, 1810–1817, he was always a Republican but for most of his life he attended the Congregational church. Later he became a Baptist, though he was not converted and baptized until 1819. See his obituary in the *Baptist Missionary Magazine,* n.s., III (1822), 318, and the clippings from the *Lowell Courier* in the MHS which contain a biographical sketch by F. W. Coburn.

son to be entitled to exemption in a parish where he resided, should belong to some other religious society in which he usually attends public worship and contributes towards the support thereof." [29]

Williams saw no objection to this clarification of his proposal; he rewrote it:

> And every person shall have and enjoy the full liberty of uniting with and paying to the support of whatever religious society he may choose, in which the public worship of God shall be maintained, whether incorporated or not, provided he usually attends public worship therein, *and contributes towards the expenses thereof*; and every person neglecting to unite himself with some religious society for the purposes aforesaid, shall be liable to be taxed for the support of public worship in the parish or precinct in which he may reside.[30]

This revision satisfied Parker, Dawes, and Wilde and a number of other leading Federalists, but it aroused fierce opposition from Daniel Webster, George Blake, Samuel Hoar, and many of the supporters of the status quo. The debate over Williams' compromise proposal was the most hotly contested in the convention.

Webster said he was shocked at the turn of events. Williams' proposal as modified by Parker was "the worst proposition that had been submitted" so far. It was "totally subversive" of all that Article Three stood for. He preferred Childs's resolutions to the one which Parker and Wilde now endorsed.[31]

> He protested that the Convention having resolved that the people have a right to compel every one to pay for the support of public worship according to his ability, and that this is essential to the good order and happiness of the community, cannot consistently with this resolution pass a resolve by which every individual can avoid paying under a plea of having joined a society where there is no security for the maintenance of public worship.

Although, he said, "it was hard to defend a fortress after those who had been principally relied upon had abandoned the defense [i.e., Parker and Wilde]," he proposed to do so.

Webster had two principal objections. First, he did not see how under this resolution "it would be determined what was the maintenance of public

29. *Journal of Debates*, p. 429.
30. *Ibid.*, p. 430. Italics are mine. Levi Lincoln later told Williams that this revision conceded more than he realized, primarily because the courts would have to define for each dissenter what regular attendance and contribution meant (p. 589).
31. *Ibid.*, pp. 447, 448, 460.

worship. Three men, the richest in the community might form a society, pay a shilling apiece, and have a sermon once a year, and this would be maintaining public worship." Thus "it would be impossible to define public worship in such a manner that this provision would not entirely do away with the effect of the third article." [32] Second, it would prevent what he strenuously contended for, "an equality in the amount of contributions for the support of public worship, and religious instruction in proportion to the ability of each individual to pay." Here Webster struck a fundamental aspect of compulsory taxation in terms of civil obligations toward the general welfare. Williams' resolution would mean, "that every person shall contribute what he pleases, and be exempt from taxation on such terms as he pleases." If this was what "the honorable member from Boston [Parker] and the honorable member from Newburyport [Wilde]" considered "a compromise," "an amicable arrangement," or "a treaty for reconciling . . . different opinions," he, Daniel Webster, "wished not to be bound by the treaty." It was an old maxim, "not to put the child to an enemy to be nursed" and yet here the supposed friends of Article Three "proposed to receive from the member from Beverly [Williams], a mode of executing and effecting a provision, to which provision that gentleman was known to be entirely hostile."

Webster's argument concerning "equality" of contribution was pretty clear proof that the supporters of Article Three were concerned more about money and taxes than they were about liberty of conscience, a charge which they frequently leveled at their opponents. What Webster meant by equal was that "one man of a given amount of property should pay as much as his neighbor of the same amount of property." Under the terms of the resolution, however, it is "in the power of half a dozen rich men in a parish to form one of these new created societies and pay a dollar a year while all the expense of maintaining public worship and religious instruction" in the parish would be thrown upon the poor or those "well disposed" to the parish system. Webster here argued consistently with his stand at other points in the convention regarding the necessity for a property qualification for the suffrage. He insisted that the rich, with their privileges, had certain obligations to the poor; one of these was the duty to provide a greater proportion of the support for public worship. After all, they had more property at stake in preventing immorality, crime, and anarchy. He stated it as axiomatic "that religion should be supported for the good of society — that it was a duty on society which divided itself among individuals, in proportion to their interest in society, and their ability." And he objected to the "growing sentiment, that religion had

32. Webster's argument involved several speeches on the floor which I have condensed here. See *ibid.*, pp. 447–449, 458–460.

nothing to do with society." On this issue Webster stood for the old corporate view of society as opposed to the increasing atomism and individualism of the times.

In answer to Webster, Parker defended the compromise on the grounds that it was consistent with the guarantee of religious liberty in the constitution, and it was the best practical method of attaining harmony within the community on this controversial issue. "What interest have the parish in taxing ten or fifteen persons who the next day after the money was paid would carry it away to their own minister [as Article Three currently provided]. If there were persons who belonged to another society, was it not better to stop in the outset and let them tax themselves?" [33] This he found far more satisfactory than the law of 1811. "By this law a person who does not attend worship in the parish where he dwells, by getting the certificate of a committee of any other society shall be exempt from taxation." [34] And such a society need not even have a minister to give a certificate nor did it need to provide regular worship. Parker believed that Williams and the dissenters were really giving up more than they gained. Certainly they were assisting those who wished to enable courts and juries to distinguish bone fide dissenters from tax dodgers: "It could easily be shown whether public worship was maintained in a suitable manner" because "it would undoubtedly be required that it should be maintained constantly." Under this resolution the courts could declare fraudulent any society like that involved in Adams *vs.* Howe and Webster's fears were, to Parker's mind, groundless.

Webster did recognize that there was one aspect of Williams' proposal which attracted supporters and which he was willing to accept. He was willing, he said, to alter Article Three to the extent of allowing a man to apply his religious taxes to the teacher of his choice even though he were of the same denomination. In proposing this as an amendment Webster brought forth a precise division of the delegates into two equal groups. The amendment lost on a tie vote of 196 to 196. Had it passed it would have brought the Trinitarians and Unitarians who sided with Williams' compromise back into Webster's camp and put a quick end to that compromise. As it was, when the vote came on Williams' proposal it was almost as close. It lost by 186 to 179. Significantly, although Governor Levi Lincoln favored it, Rev. Edmond Foster of Littleton opposed it. The next day, December 28, with Hoar's minor revisions of Article Three once again on the floor, the convention, as a committee of the whole, voted 181 to 120 to end debate on Article Three for the present.

On January 6, three days before it adjourned, the convention again resumed debate on Article Three. The dissenters tried once again to obtain

33. *Ibid.,* p. 447.
34. Williams' resolution said nothing about certificates but this was undoubtedly assumed by both sides to be an inevitable part of the system.

some more significant revisions than those which the Federalists had conceded. Henry H. Childs offered a new amendment which he admitted was "in substance the same as the one he had offered before." The debate on this motion was short. It was defeated by 246 to 136.[35]

The same day Elder Baldwin made the dissenters' fourth and final attempt to gain some advantage from the convention. He proposed to insert the second section of the law of 1811 into the constitution with the following amendment:

> Whenever any person shall become a member of any religious society, corporate or unincorporate, within this Commonwealth, such membership shall be certified by a committee of such society, chosen for this purpose, and if filed with the clerk of the town where he dwells, such person shall forever after be exempted from taxation for the support of public worship and public teachers of religion in every other religious corporation whatsoever, so long as he shall continue such membership.[36]

All this gained for the dissenters was insurance that the legislature would not revoke the law of 1811. But that Baldwin would want the certificate system imbedded into the constitution was strange. Presumably he believed half a loaf to be better than none. Or perhaps by this he hoped to end annual certification. Joseph Story, for one, saw no need for the amendment and spoke twice against it. Joseph B. Varnum spoke on behalf of it and mentioned the case of a man who "was taxed four dollars which he paid to the parish treasurer, and it was only after a series of lawsuits which lasted four years, at an expense of one hundred dollars to him and as much more to the parish, that he succeeded in having it appropriated to the teacher of his own society." [37] He too feared that the law of 1811 might be repealed.

Wilde opposed the amendment. This was precisely what he and Parker had sought to avoid by supporting Williams's compromise resolution: he did not want the law of 1811 in the constitution. He recognized that

35. *Ibid.*, pp. 557, 559–560. This amendment, like Childs's first one, was very similar to the Eleventh Amendment adopted in 1833 which finally put an end to compulsory religious taxes. The speakers made two interesting points during this brief debate. Heman Lincoln pointed out that "last year two thousand persons were added to the churches" in Rhode Island. This meant, he said, "there was as great a proportion of real Christians there as in any other part of the country" (p. 559). This was symbolic that Rhode Island had at last ceased to be a total embarrassment to the Massachusetts dissenters. David Colby of Manchester raised the second point in opposing the resolution. He described a new technique used by some dissenting ministers, though he did not say of which sect: "The town in which he lived had lost $10,000 by the law of 1811. Sectarians came there with their certificates of membership, selling them for a quarter of a dollar apiece; and if they could not get that they would let them go for ninepiece" (p. 559). The sect he referred to was probably Methodist.
36. *Ibid.*, p. 560.
37. *Ibid.*, p. 563.

Baldwin was not trying "to exempt profligates from contributing to the support of religion and morality" but he felt that was the result this amendment would produce. Levi Lincoln joined Story in opposing Baldwin: "If the proposition of the gentleman from Boston should be adopted there would be subordination . . . of the Congregationalists; if you compel them to pay for the support of religion and exonerate every other denomination of Christians" that would be unfair.[38] When the question was finally taken on January 8, the day before the convention adjourned *sine die,* Baldwin's motion lost, 218 to 74. Apparently even many of the dissenters did not want to write a certificate system into the constitution.

At the same time that Baldwin's last effort was being considered, the Trinitarians, aided by Judge Samuel Fay, an Episcopal church warden of Christ's Church, Cambridge, were again trying to have an amendment passed which would enable persons to sign off from one society to another of the same denomination. Hoar, Saltonstall, and other Federalist-Unitarians strongly opposed Fay's proposal, saying that the convention had already considered this point and agreed that it would be the ruination of the parish system. Story, Levi Lincoln, and Baldwin favored it. Story argued that "No gentleman would say that the difference of sentiment was not as great between a Unitarian and a Trinitarian as between a Trinitarian Congregationalist and a Baptist. Why should not this difference be entitled to the same indulgence." Lincoln agreed, saying that because he was a Unitarian living in a Unitarian parish he was perfectly content, but he readily recognized how unhappy a Trinitarian might feel in such a parish. Elder Baldwin supported the Trinitarian position for the same reason: "A person cannot worship with any profit with a teacher from whom he differs in the essential points of faith." [39] With the support of the dissenters and of the liberal Unitarians like Lincoln and Story, Fay's measure on behalf of the Trinitarians passed 214 to 116.

This and the other revisions of Article Three passed by the convention were lumped together with proposed revisions of other articles in the Declaration of Rights as one amendment. Together they were entitled "Article The First" of the proposed amendments and referred to the voters for acceptance or rejection *in toto.* This conglomerate Article read:

> The power and the duty of the Legislature to require provision to be made for the institution of the public worship of God, and for the support and maintenance of public teachers, shall not be confined to Protestant teachers but shall extend and be applied equally to all public Christian teachers of piety, religion and morality; and shall also extend and be applied equally to all religious societies, whether incorporated or unincorporated.

38. *Ibid.,* p. 585, 590.
39. *Ibid.,* p. 578, 582.

All moneys paid by the subject for the support of public worship and of the public teachers aforesaid, shall, if he require it, be applied to the support of the public teacher or teachers, if they be any on whose instructions he attends, whether of the same or of a different sect or denomination from that of the parish or religious society in which the said moneys are raised.[40]

Provided that all taxes assessed for the support of the public worship and of the public teachers aforesaid, upon the real estate of any non-resident proprietor or proprietors, shall be applied towards the support of public worship in the town, precinct, or parish, by which such taxes are assessed; unless such proprietor or proprietors shall be resident within this Commonwealth and shall be of a different sect or denominations of Christians from that of the town, precinct or parish by which such taxes are assessed.[41]

The clause in the third article of the declaration of rights which invests the Legislature with authority to enjoin on all subjects of the Commonwealth an attendence upon the instructions of public teachers, shall be and hereby is annulled.

No person shall be subjected to trial for any crime or offence for which on conviction thereof he may be exposed to imprisonment or to any ignominious punishment, unless upon presentment or indictment by a grand jury; except in cases which are or may be otherwise expressly provided for by the statutes of the Commonwealth. And every person charged with any crime or offence shall have a right to be fully heard in his defence by himself and his counsel.[42]

In short, the convention changed the word "Protestant" to "Christian"; it included that portion of the law of 1811 which exempted persons of unincorporated as well as corporate religious societies; it allowed persons to have their religious taxes transferred to another religious society of the same denomination (i.e., it allowed Trinitarians to split from Unitarians and vice versa); it required that religious taxes on nonresident proprietors be used to support the parish in which these lands were located unless the proprietor was of a different denomination (thus permitting parishes to derive support from nonresident Congregationalists); and it repealed the clause requiring all citizens to attend church (though this was already a dead letter).

In addition to these changes in Article Three regarding compulsory

40. This clause allowed Unitarians and Congregationalists to sign off from a parish and to form their own dissenting congregations.

41. This clause had been added as an amendment to the resolution by a vote of 165 to 89 on the last day of the convention; it was a modification of Saltonsall's determined effort to gain needed tax support for parishes by allowing the taxing of nonresident property for religious purposes. *Ibid.*, pp. 603–606.

42. *Ibid.*, pp. 613–614. Since the right to a jury trial was a matter concerning revision of the Declaration of Rights, it was included with the revisions of Article Three. Some reformers considered this indiscriminate combining of religious and civil reforms in one conglomerate amendment as a Federalist device to sabotage revision of Article Three.

religious taxes, there were three other issues with religious aspects about which the Baptists expressed concern at the convention. First, the Baptists favored the proposed amendment to make ministers of any denomination (not only Congregationalists) eligible for the board of officers of Harvard College. Elder Baldwin mentioned that Thomas Hollis, the great benefactor of Harvard was a Baptist and that Brown University had set an example by requiring that ministers of various denominations be represented in its corporation and on its board of fellows.

Second, they favored abolishing the requirement that the governor, lieutenant governor, counselors (that is, Senate) and members of the legislature must declare their belief in the Christian religion to be eligible for office. They referred to Isaac Backus's speech at the ratifying convention of 1788 opposing test oaths. Elder Baldwin even recommended that not only Quakers, but anyone who wished, should be permitted to affirm rather than make an oath of office.[43] Baldwin claimed that many persons besides Quakers had scruples about taking an oath; "he had religious scruples himself about taking oaths and had not taken one these forty years."

And, third, the Baptists approved of the convention's decision to abolish the legislature's right to require attendance at public worship on the Sabbath. Elders Nelson of Malden and Williams of Beverly both spoke in favor of abolition.[44] In 1780 the Baptists had not been so clear about this issue, but in 1820 they had no doubts about it.

The Convention adopted all three of these measures (excluding Baldwin's desire to permit anyone to affirm rather than swear an oath) and then presented them to the voters for consideration.[45] On April 9, 1821 the

43. *Ibid.*, pp. 167, 197.
44. *Ibid.*, p. 352.
45. Several points of historical interest were brought out in the debates. John Adams, who was a delegate, took no active part in it. His only contribution to the discussion of church and state was a proposal that the term "all men of all religions" be substituted for the term "Protestants" to give the broadest possible interpretation to tax exemption. Judge Parker proposed this amendment from Adams in his absence, but he withdrew it almost immediately (p. 427). One of the debaters noted that over twenty-five cities and towns had abolished religious taxes entirely including Dorchester, Salem, Newburyport, and Sutton. This was probably a very low estimate (pp. 563, 580). During the debate both Judge Parker and Joseph Story noted casually that they considered Judge Parsons's decision in Barnes *vs.* Falmouth an erroneous reading of Article Three (p. 561). Judge Parker also said that the Massachusetts Courts, like those of New Hampshire, were free to judge the honesty of any man's claims that he was a dissenter and noted that a man who was immersed as a Baptist and who boasted that he had been immersed "to wash away his taxes" had been adjudged really a Congregationalist and forced to pay his taxes to the parish (p. 576). Reportedly, the Baptists in one town in Middlesex County had to fight fourteen lawsuits to recover their taxes from the town treasurer (p. 365). And Elder Zenas Leonard was said to have been hired to preach by a group of Baptists in Sturbridge whose terms of agreement with him were that he would preach to them only in months which had five Sundays, and the courts had been forced to uphold this as a bona fide tax exempt religious group (p. 452).

people of Massachusetts met in town meetings and voted on each of the fourteen proposed articles of amendment. A committee of the convention met on May 24 to count the returns. The vote on the first article was overwhelmingly against adoption, 19,547 to 11,065. The vote on Harvard was also negative, 20,123 to 8,020. However, the votes on abolishing religious tests and the oath of allegiance were affirmative.[46] Apparently the moderate alterations in Article Three proposed by the convention satisfied very few people on either side. Thus, for another thirteen years the ecclesiastical system remained as it had been. The Baptists lapsed into anoher decade of political apathy on the issue; they never really returned to the fight. The Universalists took the lead in the final phase of disestablishment.

46. *Ibid.*, p. 634.

PART XIII

The Final Downfall of the Massachusetts Establishment,

1820–1833

"The Unitarians are the only party in favor of *compelling people by law to support religion.*"

The Universalist Trumpet, July 2, 1831

Chapter 60

The Dedham Case and the Amendment
of the Religious Liberty Act,
1821–1824

No citizen of this Commonwealth, being a member of any Religious Society in the Commonwealth, shall be assessed or liable to pay any tax for the support of Public Worship or other Parochial charges to any Parish, Precinct or Religious Society whatever, other than that of which he is a member.

Religious Liberty Act of 1824

Shortly after the convention adjourned, the state Supreme Court handed down its decision in the Dedham case (Baker *vs*. Fales). This case was not directly concerned with the Baptists or with any other dissenters. But it was a crucial issue in the separation of church and state nonetheless, for it split the Congregational denomination into two irreconcilable camps. The court's decision was the final blow for many Trinitarians in a rapidly deteriorating situation. Before this the Trintarians (or "Orthodox" as they preferred to call themselves) had quarreled with their Unitarian brethren primarily on theological grounds or over the infidelity of Harvard College. Now the issue became a contest over the autonomy of the churches, the choice of ministers, and the control of property. And once the Trinitarians lost faith in the establishment, it could no longer stand. Only the possibility of reversing this decision kept the system struggling along for another decade.

The Dedham Case began in February 1818, when the Rev. Joshua Bates, pastor of the first parish church in Dedham, was granted a dismission to accept the presidency of Middlebury College in Vermont.[1] The church, most of whose members were Calvinists and Trinitarians, refused to concur in the parish committee's choice of Alvan Lamson as Bates's successor.

1. Both contemporary and scholarly comment on this case are extensive. For a good summary of the literature and the significance of the case see Douglas Shaw, "Unitarians, Trinitarians, and the Massachusetts Establishment, 1820–1834," unpublished master's thesis, Brown University archives, 1967

Lamson, a recent graduate of the Harvard Divinity School, was a Unitarian. Twice the church refused to concur with the majority of the parish, and by custom this should have ended Lamson's candidacy. The parish, by a majority of 81 to 44 wanted a Unitarian; the church members, by a majority of only 17 to 15 (with six not voting), wanted a Trinitarian.[2] The two views were irreconcilable, and the parish therefore assumed that since it had the legal right to make the contract with the minister, it need not let the church veto its choice, and Lamson accepted its call. A committee of thirteen ministers and lay delegates was called to investigate Lamson's qualifications and to hear the Trinitarians' protest against him. The council consisted overwhelmingly of Unitarians, led by William Ellery Channing, President John Kirkland of Harvard, the Rev. Henry Ware, Professor of Divinity at Harvard, and the Rev. James Walker, later to succeed Kirkland as President of Harvard. On October 28, 1818 it listened patiently to the complaints of Trinitarians that they had the right to a concurrent voice in the selection of the pastor of their church. It then ruled that although "well-known usage" did give them this right, the right was not one established in law and in this case the circumstances justified the parish's proceeding without the church's concurrence. On October 29 the council, having found Lamson pious and orthodox by its standards, ordained and installed him.

Rather than allow a Unitarian to become their pastor, the Trinitarian majority, including one of the deacons, withdrew from the church taking their records, communion service, trust deeds, and securities with them. The Unitarian remnant then excommunicated the Trinitarians for disorderly walking and schism. The Unitarians' next step was to go to the courts for the return of the property which they said rightly belonged to the parish, not to the church. Deacon Eliphalet Baker, for the Unitarians, brought suit in replevin against Deacon Samuel Fales, of the Trinitarians, for recovery of the church property — especially the sizable trust funds which had accumulated over the years by gifts for the support of the church (presumably made by Calvinists for the support of Calvinism). The first pleadings in the case took place before the Norfolk circuit court on a writ of replevin in August 1819. It was then heard before a jury in February 1820 with Judge Samuel Wilde presiding. The jury, accepting Wilde's charge that Fales's schismatics were not entitled to the church's property, gave its verdict in favor of the parish. Fales claimed a mistrial and it was up to the full Supreme Court to decide whether Wilde's instructions to the jury had been correct. Fales and the Trinitarians had retained Daniel Webster and Theron Metcalf as their lawyers (Daniel Davis, the Solicitor General of the state, and Jabez Chickering argued the case for the parish). The arguments took

2. One of the church members later changed his vote so some accounts give it as eighteen to fourteen against Lamson. Frank Smith, *History of Dedham* (Dedham, 1936), p. 80.

place in October 1820, but Chief Justice Isaac Parker did not hand down the court's unanimous opinion until April 1821.[3]

The court was faced with two fundamental questions in the case. First, did the constitution of 1780 (in Article Three) give the majority of a parish the right to choose a minister over the objection of (or without even consultation with) the majority of the church members? Second, did the majority of the church members (or their deacons) have the corporate power to hold property even if they seceded from their connection with the parish; that is, were the old deacons of the Trinitarian majority really the deacons of the First Church of Dedham, or were the new deacons elected by the minority of the Unitarians the legal deacons of the First Church of Dedham? [4]

In rendering its opinion sustaining the jury's verdict and Wilde's charge, the court relied on two lines of argument: first, the historical evidence concerning the evolution of the Massachusetts ecclesiastical system and second, the legal interpretation of Article Three and of certain judicial precedents based upon it. The court decided both of the basic questions in favor of the Unitarian deacons. The court had to admit that historically the majority of the church had taken precedence over the majority of the parish and that even after 1780 the custom generally prevailed that the church took the initiative in choosing a new minister and the final decision was made on the basis of the mutual concurrence of church members and parish voters. But here the wording of Article Three seemed to the court to be "too explicit to admit of cavilling or to require explanation":

> that the several towns, parishes, precincts, and other bodies politic or religious societies, shall at all times have the exclusive right of electing their public teachers, and of contracting with them for their support and maintenance.

"All pre-existing laws or usages must bow before this fundamental expression of the public will." That for forty years since 1780 the old practice

---

3. *Reports of Cases Argued and Determined in the Supreme Judicial Court of the State of Massachusetts,* ed. Ephraim Williams (Northampton, 1805), XVI, 147–157, 488–522. (Hereafter referred to as *Massachusetts Term Reports.*) The decision is also printed in Mark De Wolfe Howe, *Cases on Church and State in the United States* (Cambridge, 1952), pp. 40 ff. Also Edward Buck, *Massachusetts Ecclesiastical Law* (Boston, 1865), pp. 50–59.

4. The Trinitarians planned to continue as the first Congregational church of Dedham and eventually did hire its own minister and erect its own meetinghouse. So far as they were concerned, the parish could go its own way and the Unitarians would be the second church (Congregational or Unitarian). This had already happened in the town of Princeton where no lawsuit was involved. Technically, of course, this would have made the Trinitarians dissenters from the parish majority, and it was the psychological shock of finding themselves among the dissenters which, as much as anything, turned the Trinitarians against the prevailing system.

had been retained "by courtesy" in most towns could not deny the exclusive right granted by Article Three to the parish of Dedham if the parish chose to exercise it: "Whenever a parish determines to assert its constitutional authority, there is no power in the state to oppose their claim." [5]

This aspect of the decision could be, and was, severely criticized because no evidence exists that the framers of Article Three intended to subvert the ancient custom and usage. No one raised this argument at the time; the framers were in no way impelled toward such an action; and it seems clear that the voters would never have ratified the article had this been generally understood as the interpretation of it.[6] Had the framers of Article Three been asked to explain the phrase quoted by the Court, they probably would have said that they meant only to exclude any right of the state legislature to overrule the choice of ministers made in the towns or parishes, and not to exclude a Congregational church from its time-honored right of taking the initiative in choosing a minister and concurring with the parish in his call. The phrase was a product of the extreme jealousy of the town governments vis-à-vis the state at the time; it may also have reflected the dissenters' problems in towns like Dartmouth, Haverhill, Leicester, Brimfield, Rehoboth, Swansea, Bellingham, and Ashfield. There were no quarrels with the established practice on this point among the Congregationalists at that time which would have indicated a desire to alter the system, and there were no acknowledged (and few covert) Unitarians in Massachusetts in 1780.

As for the corporate rights of the majority of the church, the court held that here both history and legal precedent were against the Trinitarian deacons. Legally the court sustained the charge which Judge Wilde had made to the jury in the previous hearing of the case:

> Although the grants of land and donations to the church in Dedham purport to be for the use of the church, yet the church could not hold the same as a corporation, never having been incorporated as a body politic.

And moreover, Wilde had continued,

5. The Court also pointed to certain precedents which prefigured its decision here, notably Avery *vs.* Tyringham in 1807 (3 Mass. 181) and Burr *vs.* Sandwich in 1812 (9 Mass. 277) in both of which the Court had upheld the superior right of the parish over the church. See also Douglas Shaw's discussion of the similar situation in the town of Princeton in 1815–1817.

6. See the argument put forth on this point in the Trinitarian journal, *The Spirit of the Pilgrims* (of which Lyman Beecher was the editor), II (1829), 379. For an answer to this argument see the article by John Lowell in the Unitarian journal, *The Christian Examiner,* V (1828), 298. The Trinitarians claimed that in this clause the term "religious societies" was used to designate the right of the churches to exclusive choice as well as the town (in the case where no church was organized). The problem involves whether the framers of Article Three distinguished between a parish and a religious society or whether they thought the terms synonymous.

said lands and other property did vest in the deacons of said church by virtue of the statute of 1754; and that the deacons were to hold the same in trust for supporting the ministry and for defraying charges relating to public worship; and that by the true construction of that statute and other acts relating to the same subject, said grants and donations must be considered as made for the whole town of Dedham, for the purpose of supporting and maintaining public worship.

The first ground seems extremely shaky, since it is not clear that the law of 1754 meant to say that a parish or congregation could be incorporated while a church could not. Its prime concern was to define more clearly the precise persons (deacons) and methods by which corporate property for the support of the ministry and of public worship was to be legally held and administered.

What struck the Trinitarian majority in Dedham even harder was the court's claim that once they had seceded from the parish they ceased to exist, at least in the eyes of the law (a view consistent with the old view that unincorporated religious congregations had no legal standing). Starting from the assumption that "Churches as such, have no power but that . . . of divine worship and church order and discipline" in any parish, the court went on to declare "The authority of the church" is "invisible" and "as all to civil purposes, the secession of a whole church from the parish would be an extinction of the church; and it is competent of the members of the parish to institute a new church or to engraft one upon the old stock if any of it should remain; and this new church would succeed to all the rights of the old, in relation to the parish." Somehow the Congregational churches had become nothing but the creatures of the majority of qualified voters in the parish. This would have shocked the founders of the Bay Colony.

As for the second argument — that the grants to the church of Dedham which gave certain lands and funds to it for the support of the ministry were really grants to the whole of the town or parish and not to the church — the court relied on dubious historical evidence and read its own ecclesiastical predilections back into history. The court claimed that most, if not all, of the inhabitants of Massachusetts Bay in the early seventeenth century were church members and that there was no distinction therefore between the parish and the church at the time when the first grants were made to the church. The grants, consequently, were made to the church only on behalf of the parish and the deacons were not trustees for the church but for the parish; the gifts were designed, said the court, to support the ministry in the parish and not any particular denominational form of Christianity. "The equitable title" was vested in the parish and could not be taken from it by the Trinitarian trustees relying on the ancient wording of the gifts.

What the court did not consider was the historical temper of Puritanism. It read its own nineteenth century secularistic and Erastian spirit into the past. The Puritans had clearly considered the church (the visible saints or the members of the mystical body of Christ) as the superior body over the parish (this was written into the law in 1695 when the church's choice of a minister was assumed to have priority over that of the parish in case of conflict). Land granted or gifts made to a church in Massachusetts Bay were gifts for the perpetuation of the true gospel, for the support of the visible church, for the preaching of the Word in its purest (i.e. Calvinist) form; they were not simply a means to make the support of religion less onerous or to lower parish taxes. No Puritan would have considered a trust properly administered which granted the income from his gift "to the church" to support or inculcate the mere morality of Unitarianism. Had the founders of Massachusetts Bay returned to find the magistrates so remiss in their duties as "nursing fathers to the church" as to allow it to be assailed from both without and within by heretics, they would certainly have believed that their trust funds ought to be used as the "Orthodox" deacons said, for the maintenance of the true church in its inculcation of the true gospel. Yet in seceding from the parish the Trinitarians were following a Separatist logic equally abhorrent to the Puritans while the court's Erastian temper clearly subverted the Puritan conception of a corporate Christian commonwealth into a utilitarian and latitudinarian corporate commonwealth. Both positions were contrary to the spirit of the founders. Obviously, the historical evolution of church, state, and theology in New England had silently and subtly disestablished the Congregational churches without anyone's realizing it had happened. A social and intellectual revolution had already occurred; the legal pronouncements of the Dedham Case merely acknowledged these. The court showed a somewhat better sense of history when it discussed the gradual shift in sentiment which led to the decline of the church's superiority over the parish as it had originally been expressed in the law of 1693: "The public sentiment was gradually verging towards the broad and liberal principle which was adopted in the constitution," said the court. But the court was wrong to pinpoint this revolution in 1780; it came in 1824.

Judge Parker expressed in his decision the same position which he and the Federalist-Unitarians had expressed in the convention of 1820. That a broad Erastian policy would have to be allowed if the established system were to survive. "Nothing would tend more directly to break up the whole system of religious instruction," he said in the decision, than for the churches to try to assert a right to veto the decision of the parish,

> for the people never would consent to be taxed for the support of men in whose election they had no voice. It is an undoubted fact, that the male members of the churches form but a small part of the corporation which makes the contract, and is obliged to perform it; and it is not at all consistent with the spirit of the times that the great majority should, in this particular be subject to the minority. To arrogate such a power,

would be to break up, in no distant period, every parish in the common-wealth.

Parker's concern for majority rule was admirable to Jeffersonian ears and in a way more forward-looking than was the Trinitarians' effort to maintain the system in its original terms. However, the Federalists as usual revealed little understanding of the religious intensity of the evangelical temper. And unfortunately the court's desire to preserve the parish system at the expense of the Trinitarians in Dedham left them open to charges of prejudice in favor of their own Unitarian feelings. This charge was unjust, however. Parker would have given a decision against a Unitarian church majority had a Trinitarian parish majority disagreed with it. He had gone even farther in the case of Adams *vs.* Howe. He may have been short-sighted in thinking that his decision in 1821 would help to maintain harmony and preserve the unity of the parish system, but he was not prejudiced in the overt manner of which he was accused.

In one sense the Unitarian position in this was more consistent with the definition of the established system current after 1750 than with the Trinitarians' arguments. For years the Trinitarians (and Unitarians) had argued against the dissenters that Massachusetts had no establishment because the parish minister was really a civil servant. And they had insisted that the minority of dissenters in any parish had no just complaint against taxes levied by the majority for the benefit of the general welfare (because these were civil taxes and not, as the dissenters claimed, religious taxes). But now that the Supreme Court had ruled that the majority of the parish could overrule the "Orthodox" church members and that the church's only role in the parish was that of inculcating morality, the Trinitarians suddenly began to see what the dissenters had been driving at all along. Now *they* were a minority forced to support (or at least to leave its property in the hands of) a parish church which they considered unorthodox. It was a blow to them to hear the court say of their own position, "The condition of the members of a church is thought to be hard where the minister elected by the parish is not approved by them. This can only be because they are a minority; and it is one part of the compensation paid for the many blessings resulting from a state of society." The minority, said Parker, as earlier judges had said to the Baptists, could not claim liberty of conscience against the parish majority.

The Trinitarians' protests against the decision was quite similar to those which the Baptists and Separates had used ever since the First Great Awakening. Now they too proclaimed that the ecclesiastical system was perverted by the courts, permitting the world to invade the church. They too appealed to Scriptural truth and the law of God against corrupt man-made laws. They too denounced a majority of visible reprobates, entitled to vote in parish affairs only because of their property qualifications, who were usurping the powers of Christ's kingdom. Just like the Separates in the 1740's, the Trinitarians were incensed by the arrogance with which the Unitarians (the Old Lights of the Second Great Awakening), supported by the courts, had abetted minorities of their own religious outlook in wresting away the property of the majorities simply because a council of Unitarians encouraged by the secularistic vote of the parish was allowed to define who was or was not a proper minister of the Word of God.

Daniel Webster should have known better than to argue the case for the Trinitarians in this affair. He had often said, and staunchly defended the view, that "power follows property." Because the property qualification for voting in parish affairs was low, the power of controlling the parish went to the voters who qualified. In this case, as in so many others, Webster's conservative distaste for majority rule under a low suffrage requirement made him take refuge behind the sacredness of contract. As Leverett Saltonstall had said to prevent alteration of Article Three in the convention, "Corporate rights and privileges are sacred things" — the trouble was that Webster could not convince the court that the law of 1754 made the churches corporations. The Unitarians merited their claim to liberalism at least in one respect. The judges preferred to side with the general welfare in terms of majority rule against the property rights and hallowed traditions of a vested minority interest in this particular instance. But Judge Parker's hope of saving the ecclesiastical system by this strategic retreat in the face of adverse sociological and political facts served only to throw into sharp relief the ecclesiastical system's shortcomings and the Federalists' failing vision. The Dedham Case produced the final and fatal crack in the wall of the Standing Order in Massachusetts.

After 1821 the Trinitarians slowly but steadily moved toward disestablishment — not from principle but from expediency. By 1828 they were ready to join the dissenters in dismantling the ecclesiastical system of their pious forefathers (a dismantling process which they blamed on Parker and not on themselves or "the spirit of the times"). The truth was that by 1820 both the Trinitarian and the Unitarian positions were impossible to sustain regarding an establishment and so, by default, the voluntarism of the dissenters prevailed.

However, the consequences of the Dedham case were not immediately apparent to the Trinitarians. They were not sure whether they had lost the war or just a skirmish; perhaps the decision was only a temporary and aberrant miscarriage of justice. But in the years that followed the hope for a reversal of the decision remained unfulfilled. In parish after parish in eastern Massachusetts the Unitarians continued to outvote the Trinitarians, to ignore the concurrent right of the church in choosing new pastors, and to seize control of the parish churches' records, meetinghouses and trust funds. Between 1820 and 1834, nearly one hundred parishes by estimate, fell under Unitarian control, driving the Trinitarians into exile from their own meetinghouses and forcing them either to support Unitarian ministers or to proclaim themselves dissenters and certificate men.[7] And in every case brought before the courts to prevent these occurrences, the precedent set in the Dedham case was sustained. To the conspiratorial minds of the "Orthodox" — like Jedidiah Morse and Lyman Beecher — this was clear evidence of a Unitarian plot designed to eradicate them and to subvert the commonwealth.

But before the Trinitarians' final decision to abandon the establishment, several other events occurred which made this decision easier. The first of these was the Federalists' decision to nominate Harrison Gray Otis for Governor in 1823. The second was the major revision in 1824 of the Religious Liberty Act of 1811. The third was the Republicans' decision to present a moderate Union-Ticket in 1825 in order to split off dissident Trinitarian-Federalists in rural and western Massachusetts. The defeat of Otis and the victory of the Republican William Eustis in 1823 was attributed by the *Independent Chronicle* to two circumstances: first, that the Federalists had repeatedly refused to grant a charter to incorporate Amherst College, and second, that Otis was intimately associated with Harvard and the Unitarians. The Republicans had repeatedly assailed Harvard College as "A Party Engine in Politics and Religion" run by a family oligarchy which was virtually the same as the ruling oligarchy of the Federalist Party.[8] Eustis and the Republicans specifically campaigned against this oligarchy and favored chartering more colleges as a counterweight to Harvard. Lyman Beecher, who was in Boston shortly after Otis's defeat, wrote back to Connecticut an analysis of it which indicated that the Trinitarians were no longer willing to subject themselves to this Unitarian control, even if it meant voting against the Federalist Party:

> The numerical and political and secular influence of the evangelical population is becoming powerful in this city, compelling Unitarian ambition to show less contempt and more courtesy to the orthodox.
> The late election has broken and will, in its consequences, break forever their power as a Unitarian political party to proselyte and annoy and defeat by perverted legislative and judicial influence. This at least is the opinion here.[9]

By "the evangelical population" and "the orthodox" Beecher of course meant primarily the Trinitarian-Congregationalists, but evidence persisted

7. The standard figure given is eighty-one, but Williston Walker cites a careful study which revealed "that 96 churches in all were lost from the Congregational rolls" as a result of the Dedham case. Williston Walker, *A History of the Congregational Churches in the United States* (Boston, 1894), p. 343.

8. *Independent Chronicle*, May 3, 1823, pp. 1, 2; March 17, 1821, p. 1.

9. Jacob Meyer, *Church and State in Massachusetts* (Cleveland, 1930), pp. 204–5. Beecher wrote this on April 16, 1823. The Trinitarians still were hoping for a reversal of the Dedham decision.

that the "Orthodox" party was trying to make overtures to the Baptists and to other Calvinistic dissenters. An article in the *Christian Watchman* a few months before the election called attention to this and issued a warning that in making these overtures the Trinitarians might have ulterior purposes which were not necessarily benign. Entitled "Thoughts on the popular cry of Union," the editor (presumably John Weston) noted that a number of Baptists (like David Benedict and Charles Brooks) were calling for union between the Baptists and Congregationalists and that some Congregationalists were encouraging such a policy. But, the editor said, there may be insidious designs behind this movement and the Baptists should beware of the "political cunning" of the Trinitarians.

> Had the proposal for the union with the Baptists been made at any other time than when they seem to be upon the eve of breaking with the Unitarians, there would perhaps have been no solid ground for suspicion. If that separation takes place it will diminish their political influence. If on political questions the Unitarians and Baptists should concur, their [the Trinitarians'] case may be desperate. If union with the Baptists should tend to prevent this, the step will be an act of deep policy.

The editor noted that the Trinitarians might also hope that through such a union many Baptists, unsophisticated folk, would be persuaded by the clever Trinitarian clergy to give up their allegiance to adult baptism by immersion and return to the pedobaptist fold. And finally, the editor noted that "much of that which passes for candour in our day is indifference to principle" and the movement for union with the Congregationalists indicated a breaking down of denominational commitment. He urged the Baptists to be cautious about any such blandishments which the Trinitarians proposed.[10]

The editor need not have worried, for there was still little possibility of ecumenical union. But the article indicated that the Standing Order was breaking up. A new alliance of some kind among evangelicals was in process as well as a new alignment of political parties. Just as the Trinitarians were now ready to abandon the Federalist party, so many Baptists (at least in New England) were ready to switch from anticlerical Jeffersonianism to anti-Jacksonian Whiggism.

An illuminating insight into this shift was provided by a comment in the *Christian Watchman* on February 1, 1823, berating both Thomas Jefferson and John Adams for their failure to speak in evangelical, or even Christian, terms of death and immortality in their recently published correspondence on this subject. The article also noted ironically that the New England Unitarians and Federalists who had once been so hostile to Jefferson for his religious infidelity were now praising him for his religious

10. *Christian Watchman,* September 14, 1822, p. 157. Several weeks later the editor attacked Elder Charles Brooks of New Hampshire for writing a book advocating open communion with pedobaptists. December 28, 1822, p. 11.

liberalism: "the 'old jacobin' and 'infidel' has become a very good, sensible man in the view of some of our New England divines" precisely because he, as they, had attacked Calvinism and the doctrine of the Trinity and because he praised Unitarianism and founded a secular university in Virginia. But, said the Baptist editor reprovingly, "How heathenish" were the terms which Jefferson and even Adams used to describe God in their correspondence — "the Great Teacher" and the "Ruler of the skies." This was not the kind of Christian to whom the country should trust its future.

A year later, the same editor expressed the Baptists' (and general Northern evangelical) dislike for Andrew Jackson:

> It is said that the Kentuckians have complimented the General with a ball . . . We suspect that his religious friends, who have put in circulation reports of his piety may now hesitate in placing him on the list of evangelical Christians provided he countenanced by his presence such a manner of consuming time . . . Should it ultimately appear that General Jackson is a man of real religion, we doubt not that some substantial evidence will be given on which to ground the opinion; but for the present we must be excused from considering the fact of his piety established.[11]

The Baptists never did become convinced of Jackson's piety, though they noted with great praise that John Quincy Adams acknowledged "the divine superintendence" of God over the nation in his first message to Congress. After printing this news item the editor of the *Christian Watchman* wrote, "In our happy country we have reason to rejoice that the basis of all our political institutions is the Christian faith and that the perpetuity of our splendid republican fabrick is known to rest on no other basis. When the righteous are in authority, then well may the people rejoice." [12] Righteous John Quincy Adams and the Whigs thus won over many of the Baptists from the infidelity of Jefferson and the anti-evangelicalism of Jackson.

The Baptists had a specific reason for voting against Otis and the Federalists in 1823, and it may well have influenced many Trinitarians as well. For in February 1823, just two months before the election, the Federalist-dominated legislature defeated a new tax exemption bill which was designed to put into effect some of the measures which the dissenters in the convention had favored but which they had not succeeded in obtaining. This bill included also the measure which many Trinitarians had supported at the convention but which was defeated in the omnibus amendment to the Declaration of Rights presented to the voters for ratification, i.e., the right of a person of the same sect as the parish majority to sign off and become exempt from supporting the parish minister.

Some of the impetus for this bill may have come from the act passed by the new state of Maine in 1821 at the first meeting of its legislature. This

11. *Ibid.*, December 11, 1824, p. 3.
12. *Ibid.*, December 16, 1825, p. 7.

act, "An Act Concerning Parishes," was Maine's act of disestablishment. Its passage was a foregone conclusion from the moment Maine achieved its independence and would have been passed by the inhabitants of that area much sooner had they had the power to do so. This act was printed in the *Christian Watchman* on March 24, 1821, and it contained one of the provisions which was included in the new "religious freedom" bill put forward in Massachusetts in 1823. This was a clause to enable any group of inhabitants in any parish to apply to a Justice of the Peace to incorporate themselves. However, the Massachusetts bill of 1823 did not include the clause in the Maine act which enabled any man to sign off from any society by writing his own certificate without requiring that he join any other society. (This was in effect the way the parishes were disestablished in Maine.)

The person who seems to deserve the credit for introducing the new religious freedom bill in the Massachusetts legislature in 1823 (really an amendment to the act of 1811) was Elder Charles Train of the First Baptist Church of Framingham. But whether Train acted through a group of Baptists representing the denomination or whether he acted entirely on his own is unknown. No petitions to the legislature by any groups advocating this measure exist in the archives, nor is there any notice in any periodical or in the minutes of any Baptist or other dissenting associations on the subject. The first public mention of the bill came in the *Christian Watchman* on February 1, 1823 when the editor reported that the House of Representatives had passed and sent to the Senate a new religious freedom bill. The editor printed the bill and stated, as though it were all news to him:

> As it enlarges the religious privileges of our country brethren, we wish it may meet a favourable reception in the Senate. We hope the time is not far distant when they will be as unshackled and as free in their worship as are the inhabitants of Boston.

The bill had five sections.[13] The first section stated that every parish and religious society "may" provide for the support of public worship provided that no person should be taxed by any religious society other than that to which he belonged. The substitution of "may" for "shall" (a modification of the Public Worship Act of 1800) was one of the changes in the system which Thomas Baldwin had tried unsuccessfully to have the convention endorse. The requirement that no one be taxed except by the society to which he belonged would put an end to the general assessment of parish taxes on all inhabitants required under Article Three and implemented in the Public Worship Act of 1800.

13. A manuscript copy of this bill, with sections four and five transposed from the way it was published in the *Christian Watchman* and with a sixth section added, is in the files of the Massachusetts State Legislative Archives filed with the bill as it finally passed in 1824.

The second section of the bill stated that "any person may separate from one parish or religious society and join another either of the same or of a different denomination" by filing a certificate from the society he wished to join. This was the clause which the Trinitarians had persuaded the convention to pass at the last minute to enable them to sign off of Unitarian parishes. It had been voted down by the public along with the other proposed amendments of the Declaration of Rights.

The third section stated that any person moving into a town was free to join himself to whatever society he wished by May first after he moved into the town; but after May first he would automatically become "a member of the oldest religious society within the town or parish wherein such person dwelleth." This would end the old assumption that all new inhabitants of a parish were automatically members of the parish until such time as they obtained a certificate of membership in some dissenting congregation.

Section four required every parish and religious society to keep a correct list of all its members and imposed a fine of ten dollars on any clerk who refused to exhibit this list on request. This was intended to assure that only bona fide members of any society would be taxed.

But the heart of the act was section five:

> Be it further enacted That every parish, precinct and religious society in this Commonwealth may organize itself agreeably to the act referred to in the first section hereof and the acts in addition thereto. And any Justice of the Peace within the county wherein any parish, precinct or religious society may be, which is not organized agreeably to said acts, is hereby authorized upon application therefor, to issue a warrant for calling the first meeting thereof, directed to some suitable member of said parish, precinct, or religious society, requiring him to notify and warn the members thereof, qualified to vote in parish and precinct affairs, to meet at such time and place as shall be appointed in such warrant to choose all such officers and transact all such business as parishes are by law entitled to choose and transact in the months of March and April annually.[14]

By this section any group of people could organize themselves into a society and obtain the corporate powers necessary to support religious worship simply by applying to a Justice of the Peace instead of applying to the legislature.

This bill was by no means intended to disestablish church and state, for it explicitly continued the basic assumption that the state should support religion by law. But it was definitely the most extensive liberalization of the establishment which had ever been put before the legislature, and it is surprising that the House seems to have passed it so quickly. The vote in its favor was 67 to 41, and the *Christian Watchman* printed the yeas and

14. *Christian Watchman*, February 1, 1823, p. 31.

nays.[15] The *Christian Watchman* also printed the speech which Elder Train (as representative from Framingham) made to the House supporting his bill. He spoke from the same conservative evangelical viewpoint which Baldwin and Williams had maintained at the convention in defending their compromise measure. "We are all agreed," he began, "in establishing the Christian Religion as the only true religion and the very basis of all moral obligation. On this imperishable basis our Civil Government is erected." We are also agreed, he continued, that every citizen "ought to be left to judge for himself what the Christian religion is." He was convinced that in Massachusetts "We have no Dissenters because we have no religious establishment." However, he did feel that some were less dissenters than others and therefore certain improvements were needed on the Religious Freedom Act of 1811 "to place all denominations upon an equal and satisfactory ground."

The first thing his bill would do, said Train, would be to let every religious society support religion in its own fashion:

> I believe the mode of defraying parochial expenses among the Congregationalists, so called, is almost invariably by a tax on their polls and estates or upon the pews . . . This I believe to be the most easy and equitable way. But this mode I believe has not been generally adopted by other denominations, especially in the country . . . These persons choose to support the Gospel by voluntary subscription. This mode, however, is gradually going out of use.

Train was clearly on the side of those Baptists who favored incorporation so that they could tax their own members, and this bill made that easier.

The second part of the first section was designed, he said, to help Congregationalists (by which he meant Trinitarians). Under this section

> no person who is a member of one religious society can . . . be taxed for the support of another to which he does not belong. This exemption by the law of 1811 was not extended to Congregational societies . . . Under the existing law it has been pretended that those who withdrew from the Congregationalists are exempted only from the minister tax and not from other parochial charges [like building and repairing meetinghouses]. Such a construction of the present law is, no doubt, a mere pretence, but should this bill become a law such pretensions must cease.

The second section of his bill clarified the process of certification or signing off. To the third and fourth sections "no reasonable objections have been nor can be made." Section four "supercedes the necessity of transmitting annually a list of society members to the town assessors."

But "the marrow of the bill," according to Train, was section five. This "is calculated to prevent a great deal of trouble, difficulty, and expense."

15. *Ibid.,* February 8, 1823, p. 33.

Under its provisions "Any parish and religious society . . . may legally organize by applying to a Justice of the Peace for a warrant to call the first meeting without the trouble and expense of applying to the Legislature [for incorporation]." This would be "especially useful when a new parish splits off and wants to conduct parish business separate from town meetings." Train declared emphatically that "The old practice of vesting towns with corporate powers as a parish is one of the greatest evils that ever infested Massachusetts." It would be best were "every parish to consist of the polls and estates belonging thereto without regard to territorial limits." "Why should a religious society be set off by metes and bounds any more than in the city of Boston?" The great evil of this system was that "it gives the town or parish the overbearing, the enormous power of stretching a drag net all around its territorial limits and of scooping together all the inhabitants who do not jump over, creep under, or through the meshes. A kind of dodging that is becoming unpopular in Massachusetts." (Or, he might have said, too popular.) Another evil is that "it makes the whole town or parish security for the payment of parochial taxes . . . although many of different denominations reside within the same." A third evil is that "it gives to one denomination a superiority over others and consequently brings them [the dissenters] into a state of subordination." [16] Train's bill, then, was really a general incorporation act for ecclesiastical societies.

The large vote in favor of this radical measure can only mean that many Trinitarians were persuaded by the Dedham Case and its aftermath (as well as by the bigotry of the Federalists regarding Harvard, Amherst, and similar issues) to side with the dissenters in a serious modification of the establishment. However, the bill failed to pass in the Senate because of Federalist opposition. The *Christian Watchman* regretted the failure but commented mildly that "the mere discussion of the subject always increases its friends." The time was not far off the editor thought, when total disestablishment would come.[17]

One cannot attribute the Republican victory in the election two months later to the failure of this bill. No publicity was given to the bill and the Republicans made no attempt to capitalize on it as a party question. But significant change did occur in the party politics of Massachusetts between 1823 and 1825 which contributed to the downfall of the Standing Order. In effect, though not in detail, it was similar to what happened in Connecticut — the reactionary intransigence of the Federalists antagonized so many who had previously supported the establishment that the Republicans, by an adroit show of moderation and flexibility, were able to persuade a large segment of discontented Federalists to break with their party and join a coalition party. In Massachusetts, however, it was Trinitarian-Congregationalists, not Episcopalians, who bolted, and it was a Union Party (the basis

16. *Ibid.*, February 8, 1823, p. 33.
17. *Ibid.*

of the incipient Whig Party) and not a Toleration Party which provided the bridge between the old and the new political alignments. Although a wide range of issues was involved, any careful study will indicate that the religious issue, however understated, was central. The issue was muted because most Trinitarians could not yet bring themselves openly to attack the concept of public support for the maintenance of religion. As Beecher's letter indicates, the Trinitarians in 1823–1825 clung wistfully to the hope that by switching their votes to the Republican Party (in its moderate "union" form) they could still revitalize and patch up the established system, either by bringing the Federalists to their senses or by using their influence with the Republicans to reverse the Dedham case, reform Harvard, bolster Amherst, and otherwise shore up the old New England relationship of church and state which stood as the last bulwark against Jackson's barbarian hordes.

The Republicans shrewdly played on these hopes and fears, putting forward their most conservative, respectable, prestigious statesmen as candidates, by pointing out the rigid intolerance of the Unitarian-dominated Boston-and-Essex Junto, and by at last making religious differences between Unitarians and Trinitarians a central feature of their political propaganda (without, of course, ever suggesting that they were advocating disestablishment). It was bigotry they wished to overthrow, not compulsory religious taxation — the bigotry of an eastern, urban, snobbish, infidel elite. In 1821, the *Independent Chronicle* had been appealing primarily to dissenters dissatisfied with the convention results when it said,

> Religion enforced by law leads to craft, fraud, deceit, treachery, hypocrisy, and every other evil thing. Left to God and the operation of his providence, [it] produces purity, honesty, uprightness, humility, sincerity.[18]

But by 1823 the *Chronicle* was appealing to the Trinitarians when it contrasted the "Calvinism" of its candidate, William Eustis, to the "Socinianism" of the Federalist Otis.[19] The Republicans played on the conspiratorial fears of the Trinitarians, claiming that the Harvard corporation was "aiming at undue influence in matters of religion." [20] It reported (*pour encourager les autres*), that "some [ministerial] associations of orthodox clergy in the State have resolved not to vote for the federal candidate for Governor." [21] That this approach did encourage Trinitarians to speak out against the Federalist Party is evident in the letter printed in the Worcester *National Aegis* just before the election; it was attributed to the Rev. Austin

18. *Independent Chronicle*, February 28, 1821. I am indebted to Douglas Shaw's thesis (see n. 1 above) for insights into this shifting political situation in Massachusetts in these years.
19. *Independent Chronicle*, March 15, 1823.
20. *Ibid.*, March 26, 1823.
21. *Ibid.*, March 29, 1823.

Dickinson, of Amherst. Dickinson denounced Otis for being connected with the "Boston and Harvard College aristocracy" which was "dangerous to the civil and religious privileges of the great body of the Congregationalist, Baptist, Methodist, and Episcopal friends of true religion in the State." And he concluded, "We are disposed to support the Republican candidates for the present year because we regard them as gentlemen of distinguished ability, integrity, patriotism, and truly liberal sentiments." [22]

The Republicans' victory in 1823 led to the passage of the so-called Religious Liberties Act of 1824, a slight modification of Charles Train's bill of 1823, though the Republican press did not feel it well-advised to stress the matter. The first mention of the bill in the Republican press did not occur until it was introduced into the Senate in January 1824. Even then the *Independent Chronicle* merely noted its passage in the Senate and in the House and printed it when it became law on February 18, 1824. For some reason the *Christian Watchman* made no mention whatsoever of its passage, an indication perhaps that it was in no sense a Baptist-sponsored measure.

The bill as finally enacted contained the provision for self-incorporation of religious societies before a Justice of the Peace, the provision enabling any person to sign off from a parish or dissenting congregation on presenting a certificate from the society he was joining, and the provision granting all newcomers to a town or parish to decide by the following May first what congregation they wish to join (or otherwise be considered a member of the oldest — and consequently Congregational — society in the town).[23] The bill as it was passed did not contain the section which said that religious societies "may" provide for the support of religion in any form they chose nor the section requiring every society to keep a list of its members and to make that list readily available. Parishes therefore were still required under Article Three to provide public support for their churches. But the act did end the system of general taxation by a town or parish on all inhabitants, for it said that "No citizen of this Commonwealth, being a member of any Religious Society in the Commonwealth, shall be assessed or liable to pay any tax for the support of Public Worship or other Parochial charges to

22. William S. Tyler, *A History of Amherst College* (Springfield, 1873), pp. 662–3. Austin Dickenson (1791–1849), son of Zachariah Dickenson and Dartmouth graduate (1809), was a fund-raising agent for Amherst in 1822–1823. He is not to be confused with Emily Dickinson's brother.

23. *Massachusetts Laws,* IX, 347. One important change was made in the bill before it passed in 1824. A clause was added to the section dealing with incorporation of religious societies by a Justice of the Peace; this said that any such society must consist of "ten or more of the legal voters of such Parish, Precinct or Religious Society." The adition was to prevent groups of smaller than ten from claiming the rights of a legal corporate ecclesiastical society; presumably the dissenters accepted this minimal limitation on size for legal reasons. Otherwise the question could arise as to whether one man or two could claim to be a dissenting congregation.
The order of the sections of the act was also altered in passage, and the incorporation section became the first section of the act.

any Parish, Precinct, or Religious Society whatever, other than to that of which he is a member."

This was, as Train had said, an advance over the previous system, but it was one which chiefly benefited the Trinitarians and those who were willing to take advantage of corporate privileges. It accomplished more or less what the proposed amendment to Article Three by the constitutional convention would have effected if it had been ratified. It left dissenters off parish tax lists and enabled Trinitarian or Unitarian Congregationalists to sign off from their parish church if they did not mind becoming "certificate men."

For such an important modification (if not dismantling) of the system, this act received surprisingly little comment either at its passage or immediately afterward. The Republican and Trinitarian newspapers merely mentioned its enactment; the dissenting newspapers and the Unitarian press said nothing. Apparently there was a certain uneasiness on all sides as to precisely what they had done. The primary significance of the bill in the broader perspective was that it marked the turning point which Judge Parker's decision in the Dedham Case indicated had been reached in 1780. Now at last the majority of the people (who had not favored the alterations proposed by the convention in 1820) were ready to enact serious revisions in the establishment — revisions which made its downfall inevitable.

At the same time, in 1824, the accession of John Quincy Adams to the Presidency in a bitterly contested national election further encouraged the alliance of moderate Federalists and Republicans which had begun so auspiciously in 1823. A year later this new coalition (the proto-Whig Party) put forward the Union Party ticket supporting Levi Lincoln for Governor and Marcus Morton for Lt. Governor. Lincoln, whose respectability was unquestioned and who had endorsed public support of religion in the convention of 1820, was elected overwhelmingly against a weak Federalist ticket — the last time the Federalist Party seriously contested an election in Massachusetts.

The next question was how many of the dissenters would become Whigs and how many Jacksonian Democrats. The choice for them after 1825 was as difficult as was the Trinitarians' decision to abandon the Federalists in 1823. How many Baptists went in either direction it is impossible to determine, but the choice was sufficiently divisive so that it kept the Baptists from leading the final assault on the establishment. Or perhaps it would be more accurate to say that for the Baptist leaders the issue of disestablishment no longer seemed a politically partisan one. In any case, the Universalists who remained more anticlerical (and less respectable) than the Baptists and thus had less to lose, were the ones who finally pushed through the amendment to the constitution which ended compulsory religious taxes.

Chapter 61

The Trinitarian-Congregationalists Abandon the Establishment, 1824–1830

If the friends of religious freedom will do their duty, the time will soon come when these unjust decisions of our courts will be reversed, or what will be more favorable to the cause of truth, all laws requiring a tax for the support of the ministry will be repealed and thus every sect will be left to stand on its own merits.

The Rev. Parsons Cooke, Trinitarian-Congregational pastor
in Ware, Massachusetts, 1828

The breakdown of the Unitarian-controlled Federalist Party, the union of Trinitarians and Republicans, the passage of the Religious Liberties Act of 1824, and the chartering of Amherst College in 1825 temporarily met the Trinitarians' demands for reform in the religious system. But gradually, over the next five years, their discontent built up again until this time it could not be assuaged without total disestablishment. Although the Universalists took the initiative for this in 1830, the Trinitarians' willingness to cooperate with the Universalists' effort assured its success.

A combination of factors brought the Trinitarians to this point where some of them not only acquiesced in the Universalists' effort, but also actually welcomed and abetted it. The three most important of these factors were the continued acceleration of Unitarian gains; the failure of the Religious Liberties Act to alleviate the difficulties of the Trinitarians; and the failure of either the legislature or the courts to reverse the Dedham decision. Coupled with these negative factors were three others which gave positive support to the voluntaristic approach. First was the success of the new revivalistic techniques of the Second Great Awakening; second was the success of the new moral reform societies, and the third was the dynamic leadership of men like Lyman Beecher, Richard S. Storrs, Edward Dorr Griffin, Calvin Stowe and Leonard Woods.

A detailed examination of these forces lies outside the scope of this study and has been already undertaken by other scholars.[1] These forces evolved and developed with a dynamic quality of their own — theological, social, and institutional — and the breakdown of the system of compulsory religious taxation in Massachusetts was only one of the stimuli behind them. Disestablishment itself is better seen as a by-product than as a goal of this new pietistic-perfectionist upsurge in America. But the connection was real, and it has not been made as clear as it might.

Lyman Beecher first invaded Boston in 1823. The revivals he launched in the Park Street Church, one of the four remaining Calvinist churches in that Unitarian stronghold, were the most conspicuous aspect of the Protestant Counter-Reformation in eastern Massachusetts. They were followed by Beecher's call to the newly formed Hanover Street Congregational Church in Boston in 1825. The spectacular success of his evangelism, his moral reform societies, and his propaganda in the following six years confounded the Unitarians and heartened the Trinitarians. Beecher's theology (based on the "New School" or "New Haven" Divinity of Nathaniel W. Taylor at Yale) conceded a great deal to the Arminian temper of the times, as did his encouragement of sudden conversion with its stress on the individual sinner's initiative. At first both of these aspects of his work aroused the suspicion of the more orthodox Calvinists of Massachusetts, but his success in attaining new converts and arousing new enthusiasm (and funds) for the Trinitarian cause soon won them over. He succeeded in proving to his demoralized and discouraged brethren that the people of New England were still deeply committed to the experimental, evangelical pietism (the moving of the Holy Spirit) which flowed deeply, though intermittently, in New England from the seventeenth century. Utilizing techniques which he and Timothy Dwight and Asahel Nettleton had developed in Connecticut, Beecher succeeded in turning the defeatism of the Trinitarians (who had begun to see themselves as a persecuted minority in a Unitarian dominated system) into a new self-confidence and a new dedication to action. Most important, he demonstrated how the emotional fervor and commitment of his revival converts could be transformed into the constructive social and ecclesiastical institutions of the great moral reform crusade.[2]

In 1826 Beecher addressed himself in characteristic fashion to the problems the Dedham case raised. Invited (at his own suggestion) to participate

1. Sidney E. Mead, *Nathaniel W. Taylor* (Chicago, 1942); Frank Hugh Foster, *A Genetic History of New England* (Chicago, 1907); John Bodo, *The Protestant Clergy and Public Issues* (Princeton, 1954); Clifford S. Griffin, *Their Brothers' Keepers* (New Brunswick, 1960); W. G. McLoughlin, *Modern Revivalism* (New York, 1959); Charles J. Foster, *An Errand of Mercy* (Chapel Hill, 1960); and Charles C. Cole, Jr., *The Social Ideas of the Northern Evangelists* (New York, 1954).
2. One indication of the success of Beecher's methods was the increase of Trinitarian churches in Boston from four, in 1823, to nine, by 1830. Other statistics which encouraged the Trinitarians in these years was the steady decline in the enrollment at Harvard College and Harvard Divinity School and the steady increase of students at Amherst and Andover Seminary.

in a council to resolve a typical Unitarian-Trinitarian quarrel in the town of Groton, Beecher wrote and published the "result" or conclusions of the council of which he had been chosen moderator. His defense of the rights of the church over those of the parish was forceful but not new. What was new was his conclusion that if the parish system in Massachusetts could not be made to work to support the divine rights of the churches against the secular control of the non-church members, then perhaps it was time to abandon the parish system. "More will be lost" he said, by maintaining such an establishment than by abandoning it.[3] Beecher had the experience of Connecticut's disestablishment behind him and although he was not denying in principle the superiority of public support for religion, he was sufficiently pragmatic to recognize and to acknowledge what many Trinitarians in Massachusetts still hesitated to accept.

His tract was widely reviewed in the Trinitarian and Unitarian journals, but the reviewers, missing the thrust of his argument (because he had himself understated it), merely took it as another attack upon the Dedham decision; Unitarian reviewers therefore reiterated the arguments in favor of that decision, and Trinitarians complimented him upon seeing its failings.[4] Two years later, however, two leading Massachusetts Trinitarians, William Cogswell and Parsons Cooke, set forth Beecher's point even more forcefully.

Cogswell was the pastor of the Congregational parish church in South Dedham where he was engaged in a bitter fight with the Unitarians. Cooke was pastor of an "exiled" or dissenting Trinitarian church in the Unitarian town of Ware. Cogswell's tract, *Religious Liberty,* roundly denounced the ecclesiastical system as it had been "perverted" by the courts in Baker *vs.* Fales, Avery *vs.* Tyringham, and Burr *vs.* Sandwich.[5] He called it "usurpation" for the parish "to impose a pastor upon the church" and "high sacrilege" for the courts to "pervert such funds or appropriate them to other uses than those specified by the donor."

> All that civil government has a right to do in matters of religion is to protect its subjects in the enjoyment of their religious rights and privileges . . . Neither do we believe that any civil power can ever interfere directly or indirectly with the concerns of the church . . . without violating one of the first principles of the liberty of the United States. We, whose

3. Lyman Beecher, *The Rights of the Congregational Churches of Massachusetts* (Boston, 1827) and his *The Autobiography of Lyman Beecher,* ed. Barbara Meyers Cross (Cambridge, 1961), II, 57.

4. Douglas V. Shaw, "Unitarians, Trinitarians and the Massachusetts Establishment, 1820–1834," unpublished master's thesis, Brown University, 1967. I am indebted to Shaw for many of the facts and quotations in this discussion of the shift of Trinitarian attitudes toward the establishment.

5. For Baptist praise of Cogswell's tract see the *Christian Watchman,* August 1, 1828, p. 123. The Baptists may have mistaken the Trinitarians' expedient arguments against compulsory religious taxes for a shift toward the principle of voluntarism. The latter did not come until many years later.

birthright it is to enjoy religious freedom, would rise against all civil and ecclesiastical domination.

But the most striking statement was this: "We believe in no alliance between Church and State except that which is voluntary . . . It is opposed to the genius of our government to have a civil or ecclesiastical establishment in matters of faith or a national or state religion." [6] In the context of the times this was not the same plea Charles Chauncy made in 1769 that the people of Massachusetts had no establishment and wanted none. Chauncy was defending the Standing Order; Cogswell was *attacking* it. He concluded by saying that it was the "Liberals" — the Unitarians — who at the constitutional convention of 1820 "were in favor of something like a civil establishment in matters of religion. They would blend Church and State, annihilate any distinctions between them, wrest all power and authority and immunities from the Church and give them to the State and thus destroy those religious liberties for the enjoyment of which our Fathers fled to this land as an asylum." In short, the Unitarians had become Erastians.

Cooke's tract, *Unitarianism an Exclusive System,* was equally blunt. He declared that Unitarianism was a "false gospel" seeking to control "the springs of civil power" in order "to promote sectarian purposes." He noted that "the chief offices of trust and profit have been for a long time monopolized by one denomination of religionists" and he asked "How comes it that all the higher offices of government have been filled by men selected from one denomination and that embracing not more than one-quarter of the citizens of the state?" The answer, he said, was simple: "the liberalists . . . have used the influence which their offices gave them to exalt those who would favor the influence of their sect" — "Liberalism has been held an indispensable qualification to receive any gift [of office] from the executive." [7] No anticlerical Jacksonian could have made a more partisan attack on the ruling elite.

What amazed Cooke was that until very recently the people had been unaware of this elitism. "Acts of incorporation have been withheld from literary institutions for no other reasons than their orthodoxy. Trustees of the liberal class have been thrust" on Harvard. And legal decisions of the courts have taken away the corporate powers of the Congregational churches: "If the legislature had passed an act that no church should celebrate the Lord's Supper such an act would not be more oppressive in principle."

The "unjust decision" in Baker *vs.* Fales was wrecking the churches: "The effect of this law is virtually to hire the opposers of the church to acquire the majority in the parish and to reward them with all the property in possession of the church and leave them to divide the spoil." Cooke's

---

6. William Cogswell, *Religious Liberty* (Boston, 1828), pp. 10–17.
7. Parsons Cooke, *Unitarianism an Exclusive System* (Boston, 1828), p. 12.

purpose in this tract was to arouse the voters to throw the Unitarians out of office and to end the perverted or subverted ecclesiastical establishment. "If the friends of religious freedom will do their duty the time will soon come when these unjust decisions of our courts will be reversed, or what will be more favorable to the cause of truth, all laws requiring a tax for the support of the ministry will be repealed and thus every sect will be left to stand on its own merits." Cooke did not, however, give up the principle of tax support. He favored disestablishment, as Beecher did, "not because the gospel has not a right to claim from civil authority a support in consideration of the support it gives [to the State], but because then civil authority will not minister so much to the cause of error." To a Baptist this was totally inconsistent; all civil support inevitably became corrupted and supported error. But the Trinitarians were not yet ready to acknowledge this.

Judge Isaac Parker answered Cooke's tract in a public letter in which, ironically, he upheld his Unitarian Erastinianism as a greater support to religious freedom than Cooke's evangelicalism. Parker denounced "those who would overthrow the institutions by which the state is upheld in order to erect on their ruins a power [an established religion] which in all ages has been found to be a curse." [8] In short, Parker and the Unitarian liberals agreed with the denunciation of Cook's tract which the Universalist-liberals published in the *Universalist Trumpet*. The Universalists called it a political device by the evangelicals (Trinitarian, Presbyterian, Methodist, and Baptist) who wanted to control the state for their own special purposes.[9] To this Cooke replied in *A Remonstrance Against An Established Religion in Massachusetts* that it was the Unitarians who had constructed an established religion and received all the benefits of it.

The Unitarians, smarting under the new aggressive fervor of the Trinitarians, had some cause to believe that the Trinitarians under Beecher's leadership were indeed seeking a new kind of establishment — the domination of a Christian party in politics. Beecher's temperance reform, his assaults on theatregoing, dueling, swearing, Sabbath breaking, and the delivery of the United States mail on Sunday had led to the formation of a dozen reform societies dedicated to arousing the public to the dangers of increasing liberalism, secularism, and irreligion. Rationalists (like the Unitarians, Universalists, and anticlerical Jeffersonians and Jacksonians) looked on this as ecclesiastical demagogy of the worst sort — an effort to inflame the passions of the simple and unsophisticated churchgoers and to tyrannize the mind of man by legislative majorities. In this the liberals were correct. A new kind of national establishment did emerge from the zealous moral crusading of the evangelical pietists in ensuing years.

8. Parsons Cooke, *A Remonstrance Against An Established Religion in Massachusetts* (Boston, 1831), p. 4.
9. *Universalist Trumpet,* May 28, 1829, p. 1.

Still, by the old definition of an establishment, the Unitarians were hardly being consistent. In truth, neither side was in a position to claim liberalism. But in the struggle between the religious elitists and the religious demagogues the bitterness engendered gradually caused both sides to abandon the struggle to maintain the parish system. The Religious Liberties Act of 1824 proved to be an unworkable compromise. Before the act Trinitarians only felt sufficiently upset to withdraw from a parish when a church majority was overruled by a parish majority. After 1824 many Trinitarian church minorities could, and did, withdraw when a Unitarian minister was called; and Unitarian minorities began to feel the same way. The parish system disintegrated either way.

Even more exasperating for both sides was the increasing evidence of chicanery and perversion of the law as one group or the other sought to pack the parish meetings with their own supporters. Scandalous stories began to circulate about Unitarians who bribed dissolute Nothingarians to attend parish meetings to vote against the hiring of a Trinitarian or about Trinitarians who persuaded nominal Baptists or Methodists to sign off their own congregation just long enough to attend a parish meeting and vote against the hiring of a Unitarian. The dissenters found themselves being used as pawns in the game of parish stealing; sometimes dissenting allies against the establishment were forced to choose sides in support of the system, as for example, when the Universalists or Christians came to a parish meeting to support a Unitarian and faced across the aisle the Baptists and Methodists who had come to support the Trinitarian candidate.[10]

As the decade ended the war between the Trinitarians and Congregationalists was bringing disgrace to the leaders of both parties. This, as much as anything, probably persuaded the Unitarians finally to give in: the battle with demagogues like Beecher was beneath their dignity. The Trinitarians in turn found it difficult to denounce the political machinations of the Unitarians in the legislature, Boston, Essex, or Harvard while engaging in similar machinations in defense of dozens of parishes in eastern Massachusetts. For the Trinitarians the game ceased to be worth the candle when the Supreme Court in a notable case in 1830, reviewed the whole issue raised in the Dedham Case and then voted again to affirm the decision.[11] With no hope for repeal in the courts, the matter at last had to come to the legislature.

In this final phase of the long fight for disestablishment, the first petition to the legislature calling for the abolition of compulsory religious taxes

10. See *ibid.*, November 13, 1830, p. 78, February 26, 1831, p. 138 and Shaw, "Unitarians, Trinitarians and the Massachusetts Establishment" for documentation of such incidents.
11. This was the case of Stebbins *vs.* Jennings, 10 Pickering, 172, which took place in Brookfield and in which Chief Justice Lemuel Shaw, the successor to Isaac Parker, rendered the decision. See Edward Buck, *Massachusetts Ecclesiastical Law* (New York, 1866), pp. 60–61.

came early in the year 1830, though it had obviously been circulating during the closing months of 1829. Dated January 8, 1830, it was signed by Oliver Estey and ninety-seven other inhabitants of the town of Westminster. The petitioners said that

> they have seen with regret the disinclination of the Legislature for years past to take into consideration a subject which has been frequently presented to them which your petitioners humbly conceive to be of vital importance to the general welfare and happiness of the whole community.
>
> Believing that religious liberty or freedom is the unalienable right of man and that all attempts towards the establishment of a governmental religion are unjust and impolitic and in the end subversive of that pure worship which we wish to have cherished and supported;
>
> Believing also that the virtue and intelligence of our enlightened community when left free will more efficiently (and peaceably too) support all the venerable and religious institutions of our beloved country;
>
> Knowing as we do that all our cities and larger towns in effect now enjoy this freedom in relation to their religious privileges. And that this ancient Commonwealth is the only State in this confederacy which has anything in its policy that even looks like an attempt to enforce religion upon the consciences of men by the aid of statute law;
>
> Believing as we do that law will not make a man religious or pious in these enlightened days and that all law in relation to that subject is altogether obnoxious to far the greatest portion of the citizens of this commonwealth;
>
> Believing also that at the time of the adoption of the third article of the declaration of rights it might have been proper but still in the progress of time and as the circumstances of the community change what was once wisely deemed proper may become most manifestly improper and absurd sufficiently so to command and require the wisdom and the energy of the Legislature to apply a corrective;
>
> Having a full belief that these propositions are almost self evident, your petitioners therefore pray that your honors would take the subject into consideration and propose such an alteration in the third article of the declaration of rights as to leave every Christian free to worship God according to the dictates of his own conscience.[12]

The significance of this petition is not only that it apparently came from persons who had formerly accepted the principles of Article Three, but also that it contained none of the emotional overtones which would have marked its signers as partisans in the matter. They spoke not with the accents of Unitarian defenders of the status quo, nor as evangelical opponents, nor as liberal anticlericals. The tone throughout was one of enlightened Congregationalists of no particular partisan tinge; men who had

---

12. Massachusetts Legislative Archives, Senate Files, 9038, Actions in Sessions of 1830–1831. Not a great deal is known about Estey. He was a successful druggist in Westminster and served at times on the school committee and as selectman. He himself may not have been the prime mover of the petition.

the good of the community at heart, and whose rationale for disestablishment was sociological accommodation — "the progress of time and as the circumstances of the community change what was once wisely deemed proper may become most manifestly improper" and therefore ought to be changed. There was a new temper of pragmatism upon the subject of church and state implicit in this petition which marked an important turning point in the whole approach to the problem. For many people, religion was not only an individual matter, but a matter so private as to have almost no public relevance in the eyes of the law.

There is no record of the legislature's taking any action on this petition. But in the next session, it did take action on several other petitions which raised the same issue. One of these, dated May 10, 1830 and signed by Asa Hopkins and thirty-seven others from Orleans, was couched in the usual terms of Baptist protests. It argued that the system was "contrary to the principles of the Glorious Gospel as exhibited by its divine author who has said that his kingdom was not of this world and who expressly commanded his disciples to call no man Master on earth." But a more interesting and novel petition was the one from the town of Brookfield where a legal case in the Superior Court was about to be decided on the precedent set in Baker *vs.* Fales. Dated June 1, 1830, and signed by Alanson Hamilton and fifty-seven others, this petition protested that under the present laws

> much uneasiness and disaffection are excited both towards religion and its teachers. However beneficial religion and morality may be to the secular interests of Society and to the maintenance of civil government, yet it is by many considered as a separate and distinct concern between the individual and his maker and ought therefore to be supported by voluntary contribution or contract and not by the compulsory power of the Law.

Citing the precedents set for voluntarism "in several of our Sister States" in New England, these petitioners argued that it would be to the "best secular interest of the community" to abolish the Third Article and to make the support of religion "wholly voluntary." This request bore the earmarks of Trintarian disillusionment with the system and may be the first such petition from a Congregational group ever to have been presented to the legislature.[13]

All of these petitions presented at the summer session of 1830 were referred to the Committee on Parishes and Religious Societies for action at the winter session. When that session opened in January 1831, nine more petitions had arrived. These came from the towns of Eastham, Princeton, Stow, Pepperell, Barre, Marlborough, Acton, Westford, and Littleton. Except on the basis of uncertain internal evidence it is impossible to tell

13. *Ibid.*

whether these came from Trinitarians, Baptists, Universalists, anticlericals, or any combination of them.[14] However, significantly, five of the nine petitions presented in January 1831 were identical in their wording, which was indicative that a concerted petition movement was under way and that some group was circulating a single petition over a wide area. No doubt this was the same group, or certain members of it, who in August 1831 met in Boston to draw up the petition which was responsible for uniting the movement leading to the Eleventh Amendment to the Constitution of Massachusetts.[15]

The legislature received the new petitions in January 1831. These were also referred to the Committee on Parishes, and in March George Blake reported to the legislature for this committee. Blake said that the committee had "partially considered that subject and report that in their opinion it is expedient that the further consideration thereof be referred to the next session of the General Court." The *Independent Chronicle* was the only newspaper which took any note of these petitions, and it merely mentioned that they had been presented and that consideration of them had been postponed.[16]

When the session of June 1831 opened, more petitions calling for the repeal of Article Three were on hand. The most important of these was one signed by the Rev. Thomas Whittemore, pastor of the Universalist church in Cambridge, and sixty-four others. Whittemore was that year a member of the House of Representatives and was reelected for the next two years. In this capacity he played a crucially important role in the amendment of Article Three. His petition is therefore of interest:

> the provision of the Bill of Rights in the third article beginning "the Support and maintenance of public protestant teachers of piety, religion and morality . . ." [is] in the opinion of the undersigned subversive of the rights of the people, inconsistent with the genius of Christianity and oppressive in their operations. Civil government in a free country cannot consistently intermeddle with the affairs of a religion which is

14. The petition from Littleton, signed by Samuel Smith and 113 others on February 7, 1831, stated that Article Three and the laws based on it were "unjust, unequal and oppressive" and they prayed "that the constitution may be so amended that no subordination of any person, sect, or denomination of Christians to another shall ever be established by law and that all laws heretofore made in relation to the subject may be repealed and a general law enacted giving to all denominations of christians equal right and priviledge." Seth Lee and fifty-five others from Barre stated that they believed "the Public worship of God will ever meet with an ample support from an enlightened community, and it is unnecessary in this as well as in other States of the Union to resort to taxation and compulsion to promote and maintain liberally the public worship of our common Parent." *Ibid.*
15. The petition and its proponents is discussed in chapter 62.
16. *Independent Chronicle,* January 29, 1831, p. 1, and March 19, 1831, p. 2. The item in the latter issue stated that a bill on public worship and religious freedom had been presented to the legislature and dismissed. If so, no record of this bill exists.

spiritual in its character as is the religion of Christ, and which acknowledges none as lord and Judge but him only.

The Universalists, in short, differed little from the Baptists and other dissenters in the grounds of their objection. If they were liberal in doctrine and anticlerical in temper, they were also pietistic in their defense of freedom of conscience. That this petition was worded exactly the same as several submitted at the previous session indicates a link between the earlier petition movement and Whittemore, which is the best evidence for giving the Universalists credit for the petition movement.[17]

At first the legislature referred these and the earlier petitions to the committee which had been for some time considering amendments to the constitution, though this committee had been concerned primarily with changing the basis of representation in the legislature. Whittemore, "fearing that said Committee had before them more business than they would find time to attend to . . . moved a reference of this subject [Article Three] to a special committee. The House thereupon recalled the petitions [from the committee on amendments] and referred them" to a select committee on the Third Article of which Whittemore was made chairman. This committee consisted of Patten of Amesbury, Frothingham of Salem, Webster of Boston, Brainard of Nantucket, Parker of Plympton, Hooper of Troy, Loud of Dorchester, Brown of Winchendon, Fay of Southboro. Stedman of Springfield, Porter of Buckland, and Sherrill of Richmond. According to Whittemore "at first a majority were opposed to reporting any alteration [in Article Three]. After several meetings, however, a change was effected in the minds of some and a majority reported in favor of totally annulling the article. Messrs. Webster of Boston, Parker of Plympton, and Loud of Dorchester steadfastly opposed the alteration from beginning to end of the discussion." [18] On June 3, 1831 this committee submitted the following report:

> The select committee to whom were referred the numerous petitions which have been presented to this House praying for an amendment to the constitution . . . have considered this subject. Your committee entertain the sincerest respect for religion and religious institutions, nor have they any doubt that the same respect glows in the bosoms of the large body of petitioners on this subject; they all believe that the happiness of the people and the good order and preservation of civil government essentially depend on genuine principles of piety, religion, and morality, but as the Articles in question and the laws founded upon it have a very unequal operation in the commonwealth, as in some places they are in force and in others a mere dead letter, as in many places their operation is judged

17. Whittemore's petition is worded the same as the petition from the town of Acton submitted on January 20, 1831. For further discussion of Whittemore and the Universalists, see chapter 62.
18. *Universalist Trumpet*, November 12, 1831, p. 78.

to be oppressive by the petitioners, tending to discontent and ill feeling among the people, therefore your committee beg leave to report that it is expedient so far to amend the Constitution of this commonwealth as to expunge therefrom in full, the third Article of the Bill of Rights.[19]

According to Whittemore, when this resolution was brought to the floor "an attempt was made by Mr. Dewey of Williamstown to postpone it, but the house refused to sustain the motion. There was little debate for a large majority were in favor of the alteration. Mr. Holden of Charlestown, Jackson of Newton, Kendall of Boston, Case of Lowell, Foster of Brimfield, and Whittemore of Cambridge took part in the debate in favor of the alteration." [20] The *Independent Chronicle,* however, reported the discussion as follows:

> On motion of Mr. Whittemore of Cambridge the Resolution proposing to amend the Constitution of the Commonwealth expunging the 3rd article of the Bill of Rights was taken up for consideration [on the morning of June 16]. Mr. Dewey of Williamstown moved that said Resolution and accompanying Article of Amendment be referred to the next General Court, and after discussion thereon the previous question was called for by Mr. Adams of Marblehead and the question was determined in the negative. Said article of amendment was then amended on motion of Mr. Holden of Charlestown in such manner as to retain certain portions of the third Article and after further Amendment it was recommitted to the same committee with instructions to report this afternoon.[21]

The amended article as reported that afternoon read:

> The third Article of the Bill of Rights is hereby so far amended and modified as to stand in the words following: — As the happiness of a people and the good order and preservation of civil government essentially depend upon piety, religion, and morality and as these cannot be generally diffused through a community but by the institution of the public worship of God and of public instructions in piety, religion and morality — therefore to promote their happiness and to secure the good order and preservation of their government, the people of this commonwealth have a right to make suitable provision at their own expense for the institution of public worship of God and for the support and maintenance thereof. Provided that all religious societies shall at all times have the exclusive right of electing their public teachers and of contracting with them for their support and maintenance. And provided also that the obligation of no existing contract shall be hereby impaired.
> And all religious sects and denominations demeaning themselves peaceably and as good citizens of the commonwealth shall be equally under the

19. Massachusetts Legislative Archives, Senate Files, 9038, 1831.
20. *Universalist Trumpet,* November 12, 1831, p. 78.
21. *Independent Chronicle,* June 18, 1831, p. 1.

protection of the law and no subordination of any one sect or denomination to another shall ever be established by law.[22]

This article was adopted by a vote of 272 to 78.[23] At the same time the House also approved of a resolution which specified the manner in which this proposed amendment should be presented to the people for ratification. This was the first amendment to be adopted under the rules adopted at the convention of 1820, and the procedure was rather complicated:

> *Resolved:* by both Houses, the same being agreed to by a majority of senators and two-thirds of the members of the House of Representatives present and voting thereon, that it is proper and expedient to alter and amend the Constitution of this Commonwealth by adopting the subjoining article of amendment & that the same as thus agreed to, be entered on the journals of the two Houses with the yeas and nays taken thereon and referred to the General Court next to be chosen and that the same be published, to the end that if agreed to by the General Court, next to be chosen in the manner provided by the Constitution, it may be submitted to the people for their ratification in order that it may become a part of the Constitution of this Commonwealth.[24]

The most important feature of this cautious amending procedure was that the article had to be passed by two successive legislatures and that it could be thwarted by a majority of the Senate or by a minor revision in the wording.

On June 17 the Senate referred the resolution and article as adopted in the House to a committee of Nathan Brooks, Levi Lincoln, Jr., and Enos Foote. On June 20 this committee reported that it had "considered the same and report that the same ought to pass." The resolve passed its first reading in the Senate but after the second reading "Mr. Everett moved that said resolve be referred to the next General Court; and on motion of Mr. Turner it was ordered that this question be taken by yeas and nays — and it being so taken it was determined in the affirmative" by a vote of 18 to 15.[25] This narrow margin of three votes meant that the measure had to start all over again in the succeeding legislature.

As a result the question of disestablishment became a political issue in the next election. Since 1824 the National Republican (or Whig) Party, the conservative Jeffersonian Republicans and the moderate Federalists, had dominated Massachusetts politics. They dominated the legislatures of 1831–1833 under the leadership of Levi Lincoln. And their leading spokesmen were men like Edward Everett, Alexander H. Everett, and John Davis (who was to succeed Lincoln as Governor after 1834). The *Independent*

22. Massachusetts Legislative Archives, 1831.
23. *Universalist Trumpet,* June 25, 1831, p. 206.
24. *Ibid.*
25. *Ibid.,* and *Independent Chronicle,* June 22, 1831, p. 2.

Chronicle, the official organ of the party, estimated that in June 1831 there were sixty to seventy Jacksonians in the legislature, a handful of Anti-Masons and incipient Workingmen's Party delegates, and all the rest were National Republicans. The *Chronicle* admitted that the Jacksonians had probably voted unanimously to amend Article Three in June 1831, but they pointed out that it was the support of the National Republicans which had given the amendment its two-thirds majority. What the *Chronicle* found difficult to explain was why the Senate, also dominated by the National Republicans, had voted 18 to 15 against the resolve. When the Boston *Statesman,* the Jacksonian organ, made a campaign issue of the amendment in the fall 1831, the *Chronicle* offered this explanation: the votes of Lincoln, A. H. Everett, Blake, Phillips, Brooks, Endicott, *et al.* against the measure were based "not upon the merits of the main question but upon the propriety of acting upon it at the close of the session when several members have obtained leaves of absence" and "there was not time to give it that mature examination necessary to a full understanding of its bearings on our existing laws." According to this explanation, several Senators who favored the amendment voted to postpone its consideration for this reason alone. No party, said George Blake, the chairman of the National Republican Party, could take credit for what had been done on behalf of the amendment and no party should be blamed for the postponement.

Yet despite this implicit claim that the National Republicans were as much in favor of the amendment as were the Jacksonians, the Address of the National Republican State Convention to the voters on behalf of Lincoln's reelection in October 1831, concluded its remarks on the amendment with this defense of the prevailing system:

> The steady and liberal support of the Ministration of the Gospel has ever been the pride and boast of our State, and we have yet to learn of the amount paid for support of the clergy even by two millions annually, that it will be any recommendation to a candidate for Governor that his partisans would reduce that amount and deprive the clergy of an honorable support; and still less are we ready to believe that the mere assertions of interested partisans can convince the intelligent people of this State that their voluntary contributions for the support of the Gospel in its purity, according to the dictates of their own consciences, is to be regarded as an onerous tax; — relief from which is to be sought in new and untried administration of our State Concerns.[26]

In short, the Whigs were ready to campaign on behalf of preserving the status quo.

The Jacksonian Democrats (who considered themselves the true heirs of Jeffersonian's Democratic-Republican Party) had a different explanation

26. *Independent Chronicle,* October 26, 1831, p. 4.

for the failure of Whittemore's resolve to pass the Senate in June 1831. In the first place, the Jacksonians pointed out, Levi Lincoln, "the apostate [Jeffersonian] Republican," had frankly stated at the Constitutional Convention of 1820 that "It was more congenial to his own feelings that religion should be supported by a tax than in any other mode" and therefore he was not likely to put any pressure upon his party to support this amendment. Secondly, they maintained in 1831, as they had maintained since the Jacksonian party came into existence in Massachusetts in 1824, that the National Republicans had in reality sold out the party of Jefferson to the Federalists. (The Jacksonians habitually referred to the party of Levi Lincoln as "the Federalist Party." The National Republicans, however, admitted only to a merger which had granted a parity of offices and patronage to those Federalists who had seen fit to abandon their old Tory views and to accept the principles of the Republican Party as they had stood since Jefferson.) The Jacksonians pointed out that in reality the National Republicans were dominated by former Federalists and that they appointed members of the Harvard-Unitarian-Boston aristocracy to all of the leading positions and followed their views in all of their policies. As proof that the earlier Republican Party had been taken over by the Federalists, the editor of the *Statesman* declared in March 1831,

> We have received a letter from a friend in the country, a Universalist, who complains of the almost entire proscription from office of that numerous and respectable class of citizens. He says that the Universalists, Baptists, and Methodists are kept out of office by the influence of Harvard College, while Unitarians are promoted to stations of honor and profit thereby obtaining an undue influence in the State Government. Our correspondent is in favor of an equal distribution of government favours without regard to religious sentiments.[27]

The opponents of the amendment of Article Three, said the *Statesmen,* were hard core Federalists and Unitarians who had, since 1780, opposed any alteration in the ecclesiastical system, and who had no intention of giving in to the dissenters at this time. To say that the question of the amendment needed more time for consideration was ridiculous. All of the aspects of the issue had been debated for decades. Now it was time to act on the people's clearly expressed will to overthrow the establishment. Comparing the system of parochial taxation to the tithing system of England, the Jacksonians linked the opposition to amending Article Three to the National Republican administration's consistent refusal to accede to the Jacksonian requests for extending the suffrage and for redistricting the representation in the legislature. Boston and the large cities of the state, the Jacksonian said, had long since granted complete religious liberty to

27. *Boston Statesman,* November 5, 1831, p. 2; March 26, 1831, p. 2.

dissenters. The people of the small country towns asked only that they might enjoy the same privileges and rights as the "aristocratic" and "literary" people of the eastern cities. "We hope they will abolish the third article." [28]

The Jacksonians were themselves split on the issue of religion and although the *Statesman* spoke for the anticlerical wing of the Party, the Pittsfield *Sun,* which was equally devoted to Jackson, eschewed the anticlericalism of the party and refused to take any public stand on Article Three in these years. Its pages were filled with articles concerning the Bible Societies, the Sunday School Union, Temperance, Missions, revivals, which appealed to the Trinitarian and evangelical dissenting members of the Jacksonian party in the western part of the state. The *Sun* was so evangelical in sentiment that in December 1831 it sided with the evangelical-dominated legislature of South Carolina when the legislature dismissed that old Jeffersonian stalwart, Dr. Thomas Cooper, from his position as President of the state university because of his hostile attitude toward the evangelical clergy.[29]

The Anti-Masonic Party, never strong in Massachusetts, entered the campaign of 1831 with its own cadidate for governor. It had broken with Levi Lincoln, whom it had backed in 1830, because he refused to accede to its radical demands for evangelical reform. Samuel I. Lothrop was the man whom they nominated on "The Anti-Masonic Republican" ticket. Lothrop had been President of the state Senate in the session of 1830–31, but he retired before the Senate took any action on the third article. However, his parting speech to the Senate contained a paragraph which left no doubt about his position on the issue:

> Whenever any provision of the Constitution ceases to have any obligatory effect — when public opinion clearly and unequivocally demands of the legislature a disregard of its injunctions — when we are obliged to frame our laws in such a manner as to evade it, directly to contravene it, and when our judicial tribunals give the sanction of constitutionality to such enactments, the continuance of the article remains not merely useless — it tends also to diminish our veneration for the whole instrument and necessarily leads to a practice of immoral tendency. Will not these observations apply to the third article in our Bill of Rights? It is not too late to agitate the question whether the enforcement of the provisions of that article would be an infringement of the liberty of conscience. The question is settled both by the legislative and judicial tribunals — and it is settled by a still higher tribunal, by the people themselves. No legislature can enforce its provisions and obey its requirements.

28. *Ibid.,* January 14, 1832, p. 2. Also *Independent Chronicle,* January 7, 1832, p. 2.

29. *Pittsfield Sun,* December 29, 1831, p. 2. Even when the amendment finally passed both houses of the legislature and was submitted to the people for ratification, the *Sun* would do no more than mention the fact in two lines without editorial comment.

There is perhaps no subject on which a free and enlightened people are more jealous of the interference of the government than that of religion . . . Our legislation for a long period has been fruitful in devices by which we the people may evade an obligation expressly but unwisely enjoined. Is it not better that the article be wholly expunged rather than that our statute book should exhibit such glaring inconsistencies between the provisions of the law and the duties enjoined by the constitution? It will scarcely be contended by any one at the present day that there will be less of vital piety or genuine religion and of practical morality where they derive their support from voluntary association and free contribution than from constitutional provisions and legal enactments.[30]

In short, Lothrop and the Anti-Masons represented those Trinitarians who were most disgruntled with the Standing Order; the Anti-Masonic movement was for them a convenient position between the anti-disestablishmentarian Whigs and the anticlerical Jacksonians.

The Boston *Christian Herald* was the journal of the Anti-Masons in Boston. Its pages gave support to the disestablishment movement from November 1831 when the Committee of the American Sunday School Union offered a prize of one hundred dollars for the best essay on the necessity and importance of the separation of church and state. The Anti-Mason's party platform itself did not mention this issue, but the *Christian Herald* gave full coverage to Lyman Beecher's Evening Lectures in January and February of 1831 in which he made clear his own opposition to Article Three. And in February 1832, the editor wrote that Article Three "will undoubtedly be altered. The Amendment or destruction of the article leaves every man to pay when or where he pleases or not at all, which we prefer to the law as it now is, which is easily evaded and is made the subject of continual complaint and discord." [31]

It was apparent, however, that the Anti-Masons, composed as they were primarily of devoutly evangelical — if not fanatical — Congregational-Trinitarians, had reached this position reluctantly and not from any commitment to the Baptist principles of separation. To them it was an unfortunate necessity under the existing circumstances, not the realization of a desirable status for the church. An editorial in the *Christian Herald* on March 7, 1832 pointed out that the system of religious taxation began when New England had only one denomination and at that time "it was doubtless both just and expedient. It contributed to the general welfare. It was the only certain method of establishing the morals of the community on a good foundation." However, in recent years many new denominations had arisen and so had infidelity. Complaints against the old system arose chiefly from "those who were opposed to religion in any shape." But since God would preserve

30. *Universalist Trumpet*, October 29, 1831, p. 70.
31. Boston *Christian Herald*, November 23, 1831, p. 146; February 2, 1831, p. 19; March 9, 1831, p. 2; February 1, 1832, p. 13.

his church against "the gates of hell," it would be less harmful to true religion than to false religion to end religious taxes, for under a voluntary system "these false systems will of course go to decay and fail." Infidels would give nothing to support their views and Unitarianism and Universalism would survive only while they were able to divert some of the taxes to themselves. (They probably referred here to the kind of Universalism which Charles Chauncy had initiated among the Congregational churches.) The editor therefore approved of the amendment to abolish Article Three "though we cannot approve of the motives and spirit by which a part of its advocates appear to have been actuated — an opposition to religion itself." True, "The proposed change may increase the burden of supporting public worship — but if we mistake not, it will do much to establish in the societies [congregations] of real christians, peace, harmony, brotherly love, and spirituality." [32]

In this respect the views of the Anti-Masons differed little from those of the Trinitarians who remained within the National Republican Party. The two journals which spoke most loudly for this group were the Boston *Recorder* (edited weekly by Asa Rand from 1828 to 1830 and by Calvin Stowe in 1830–31) and *The Spirit of the Pilgrims* (edited monthly by Lyman Beecher). From its first issue in January 1828, the *Spirit of the Pilgrims* was dedicated to promoting the cause of "Orthodoxy" against Unitarian infidelity. It was filled with attacks on the court decisions of Unitarian judges, on the Unitarian trustees and corporation of Harvard, and on the Unitarian-dominated politicians who refused incorporation to Trinitarian parishes and institutions of learning. Since it consistently defended Parson Cooke's views, this journal may be said to have favored disestablishment from its beginning.[33] But not until December 1831 did it devote an article specifically to this question.

This essay, entitled "Third Article in the Declaration of Rights" is unsigned. It may well have been written by Beecher himself, though it sounds more like Stowe or Cooke. Although it did not adopt the position that separation was good or essential in and of itself, it nevertheless utilized every one of the Baptist arguments in favor of abolishing Article Three and even quoted Baptist authors like Isaac Backus to justify these arguments. For example, the anonymous writer stated flatly what the Congre-

32. *Ibid.,* March 7, 1832, p. 3. To what extent the Baptists were anti-masonic is not clear. That many of them shared the distrust of freemasonry (a distrust which, for them, began in the 1780's) is obvious. The *Christian Herald* reported on February 2, 1831, that the Baptist church in Reading had voted to exclude masons from membership. But the *Christian Watchman* contains very little about anti-masonry, and the movement seems to have had an aura of fanaticism about it which made the more respectable Baptists and Trinitarians shy away. It also had the serious possibility of splitting these denominations and thereby weakening them before their common enemies (Unitarians and Universalists).

33. For a typical defense of Cooke by Beecher's journal see *Spirit of the Pilgrims,* III (1830), 25–35, 641–650.

gationalists had denied for two centuries — that the ecclesiastical system of tax support for public worship as it was imbedded in Article Three "goes to create a legal, religious establishment." [34] However, it was not the Congregational denomination which was established: "It established the Protestant religion by law as the religion of the state." And the reason this was wrong, as the Baptists had said, was "it is altogether unscriptural. Where did Christ or his Apostles ever intimate that they wished their religion to be incorporated with the state and to be supported by civil enactments? . . . a legal establishment of the Christian religion . . . tends invariably to secularize and corrupt it . . . we have it on the authority of Christ himself, that his kingdom is not of this world." This had been the standard Baptist argument for generations. Moreover, the writer granted also what no Congregationalist had before been willing to admit to dissenters, "The spirit of this article and of the laws which have grown out of it is repugnant in many ways to the right of conscience." [35] Unlike the Baptists, however, the writer professed to be upset primarily because the establishment of the Protestant religion denied religious freedom both to the thousands of Roman Catholics now in the state and to those who belonged to no Christian society: "Shall we compel them to support and to frequent our worship, contrary to what they declare are the dictates of their consciences?"

The author of this article quoted Backus in defense of those who felt that "the act of giving and obtaining a certificate" was in itself an infringement of conscience because it constituted "a virtual acquiescence in the propriety of the tax." [36] He also quoted Elder Thomas Baldwin and Joseph B. Varnum concerning the difficulties dissenters often had in recovering their taxes when they did pay them. Despite the laws of 1811 and of 1824, "There is still the legal tax which every citizen must pay unless he makes what has been termed 'the certificate bow' or contrives some other way to evade it."

> I know it will be said that these scruples about a legal tax, and about certificates are needless and childish; and perhaps they may be so. But that they exist in the minds of many of our citizens and of some of our most worthy citizens, there can be no doubt; and the question is whether a provision shall be retained in our Constitution and incorporated with our laws which goes (to make the best of it) *needlessly* to violate them; or whether it shall be set aside.

Like the Baptists, the writer pointed out that Article Three was inconsistent

34. *Ibid.*, IV (1831), 630. Since this article is listed under "Communications" it is even possible that it was submitted to the editor by some Baptist. But if so, Beecher made no editorial comment to disavow any aspect of its argument. The article was later printed as an anonymous tract.
35. *Ibid.*, p. 631.
36. *Ibid.*, p. 632.

with itself, that it was "unequal in its operation" (because towns like Boston, Newburyport, and Salem had no religious taxes), that "the example of her sister states" proved that religion could be supported just as well by a voluntary system. He also quoted George Washington, James Madison, and John Locke on behalf of separation.[37] And finally he pointed out that the system was "a source of perpetual strife and litigation" which did not conduce to the peace and welfare of the community. He concluded, "The third article ought to be essentially modified or abolished because it is already to a great extent abandoned in practice and cannot longer be enforced." Moreover, "religion can be better supported and lend a more efficient aid to government without laws than with them." The article was, taken in all, as forceful a statement for separation as any which the Baptists had ever made, and it indicated the high level of agreement which the two groups had reached.

The *Boston Recorder,* which began publication in 1816 (and more or less defended the system in 1820), first began to call for the abolition of Article Three in April 1831, when it reprinted a series of articles on "Religious Laws" which had appeared in the *Essex Gazette* in January. The writer of these letters signed himself "C," and the first was dated from West Haverhill, December 25, 1830. His position was quite similar to Samuel Lothrop's:

> I have in view that old patched and superannuated system of religious laws in this State which in theory professes to provide for the support of piety, religion and morality, but which in practice is imposing a most deadly weight on all the free and healthful operations of religious society. It claims to be the legitimate offspring of our excellent Constitution, but it bears every mark of a degenerate plant. It has undergone an almost infinite number of changes and it appears to have been waxing worse and worse at every step. It has outlived all similar institutions in other States and is quite behind the spirit of the age; but it is still in vigorous though crazy operation in this Commonwealth. I regard it as no longer needed; nay, as a heavy burden on the Christian Community . . . we look upon it as presenting a most singular compound of despotism and toleration.[38]

The writer claimed that although Article Three was clear and distinct in itself, the laws and legal decisions based on it since 1780 had rendered its meaning "vague and indefinite," "strained and awkward." As a result of the laws of 1811 and 1824 and the Dedham Case, it was impossible any longer to answer the question "What is a parish?" The law of 1824 completely confused the state's assessors about the meaning of the term "the oldest religious society" in a town. Some took it literally to mean

37. Others he quoted were the Baptist historian David Benedict, Isaac Watts, Bouge, and Bennett's *History of the Dissenters.*
38. Boston *Recorder,* April 27, 1831, p. 66.

the first parish set up in a town (assuming a town had more than one parish). "But others and by far the greater part . . . suppose that the 'oldest society' in any town means each and every parish in that town." That is, as parish assessors, they assessed religious taxes on persons who failed to sign off the parish in which they lived not to the oldest parish in the town but to the oldest parish in which they lived.

Furthermore, the law said that qualified voters in town meetings could vote in parish meetings. Where did this place the general qualification that six months residence in a town was needed before a man could be a legal voter? Did that apply to his right to vote in town meetings but not in parish meetings? And how could a man establish six months' residence if he attended a church in a parish in another town (having signed off his own parish because he did not like the minister there)? "It has literally come to pass that men are unblushingly seen as parish polls and are actually received as legal parish voters in one county whose right to vote in town affairs depends upon their residence in another county." Nor did the law explain how a parish could keep voters known to be of another denomination from voting in parish affairs to frustrate the will of the bona fide members of that parish. And precisely by what means did a religious society or parish get the religious taxes of its members back from another parish or society in a different town or county?

The worst of all confusions in the religious laws, said "C," resulted from the court's decision "that it is lawful for a man to continue his actual residence in one part of the State and still be a parish voter in any other part of it. Thus a man, for instance, who lives in the county of Barnstable may poll off to the west and become a legal parish voter in Berkshire County." This wreaked havoc with the settled ministers and the levying of parish taxes. "It puts the whole control of all parish affairs in the State directly into the hands of the avowed enemies of all divine institutions." This "is doubtless a gross perversion of the true intent and meaning of the law" which intended only that a man might sign off to a church or parish contiguous to his residence or to a poll parish within the same parish of his residence. Now the religious infidels "come up from the east and their flight is towards the west" wrecking parishes as they go. And "the power of admitting new members is vested solely in the clerk." Because of the court's decision "these shameless invaders" cannot be expelled once they get in. "Consequently the entire concerns of the parish must now be controlled year after year by the influence and suffrages of a host of non-residents." [39] In the seventh of these letters, published in the *Boston Recorder* on June 15, 1831, the writer stated that the solution to the problem lay with the voters: "In the future exercise of their elective

39. *Ibid.*, May 11, 1831, p. 1; June 8, 1831, p. 1. The writer was concerned here primarily with Unitarians and Trinitarians, not with Baptists, Methodists, or other dissenters.

franchise they will therefore keep an eye on the present religious policy of the State and aim to effect as soon as possible an entire abolition of the taxation system." We need "an entire demolition of our present fabric of religious laws."

Compared to these forthright statements by the Trinitarians, the Baptists at this time were strangely inarticulate. The *Christian Watchman,* their chief public organ, was very slow to recognize that the long battle was reaching its final climax. Even John Leland, who talked about separation in 1830 in a Fourth of July oration in his hometown of Cheshire, did so in general terms, making no mention of any new movement on foot and offering no arguments that he had not advanced forty years earlier.[40]

In June 1831 the *Christian Watchman* printed Whittemore's resolution and noted under the heading of legislative business that the House had passed it. But it was not until December 23 of that year, that any editorial comment appeared on the issue. Not even the election that fall had caused the journal to notice the situation. The editorial on December 23 stated that the alteration of Article Three was an item which would come before the legislature in January and "It is a very important subject; for no part of our State Constitution has occasioned so much litigation as this or been the cause of such oppression for the last 50 years." The editor preferred complete abolition of the article rather than the alteration offered by Whittemore's committee:

> For ourselves, we should prefer that no substitute should be offered but that the "third article" the bone of contention, should be entirely repealed and obliterated from our Constitution. Our idea is that the concerns of religion be left to every man's conscience and that the attempts of civil governments to regulate its administration only tend to pollute it . . . This is the philosophy of our Federal Constitution and this, in our opinion, is right and proper.

Having finally awakened to the issue just as it was about to be settled, the *Christian Watchman* became one of the most ardent voices of opposition to Article Three. Two weeks after this editorial another declared that "the operation of this third article has been such as to oblige a minor denomination of Christians in a country town or parish besides supporting their own Minister to pay also towards the support of the Minister of the ruling or most numerous sect." [41] And in the two years that followed, as the amendment worked its way through the legislature, the *Watchman* continued to stress that "it is time that the relics of an odious establishment of religion which the people will not submit to, were totally destroyed." [42]

40. John Leland, *The Writings of Elder John Leland,* ed. L. F. Greene (New York, 1845), pp. 578 ff.
41. *Christian Watchman,* January 6, 1832, p. 2.
42. *Ibid.,* January 18, 1833, pp. 9–10.

The editors were particularly quick to pick up and answer every argument offered by opponents of the amendment, regarding as "mere sophistry" the claim that "sufficient liberty . . . is now given" to all under the terms of the law of 1811. That law, said the *Watchman,* not only "contravenes and is inconsistent with this third article" but it might be repealed at any time." [43]

Generally the arguments the *Watchman* used for disestablishment were the same ones the denomination had used since 1780. But there were two points about the Baptist position on separation of church and state at this time which need emphasizing. First, the Baptists seldom, if ever, mentioned disestablishment as essential to provide religious liberty for Roman Catholics, Jews, deists, atheists, and Nothingarians. They spoke almost entirely in terms of their own consciences, their own persecutions, and the freedom commanded by Christ for the best promotion of his Church — the evangelical Church. "The yoke must be broken for it is one which neither we nor our fathers have been able to bear." [44] The yoke was to be broken, it seemed, to give the Baptists the freedom to achieve their manifest destiny and not for any abstract concept of religious liberty to all men.

The other significant point in the Baptists' argument at this time was their abandonment of prooftext Scripture for the hard facts of historical evidence (with particular reference to Backus's *History*) and the heavy (though not new) reliance on James Madison's *Remonstrance* of 1785.[45] The parts of the *Remonstrance* which were most congenial were naturally those in which Madison specifically pointed out the shortcomings of a system of religious taxation.

> Who does not see that the same authority which can establish Christianity in exclusion of all other religions may establish, with the same ease, any particular sect of Christians in exclusion of all other sects? that the same authority which can force a citizen to contribute threepence only of his property for the support of any one establishment may force him to conform to any other establishment in all cases whatsoever.

Of course the Baptists did not share Madison's rationalist outlook, nor did they share his belief that America was and should remain a secular rather than a Christian nation. But as always, they made use of those arguments which seemed best suited to meet their particular needs at the moment. Here, at least, the two disparate strands of separationist thought in America, the rationalist and the pietist, came together. The essential antinomy of the two viewpoints was conveniently blurred in the interest of

43. *Ibid.,* January 13, 1832, p. 6.
44. *Ibid.,* January 6, 1832, p. 2.
45. For quotations from the *Remonstrance* see *ibid.,* January 2, 1832, p. 2; January 13, 1832, p. 6; January 20, 1832, p. 9.

a general consensus on the doctrine of separation for the secular well-being of the nation and the spiritual freedom of the Truth.

Perhaps more significant than this use of Madison's *Remonstrance* was the rise in Roger Williams' status as martyr and prophet of the Baptist cause. Ever since his rediscovery by Isaac Backus in 1770, the Baptists had found Williams an intriguing figure. But with the denomination's rise to national importance after 1800, Williams suddenly assumed added significance — he became the Baptists' Bradford, Winthrop, Jefferson, and Washington — all rolled into one: the founder of the Baptist denomination in America and the greatest expositor of religious liberty in Western Christendom. Not an unmerited estimate, perhaps, but the Baptists were late in their acknowledgment with perhaps too proprietorial a claim on a man whose commitment to their denomination had lasted a scant six months in a long life.[46]

The key to the Baptist viewpoint in the 1820's was the implicit faith that disestablishment was the best, the only, way to obtain a Christian society. And the proof that this was so, as the Baptists never tired of pointing out, lay in the great outpourings of divine grace that were sweeping over the rest of America: "Remarkable Revivals of true religion which have occurred in the South are evidence direct [from Heaven] that liberty of conscience is promotive of genuine liberty." [47] Disestablishment did not really mean liberty for every man to think as he pleased, but Christian liberty for the nation to follow God's will. In other words, unless it abolished Article Three, Massachusetts would continue to be plagued by Satanic influences, by Unitarianism, Universalism, deism and other forms of infidelity which thrived on the polluted and antichristian system of religious taxation and favoritism. Consequently it was a mystery (to which the Baptists offered no answer) that the most sustained and vigorous political effort for disestablishment between 1830 and 1833 was not by purveyors of evangelical truth but by the Universalists.

46. For a good example of the Baptists eulogies of Williams at this time see "Tribute to Roger Williams," *Christian Watchman,* October 17, 1828, p. 166, which was frankly directed against the efforts of the Trinitarians to eulogize the Pilgrim fathers and the Unitarians to eulogize the Puritan forefathers. Unfortunately for Isaac Backus, whose commitment to the Baptist cause was far greater than Williams' was, he was still too recent and too well remembered to be a useful mythological hero.

47. *Ibid.,* September 21, 1832, p. 150.

Chapter 62

The Universalists and the Eleventh Amendment
to the Massachusetts Constitution,
1830–1833

The Orthodox, the Baptists, the Episcopalians, the Methodists, and the Universalists are all desirous of leaving religion to stand on its own foundation without the aid of law and, using general terms, the Unitarians are the only party in favor of *compelling people by law to support religion*.

Universalist Trumpet, July 2, 1831

The irony of the pietistic Baptists'-Congregationalists' quoting Madison's rationalist *Remonstrance* in 1832 was matched by that of the Trinitarians' public recognition that the Universalists were among the most dedicated of those attacking the corrupt Unitarian establishment. And this in turn was matched by the irony of the Universalist liberals attacking the Unitarian liberals for being untrue to liberalism.

The Trinitarians considered the Universalists enemies, not friends or allies, and although they welcomed the Universalists' help against the perverted old system, the Trinitarians denied that the Universalists had anything constructive to replace it. The evangelicals — Trinitarian, Baptist, and Methodist — comforted themselves as they watched the Universalists demolish the dam of the establishment which held back the floodtides of evangelical truth because they knew that the Universalists were digging their own graves. Disestablishment would be the undoing of infidelity in all its forms.

The Universalists, on the other hand, saw themselves as fighting for the freedom of thought, speech, and conscience against the remnants of a feudal and tyrannical priestcraft. Associating themselves in spirit with the liberal religion of the Unitarians, they were highly embarrassed, and said so, that their fellow liberals were so misguided as to defend the old system. They could not understand how men so enlightened in fighting Calvinism could be so unenlightened as to defend the institutions which Calvinism had built to enhance itself. If the Puritans's religious premises were false, so were their religious institutions.

The Universalists also saw themselves as allies of the Unitarians in opposing the fanatical bigotry and lust for power of the evangelicals. They fully believed that the evangelicals were trying to use their revivals and their benevolent societies to forge a Christian Party in politics which would ultimately demand a uniformity and conformity of belief and practice equal to the tyranny of the Inquisition and of the Puritan persecutions of the seventeenth century.[1] The Universalists tended to be Jacksonian democrats and to dislike the aristocratic snobbery and political conservatism of the Unitarians.[2] And their journals gave grudging credit to the Trinitarians after 1829 for finally seeing the light on this issue at least.[3] But from 1830 to 1833 the Universalists seemed to stand virtually alone among denominations in defending human reason and goodness against bigotry and persecution. Their chief allies were anticlerical Jacksonians, Nothingarians and deists.

Thomas Whittemore of West Cambridge was the leading figure in the Universalist camp in these years. Whittemore led the fight for disestablishment in three areas. He led it as a Universalist minister who coordinated the ranks of his own denomination. He led it as editor of the *Universalist Trumpet* (or *Trumpet and Universalist Magazine*) with his vigorous editorials and publicity for the campaign. He led it as a politician, organizing petition campaigns and then, through his role in the House of Representatives, speaking on the floor of the legislature and acting as chairman of the special committee to reconsider Article Three. His role in this battle has not yet been properly appreciated by historians.

Whittemore was born in 1800 on Copps Hill in Boston. He attended the common schools in Charlestown. His father died when he was fourteen, and the boy was apprenticed to a bootmaker. His parents had been Congregationalists but as an apprentice he sang in the choir of the Universalist church led by Elder Edward Turner in Charlestown and came to admire his doctrines. He did not join the church at once, however, and after learning to play the bass viol he took his talents to the First Baptist Church in Boston where he stayed for two years. Then he met Hosea Ballou and through Ballou he joined the Universalists and became an editor with Ballou of the *Universalist Magazine*. In 1821 he became a minister and

1. For articles on this see *Universalist Trumpet,* July 25, 1828, p. 1; July 19, 1828, p. 12; November 29, 1828, p. 86; February 6, 1830, p. 126; June 5, 1830, p. 193; and June 26, 1830, p. 26.
2. For defenses of Jackson see *ibid.,* May 1, 1830, p. 174 and July 10, 1830, p. 6. For a typical attack on "high toned" Unitarians like Governor Levi Lincoln see April 2, 1831, p. 158.
3. *Ibid.,* December 10, 1831, p. 94.

preached his first sermon in Roxbury. He was then pastor of the Universalist church in Milford for a year before he moved to Cambridgeport where he remained as pastor from 1823 to 1831. Meanwhile he kept writing for the *Universalist Magazine* and, in 1825, engaged in a prolonged and celebrated debate with the Methodist preacher, Orange Scott, in which he attacked both the autocratic episcopacy of Methodism and its fanatical conception of "experimental religion." [4]

In 1828 Whittemore joined with Russell Streeter to establish the *Universalist Trumpet* in Boston, the first weekly journal of the sect and a proof of the denomination's coming of age. He had to mortgage his house to raise the funds for the enterprise but eventually the paper and other publishing ventures became very profitable. He bought out Streeter in 1829; by the 1840's he was a wealthy man, President of the Cambridge Bank and of the Vermont and Massachusetts Railroad. He published a history of Universalism, but he resigned his pastorate in 1831 to devote his full time to publishing and banking. That year he was elected to the legislature from West Cambridge and was reelected for several years thereafter.

Whittemore was assisted by a group of able Universalist leaders, most of them ministers of the denomination at one time or another. These included Hosea Ballou, Russell and Sebastian Streeter, Ezra Leonard, Paul Dean, Joshua Emmons, Robert Killam, Edward Turner, Charles Hudson (who served the town of Westminster in the state legislature from 1828 to 1831), Dr. John Brooks, Sylvanus Cobb, Amasa Nichols, Abner Kneeland, and Richard Carrique.[5] The Universalists were not numerous in these years (in 1820 they had only twenty-one congregations in Massachusetts which was fewer than the Methodists, Quakers, and Episcopalians, to say nothing of Baptists, Trinitarians and Unitarians). Nor were they wealthy or influential. As anti-Calvinists they were competing with the Methodists and Freewill Baptists at one end of the social scale and with the Unitarians at the other. Theologically they fell between outright deism and a very loose Arminianism. Their tendencies were toward a humanitarian rationalism, and they attracted persons of independence and spirit. In several towns the Universalists were able, with the help of other opponents of the establishment, to take control of parishes and meetinghouses. In the late 1820's this occurred in the towns of Malden, Acton, Saugus and Reading, and perhaps elsewhere.[6] Generally Jacksonians in politics, the Universalists thought of themselves as the rational voice of the common man engaged

4. John G. Adams, *Memoir of Thomas Whittemore, D. D.* (Boston, 1878), and Thomas Whittemore, *The Early Days of Thomas Whittemore* (Boston, 1859).
5. For biographical details of these Universalist leaders, see Richard Eddy, *Universalism in America* (Boston, 1886), II. For some unaccountable reason Eddy does not mention the final passage of the Eleventh Amendment and the part these men played in it.
6. For accounts of the parish quarrels in these towns see the *Universalist Trumpet,* April 2, 1831, p. 158; May 5, 1832, pp. 177, 178; May 12, 1832, p. 182.

in destroying the last remnants of religious superstition and ushering in the golden era of enlightened humanitarianism.[7]

The relationship between the Universalists and the Baptists, as it was reflected in Whittemore's editorials and the articles in the *Trumpet,* was no more cordial than the relationship between the Universalists and the Trinitarians — although the Trinitarians generally came in for heavier blows as the more powerful and dangerous foes. The Baptists were considered the Trinitarians's potential allies or partners and were denounced for their adherence to the superstitions of Calvinism, their revival enthusiasm, and their evangelical philanthropies. Whatever virtue the Baptists had had in former times when they fought pietistically for religious liberty against Puritan intolerance was now gone: "We had hoped that they would longer have kept themselves clear from the evil there is in the world," said Whittemore in an article entitled "Money! Baptists Begging Money!" The Baptists, he said, "separated from the sects at first to distinguish themselves by a purer practice" and suffered persecution for their faith. "But pride and love of power and wealth soon allured them, and they have now entered the ranks of that enemy whom they once so valiantly opposed." Like the Papists, they used the fear of hellfire and damnation to frighten people into giving money to support their priestly activities. "The Baptists who have so long pleaded for the closest adhesion to the principles and practices of the early Christians have now embraced the money-begging system and joined the sects who take the lead in it . . . God save us from the approaching evil." [8]

Because the Universalists received so many of their converts from the Baptists and were so often entangled with them in local disputes over "sheep stealing," the rivalry between them was intense and bitter. In a series of articles entitled "The Orthodox [Trinitarians] and the Baptists," which began in January 1830, the *Universalist Trumpet* declared that there was little to choose between the two groups any more. They had joined forces to engineer a national religion from their fear of the rapid spread of Universalist and Unitarian liberalism and the only hope for liberal Christians was to unite against them and to hope that in their selfish rivalry for power and the spoils of revival meeting conversions, the evangelicals would quarrel so much among themselves that they would ruin their own unity. With great glee the journal printed the words of John Leland supporting the Sunday mails and praising Col. Richard Johnson's report: "and will our Baptist brethren give heed to his faithful admonition?" [9] They recognized a good Jacksonian anticlerical when they saw one.

7. The Universalists were not generally favorable to Frances Wright's and Robert Owen's views, though Abner Kneeland defended them. See *ibid.,* January 8, 1831, p. 10, and March 5, 1831, p. 141.

8. *Universalist Trumpet,* July 12, 1828, p. 6.

9. *Ibid.,* February 6, 1830, p. 126; December 18, 1830, p. 99.

Whittemore printed a letter signed "Observer" on December 4, 1830 severely critical of the Baptists: though "formerly persecuted and despised" they have now "become one of the most numerous sects in Massachusetts and perhaps in the New England states." And because they were Calvinists they "have at length arrived at the distinguished honor of being admitted as auxiliaries in the holy war which their former persecutors, the Orthodox [Trinitarians] are carrying on against Unitarians and Universalists." The Baptists "appear to be zealously aspiring after further and higher degrees of respectability and have recently established an expensive Theological Seminary for the undoubted, if not avowed, purpose of manufacturing adroit and honorable priest-riders." This Universalist was convinced that "had they sufficient power it can hardly be doubted but their Calvinistic principles would goad them on to persecute." He quoted a Baptist deacon in Boston who "lately said that he thought all religious sects ought to be tolerated excepting the Universalists. Them he thought insufferable!"

But the Universalists themselves were becoming numerous and respectable by 1830. In 1820 there had been only twenty Universalist churches in Massachusetts; by 1830 there were between seventy and eighty.[10] The *Trumpet* revealed in 1831 that the denomination had its own ambitions for respectability. One of their ministers was supposed to be chosen to give the annual election sermon that year. But unfortunately the legislators could not agree on which Universalist to honor. The votes were split between Paul Dean of Boston (a Restorationist) and the Rev. Linus E. Everett of Charlestown. Between them they received a majority of 172 and only 171 votes were needed to win. But because of the division, the legislature postponed the decision.[11] Perhaps in chagrin the *Trumpet* urged that the whole ritual of election sermons should be abandoned as a needless expense.

The Universalists had good reason to oppose the established system. From the origin of their denomination in New England they had been subject to taxation by the Standing Order, to discrimination in the courts, to social prejudice and bigotry by the established clergy. The Murray case in 1786 established their right to be considered a separate sect and gave their ministers the right to recover the taxes of their members, but they were subject to the same difficulties as the Baptists regarding certificates and the recovery of taxes by court action. Disestablishment, therefore, was a part of their creed from the beginning. However, not until April 1831 did they take an active role as a denomination in the matter.

Whittemore had a seat in the legislature. The denomination had a well-edited popular organ. The moment seemed propitious for a final thrust against the Standing Order. On April 2, 1831 the *Trumpet* printed and

10. Thomas Whittemore, *Modern History of Universalism* (Boston, 1830) p. 401.
11. *Universalist Trumpet,* June 18, 1831, p. 202.

praised Samuel Lothrop's (Lathrop's) farewell address as President of the Massachusetts Senate which urged the abolition of Article Three. "The voice of the people cries aloud for the suppression of the third article of the Bill of Rights," said Whittemore. "Universalists, Baptists, Methodists and most of the minor sects are against it — many of the orthodox, and the Unitarians almost entirely, are in favor of it." "Massachusetts stands almost if not quite alone in the United States in compelling her citizens to support religion." A month later the *Trumpet* began a series of articles, "Legal Support of Religion," which gave close attention to the progress of the new petition campaign to amend the state constitution to abolish compulsory religious taxes.

Some of the grounds on which the Universalists supported disestablishment were no different from the Baptists's. The Baptists and Trinitarians considered the Universalists infidels but the Universalists considered that they were the true Christians and that the Bible provided them with the doctrines of separation. As Elder Paul Dean said in the convention of 1820, "the kingdom of this religion [the Christian] was different from the kingdom of this world and ought not to be governed by the laws of this world. Civil governors do not know what belongs to the Christian religion and are therefore incapable of bestowing their rewards and imposing restraints in regard to it." Establishment had always led to persecution and hurt the church. Christ had ordained only a voluntary support for his ministers. And, Dean concluded, Article Three "made the teachers [of religion] too independent of those who were instructed. A mutual dependence was productive of mutual benefit." [12] Whittemore put the matter more bluntly in his columns: "By this article and the statutes founded upon it, we have in Massachusetts "a law religion and every man is obliged by law to pay to the support of some creed." And

> the history of this commonwealth for fifty years has proved that the third article and the statutes founded upon it have been a source of ill feeling, contention and litigation . . . The obnoxious third article of the Bill of Rights was a sacrifice which the framers of the constitution in 1780 made to the clerical part of that body who were fearful that their support might be endangered if people were not compelled to belong to some parish and pay taxes thereto. It was through *their* influence that the third article was obtained and the second, which every man knows is contrary in its operation to the third was inserted to keep the parishes and the clergy from oppressing the minor denominations.[13]

12. *Journal of Debates, and Proceedings of the Convention of Delegates Chosen to Revise the Constitution of Massachusetts* (Boston, 1853), pp. 383, 384.

13. *Universalist Trumpet*, October 29, 1831, p. 70. The Universalists were also willing to defend the right of Nothingarians to be free of religious taxes: "If a man cannot conscientiously join any body of men in worshipping God, let him have the

These, however, were the external or social arguments against the Standing Order. There was also a philosophical basis for their opposition to an establishment which differed from the Baptists's. This received its most clearcut statement in the pages of the *Universalist Magazine* in 1832. In an unsigned article entitled "Church and State" (perhaps written by the editor, Sebastian Streeter) not only was the conventional argument used that "Our Saviour . . . declared that his kingdom was not of this world . . . the reign of the Messiah is purely spiritual," but true to their anti-Calvinist and anti-evangelical reliance on reason rather than "experimental religion," the Universalists offered the following reason against an establishment:

> Religion is an inward principle. It exists in the human heart or it exists nowhere . . . The human mind is conscious of its own independence . . . It is useless to legislate upon it or upon its affairs . . . There is one and only one way in which the human mind can be influenced in respect to its opinions and that is by bringing argument and fact to bear upon it . . . religion has only to be left to itself to work its way to the hearts, conscience, and affections of mankind.[14]

The Universalists thus shared the common view that religious truth would prevail best in a free environment, but they relied on "bringing argument and fact to bear" on men, rather than on the irresistible grace of God through the Holy Ghost. Human reason and moral conscience, not the religious affections or emotions were the source of regeneration. Thus religion was to be advanced not by revivals, missions, and hellfire preaching but by freeing the human mind and heart from superstition and fear, by making reason supreme over the emotions, by letting the inner goodness and reasonableness of man prevail.

As Whittemore put it, "Religion to do any man good must operate in his heart . . . but this a mere artificial support can never do." Religion, like eating or marriage, was doing what comes naturally: "It is for the benefit of society that persons should enter into the marriage relation; but we make no laws to compel them." There is an "irresistible force — far above the power of formal statutes" which make men religious and benevolent; "laws of the human mind and conscience will regulate religion with as much certainty" as any man-made laws. "Religion is the aliment of the soul — the bread and water of life — we cannot live without it. The matter is made certain by the laws of the human constitution. . . . People will support public worship liberally when religion is left to their consciences." [15] In short, the Universalists, like the Jacksonian anticlericals, were optimistic

---

privilege of remaining in his own dwelling and never be compelled to support any minister or church on earth." *Ibid.*, December 10, 1831. This was signed "C. S."

14. *Universalist Magazine*, I (May 19, 1832), 5–6.
15. *Universalist Trumpet*, March 3, 1832, p. 142.

about the inherent goodness and reasonableness of man and were thus willing to release him from all institutional restraints, all hellfire and damnation preaching, all compulsion of any kind whatsoever.

The fight for the adoption of the Eleventh Amendment to the Massachusetts constitution was therefore a confederated and not a coordinated one. Its supporters fought with different weapons, from different motives, from different principles, and for different ends. And while the petitions against Article Three were signed by men of all sects and of no sect, there was no unity beyond the immediate abolition of compulsory religious taxes. As Whittemore wrote in October 1831, "This, we are happy to say, is a subject which can be discussed without reference to party and without calling forth any party feeling. Good men, sincere and pious christians of all denominations, Orthodox, Baptists, Methodists, Universalists, all unite in the desire to have this offensive article stricken from the constitution." [16] Yet so strongly entrenched were the defenders of the system that though they constituted a very small fraction of the population (roughly one person in ten if the ratifying vote was representative), they were able to stave off the final success of the movement until all of their opponents united against it.

The Unitarians were, for all practical purposes, the principal defenders of the establishment in this last phase, though a number of moderate Trinitarian-Congregationalists (the kind who found Lyman Beecher and Jedidiah Morse offensively vulgar, demagogic, and aggressive) sided with them just as a few liberal Unitarians sided with the dissenters. What made the minority hard to beat in the first instance was, as the dissenters pointed out, their dominant influence in the executive, senatorial, and judicial branches of the government. But they owed this position not only to wealth and ambition but to a long tradition of leadership, to well-earned prestige, and to widespread respect for their superior education and talent. That the average man continued to respect the old aristocracy as his betters long after he ceased to believe in the doctrine of the elect or the virtues of a corporate, class-structured social system was a measure of New England conservatism.

The religious journals which spoke for the Unitarians at this time were the *Christian Examiner,* the *Christian Register,* the *Christian Disciple*, and the *Christian Advocate.* The political journals which ostensibly spoke for

16. *Universalist Trumpet,* October 29, 1831, p. 70. One of the many anomalies of the moribund parish system which gave an added boost to the final drive for disestablishment was that even business firms owning property in a parish were subject to parish taxes. In 1821 the Amesbury Nail Factory failed to win a case for exemption from support of the East Parish church of Amesbury (17 Mass. Reports 54), and in 1831 the Goodell Woollen Manufacturing Company failed in a similar suit in Milbury (11 Pickering 515). Rising businessmen did not relish the thought of becoming the main source of tax support for the Congregational churches even though, by the court's interpretation, they benefited from the morality and good order which the established system provided to men of property. See Edward Buck, *Massachusetts Ecclesiastical Law* (Boston, 1865), pp. 27–28.

the National Republicans or Whigs as a whole but which in reality echoed the views of the Republican Unitarians who led the party, were the *Independent Chronicle* and the *Daily Advertiser*. The political journals virtually ignored the issue as they always had. Previously the *Independent Chronicle* had kept silent to avoid a split between the dissenting and Congregational wings of the Jeffersonian movement. In this period the paper was silent because it feared a party split between the Unitarians and the Evangelicals. Many of the more radical Trinitarians had already split off to join the Anti-Masonic Party and many more found it difficult to support a party which showed such favoritism to the Unitarians. On the same grounds many Baptists and Methodists supported the Jacksonians. Politically disestablishment remained a touchy issue to the end, even though there was overwhelming popular support for it among the most vocal groups and general apathy toward the issue among the large mass of the people.

The closest the *Independent Chronicle* came to taking an editorial position on the amendment was in an article on June 18, 1831:

> An article of amendment was passed in the House yesterday making a material alteration in the third article of the Bill of Rights, which goes to take from the Legislature the power to require the people to support religious worship and merely makes a declaration of the rights of the people to support religious worship at their own expense. This amendment will operate if finally adopted, so as to secure any person from a ministerial tax who does not choose to join some religious society and to incur the obligation voluntarily. This change in the Constitution has been long petitioned for from various quarters of the state and will probably be satisfactory to a majority of the people.

If not endorsing the movement, it seemed to acquiesce in it. But when the Senate, a few days later, postponed action on the amendment, the paper made no comment and by October it was vigorously defending the postponement as a wise move. The only subsequent comment by this paper was a letter signed "Spirit of Liberty" in January 1832, which defended Article Three:

> Let the constitution, an instrument that the people are ever accustomed to hold sacred, declare all exempt from obligation to support Public Worship, and will not multitudes boldly avail themselves of exemption as a sacred right because it is permitted by the constitution? The burthen of support of Public Worship will be increased on the poorer class until they become discouraged, and in a few years the Sabbath will be turned into a holiday for profane and demoralizing sport.[17]

After January 1832 the Whig newspapers contented themselves with printing selections from the debates in the legislature on the amendment. Even

17. *Independent Chronicle*, January 7, 1832, p. 2.

when the amendment was passed and ratified, they offered no editorial comment.

The Unitarian religious journals in these years were, however, filled with comments in outright defense of the system. And many of the leading Unitarian ministers published sermons and tracts on behalf of the Standing Order. Though the legislature found it increasingly difficult to follow its unwritten rule of electing alternately Unitarians and Trinitarians to give the election sermons, whenever a Unitarian was chosen he usually found some way in which to indicate that it was the duty of the legislature to maintain the system. Even William Ellery Channing's carefully phrased election sermon of 1830 was attacked by the Trinitarians and dissenters as a blatant defense of the old order.[18]

Probably the most thorough and forceful defense of the system by a Unitarian during the debate was a series of seven articles printed in the *Christian Register* in October and November, 1832. They were signed "A.B.M." and they tried to answer all of the objections raised by those who wanted to abolish Article Three. The author did not produce any arguments in its defense which had not been stated many times before, yet he revealed a great deal about the nature of Unitarian conservatism in the face of Jacksonian innovation. "Every innovation is accompanied with danger," the writer began. "Change is by no means always improvement. Yet there is a restlessness under republican institutions which not seldom prompts to alterations of law and government from a mere desire of exercising power." [19] He asked who was hurt by the present system since all who objected to religious taxes were allowed exemption: "Many conceive that the existing requirement infringes on the *conscience* of the Deist, the Jew, and all who deny the Christian religion by compelling [them] to aid in its defense." But

> no public institution in our land operates to the equal advantage and satisfaction of all the individuals it effects. Every man must help in the support of our free schools . . . And is the conscience of any more infringed (in our State) by the present statutes on religion, than by the law allowing prayers in public schools? or especially by the law that specifies the kind of books that parents must purchase for their children at school? If this matter is to be so closely sifted must we not seal our school-teachers' lips on everything religious while with his scholars?

This was some "close sifting" which the evangelicals were not yet prepared to undertake, and they may well have thought the Unitarian proponents of such arguments were grasping at straws and going to ridiculous lengths to defend the establishment. Yet within a few years Horace Mann was to raise

18. For an indication of the difficulties involved in choosing the ministers to give the election sermons in these years see *Christian Register*, June 18, 1831, p. 98.

19. *Christian Register*, October 6, 1832, p. 158.

just this issue — much to the dismay and anger of the Trinitarians and other evangelicals in Massachusetts.

In one sense, said this Unitarian, "The simple question is, are you a man who wishes to be 'happy'?" If so, you would recognize that there were only two choices open to the government: either the state could support religion and promote the general happiness of the people or it could cease to do so and become "an ally of the irreligious and unbelieving." Without tax support the churches would surely fail. The rich, on whom the burden of religious taxes fell most heavily, would certainly no longer give their full proportion: "We have in mind instances where one individual pays an 8th, a 6th, or even a 4th part of the whole ministerial tax on the parish he has joined." When this man is not compelled to pay and therefore does not, the remainder of the parish will not be able to make up for it even if they wished to increase their own contributions. And then what will happen to the poor and destitute for whom the consolations of religion are the most important? "Religion is of peculiar value to those destitute of this world's goods. It gives them comforts which no other source does," and the Sabbath "has well been called 'the poorman's day.' " But if the poor man is so foolish as to vote for this amendment, he may well lead himself into a week of seven days of labor and will certainly "lead himself and his family into a spiritual poverty" which will destroy "his chief solace" for his lot in life. Compulsory taxes, far from being a burden on the poor, were part of the *noblesse oblige* of the rich.

Protection of their property was the appeal offered by this defender of the establishment to those of the middling and wealthy class:

> Sometimes the most dangerous members of society must be kept in awe through the influence of worship toward which they give not a mill. We knew a man of wealth who, objecting to his ministerial tax said, 'Why should I pay more than my neighbors for preaching? I have only two ears.' True, this man did not hear any more on the sabbath than they did. But he had more houses and lands than they and this was protected by the moral and religious influences of the preaching they heard in common . . . If he was compelled to contribute to his clergyman's salary, he was not compelled to hire men to watch his house and grounds as he might have.[20]

The patronizing tone of this conservative defense of religion seemed to the Universalists just as offensive as the Trinitarians's moralistic self-righteousness. It was equally offensive to Jacksonian democrats and to republicans.

Because the Unitarian aristocrats looked on the clergy as brethren in the ruling elite they professed a brotherly concern for their welfare: "Their independence and faithfulness would be greatly tried by the new order of things." How could a minister admonish "the faults of the one, two, or three

20. *Ibid.,* October 27, 1832, p. 170.

leading men in his parish" who perhaps are rich enough to supply the bulk of his salary? "This constraint would render the office of a preacher so servile that not a few would flee from it." The clergy should be as independent and secure in their position of authority as the aristocrats with whom they shared power. The clergy under a voluntary system, if they were not under the thumbs of their rich deacons, might become as grasping after money as those whom they served or they might become even more poorly paid than they were at present. "Look at New Hampshire. The Baptists and Methodists were earnest for the like change in that State. They finally accomplished their end. Did they gain all they expected? The amendment operated, we have been credibly informed, directly against them. Their clergymen had previously received little. It then became respectable to pay less and the sum was uncertain as the wind." [21] And as for the Congregationalists, "It is a well known fact . . . that many clergymen were dismissed and many parishes destroyed" when New Hampshire abandoned its establishment.[22]

But the fundamental issue was the maintenance of a Christian society, which even most of the opponents of an establishment agreed was essential. The Unitarian who signed himself "A.B.M." emphasized that the evangelicals really had not thought through the logic of their premises. Not only did they still demand prayer in the public schools and the use of school textbooks chosen to suit the outlook of the majority in the school district (usually including the Westminster shorter catechism), but they demanded that the state uphold revealed laws of morality. "Have they forgotten that blasphemy, sabbath-breaking and profaneness are prohibited by our laws? . . . If there be a statute punishing the sabbath breaker, surely it is right there should be another enforcing the observance of that day and specifying in some general terms the manner in which it shall be observed? This the third article now does." But if that article were abolished, or that clause in it omitted, would the evangelicals be happy to have a state which did not enforce these moral laws? Was that what they meant by separation of church and state? [23]

When this Unitarian came to explain the cause for the movement to abolish Article Three, he naturally found it in a general revulsion against revivalistic religious and fanatical sectarianism, just as the evangelicals found the necessity for abolition in the rise of Unitarianism and latitudinarianism. The movement, he wrote,

> has originated in no slight degree, we believe, from a disgust at the religious contention of the day [caused by sectarian rivalry]. Not a few have been driven to scepticism, others to infidelity, by the measures re-

21. *Ibid.*
22. *Ibid.*, October 13, 1832, p. 162.
23. *Ibid.*, October 20, 1832, p. 166.

cently adopted in this Commonwealth and elsewhere under the name of 'revivals of religion.' It is thought by them that if Christianity is to go on dividing towns, neighborhoods, families and friends, as it has for the last two years, we had better utterly explode it [for] . . . an agent which produces such incalculable mischief is unworthy [of] our support.[24]

He went on to emphasize the kind of pressure which evangelicals exerted on their members to adhere and conform to a particular sect. "It is well known that in many of our towns no man will be patronized in his profession, trade, or business unless he worships with his employers." And

> We have known in an adjoining State [Connecticut] mothers and inmates [children, apprentices] continue their appearance at [a Trinitarian] church for a few weeks or months after the husband has 'signed off.' But sidelong smiles, the withering taunt, added to the comfortless feeling in their own consciences, compelled them at length to withdraw wholly from the house of God.[25]

This writer concluded unrealistically: "we believe that but a small proportion of the citizens of the Commonwealth truly and heartily desire the alteration" of the system.[26]

In contrast to this extravagant statement of the Unitarian position is a more responsible article in the *Christian Examiner* in January 1833. Although this writer was just as much opposed to abolishing Article Three, he omitted all of the fearsome predictions, snide inferences, and horrified hand wringing. The only new point he raised was that if religious taxation ceased, one of the alternatives would have to be pew rents, and in his opinion pew rents fell more heavily upon the poor than the rich. He noted that "In Boston, where worship is supported [in most churches] by a pew-tax, there are thousands of people who never enter a meeting-house . . . Because the ministers receive high salaries which are raised by assessing upon each pew-holder an annual tax . . . large enough to discourage persons of very limited income from purchasing or hiring pews." True there were "free or poor seats" for those who could not afford pews, but this produced invidious distinctions which neither the poor nor the lower income

24. *Ibid.*, October 27, 1832, p. 170.
25. *Ibid.*
26. *Ibid.*, November 18, 1832, p. 178. The writer contended that the oppressions under the prevailing ecclesiastical system "are the dust of the balance." At most all that needed to be changed was to alter the word "Christian" in Article Three "and give not only the Catholic but the jew and the Deist all they desire" — a concession which seemed designed more to provoke the evangelicals than to conciliate them, but which nevertheless marked a decided advance over the Unitarian attitude in 1820. If the amendment passed, "The sweet sounds of the church-going bell on the sabbath shall be gradually exchanged for voices of rioting and mirth . . . We stand . . . on the brow of a precipice."

middling class cared to accept. The only alternative to this system was that of voluntary subscription and here he agreed with the writer in the *Christian Register* that this would prove precarious and inadequate and result in a lowering of ministerial standards.[27] These were serious questions which the voluntarists had not adequately thought through. By the end of the nineteenth century evangelical leaders were voicing grave concern because the churches had lost touch with the poor and because the best young men were no longer interested in the ministry as a career.

I have found only one statement by a Massachusetts Unitarian at this time opposing the concept of public support for religion and the abolition of Article Three. There may have been others, undoubtedly there were, who believed that the system had outlived its usefulness, but they did not say so publicly. And it is perhaps significant that this attack was published in a Hartford, Connecticut, newspaper, the *Christian Secretary*. The author, Francis W. P. Greenwood, a graduate of Harvard (1814), had attended the Harvard Divinity School and served as pastor of the New South Church in Boston from 1818 to 1820. In 1827 he succeeded James Freeman as minister of King's Chapel in Boston. Freeman had considered this an Episcopal Church and it therefore stood somewhat outside the Standing Order; yet because of its Unitarianism, it had never been officially recognized by the Episcopalians after the Revolution. Greenwood delivered these views in an ordination sermon in Salem in 1832, and although the sermon as a whole is cautious and diplomatic in indicating the failings of an established system, some of its statements were as forthright as anything the dissenters were saying. The title was "Establishments Degrade the Church," and the main line of argument was that "The entire disjunction of the church from the state is, in this country, and every where else where Christianity is founded upon reason and conviction rather than authority and ancient custom, vastly better for all concerned than any direct union between them." By this disjunction religion "escapes the degrading associations, compliances, pollutions and assaults to which a political alliance must inevitably subject her." Greenwood's article revealed that some Unitarians at least had passed from the older defense of a corporate Christian commonwealth to an individualistic, self-reliant, laissez-faire society. "Her [the church's] support is better when she is thrown wholly upon the hearts of men. . . . The very fact that she stands alone is an increase of respectability. Independence is always respectability." No more was there to be a legal recognition and requirement of religion as a mutual concern of the community. Like Whittemore and the Universalists, Greenwood believed that "Man was created a religious being. Religion is an inherent disposition and want within him and a certain blessing to him." Nothing was left of the

---

27. *Christian Examiner.* XIII (January 1833), 351–356.

old Puritan concept of the depravity of man, and predestination was clearly on the side of progress onward and upward.[28]

When the New England Standing Order reached this position, compulsory religious taxes became a sin against the laws of God rather than an essential prop to the order and safety of the community.

28. *Christian Secretary,* June 2, 1832, p. 77. In commenting on it, the *Universalist Trumpet* did not find the sermon as forthright as it seemed, but the *Universalist Trumpet* acknowledged that Greenwood "differs essentially from many of his brethren on this point." May 12, 1832, p. 182.

Chapter 63

The Abolition of Compulsory Religious Taxes in Massachusetts, 1832–1834

Religion will be abundantly supported without compulsion. People are willing always liberally to support their own views; this is a fact which cannot be denied; and provided it were not so, no person has a right to compel them.

The Universalist-sponsored petition of 1832

When the Massachusetts Senate voted to postpone discussion of Thomas Whittemore's resolution which the House had passed by such an overwhelming margin in June 1831 the *Universalist Trumpet* commented bitterly,

> This procedure will be a subject of very deep and very general regret among the citizens of Massachusetts. Had the Senate permitted the passage of the amendment, it would have come before the legislature in June, 1832, been submitted to the people probably on March following, and gone into effect immediately. Those members of the Senate who voted for the indefinite postponement of the subject did the same as though they had voted against the amendment, since it had precisely the same effect . . . The gentlemen who were principally influential in obtaining the postponement were Messrs. [George] Blake and A. H. Everett of Suffolk, and [Asahel] Strong and [Nathan] Brooks of Middlesex . . . it is well known that these gentlemen are members of the Unitarian denomination and that denomination is the only one which has opposed the amendment of the Third Article. The Orthodox, the Baptists, the Episcopalians, the Methodists, and the Universalists are all desirous of leaving religion to stand on its own foundation without the aid of law, and using general terms, the Unitarians are the only party in favor of *compelling people by law to support religion.*[1]

1. *Universalist Trumpet*, July 2, 1831, p. 2. The editor noted that every one of the Senators from Suffolk County present voted against the bill. "Mr. Wells was absent when the vote was taken. We have a slight acquaintance with the gentleman and believe he is in favor of expunging the Third Article." The editorial concluded

The editorial, undoubtedly written by Whittemore himself, was in effect a declaration by the Universalists that they planned to carry the fight against the Unitarians into the public arena. They did so in two ways. The first was with constant editorial comment on the subject, in which the opponents of the amendment were pointedly named and their constituents urged to vote against them or to force them to alter their views. The second was to step up the petition campaign. This second action was begun by calling a meeting of some of the leading supporters of the amendment to inaugurate a state-wide effort to circularize a standard petition. This meeting in Boston was early in August 1831. Precisely who was asked to attend and how many did so the *Universalist Trumpet* never said, nor did any other source. But the group's work indicated that experienced leadership was available in drawing up a circular letter and a petition and setting on foot a coordinated campaign of political action designed to flood the legislature with petitions when it reconvened in January 1832 for its winter session. The circular letter sent out by the sponsors of the campaign summarized the religious, social, and political reasons the amendment was needed. In view of its effectiveness the petition probably constitutes an accurate statement of the general feeling on this subject in Massachusetts:

Dear Sir,

Several gentlemen of this city and vicinity, after consultation with persons of piety and patriotism in different parts of the Commonwealth, have adopted this method for the purpose of calling your attention in a *particular* manner to the THIRD ARTICLE OF THE BILL OF RIGHTS in our Constitution. Massachusetts stands alone among the States in the Union in making *legal* provision for the support of Religion; and notwithstanding the reverence which has by some been paid to the Third Article, it has become settled that it is a subject of vexation to many, a means of petty tyranny in the hands of a few, and altogether injurious to the cause of pure and undefiled religion. We beg leave to submit to you the following reasons why the article should be annulled or modified.

1st. Human governments should never be linked with Religion. Religion is spiritual in its nature and cannot be aided by human law. The unholy alliance between them has always debased religion and generated corruption and persecution.

2. Jesus Christ never applied to the civil power to aid him, nor has he left any direction to his followers to do so.

3. The operation of the Third Article is unequal. It has no effect in the city and large towns and the inhabitants of the small towns justly feel themselves aggrieved that they are subject to laws from the influence of which others are screened.

4. Religion will be abundantly supported without compulsions. People

by listing the counties whose Senators favored and opposed the resolution. The counties in favor were Middlesex, Plymouth, Hampshire, Hampden, Berkshire, and Barnstable. The counties whose Senators opposed the resolution by voting to postpone it were Suffolk, Essex, Norfolk, Bristol, and Worcester.

are willing always liberally to support their own views; this is a fact which cannot be denied; and provided it were not so, no person has a right to compel them.

5. The effect of compelling people to support religion is highly injurious. Men never were made to have any respect for religion by being *compelled* to support it. Such a course generates hate and opposition. Religion cannot have a good influence upon any man any further than it is a matter of conscience and choice with him. Where it is a matter of conscience it will always be supported cheerfully and abundantly and where it is not, a compulsory support produces only hatred and irreligion.

These are esteemed sufficient reasons why the alteration should be made in the Third Article of the Bill of Rights.

The desired alternation was proposed and carried in the House of Representatives by an overwhelming majority at the last Legislature; but a meagre majority of the Senate, by an unwarrantable exercise of power, saw fit to put a wanton veto on the doings of the House.

It is desirable therefor that there should be a general expression of the peoples wishes on this important subject at the session of the next General Court. The object of this Circular is to suggest to you the propriety of drawing up a petition to the next General Court, praying *for an alteration of the Constitution of this Commonwealth in the Third Article of the Bill of Rights*. It requires no labor to draw a petition and but little to obtain the signers. The reasons stated above, if thought best, may be introduced in substance into the petition. Send your petition by a representative from your town or a neighboring town. It will do the more good should two or three petitions come from each town, and the petition, after being circulated, should be sent, how few soever signers it may have. It would be well to have the petition circulated early this fall, that it may go in at the beginning of the session. By giving this an *early and efficient* attention you will assist those who are endeavoring to bring about a highly necessary alteration in the Constitution in favor of religious liberty.

This letter was unsigned. From its internal content, however, it bears the clear stamp of Whittemore's Universalist approach to the problem. The bulk of its arguments were against compulsion, inequality, and "petty tyranny in the hands of a few," but the petition also included the pietistic claim of Jesus Christ to rule his own followers. Its general appeal to "piety and patriotism" and to state pride was designed to attract a broad range of signers.

Commenting on the circular and the petition campaign in November 1832, the *Christian Register* expressed the Unitarians's opposition to it. The petitions were, said the paper, the result of a form drawn up and circulated "with great labor through the agency of a few individuals" and "by dint of much persuasion" many signed them. "Can this be termed a spontaneous, independent, universal call for redress of some oppressive burden?" [2]

2. *Christian Register,* November 10, 1832, p. 178.

But the *Christian Register* was wrong in estimating that the response would be small. The number of petitions turned in and the number of signers indicated clearly an overwhelming desire for alteration of the article. Between August 9, 1831, and January, 1832, over 142 petitions were received in Boston from over 140 different towns and these petitions contained 7690 signatures. This was a demonstration of popular concern which the legislature simply could not overlook and the Senate could not repudiate.

The vast majority of these petitions were based either on the wording in the five points of the circular letter or else were copied from a standard petition form printed on page two of the circular. This standard petition, drawn up by the "several gentlemen" from the vicinity of Boston provided the usual heading addressed to the Senate and House of Representatives "in General Court Assembled" and petitioning that "Honorable body that the Constitution of the Commonwealth may be so far altered that Religion may be supported by the voluntary contribution of the citizens and not by any *legal* process or compulsion." The main body of the petition simply listed the same five reasons in the same wording as they appeared in the circular letter. It concluded, "We believe your Honorable body, on giving this subject your serious consideration, will take the necessary measures to bring about the desired alteration in our Constitution." [3]

In the absence of any description of this petition campaign, either in the newspapers or by any of its organizers, the only method of analyzing its procedure is by means of the addresses on the back of the page containing the petition (where these pages were returned to the legislatures with signatures attached). From these addresses it is clear that the committee which sent out the circular-petition document did not send them only to the ministers of one denomination or only to dissenting ministers. Nor did they send them only to ministers, though ministers constituted the central core of the recipients. Moreover, in their effort to reach every town in the state, the forms were sent out even when no name was available of a minister or a suitable layman — these were addressed either to the religious societies known (or thought) to exist in the town or simply to the postmaster of the town. For example, one petition-circular was returned with signatures though it had been addressed simply to "Postmaster, Stockbridge, Mass." Another came in with signatures though addressed to the "Methodist

---

3. Copies of this petition and the circular letter to which it was attached are among the petitions in the Massachusetts Legislative Archives, chap. 56, Resolves, 1833, original papers, 1832–1833. At the very bottom of the page on which the petition was printed were these words in brackets: "You can draw off this petition and use it, or frame another as shall best suit you." In most cases the persons who received the printed petition copied the petition in longhand on a large sheet of paper and had petitioners sign this. In many cases, however, the recipient simply tore off the printed petition, filled the name of his town in the blank space, and pasted a piece of paper at the bottom of the form for the signatures.

Society, Peru, Mass." Others, for example, went to "Rev. Tubal Wakefield, Belchertown, Mass." to "Postmaster, Tolland, Mass.", to "Tyler Goddard, Esq., Paxton, Mass.", to "Methodist Society, Stockbridge, Mass.", "Benajah Mason, Esq., Swanzey, Mass.", "William Lewis, Harvard, Mass.", and "Rev. Mr. Luce, Westford, Mass."

The postmarks on these forms indicate that the majority of them were sent either from Boston during the week of October 2–9, 1831 or from Charlestown, during the week of October 10–17.

Although the great bulk of the 142 petitions on file in the archives followed the printed form and indicated only the name of a town as the place of the petition's origin, a number of them were original in form and reveal certain important features about the movement. For example, it is clear that petitions were received from Orthodox or Trinitarian parishes, from Methodists, and from Baptists, because these groups identified themselves by name. One petition came from "Members of the second religious society of Ashburnham," another from "members of the Methodist Society in Peru," and another from "members of the Sunderland and Montague Baptist Society." In some cases the signers indicated that though one particular denomination took the lead in obtaining the signatures in that town, many had signed who were not members of that denomination: e.g., "Members of the Methodist Episcopal Church and Society and other inhabitants of Leominster" and "members of the various Religious Societies in Newton." [4]

While most of the petitions were dated January 1 to January 7, 1832, the date on which they were presented to the local representative to be carried to Boston, a few were dated as early as October 13, 1831, indicating that the petitions were circulating throughout the state from that date onward.

Of the petitions which did not follow the form prescribed or suggested in the circular letter, the most succinct came from the town of Barnstable. It contained only one sentence praying "That the Constitution of the Commonwealth may be so far altered that Religion may be supported by the voluntary contribution of the citizens and not by any legal process or compulsion and that for this purpose the third article of the Bill of Rights may be expunged or modified."

The petition from the "various Religious Societies in Newton" began by copying the printed form but added an interesting note concerning the particular problems within that town:

4. Some of the printed petition forms differ in typography, though not in wording, which indicates a second printing. The *Universalist Trumpet* also reported that the petition was printed in local newspapers. And in some towns, according to Whittemore, the petitions were voted on at town meetings and were submitted to the legislature with the signatures of the selectmen on behalf of the town. See *Universalist Trumpet*, March 3, 1832, p. 142.

In addition to these general reasons, permit us to add that in Newton there are five Religious Societies and part of a sixth. Two of them in conformity with the provisions of the Third Article are Parishes covering the whole Territory of the Town and having a legal right to tax every man in it. Indeed it may be, as we are informed, has been a question, whether this right is not exclusively in one, that is, the 'Oldest Religious Society in the Town.' We are aware of the fact that those who do not wish to be taxed by either of these two parishes may 'sign off' as it is called. But notwithstanding this provision, members are every year caught in this trap and compelled to pay for the support of doctrine which they disbelieve and perhaps abhor. Nor is it the wish of these two Parishes to avail themselves of such aid, for they cordially unite with the other denominations in this Town in praying for the abolition of the Third Article and for such modification of the Laws as will place the support of all the Religious Societies in the Town upon the same foundation.

This petition was signed by 129 persons, headed by Elder Joseph Grafton of the First Baptist Church in Newton. Grafton was a leading figure in his denomination and probably wrote the above addendum to the petition. The signers, however, did not indicate their religious affiliations so that it is not known what proportion of them was Baptist and what from the other churches in the town.

Evidence that Whittemore and the Universalists were the leading figures in the petition movement can be found by comparing the attention which the *Universalist Trumpet* paid to the campaign and to the political aspects of disestablishment during the months from August to December 1831 to the lack of interest demonstrated by the other papers, religious and political. Although the *Trumpet* contained numerous articles on all phases of the movement, none of the other papers mentioned the petition campaign more than once or twice and most ignored it altogether.

Whittemore's hammering on the issue included personal accounts of the debates which had taken place in his committee during the preceding June session (these appeared on November 12, 1831), lists of the names of those Senators and representatives "who showed by their votes that they are in favor of retaining the offensive third Article," (these appeared October 15, 1831), arguments justifying the abolition of the article, and exhortations that "It is not too late to agitate the question."[5] He was particularly hard upon the Unitarian representatives from Suffolk County whom he considered (rightly) the nucleus of the opposition. And he also chastized some of the Trinitarians who still held back. "This is a stain on the character of Suffolk which cannot soon be washed out . . . nearly or quite all of the denominations agree in the desire to have the alteration take place. The orthodox in the western and the Unitarians in the eastern part

5. *Ibid.,* October 29, 1831, p. 70.

of the state oppose it in some measure. But among the friends of the alteration we are happy to find many of all denominations." [6]

Toward the end of November 1831, Whittemore urged his co-workers to greater efforts: "We hope our friends will not go to sleep in the subject . . . The majority of all the political parties are in favor of the alteration, but the aristocrats in all of them are opposed." He named Hoar of Middlesex and Loud of Norfolk as the leaders of the aristocratic opposition. "We hope a petition will come from every town in the Commonwealth. Let religious societies petition as such. One of the Baptist churches in the neighborhood of this city has voted to petition for that object." [7]

When *The Spirit of the Pilgrims,* in its December 1831, issue, finally gave its full and clearcut endorsement to disestablishment, Whittemore even had praise for that "high-toned orthodox publication." [8] His own tone here indicated that the editors and supporters of this magazine had not been among those gentlemen who had organized the petition movement in August.

At the same time Whittemore attacked "the editors of popular journals in this state" for their unwillingness "to canvas" this subject in their papers. This evidently brought the Baptists to take a more forthright public stand in the *Christian Watchman* than they had previously. On December 23 the editor of that magazine wrote that he did not find the resolution adopted by the House in June strong enough. He demanded complete expunging of Article Three instead of mere alteration.[9] This was the first editorial the subject of religious taxes in the *Watchman* in a decade, another proof that the Universalists had taken the lead in this final phase of the movement.

When the January session of the legislature opened Whittemore reported jubilantly that over one hundred petitions were presented against Article Three on the very first day: "We believe there has not been a more general expression of popular opinion on any subject in the House of Representatives for several years." He was probably correct.[10]

The House referred these petitions to a special committee on Article Three consisting of one member from each county. Whittemore was again appointed chairman of the committee, and by January 20 the Committee had again favorably reported a resolution for amending Article Three. The matter came up for debate on February 8. During a two-day debate two amendments were added to the resolution, and it was returned to the Committee. On February 11 it came out of Committee and was adopted by the

6. *Ibid.,* November 12, 1831, p. 87.
7. *Ibid.,* November 26, 1831, p. 87.
8. *Ibid.,* December 10, 1831, p. 94.
9. *Christian Watchman,* December 23, 1831, p. 206. This editorial is quoted in Chapter 62.
10. *Universalist Trumpet,* January 14, 1832, p. 115.

House that same day.[11] Whittemore, speaking on behalf of his committee's resolution, which was essentially the same as the one adopted by the House in June 1831, noted that as of January 20 when the committee was formed, 150 petitions had been received with nearly 8000 names, and since that date another 50 petitions containing 4000 more names had been presented.[12] He then described the resolution:

> The great alteration here proposed is that which abolishes the compulsory support of religion. It is herein provided that any person may dissolve his membership with the society to which he belongs at any time — not by joining some other society, as he is now obliged to, but by filing with the clerk of the society to which he belongs a written notice of the dissolution of his membership. He will not be compelled to be a member of any society. The support of religion will be left where it is just and expedient that it should be, to his conscience and inclination. No society will be compelled to receive members against their wishes nor will any person be compelled to join. Thus each society is protected in their rights and each individual in his right; and pure religion must flourish under so happy a state of things.[13]

According to the *Universalist Trumpet,*

> The Report of the Committee was opposed in the House principally by Messers Buckingham of Boston, Gardner of Roxbury, Doane of Cohasset, and Hobart of Leicester. It was sustained by the chairman [Whittemore], Messrs. Hudson of Westminster and Foster of Brimfield. There were several in favor of annulling the third Article entirely who would not vote for the report of the Committee.

Nevertheless the amendment easily obtained the required two-thirds majority. The vote was 347 to 90. Every county except Suffolk, the center of Unitarianism and "aristocracy," had a majority of its representatives favoring the motion. What was more, the Suffolk County representatives gave a larger majority against the resolution than they had at the preceding session, an indication that the Unitarians had not been inactive in the meantime. The *Universalist Trumpet* claimed that "probably thirty negative votes" were "given by those who would have voted for annulling" the third article. These may have been Baptists following the lead of the *Christian Watchman.* From the Universalists' viewpoint, the resolution was "far preferable" (probably from a tactical viewpoint) to complete abolition.[14] Some of the Trinitarians opposed the measure because it did not go far enough in denying the right of the society to control the church even among voluntary societies. The Trinitarians wanted the church members in all religious so-

11. *Ibid.,* February 18, 1832, p. 134.
12. *Ibid.,* and March 3, 1832, p. 142.
13. *Ibid.,* February 18, 1832, p. 134; March 3, 1832, p. 142.
14. *Ibid.,* February 18, 1832, p. 134.

cieties to be guaranteed the exclusive right of choosing the minister for the society.[15]

The resolution adopted by the House was sent up to the Senate on February 14 and referred to a special committee of which Leverett Saltonstall was chairman. On February 16, this committee brought in an adverse report on the amendment:

> The permanency of the Constitution is of the utmost importance. An instrument of this solemn nature, the foundation of the Government, should not be liable to change with temporary incitements or fluctuations of opinion. Frequent changes must necessarily impair the respect due to that instrument.
>
> In the opinion of the Committee it is a settled principle that the Constitution ought not to be changed *except for practical purposes* and when an evil exists which can only be remedied by that extraordinary measure. The Committee are not aware that any such evil exists under the third article of the Bill of rights. They believe that perfect religious freedom is now enjoyed under the Constitution and laws of this Commonwealth and that no citizen can justly complain of oppressions. And further, if any evil does exist under that part of the Constitution, they believe that it is now in the power of the legislature to provide relief.
>
> The constitutional provision for the support of public worship and for instruction in piety, religion, and morality, has in their opinion had a most important and salutary influence in promoting 'the happiness of the people and in securing the good order and preservation of the Government.'
>
> Under these circumstances they believe it to be their duty to report, That it is not necessary nor expedient to adopt the proposed 'Article of Amendment.' [16]

Whether the conservative Unitarians for whom Saltonstall spoke were really worried about the innovating tendencies of Jacksonian democracy and feared that the whole constitution was in danger of continual revision, or whether this was simply a subterfuge to avoid facing the religious issues, nonetheless these men were prepared to hold out to the bitter end against the change.

The resolution was vigorously debated in the Senate, and as in the House, some who favored alteration of Article Three did not approve of the form of the Whittemore resolution. On February 24, therefore, Barker Burnell, the Senator from Nantucket, moved the substitution of the following resolution:

> All men have a natural and indefeasible right to worship Almighty God according to the dictates of their own consciences and no citizen shall be hurt, molested or restrained in his person or liberty or estate for worship-

15. See the article from the *Yeoman's Gazette* quoted in the *Universalist Trumpet,* February 25, 1832, p. 138.
16. Massachusetts Legislative Archives, 1832–1833.

ping God in the manner and season most agreeable to the dictates of his own conscience; or for his religious profession of sentiments; provided he doth not disturb the public peace, or obstruct others in their religious worship. No man can of right be compelled to attend any place of public worship or to pay tythes or taxes to erect or support any place of worship or to maintain any ministry. No preference shall ever be given by law to any religious establishments or modes of worship nor shall any person be denied the enjoyment of any civil or political right merely on account of his religious principles.[17]

This was an attempt to end the whole ecclesiastical system merely by stating, as the Federal Constitution did, the essential aspects of religious freedom, taking no account of any existing ecclesiastical structure. The resolution was voted down in the Senate as had a similar amendment in the House.

Finally the question was called in the Senate on March 9, and the vote recorded twenty-five for the resolution and thirteen against. Of the thirteen opponents, six were the representatives from Suffolk County; the others were Saltonstall and William Jackson, Jr. from Essex County; Elihu Cutler and Samuel Hoar, Jr. from Middlesex; Joseph Hawes from Norfolk; John W. Lincoln; and David Wilder from Worcester. In no county except Suffolk did the opponents have a majority. The *Universalist Trumpet* printed the yeas and nays with this comment:

> The majority was larger than was anticipated. In opposition to the amendment Mr. Saltonstall of Salem took the lead. He is a lawyer and by religion a Unitarian. Mr. Hoar of Concord, another Lawyer and a Unitarian also followed in Mr. Saltonstall's steps. James T. Austin of Boston, a lawyer and we believe a Unitarian, opposed the amendment. Mr. Wilder from the county of Worcester and Mr. Cutler from Middlesex joined in the opposition . . . In favor of the Amendment we must name first Mr. Burnell of Nantucket, who although he did not like the exact form of it espoused the cause of unrestrained religious liberty in a fearless and powerful manner. Mr. Hastings of Mendon, in Worcester District, advocated the amendment . . . as did also Mr. Cummings of Hampshire District . . . Mr. Austin of Middlesex spoke in favor . . . His speech was the most lively of all.[18]

According to the constitutional provisions for amendment, it was necessary for the legislature to pass the article of amendment as a resolution twice in two succeeding years. In each year it was necessary that the resolution pass the House by a two-thirds majority and the Senate by a majority vote. Hence another year had to go by and another legislature in the succeeding winter session had to reconsider the amendment.

Except among a few die-hard Unitarians, however, the matter was con-

17. *Ibid.*
18. *Universalist Trumpet,* March 17, 1832, p. 150.

sidered settled. In September 1832, the *Christian Register* protested the amendment in an article deploring the rising multiplicity of sects, the increasing religious taxes on the faithful parishioners, and the growing number of churches in every town, none of which had sufficient members to support a regular minister. The amendment of Article Three was "another evil which now threatens us:"

> We have no doubt that this measure was resorted to as a means of obtaining relief from what was felt as a grievance. Others have joined in it to promote party purposes. For ourselves, we should view its success as a serious calamity to our Commonwealth. We should view it with sorrow, not as Unitarians, but as friends of virtue and good morals. How many are there who, if the law did not require it, would not contribute anything to the support of religion? How many more whose consciences would be satisfied by contributing much less than their proper proportion!

The paper blamed the Orthodox primarily for the difficulties arising under the prevailing system. "These apostles of discord" had promoted all of the schisms in parishes, not the Unitarians. And "An Orthodox leader is reported to have declared that an Orthodox house of worship should be erected beside every Unitarian church throughout the State." And they were trying to do it.[19]

The *Christian Watchman,* in a long and sarcastic comment on this article said "We had not expected from a denomination claiming to be the enlightened friends of religious freedom such observations." And without being aware of any contradiction concerning the Baptists' advocacy of legislation for the preservation of the Sabbath and other moral virtues, the paper deplored the *Christian Register*'s defense of religious taxation in terms of the public good: "This theory of doing things by law for the public good has been the grand pretence of tyrants in all ages." [20]

The *Watchman* also took Judge Joseph Story to task in November 1832, for "speaking against a repeal of the third Article" at a "recent public meeting of Unitarians." Story was quoted as saying at this meeting that "the great question was whether the Christian Religion is not of sufficient value to be supported by law." But the question, said the *Watchman,* was not the value of the Christian religion, but whether God had given the government the right to support it by law. The answer was, "No government nor any religious sect has the power of toleration in the accurate or strict sense of the word, and that all governments ought to be so constructed and administered as to render its exercise unnecessary. This principle is thoroughly recognized in the Constitution of the United States and ought to be so in all the Constitutions of each State." [21]

19. Quoted in *Christian Watchman,* September 21, 1832, p. 150.
20. *Ibid.*
21. *Ibid.,* November 16, 1832, p. 182. Story, formerly a Jeffersonian, has some-

As the time drew near for the second and final debate on the amendment, the *Universalist Trumpet* published a report that "a great effort has been making for some time past to defeat the proposed amendment of the Third Article of the Bill of Rights . . . by means of secret operations. Certain gentlemen residing in towns where the law has no effect" (obviously Boston and Salem) had repeatedly been actively engaged in formulating measures for defeating the resolution at the next session. But the *Trumpet* offered no details of this plot.[22]

Apart from verbal skirmishes like these, there was no action taken during the time between the first passage of the act and its reconsideration in 1833. When the legislature assembled in January 1833 the matter was immediately referred to a select committee headed by Whittemore. On January 16, the committee reported it saw no reason not to pass the resolution adopted the year before since the public seemed more in favor of it than ever. The committee also stated its belief that many parishes "who have the legal power to tax all such as do not sign off to other societies have of late declined to make use of that power from the belief that compulsory taxation is injurious to the cause of religion and to the best interests of the parishes." [23] The next day the House passed the resolution by a vote of 431 to 75.[24]

The resolution then went to the Senate where it was referred on January 18 to a committee of which Samuel Hoar was the chairman. According to the *Universalist Trumpet* Hoar was "opposed to its passage and he made no effort therefore to have it early passed upon." [25] The report of this committee, submitted on January 30, stated that the committee regretted that the resolution as it was now worded omitted the phrase in Article Three which stated that piety, morality, and religion were "essential to the happiness of the people and the good order and preservation of civil government." This was obviously an attempt to stall consideration, for such a rewording would have meant another year would have to pass before the amendment could be passed. The majority of the committee agreed that it was too late to change the wording, "The chairman dissenting." [26] When the resolution reached the floor of the Senate "The three principal opponents

---

times been portrayed as a supporter of disestablishment but there is no evidence of this at any point in his career. As a liberal Unitarian his views on the subject were like those of James Sullivan and the Rev. William Bentley — willing to give the dissenters every modification in the system to avoid oppression so long as the system itself was retained.

22. *Universalist Trumpet,* November 10, 1832, p. 78.

23. Massachusetts Legislative Archives, 1832–1833. As usual, no one made any effort to produce any statistical evidence as to how many towns or parishes had ceased to levy religious taxes.

24. *Independent Chronicle,* January 19, 1833, p. 1.

25. *Universalist Trumpet,* March 9, 1833, p. 146.

26. Massachusetts Legislative Archives, 1832–1833. The resolution as it was adopted contained substantially this wording.

of the amendment were Messrs. Samuel Hoar, Alexander H. Everett, and George Blake." [27] On March 1, the Senate voted 28 to 9 to pass the resolution a second time. The amendment then went to the judiciary committee which determined the proper method for its ratification by the people.

The *Universalist Trumpet* could not resist a final bitter comment against the Unitarian opponents of the bill and listed the names of the nine Senators who voted nay: Lee, Hawes, Cutler, Merrill, Blake, Everett, Motley, Wilder, and Hoar.

> The public will very naturally inquire to what denomination of christians these gentlemen belong who opposed the amendment. We answer, they are *Unitarians*. This fact will be remembered. The Unitarians are the only sect who have opposed this measure. It will go down to posterity and be always connected with the history of that denomination in New England . . . The Orthodox, the Baptists, the Methodists, the Universalists, combined to rid the Constitution of the offensive Third Article . . . The leading opponent of this measure in the House of Representatives was Mr. Phillips of Salem, one of the principal Unitarians in the Commonwealth. In that branch the Unitarian city of Boston gave 21 negative votes, more than four times as many as were given in the county of Essex. We do not deny that there were some Unitarians who voted for the amendment. We mention with pleasure that Mr. Robinson of Lowell not only voted in the affirmative but used his exertions to have the amendment passed . . . But the Unitarians as a body were opposed to the measure. They had no hope of success in the House; in the Senate, however, they made their final desperate effort to arrest it, but they failed.

The Universalists were not willing to concede that a matter of principle or conviction underlay this effort. To them it was pure self-interest and a will to dominate the many for the few. The paper concluded its remarks with the happy thought that the "fashionable" religion of the aristocratic Unitarians would scarcely flourish under the new system.[28]

But the Unitarians had not, as a denomination, opposed the amendment to the last ditch. Early in January 1833, before the resolution came before either house, the editors of the *Christian Examiner* published a statement in which they stated their acceptance of the inevitable with good grace:

> We take much less interest in the determination of this particular question than is commonly expressed by those who advocate or those who oppose the amendment under consideration. The former can hardly make out, as it seems to us, a very strong case of oppression or hardship . . . The cry of 'aristocracy' and 'church and state' as a means of exciting popular prejudice against the Third Article can hardly be raised in good faith . . . At the same time, if it is the will of the people, acting in their sovereign capacity, that the proposed amendment should go into effect,

27. *Universalist Trumpet*, March 9, 1833, p. 146.
28. *Ibid.*

we are entirely content . . . Every body knows that governments, as such, have lost much of the power they once had over the *minds* of men; and that laws in respect to religion in particular and religious institutions have become, generally speaking, obnoxious. Under these circumstances it may well be doubted whether it is expedient to keep up the semblance of an authority, which has ceased to be either respectable or formidable.

The editors continued that they certainly believed it was time to expunge from the Constitution "the odious distinction there recognized in favor of Protestantism and the clause authorizing the legislature to enjoin attendance on public worship." And "what very important practical purpose can be gained by requiring that the Constitution shall continue to read as if religious institutions were supported by a general and equitable tax while everybody knows that in practice this is now and long has been as contrary to fact as it ever can be should the proposed amendment pass?" After answering all the objections of those who opposed the amendment, the editors stated, "we are more and more convinced that those who are most eager and zealous in opposing the amendment under consideration are contending for a mere semblance of what they want." If people felt certain religious institutions were oppressive and wrong, then to persist in them would only harm religion. "Better have no religious institutions than to have them as objects of general suspicion, reviling and blasphemy." Here the editors spoke for the more liberal Unitarian clergy. They were correct that the laymen in the Senate who argued so vehemently for retaining Article Three were contending for the shadow rather than the substance. So little was left of the old system, either in theory or in practice, that the editors rightly concluded that little harm would occur to their churches or the commonwealth from its abolition and much might occur if it were pointlessly retained.

"In the present diversity of sects," said these Unitarian ministers, "it must certainly be more agreeable, and equitable, and in our judgment more practicable and convenient and equally safe, to let each sect adopt its own method." Some Unitarians, they said, fear "that if the legislature withdraws its patronage from the territorial parishes, everything will be thrown up to the zeal and activity of the contending sects. We answer, that it is so now, at least virtually." On the other hand, matters were not and would not be so horrendous as the "alarmists" like Saltonstall, Hoar, Blake and the editors of the *Christian Register* believed. The article concluded by labelling these opponents of the amendment men of little faith in God or man:

> For the future support of christian worship we rely much less on human legislation than on human nature. We rely, moreover on the intelligence and virtue of the people, being convinced that they will not suffer institutions to fall into the decay and ruin to which this community is indebted for almost every thing by which its character is so honorably distinguished.

We rely on the intrinsic vitality and energy of the religion itself, which, though overlaid as it is by such masses of error and corruption, the error and corruption cannot kill. Above all, we rely in the over-ruling providence of God.[29]

The final sentence was a reference to a text the Baptists often used in the past to justify the system of voluntarism: "He [God] will not suffer the church, which was planted by the care and watered by the tears and consecrated by the prayers of our fathers, to be prevailed against by the gates of hell." It was a fitting symbol of the transformation of Puritanism. Now both the Orthodox and the Liberal wings of the Puritan church had conceded the correctness of the Baptist position. Two centuries after the first Baptist raised his voice in Massachusetts Bay, the Puritan Bible Commonwealth capitulated. The Separatist seekers after religious freedom had triumphed in the free soil of the New World over the Puritan seekers after corporate conformity. Or, better, a new form of corporate conformity, based on voluntaristic and individualistic principles, had replaced the old. For it would be hard to deny that for the next fifty years or more, the United States accepted the religious and moral principles of Evangelicalism as the National Establishment.

Following advice from the legislature's judiciary committee, Governor Levi Lincoln set the second Monday in November 1833, as the date on which the voters in each town were to register their opinions for or against the proposed amendment to the constitution. And on November 11, 1833, the people voted 32,234 to 3,273 in favor of it. The vote was accompanied by almost no comment either before or after November 11. No one doubted the outcome and no newspaper — not even the *Universalist Trumpet,* the *Christian Watchman,* or the *Christian Register,* to name the three which had been most intensely concerned with the measure before March 1833 — considered the results of the election even worth reporting. The Baptists' position on their victory is evident in a comment in the *Christian Watchman* a month before the ratification:

This Amendment is a halfway measure; we should have been better pleased if it had extended further. It's practical effect will be as follows — Under our present constitution and laws every man may select what society he pleases but he must belong to some society. Under the Amendment it will not be necessary for him to be a member of any society; he may *sign off* from one society and remain off, without being obliged to *sign in* to another. We trust that this amendment will be adopted although it does not go so far as we could wish.[30]

On this point, at least, the Baptists remained pietistic enough to wish a clean

29. *Christian Examiner,* XIII (January, 1833), 345–350.
30. *Christian Watchman,* October 11, 1833, p. 164.

break with the old system. Merely that the constitution recognized that a man had to sign off or opt out of a religious society was to them an assertion of human law over Christ's church and over the individual conscience. The Eleventh Amendment to the constitution, as it was finally adopted, read:

> As the public worship of God and instructions in piety, religion, and morality, promote the happiness and prosperity of a people, and the se-curity of a republican government; therefore, the several religious societies of this commonwealth, whether corporate or unincorporate, at any meeting legally warned and holden for that purpose, shall ever have the right to elect their pastors or religious teachers, to contract with them for their support, to raise money for erecting and repairing houses for public wor-ship, for the maintenance of religious instruction, and for the payment of necessary expenses; and all persons belonging to any religious society shall be taken and held to be members, until they filed with the clerk of such society a written notice, declaring the dissolution of their membership, and thenceforth shall not be liable for any grant or contract which may be thereafter made, or entered into by such society; and all religious sects and denominations, demeaning themselves peaceably and as good citizens of the commonwealth, shall be equally under the protection of the law; and no subordination of any one sect or denomination to another shall ever be established by law.

The Baptists were correct in understanding that this amendment did not break all the ties between church and state. The same kinds of complications in ecclesiastical law remained to plague the courts and to require new legis-lation over the years as in New Hampshire, Connecticut, and Vermont. The courts had to decide many cases involving religious taxes levied by voluntaristic societies on men and property by a majority vote but to which some of the minority, for one reason or another, objected. There were cases involving trust funds and endowment funds left for the support of the ministry in a town or parish where it was difficult to decide which voluntar-istic society in the multiplicity which had subdivided the town was the rightful recipient. Most troublesome of all were the so-called "blue-laws," like that against blasphemy, a crime for which Abner Kneeland served two years, 1838–1840, in prison.[31]

One important aspect of religious taxation which the Eleventh Amend-ment failed to settle, though Thomas Whittemore had pointed it out at the time, was the status of young men who came of age without having formally presented a certificate either signing off from their parish or attesting to their membership in some dissenting society. Whittemore had said in 1832 that "young men becoming sixteen years of age and people moving into this Commonwealth not being used to the effect of such laws, do not think to attach themselves to a society of their own denomination and before they

31. Henry Steele Commager, "The Blasphemy of Abner Kneeland," *New England Quarterly*, VIII (1935) 29–41.

are aware of it a tax is clapped on them and applied to the support of a system of preaching which they abhor." [32] This "has proved a very profitable trap in some places where parish assessors have seen fit to use it with cunning." Henry David Thoreau fell into this trap in 1838, when he reached twenty-one, five years after religious liberty had (presumably) freed all men from compulsory religious taxes.

Thoreau recorded his clash with ecclesiastical law in a famous passage in "Civil Disobedience" in 1848: "Some years ago the State met me in behalf of the Church and commanded me to pay a certain sum toward the support of a clergyman whose preaching my father attended, but never I myself. 'Pay,' it said, 'or be locked up in the jail.' I declined to pay. But, unfortunately, another man saw fit to pay it." The same problem which had troubled the Baptists for a century still plagued a Unitarian (Transcendental) Harvard graduate five years after the Eleventh Amendment went into effect. "At the request of the selectmen," said Thoreau, "I condescended to make some such statement as this in writing: — 'Know all men by these presents, that I, Henry Thoreau, do not wish to be regarded as a member of any incorporated society which I have not joined.' " He thus made his "certificate bow" to the state, and "The state, having thus learned that I did not wish to be regarded as a member of that church has never made a like demand on me since; though it said that it must adhere to its original presumption that time." [33]

Much of Thoreau's argument in "Civil Disobedience" reflects the voluntarist principle which had been the keystone of the Baptist stand for two centuries: "I did not see," he wrote of his arrest for refusing to pay religious taxes, "why the schoolmaster should be taxed to support the priest and not the priest the schoolmaster; for I was not the State's schoolmaster, but I supported myself by voluntary subscription." [34] It is a fittingly ironic epilogue to this phase of New England intellectual history that the civil disobedience of pietistic Baptist martyrs was justified (and by America's civil religion, sanctified) by a pantheistic Transcendentalist.

But for the Baptists, the fall of the Standing Order in Massachusetts merely confirmed that they had now entered the mainstream of the new American evangelical consensus (from which Thoreau was a heinous dissenter). In New England they had ceased to be a dissenting sect and were

32. *Universalist Trumpet,* March 3, 1832, p. 142.
33. Thoreau's parish in Concord claimed the right to tax him not only because his father attended the parish church but also because Thoreau had been baptized into it as an infant. However, a statute law of 1836 had declared that "no one can be made a member of a religious society without his consent in writing." If Thoreau had taken his case to court, he might have won. For this and other ecclesiastical legislation and judicial rulings on ecclesiastical matters after 1833, see Edward Buck, *Massachusetts Ecclesiastical Law* (Boston, 1865) rev. ed., p. 31 and *passim.*
34. Thoreau also made use of the favorite Baptist text "Render unto Caesar . . ." in his argument for voluntarism.

now fully the equal of the Congregationalists and clearly more important than the Unitarians — who had been dwindling in force since 1825 when they became an acknowledged sect themselves. The beginnings of this accession to respectability have already been noted. It remains only to demonstrate briefly its fulfillment from 1828 to 1835.

Chapter 64

The Baptists Enter the Mainstream

They [the Baptists] see as clearly as their Presbyterian, Episcopal and Methodist brethren that a law requiring the mail to travel and post offices to be opened on Sunday in defiance of the religious creed of all the leading denominations is an alarming invasion of the rights of the people.

New York *Observer* (Presbyterian) quoted in Boston *Christian Watchman* (Baptist), October 16, 1829

There were no celebrations in New England when the Eleventh Amendment to the Massachusetts Constitution finally ended forever the system of compulsory religious taxes which had for two centuries been the cornerstone of New England's religious life. The strategic retreat by the defenders of the establishment had been so adroit, so drawn out, so piecemeal that the establishment was not really overthrown, it simply withered away. It had ceased to be significant in most towns and parishes long before the state took action against it. Victory for the Eleventh Amendment was as devoid of triumph as it was overwhelming; who cheers when an old, deserted barn caves in or an empty bottle breaks?

More important for the dissenters than the final demolition of the establishment (under which few of them had suffered for the preceding quarter century) was that they had at last rid themselves of the stigma of social and religious inferiority. They were now, in fact as in spirit, the equal of the Congregationalists and Unitarians. In some respects they were superior. Morally, for example, they had the satisfaction of knowing that at last the ruling sect had to acknowledge the correctness of their view of voluntarism just as previously it had had to abandon the halfway covenant and Stoddardeanism. For the Baptists and Methodists there was, in addition, the knowledge that on a national scale their denominations had long since eclipsed the Congregationalists and were clearly to be the dominant denominations of the nation in the ensuing years.

But even before the final abolition of Article Three the Baptists (who were still far more numerous, influential, and respectable than were the Methodists in New England) had ceased to feel inferior. Their vision had

1263

risen from the borders of their own region to national and world horizons. In 1814 the Baptists of America had at last united in a nationwide organization, the General Missionary Convention of the Baptist Denomination in the United States — generally referred to as the Baptist Triennial Convention. The purpose of the convention was to discuss and administer their foreign mission movement, but it had a symbolic significance for denominational unity and maturity far beyond this. It was aslo symbolic that the *Massachusetts Baptist Missionary Magazine* became in 1817 the organ for the Triennial Convention and dropped its state identification, though Thomas Baldwin remained its editor. In the 1830's the denomination formed the American Baptist Home Mission Society, the Baptist General Tract Society and the American and Foreign Bible Society. These organizations raised funds on a nationwide basis for international activities. By refusing to yield their denominational identity and to join with those benevolent societies led chiefly by the Presbyterians and Congregationalists, the Baptists demonstrated their ability to compete effectively with those who had formerly lorded it over them. In 1825 the Baptists formed their own divinity school in Newton, Massachusetts to compete with the Harvard, Yale and Andover divinity schools. The Baptist college in Rhode Island was supplemented by the Baptist college in Maine (Colby) in 1820 and one in New York (Hamilton) in 1821 which served western New England. With a faith that for a time exceeded their financial resources, the Baptists even formed a national Baptist University (Columbian College) in Washington, D.C. in 1822.[1]

At the same time that their numerical and institutional strength provided greater unity and self-confidence, the New England Baptists found an increasing number of evangelical activities in which they could lend support to the established churches. One of the first enterprises in which the Baptists and Trinitarian-Congregationalists were willing to join forces had been the fight against deism, rationalism, and Unitarianism. Then after 1820 came the joint efforts against the delivery of the mail on Sundays, the temperance movement, the crusade against lotteries, the effort to outlaw dueling, anti-Popery, anti-Mormonism, and finally antislavery. In each of these evangelical efforts the Baptist leadership and publications revealed a growing middle class conservatism which contrasted sharply with their former radical Jeffersonianism. Proportionally more Baptists than Trinitarians were Jacksonians, but like their evangelical brethren, the better educated, more sophisticated urban and suburban leaders tended to be Whigs. The *Christian Watchman* in the 1820's provides graphic evidence of this pietistic hardening of the spiritual arteries. Not only did the paper declare Jefferson, John Adams,

---

1. A. H. Newman, *A History of the Baptist Churches in the United States* (New York, 1894) pp. 393–435. Statewide Baptist conventions were also formed in Connecticut (1823), Massachusetts (1824), Vermont (1825) and New Hampshire (1826); these joined together the various Baptist associations within each state.

and Jackson beyond the pale of Christian respectability, it even criticised foreigners like the Marquis de LaFayette for setting "so pernicious an example" during his United States visit in 1825 as to travel on the Sabbath.[2] With mingled horror and delight the Baptists found two new infidels on whom they could vent the wrath they once levelled against Thomas Paine and Voltaire: Robert Owen and Frances Wright, two of the ungodliest foreigners ever to taint American soil and threaten its moral fibre. In 1826, in an article entitled "The Duty of Reproving the Ungodly" the *Christian Watchman* delivered its first stern rebukes to Robert Owen and in 1828 and 1829 it looked "with disgust and horror" on Frances Wright's awful opinions which were "dishonoring to God and tending to confusion and anarchy." [3]

> A bold and adventurous woman, known to entertain and publicly propagate opinions, to particularize which would offend the ear of decency, has been permitted to come into the heart of our city, with the avowed object of contesting the dearest principles of our social state and to enter and tarry without being interrupted . . . She has come indelicately assuming the province of a teacher, with the masculine airs which dishonor and degrade her own sex.

The paper would not desecrate its columns with any quotations from her lectures: "Her principles appear to be as infidel and of course as lewd as those of the famous but visionary Robert Owen . . . We are pleased to learn, for the honour of American ladies, that she is not a native of the United States." [4]

The *Christian Watchman*'s attacks on "rational religion" (Unitarianism) and Universalism throughout this period were almost as vehement.[5] The paper also reflected accurately the Baptists' growing interest in the various moral crusades of the age. Like Lyman Beecher, the editor of the *Christian Watchman* talked of "the Church" with a kind of proprietorial ownership which assumed that all evangelicals were at one in desiring to convert the world and bring on the millennium: "An experiment is now making in the Christian world upon a more extensive plan than was ever before adopted of uniting different denominations of Christians in objects for the general interests of the Church." [6]

In 1826 the *Christian Watchman* published an article urging the legislature to pass a law then under consideration in the legislature for the outlawing of lotteries.[7] To the Baptists "The immorality of lotteries" was

2. *Christian Watchman,* August 12, 1835, p. 141.
3. *Ibid.,* August 18, 1832, p. 150; August 14, 1829, p. 130.
4. *Ibid.,* August 1, 1828, p. 122.
5. For an attack on Universalism, see *ibid.* March 16, 1822; for an attack on rational religion see September 2, 1825.
6. *Ibid.,* July 13, 1822, p. 123.
7. *Ibid.,* February 3, 1826, p. 35.

based on their being simply a species of "public gaming" encouraged by the state and tempting the minds of the weak away from industry and frugality.[8] Like Beecher, the Baptists at this time also favored a law against dueling and laws against drunkenness.[9] An article in 1826 praised the Puritans for their laws against drunkenness and suggested that it might be well to compel habitual drunkards to wear a red letter "D" upon their clothes.[10]

But it was in the drive against the Sunday delivery of the mails that the Baptists first really let themselves go in this area. On May 29, 1828, a meeting of Baptist delegates from all over New England met in the Second Baptist Church in Boston and passed a series of resolutions calling for maintenance of Sabbath observance by the state. One of the resolutions stated "We consider the transport of the mail and delivery of letters . . . on the Sabbath-day to be a national sin." Another pledged the Baptists to patronize only stages and packets which did not operate on the Sabbath. The Baptists joined the Congregationalists in circulating, signing, and sending petitions to Congress to pass a law against the Sunday mail.[11]

As the decade drew to a close the *Christian Watchman* suddenly became aware of the increasing inroads of Popery. And then the editor rediscovered the evils of Masonry. As the 1830's began, the new heresy of Mormonism attracted their barbs. The stronger the evangelicals grew the more Satan seemed to be aroused to thwart them by raising new menaces to the Christian faith and the rising glory of America.[12] In 1829 the paper published a long paraphrase of Lyman Beecher's Thanksgiving Sermon entitled "The Dangers of Our Country," which indicated very clearly the extent to which the Baptists, once eager for change and reform, were now content with the direction the nation was taking and fearful of those forces which might alter its course. Or, as the editor said in commenting on Beecher's sermons, he was fearful of "these dangers which now obscure the fair prospects of our country" — meaning that he feared the forces which might prevent the growing domination of evangelical religious and social views as the new national establishment.[13]

The seven dangers which Beecher and the Baptists agreed on were first, "Sectional jealousy" which might divide the nation (and weaken the influence of New England); second, "Excess of liberty," which was the Whig

8. *Massachusetts Baptist Missionary Magazine*, n.s. IV (1814–1816) 14.
9. *Christian Watchman*, February 3, 1826, p. 108. For a Baptist tract against dueling see Thomas Baldwin, *The Dangers of Living Without the Fear of God* (Boston, 1819).
10. *Christian Watchman*, November 10, 1826, p. 198.
11. *Ibid.*, June 26, 1828, p. 90.
12. For attacks on "the Papists" see *ibid.* December 11, 1829, p. 197; February 19, 1830, p. 30, also *Massachusetts Baptist Missionary Magazine*, n.s. XII, 66. For an attack on the Masons see *Christian Watchman*, January 9, 1829, p. 7. For a typical attack upon the Mormons see *ibid.* November 9, 1832, pp. 177–178.
13. *Ibid.*, December 4, 1829, p. 195.

term for Jacksonian democracy and expansion of the suffrage; third, "Easy access to literary advantages," which would educate the mind but not re-generate the heart — "unless our schools of education are subjected to the control of moral principle they can be no security to our liberties" (the old anti-intellectual distrust of a learned ministry was now turning against the secularized public schools and state universities); fourth, "Infidelity," "atheism," and "mobs" — an obvious throwback to the New England fear of Jacobinism now leveled against Owenites and labor unions; fifth, "Wealth and luxury" which would corrupt the morals of the better classes as well as of social climbers (a fear of their own loss of innocence); sixth, "An established religion" — the Trinitarians and Baptists were at last agreed on this; and seventh, "The perils from the spread of Popery" — if the one million Roman Catholics in the nation "should unite in some favourite but corrupt election" they could perhaps "overthrow our republican institu-tions;" since all Catholics "are the obedient subjects of a foreign prince," they had no allegiance to American Protestant leaders; and "it must of course be a leading object with Catholics to destroy our republican govern-ment and overthrow our institutions" since all Catholics believed in mon-archy and absolutism.

If this is a fair summary of the outlook of the Baptists in 1829, and the editor of the leading Baptist journal in New England seemed to think it was, the denomination was obviously badly torn between its optimistic faith in the approaching millennium under Baptist leadership and its pessimistic fears that Satan and the innate depravity of man would frustrate "the Church" in its divine mission. Hence it is not surprising that the Baptist conservatives, like the "theocrats" in the Congregational and Presbyterian churches, felt compelled to call on the power of the state to pass laws to maintain order until the work of evangelism could regenerate the nation. They apparently saw no inconsistency between this use of the state to pre-serve moral order (and a Christian environment) and their claims that Christ's kingdom was not of this world (and that the church needed no assistance from the state to preserve it against the gates of Hell). They were therefore surprised when anticlericals like Leland and Jacksonians generally opposed the ban on the Sunday mails and objected strongly to the Rev. Ezra Stiles Ely's call for "a Christian Party in Politics." The Baptists could see no danger of a new kind of establishment of religion because this time they were themselves to be part of that establishment. And could anyone doubt that they stood for voluntarism and separation of church and state, for all that was good in religion and republicanism?

The *Christian Watchman* professed astonishment at "the foolish charge that orthodox Christians were endeavouring by Memorials to Congress to Unite Church and State" when all they were trying to do was preserve the Sabbath? [14] Assuming that an establishment meant the granting of special

14. *Ibid.*, March 13, 1829, p. 41.

privileges to one particular denomination, the editor pointed out that many different denominations were supporting the petitions against the Sunday mail. Even Unitarians like William Ellery Channing had signed the petitions. Did the opponents of this measure seriously conceive of the possibility that the Baptists would unite with the Unitarians and other denominations to seek some special establishment for themselves? [15]

The most outspoken criticism of the Sunday mail crusade in New England came from the *Universalist Trumpet*. It is not exaggeration to say that the Universalists founded this paper to provide an organ for anticlericalism against the aristocratic Unitarians on the one hand and against the evangelical demagogues (Trinitarian-Congregationalists and Baptist) on the other. The *Universalist Trumpet* stood squarely behind the views of John Leland against institutionalized religious and moral reform and in favor of Jacksonian democracy. In this respect the journal spoke for many Jacksonian radicals (anticlerical dissenters as well as rationalist liberals) among the lower and middle classes.

Only a few weeks after its first issue appeared on July 5, 1828, the editors of the *Universalist Trumpet* began to attack the Calvinist-dominated Union for Promoting the Observance of the Sabbath. They particularly disliked its instructing its members not to patronize those transportation and packet companies which carried freight or passengers on Sunday. This they said portended the creation of a political test for candidates for office; it was a pressure group which demanded that a man pledge himself to the views of the Union or else be deprived of the votes of their members.[16] And when Col. Richard M. Johnson issued his report defending the right of the government to deliver the mail on Sunday, the *Trumpet*'s editor showered him with praise.[17] *Trumpet* editorials opposed all Sabbath laws and hoped they would soon be repealed "suitable to the liberal spirit of the age." [18] When Lyman Beecher published his answer to Col. Johnson, the editors found in it proof for what "we have said, that the orthodox are aiming at a union of Church and State" because Beecher obviously expected Congress to enforce the religious views of the evangelicals.[19]

The Baptists expected this kind of attack from Universalists, but they were shocked when one of their own eminent leaders in the South echoed them. Professor James M. Staughton, M.D. of Georgetown College in Kentucky, a man with a D.D. from Princeton, who for some years had been pastor of the First Baptist Church of Philadelphia, wrote a letter in 1829 to

15. *Ibid.*, April 17, 1829, p. 62. For Channing's equivocal position on Sunday mail deliveries, see his article in the *Christian Examiner*, VII (1829) 135 ff. and the review of it in *The Spirit of the Pilgrims*, III (1830) 135 ff.
16. *Universalist Trumpet*, August 2, 1828, p. 20. For the *Trumpet*'s attack on Ely's call for "a Christian Party in politics" see February 6, 1830, p. 126.
17. *Ibid.*, January 31, 1829, p. 123; February 6, 1830, p. 126.
18. *Ibid.*, March 14, 1829, pp. 145–146.
19. *Ibid.*, March 28, 1829, p. 154.

the Rev. Joseph Ivimey, the renowned Baptist historian in London, in which he said that Col. Johnson's report "has met the views of our denomination exactly." When this was published, the *Christian Watchman* issued a vigorous denial: "The brethren here [in New England] of this denomination . . . very generally consider Col. Johnson's Report as an uncandid intimation of views foreign to the minds of the Memorialists against Sabbath Mails." Among those memorialists in the Baptist denomination were Elders Francis Wayland, Lucius Bolles, Daniel Sharp, and many other New England leaders. "The Baptists of our section of the country are as decidedly opposed to every measure which would have a favourable aspect to a religious establishment" as they are to the Sabbath mails.

> They therefore consider that part of the Report which suggests the danger of an 'extensive religious combination to effect a political object' and applies this contemptible motive to the Memorialists against Sabbath Mails as an intimation unfounded in fact . . . We are told it is dangerous to our religious liberty to lay before Congress their violation of the Sabbath and that it implies their [Congress's] authority to legislate about religion. Now we can see no such implication. We only ask Congress to cease their legal profanation of the Sabbath . . . We hope the time will never arrive when Christians shall fear to combine their efforts in sustaining in an argumentative and religious manner and with all due deference their opinion of the moral tendency of the laws or the legal conduct or proceedings of our highest authorities. When we shall fear to do this lest we should be considered bigots, or as acknowledging the civil authority in matters of conscience, we shall cease to deserve a continuance of our immunities.[20]

To clinch his argument, the editor could think of no better method than to quote a paragraph from the *New York Observer,* a staunchly evangelical Presbyterian journal in New York City which also refuted Staughton's letter:

> They [The Baptists] see as clearly as their Presbyterian, Episcopalian, and Methodist brethren that a law requiring the mail to travel and post-offices to be opened on Sunday in defiance of the religious creed of the leading denominations is an alarming invasion of the rights of the people; that like the infamous Test Act of Great Britain, it necessarily excludes under the government [in the Post Office Department] the most conscientious men in the land; that to submit to it quietly is to sanction a principle which may be used to rob religious men of all their rights and to convert our happy republic into an infidel despotism. The principal Baptists, we repeat it, see this clearly.[21]

To endorse the argument that the government must always act in conformity to "the religious creed of the leading denominations" was to use

20. *Christian Watchman,* October 16, 1829, p. 166.
21. *Ibid.*

the old argument of the Standing Order that the religious views of the minority must yield to those of the majority. And for the Baptists to claim that any government action that did not agree with their consciences was an infringement of their rights of conscience was to put the state at the beck and call of the evangelical majority.

The entire controversy made it perfectly plain that the New England Baptists had never advocated the kind of separation of church and state which Jefferson, Madison, and Leland stood for. They demanded a Christian state, and by Christian they meant their own brand of evangelicalism. "It would be folly, nay, hypocrisy, for us to deny that we should rejoice to see all Christians become Baptists, all Christian churches Baptist churches and all Christian ministers, Baptist ministers." [22]

After 1828 instead of urging their members to remain aloof from politics the Baptists berated them because too many "professors of vital godliness . . . prefer to stand almost entirely neuter" on vital issues. "This, however, is wrong." It leaves the government of the republic in the hands of the godless and profligate. True, a devout Christian should never sully himself by entering party politics but — the *Christian Watchman* argued rather inconsistently — "we can see no good reason why Christians should not make it a general rule to vote for no man, however splendid his name or imposing his talents, who is known to be a duellist, an adulterer, a gambler, a swearer or an intemperate man." So much for General Jackson! The political hero of the Baptists after 1828 became Senator Theodore J. Frelinghuysen of New Jersey — a true Christian who, it would appear, never let party loyalty stand above evangelical duty.[23]

For all their certitude about Sabbatarian legislation and personal moral reform, the Baptists found themselves as confused about the most serious moral and social problem of the period as were most other Americans. This was the issue of slavery, a problem which only the Quakers had found sufficiently clear-cut to merit a precise moral stand. The Baptists' ambiguity on the problem from 1820 to 1833 can be briefly but accurately traced in the comments on the subject which appeared in the *Christian Watchman* during this period.

After denouncing the Missouri Compromise as a "deed of horror" in March 1820, the *Watchman* portrayed slavery itself as "degrading and cruel . . . cursed of God and abhorred of men." [24] However, in December 1823, an article expressed equal horror at the thought of immediately emancipating the one and one-half million slaves then in the United States; it argued that it was first necessary to educate these slaves, and it proposed that this

---

22. *Ibid.*, October 16, 1829, p. 168.
23. *Ibid.*, January 29, 1830. Praise of Frelinghuysen is scattered throughout this newspaper after 1828. Their heroines in these years were Hannah More and Mrs. Adoniram Judson.
24. *Christian Watchman*, March 11, 1820, p. 3.

be undertaken in African (i.e. Black) schools under converted African teachers.[25] Two years later an article on the Negro proclaimed "The human family are all brethren and as brethren they ought to love and protect one another. All the differences that exist among them are merely accidental . . . When the master lashes his slave he lashes his brother." [26] In August 1828, an article praised Benjamin Lundy's address in the Federal Street Baptist church in Boston advocating abolition of slavery.[27] Yet a year after this the editor commented negatively upon "A spirited letter on involuntary slavery" which he had received. The letter called for "its entire abolition," but the editor stated, "Our columns bear witness that the odious sin of the Slave Trade has been long reprobated by us and that we are in favour of as speedy an emancipation of all who are in slavery as their best interest will admit. The immediate liberation of all would neither be a blessing to them nor to our country." [28] A few months later the editor defended the good work by the African Colonization Society against some unjust attacks.[29] But on July 26, 1833, he suggested that a national loan be undertaken, or else that direct taxes be levied, for the express purpose of buying the freedom of all of the slaves in the South from their masters and then educating them. Six months later the editor defended William Lloyd Garrison for his defense of Prudence Crandall's school.[30] And by December 1833, the editor was saying that the Colonization Society's efforts were entirely inadequate.[31] However, a few years later the New England Baptists were trying to quiet the abolitionists within their ranks. In 1844 Francis Wayland, one of the acknowledged spokesmen for the northern Baptists, engaged in a debate with Richard Fuller, one of the leading spokesmen for the southern Baptists. In this debate Wayland took virtually the same cautious antislavery position as William Ellery Channing had for the Unitarians and Lyman Beecher had for the Congregationalists: that slavery was a moral evil which was politically insoluble.[32] Then in 1845 the denomination split into a northern and southern wing which have not yet reunited.

The Baptist position on slavery was cautious and vacillating, but this was not so on other issues. In 1824 the Baptists spoke up for the independence of Greece, urging all Baptists to work for its accomplishment.[33] A year later the editor praised "the New Republics of South America," while

---

25. *Ibid.,* December 27, 1823, p. 11.
26. *Ibid.,* February 12, 1825, p. 37.
27. *Ibid.,* August 15, 1828, p. 130.
28. *Ibid.,* June 12, 1829, p. 94.
29. *Ibid.,* October 23, 1829, p. 170.
30. *Ibid.,* November 15, 1833, p. 184.
31. *Ibid.,* December 15, 1833, p. 198.
32. It is interesting that Fuller sought to defend slavery by quoting from Wayland's *Elements of Moral Science.* See Newman, *Baptists,* pp. 445–446.
33. *Christian Watchman,* January 3, 1824, p. 31.

deploring their establishment of the Roman Catholic Church.[34] In 1829 the paper hailed the passage of the Catholic Emancipation Act in England as "a triumph of principle over superstition and ecclesiastical tyranny." [35] That same year the journal spoke up for the Georgia Indians against the actions of the state of Georgia and the policy of Andrew Jackson.[36] Two years later it praised Jackson for his strong stand against South Carolina's Nullification Proclamation.[37] But it noted that Jackson should be consistent and also take a strong stand against Georgia regarding the Indian treaties.[38]

While it seems clear enough now that the Baptists were predominantly motivated by an individualistic laissez faire conception of society and an overemphasis on the direct personal relationship between man and God, this was not the way they saw their position in 1820. When William Ellery Channing delivered a sermon that year entitled "Religion A Social Principle," the Baptists felt called upon to disown the narrow individualism which he accused the evangelicals of acting upon. Channing was here wrestling with the great problem of nineteenth century Christianity — the breakdown of the corporate ideal of the state and its replacement by the atomism and intensely individualistic quality of economic laissez faire and evangelical religion. Channing himself, like Emerson, was torn on this point and never sufficiently reconciled the dual obligations of self-reliance and social responsibility. But he did see clearly the dangerous implications of individualistic evangelicalism, and he pointed them out in this sermon. This sermon, coming on the eve of the constitutional convention, was taken — probably rightly — as a defense of the established church; many people claimed that it helped significantly in preventing the convention from making any major alterations in Article Three. The editor of the *Massachusetts Baptist Magazine* said that the Baptists had read the sermon "with feelings of surprise and grief. We naturally supposed that he would urge the importance of supporting religion by law, but we did not expect to find so many illiberal remarks on other circumstances." One of these illiberal remarks was Channing's claim that evangelicals (Trinitarians, Baptists, Methodists) believed "that religion is a private affair between Man and his Maker." Another was his implication that they were "fanaticks." Channing holds, said the editor, that "religion is a social principle intimately united with social duty, operating upon us as social beings, and that it is not a secret to be locked up in our own hearts but a sentiment to be communicated, shared, and strengthened"; thus "a community once convinced of this great truth is bound to incorporate it into its public institutions." The Baptists thought this a poor excuse for an establishment, but on the

34. *Ibid.,* March 5, 1825, p. 51.
35. *Ibid.,* May 15, 1829, p. 78.
36. *Ibid.,* September 4, 1829, p. 141. Their principal interest was in the missionary activities among these Indians.
37. *Ibid.,* December 21, 1832, p. 202.
38. *Ibid.,* January 4, 1833, p. 2.

other hand it is precisely the reason behind the benevolent Christian activities in which they were so mightily engaged on a voluntary basis. If Channing meant to blame them for advocating separation of church and state, if that was what he meant by saying their religious individualism was atomistic, they would own it. But otherwise they claimed to believe as well as he that religion was a social principle.

However, they defined the term differently. "As a social principle religion not only binds man to his family and country but to the whole human race. It awakens sympathies for the wants and sorrows of mankind." And what are their wants and sorrows? The great want of mankind is to hear and accept the gospel. "It is to religion operating on the social affections that we are indebted for the exertions which have been made for the conversion of the heathen. Bible societies, missionary societies, and many other benevolent institutions are all the fruits of religion operating as a social principle on the hearts of men." The essence of the social principle of religion then, was the effort to regenerate sinners and to save their souls. How could any man show his love for his neighbor better than to be concerned for his eternal welfare? If that was excessive individualism, let Channing make the most of it. To the Baptists it was the only true Christian principle and to them it was a social one.[39]

In addition to the Christian nationalism or patriotism evidenced in the Baptists' support of missions and moral reforms, the New England wing of the denomination closely identified itself with the honor and destiny of the nation in other ways. I have already mentioned, for example, that the editors of the *Christian Watchman* found the infidelity of certain foreign visitors (Robert Owen, Frances Wright, Lafayette) an affront to national honor, not just to Baptist doctrines. The *Watchman* also found the secularism of the University of Virginia "discreditable to the nation" and to "our" reputation "abroad." The Missouri Compromise caused the *Watchman* to say "we blush for our country," and the delivery of the mail on Sunday was equally "a national sin." And conversely, the Second Great Awakening was a national blessing: "There is undoubtedly no one circumstance more favorable to the best interests of our beloved country than revivals of genuine religion . . . As therefore Christians love their country" let them "pray for revivals." [40] This identity of Baptist evangelical values with patriotic national values was in one respect compensation for their regional inferiority, but in another it was a sign that the Baptists of New England had found the means to transcend their inferiority feelings. Throughout the colonial period they had viewed the majority of their "country" (their

<hr/>

39. *Massachusetts Baptist Missionary Magazine,* n.s. III, 57 ff. For Baptist praise and criticism of Channing's election sermon of 1830 see *Christian Watchman,* May 29, 1830, p. 86.

40. *Christian Watchman,* December 4, 1819, p. 3; March 11, 1820, p. 3; June 6, 1828, p. 90; and April 14, 1821, p. 71.

colony) as the enemy, the oppressor, the corrupters of Christian Truth; what happened to "them" might or might not be good for "us." In many instances before 1776, the more trouble the Standing Order had with the home country, the happier the Baptists were. But in the 1820's (and after) the Baptists saw the United States of America as *their* country and felt themselves wholly in harmony with its ideals and its future. Since they had this stake in society and felt that its values were their values, whatever hurt the nation hurt the Baptists and whatever was good for the Baptists was good for the nation. Feeling they were no longer outsiders, an outgroup in a closed society, they doubtless overcompensated for their previous low status. In any case, the alteration in their perspective was highly significant for them and for the nation in the years ahead.

Of all the evidence that the Baptists in New England had entered into the mainstream of American life in the 1830's none is more dramatic and convincing than the career and writings of Francis Wayland, a graduate of Union College (1813) who had attended Andover Seminary and who was chosen the fourth President of Brown University in 1827. He not only made Brown the most dynamic and forward-looking evangelical college in New England (basing much of his reforms, curiously enough, upon Jefferson's curriculum for the University of Virginia), but in his nationally famous textbooks in *Moral Science* (1835) and *Political Economy* (1837) he put into eloquent form the essence of the American nineteenth century Evangelical temper.[41] Wayland's volumes went into many editions and became the most popular textbooks for the required course in moral philosophy in colleges across the nation for the next thirty or forty years. The important point is that no one thought of them as Baptist works — certainly Wayland did not. They were simply the best statements of the common American consensus on religion, philosophy, ethics, and political economy. Thus in the nineteenth century a Baptist became the philosopher and school teacher for the nation.

When this could happen, the New England Baptists were no longer dissenters. They belonged to the new establishment — the Evangelical Protestant establishment which dominated the national morality, directed the nation's destiny, and fostered its culture for the rest of the century. Those who disagreed with Wayland's principles became the dissenters in New England and the nation after 1835.

41. Even the Unitarians had high praise for Wayland; see the *Christian Register,* September 10, 1831, p. 147. For my interpretation of Wayland's contribution to the American Evangelical consensus of the nineteenth century see the introduction to *The American Evangelicals,* ed. W. G. McLoughlin (New York, 1968).

PART XIV

Epilogue

"Union of Christians will hereafter regulate political power in this and every other country."

Elder James Knowles, Second Baptist
Church of Boston, July 4, 1828

Epilogue

Thirty-five years ago, Perry Miller describing the "unwritten chapter" on religious liberty in America, said that "the Protestant churches did not so much achieve religious liberty as have liberty thrust upon them." [1] As Sidney Mead has recently shown [2] this is still a persuasive argument and a necessary corrective to those nineteenth-century religious historians who saw such a clear, straightforward march from Roger Williams to John Leland and the downfall of the final bastion of religious tyranny in Massachusetts in 1833.

But if the story I have told in these chapters is at all accurate, the history of religious liberty, at least in New England, is neither so fortuitous and unsought for as Perry Miller implied nor so triumphant and inevitable as his predecessors had said. However clearly Roger Williams, John Clarke, and Obadiah Holmes saw the principle in the seventeenth century, their efforts in Rhode Island did little to advance religious liberty elsewhere in New England. If anything, "the licentious republic" of Rhode Island was a detriment to the separation of church and state in the Puritan colonies — cited with contempt by its opponents and avoided with embarrassment by its friends. Voluntarism, said a defender of the establishment in Connecticut in 1818, was nothing but a return to "a state of nature"; i.e., it was license, not liberty, as the retrograde course of civilization in Rhode Island had demonstrated. [3]

Those Baptists who remained in Massachusetts to battle for their right to ignore infant baptism eschewed the rash course of Separatism as vehemently as they denied any kinship with Anabaptists or Munsterites. They did not even start the struggle for religious liberty in the name of toleration. They considered the ordinance they opposed a mere "inconsequential" or "nonessential" — a rite of no significance to salvation or to gospel truth (however necessary its abolition was to the complete reformation of gospel practice). "We do not separate from you," said Thomas Goold and his brethren

1. Perry Miller, "The Contribution of the Protestant Churches to Religious Liberty in Colonial America," *Church History*, IV (March, 1935), 57–66. Miller says that the Protestant churches by and large "did not [willingly] contribute to religious liberty, they stumbled into it, they were compelled into it, they accepted it at last because they had to, or because they saw its strategic value."

2. Sidney E. Mead, *The Lively Experiment* (New York, 1963), p. 19. Mead, however, seems to find more of a "positive ideological thrust" for religious liberty "by the Baptists" than I do.

3. Governor John Treadwell, quoted in the *Connecticut Courant*, September 22, 1818, p. 2.

to the Puritan magistrates and the church of Charlestown; you have forced us to leave. The difference, as the non-separating Congregationalists well knew, was one of vital importance.

At the same time that Goold and his friends felt compelled, against their wishes, to establish their own church on Noddles Island and to request the privilege of toleration, another and more eminent Baptist minister in Plymouth blandly followed the course he had practiced in England of open communion with pedobaptists. Neither John Myles nor Thomas Goold questioned the need for public support of religion. Neither demanded religious liberty for all Protestant dissenters — let alone for Roman Catholics or atheists. This early phase of religious toleration was largely an attempt to differentiate the protesters within the churches from schismatics and separatists. With the coming of toleration for dissent (within limits) in 1682, the schismatics became sectaries.

From 1690 to 1727 the Baptists in the old Plymouth area sought shelter within the establishment (seeking to manipulate the system to their own advantage), while those in Boston rested content with the good fortune which made that city an exception to the general system of religious taxation. For fifty years after the granting of the new charter to Massachusetts, the main thrust of the Baptist movement was toward assimilation or integration with the establishment, and by 1740 they had gone a long way in that direction. Cotton Mather felt certain that "the syncretism of piety" could be stretched to include fellow Calvinists like the Baptists so long as they strove to imitate their betters and be guided by them.

Not until the First Great Awakening forever wrent the Puritan social and religious order was there anything that might be called a struggle for religious liberty as that term later came to be understood. And even between 1740 and 1770 the Baptists fought primarily for toleration for themselves; they wished the tax exemption laws to be executed fairly and consistently, but they had no vision of the overthrow of the establishment nor any definition of what that overthrow would mean. Some of the Separates and the Rogerenes saw new light in this direction. The Rogerenes, of course, were fanatical visionaries whom no one — not even the Separates or Baptists — took seriously. The Separates came to their radical stance only when they found that they were not to be granted the privilege of tax exemption already granted to the Baptists, Quakers, and Episcopalians. Religious liberty in terms of disestablishment was not one of the causes of their separation any more than it was for the followers of Thomas Goold.

Finally, in 1773, the light of religious liberty dawned for Isaac Backus and his friends, but even then it was a dim and cloudy dawn. The abolition of the unfairly applied tax exemption laws was defended in grandiose terms, but the principle failed in application. The Baptists were no more consistent in defining religion liberty in the Revolutionary era than were the Congregationalists. For how could the Calvinistic defenders of religious truth exert themselves on behalf of heretics like the deists, the Shakers, the Methodists, the Universalists, or even the Freewill Baptists? The emergence and the success of new non-Calvinistic sects threw the Baptists completely off balance, and they maintained a teetering posture in regard to religious liberty for another generation. As late as 1820 the leading Baptists in Massachusetts were willing that Nothingarians and infidels should be taxed to support parish churches they did not attend. It had never been their intention to grant equal religious liberty to nonbelievers.

Yet to say that religious liberty was "thrust upon" the Protestant churches is to belittle both the battle the dissenters waged and the sufferings they endured. It is not even to damn with faint praise the significant accomplishments they courageously strove for and were generously granted. The eighteenth-century Congregationalists were not deaf or instransigent toward the claims of religious minorities in their midst. If their Congregational neighbors could sometimes be petty and vindictive, they could also be — and often were — willing to yield in the end to conscientious dissent. The Baptists' courage and persistence in seeking liberty for their consciences were not, as their opponents claimed, sheer fanaticism. If their Calvinistic version of Truth is not ours, their victories were nonetheless victories for religious liberty. One does not have to accept the doctrines of Jehovah's Witnesses to applaud their challenge to compulsory flag salutes in the classroom.

It is difficult to establish a meaningful criterion by which to judge the degree of oppression the New England Baptists suffered. Compared to the dissenters in Rhode Island or in Pennsylvania in the colonial era, they were indeed oppressed; but compared to dissenters in Virginia or in the British Isles, they enjoyed extraordinary freedom. Their legal status as citizens, contrasted to that of Roman Catholics and other dissenters (like the Rogcrenes, the Separates, the Shakers, the avowed deists or atheists) was also extremely favorable. Yet the amount of social prejudice and discrimination against them was considerable. A wide variety of legal technicalities was used to harass them. They were subjected to mob violence as late at 1782 and were treated with general scorn in many towns well into the nineteenth century. Even in the courts of justice they were often discriminated against by judges and juries. I am nevertheless inclined to conclude that the Baptists probably achieved their gradual emancipation about as fast as could be reasonably expected in their circumstances (i.e., relative to their numbers, the justice of their complaints, the effort they were willing and able to make, and the political situation at the time).

Whether the Baptists epitomized in their beliefs and actions (consciously or unconsciously) the transformation of New England from a conformist, elitist, corporate Christian Commonwealth to an atomistic, individualistic, laissez faire, quasi-secular democracy the reader must judge for himself. Certainly the tyranny of the nineteenth-century evangelical majority was far from a Jeffersonian ideal. In a liberal, open society like America where the forces of change are habitually accepted as the forces of progress, the Baptists had a vested interest in the downfall of the Standing Order and the Federalist Party which upheld it. Significantly, in New England, unlike Virginia, the dissenters were unable to enlist the rationalist liberals of the eighteenth century in their support. John Adams and Robert Treat Paine make, as we have seen, a significant contrast to Thomas Jefferson and James Madison in this regard, for their Unitarianism did not at all constrain them toward disestablishment. And even the Democratic-Republican Party in New England was unable to do what Jefferson and Madison had done earlier in Virginia. Still, I am convinced that the rise of the Baptists and the rise of Jeffersonian democracy is more than mere coincidence. Their adherents aided and abetted each other for reasons that they did not entirely agree upon. Nevertheless they both opposed what to them seemed aristocratic and paternalistic aspects of the old order in the name of republicanism and equality. If Jefferson and his dissenting allies were sometimes pretentious and self-righteous, they were on the whole less so than their opponents.

For John Leland to become a spokesman for the Baptists in New England (as he had earlier for this sect in Virginia) is as anomalous as for Theophilus Parsons to be the spokesman for liberal religion. Leland was not conservative enough to be a good evangelical Baptist, and Parsons was not liberal enough to be a good Unitarian (in Jeffersonian terms). The anomaly is not unlike the many inconsistencies which the Baptists themselves demonstrated in their struggle for religious liberty. Not only did they make many compromises with the establishment and show little concern for the religious liberty of other dissenters, but as advocates of voluntarism they by no means abandoned their belief that the nation was and must remain Christian (that is, evangelically Protestant). And if George Blake was self-contradictory in 1820 in opposing disestablishment (though he was a Jeffersonian Republican) because it meant "everything might be safely left to each individual," the Baptists were equally self-contradictory in seeking in the early nineteenth century, government aid for missions, for accurate Bibles, for religious education, and for moral legislation to uphold the Sabbath and temperance, or to punish blasphemy, theater-going, card-playing and other evils. Baptist religious laissez faire was no more consistent than business and mercantile laissez faire which demanded subsidies, monopolistic charters, internal improvements, and protective tariffs from a government which was supposed to let each man advance his own self-interest.

Essentially, the dissenters and the defenders of the establishment had throughout the course of the two centuries, from 1630 to 1830, a far greater harmony of interest than they had in opposition. It is wrong to see the two as essentially pitted against each other in a life or death struggle. True the old Standing Order was destroyed (or, more accurately, transformed) but from its ruins the evangelical Congregationalists emerged unscathed to become leaders in the new evangelical moral reformation of the Second Great Awakening and the Age of Jackson. The Baptists of New England did not become Loyalists in 1776, but many of them became Whigs after 1824. Lyman Beecher and Thomas Baldwin were equally convinced that the Second Great Awakening and the missionary and moral reform movements which it spawned would provide an even better means than an establishment to unite the nation and usher in the millennium.

For the Baptists the accomplishment of religious liberty was always a secondary goal (just as it was secondary to the Puritans' emigration to Massachusetts). The primary goal was the triumph of the Truth of God and the establishment of His Kingdom on earth. In their desire to produce a Christian nation and to Christianize the world, the standing Order and the dissenters were arguing about means not ends, much as the Presbyterians and the Independents in England did in the mid-seventeenth century. The Baptists in New England must not be equated with the Levellers and Diggers, the Fifth Monarchy Men, and the other radical revolutionaries of the Interregnum. They were conservatives, and they rightly insisted that they had no quarrel with the civil, social, and intellectual ideals of the New England community. They fought not to overthrow the New England system but to purge it of its errors and to establish it on a more correct foundation. The quarrel was an intramural one, a domestic squabble in the house of pietism. As it turned out, the new architectural designs could not be effected simply by renovations in the old structure. But both groups went out of the old house to build the new one together. The Trinitarian-Congregationalists became as disgusted with their old and constantly remodeled living quarters as did the Baptists. Again contrast with the downfall of the establishment in Virginia is significant. The Episcopal church was almost destroyed when its house was brought down on its head. But the Congregationalists emerged stronger than ever (only the Unitarians suffered and, having control of their neighborhood of Boston, their suffering was not noticeably great).

The established system in New England died, as in any conservative evolution, by being whittled away. That is probably the safest way to dismantle an old institution, no matter how frustrating it is to those who chafe at the slowness of change. I draw no lessons about a usable past. I only conclude that America, even at its most liberal or pietistic, has been an essentially conservative community; the history of religious liberty chronicled here was a conservative transformation not a revolution.

To me the most important aspect of the saga of the Baptists is not, in the end, the doctrine of separation of church and state which they evolved, but the way in which they took advantage of the flexibility and opportunity of the New World experience to make their dissent respectable. In seeking Christian liberty for themselves, they helped (almost in spite of themselves) to expand the concepts of freedom and equality for everyone. The radical Reformation doctrine of the supremacy of private judgment in religion became united, after 1775, to the democratic concept of a higher law than that of any church or state constitution; together they eventually produced the anti-institutional individualism which dominated American life in the nineteenth century (even though many Baptists in New England pulled back from the anarchistic implications of this trend when they realized that it gave license to atheism and thus fatally undermined the Biblical injunction that civil government was ordained of God for the enforcement of His will, not the majority's.)

The war against privilege, aristocracy, and institutions in America was waged in three overlapping phases. First, it was a war against an established, tax-supported church system — a war begun in 1740 and ended in 1833. Second, it was a war against King and Parliament, begun in 1765 and ended in 1783. And third, it was a war against financial and mercantile monopoly, begun in 1792 and ended in 1832 (with the veto of the bank charter). And while these phases of revolt were taking place in the external world, a similar threefold revolution was taking place in the inner world of American thought. From 1740 to 1776 the people fought for a new definition of liberty of conscience: from 1776 to 1800 they fought for a new concept of republican government; from 1800 to 1835 they fought a two-sided battle for a redefinition of human nature, rejecting Calvin's theory of total depravity on the one hand and deism's theory of inherent goodness and rationality on the other, to emerge with an evangelical Christian conception of freedom of the will.

As this study has tried to show, the continuous search for liberty and equality in religion, politics, and economics owes much more than we have realized to the pietistic doctrine of the priesthood of all believers — the notion that God, through the Holy Spirit, often employs the weak and foolish of this world to confound the learned and powerful. As instruments of God the sectaries in America fought a two hundred year's war against established authority in church and state to emerge in the Age of Jackson with their slogan a reality: "The voice of the people is the voice of God; all power to His lambs!"

Free grace for a free society. Religion, the moral control of God's grace operating through the regenerated individual heart, became the only acceptable authority in a "new world" of unbounded space and opportunity.

Then it was that American pietism, assuming power, learned corruption.

Bibliographical Essay   Index

Bibliographical Essay

Because the dissenters' efforts to gain religious freedom in New England began at the local level and were so often resolved (for or against them) by local circumstances, the basic sources for this study had to be local records. One of the first steps in my research therefore entailed visits to over one hundred towns throughout New England where I knew or suspected that there had been quarrels at various times between the established church or parish and dissenters of one sect or another. In each of these towns I tried to locate and to look at four different sets of records: those of the established (Congregational) church or churches; those of the parish or official ecclesiastical society; the records of town meeting, and those of the Baptist and other dissenting churches and societies.

From the Congregational church records I was able to discover when the dissent had begun as a pietistic movement within the established system, who the leaders were, what their arguments were, and how the church dealt with them. From the parish records I discovered when and what taxes had been levied and collected for the support of the established church and how and when exemptions (or applications for exemption) from these taxes were made. From the town records (often the town meeting also served as the parish meeting) I discovered how ministers were chosen and paid, what local offices were held by dissenters, how certificates were recorded, how quarrels between the church and the town (or parish) were resolved regarding a choice of minister or meetinghouse site, and how the town reacted to lawsuits, to civil disobedience, or to other disturbances of the peace by dissenters. From the dissenting church and society records I learned when and how these churches were formed, what were their articles of faith, how their meetinghouses were built and their ministers paid, which churches they had fellowship with, how they disciplined their members, and whether they thrived or broke up.

The search for local records was easiest in Connecticut, for there almost all of them have been gathered into the State Library in Hartford. Although few towns have all four kinds of records available (the parish records are the most difficult to find), there are sufficient numbers surviving to provide what seems an adequate sampling. Some day perhaps scholars will be more systematic in dealing with these records from a statistical point of view. Imaginative use of tax records, land records, and probate records in conjunction with these other local records could provide a more precise evaluation of the wealth, family structure, and social position of the members of the various dissenting bodies over the years.

The search for local records in other New England states was far more difficult. While the town records, by law, are kept in the office of the town clerk, the records of churches and parishes are often still in the churches or in private hands. It would be helpful if state and denominational historical societies would undertake a systematic process of locating and making copies of these church records before more of them disappear. At the very least it would be valuable to have a list of the current location and ownership of these records to update the now almost useless WPA historical survey lists compiled over thirty years ago. A few, but not many, early church records have found their way into university libraries and local and state historical societies.

In addition to the church and society records, the records of denominational associations are sometimes helpful. No such records exist for the Rhode Island Association of General Baptists formed in 1692, though a few scattered documents referring to it are among the Isaac Backus Papers at the Rhode Island Historical Society. A good proportion of the manuscript papers of the Warren Baptist Association for the years 1767 to 1800 are among the Backus Papers at Andover Newton Theological School in Newton Centre, Massachusetts, including an unpublished history of the association which Backus wrote. But I have been unable to locate the manuscript papers of any other Baptist Association for the years before 1830. To some extent the published "minutes" of each of the associations fill this gap. There are more or less complete files for all of these; they contain not only annual lists of churches, ministers, deacons, and membership statistics but also important quotations from letters sent to the association seeking answers to church problems and an annual circular letter exhorting the member churches upon important issues of the moment. A close, comparative study of their association minutes would, I think, produce interesting new insights into the Baptists' development.

The single most important collection of papers for this study is the collected papers of Isaac Backus at Andover Newton Theological School. Other important parts of Backus's unique and remarkable collection of manuscripts are at Brown University, the Rhode Island Historical Society, and the Western Reserve Historical Society in Cleveland. As the first major historian of the New England Baptists and a man who played a leading role in the denomination for over half a century, Backus collected or was given over 10,000 items — letters, petitions, official statements, affidavits, records of the Grievance Committee and the Warren Association, and church council results. In addition there are copies and notes which he himself took from now lost church, private, court, and state papers. Backus's papers also include his own Separate church records, his diary (covering the years 1748 to 1806), his sermon notes, unpublished tracts, and many of his private letters. In 1856 the Backus Historical Society was formed in Newton, Massachusetts and over the years it added other papers to his collection. The bulk of these papers are now at Andover Newton Theological School. Efforts are being made to publish these with the help of grants from the National Historical Publications Commission, and Brown University is preparing a detailed index of them. A large part of the collection is available on microfilm from the Southern Baptist Historical Commission in Nashville, Tennessee. William Henry Allison made a rough calendar of the documents for his *Inventory of Unpublished Material for American Religious History in Protestant Church Archives and Other Repositories* (Washington, 1910.)

Miscellaneous items of New England Baptist primary material can be found in the well-indexed collections of the Baptist Historical Society (Rochester, New York), the Brown University Library, the Rhode Island Historical Society, the Massachusetts Historical Society, the Connecticut Historical Society, the New York Public Library, the Pennsylvania Historical Society, the American Antiquarian Society, the Vermont State Library, the Newport Historical Society and the New Hampshire Historical Society. A few of Backus's early manuscripts have been recently discovered at Regents Park College Library in London (a microfilm is at the Brown University Library) and the Western Reserve Historical Society.

Except for the Backus papers, no other colonial Baptist leader appears to have left any significant collection of his private or public papers. The Backus Papers contain a few items by John Davis, Hezekiah Smith and Samuel Stillman. The diary of John Comer is at the Rhode Island Historical Society with a group of papers relating to Elder Nicholas Eyres of the Newport Baptist church and the manuscript of Morgan Edwards "Materials for a History of the Baptists in Rhode Island" (1771). A few records of John Clarke and Obadiah Holmes are at the Newport Historical Society with the diary of Elder Peleg Burroughs of Tiverton, Rhode Island and some early Baptist church records. The papers of Elder Daniel Hix of Dartmouth, Massachusetts are in the Free Public Library of New Bedford, Massachusetts. The diary of Elder Joseph Dimock is at the Maritime Baptist Historical Collection, Acadia University Library, Nova Scotia. The Moses Brown Papers at the Rhode Island Historical Society and the Brown Family Papers at the John Carter Brown Library, Brown University contain a few items relating to the Baptists. Almost nothing is known to have survived of the papers of John Leland, Samuel Stillman, Hezekiah Smith, James Manning, Thomas Baldwin, or of any of the lesser figures among the Baptists. The Library of Congress does have the diary of Hezekiah Smith (parts of which are also in the Massachusetts Historical Society). Brown University has some letters of James Manning, Samuel Jones and David Howell relating to the college. The James Terry Collection at the Connecticut Historical Society is the only significant collection of Separate manuscripts, mostly relating to the Canterbury Separate Church and its leaders Solomon and Elisha Paine. (There are some Separate church records at the Connecticut State Library and the New London County Historical Society.) The scarcity of private papers and dissenting church records is good indication of how insignificant the dissenters were, or thought they were, and how little interest New England's collectors of antiquities showed in these.

Next in importance to local records and private papers, the most important primary sources for this study have been the county court house records and the state supreme court records of the New England states. These are a largely untapped but marvelously rich source' for American religious and social history and I have utilized only a scant proportion of what they contain. Like my approach to local records, my use of court records was based on a list of some two hundred incidents in Baptist history (and that of other dissenting groups) which involved legal adjudication. Starting with those cases which reached the supreme courts, I then worked back to county courts. If a case reached the supreme court, usually all of the papers relating to the case are in the supreme court files. The published *Reports* of supreme court cases also were very helpful in supplementing this research, but these were not begun until the nineteenth century. For my purposes the richest manuscript materials are those in the Middlesex, Bristol, Suffolk, and Worcester county court houses and the files of the Massachusetts Supreme Court in Boston. Many of the early court records for Connecticut are in the State Library in Harford though some of these, especially those for New London County, are in very bad condition.

Legal history, like the statistical study of local records, is just beginning to arouse new interest among historians. Edward Buck's *Massachusetts Ecclesiastical Law* (Boston, 1865) is greatly in need of revision, and so is Emory Washburn's *Sketches of the Judicial History of Massachusetts* (Boston, 1810). George Lee Haskins, *Law and Authority in Early Massachusetts* (New York, 1960) is helpful for the earliest years of the colony. The introduction and annotation done by L. Kinvin Wroth and Hiller Zobel for John Adams's *Legal Papers* (Cambridge, 1965) is perhaps the best work on Massachusetts law available in this field, but they treat only three of John Adams's cases in ecclesiastical law. John D. Cushing has written several good articles in this area; see especially his "Notes on Disestablishment in Massachusetts," *William and Mary Quarterly*, XXVI (1969) 169–190. I have also found useful the chapter on ecclesiastical law in Nathan Dane's *General Abridgment and Digest of American Law* (Boston, 1823–29) and Jeremiah Smith, *Decisions of the Superior and Supreme Courts of New Hampshire* (Boston, 1879). On Connecticut law the most useful book is still Zephaniah Swift's, *A System of the Laws of the State of Connecticut* (Windham, 1795–1796). Some indication of the imaginative new ways in which legal records can be used to study religious history can be seen in Kai T. Erikson's recent study, *The Wayward Puritans* (New York, 1966).

In many respects the most valuable and frequently used primary source for this study has been the legislative archives of each state. These records are on the whole well-ordered and well-indexed and are located in the office of the secretary of state or in the state library or state archives room of each state capitol. They contain petitions to the legislature from dissenters of all kinds (singly, by churches, and by denominations) seeking redress of grievances, reports of legislative committees directed to investigate religious problems, counterpetitions defending the established system (usually by selectmen or parish officials), petitions for the setting off of new parishes or ecclesiastical societies, drafts of legislation to cope with these problems, petitions for incorporation and for lottery privileges, and often excerpts from now lost local records relevant to local quarrels. Since dissenting groups did not, until late in the eighteenth century, put their arguments for toleration, religious liberty, and disestablishment into learned tracts, sermons, or pamphlets, these petitions often provide the only source for discerning their attitudes on these questions. A detailed study of all these petitions, comparing the various arguments over the years in each colony and state by each dissenting denomination, would be a very valuable book, especially if it included some of these petitions in an appendix. Because the legislature often was obliged, or felt obliged, to settle local problems which a congregational polity could not resolve, these records deal with the most minute aspects of ecclesiastical law as well as the broad general policies of the establishment. After 1780, however, these problems were generally resolved by the courts.

Any list of printed primary sources would be too extensive to include here. I have tried to read every extant tract written by New England dissenters in these years, particularly those which touch in any way on the question of religious liberty and disestablishment. This also entailed reading the Congregationalists (lay and clerical) defenses of the establishment. The literature is not as extensive on this issue as one might expect, for the "illiterate" dissenters seldom felt able to argue these points with their learned opponents. However, since I have also been concerned in this study with church polity, the arguments over infant baptism, the qualifications for the ministry, and the changing nature of Calvinist theology, the number of tracts I have consulted on these polemical topics has been much greater. Edward C. Starr's bibliography of tracts relating to the Baptists is basic for this. The bibliographies included by M. L. Greene, C. C. Goen, and Richard L. Bushman in their works (cited below) give the most important titles which I have cited in my footnotes.

Newspapers and magazines became relevant for this study only after 1765, and even then their usefulness was limited to specific occasions when, for peculiar reasons, a religious issue assumed political importance. By and large the newspapers eschewed religious issues (Thomas Prince's *Christian History,* 1743–1745, was the notable exception), particularly those regarding dissenters: First, because the newspapers (outside Rhode Island) were, like everything else, run by members of the establishment, second, most newspapers, especially after 1795, took on a party bias and as official or semi-official organs of a party they refrained from commenting on issues on which the party did not wish to take a stand — religious liberty was (as I have indicated) one of the least fashionable political issues for any party. But probably even more important, newspapers considered their prime purpose to be the conveyance of political, economic, and literary "intelligence" — religion was left to the ministers and churches. Nowhere is the separation of the sacred and the secular more evident. One can read scores of issues of almost any New England newspaper between 1765 and 1830 without finding one mention of the question of dissent or religious liberty.

However, on those occasions when a religious issue did become central to a political struggle, such as during the constitution-making process in each state or during the final disestablishment process, then the newspapers assume central importance for historians of religion. As my footnotes indicate, the lengthy "communications" and epistolary warfare by contributors in the press (usually and unfortunately anonymously written) present some of the most important sources of public opinion on both sides. An anthology of these pseudonymous letters would be a valuable addition to our understanding of church-state issues. In addition, when newspapers began, after 1790, to report debates in the state legislatures, their pages represent the best, sometimes the only, source for discovering which individual legislators voted on which side and for what reasons on religious bills.

In the early nineteenth century the various denominations began to publish their own magazines and newspapers, and these are fundamental to this study for 1800 to 1833. I have made particularly heavy use of the following:

SECULAR NEWSPAPERS: Columbian Centinel (Boston), *Boston Statesman, Boston Independent Chronicle, Eastern Argus* (Portland), *Providence Gazette, The Phenix or Windham Herald, New London Bee, Connecticut Journal* (New Haven), *New London Gazette, The Farmers Journal* (Danbury), *Middlesex Gazette* (Middletown, Conn.) *Norwich Packet and Country Journal, Columbian Register* (New Haven), *American Mercury* (Hartford), *Hartford* (or *Connecticut*) *Courant, The Pittsfield Sun, The Western Star* (Stockbridge) *Boston Evening Post, Boston Gazette and Country Journal, Boston Independent Ledger and American Advertiser, Massachusetts Gazette and Boston Weekly Advertiser, Continental Journal and Weekly Advertiser* (Boston).

RELIGIOUS JOURNALS: Christian Secretary (Baptist, Hartford), *Christian Watchman and Baptist Reflector* (Boston), *Massachusetts Baptist Missionary Magazine* (Boston) *Universalist Trumpet and Magazine* (Boston), *Boston Recorder* (Trinitarian), *The Spirit of the Pilgrims*

(Trinitarian, Boston), *Christian Register* (Unitarian, Boston) *Christian Examiner* (Unitarian, Boston) *Herald of Gospel Liberty* (Christ-ian, Portsmouth, N. H.).

In addition to these primary materials, I have relied greatly on local town and county histories, gazetteers, and the yellowing files of long-defunct local historical society journals. But I wish to enter a caveat to historians who do not check these accounts against official records wherever possible. The historian of today owes a great debt to those amateur historians of the nineteenth century who compiled most of these massive tomes, often quoting at length from local town and church records which now have disappeared (often one suspects, into the attics of the local historians who used them). But it is important to make allowance for the cultural and religious biases of these writers. Almost all of them were members of the Congregational or Unitarian church in their towns and many of them were clergymen of these churches. These authors were intensely filiopietistic and loyal to their Puritan or Pilgrim forefathers. A large proportion of these histories were written when Americans were facing the new pluralism of "foreign" immigration which did not share the old Yankee or WASP values and traditions and certainly did not share its religious heritage or admire it. Partly therefore to build up their Puritan forebears and partly to enhance their own declining status, these local historians often gave short shrift to the dissenters and social deviants of earlier days. In addition, today's scholarly criteria for fidelity to the original sources were seldom adhered to and very few quotations from original manuscripts were transcribed with what is acceptable accuracy today.

Almost every town in New England has at least one official history, and it is a great virtue of the older ones that they devote considerable space to ecclesiastical history — often trying with great care to establish the first members and founding dates of every church and congregation. These local histories are also valuable for putting the dry legal or legislative records into more human form and contexts, so that the local issues stand out as intense and vital episodes in the story of that town. Among older local histories, the works of Ellen Larned, Arthur E. Wilson, Thomas Weston, Francis M. Caulkins, Josiah T. Paine, Richard L. Bowen, George F. Clark, J. E. A. Smith, John Daggett, and D. Hamilton Hurd are outstanding. Among newer local histories, the books and articles of Philip J. Greven, Sumner C. Powell, Richard Birdsall, Charles S. Grant, Benjamin W. Labaree, Darrett B. Rutman, and George D. Langdon deserve special mention. I am also much indebted to John M. Bumsted's excellent doctoral dissertation, "The Pilgrim's Progress: the Ecclesiastical History of the Old Colony, 1620–1775," Brown University, 1965.

Baptist historians's works have had some of the same failings as have those of local historians. The older ones in particular tried too hard to establish the uniquely important role of their denomination in the history of Christianity and of America. As well as arguing the case for the scriptural truth of infant baptism and worrying over Baptist quarrels regarding Calvinism and Arminianism, open and closed communion, and seventh and sixth day worship which were so vital to their own history, they have consistently glorified their heroes of religious liberty and denigrated their Puritan "persecutors." Nevertheless, like local historians, their intense concern for details, names, dates, church foundings, ordinations, and other institutional data — have provided information on which any historian must build and for which he must be grateful. The earliest Baptist historians of New England are of course primary sources — John Callendar, Morgan Edwards, Isaac Backus, David Benedict, Richard Knight. Of the nineteenth century Baptist historians have drawn upon H. M. King, Henry S. Burrage, Nathan E. Wood, Henry C. Crocker, William Cathcart, Frederick C. Denison, and A. H. Newman. Newman's volume on *The Baptists* (New York, 1894) is still the most scholarly institutional history of the denomination, but it is badly out-of-date; it is surprising that no one has sought to revise him. Among modern Baptist historians, who fortunately have none of their predecessors's axes to grind, I have been greatly helped by the works of Winthrop S. Hudson, Edwin S. Gaustad, and Norman H. Maring.

Biographies of most of the Baptist leaders are considerably out-of-date (with the exception of Roger Williams for whom Perry Miller and Edmund S. Morgan have written outstanding interpretative studies in recent years). I have tried to update Alvah Hovey's old biography of Isaac Backus in a short biography of my own (Boston, 1967) but readers interested in Backus should also see the doctoral dissertations about him by Thomas B. Maston (Yale, 1939) and Milton V. Backman (University of Pennsylvania, 1962). Reuben A. Guild's old biographies of James Manning and Hezekiah Smith are solid but narrow. Thomas W. Bicknell's biography of *John Clarke* (Providence, 1915) contains all the known facts but pushes its thesis too hard. Henry M. King's biography of *John Myles* (Providence, 1905) is brief but useful. There is no good biography of Samuel Stillman, though he deserves one. Jeremiah Chaplin's *Life of Henry Dunster* (Boston, 1872) deals adequately with Dunster's antipedobaptism. Lesser Baptist figures sometimes have memorial sermons or historical sketches about them. A good biography of John Leland would be welcome, though it would have to draw heavily on the fine article by Lyman Butterfield in American Antiquarian Society *Proceedings,* LXLL (1952) 156–242. Short sketches of major Baptist figures appear in William B. Sprague's *Annals of the American Pulpit,* VI (New York, 1860) and in *The Baptist Memorial and Monthly Chronicle* (New York). Often the minutes of the various Baptist associations contain memorial sketches of early leaders; see especially Stephen Wright, *History of the Shaftsbury Association* (Troy, 1833). Henry C. Crocker, *History of the Baptists in Vermont* (Bellows Falls, 1913) and Henry S. Burrage, *History of the Baptists in Maine* (Portland,

1904), which provide valuable biographical and historical material supplementing the sketches in the histories of Backus and Benedict.

Some of the dissenters wrote their own autobiographies (John Gano, Elias Smith, Dan Young, Billy Hibbard, Lorenzo Dow, Orange Scott, and Francis Asbury's journals), but these are usually the products of old age when factual details were only dimly recalled. For the other side of the picture, the Congregationalists' great clerical diaries and autobiographies are useful for the tone they take toward dissenters (when they deign to mention them).

The most important monographs on disestablishment in New England are M. Louise Greene, *The Development of Religious Liberty in Connecticut* (Boston, 1905), Susan M. Reed, *Church and State in Massachusetts, 1691–1740* (Urbana, Illinois, 1914), Jacob C. Meyer, *Church and State in Massachusetts, 1740–1833* (Cleveland, 1930), Charles B. Kinney, Jr., *Church and State: The Struggle for Separation in New Hampshire* (New York, 1955), and David B. Ford, *New England's Struggles for Religious Liberty* (Philadelphia, 1896). Richard J. Purcell's *Connecticut in Transition 1775–1818* (Washington, 1918) also deals at some length with this problem but he is interested primarily in social and political affairs. On the whole, all of these are unsatisfactory because they do not deal with the local situations and seldom have they utilized the relevant legal, legislative, and local archival sources. None of them used church records, for instance, or utilized the Isaac Backus papers. Reed's is the best of the lot in this respect though she is not especially interested in social or intellectual history. Kinney's book is devoted to a broader historical picture and almost half of this volume deals with events since 1819; it is, however, solidly researched. Ford's book relies heavily on Backus and is written from the Baptist viewpoint. Meyer is skimpy and superficial throughout, Greene's makes the most concerted effort to treat the whole story (at least for Connecticut) but her omission of denominational local and court records results in too abstract an approach. The best general study of this subject is Sidney E. Mead, *The Lively Experiment* (New York, 1963). Much more can and needs to be done in this area. Detailed monographs of dissent in each colony, even if they deal only with small chronological or denominational segments, will ultimately be the only way to tell the whole story of dissent and disestablishment in America.

There is nothing in recent scholarship immediately pertinent to this study, but there are a number of valuable studies which are essential to understanding the background of it. Perhaps the most closely related to this book is Clarence C. Goen's *Revivalism and Separatism in New England* (New Haven, 1962). Goen's study of the Separates and Separate-Baptists is concerned primarily with theology, and ecclesiology and as such it is extremely perceptive. It does not concern itself very directly with the social and political issues involved in this movement and has little to say in concrete legal terms about the efforts to overthrow the establishment. But it does provide valuable insights into the religious issues at stake in the Awakening. Richard L. Bushman's *From Puritan to Yankee* (Cambridge, 1967) concerns Connecticut's transition from a Puritan theocracy to a Yankee republic in the years 1690 to 1765 and the Great Awakening is for him the pivotal point. Heimert's *Religion and the American Mind from the Great Awakening to the Revolution* (Cambridge, 1966) treats the whole colonial experience in terms of the intellectual impact of the Awakening. Bushman's book is more carefully anchored in social and political history and its emphasis on the crisis in the definition or redefinition of authority in Connecticut seems to me extremely important. Heimert's book has performed an equally valuable service in emphasizing the radical potential inherent in the evangelical theology, philosophy, and fervor of the Great Awakening. I would link all three of these books to the contributions made by Norman Pettit, *The Heart Prepared* (New Haven, 1966), Edmund S. Morgan, *Visible Saints* (New York, 1963), Geoffrey Nuttall's *The Holy Spirit in Puritan Faith and Experience* (Oxford, 1946) and Nuttall's *Visible Saints* (Oxford, 1957). What these books seem to me to have done is to open up for new consideration the psycho-theological facets of Puritan mysticism or, if you will, Reformation pietism. Since, as I have indicated in this study, I believe America to be a pietistic nation which has its roots in the pietistic aspects of the Reformation and its aftermath (Anabaptist, Puritan, Separatist, Congregational, Methodist), I consider the works of Morgan, Pettit, and Nuttall fundamental to any understanding of the American religious experience in the colonial period. These works also give added prestige to H. Richard Niebuhr's ground-breaking book, *The Kingdom of God in America* (Chicago, 1937).

We need a great deal more research in specific chronological, geographical and denominational areas to pin down this concept. I have tried here to pin it down concerning the Baptists, to indicate how the Baptist schism turned into a sect and then to a respectable denomination primarily from pietistic motives or assumptions about the nature and destiny of man. I have tried to show (as I think the works of Heimert and Bushman show) that there is an important correlation between the American Revolution and the Great Awakening in terms of evangelical pietism. To understand what happened to the theocratic, aristocratic, stratified and paternalistically controlled social order in New England between 1630 and 1833 requires an understanding of the pietistic elements within Puritanism — elements which the Puritans were unable, in the New World environment, to control as they wished.

Index

Abbott, F. E., II, 911
Abington, Mass., I, 641
"A. B. M." letter of, II, 1239–1242
Abrahamic Covenant, I, 28–29, 31–48, 58,
  69, 315–317, 351, 427, 434; II, 1017–
  1018
Abyssinian Baptist Church of N. Y., II,
  766 n. 48
Act for the Support of Religion and Lit-
  erature, II, 1034–1042
Act of Uniformity (1662), I, 130, 216
Act of Union (1707), I, 216, 220
Acushnet, Mass., I, 186, 197
Adams, Daniel, II, 1105
Adams, Eleazar, I, 463
Adams, John, I, 463, 572, 785, 1012,
  1017, 1109, 1198–1199; and Nathaniel
  Green's case, I, 517–520; and John
  White's case, I, 521; and Baptist peti-
  tion, I, 558–565; and Mass. Constitu-
  tion, I, 602, 604, 607
Adams, John Quincy, II, 113, 117, 1199,
  1206
Adams, Patience, I, 427
Adams, Samuel, I, 557, 559–562, 572; II,
  1075; and Mass. Constitution, I, 602–
  603
Adams v. Howe, II, 1105, 1107, 1180,
  1195
Address to the Charitable Society, II,
  1029, 1138
Address to the Clergy, An, II, 891
Address to the Inhabitants of New Eng-
  land, II, 779
African Baptist Church of Boston, II, 765–
  766
African Colonization Society, II, 1271
Age of Inquiry, The, II, 1011–1012
Age of Reason, The, II, 804, 972
Aikin, Solomon, II, 1074
Akin, John, I, 170, 188
Alden, Noah, I, 438, 443, 475, 504, 505,
  533, 548 n. 2, 550; II, 703, 704, 705,
  734, 770, 782, 949, 951, 1094; and
  Mass. Constitutional Convention
  (1780), I, 599, 600, 602–603, 686
Alden, Samuel, I, 378, 432–433, 559–565
Alien and Sedition Acts, II, 1012
Allen, Ethan, I, 610; II, 718, 737, 976,
  1022

Allen, Ichabod, II, 955
Allen, John (of Dedham), I, 62, 63
Allen, John (Elder), I, 584; II, 723, 766
Allen, John (of Litchfield), II, 980
Allen, Joseph, I, 168
Allen, Samuel, II, 835
Allen, Thomas, I, 608, 663; II, 714, 1023,
  1074
Allen, Timothy, I, 364
Ambrose, Samuel, II, 860
American Alarm, I, 584
American Baptist Home Missionary So-
  ciety, II, 1264
American Baptist Magazine. See Massa-
  chusetts Baptist Missionary Magazine
American Bible Society, II, 1099
American Education Society, II, 1137–
  1138
American Mercury, II, 918, 941, 974, 975,
  980, 997, 1019, 1032, 1060
American Revolution, see Revolution,
  American
American Sunday School Union, II, 1222
Ames, William, I, 65
Amesbury, Mass., II, 1090–1091; Ames-
  bury Nail Factory, II, 1237 n. 16
Amherst College, II, 1203–1204, 1207
Amherst, Mass., I, 528, 547
Amherst, N. H., II, 863
Anabaptists, I, 3–24, 59, 60, 70, 71, 102,
  254, 462, 483; law banishing, I, 24–25;
  See also Munsterites; Baptists
Andover, Conn., II, 1040
Andover Theological Seminary, II, 890,
  891, 1030, 1121
Andrews, Elisha, II, 803, 804, 1114
Andrews, Samuel, I, 285
Andros, William, I, 108–110, 123, 158,
  272; II, 835
Angier, Samuel, I, 149, 150
Anglicans (Episcopalians), I, 8, 50, 53,
  60, 65, 66, 76, 97, 114, 122, 134, 153,
  161, 193, 199, 200, 268, 275, 286, 339,
  367, 372, 392, 398, 413, 492, 597, 607 n.
  33, 655; II, 760, 865–866, 881, 1013 n.
  8, 1020; Baptists seek aid of, I, 158–
  159; Bishops for America, I, 277, 288,
  557, 562, 571, 576–577; II, 724; Bishop
  of London, I, 200, 202, 207–208, 211,
  214–224, 234, 265; and Childe Remon-

strance, I, 118; in Connecticut, I, 253–
254, 263, 265; II, 919, 927, 1020–1021,
1023, 1024–1062; in Freetown, Mass.,
I, 207–213; glebelands in Vermont, II,
816–820; growth of, I, 120–122, 200,
265, 276–277; King's Chapel, I, 76, 126,
158, 202, 208, 215; laws exempting
from support of Congregationalism, I,
221–224, 238–239, 269–270; lawsuit
against Massachusetts (1733), I, 236–
237, 238; in Massachusetts, I, 76, 114,
120, 126, 158, 165, 200–224, 238–239,
265, 276–277; in New Hampshire, II,
833, 839–840, 859, 903; and religious
taxes, I, 113, 220–224, 265; and Society
for the Propagation of the Gospel, I,
114, 120, 200–224, 254, 265, 283, 296,
396; II, 816–817, 840; in Southington,
Conn., II, 1044–1045; and Synod of
1725, I, 165, 214–224; and Thirty-nine
Articles, I, 125, 217, 254; II, 865; and
Toleration Party, II, 1024–1062; in Vir-
ginia, I, 591–592, 600–601; and Yale
College, I, 265, 482
Annan *v.* Salisbury, II, 871–872
Anomie, I, 333–335
Anthony, Joseph, I, 181, 188
Anti-Catholicism. See Papists, Roman
Catholics
Anticlericalism, I, 56, 403–405; II, 976–
977, 983, 1076, 1221
Anti-Masonic Party, II, 1219, 1221–1223,
1238
Antimasonry among Baptists, II, 759–760,
829, 1016, 1266
Anti-mission Baptists, II, 1141, 1143, 1171
Anti-Mormonism, II, 1266
Antinomians, I, 3, 6, 7, 9, 10, 11, 12, 30,
48, 65, 76; II, 834
Antipedobaptists. *See* Baptists
Appeal to the People of Massachusetts, I,
617
*Appeal to the Public for Religious Lib-
erty,* I, 553–554, 561, 614
Apologeticall Narration, I, 100, 103
Appleton, Nathaniel, I, 285, 294
Arianism. *See* Unitarianism
Arminianism, I, 3, 5, 11, 287, 323, 352,
406–408, 496–497, 499; II, 710–711,
718, 876, 1115, 1139; among educated
Baptists, I, 277–299, 304–325; in First
Baptist Church of Boston, I, 319–322;
423; and General Atonement, I, 304–
305, 321–322; and Great Awakening, I,
304–305, 321–322, 323, 349–350;
Daniel Martin defends, II, 728–729. *See
also* Free Will Baptists; Methodists; Six
Principle Baptists; Unitarians; Universalists

Arnold, Thomas, II, 738
Article Three of Mass. Constitution: debate over, I, 594–635 (esp. 602–620);
Isaac Backus on, I, 613–614, 616, 633–
634; vote on, I, 630; court cases over, I,
636–659; and the Cutter Case, I, 644–
646; and the Universalists, I, 654–658;
local compromises over, I, 660–684; in-
terpretations of, I, 662–663; in Medfield, I, 673; in Pittsfield, I, 668; efforts
to abolish, II, 1147–1185. *See also*
Barnes *v.* Falmouth; Dedham Case;
Disestablishment; Incorporation; Religious Taxes
Article Two of Mass. Constitution, I, 603,
623–624, 635
Articles of Confederation, II, 768, 780
Asbury, Francis, II, 723, 724, 995–996
Ashburnham, Mass., I, 671–672, 690–691;
II, 779, 780
Ashby, Mass., I, 598
Ashfield Law, I, 535–546, 560, 562
Ashfield, Mass., I, 516–517, 521, 530, 552,
559, 571, 580, 628; Persecutions in, I,
531–546, 628; Baptists seek incorpora-
tion in, I, 649; quarrel over ministerial
lot, II, 688–690. *See also* Smith;
Chileab; Smith, Ebenezer
Ashford, Conn., II, 1039
Ashford, Mass., I, 323
Associations: of Baptists, I, 130, 281, 502–
503, 508; II, 700–704, 826–832, 920.
See also under names of; of Congrega-
tionalists, I, 365, 407–408, 412, 505; of
Separates, I, 411–412; *See also* Six
Principle Baptists
Attleboro, Mass., I, 122, 200, 241, 302,
378, 391, 690; II, 710, 756, 859
Austin, Benjamin, II, 1067
Austin, David, II, 747
Austin, James T., II, 1254
Avery, Benjamin, I, 396
Avery, Joseph, I, 208
Avery, Thomas, II, 957
Avery *v.* Tyringham, II, 1192 n. 5, 1209

Babcock, Amos, I, 478, 480
Babcock, Rufus, II, 991
Babcock, Stephen, II, 763, 842
Backus, Ebenezer, I, 373
Backus, Elizabeth, I, 374–375
Backus, Isaac: mentioned, I, 134, 287,
337 n. 8, 348, 358, 399, 413, 428, 438,
465, 466, 470, 475, 520, 545, 548, 549,
631, 668, 669, 670, 682, 683; II, 701,
761, 771, 814, 936, 985, 1014, 1085,
1091, 1113, 1139, 1184, 1223, 1278;
conversion of, I, 356–357; founds
Separate church in Titicut, I, 376–384;

becomes an open communion Baptist, I, 384, 432–435, 436, 447–448; lawsuit by his church, I, 382–384; and Separate petitions, I, 391–392; on the Awakening, I, 421, 422; schism over baptism in his church, I, 431–433; on Mass. certificate law of 1758, I, 462; on petitions to the legislature, I, 477–478; and R. I. College, I, 498–499, 500, 501; joins Warren Assoc., I, 504–511; *History of New England,* I, 510, 520; II, 715, 724, 738, 742, 774–776, 783; on right of Baptist ministers to exemption from civil taxes, I, 520–521; on right of Baptist ministers to perform marriages, I, 520–521; on John White's case, I, 524–525; and Joshua Emery's case, I, 526–527; and Grievance Committee, I, 529, 549–568; and Ashfield Case, I, 537–546; *Appeal to the Public for Religious Liberty,* I, 553–554, 561; refuses to write certificates, I, 554; on Tea Act, I, 564–565; on Stamp Act, I, 569–570; and Revolution, I, 583; II, 776; on Battle of Lexington-Concord, I, 586–587; *Door Opened for Equal Christian Liberty, A,* I, 594, 640, 642, 669; *Government and Liberty Described,* I, 597–598; attacks Charles Chauncy, I, 597–598; arguments against religious establishment, I, 597–599, 604–635 (esp. 613–614, 616, 617, 631–632); instructions to Middleborough Constitutional delegates, I, 599–600; drafts Bill of Rights for Mass. Constitution, I, 600–601; on compulsory Sabbath attendance, I, 605; favors a Christian Commonwealth, I, 605–606; attacks "Hieronymus," I, 616; attacked by "Swift," I, 625; *Truth Is Great and Will Prevail,* I, 632–633; on Incorporation, I, 646–648; silent on Murray case, I, 656; and Barnstable, Mass., I, 674; efforts to petition legislature (1788), II, 697; optimistic about end of persecution (1795), II, 698; on Baptist growth, II, 698–699; and Stonington Assoc., II, 702; tries to convert Six-Principle churches to Five-Principle Calvinism, II, 704–706; *Liberal Support of Gospel Ministers,* II, 706–707; attacks Shakers, II, 714–716; attacks Universalists, II, 718–722, 732; attacks Wesley, II, 724–726; attacks Free Will Baptists, II, 727, 728; defends Calvinism, II, 728–733; defends Jonathan Edwards, II, 730–731; attacks Hopkinsians, II, 731–734; on infant damnation, II, 735–736; attacks Sandeman, II, 741; receives

A. M., II, 743; criticized by Elias Smith, II, 747–748; and politics, II, 752; on theatre-going, II, 755; on Sabbath laws, I, 605–606; II, 757–758; on fornication, II, 759; and Indians, II, 763; and slavery, II, 767–768, 781; on science and history, II, 772–777; and revival of 1779–1780, II, 776; and Shay's Rebellion, II, 777–778; *Address to the Inhabitants of New England,* II, 779; and Mass. Ratifying Convention (1780), II, 780–783; on national and international affairs, II, 784–786; on Jefferson, II, 784–786; on Vermont, II, 795; and Eden Burroughs, II, 847–848; and John Leland, II, 928–935; on legislative chaplains, II, 931; William Bentley on, II, 1068

Bacon, Ezekiel, II, 1023, 1074, 1079, 1082, 1093
Bacon, John, II, 1074
Baillie, Robert, I, 101–102, 103
Baker, Eliphalet, II, 1190
Baker, William, I, 18 n. 21
Baker *v.* Fales. *See* Dedham Case
Baldwin, Ebenezer, I, 375
Baldwin, Thomas, I, 687; II, 745–747, 847–848, 859, 860, 1097, 1130 n. 3, 1137, 1138, 1157, 1264; favors incorporation, II, 1015, 1030, 1091 n. 13; William Bentley on, II, 1069, 1071 n. 17; sketch of, II, 1114–1115; at Mass. Constitutional Convention (1820), II, 1163, 1170, 1172–1175, 1177, 1181, 1182, 1184, 1202, 1224
Balkcom Case, I, 637–640, 655, 670
Balkcom, Elijah, I, 638–640
Ball, Deacon, I, 550
Ballou, Hosea, II, 718, 1001, 1231, 1232
Ballou, Matturin, II, 718, 861, 1001
Banishment of Dissenters, I, 24–25
Baptism, among early English Baptists, I, 5–6; first antipedobaptists in Mass., I, 9–24; Henry Dunster on, I, 21–22; early debates over antipedobaptism, I, 26–48, 62–70, 79–91; John Walton on, I, 312–317; immersion, I, 5, 316–317, 1129–1133, 1134; Separates divide over, 422, 424–439; Patience Adams on, I, 426; problem in Woburn church over, I, 84–89; claims that Baptists practised immersion in the nude, I, 313; dispute over in Titicut, I, 431–433; ridiculed, I, 550, 1071; Nehemiah Dodge on, II, 1017–1018; William Bentley on, II, 1071–1072; dispute with Trinitarians over, II, 1129–1133
Baptism Discovered, I, 317
Baptist College. *See* Brown University

Baptist Education Society, II, 707, 1120–1121
Baptist Evangelical Tract Society, II, 1117
Baptist General Tract Society, II, 1264
Baptist Missionary Society, II, 766 n. 48
Baptist Petition, The (Conn.), II, 985–1005
Baptist Repository and Christian Review, II, 1118
Baptist Triennial Convention, II, 1115, 1264
Baptistes, I, 317
Baptists, first churches in England, I, 5–6; early persecution in Mass., I, 3–91; compared to Munsterites, I, 5, 6, 8–9, 23–24, 29 n. 4, 32, 37, 58; first exponents of, in Mass., I, 8–29; non-separating position, I, 5, 62–70, 79–90, 99; opposition to covenant theology, I, 28–48; opposition to learned clergy, I, 30, 37, 56, 84; Calvinistic (Five Principle or Particular) Baptists, I, 5, 190, 198, 273 n. 17, 280–281, 304–306, 309–311, 320–325; General (or Six Principle) Baptists, I, 5, 254, 280–281, 304–306, 309–311, 442, 446; and Quakers, I, 30, 89, 151, 318; II, 737–738; attain toleration in Mass., I, 91–1113; in Rhode Island, I, 3, 7–8, 492; II, 758; as social deviants, I, 3–91, 550, 555–556, 572; II, 779–780, 1068–1073; in Rehoboth, I, 149–162; in Swansea, I, 129–148; membership growth, I, 120–122, 279–281, 421, 425, 436, 437–438, 555; II, 698–699; in Vermont, II, 791–794, 826; in New Hampshire, II, 843, 855–860, 875–876; in Conn., II, 919–920; in New England, II, 1113; in Mass., II, 1113; as defenders of local home rule, I, 142–143, 148, 441–442, 466, 487; early years in Conn., I, 250–281; use of state aid to religion, I, 134–136, 470–473, 475–476, 685–695; II, 803, 816, 860, 1280; oppose religious taxes in Dartmouth and Tiverton, I, 165–199; on support for ministry, I, 198, 509; first exemption acts in Mass. 1728–1734, I, 225–247; in Conn., I, 269–277; efforts to renew exemption act in 1739, I, 239–240; on compulsory church attendance, I, 272–273; II, 803; "Old" Baptists and "New" Baptists, I, 277, 282, 320–325, 421–422, 437, 439–442, 455–476; Seventh Day, I, 261, 268; II, 758; efforts toward fraternal union with Congregationalists, I, 277–299, 301–323, 324–325; rural Baptist conservatism, I, 277–299, 301–325, 422; Indian churches of, I, 279, 281; college-educated ministers,

I, 282–285, 301, 422, 491–502; II, 703–704, 1119, 1122; relations with English Baptists, I, 190, 304–306, 478–480, 501–502, 582–583; support permanent salary for royal governors, I, 227; reluctant to proselyte before 1740, I, 314, 317; on hymn singing, I, 318; reactions to Great Awakening, I, 319, 320–325, 408–409, 421–439, 479–480, 488, 491; ministers seek exemption from civil taxes, I, 470–473, 515–521; II, 886, 946–947; first threaten to petition King 1753–1758, I, 480–487; anti-intellectualism, I, 30–31, 492, 499; as antifederalists, I, 505, 557; II, 753, 780, 784, 1001; functions of associations, I, 508–511; II, 700–704, 826–832; ministers' right to perform marriages, I, 514; II, 946–947; subject to ridicules, I, 541, 550, 599; II, 1068–1073; mob action against, I, 550, 578, (in Pepperell) 579, 598–599, (in Hingham) 640–642; and civil disobedience, I, 547–555; tend to be apolitical, I, 555, 569–572; II, 751–752, 1107–1109; suspected of Toryism, I, 556–561, 569–575, 599; and the Revolution, I, 555–568, 569–587; and Jeffersonian party, I, 556; II, 751–753, 988; II, 1066, 1107; and Anglican episcopate, I, 557, 562, 571, 574–578; and foreign missions, I, 568; II, 1066, 1115–1117, 1143; and pacifism, I, 580–587; and Mass. constitution, I, 591–635; division over Incorporation, I, 645–650; II, 1088; become a denomination, I, 693; II, 698–788; attacked by Noah Worcester, II, 699–700; efforts for ministerial support, II, 706–707; inroads of competing sects, II, 701–702, 709–750, 1139–1140; ask Congress to regulate Bible publication, II, 711; and Second Coming, II, 741–742; seek respectability, I, 115, 288–299; II, 742, 744–748, 1066, 1107–1127; views of government, II, 751–753; views on morality, II, 752–764, 829–830; views on slavery, II, 764–767, 829, 1269–1271; and church discipline, II, 753–764, 829–830; not teetotalers, II, 756–757; and Masons, II, 759–760, 829; and women, II, 762, 829; on education, I, 606, II, 770–772, 1118–1126; on Indians and Blacks, II, 763–766; and science, II, 772–773; and Shays's Rebellion, II, 777–780; and Protestant Ethic, II, 779–780, 828–829; and official fast days, II, 1013–1014; belittled by Lyman Beecher, II, 1029–1032; and the Connecticut Act for the Support of Religion and Literature, II,

1034–1042; and moral reform, II, 1107–
1112; and Sunday mail delivery, II,
1112, 1264, 1266, 1267–1268; and
Andrew Jackson, II, 1113, 1198–1199;
and revivals, II, 1138; and Unitarians,
II, 1142–1143; combine with Trinitari-
ans for disestablishment, II, 1198–
1262; begin to vote Whig, II, 1198–
1199; and temperance, II, 1264, 1266;
oppose lotteries, II, 1265–1266; and
Christian patriotism, II, 1273, 1281. *See
also* Separate Baptists; Six Principle
Baptists; Free Will Baptists
Barker, Joseph, II, 1074
Barlow, Joel, II, 1022, 1073 n. 24
Barnes *v.* Falmouth, I, 650, 653 n. 39,
692; II, 1084–1094, 1105
Barnstable, Mass., I, 392, 595, 674; II,
1249
Barre, Mass., II, 1105
Barrington, John Shute, I, 293
Barrington, (R. I.) Mass., I, 122, 132;
quarrels with Baptists, I, 139–146; An-
glicans in, I, 200
Barrows, Oliver, I, 548
Barrowists, I, 65
Barstow, Jeremiah, I, 363 n. 8, 507
Bartlett, Enoch, I, 523
Bartlett, Isaac, II, 908
Batchelder, Thomas, II, 873
Batchelder, William, II, 1114
Bates, Joshua, II, 1189
Bath, N. H., II, 861
Bavarian Illuminate, II, 918, 971
Baylies, William, I, 638
Bealls, Isaac, II, 778, 827
Bean Hill Separate Church, I, 373–375,
377, 437
Beccaria, Cesare, II, 773
Becket, Mass., I, 528–529, 547
Beecher, Lyman, II, 882, 918, 1019,
1029–1032, 1038, 1061, 1138, 1207–
1208, 1223, 1268, 1271; and Dedham
Case, II, 1197; praised by Baptists, II,
1133–1134, 1266–1267; favors disestab-
lishment in Mass., II, 1209; and Anti-
Masonic Party, II, 1222; and Whig
Party, II, 1223
Beers, Isaac, II, 1023
Belcher, Jonathan, I, 302, 482, II, 839
Belden, Samuel, I, 539
Belknap, Jeremy, II, 1078 n. 34
Bell, Samuel, II, 879, 898
Bellamy, Joseph, I, 445; II, 730; attacks
Halfway Covenant, II, 735
Bellingham, Mass., I, 165 n. 1, 296, 463,
474–476, 481, 516, 528, 529, 530, 550,
599, 619 n. 10, 628, 675, 685–686; II,
734, 770, 810, 1192

Bellingham, Richard, I, 53, 62, 64, 73 n.
47, 74, 103
Benedict, David, I, 287; II, 789, 795, 811,
849, 937 n. 35, 952, 1102, 1198; and
open-communion, II, 1131, 1135; and
the American Education Society, II,
1137–1138
Benedict, Joel, II, 961
Benedict, Thaddeus, II, 981–982
Bennet, John, II, 814
Bennett, Francis, II, 822
Bennington, Battle of, I, 581
Bennington, Vt., II, 792, 795
Bentley, William, II, 1067; contempt for
Baptists, 1068–1073, 1074; on the
Worship or Infidel Bill, II, 1082, 1102
"Berean" letters of, concerning church
and state, II, 1091–1094, 1096–1097
Bernard, Francis, I, 545
Berwick, Me., I, 526–527, 547; II, 1074
Bester (Bestor), Daniel, II, 987, 990, 991,
996, 998, 999, 1000
Bethel, Vt., II, 814
Bible Commonwealth ideal. *See* Corpo-
rate Christian Commonwealth
Bidwell, Barnabas, II, 777–778
Bigelow, Samuel, II, 778
Bill of Rights, in Mass., I, 593. *See* Article
Three, Mass. Constitution; in U. S., *see*
First Amendment; in Virginia, *see*
Madison, James, Mason, George
Billerica, Mass., I, 89
Bishop, Abraham, II, 1004, 1006, 1022,
1073 n. 24
Bishop of London. *See* Anglicans
Bishop's Fund (Conn.), II, 1027, 1034–
1035
Blacks. *See* Negroes
Blackwood, Christopher, I, 27
Blake, George, II, 1074, 1158, 1164, 1170,
1173, 1177, 1178, 1215, 1219, 1245,
1254
Bliss, George, II, 1163
Blois (Bloice), Abraham, I, 458, 459 n.
11, 504, 507
Blood, Caleb, II, 767, 770, 793, 822, 827,
1015 n. 11, 1114; election sermon of, II,
803, 829–830
Blow at the Root of Aristocracy, A, II,
1103–1104
Blunt, John, I, 457–461, 478, 480
Board of Trade (London), I, 173, 191–
195, 220
Boardman, Elijah, II, 1020–1021, 1023
Boardman, Richard, II, 723
Bolles, David, Jr., II, 987, 990, 991,
1000, 1002–1003, 1022, 1024, 1047
Bolles, John, II, 987, 988, 1015 n. 11

Bolles, Lucius, II, 1002, 1069, 1071 n. 17, 1072, 1098, 1114, 1269
Bond, Benjamin, I, 519
Borden, Richard, I, 171, 175, 176, 180, 181, 224
Boston Baptist Association, II, 1110, 1113, 1121
Boston Christian Herald, II, 1222
Boston Continental Journal, I, 625
Boston Evening Post, I, 529, 537
Boston Gazette, I, 614, 616; II, 1103
Boston Independent Chronicle, I, 604–605, 617; II, 1078, 1081, 1082, 1091, 1093, 1102, 1103, 1197, 1204, 1205, 1215; and Mass. Constitutional Convention (1820), II, 1149–1150; and Eleventh Amendment of Mass. Constitution, II, 1217, 1219, 1238
Boston, Mass., I, 42, 481; exempt from religious taxes, I, 118, 126; North Church opposes learned ministry, I, 119–120; First Baptist Church of, I, 9, 14, 48, 49–78, 82–83, 283–297, 302, 320–322, 421, 422, 456, 617; II, 755, 1111; Second Baptist Church of, I, 320–322, 423, 432, 464, 507, 584, 631; II, 782, 1173
Boston Massacre, I, 530
Boston Ministerial Association, I, 301–302
Boston Recorder, II, 1138, 1146–1149
Boston Statesman, II, 1219–1221
Bosworth, Ephraim, I, 482
Bosworth, Jonathan, I, 229, 231
Botsford, Edmond, II, 726
Boucher (Butcher), Thomas, I, 322, 482
Bound, Ephraim, I, 320–322, 422, 457, 475, 478, 480; owned a slave, II, 766
Bound, James, I, 239 n. 42, 320
Bowditch, Mrs. William, I, 19
Bowdoin College, II, 1124–1125
Bowdoin, James, II, 1075
Bowdoinham Association, II, 701
Bowers, Benanuel, I, 17, 22, 62–70
Bowers, George, I, 17
Boylston, Zabdiel, I, 286 n. 11
Brackett, Alpheus, II, 1044
Bradbury, Theophilus, I, 655, 657
Bradford, Mass., I, 528–529, 547
Bradford, Vt., II, 823–824
Bradford, William, I, 638–639
Bradley, Joshua, II, 1045–1046, 1108
Braintree, Mass., 200–202
Brandon, Vt., II, 823
Branford, Conn., I, 364, 445, 446
Branford, Joseph, I, 274
Brattle St. Church, II, 1074–1075
Brattle St. Manifesto, I, 288
Brattle, William, I, 170, 541–542
Brett, Silas, I, 376, 377

Brewster, William, I, 9 n. 1
Bridge, Matthew, I, 407
Bridges, Robert, I, 19
Bridges, William, I, 100
Bridgewater, Mass., I, 392, 670. *See also* Titicut Parish
Brief Answer, A, I, 98
Brief Narrative, A, I, 82, 104
Briggs, Josiah, II, 729
Briggs *v.* Stoughton, II, 1094
Briscoe, Nathaniel, I, 27 n. 1, 117
Bristol, Conn., II, 963
Bristol County, Mass., I, 113, 121–243
British Foreign Bible Society, II, 1169
Brookfield, Mass., I, 458, 649; petition of, II, 1214
Brooks, Charles, II, 1131, 1198
Brooks, John, II, 1232
Brooks, Nathan, II, 1218, 1245
Brown, Arthur, II, 840
Brown, James (of Providence), I, 309–311
Brown, James (of Rehoboth and Swansea), I, 130–132, 134
Brown, Jeremiah, I, 1050
Brown, John (of Providence), II, 768
Brown, Moses, I, 310 n. 19; II, 738, 768
Brown, Samuel, II, 955–956
Brown, Simeon, II, 988
Brown University (Rhode Island College), I, 284, 285, 487, 545, 558, 565, 579; II, 852, 920, 1122–1123, 1184; founding of, I, 491–502, 510, 522; and the Revolution, I, 584, 585; hostility toward, II, 703–704; support of, II, 707; and James Manning, II, 770, 810
Browne, John (of Rehoboth), I, 119, 130
Brownists, I, 3, 46, 65, 69
Buckland, Mass., I, 650
Bucklin, Joseph, I, 478, 480
"Building up the Waste Places," II, 1029–1030
Bulkley, Job, I, 446
Bulkley, John, I, 266, 294, 313
Bulkley, Nathan, II, 999
Bunyan, John, I, 425, 434
Burnell, Barker, II, 1253–1254
Burnet, William, I, 228
Burr, Aaron, II, 758
Burr *v.* Sandwich, II, 1192 n. 5, 1209
Burroughs, Jeremiah, I, 100–101
Burroughs, Peleg, I, 582; II, 774
Burrows, Daniel, II, 996, 1024, 1037, 1047, 1050, 1054
Burrows (Burroughs), Eden, II, 846–848; 1036
Butler, Ezra, II, 803–804, 806, 809–810
Butters, William, II, 907
Buxton, James, II, 1086

Byfield, Nathaniel, I, 170 n. 2, 172–174, 197
Byram, Eliab, I, 376

"C" letters for disestablishment, II, 1225–1227
Call, Joseph, II, 809
Callender, Elisha, I, 115, 283, 284, 285, 293–297, 311, 317, 438, 496; and Increase Mather, I, 288–290; and John Comer, I, 308
Callender, Ellis, I, 75, 283, 288–289, 290, 296
Callender, John, I, 115, 283, 285, 293, 303, 318, 319, 322; "Century Sermon" of, I, 298, 317
Callender, Joseph, I, 240 n. 42
Calvin, John, I, 4, 29, 574
Calvinism, I, 3, 5, 27–48, 63, 124, 304–306, 319–322, 421, 424, 488, 491; II, 718, 722, 727–733, 736–737
Cambridge, Mass., I, 9, 21–22, 642; II, 708, 1215
Cambridge Platform, I, 9 n. 2, 13, 38, 45, 55, 86, 96, 100 n. 20, 118, 125, 352, 361, 364, 366, 368
Canaan, Conn., I, 424–425; II, 821
Cannon, Josiah W., II, 1099, 1100–1101, 1102, 1139
Canterbury, Conn., I, 346, 364, 368, 426
Carey, William, II, 1115
Carpenter's Hall Meeting (1774), I, 559–568
Carpenter, William, I, 465, 504
Carr, Esek, II, 756
Carrique, Richard, II, 1232
Carter, John, II, 873
Carter, Thomas, I, 85
Century Discourse, I, 298, 317
Certificates, see Religious Taxes
Chandler, James, I, 625; II, 860
Chandler, John, I, 549
Chandler, Thomas B., I, 528, 597–598
Channing, William Ellery, II, 1190, 1239, 1268, 1271, 1272–1273
Chapman, Asa, II, 1023
Charitable Society for the Education of Pious Young Men, II, 1029
Charleston, S. C., I, 96, 294, 310 n. 20
Charlestown, Mass., I, 16, 17, 49–78, 118, 200
Charlton, Mass., I, 628, 692; II, 709, 719
Charter of Mass. (1629), I, 59, 81, 106–108
Charter of Mass. (1691), I, 109–118, 145, 150, 191, 239, 482, 594
Chase, Benjamin, I, 232
Chase, Richard, II, 756

Chauncy, Charles (1586–1671), I, 9, 22 n. 30, 45, 46–47
Chauncy, Charles (1705–1787), I, 319, 323, 355, 368 n. 16, 410, 422, 537; II, 864, 868, 1210, 1223; opposes "establishments," I, 597–598; on Article Three, I, 609; against Backus, I, 614–616; universalism of, II, 718, 719–720
Checkley, John, I, 214 n. 1, 293 n. 29
Chelmsford, Mass., I, 547–548, 551, 552, 568, 598; II, 741, 778
Cheney, Thomas, I, 481, 482
Cheshire, Mass., I, 423, 599; II, 760, 928, 930
Chester, Mass., I, 650; II, 886, 1088
Chester, N. H., II, 840
Chester, Vt., II, 810
Cheverus, Jean, I, 658
Chickering, Jabez, II, 1190
Childe, Robert, I, 14, 118
Childs, Henry H., II, 1157, 1162, 1163, 1166, 1167, 1168, 1170, 1171, 1178, 1180
Christian Examiner, II, 1140, 1242, 1257
Christian Loyalty, II, 1014
Christian Register, II, 1239, 1243, 1247–1248, 1255, 1258, 1259
Christian Secretary, II, 1243.
Christian Watchman, II, 1109, 1110, 1117, 1118, 1123, 1129, 1138, 1145, 1198, 1199, 1200, 1202, 1203, 1205, 1273; and Mass. Constitutional Convention of 1820, II, 1151–1152; on disestablishment, II, 1227–1229, 1251, 1255, 1259
Christ-ians, II, 745–752, 825, 827, 855, 878–879
Christopher, Richard, I, 257–258
Church covenants, I, 57–58, 131
Church of England. *See* Anglicans
Circumcision, I, 316–317. *See also* Abrahamic Covenant
Civil disobedience, I, 38, 49, 409, 464, 485, 547–555, 575, 613–614; II, 796, 1014, 1261
Civil Government, the Foundation of Social Happiness, I, 414–415
Civil Right of Tithes, The, I, 153
Civil taxes and dissenting ministers, I, 467–473, 515–521, 650, 654–658; II, 884–888, 894–895, 946–947
Clap, Nathaniel, I, 293
Claremont, N. H., II, 870
Clarendon Code, The, I, 6, 50, 55, 151, 221, 291, 395, 575
Clarendon, Vt., II, 803
Clark, Ezenezer, I, 672
Clark, Jonas, II, 1093
Clark, Peter, I, 294, 314–317, 323 n. 45
Clark, Seth, I, 520–521

Clarke, Harry, II, 1071
Clarke, James, I, 285
Clarke, John, I, 11, 14, 16, 19–21, 27,
  44 n. 59, 50, 56, 61, 68, 79, 83, 92, 96,
  99, 109, 129 n. 2, 134, 166; compared to
  Roger Williams, I, 97–98; on ministe-
  rial support, I, 198 n. 44; in N. H., II,
  834
Cleaveland, Ebenezer, I, 378
Cleaveland, John, I, 522
Cleaveland, Moses, II, 979
Clinton, DeWitt, 772
Close (Closed) Communion. *See* Open
  Communion
Cobb, Sylvanus, II, 1232
Cobbett, Thomas, I, 12, 19, 27–48, 62, 97,
  98–99, 104, 118, 294
Cogswell, James, II, 924, 925
Cogswell, William, II, 1208–1209
Colby College, II, 1264. *See also* Water-
  ville College
Colburn, Josiah, I, 504
Colchester, Conn., II, 953–961
Cole, Hugh, I, 227
Coleman, Benjamin, I, 317–318
Colerain, Mass., I, 547
Collins, Joseph, I, 482
Columbian Centinel, II, 1151, 1152–
  1156
Columbian College, II, 1264
Columbian Register, II, 1027, 1032, 1037,
  1043, 1044
Comer, John, I, 115, 285, 294, 296–297,
  304–307, 317, 381
Common Sense, I, 608
Condy, Jeremiah, I, 283 n. 7, 284, 293, 294,
  296, 317, 318, 319–320, 422, 423, 438,
  456; II, 1071; and R. I. College, I,
  496–497, 499, 500; owned a slave, II,
  766
Confederation of Strict Congregationalists, I, 411–412
Connecticut, early Baptists in, I, 247, 255;
  early laws against dissent, I, 247–248;
  Toleration Act of 1708, I, 249, 254–
  262, 345; and Rogerenes, I, 251–254;
  first Baptists in, I, 254–281; petition
  from New London, I, 268–269; growth
  of Baptists in, I, 279–280; suppression
  of Separates, 360–365; disestablishment in, II, 1043–1062
Connecticut Baptist Education Society,
  II, 1042 n. 36
Connecticut Constitutional Convention
  (1818), II, 1050–1062
Connecticut Courant. See *Hartford Courant*
Connecticut Gazette, II, 1008
Connecticut Journal, II, 936–937, 977

Conscience, the, I, 7, 26, 92–96
Consociations, I, 264, 363, 364, 403–405,
  407–408, 412
Constitution, ratification of U.S., II, 767–
  768, 780–784
Constitution of Mass. *See* Mass Constitu-
  tion
Continental Congress, I, 510, 556–558
Cook, Phineas, II, 1038
Cooke, John, I, 166–167
Cooke, Parsons, II, 1209–1211, 1223
Cooley, Elder, II, 261, 285
Coolidge, Elisha, I, 671
Coombs, Simeon, II, 823
Cooper, Samuel, II, 1075
Cooper, Samuel, Rev., I, 633
Cooper, Thomas, II, 1221
Corbin, Ebenezer, II, 949–950
Cornell, Joseph, II, 827
Cornish, N. H., II, 857
Corporate Christian Commonwealth, I,
  7, 12–13, 26, 28, 29, 30, 34, 69–70, 123,
  178, 412; II, 832, 872, 1033, 1056,
  1065, 1180
Cottle family, II, 793–794
Cottle, Jabez, II, 804
Cotton, John, I, 9 n. 2, 12, 27–48, 65, 66,
  101, 103, 117, 154, 292, 514; and Roger
  Williams, I, 92–96
Cotton, John, Jr., I, 135 n. 22
Covenant Theology, I, 28–48, 315–316,
  351, 434
Coventry, R. I., 505
Cowles, Whitfield, II, 1024
Cragin, Samuel, I, 547
Craighead, Thomas, I, 209–211
Crandall, John, I, 19–20, 62–70, 250
Crandall, Prudence, II, 1271
Cranfield, Edward, II, 834, 835
Cromwell, Oliver, I, 4, 55, 74, 130, 198,
  354, 432
Crosby, Nathan, I, 548
Crosby, Parson, II, 1001
Crosby, Thomas, II, 729
Crossman, Abishai, I, 650 n. 34; II, 778
Culver, John, Sr., I, 255, 260
Cushing, John, I, 658
Cushing, Nathan, II, 1095
Cushing, Thomas, I, 559–560
Cushing, William, I, 657, 668
Cushman, Elisha, II, 1022
Cushman, Joshua, II, 1101 n. 30
Cutler, Elihu, II, 1254
Cutler, Timothy, I, 174, 215, 219, 236,
  265
Cutt, John, II, 835
Cutter, Gershom, I, 642, 644
Cutter *v.* Frost, I, 642–644, 650, 654; II,
  1077

Daboll, John, II, 1050
Daggett, David, II, 1024, 1045
Daman, George, II, 825
Dana, Francis, I, 655, 657, 666, 668, 670; II, 1094
Dana, James, I, 407–408
Danbury Baptist Association, II, 701, 743, 1016; and Baptist Petition, II, 986–1005; on certificates, II, 1014
Danbury, Conn., II, 1027, 1041
Danbury Farmers Journal, II, 916
Danby, Vt., II, 823
Dane, Nathan, I, 611, 650; II, 1084–1085
Danforth, John, I, 302
Danforth, Samuel, I, 207, 208, 285
Danforth, Thomas, I, 18, 62, 68
Danville, Vt., II, 745
"Dark Day," II, 773
Darrow, Lemuel, II, 1003
Darrow, Zadock, II, 702, 987, 988
Dartmouth College, I, 501; II, 846, 883, 887–893, 894, 895, 1028
Dartmouth Gazette, II, 811
Dartmouth, Mass., I, 10, 113, 121–122, 516; opposes religious taxes, I, 119, 165–199, 626
Davenport, James, I, 323, 340–341, 345, 356, 358, 363, 422
Davenport, John, I, 47
Davis, Aaron, I, 167
Davis, Daniel, II, 1190
Davis, John (Whig leader), II, 1218
Davis, John (Baptist agent), I, 14 n. 14, 438, 500, 518; II, 739; and Ashfield Case, I, 536–546, 547 n. 1, 549, 550; considered a Tory, I, 578, 584
Dawes, Thomas, Jr., II, 1095, 1158, 1177, 1178
Dean, Paul, II, 1158, 1232, 1234, 1235
Debates, in Boston (1668), I, 61–70; in Lyme, I, 266
Declaratory Act, I, 571, 586
Dedham Case, I, 632; II, 1076, 1127, 1189–1199, 1203, 1208, 1209–1211, 1212
Deerfield, N. H., II, 874
Deism, I, 166, 316, 388, 407, 416, 611; II, 737, 800, 932, 1011–1012, 1147, 1239
Democratic-Republican Party, I, 556; II, II, 751, 784–786; in Vt., II, 808–810, 814, 831; in N. H., II, 874, 875, 877–911; in Conn., II, 971, 989, 997, 998–1062; in Mass., II, 1065–1204, 1219–1221, 1222; and Mass. Constitutional Convention (1820), II, 1145, 1149–1150, 1158; forms Union Party, II, 1197, 1203, **1204,** 1206; merges with Whigs, II, 1218–1219
Den, Henry, I, 27

Denison, Thomas, I, 322–323; II, 954
Denny, Daniel, I, 467, 478, 480
Devil, The, I, 335, 426; II, 828 n. 34, 897
Devotion, Ebenezer, II, 925
Devotion, Ebenezer, Rev., I, 297
Dickinson, Asher, II, 1044
Dickinson, Austin, II, 1205
Directorenes, The, II, 830–831
Disallowance by King of religious laws, I, 115, 123, 253
Discourse Concerning the Maintenance Due to Those That Preach, I, 152–154
Discourse on Some Events, II, 918
Disestablishment, in Vt., II, 787–832; in N. H., II, 877–911; in Conn., II, 1043–1062; in Maine, 1199–1200 in Mass., II, 1245–1262
Dissenting Deputies, The, I, 293, 395, 396, 487
Distraint for religious taxes. *See* Persecution
Divine Right of Infant Baptism, The, I, 82
Doctrine of Particular Election, II, 725
Doctrine of Sovereign Grace Defended, II, 728–729
Doctrines of Universal Salvation Examined, II, 719
Dodge, Nehemiah, II, 930, 998, 1006–1008, 1017–1019, 1024
Dodson, Jonathan, I, 208, 232
Door Opened for Equal Christian Liberty, A, I, 594, 640, 642, 669
Douglas, John, Jr., II, 956
Douglas, Mass., I, 547
Drake, John, II, 756
Drake, Nathaniel, Jr., II, 947–948
Drinker, Edward, I, 55, 58, 62–70, 72, 73, 74, 77
Dublin, N. H., II, 892
Dudley, Joseph, I, 150, 152, 173, 176, 184 n. 5, 185; II, 835; and Anglicans, I, 201, 202, 203, 217
Duelling, II, 758
Dummer, Jeremiah, I, 185
Dummer, William, I, 204, 215, 219, 220, 482
Dunkers, I, 573
Dunstable, N. H., II, 884
Dunster, Henry, I, 9, 14, 21–22, 26, 46, 50, 52
Durfee, Robert, I, 205
Durfee, Thomas, I, 638
Durkheim, Emil, I, 329
Dutton, Warren, II, 1170
Dyar, John, II, 755
Dyer, Eliphalet, II, 925, 937
Dwight, Sereno, II, 1137
Dwight, Timothy, II, 882, 917–918, 970, 982, 1021, 1024, 1208

East Lyme, Conn., I, 261, 441 n. 2, 448–450
East Swanton, Vt., II, 824
East Waterford, Conn., I, 437
East Windsor, Conn., I, 547; II, 811, 947–948
Eastern Argus, II, 1089–1090, 1124
Eastman, Hezekiah, II, 823
Easton, Lilley, II, 1097
Easton, Mass., I, 465, 521, 626
Ecclesiastical laws, in Plymouth, I, 118–119, 212; in Massacuhsetts, 1692–1695, I, 114–127, 136 n. 26; Anglican opposition to, I, 200–224; Quaker opposition to, I, 165–199; religiously indifferent resist, I, 207–213; Anglican exemption acts, I, 221–224; Exemption Acts of 1728–34, I, 225–247; in New Haven Colony, I, 247–248 in Conn., I, 247–250 (against Rogerenes, I, 250–253; against Quakers, I, 253; Toleration Act of 1668, I, 254; Toleration Act of 1708, I, 254; to exempt dissenters from religious taxes, I, 268–277, 443; against Separates, I , 362–363; after 1770, II, 921–923; exemption laws of 1790–1791; II, 925–928, 935–938; attacked in Baptist Petition, II, 988–994); designed to suppress Separates, I, 362–363, 410; Separate opposition to, I, 360–385, 386–398, 399–415; Separate-Baptist problems with (in Conn.) I, 440–453, (in Mass.) I, 453–476, 481–488; and Wallingford, Conn., I, 407–408, 421, 423, 444–446; regarding "settled ministers," I, 472–473; 650; appeal to Continental Congress against, I, 556–568; and Mass. Constitution, I, 591–635; Mass. Public Worship Act of 1800, I, 651–653; in Vermont, II, 795–827; in N. H., II, 835–853; and Barnes *v.* Falmouth, II, 1086–1093; and Dedham Case, II, 1189–1199; in Mass. Convention, 1820, II, 1145–1185. *See also* Learned Ministry; Religious taxes; Saybrook Platform
Ecclesiology, I, 7, 28–48, 58, 100, 127; as seen by Thomas Goold et al., I, 62–70; as seen by New Lights and Separates, I, 340–359
Ecumenicalism (or fraternal union), I, 115, 116, 166; in 1710–1742, I, 277–299; after 1776, II, 917. *See also* Open Communion
Edmonds, William, II, 979, 980
Edwards, Jonathan, I, 286, 351, 352, 355, 422, 488, 532, 607; II, 729, 730, 734, 869, 929
Edwards, Jonathan, Jr., II, 730, 805, 1021
Edwards, Morgan, I, 493, 496, 500, 537,

545, 559; II, 721; Toryism of, I, 576–578
Edwards, Pierpont, II, 1004, 1022, 1073 n. 24
Eldridge, Matthew, I, 236, 238
Eleventh Amendment to Mass. Constitution, II, 1065, 1216–1262
Eliot, Andrew, I, 496–497, 498, 578, 583
Ellis, Caleb, II, 871
Ellis, John, I, 682–683
Ellis, Matthew, I, 236, 238
Ellsworth, Oliver, II, 989
Ely, Ezra Stiles, II, 1267
Embargo Act, The, II, 831, 879
Emery, Joshua, I, 526, 527
Emmons, Joshua, II, 1232
Emmons, Nathaniel, II, 730, 733, 1021
Endicott, John, I, 20
Enfield, Conn., I, 437, 443, 547
Enlightenment, The, I, 166, 330–332, 388, 400, 593, 611; II, 915
Enthusiasm, I, 30–31, 100. *See also* Holy Spirit, The
Episcopalians. *See* Anglicans
Erastianism, I, 13, 41, 123, 178, 180, 408, 424; II, 1092, 1193–1194
Erikson, Erik, I, 329
Erikson, Kai T., I, 48
Erskine, Christopher, II, 870–872, 880
Essays to Do Good, I, 318
Essays of Fevers, I, 317
Established church, I, 40, 88, 122–127, 152, 178, 195, 200–201, 214–224, 264, 559–560, 614–617. *See also* Ecclesiastical laws; Standing Order
Estey, Oliver, II, 1213
Eustis, William, I, 665; II, 1197, 1204
Everett, Alexander H., II, 1216–1217, 1245, 1254
Everett, Daniel, I, 311
Everett, Linus E., II, 1234
Ewing, William, I, 461, 507, 599, 631, 680
Exemption from religious taxes. *See* Religious taxes
Exeter, N. H., II, 766 n. 48
Exeter, R. I., I, 423, 428–429, 433, 435
Exhorting, I, 30, 56, 361, 404. *See also* Itinerant preaching, Prophesying
Eyres, Nicholas, I, 286–287, 294, 317, 324

Faculty psychology, I, 93–95
Fairfax, Vt., II, 831
Fairfield, Conn., I, 265, 270
Fales, Samuel, II, 1190
Familists, I, 3, 6, 65, 70
Farley, Michael, I, 654, 657
Farnam, John, Sr., I, 71, 72
Fast days, II, 846–847, 1013–1014
Fay, Samuel P. P., II, 1158, 1182

Federalists, the, I, 660; II, 785–786; in
Vt., 808–809, 811, 831; in N. H., 877–
911; in Conn., II, 935, 989, 990, 991,
994, 997, 999, 1008–1024; in Mass.
Constitutional Convention (1820), II,
1152–1156; oppose Religious Liberty
Act, II, 1093–1105; and Dedham Case,
II, 1194–1195; decline of in Mass., II,
1197–1199, 1202, 1206, 1207
Fessenden, Samuel, II, 1125
Finney, Charles G., II, 1134
First Amendment to U.S. Constitution, II,
783–784, 918
First Baptist Church of Boston, I, 9, 14,
48, 49–78, 82–83, 126, 319–320
Fish, Joseph, I, 368 n. 16, 404, 415, 492
Fisk, Daniel, I, 320, 460, 595 n. 5
Fisk, Henry, I, 458–461, 478, 480
Fiske, John, I, 139–140
Fitch, Ebenezer, II, 890
Fitch, Thomas, I, 396
Fitchburg, Mass., I, 691
"Five mile" acts in Mass., I, 221–223, 226–
227, 235, 237
Five Principle (Calvinistic) Baptists. *See*
Baptists
Flagg, Ebenezer, II, 840
Fletcher, Asaph, I, 552, 567, 599; II, 800
Fletcher, Samuel, I, 598
Flying Post, The, I, 293
Fobes, Joshua, I, 376, 378
Fobes, Perez, I, 674–675
Folger, John, I, 313
Foote, Enos, II, 1218
Forman, Samuel, I, 211
Foster, Edmund, II, 1158, 1170, 1171,
1172, 1180
Foster, Thomas, I, 84, 89–90
Fowler, Benjamin, II, 1050
Fox, George, I, 251, 319
Fox, Joseph, I, 558–559
Foxcroft, Thomas, I, 323
Framingham, Mass., I, 407
Franklin, Benjamin, II, 718
Free Will Baptists; rivals of Calvinistic
Baptists, II, 709, 726–728; growth of,
II, 726–728, 827; compete with Shak-
ers, II, 727–728; in N. H., II, 852, 855,
875; in Conn., II, 1024. *See also* Ran-
dall, Benjamin
Freeman, Edmund, II, 1050, 1059
Freeman, James, II, 1158, 1170, 1243
Freeman, Philip, I, 482, 504
Freetown, Mass., 121–122, 200, 204–213,
232, 377, 516
Frelinghuysen, Theodore J., II, 1270
French and Indian War, I, 486, 532
French Revolution, I, 583; II, 752, 784,
919, 1010, 1073

Friends. *See* Quakers
Frost, Ephraim, I, 642–644
Frothingham, Ebenezer, I, 341, 343 n. 2,
355, 363 n. 8, 371, 395, 396 n. 14, 399–
416, 426–427, 429; II, 703
Fuller, John, I, 370
Fuller, Richard, II, 1271
Furneaux, Philip, I, 544, 618
"Further light," I, 29–30, 79, 99–102, 424,
466

Gair, Thomas, I, 672; II, 782
Galloway, Joseph, I, 559
Gallup, Amos, II, 1050
Gammell, William, I, 687
Gano, John, I, 505, 558, 559
Gardiner, Samuel, I, 468
Gardner, Cato, II, 766 n. 48
Gardner, James, I, 311
Garner, Benjamin, II, 822–823
Garrison, William Lloyd, I, 542; II, 766 n.
48, 1271
Gay, Ebenezer, I, 641
George, John, I, 55, 58, 60, 77
Georgia, Vt., II, 825–826, 829
Gerry, Elbridge, II, 1067, 1089, 1098,
1102
General Assessment tax for religion, I,
593–594, 800, 924, 967
General Baptists, see Six Principle Bap-
tists, Baptists
General Missionary Convention of the
Baptist Denomination, II, 1264
Gibson, Edmund, I, 214–224, 265
Gill, John, I, 305, 501, 502; II, 930
Gilmanton, N. H., II, 727
Glas, John, II, 740
Glebelands, I, 660, 685; II, 813–832. *See
also* Ministerial lots
Gloucester, Mass., I, 654–658
Glorious Revolution, I, 108, 272
Goddard, Beriah, I, 189, 196
Goddard, David, I, 467
Goddard, Edward, I, 407
Goddard, Tyler, II, 1249
Goffstown, N. H., II, 835
Goodall, Richard, I, 55, 77
Godfrey, George, I, 638
Goodman, Paul, II, 1067, 1074
Goodwin, David, II, 1080, 1082
Goodwin, Thomas, I, 94, 100, 102
Goodwine, Christopher, I, 16–17
Goold, Mary, I, 51, 57
Goold, Thomas, I, 14 n. 14, 49–78, 80, 83,
87, 92, 95, 96, 129, 289, 299, 485, 542;
II, 1277
Gorham, Maine, I, 528
Gorton, Stephen, I, 260–261, 271, 275,
446

Goshen, Conn., II, 961
Gould, Joseph, I, 482
Government and Liberty Described, I, 597, 614
Gowen, John, I, 526
Grace, preparation for, I, 28
Grafton, Joseph, II, 747, 1114, 1250
Graham, John, I, 474; II, 948
Granger, Gideon, II, 977, 1022
Granville, Mass., I, 626
Great Awakening, The, I, 8, 10, 116, 198, 264, 274, 304, 319, 320, 329–339, 514, 569, 592, 611; II, 776, 841–842, 1278. *See also* Second Great Awakening.
Greek Independence, II, 1271
Green, Amasa, II, 814
Green, Henry, II, 820–821
Green, Nathaniel, I, 507, 517–520, 541; II, 704, 719
Green, Thomas, I, 320–322, 323, 470, 482, 498–499; exempted from civil taxes, I, 516 n. 3; and Cutter Case, I, 642–645, 654
Greenwood, Francis W. P., II, 1243–1244
Greenwood, John, I, 301
Greenwood, Thomas, I, 155
Grew, Henry, II, 1013–1015
Grievance Committee of the Warren Association, I, 463, 510–511, 512, 580, 617, 634; founding of, I, 529–530; and Ashfield Case, I, 536–546; and Warwick Case, I, 549–550; recommends civil disobedience, I, 551–553; petitions Continental Congress, I, 553–564; and Mass. Provincial Congress, I, 564–566; and Hingham Riot, I, 641; and incorporation, I, 645; and Barnstable, Mass., I, 674; and Harwich, Mass., I, 676
Griffin, Edward Dorr, II, 1131–1133, 1207
Griffith, Abel, I, 505
Griswold, George, I, 449
Griswold, Roger, II, 1020, 1023
Griswold, Stanley, II, 1011 n. 6, 1023
Groton, Conn., I, 254–262, 263, 266, 319, 421, 423, 441; II, 966, 1039–1040
Groton Union Conference (or Association), I, 435 n. 35; II, 702–704, 920, 1061
Grounds and Ends of Baptisme, The, I, 27–48
Grow, William, II, 745, 825
Guild, Joseph, I, 638
Guilford, Conn., I, 361

Hadley, Mass., I, 528
Haiti, II, 766 n. 48
Hale *v.* Everett, II, 871 n. 37, 911
Hale, James, I, 208, 224
Hale, Moses, II, 840

Halfway Covenant, I, 43, 45–47, 49, 55, 59, 67, 71 n. 42, 80, 87, 107 n. 37, 291, 315–316, 358, 410, 412, 424, 437; II, 735, 1031
Halifax, Vt., II, 831
Hall, Elihu, I, 413, 415, 416 n. 55
Hall, Robert, I, 583; II, 1131
Hamilton, Alexander, II, 758
Hamilton College, II, 1112, 1264
Hammond, Noah, I, 505
Hampshire *v.* Taylor, II, 886
Hampton Falls, N. H., II, 841, 861–862, 879
Hampstead, N. H., II, 858
Hancock, John, I, 565; II, 780, 1075
Hancock, Mass., I, 581
Hanover, N. H., II, 846
Hardwick, Vt., II, 822
Harris, Henry, I, 217
Hart, Oliver, I, 522
Hart, Samuel, II, 1058
Hart, William, II, 982
Hartford Baptist Association, II, 921
Hartford, Conn., 441 n. 1; II, 966, 986, 1010, 1013–1015, 1034, 1039, 1050
Hartford Convention, II, 888, 916, 1025
Hartford Courant, II, 805, 926, 927, 935, 939, 967, 972, 975, 978, 979, 981, 994–995, 1003, 1008–1009, 1019, 1060
Hartford, Vt., II, 814
Harvard College, I, 21–22, 76, 114, 119, 171, 205, 217, 224, 282, 283, 284, 285, 295, 296, 318, 352, 471, 473, 499, 519, 523, 597, 643, 674; II, 743, 862, 890, 1123, 1149, 1156, 1184, 1185, 1189, 1190, 1203–1204, 1205, 1220; and Separates, I, 363; and Separate Baptists, I, 491, 492
Harvard, Mass., I, 548, 692; II, 713, 739
Harvey, Samuel, I, 527–528
Harwich, Mass., I, 392, 649, 675–678; II, 725
Hastings, John, II, 951, 987
Hastings, Joseph, I, 450–451, 948
Hathaway, John, I, 207
Haverhill, Mass., I, 521, 526, 528, 547, 629–630, 649, 690; II, 1089–1090
Hawes, Joseph, II, 1254
Hawley, Joseph, I, 527–528, 567, 607–608; II, 1022, 1073 n. 24
Haynes, Jonathan, I, 261
Haynes, Sylvanus, II, 824
Hazel, John, I, 21 n. 28
Heads of Agreement, I, 264
Heald, Amos, II, 892
Hebbard, Jedidiah, II, 847–848
Hebron, Conn., II, 1037
Hedge, Lemuel, I, 550, 678
Helwys, Thomas, I, 5

Henderson *v.* Erskine, II, 870–871
Henry, Patrick, I, 593 n. 3, 607; II, 967, 1023
Herald of Gospel Liberty, II, 749, 878
Hibbard, Ithamar, II, 821
Hicks, John, I, 507
Hicks, Joseph, I, 170
Hide, Jedidiah, I, 373, 378
"Hieronymus" letters on Article Three, I, 609, 614–617
Higginson, John, I, 62
Hill, Abraham, I, 680
Hill, Isaac, II, 881, 887–893, 895, 896, 898, 899, 900, 902, 909
Hillhouse, James, II, 1023
Hillsborough, N. H., II, 858, 861
Hinds, Ebenezer, I, 431–433, 447, 478, 480, 498–499, 504, 505, 506, 636–637, 647 n. 23, 648; II, 703
Hingham, Mass., I, 640–642
Hireling ministry, I, 56, 151, 198
Hiscox, Thomas, I, 250
Hiscox, William, I, 62, 309
Historical Narrative and Declaration, I, 411–412
History of New England (Backus), II, 774
Hix, Daniel, II, 749
Hoar, Samuel, II, 1158, 1165, 1166, 1167, 1168, 1169, 1173, 1175, 1177, 1178, 1180, 1182, 1254, 1256, 1257
Hobart, Noah, I, 414–415
Holden, Mass., I, 628
Holland, Mass., I, 691
Holliman, Ezekiel, I, 10
Hollis, John, I, 294
Hollis, Thomas, I, 190, 224, 283, 284, 294–296, 318, 496, 501; II, 1184
Hollis, Mass., I, 708
Holliston, Mass., I, 547
Holly, Israel, I, 387 n. 1, 399, 411, 413, 416 n. 56; II, 775 n. 11, 922
Holmes, Abraham, II, 1174
Holmes, Obadiah, I, 14, 19–21, 50, 61, 71, 93, 97, 103, 128–129, 298, 571
Holmes, William, I, 638
Holy Spirit, I, 30–31, 69–70, 99, 197, 323, 337, 349, 351, 390, 444; II, 1208
Hooker, Thomas, I, 117
Hooper, William, II, 727, 843, 850–852, 853
Hopewell Academy, I, 500
Hopkins, Asa, II, 1214
Hopkins, Samuel, II, 730, 733, 734, 768, 917, 930. *See also* Hopkinsians
Hopkins, Stephen, I, 559
Hopkinsians, I, 593; II, 709, 730–732, 794, 883, 888–893, 917, 976, 1070–1071
Hovey, John, I, 346

Hovey, Samuel, I, 587; II, 734
Howard, Nathan, I, 437
Howe, Estes, II, 1099
Howell, David, I, 500
Howland, Nathaniel, I, 188
Hubbard, Henry, II, 905–907
Hubbard, Samuel (of Boston), II, 1158
Hubbard, Samuel (of Newport, Westerly), I, 62, 250
Hubbard, William, I, 6, 77–78, 80–81, 101 n. 23
Hudson, Charles, II, 1232
Hull, John, I, 49, 74
Hunn, Zadock, I, 677–678
Hunt, Asa, I, 595; II, 761–762, 764
Hunt, Ephraim, I, 531
Hunt, Samuel, I, 174, 184, 186, 187, 188, 197, 210, 224
Huntington, David, II, 960
Huntington, Joseph, II, 722
Huntington, Samuel, II, 925, 937
Huntstown. *See* Ashfield, Mass.
Hussey, John, II, 1158
Hutchinson, Anne, I, 9, 10, 14, 22, 30, 50, 92, 299, 542. *See also* Antinomians
Hutchinson, Elisha, I, 182
Hutchinson, Elisha (Rev.), II, 816
Hutchinson, Thomas, I, 537–538, 543, 544, 560, 580
"Hushai," letters of, II, 935–936
Hyde, Elihu, II, 858–859
Hyde, Elisha, II, 1023

Illiterate ministry, I, 30, 37, 56. *See also* Learned ministry
Ill-Newes from New England, I, 21, 97
Immersion, I, 3, 313; in Providence (1639), I, 10; of children, I, 9. *See also* Baptism
Immortalists, I, 358, 389; II, 739. *See also* Ireland; Shadrack
Impartial Inquiries Concerning the Progress of the Baptist Denomination, II, 699–700
Incorporation of dissenting churches, I, 442; of Ashfield, I, 535–538; problem raised by Cutter Case, I, 644–646; Backus and Smith on, I, 646–648; Mass. law of 1755, I, 644–645; Act of 1786, I, 647–648; court decisions conflict, I, 649–651; and Act of 1800, I, 653; in Pittsfield, Mass., I, 668; in Medfield, I, 673; in Becket, I, 677–678; in Warwick, Mass., I, 678–679; in Vermont, II, 797, 801–803, 828; in N. H., II, 840–841, 874, 876, 880, 894; in Conn., II, 966, 1015–1016; Test cases in Mass., II, 1084–1106. *See also* Dane, Nathan; Parsons, Theophilus

Independents, I, 29 n. 4, 100–101, 110, 216, 295, 314
India, II, 1114; Serampore, II, 1115, 1171
Indians, I, 204, 279, 316, 484; II, 763, 1272. *See also* King Philip's War
Individualism, Baptists and, I, 69–70
Infant baptism. *See* Pedobaptism
"Infidel Bill," II, 1079–1082, 1084
Ingalls, Elkanah, II, 721
Ingersoll, Jared, I, 569
Ingersoll, Jonathan, II, 1023, 1025, 1036, 1043
Ingols, Edmund, I, 228 n. 5, 229, 231
Inner Light, I, 30, 99, 197. *See also* Quakers
Intolerance. *See* Persecution; Baptists; Quakers
Ipswich, Mass., opposes religious taxes 1657, I, 118, 200; New Lights in, I, 365, 367
Ireland, Shadrach, I, 358; II, 736, 738–739
"Irenaeus," see West, Samuel
Irenicum, I, 101
Itinerant preaching, I, 340–341, 343, 361; outlawed in Conn., I, 362–363, 366, 410, 413 n. 44, 465, 522; by Methodists, I, 658; II, 725; in N. H., II, 855; in Conn., II, 920, 924, 979
Ivimey, Joseph, II, 1269

Jackson, Andrew, II, 1002, 1027, 1073, 1109, 1113, 1198–1199, 1204, 1206, 1272. *See also* Democratic Party
Jackson, William, II, 1254
Jacob, Henry, I, 5, 11 n. 7
Jacobs, Wightman, I, 363 n. 8, 478, 480, 502, 533, 549; II, 704, 705
Jamaica, Vt., II, 823
Jefferson, Thomas, I, 292, 330, 401, 511, 556, 563, 576, 591–593, 605, 607, 610, 618, 619; II, 718, 751–753, 772, 784–786, 792, 879–880, 1001, 1003, 1004, 1007, 1010–1013, 1017, 1067, 1073, 1108, 1109, 1112, 1113, 1123, 1198–1199
Jeffries, Jonathan, I, 676
Jenckes, Daniel, I, 494
Jenckes, Joseph, I, 267; and John Walton, 309–311
Jessey, Henry, I, 5–6, 54
Jews, The, I, 93, 132, 316, 389, 400, 414, 434, 610, 657, 658; II, 800, 848, 945, 1017–18, 1228, 1239. *See also* Abrahamic Covenant
Johnson, John, I, 62–70
Johnson, Matthew, I, 84–85
Johnson, Richard M., II, 932, 1233, 1268
Johnson, William Samuel, II, 1023

Jones, Abner, II, 749
Jones, Ebenezer, I, 507, 528
Jones, Jabez, Jr., II, 954–961
Jones, Jabez, Sr., II, 954–961
Jones, John Pierce, I, 683
Jones, Robert Strettle, I, 494, 558–559, 566, 585
Jones, Samuel, I, 494, 559, 631
Joslin, Joseph, II, 1001–1002
Judd, William, II, 975, 1004, 1023
Judson, Adoniram, II, 1114, 1115, 1135
Judson, Agur, II, 1046
Judson, Ephraim, II, 1074
Just Vindication of the Covenant, A, I, 27–48

Kelley *v.* Bean, II, 886
Kelly, Erasmus, I, 581
Kendall, Ezra, II, 1085
Kendall *v.* Kingston, II, 1085
Kendrick, Ariel, II, 825
Kendrick, Clark, II, 821–822
Kendrick, Nathaniel, I, 687
Key to Unlock the Door, I, 399–409
Kidder *v.* French, II, 883–888
Kiffin, William, I, 5–6, 55, 82
Killam, Robert, II, 1232
Killingly, Conn., II, 962–963
Killingsworth, Conn., I, 446
King, Joshua, II, 1023
King, Rufus, I, 655
King Philip's War, I, 42, 74, 82, 84, 122, 136, 161, 253
King's Chapel. *See* under Anglicans
Kingston, Mass., II, 1085
Kinsey, James, I, 559
Kirby, Ephraim, II, 978–979, 1004, 1023
Kirkland, John, II, 1190
Kissites, the, II, 740
Kittery, Maine, Baptists in 1682, I, 76
Kneeland, Abner, II, 1232, 1260
Knight, Amos, II, 1086
Knollys, Hanserd, I, 5–6, 82; II, 834
Knowles, James D., II, 1114, 1134

Lafayette, Marquis de, II, 1265
Lakeville, Mass., I, 436
Lamb, Elizabeth, I, 255, 260
Lamb, Isaac, I, 255, 260
Lambe, Thomas, I, 27–48
Lambert, Robert, I, 55
Lambton, John, I, 202
Lamson, Alvan, II, 1189–1190
Lamson, Ebenezer, II, 721, 965
Lancaster, Mass., I, 598
Lancaster, N. H., II, 861
Lanesboro, Mass., I, 675
Langdon, John, II, 879
Larned, Ellen, II, 1045

Lathrop, Benjamin, II, 1045
Latitudinarianism, I, 166, 276, 279, 301, 312, 318–319, 408; of Jeremiah Smith, II, 867–872, 943, 945; of Zephaniah Swift, II, 916, 943–946; of James Sullivan, II, 1076–1083
Law, Jonathan, I, 355, 396
Lawrence, James, I, 470–472
Laws governing religion. *See* Ecclesiastical laws
Lay participation in churches, I, 353, 388, 403–405. *See also* Prophesying
Laying on of hands. *See* Sixth Principle.
Learned ministry, I, 30, 37, 56, 76, 84, 617; laws requiring, I, 114–127, 155, 160, 169, 171, 178, 183; New Lights criticize, I, 343, 353; opposition to in Plymouth, I, 119–120; attacked by Separates, I, 403–408; Baptists encourage, 606, II, 770–772, 1118–1126
Leaselands (Vermont). *See* Glebelands
Ledoyt, Biel, II, 949
Lee, Ann, II, 712–717
Lee, Jacon, II, 745
Lee, Jesse, II, 723, 897
Lee, Richard: mobbed in Hingham, I, 640–642
Lee, Richard Henry, I, 593, 607
Lee, Mass., I, 626
Leicester, Mass., I, 296, 297, 317, 421, 423, 464, 467, 516, 628; II, 778; Green case in, I, 515–520, 528, 547
Leland, Aaron, II, 809–810, 832
Leland, John, I, 406, 438; II, 1024, 1048, 1109, 1171, 1176, 1227; and slavery, II, 767 n. 53; on Conn. tax laws, II, 926–938, 942; compared to Backus and Jefferson, II, 928–935, 1013; opposes missions, II, 932; opposes Sabbath laws, II, 932, 1112, 1142, 1267; on education, II, 935; opposes Western Lands Act, II, 983, 989 n. 7; helps Baptist Petition, II, 999; and Religious Liberty Act, II, 1099–1101; and Jackson, II, 1113; opposes Sunday Schools, II, 1141–1142, 1233
"Leo" on Article Three, II, 1150
Leonard, Daniel, I, 536, 572
Leonard, Ezra, II, 1232
Leonard, George, II, 1050, 1052
Leonard, Samuel, II, 821
Leonard, Zenas, II, 1105, 1114, 1158, 1173
Letter from the Associated Ministers of . . . Windham, I, 368
Letter on Communion, II, 1131
Letters Concerning Toleration, I, 387, 520, 614
Letters on Theron and Aspasia, II, 740

Leverett, John, I, 74, 103
Leverett, Mass., I, 599
Lewis, Abner, II, 725
Lewis, Timothy, I, 539
Lewis, William, II, 1249
Lexington and Concord Battle, I, 566, 579, 597
Leyden Baptist Association, II, 701, 826
Liberal Support of Gospel Ministers, The, II, 706–707
Liberty of Conscience, II, 846
Liberty of Conscience, I, 59, 75, 92–96, 150–151, 161–162, 183, 212, 239, 299, 376, 381, 388, 390, 392, 401, 479, 552; as seen by the Mathers, I, 108–110, 123–124, 291–292
Licensing of dissenting ministers, I, 441–476. *See also* Toleration Act
Lincoln, Benjamin, I, 641
Lincoln, Heman, II, 1158, 1173, 1175, 1177
Lincoln, John W., II, 1254
Lincoln, Levi, I, 642; II, 1023, 1067, 1150, 1158, 1172, 1180, 1182, 1206, 1218–1221
Lillebridge, David, II, 951
Little, Ephraim, II, 954
Little Compton, Mass., I, 10, 121–122, 200, 231–232
Littleton, Mass., petition, II, 1215 n. 14
Littleton, N. H., II, 857
Livermore, Arthur, II, 863, 868
Llewellyn, Thomas, I, 501, 530
Local home rule, I, 114–115, 129, 142–143, 148, 178–179, 203, 211–213, 441
Lock, Edward, II, 727, 766 n. 48
Locke, John, 79, 109, 292, 316, 387, 388, 400, 405, 519–520, 559, 575, 597, 600–601, 614; II, 752, 773
London Confession of Faith, I, 83, 508; II, 710
London, N. H., II, 873
Londonderry, N. H., II, 840–841
Lord, Abraham, I, 526
Lord, Benjamin, I, 346, 373–376
Lord, Tozier, II, 727
Lord's Day Schools Association, II, 1117
Loring, James, II, 1118, 1129
Lothrop, Samuel I., II, 1221–1222, 1235
Lotteries, II, 758–759, 962–963, 965–966, 1265
Lovell v. Byfield, II, 1084
Lovett, Joseph, II, 953–954
Low, Samuel, I, 140–145
Loyalists, Baptists accused of being, I, 485, 569–585
Ludlum, David, II, 792, 794
Lukar, Henry, I, 11
Lundy, Benjamin, II, 1271

Luther, Martin, I, 4, 29, 574
Luther, Samuel, I, 136–146, 155, 206
Lyme, Conn., I, 266, 313, 364
Lynde, Simon, I, 49, 74
Lynn, Mass., I, 14, 18–19, 62, 96

McClary, Michael, II, 874
McCollum Case, I, 664 n. 3
Mack, Ebenezer, I, 438, 448–450
Mackenesse, Thomas, I, 583
Macomber, Ann, II, 765
MacSparran, James, I, 211, 223 n. 18, 239
Madbury, N. H., II, 727, 852
Madison, James, I, 401, 556, 563, 592, 601, 607, 624; II, 881, 928, 967, 1008, 1022, 1092, 1099; *Remonstrance* cited, II, 1228–1229, 1230
Magistrates, role of in religious affairs, I, 7, 11, 12–13, 30, 36, 58, 68, 92–96, 154, 387, 389, 414–415. *See also* Erastianism
Magna Charta, I, 257
Maine, II, 1122–1127, 1145, 1199–1200
Maine Literary and Theological Institution. *See* Waterville College
Malden, Mass., I, 125
Manchester Association, II, 826
Mann, Horace, II, 1239
Mann, Richard, I, 252 n. 7
Manning, James, I, 438, 522, 530, 545, 582, 583, 584; II, 1113, 1130; founds R. I. College, I, 493–502, 512; petition to Continental Congress, I, 558–568; attacked as Tory, I, 579–580; in Congress, I, 675; on the Shakers, II, 716; on Universalism, II, 74; on Jemima Wilkinson, II, 740; obituary, II, 743; on lotteries, II, 758–759; owned a slave, II, 766, 768; joins abolition society, II, 768; on education, II, 770–772; and ratifying convention, II, 780–784; debates in Conn., II, 920; William Bentley on, II, 1069
Mansfield, Conn., I, 346, 424–452, 1045
Manwaring, Christopher, II, 1022
Marblehead, Mass., I, 200, 203
Marcy, Moses, I, 459–461
Marriage privileges for dissenting ministers, I, 515–521, 650, 654–658
Marsh, Benjamin, I, 507, 679
Marsh, Joseph, I, 174, 175, 176, 185
Marshall, Daniel, I, 438
Marshall, Eliakim, II, 922, 946, 1050
Marshall, John, I, 593, 941, 943
Marshall, Joseph, I, 429–450
Marshfield, Mass., I, 200, 205, 311
Marshman, David, II, 1115
Martha's Vineyard, I, 299
Martin, Daniel, II, 728–729

Martin, John, I, 507
Mascall, Robert, I, 103
Mason, Benajah, II, 1249
Mason, George, I, 563, 592, 593, 600–601, 607
Mason, Jonathan, I, 458–459
Massachusetts: Charter of 1691, I, 109–110, 113, 212, 220, 394
Massachusetts: Constitution of, I, 531, 591–635; of 1778, I, 594
Massachusetts: Provincial Congress, I, 564–566, 585
Massachusetts: Constitutional Convention of 1820, II, 1145–1185
Massachusetts Baptist Convention, II, 1115
Massachusetts Baptist Missionary Magazine, II, 1108, 1114, 1131, 1135, 1138, 1139, 1264, 1272
Massachusetts Baptist Missionary Society, II, 1115, 1117
Massachusetts Proposals, the, I, 179, 219, 288
Mather, Cotton, I, 6, 9 n. 2, 79, 90, 104, 108–109, 114 n. 1, 179, 186, 214–215, 218, 283, 288, 298, 305, 314, 317, 318, 350, 352; and ordination of Elisha Callendar, I, 289–290; and "syncretism of piety," I, 115, 116, 289–293, 317; II, 1278
Mather, Eliakim, II, 951 n. 23
Mather, Increase, I, 6, 7, 12, 22, 42, 45, 47, 72, 80–81, 82, 84, 87, 90, 92, 105–106, 108, 110, 123, 152, 159, 182, 264, 283, 284, 285, 288, 289, 314
Mather, Richard, I, 45
Matignon, Francis, I, 653 n. 39, 658
Matthews, Marmaduke, I, 126
Maxcy, John, II, 721–722, 733, 759
Maxcy, Levi, I, 638
Maxson, Johnson, I, 497, 500, 581
Maxwell, Samuel, I, 285; and open communion, I, 311–312; on Thomas Denison, I, 322–323
May, S., I, 76 n. 58
Mayhew, Jonathan, II, 730
Meachem, Joseph, I, 437, 443, 507, 529; II, 947
Mead, James, I, 436
Mead, Sidney E., I, 388; II, 1227
Mears, Roswell, II, 803–804, 825–826
Medfield, Mass., I, 464–465, 481–482, 547, 551–552, 672–673
Medford, Mass., I, 236
Meetinghouse controversies, I, 472, 660, 685–695; in Pittsfield, Mass., I, 663–670; in Rehoboth, I, 682–684; in Vermont, II, 818–819, 824–826
Mellen, James, I, 470–473, 507, 517

Mendon, Mass., I, 547–548, 551
Mennonites, I, 5, 573
Mercy Exemplified, I, 318
Meredith Association, II, 701
Merrill, Daniel, 880, 889, 896
Merrill, John, I, 202
Merriman, Anson, II, 1044–1045
Merriman, George, I, 262, 444–446
Merriman, John, I, 262, 444–446; II, 1044
Metcalf, Theron, II, 1190
Methodists, I, 8, 277, 609, 653, 663, 672; Whitefield's, I, 654, 684; Washburn *v.* West Springfield, I, 658; difficulties over religious taxes in Mass., I, 658–659; in Harwich, Mass., I, 677; in Fitchburg, Mass., I, 691; rivalry with Baptists, II, 709, 711, 723–727, 1139–1141; perfectionism of, II, 725; practise immersion, II, 726; in Vermont, II, 800; in Holderness, N. H., II, 859; in Lancaster, N. H., II, 861; in N. H., II, 875, 885, 897, 909; in Conn., II, 919, 947, 1002, 1024, 1027, 1028, 1037–1038; and the Baptist Petition, II, 995–996; belittled by Lyman Beecher, II, 1029–1032; and the Act for the Support of Religion and Literature, II, 1034–1041; efforts for disestablishment in Mass., II, 1066, 1099. *See also* Wesley, John; Asbury, Francis; Lee, Jesse
Middleborough, Mass., I, 599; New Lights in, I, 365, 367, 376–384, 516; First Baptist Church in, I, 432–448; Third Baptist Church in, I, 528, 585 n. 43, 595, 636, 649; II, 710; distraint in, I, 547, 564; Ezra Kendall's case, II, 1085; and Mass. Constitution, I, 628
Middlebury College, II, 870, 890, 1189
Middletown, Conn., I, 371, 400
Miflin, Thomas, I, 559
Milford, Conn., I, 345, 366
Milford, N. H., II, 886
Millennium, the, I, 331, 336, 358, 612; II, 780–781, 1007, 1033, 1267
Miller, Alexander, I, 370
Miller, Benjamin, I, 507
Miller, Daniel, I, 504, 507
Miller, Perry, I, 32, 84, 108, 109, 388; II, 935, 1277
Millington, John, II, 721
Milton, John, I, 10
Miner, Daniel, II, 745
Ministerial lots, I, 660, 685–695; in Swansea, I, 146; in Warwick, 679; in Sutton, I, 679–680; in Shutesbury, I, 681–682; in Vermont, II, 817–832; in N. H., 860, 861. *See also* Glebelands
Ministerial taxes. *See* Religious taxes
Missions, Anglican, I, 114, 200–224

Missions, Congregational in Vermont, II, 805–806; by Vermont Baptists, II, 828–829; in New Hampshire, II, 877
Missouri Compromise, II, 1270, 1273
Mitchell, Edward, I, 320
Mitchell, Jonathan, I, 21, 62, 64, 66, 104
Mixed communion. *See* Open communion
Mohammedans (Mahometans, Muslems), I, 484, 610, 657, 658; II, 945, 1105, 1156
Monkton, Vt., II, 823
Montague *v.* Dedham, II, 1095–1096
Montague, Richard, I, 438, 527–528, 529, 599; II, 719, 742
Montague, William, II, 1096
Montague, Mass., 527–528, 547
Moody, Lady Deborah, I, 16, 22
Moody, Joshua, II, 835
Moore *v.* Poole, II, 883–888, 894, 895, 903
Moravians, I, 573
Morison, Samuel Eliot, I, 613, 630, 631
Mormons, II, 1112, 1226
Morse, Asahel, II, 990, 998, 1006, 1022, 1050, 1053, 1054
Morse, David, II, 704
Morse, Jedediah, II, 747, 773, 785, 882, 1012
Morse, Joshua, I, 363 n. 8, 478, 480
Morse, Moses, I, 395, 396
Morton, Marcus, II, 1206
Morton, Nathaniel, I, 9 n. 1
Morton, Perez, I, 642
Mosier, Hugh, I, 167, 168, 169
Moss (Morse), John, I, 256
Moulder, Joseph, I, 559
Moulton, Ebenezer, I, 320–322, 323, 422, 431, 447, 457, 469, 475, 478, 480, 481, 482
Mudge, Enoch, II, 1158, 1166
Mumford, Cass, II, 765
Munsterites, I, 3, 6, 29 n. 4, 32, 58, 82 n. 5, 133, 358; II, 1277
Murray, John, I, 521 n. 15, 643 n. 15, 668; II, 717–719, 871, 1077; wins dissenting status for Universalists, I, 653–658
Murton, John, I, 5
Muzzy *v.* Wilkins, II, 863–870, 880
Myles, John, I, 6, 74, 75, 85 n. 8, 90, 129–136, 142, 158, 160, 198, 206, 242, 283, 468, 474, 475; II, 1278
Myles, Samuel, I, 136 n. 38, 208, 215, 217, 219, 283

Nantucket, Mass., I, 299
National Aegis (Worcester), II, 1204–1205
National Congress of Baptists, I, 567–568

National establishment in U. S., II, 1020, 1211, 1259, 1274
National Republican Party, II, 1218–1219. *See also* Whig Party
Natural rights, dissenting appeals to, I, 485, 511, 539–540, 600, 626, 627; II, 751. *See also* Petitions
Nature and Necessity of an Internal Call to Preach, The, I, 356
Negro, I, 550; II, 749, 763, 767, 774, 1010, 1016–1017, 1169 n. 10, 1071 n. 17, 1269–1271. *See also* Slavery
Nelson, Ebenezer, II, 1097, 1114, 1157, 1169, 1170, 1184
Nelson, Stephen S., II, 986–987, 988, 1022
Neo-Edwardseanism. *See* Hopkinsianism
Ne Sutor Ultra Crepidam, I, 105
Nettleton, Asahel, II, 1208
Newbury, Mass., I, 76, 200, 201–203
Newcastle, Duke of, I, 216, 217, 219
New Covenant, The, I, 28–29, 31–48, 315–317, 336–339, 349–359. *See also* Abrahamic Covenant
New Divinity. *See* Hopkinsianism
New Durham, N. H., II, 727, 857
Newell, Mary, I, 55, 60
Newent, Conn., II, 961
New Gloucester, Maine, I, 648
New Hampshire; early Baptists in, I, 11; II, 833–854; first Baptist church in, II, 833, 842–843; in seventeenth century, II, 834–836; early ecclesiastical laws, II, 836–840; toleration in, 836–837; constitution of, II, 843–854; *New Hampshire Gazette,* II, 848, 851; court cases in, II, 862–876; local compromises over religious taxes, II, 855–862; and ministerial taxes, II, 884–888; Democratic-Republican Party in, II, 874, 875; disestablishment in, II, 877–911
New Hampshire Baptist Association, I, 508; II, 700, 728, 746
New Hampshire Confession of Faith, II, 876
New Hampshire Patriot, II, 881, 882, 887–893, 895, 897, 898, 900–911
New Haven Colony, I, 247–248
New Haven, Conn., I, 345, 361
New Haven Consociation, 407, 445–446
New Haven Theology, II, 1208
New Lebanon, N. Y., II, 712
New Lights, I, 329–359; in First Baptist Church of Boston, I, 320–322; criticisms of the Standing system, I, 342–344; pietism of, I, 355–356; moderates distinguished from Separates, I, 365–366; moderates oppose Separates, I, 358–359, 361; quarrels with Old Lights, I, 360–385; try to maintain

orthodoxy by law, I, 387; controversy in Wallingford, I, 407–408; ecclesiological reforms of the Standing Order, I, 410. *See also* Separates; Separate Baptists
New London Baptist Association, II, 920, 1061
New London, Conn., I, 10, 254–264, 267–268, 274, 280, 345, 361, 363
New London, N. H., II, 859
Newman, Samuel, I, 131
Newport, R. I.; Seventh Day Baptists in, I, 10 n. 3, 581; II, 763; First Baptist Church of, I, 11, 16, 18, 62, 283, 285, 286, 293, 302, 309, 421, 423; II, 710–711; Second Baptist Church of, I, 305, 307, 423, 497, 581; II, 761, 764–766; R. I. College in, I, 495; John Comer in, I, 304–309
New Reformation, the, I, 4, 5, 6, 7, 34, 99, 100, 491
New Salem, Conn., II, 952–961
New Salem, Mass., I, 547; II, 707, 778
Newton, Thomas, II, 868
Newton Theological Seminary, II, 1122–1123, 1264
Newton, Mass., I, 464; II, 767, 1249–1250
Newton, N. H., I, 457; II, 842–843
New York City, I, 265, 286; First Baptist Church in, I, 287
New York Observer, II, 1269
Nichols, Amasa, II, 1232
Nichols, John, II, 1001
Nicholson, Sir Francis, I, 158
Nickerson, Samuel, I, 676
Niebuhr, H. R., I, 329
Niles, Samuel, II, 763, 1074
Noddles Island, I, 49, 60, 71, 72, 73, 74
Norcott, John, I, 317
Northampton, Mass., I, 335, 547, 549
North Attleboro, Mass., I, 637–640
North Kingston, R. I., I, 311, 319, 423
North Lyme, Conn., I, 275
Northwood, N. H., II, 857
Norton, John, 93
Norton, Mass., I, 391
Nothingarians, I, 204, 206, 213, 437, 660–661, 669; II, 848, 928, 945, 964, 1148, 1212, 1279; see also Latitudinarians
Norwich, Conn., I, 350, 370, 373–376, 395, 569; II, 719
Norwich Packet, II, 977
Nullification, II, 1272
Nuttall, Geoffrey, I, 9 n. 1, 30–31
Nye, Philip, I, 100

Olcott, Simeon, II, 871
"Old Baptists," I, 439–441, 447. *See* Baptists; Separate Baptists

Old Lights, I, 336–338, 339; oppose Separates, I, 344–345, 358, 360, 385; considered Arians and Socinians, I, 407–408; defense of religious taxes, I, 416

Oliver, Peter, I, 524, 527, 543, 554, 572

Open (or mixed) Communion, I, 5, 6, 29 n. 5, 62–70, 79–90, 274, 287, 304, 310; practised by John Myles, I, 130–136, 161; rejected by Samuel Luther, I, 137–138; in Freetown, I, 206; in 1710–1742, I, 277–299; and John Walton, I, 309–311, 313–314; Separates and Separate Baptists on, 424–439, 447–453; after 1740, I, 467–476, 481; in Bellingham, Mass., I, 474–476; in South Brimfield, I, 470–474; declines in Groton Assoc., II, 703–704, 920; in Vermont, II, 821–822; with Trinitarians, II, 1129–1133, 1134, 1135

Oration Delivered at Winsted, II, 1006

Oration on the Beauties of Liberty, I, 584; II, 766

Ordination, in Standing Order, I, 125–126

Orleans, Mass., petition, II, 1214

Ormsby, Jeremiah, I, 229, 231

Orthodoxy, problem of defining in N. E., I, 179, 363, 616–617; imposed by New Lights, I, 407–408; imposed by Baptists, II, 710–711

Osborne, Thomas, I, 55, 57, 58, 60

Otis, Harrison Grey, II, 1197, 1199, 1204

Owen, Robert, II, 1265, 1267

Oxenbridge, John, I, 73, 86, 107 n. 37

Packersfield, N. H., II, 892

Packom (Peckom), Timothy, I, 363 n. 8, 423

Paine, Elisha, I, 333 n. 7, 346, 357, 363 n. 8, 368, 429, 433–435

Paine, John, I, 371, 392, 431, 436–437

Paine, Robert Treat, I, 559–562, 572, 602, 604, 609; II, 1023; and Balkcom Case, I, 638–639, 641; and Pittsfield Case, I, 666–667

Paine, Solomon, I, 333 n. 7, 346, 368, 378, 390, 395, 399–415; on baptism, I, 426, 429, 432–435; and marriages, II, 946–947

Paine, Thomas, I, 400, 608; II, 737, 804, 972, 976, 1009, 1011, 1073, 1156

Painter, Thomas, I, 16, 22, 50, 67

Palmer, Abel, II, 955–961, 990

Palmer, Christopher, II, 955–961, 987

Palmer, Elihue, II, 718

Palmer, John, I, 363 n. 8

Palmer's River, Mass., I, 155–160

Panoplist, The, II, 891

Papists, I, 3, 28, 38, 41, 68, 70, 89, 92, 133, 292, 389, 400, 414, 482, 484, 616; II, 933, 1266. *See also* Roman Catholics

Parish system in N. H., II, 841; in Conn., II, 939–961, 980; in Mass., I, 124–127, 306–365, 425, 593, 617, 669; II, 1191–1192; poll parishes, I, 367 n. 13, 409, 677, 683

Parish taxes. *See* Religious taxes

Park, Paul, I, 395 n. 10, 429

Park Street Church, II, 1131, 1208

Parker, Edmund, II, 907–908

Parker, Isaiah, I, 598; II, 721

Parker, Isaac, II, 1104–1106; and Mass. Constitutional Convention (1820), II, 1152–1156, 1158, 1172, 1177, 1178, 1179, 1180, 1191, 1194–1195; defends Unitarianism, II, 1211

Parker, Samuel, I, 665, 666

Parker, Thomas, I, 595 n. 5

Parsons, Jonathan, I, 364

Parsons, Stephen, I, 703

Parsons, Theophilus, II, 872, 1023; and Mass. Constitution, I, 602, 610; Barnes *v.* Falmouth, I, 650, 662, 692; II, 1086–1093; and John Murray, I, 654–658; II, 720

Particular Baptists (Five Principle Baptists). *See* Baptists

Partridge, Richard, I, 191, 224, 233, 234, 236

Paul, Thomas, II, 765–766; II, 748, 1071 n. 17

Paxton, Mass., I, 626–627

Payson, Phillips, I, 596–598, 614, 615

Peak, John, II, 748

Pearse, Miel, I, 231

Pearson, Eliphalet, II, 1138

Peck, John, II, 800

Peck, Samuel, I, 155, 156, 371–373, 392

Peckham, William, I, 260

Pees, Kingston, II, 764–765

Peirce, John, I, 76 n. 57, 84–89, 104

Pelot, Francis, I, 499, 501

Pemberton, Israel, I, 558–564

Pemberton, James, I, 558–564

Pembrook, N. H., II, 841

Penn, William, I, 253; II, 1169

Pennsylvania Chronicle, I, 577, 578

Pepperell, Mass., I, 579; riot in, I, 598–599

Perfectionism, I, 30, 37, 44, 50, 100, 357–358, 389, 408 n. 33, 437, 615; II, 723, 725, 739

Perry, Jonathan, I, 458–459

Persecution, I, 31–91; of Anglicans, I, 200–224 (in Barrington and Rehoboth, I, 238 n. 38; in Fairfield, I, 265); of

Baptists (in Boston area, I, 3–91; in Dartmouth and Tiverton, I, 165–199; in Swansea, I, 129–148; in Rehoboth, I, 149–162, 228–30, 237, 240–41; in Charlestown-Boston, 49–78; in Little Compton, I, 230–231; in Groton, I, 254–262; in New Gloucester, Maine, I, 648; in Sandisfield, Mass., I, 649; in Bridgewater, I, 670; in Harwich, I, 676; in Vermont, II, 789, 795, 804, 813–815; in N. H., II, 838–853, 861–876, 892–893; in Conn., II, 947–961, 989, 1010, 1043–1046); of Separates, 360–385, 405; of Separate Baptists, I, 440–553 (in Sturbridge, Mass., I, 457–461, 483; in Ashfield, Mass., I, 531–546); of Universalists, I, 654–658 (see John Murray, Christopher Erskine); of Episcopalians, II, 1044–1045; Roger Williams on, I, 92–96; of Rogerenes, I, 251–254; of Separate-Baptists, I, 426–439; of Thomas Goold et al., I, 49–78; of Esther White, I, 447–448; of Elizabeth Backus, I, 374–375; of John White, I, 463, 521; of Quakers, I, 10 n. 4, 22, 165–199, 228–331; of Anson Merriman, II, 1044. *See also* Ashfield; Hingham; Pepperell; other towns

Peters, John T., II, 989, 1022

Petitions; in Mass. (of Robert Childe, I, 14, 118; for leniency toward Thomas Goold, I, 71; by Baptists in 1679/80, I, 75; of John Pierce, 1679, I, 84–89; of Mass. clergy, 1694, I, 127; from Swansea and Barrington, I, 140–144; from Rehoboth, I, 150–159; from Quakers, I, 167–168, 224; from Dartmouth and Tiverton, I, 174–181, 191; against Synod of 1725, I, 215–216, 219–221; against first Anglican exemption act, I, 221–223; to Privy Council, I, 167–168, 215–216, 219, 221, 222–224, 395–397, 478–487, 531, 544–546; to Gov. Burnet, I, 228; by Baptists in 1739, I, 240–242; from Sturbridge, I, 460; to Mass. Provincial Congress, I, 564–567; by Rehoboth Separates, I, 372; by Separates, I, 386–398, II, 921–922; by Separate-Baptists, I, 454–476, 477–488; from South Brimfield, I, 470–472; from Ashfield, I, 531, 538–546; against Article Three, I, 631–632; for Religious Liberty Act, II, 1097–1102 to amend Mass. Constitution (1829–1831), II, 1213–1216, 1246–1252); in Conn. (by Quakers, I, 253–254; of William Pitkin, I, 254; from Groton Baptists, I, 255–256; by town of New London, I, 268–269; from Wallingford,

I, 271–272; from Montville, I, 273–274; from North Lyme, I, 275; by Separates, I, 386–398, 411 n. 42, 417; by Separate-Baptists, 441–453; from East Lyme, Conn., I, 441 n. 2; from Enfield, I, 443; from Wallingford, I, 444–446; the Baptist Petition, II, 982–1005); in Plymouth, by William Vassall, I, 254 n. 10; to Continental Congress, 1774, I, 553–568

Pew rental, I, 653, 661; II, 965, 966

Phelps, Charles, II, 975

Phelps, Martin, II, 1158, 1162

Phenix Bank Bonus, II, 1026–1027

Philadelphia Baptist Association, I, 305, 493, 497, 507, 530, 566, 577

"Philanthropos" on Article Three, I, 608, 609, 617–619, 623–624, 628, 640

Phillips, Benjamin, I, 539

Phillips, George, I, 27–48

Phillips, Philip, I, 539

"Philologus" on Article Three, II, 1146, 1156

Phipps, Sir William, I, 124

Pickering *v.* Harvard, I, 650 n. 34; II, 1077

Pickering, Theophilus, I, 187, 188, 196

Pickering, Timothy, II, 862, 882

Pierce, Azeriakim, I, 228 n. 5

Pierce, Benjamin, I, 423, 432; II, 842

Pierce, David, I, 256

Pierce, Nathan, II, 729

Pierce, Richard, I, 197

Pierpont, James, I, 285

Pietism, I, 6, 28, 30–32, 40, 50, 57, 69–70, 166, 277, 302, 309, 318, 398, 593; II, 707–708; and the Revolution, I, 569–577; II, 776, 1208; stimulated by the Awakening, I, 324, 325, 336, 339, 340–344, 349, 354, 356, 365, 388, 424, 426, 429, 437

Pilgrim's Progress, The, I, 434

Pilmoor, Joseph, II, 723

Pitkin, Samuel, II, 1021

Pitkin, William, I, 254

Pitman, John, II, 900–902, 905

Pittsfield, Mass., I, 663–670, 683; II, 713, 714, 717

Pittsfield Sun, II, 1221

Plain Address to the Quakers . . . , I, 536

Plainfield, Conn., I, 364, 369–370

Plumer, William, II, 848–854, 862, 863, 866, 871, 879, 881, 882, 887–893, 894–898, 908, 910

Pluralism, I, 115, 166, 353, 367

Plymouth Colony, I, 5, 6, 9, 90, 110, 113, 114, 120; connives with Baptists, I, 130–132; efforts of Mass. to force conformity in, after 1691, I, 129–213

Plymouth, N. H., II, 861
Pomfret, Conn., II, 815–816, 917
Portsmouth, N. H., II, 747–748
Poultney, Vt., II, 792, 821–822
Powell, Mitchell, I, 120
Powers, Thomas Walter, II, 842
Powers, Walter, II, 727
Pownal, Vt., II, 793, 822–823
Predestination, I, 32, 41–42, 305, 317, 358; II, 727–728, 731–736
Preparation for grace, I, 31–32
Presbyterianism, I, 89, 96, 655; in England, I, 6, 30, 65, 68, 69, 100, 101, 110, 295; Congregationalists' use of, I, 216, 482, 571; in Middle Colonies, I, 488; in New Hampshire, II, 833, 840–842, 855, 903; Muzzy *v.* Wilkins, II, 863–872
Prescott, William, II, 1173
Preston, Conn., I, 286, 395; II, 963, 1041
Price, Benoni, I, 145
Priestley, Joseph, II, 733
Prince, Nathan, I, 283 n. 6
Prince, Thomas, I, 298
Princeton, Mass., I, 528
Princeton University, I, 499, 500
Privy Council, I, 115, 124, 165, 237, 392
Proctor, Gershom, I, 548
Proctor, Henry, I, 548
Proctor, John, II, 800
Profession and Practice of Christians, The, II, 847
Prophesying, I, 30, 56, 58, 67
Protestant Episcopal Church. *See* Anglicans
Protestant Ethic, II, 752, 779–780
Providence, R. I., I, 5, 8, 14; First Baptist Church of, I, 10, 286, 299, 309–311, 497; opposition to Congregationalism, I, 301–302, Beneficent Congregational Church, I, 322; Baptist Petition conference in, I, 477–481; Abolition Society, II, 768; public education, II, 771–772
Provost, Samuel, II, 724
Public Worship Act (1800), I, 651–653, 658
Putnam, Aaron, II, 920
Putnam, John, I, 519–520

Quakers, I, 3, 6, 7, 8, 12, 14, 22, 48, 50, 55, 56, 57, 59, 70, 81, 84, 96, 99, 104, 107, 114, 119, 122, 133, 153, 161, 203, 223, 299, 318, 362, 372, 389, 390, 392, 405, 475, 482, 510, 542, 627, 655; II, 833, 874, 1132; appeals to Privy Council, I, 167–168, 224, 253; banished in Plymouth, I, 120 n. 18; in Boston, 49, 76; Baptists' opposition to, I, 66, 89; in Connecticut, I, 253, 255 n. 12, 263, 264, 265–266, 277; confused with Rogerenes,

I, 250; compared to Baptists, I, 6, 30, 31 n. 7; exempted from religious taxes (in Mass., I, 225–247, 651), (in Conn., I, 270–271); oppose hireling ministry, I, 198; declining interest in religious liberty after 1735, I, 277; London Yearly Meeting, I, 190, 191, 233, 236, 253; London Committee for Suffering, I, 183; membership growth, I, 121–122; petition to Plymouth General Court 1678, I, 167–168; resistance to religious taxes in Dartmouth and Tiverton, I, 165–199, 224, 227; New England Yearly Meeting, I, 190, 578; whipped, I, 10 n. 4, 18, 253; loss of zeal, I, 238 n. 36; attacked by Separates, I, 408–409; attacked by Baptists, II, 737–738; exemption act of 1770, I, 487; neutral in Revolution, I, 555, 573, 577–578; support permanent salary for royal governors, I, 227; join Baptists in petition to Continental Congress (1774), I, 558–561; refuse to petition Mass. legislature (1778), I, 595, 607 n. 33; and slavery, II, 768–769; in Vermont, II, 800, 814, 820; in N. H., II, 838–839, 840, 843, 855; in Conn., II, 936, 1036
Quebec Act, I, 557, 574, 586–587
Queries of the Highest Consideration, I, 100

Rand, Asa, II, 1223
Randall, Benjamin, II, 726–728, 852, 855
Randall, Joseph, II, 803
Ransom, Elisha, II, 803–804, 806, 807, 814, 859
Ranters, I, 6
Rantoul, Robert, Sr., II, 1158
Rathbun, Daniel, II, 715
Rathbun, Valentine (of Pittsfield), I, 595 n. 5, 663, 664, 665; II, 712, 714–715, 740, 782
Rathbun, Valentine Wightman (of Stonington), I, 687; II, 770
Rawson, Josiah, I, 549
Raynham, Mass., I, 447–448, 628, 674–675; II, 715
Read, John, I, 208
Reading, Mass., II, 1097
Redwood Library, I, 283, 287
Reed, Samuel, I, 678
Reed, Solomon, I, 376, 377, 384, 407 n. 29
Reeve, Tapping, II, 1029, 1032
Reformation, I, 4, 6, 7, 28, 56
Rehoboth, Mass., I, 28 n. 21, 121, 176, 200, 303, 507, 682; struggle for religious liberty in, I, 113, 128–132, 146–162, 211, 228–230, 237, 240–241, 285, 301, 516, 628, 675; Separates in, I, 371–

373, 391, 436–437; Baptists gain control of, I, 682–684. *See also* Myles, John; Luther, Samuel
Religion of Jesus Vindicated, I, 317–318
Religious Liberty, I, 212; as seen by Roger Williams, I, 92–102; as seen by Thomas Goold, I, 59–60, 63–70; as seen by John Pierce, I, 84–89; first official steps in Mass., I, 91–110; under Mass. laws of 1692–1695, I, 114–127; tax exemption laws 1728–1734, I, 225–243; Baptists in Groton, I, 256–262; in Wallingford, I, 271–273; by Quakers in Conn., I, 265; Separates' contribution to, I, 399–417; for Quakers in N. H., II, 838–839. *See also* Rehoboth; Swansea; Dartmouth; Tiverton. *See also* Toleration; Religious taxes, Liberty of conscience
Religious Liberty, II, 1209
Religious Liberty Act (1811), I, 640, 647; II, 881, 1065, 1066, 1078, 1080, 1093–1106; in Mass. Constitutional Convention of 1820, II, 1160, 1162, 1166, 1173, 1175, 1176, 1177, 1181, 1183, 1197; modified in 1824, II, 1200–1206, 1212, 1225
Religious taxes: Anglican opposition to, I, 200–224; in Connecticut, I, 117–118, 247–250, 254; in seventeenth century, I, 28 n. 3, 61, 68, 116–127; exemption from (in Mass., I, 116, 198, 201, 211; for Anglicans, I, 221–224; for Quakers and Baptists, I, 225–243; in Boston, I, 126; for Separates, I, 410–411, 414; II, 921–923, 926–938, 939–942; and Separate Baptists, I, 440–453, 454–476, 512–530; Act of 1800, I, 651–653; II, 1200; Act of 1811, II, 1093–1106; Act of 1824, II, 1200–1206), (in Conn., I, 199, 249, 268–277); struggle in Bristol County, I, 113–114, 129–199, 278; defended by Rehoboth Congregationalists, I, 160–162; Mass. law of 1702, I, 169–170; Mass. law of 1706, I, 173–174; John Cotton opposes, I, 28 n. 3; Noah Hobart supports, I, 414–415; in New York, I, 286; opposition to, among Puritans, I, 117–119; opposition to, in Swansea, Mass., I, 129–148; opposition to, in Rehoboth, Mass., I, 149–162; Thomas Hollis on, I, 295; Increase Mather on, I, 152–154; opposition to tax exemption by Congregationalists, I, 228; resistance to, in Dartmouth and Tiverton, I, 165–199, in Rehoboth, I, 149–162, in Swansea, I, 129–148, in Freetown, I, 204, 207–213, in New London, I, 268–269, in Wallingford, I, 271–272; Thomas Goold and,

I, 61, 68; Separate petitions against, I, 386–398; Laws enforcing (in Mass., I, 114–127), (in Plymouth, I, 118–119); Separate tracts against, I, 440–415; Separate-Baptists and, I, 421–424, (in Conn., I, 440–453), (in Mass., I, 454–553); Esther White jailed for, I, 447–448; levied on Separates, I, 364–385; Elizabeth Backus jailed for, I, 374–375; problem in East Lyme, Conn., I, 448–450; problem in Suffield, Mass., I, 450–451; in Mansfield, Conn., I, 451–452; Mass. exemption law: of 1740, I, 454; of 1747 and 1753, I, 455, 460, 461, 481, 483, 484; of 1758, I, 462–476, 486–487, 512–530; of 1770, I, 487, 538–539; of 1774, I, 554–555; of 1807, II, 1080; of 1811, II, 1093–1106; in Easton, Mass., I, 465–466; Lawsuits by dissenters, I, 463; in Sturbridge, I, 457–461; in Easton, I, 465; in Titicut, I, 382–384; in South Brimfield, I, 472–473; appeal to Continental Congress against, I, 556–568; in Vt., II, 797–812; in N. H., II, 833–853, 856–876
Religious test oaths, II, 781–782, 797, 848, 1147, 1155, 1156, 1160, 1184
Relly, James, I, 654; II, 717, 719
Remarks on Mr. Bulkley's Account, I, 313
Remarks on the Writings of Mr. Sandeman, I, 741
Reply to a Confutation, I, 27–48
Revolution, American, I, 115, 300, 338, 339, 417, 542, 554; Baptists' views of, I, 555–557, 569–587; II, 741, 751, 776, 1007
Reynolds, Gamaliel, I, 437; II, 719, 721
Rhode Island, I, 3, 7–8, 9, 10, 66, 158, 279–281; II, 758, 1008, 1031, 1167, 1168, 1277; law against ministerial contracts (1716), I, 198 n. 45; II, 934–942; immigration to Vt. and N. H., II, 791–792, 842
Rhode Island College. *See* Brown University
Rhodes, Samuel, I, 559
Rice, Luther, II, 1114, 1115
Rich, Elisha, I, 549
Rich, Luther, II, 1114, 1115
Rich, Thomas, I, 550
Richards, George H., II, 1023, 1040 n. 37
Richardson, Daniel, I, 638
Richardson, Joseph, II, 1158
Richardson, Thomas, I, 191
Richmond Association, II, 701, 826
Rindge, N. H., I, 547; II, 861
Ripley, Eleazar, II, 1101
Ripley, Hezekiah, II, 925, 1023
Rippon, John, I, 501, 582; II, 721

Rivington's Gazette, I, 580
Roberts, George H., II, 1024
Robbins, Ephraim, II, 987, 1015 n. 11
Robbins, John, I, 548
Robbins, Philemon, I, 364, 445–446; II, 1044
Robbins, Thomas, II, 811, 1061–1062
Robinson, John, I, 5, 65, 66, 118
Robinson, Jonathan, II, 814
Robinson, Samuel (Hardwick), I, 393
Robinson, Samuel (Guilford), II, 1047
Rodman, John, I, 265
Rogerenes, the, I, 10 n. 3, 249–252, 255 n. 12, 264, 268, 275, 277, 280, 282, 384, 389, 607 n. 33; II, 1278
Rogers, Clark, I, 581
Rogers, Daniel, I, 104
Rogers, James, I, 250, 261
Rogers, John, I, 250
Rogers, William, I, 559, 565–566, 568; II, 733, 784–785
Roman Catholics, I, 610, 653 n. 39, 658–659; II, 736–737, 785, 800, 848, 919, 923, 1011, 1058, 1074, 1077, 1112, 1119, 1152, 1160, 1168, 1224, 1228, 1267, 1272. *See also* Papists
Root, Isaac, II, 721
Root, Timothy, I, 355
Ross, Robert, I, 347, 355, 356
Round, Richard, I, 504
Rowland, David, I, 370
Rowley, N. H., II, 860
Royalston, Mass., I, 547, 549, 628, 631; II, 708, 709
Russell, John Jr., I, 28, 74, 75, 77, 82–84, 89, 104, 105
Russell, John Sr., I, 73–74, 77
Russell, Richard, I, 52, 57, 62
Russell, Thomas, II, 811, 1061–1062
Rutland, Mass., II, 1105
Ryland, John, I, 583; II, 758

Sabbath laws, in Mass. I, 124 n. 23; in Conn., I, 273, 389, 401 n. 7, 446; Baptists and, I, 514 n. 2, 605–606, 757–758, 803, 1266–1267; and delivery of mail, II, 1112, 1267
Sabin, Alvah, II, 829
Salem, Mass., I, 10, 14, 16, 18, 118; II, 1068–1072
Salisbury, Conn. I, 366
Salisbury, Mass., II, 856
Salisbury, N. H., II, 746
Saltonstall, Leverett, II, 1158, 1166, 1167, 1169, 1171, 1172, 1182, 1196, 1253, 1254
Saltonstall, Richard, I, 92–93, 95, 103, 104
Salvation for All Men, II, 718, 719

Samson, Abisha, II, 1158
Sandeman, Robert, II, 740–741
Sandemanianism, I, 437, 607 n. 33, 655; II, 728, 736, 740–741, 919, 1024, 1036
Sanders, Daniel C., II, 890
Sandisfield, Mass., I, 649
Sandwich, Mass., I, 119 n. 13
Sanford, David, I, 602; II, 1074
Sargent, Nathaniel P., I, 643, 650
Savage, James, II, 1158
Savoy Declaration of Faith, I, 81, 82, 83, 125, 264
Sawyer, Elias, I, 715
Sawyer, Isaac, II, 823
Saybrook, Conn., I, 261, 441, 446
Saybrook Platform, I, 249, 264, 368, 390, 410, 413, 505; used against New Lights, I, 344–346, 361, 364; II, 916, 921, 923, 924
Scarborough, Maine, I, 528–529, 545
Schism Act, I, 291
Scituate, Mass., I, 22, 76 n. 57, 119 n. 14, 200, 641
Scott, Job, II, 738
Scott, Orange, II, 1232
Scott, Richard, I, 10
Screven, William, I, 76
Scripture Grounds of the Baptism of Christian Infants, I, 294, 315–316
Seabury, Samuel, II, 724, 1013 n. 8
Seabury College, II, 1026
Seamans, David, I, 521 n. 13
Seamans, Job, I, 638; II, 859
Seasonable Thoughts, I, 319, 422
Sebaptists, I, 6, 9 n. 1
Second Great Awakening, I, 511, 602, 611, 661, 692; II, 699, 722, 876, 907, 918, 984, 1021, 1029, 1093, 1096, 1207, 1273, 1281
Seekers, the, I, 6, 65, 98
Seekonk, R. I., I, 10
Sentiments and Plan of the Warren Association, I, 507
Separates (or Strict Congregationalists), I, 8, 337; II, 1278; formation of, I, 340–359; suppression of, I, 344–345, 350, 360–385, 442–454; defined, I, 345 n. 10, 346, 365; in Canterbury, Conn., I, 346, 433; in Mansfield, Conn., I, 346, 424; number of, I, 346, 348–349; social status of, I, 347–348; in Norwich, Conn., I, 350, 437 (*see* Bean Hill Separate Church); criticisms of Standing Order, I, 352–359, 399–415, 437–438; criticisms of clergy, I, 353–354; apolitical stance of, I, 354; leveling aspects of, I, 355, 403–405; fanaticism of, I, 354–358, 408, 409 n. 33; not considered legal dissenters, I, 362, 365–366; expelled

from Yale, I, 363; and religious taxes, I, 366–385, 437–438, 466; petitions for religious liberty, 386–398; not sympathetic to Rogerenes or other sects, I, 388, 408–409, 414; and the Sabbath, I, 389, 401 n. 7; tracts and pamphlets, I, 399–417; attain tax exemption, I, 409–410, 414, 437–438, 453; II, 921–923; decline of, 410–415, 437–439; II, 920–921; confederation of, I, 411–412; Exeter Convention, I, 428–429, 433, 435; Stonington Convention, I, 433–435, 461; in Rehoboth, I, 436–437 (*see also* John Paine); and open communion (*see* Open communion); move to Vt. and western Mass., II, 791–794; in N. H., 842, 855

Separate Baptists, I, 339, 411, 417; rise of, I, 421–439; Backus on, I, 422; Exeter Conventions, I, 428–429, 433, 435; in Somers, Conn., I, 430–431; Patience Adams and, I, 427; in Titicut, Mass., I, 431–433; Stonington Convention, I, 433–435, 461; number of churches, I, 436; 437–438; efforts for tax exemption in Conn., I, 440–453; efforts for tax exemption in Mass., I, 454–476; as opposed to "Old" or "Regular" Baptists, I, 439–443, 447, 455–476, 487; and Rhode Island College, I, 497–498, 511; taxed in East Lyme, I, 448–451, in Sturbridge, I, 457–461, in Easton, I, 464–465; and separation of church and state, I, 466–476, 484–485; petitions of, I, 477–488; form Warren Association, I, 502–511; test certificate laws in courts, I, 512–530; the Ashfield Case, I, 531–536; judicial prejudice against, I, 512–513; right of ministers to exemption from civil taxes, I, 515–521, 650; right of ministers to perform marriages, I, 515–521, 650; and civil disobedience, I, 547–555; appeal to Continental Congress (1774), I, 555–568; and the Revolution, I, 569–587. *See also* Baptists

Separatism, I, 28, 62–70, 336
Separatists, I, 5, 6, 9, 63, 65
Seventh Day Baptists, I, 10 n. 3, 11, 250, 261, 264, 275, 280–281, 308–309
Sever, Richard, I, 392
Sewall, David, I, 641, 650, 655
Sewall, Jonathan, I, 548, 572
Sewall, Samuel, I, 185, 223–224, 283 n. 7, 290
Shaftesbury Association, I, 508; II, 698, 700, 714, 744, 760, 794–795, 829, 831–832; opposes slave trade, II, 769
Shaftesbury, Vt., II, 793, 803, 830

Shakers, I, 437, 607 n. 33, 613 n. 5, 659 n. 50, 663, 684; II, 728; Valentine Rathbun and, I, 665; rivalry with Baptists, II, 709, 712–717
Shakespeare, David, I, 583
Sharon, Conn., II, 963
Sharp, Daniel, II, 1114, 1269
Sharp, John, I, 191, 192
Sharpe, William, I, 219
Shattuck, Job, II, 779
Shaw, Crispus, II, 761
Shaw, John, I, 379
Shays's Rebellion, I, 663; II, 741, 792
Sheafe, James, II, 891, 893
Sheffield, Amos, I, 176
Shelburne, Mass., I, 690–691
Shepard, Nathaniel, I, 376, 378
Shepard, Samuel, II, 843, 850, 856
Shepard, Thomas, Sr., I, 27–48
Shepard, Thomas, Jr., I, 62, 64, 68, 69
Sherman, Elijah, II, 989
Sherwin, Jacob, I, 533–536, 688–689
Shirley, William, I, 483
Short View of the Difference, I, 399–409
Shrimpton, Henry, I, 60, 71
Shute, Samuel, I, 188, 189, 204, 217
Shutesbury, Mass., I, 547, 599, 675, 680–681, 688
Silas, Barnabas, II, 954
Simon, James, II, 763
Simple Cobbler of Agawam, The, I, 4, 41 n. 46
Simsbury, Conn., I, 441 n. 1
Sisson, John, I, 188
Six Principle Baptists (or General Baptists), I, 280, 287, 456, 477; beginnings of in R. I., I, 10–11, 302; in Conn., I, 254–262, 273 n. 17; petition to Conn. General Court (1729), I, 267; practice laying on of hands, I, 280, 305–307, 321; membership size, I, 280–281; General or Rhode Island Association of, I, 281, 320, 321, 322, 503, 504, 530; II, 705–706; and General atonement, I, 304–307; and First Church of Providence, I, 309–311; John Comer and, I, 304–307; and the Great Awakening, I, 324; James Manning's opposition to doctrines, I, 497; efforts to convert them to Calvinism, II, 704–706; in Vt., II, 793
Six Prinicple Calvinistic Baptist Association, II, 704–705
Sixth Principle, the, I, 11, 280
Skillman, Isaac, II, 771
Slavery, I, 639; II, 764–769, 829, 832, 1010, 1016, 1269–1271
Sleeper, Caleb, II, 873
Slocum, Holder, II, 1158

Smalledge, Joseph, I, 680–681
Smallpox, I, 42, 82; II, 774
Smith, Adam, I, 356, 612; II, 752
Smith, Chileab, I, 532–546, 558–559
Smith, Deliverance, I, 175, 181
Smith, Ebenezer, I, 516–517, 521, 532–
546, 552, 556, 688–690; II, 767
Smith, Elias, II, 745–750, 752, 765, 818,
878–879, 1015, 1071 n. 17. *See also*
Christ-ians
Smith, Gilbert, II, 954
Smith, Hezekiah, I, 438, 499, 504, 505,
529, 538, 558, 565; II, 743, 770, 843,
855, 1113, 1139, 1130; and Rhode Is-
land College, I, 500–501; and John
White's case, I, 521–523; and Berwick
Baptists, I, 526; agent to England, I,
530; and Mass. Constitution, I, 629–
630; favors incorporation, I, 649; on
deism, II, 737; and Elias Smith, II,
745–746; on dancing and swearing, II,
756; owned a slave, II, 766; William
Bentley on, II, 1068–1069
Smith, Isaac, II, 873–874
Smith, James, II, 704
Smith, Jeremiah, II, 845, 863–876, 881,
883–888, 894–895, 903, 943
Smith, Jesse, II, 824
Smith, John, I, 9 n. 1
Smith, John Cotton, II, 1021, 1029, 1033,
1043
Smith, Nathan, II, 1053
Smith, Noah, II, 1097
Smith *v.* Dalton, I, 650; II, 1077, 1095
Smithfield, R. I., I, 302
Snow, Joseph, I, 322, 376–377, 378
Society for the Propagation of the Gospel,
I, 114, 120, 158, 200. *See also* Angli-
cans
Socinians. *See* Unitarians
Somers, Conn. I, 430
Sons of Liberty, I, 337 n. 8, 550, 556, 576,
587
Soul liberty, I, 7, 92. *See also* Liberty of
Conscience
South Brimfield, Mass., I, 296, 319, 421,
423; II, 708, 754 n. 3; Open Com-
munion in, 467, 471
South Carolina Baptist Association, I,
580
South Hadley, Mass., I, 502, 547
South Killingly, Conn. I, 409–410
South Kingston, R. I., I, 311
Southampton, N. H., II, 856
Southey, Robert, II, 1140
Southington, Conn., II, 1044, 1046
Sovereign Decrees of God, The, II, 731
Spenser, John, II, 803
Spilsbury, John, I, 5, 11 n. 7, 27

Spirit of Liberty, The, II, 723–724
Spirit of the Pilgrims, The, II, 1118, 1223,
1257
Spooner, Walter, I, 638
Sprague, David, I, 319, 320–322, 324, 423
Sprague, Jonathan, I, 18 n. 21, 302–303
Sprague, Richard, I, 236, 238
Spur, John, I, 21 n. 28
Stacey, James, I, 465–466, 521
Stafford, Conn., I, 443, 475; II, 734, 751–
752
Stafford, Joseph, I, 320
Stamp Act Crisis, I, 337 n. 8, 338, 339,
388, 409, 417, 555, 569–570, 572, 598
Standing Order, the, I, 201, 203, 214–224,
287, 288, 301, 325, 396; codified in
Mass., I, 122–127, in Conn., I, 361, II,
1019, 1021–1022; split by Awakening,
I, 341–342, 345, 437–438; opposes
Separates, I, 360–385; opposes Separate
Baptists, I, 454–563; John Adams on,
I, 559–560
Stark, William, I, 255, 257–259
Staughton, James M., II, 1268
Stearns, Eleazar, I, 465–466
Stearns, Shubael, I, 438
Stebbins *v.* Jennings, II, 1212 n. 11
Steele *v.* Hillsborough, II, 903
Stelle, Isaac, I, 507
Stennet, Joseph, I, 190, 285, 294, 313,
501
Stennett, Samuel, I, 530, 544, 551 n. 10,
552, II, 716
Stevens, Abel, II, 947
Stevens, James, II, 1049
Stevens, Thomas, I, 370, 429
Stiles, Ezra, I, 261, 324, 524, 543–544,
605; II, 763, 805, 916, 924, 1071; and
Rhode Island College, I, 492–500; and
Baptist Toryism, I, 561–562, 576–582,
585; and Shakers, II, 716–717; on Uni-
versalists, II, 717
Stillman, Samuel, I, 438, 497, 507, 529,
583, 584, 619, 625, 631, 665; II, 743,
771, 803, 1093, 1113; and civil disobedience, I, 552–553; chosen for election sermon, I, 599, 640; opposes incorporation, I, 648–649; and Elias
Smith, II, 745–748; and Black preachers, II, 765–766; owned a slave, II, 766;
joins abolition society, II, 768; and
ratifying convention, II, 780–784; a
Federalist, II, 1068; William Bentley on,
II, 1069, 1072; favored Open Communion, II, 1129–1130
Stoddard, Solomon, I, 47, 81, 337 n. 7
Stoddardeanism, I, 31–32, 47, 67, 80, 87,
288, 291, 314, 346, 358, 410, 412, 424,
437, 532; II, 728, 1031, 1132

Stone, Samuel, I, 57
Stonington Association, II, 702, 703, 917,
    920, 1016, 1061; and the Connecticut
    Baptist Petition, II, 987–1005
Stonington, Conn., II, 961, 1040
Stonington Convention, I, 433–435, 461
Storrs, Richard S., II, 1207
Story, Joseph, II, 1067, 1150, 1158, 1181,
    1182, 1255
Stow, Joshua, II, 1022, 1052, 1054, 1055,
    1056–1058
Stowe, Calvin, II, 1207, 1223
Stowell, Cyrus, II, 1170
Stowers, John, I, 117
Stratfield, Conn., II, 741, 1046
Stratford, Conn., I, 265
Streator, John, I, 459
Streeter, Russell, II, 1232
Streeter, Sebastian, II, 1232, 1236
Strict Congregationalists. *See* Separates
*Strictures on the Rev. Mr. Thacher's
    Pamphlet,* I, 609; II, 1075–1076
Strong, Asahel, II, 1245
Strong, Caleb, I, 602
Sturbridge, Mass., I, 457–461, 483, 521,
    533, 559, 631; II, 741, 1105
Suffield, Conn., I, 369, 450–451, 547; II,
    948, 950, 1006
Suffolk Resolves, I, 557
Sullivan, James, II, 1023; and Article
    Three, I, 609; II, 1075–1079; and Uni-
    versalists, I, 609; and Cutter Case, I,
    642, 645, 1077; *Strictures on the Rev.
    Mr. Thacher's Pamphlet,* I, 609; II,
    1075–1076; and John Murray, I, 655–
    658; II, 871, 1077; and Democratic-
    Republican Party in Mass., II, 1074–
    1083; views on disestablishment, II,
    1076–1079; letter signed "Farmer," II,
    1078–1079
Sunderland, Mass., I, 528, 547, 688
Sutherland, David, II, 861
Sutton, Mass., I, 296, 297, 319, 392, 423,
    528, 678–679, 688; II, 860
Sweet, Richard, I, 311
Sweetser, Benjamin, I, 14 n. 14, 72 n. 43
Sweetser, Seth, I, 14 n. 14
Symes, Zechariah, I, 131
Symmes, Zechariach, I, 51–54, 62, 77
"Syncretism of Piety." *See* Ecumenical-
    ism; Open Communion
Synod of 1648, I, 43 n. 43
Synod of 1662, I, 45–48, 50
Synod of 1679, I, 42, 50, 81, 83
Synod of 1725, I, 165, 214–224
System of the Laws, A, II, 916, 942, 944
Swansea, Mass., I, 74, 75, 113, 122, 158,
    160, 176, 178 n. 30, 200, 283, 285, 311,
    515, 628, 675; Baptists and religious

taxes, I, 129–148; limits dissent in, I,
    133–134
"Swift," on Article Three, I, 610, 625
Swift, Zephaniah, II, 916, 922–923, 925,
    937, 942–943, 1023, 1056

Taber, Jacob, I, 189, 196
Taber, Philip, I, 167, 175, 188, 231–232
Taber, Thomas, I, 175, 181
Taft, Thomas, I, 548
Talcott, Joseph, I, 265, 274, 445
Tanner, Nicholas, I, 129, 134, 136
Tax dodging, I, 202 n. 7, 204, 271, 274,
    276, 425–426, 430, 440, 447, 456, 692;
    II, 982
Taxes and tax exemption. *See* Religious
    Taxes; Ecclesiastical laws
Taylor, John, I, 682
Taylor, Jonathan, I, 539
Taylor, Nathaniel, II, 882, 918, 1134,
    1208
Tea Act, I, 538, 564–565, 571
Temperance, II, 831–832
Templeton, Mass., II, 708
Tennent, Gilbert, I, 340–341, 422
Terry, Nathaniel, II, 1057–1059
Terry, Samuel, I, 145
Test Act, I, 396
Testimony of the Two Witnesses, II, 767
Thacher, Peter, Sr., I, 302
Thacher, Peter, Jr., I, 572; II, 1075
Thomas, Moses, I, 761
Thompson, Conn., I, 549
Thoreau, Henry David, II, 1261
Thrumbull, John, I, 55 n. 13, 62–70, 77
Thurber, Jonathan, I, 229, 231
Thurston, Gardner, I, 497, 500, 507, 581–
    582
Tillinghast, Pardon, I, 260
Tingley, Peletiah, I, 507; II, 782
Tithes. *See* Religious taxes
Titicut Indians, II, 764
Titicut Parish, Mass., I, 376–384, 391,
    432–436, 447, 554
Tiverton, Mass., I, 10, 113, 121–122, 165–
    199, 200, 210, 582
Toleration Act of 1689, I, 79, 108–110,
    123, 151, 166, 197, 216, 249, 387, 388,
    390, 391, 398, 445, 460, 482, 483 n. 8,
    615; II, 865; in Conn. (1708), I, 254–
    262, 263, 270, 275, 345, 360, 362, 388,
    442, 444, 946
Toleration Bill in N. H., II, 899–911
Toleration of dissent, in Mass., I, 60–110,
    in Conn., I, 254–263, in N. H., II, 836–
    837
Toleration Party in Conn., II, 1024–1062
Tombes, John, I, 5–6
Tomlinson, Gideon, II, 1023, 1052, 1055

Torry, Joseph, I, 62
Tracy, Isaac, I, 375
Train, Charles, II, 1114, 1200, 1202–1203, 1205, 1206
Treadway, James, II, 954
Treadwell, John, II, 1020, 1021, 1029, 1032, 1052, 1055, 1058
Tribble, Andrew, II, 1112
Trinitarian Congregationalists, II, 1081, 1120, 1126–1127; Baptists and, II, 1128–1144; and Mass. Constitutional Convention (1820), II, 1146–1149; and Dedham Case, II, 1189–1206; turn against Federalists, II, 1197–1206; favor abolition of Article Three, II, 1207–1229; and the Anti-Masonic Party, II, 1222; and Whigs, II, 1223
Tripp, Joseph, I, 171
Troeltsch, Ernest, I, 329
True Faith Will Produce Good Works, II, 728
Trumbull, Benjamin, II, 805
Trumbull, Jonathan, I, 452–453; II, 949–950
Truth Is Great and Will Prevail, I, 633–634
Tucker, Henry, I, 187
Tucker, John, I, 169, 180, 181, 376
Tuckerman, Joseph, II, 1158, 1168–1169
Tudor, William, I, 655, 657
Turner *v.* Brookfield, II, 1084, 1105
Turner, David, I, 311
Turner, Edward, II, 1231, 1232
Turner, William, I, 55, 58, 62–70, 71, 73 n. 47, 74, 83
Tuttle, Amos, II, 822, 831
Typology, I, 35–36, 38–39, 41, 153

Underwood, Nathan, I, 676–677
Union College, II, 1114, 1274
Union Party Ticket in Mass., II, 1197, 1203, 1204, 1206
Union for Promoting the Observance of the Sabbath, II, 1268
Unitarianism, I, 166, 610, 709, 868; failure of in Conn., I, 264, 1023, 1026; incipient in 1730's, I, 318, 352, 407–410; defense of religious taxes, I, 416–417, 593, 596–597, 619; and Baptists, I, 498; within the Congregational churches, I, 593; and Dedham Case, I, 632; quarrel with Hopkinsians in Fitchburg, Mass., I, 691; in Charlton, Mass., I, 692; Baptists oppose, II, 736–737; oppose disestablishment in Mass., II, 1065–1242; and Trinitarians, II, 1081, 1127–1128, 1133–1134, 1207–1229; at Mass. Constitutional Convention (1820), II, 1146, 1152–1156, 1164–

1185; and Whig Party, II, 1220; final defense of the establishment, II, 1239–1243; Socinianism, I, 8, 70, 407–408
Unitarianism an Exclusive System, II, 1209–1210
Universalism, I, 277, 436–437, 521 n. 15, 607 n. 33, 609, 684; in Norwich, Conn., I, 437; lawsuits for dissenting status, I, 653–658; founding of in Mass., I, 654–655; theology of, I, 654; quarrel with Baptists in Bellingham, Mass., I, 685–686; in Wales, Mass., I, 691; in Charlton, Mass., I, 692; rivalry with Baptists, II, 709, 711, 717–722; in Vt., II, 825, 827; in N. H., II, 870–872; in Conn., II, 1024, 1036, 1050; in Mass., II, 1065; begin petition movement to amend Mass. Constitution, II, 1215–1216, 1246–1252; lead final effort for disestablishment in Mass., II, 1230–1262; as Jacksonians, II, 1231; growth in Mass., II, 1232, 1234; religious views, II, 1235–1237; oppose Blue Laws, II, 1268. *See also* Murray, John; Winchester, Elhanan
Universalist Magazine, II, 1231–1232, 1236
Universalist Trumpet, II, 1134, 1211, 1231, 1233–1235, 1245, 1246, 1250, 1252, 1256, 1257, 1259, 1268
Upham, Edward, I, 284–285, 293, 317; opposes Awakening, I, 319, 422, 463; on religious taxes, 467–468; 491; and Rhode Island College, I, 497, 500
Upton, Mass., I, 484, 627 n. 33
Usher, John, II, 835–836
Ustick, Thomas, I, 631; II, 722

Van Buren, Martin, II, 1002
Van Horn, William, I, 558, 559
Van Schaack, Henry, I, 545 n. 28; 664–670; 672
Vane, Harry, I, 10, 102, 104
Vanity of Childish Baptism, The, I, 27
Varnum, James Mitchell, I, 638, 642
Varnum, Joseph B., II, 1073 n. 24, 1093, 1151, 1157, 1172, 1181, 1222
Vermont Association, I, 508; II, 701, 826–827
Vermont, Baptists in, II, 787–832
Vermont, University of, II, 816, 890
"Vibrating Principle, The," II, 1089–1091
Vindication of the True Christian Baptism, I, 316–317
Virginia Bill for Religious Liberty, I, 591, 600–601, 619 n. 10; II, 1008
Virginia, disestablishment in, I, 592, 610, 618

Virginia and slavery, II, 1010, 1016–1017
Virginia, University of, II, 1123, 1273
Voluntarism, I, 32, 38, 116–117, 118, 120, 149, 198, 491, 597; in Swansea, I, 136–147, 154; in Rehoboth, I, 159; in Freetown, I, 206, 211–213; among Separates, I, 355, 368–385; Separate petitions for, I, 386–398; tracts on, I, 403–415; in Virginia, I, 593–594; Separate Baptists on, I, 433, 438, 485, 610; spreads after 1800, I, 661; Eden Burroughs on, II, 847
Voluntown, Conn., II, 960–961; Separates, I, 370

Wade, Nicholas, II, 774
Wadsworth, Ebenezer, I, 392
Wadsworth, John, I, 376
Wadsworth, Recompense, I, 208
Wakefield, Tubal, II, 1249
Waldo, Zacheus, II, 1050, 1058
Wales, Mass., I, 691; *see* South Brimfield
Walker, James, II, 1190
Walker, Quock, I, 639
Wallin, Benjamin, I, 501, 530, 580
Wallin, Edward, I, 294, 295, 305
Wallingford, Conn., I, 261–262, 271, 274, 319, 407, 408, 421, 423, 444–446; II, 924, 1044, 1045–1046
Wallingford, Vt., II, 803, 819–820, 831
Walter, Thomas, I, 217
Walton, John, I, 286, 294, 309–311, 312–318, 497
Wanton, Joseph, I, 169, 171, 175, 177, 181, 187, 196, 224
War of 1812, II, 831, 881, 1002, 1021, 1024, 1034, 1108
Ward, Nathaniel, I, 4, 47 n. 46
Ward, Samuel, I, 559, 561
Ware, Henry, II, 1158, 1190
Warren, Amos, I, 642
Warren Baptist Association, I, 502–511, 512, 514, 540, 597, 613, 631, 634, 639, 674, 675, 676; II, 697, 700, 702, 741, 761, 1014, 1110; forms Grievance Committee, I, 529–530; and civil disobedience, I, 551–553; petitions Continental Congress, I, 553–564; and Mass. Provincial Congress, I, 565–567; suggests Baptist Congress (1775), I, 567–568; and the Revolution, I, 580, 584, 585–586; against incorporation, I, 649; tries to strengthen denomination, II, 706–711; opposes slave trade, II, 767
Warren, Joseph, I, 557
Warren, Moses, II, 1049, 1050
Warren, Obed, II, 827
Warren, Mass., I, 122
Warren, R. I., I, 122, 495, 503

Warwick, Mass., I, 547, 549–550, 675, 678–679
Warwick, R. I., I, 320, 423
Washburn, Robert, I, 432–433
Washburn, Seth, I, 517–520
Washburn *v.* West Springfield, I, 658
Washington Benevolent Society, II, 831
Washington, George, I, 579, 593, 607, 654; II, 747, 757, 923, 927, 1023
Waterbury, Vt., II, 809
Waterford, Conn., I, 260–262, 271
Waterman, Zebulon, Jr., II, 952–961
Waters, Timothy, I, 262
Waterville College, II, 1122–1126
Watervliet, N. Y., II, 712
Watts, Isaac, I, 618; II, 1169
Way, William, I, 205–207, 209
Way of the Congregational Churches Cleared, The, I, 65
Wayland, Francis, II, 111, 1114, 1130 n. 2, 1269, 1271, 1274
Wealth of Nations, The, I, 612
Weare, N. H., I, 852
Webb, Christopher, II, 1101
Webb, Isaac, II, 823
Webb, John, I, 289, 323
Webster, Abel, II, 861
Webster, Daniel, II, 887, 1158, 1177–1180, 1190, 1196
Webster, Jonathan, I, 523
Webster, Noah, II, 1021
Welch, Moses C., II, 1045
Wells, Amos, II, 985–986, 990, 1001, 1002, 1022
Wells, Elijah, I, 537
Wells, Sylvester, II, 1024, 1050
Wells, Thomas, II, 805
Wentworth, Benning, I, 816–817, 843
Werden, Peter, I, 423, 507, 599; II, 842
Wesley, John, I, 336, 351; II, 723–726, 1140
West Ashford, Conn., II, 965, 966
West, Richard, I, 192
West, Samuel (of Conn.), II, 990
West, Samuel ("Ireneaus") I, 609, 619–623, 624, 636, 640; II, 864
West Deerfield, Mass., I, 690–691
Westerly, R. I., I, 10, 250, 255
Western Lands Act (Conn.), II, 967–984, 1036
Western Star (Stockbridge), I, 668–670
Westford, Mass., I, 599
Westford, Vt., II, 826
Westgate, John, I, 104
Westminster Confession of Faith, I, 125, 254, 273, 606; II, 771, 1167
Westminster, Mass. petition, II, 1213
Weston, John, II, 1118
Weston, Mass., II, 725

West Springfield, Mass., I, 285, 296, 297, 463, 467–468, 547, 628

West Woodstock, Conn., I, 547, II, 949–950

Wetherell, Daniel, I, 257, 258

Wheaton, Ephraim, I, 146–148, 156

Wheelock, Eleazar, II, 846–847, 883

Wheelock, John, II, 883, 888, 889, 890

Wheelwright, John, I, 96, 299, 834

Whipple, Daniel, I, 320–322, 323, 376

Whipple, Samuel, II, 1095

Whipple, Thomas, II, 898–911

Whiskey Rebellion, II, 784

White, Benjamin, I, 378, 379, 382

White, Esther, I, 447–448

White, John, I, 438, 463, 521–526

White, William, I, 599; II, 924

Whitefield, George, I, 319, 335, 340–341, 351, 355, 422, 488, 492, 522, 654; II, 717, 726, 739

Whitman, Benjamin, II, 1082

Whittemore, Thomas, II, 1158, 1215–1217, 1220; attacks Baptists, II, 1233–1234; efforts for disestablishment in Mass., II, 1231–1262

Whittlesey, Chauncy, I, 444–445

Wickenden, William, I, 14

Wight, Elnathan, I, 474–476, 685–686

Wightman, Daniel, I, 287, 311

Wightman, Edward, I, 256

Wightman, Timothy, I, 529

Wightman, Valentine, I, 115, 256–262, 266, 287, 318, 320–322, 446

Wilbraham, Mass., I, 520–521

Wilcox, Asa, II, 1022, 1056

Wilcox, Nathan, II, 989

Wilde, Samuel S., II, 1158, 1177, 1178, 1181, 1190–1193

Wilder, Theophilus, I, 641

Wildman, Daniel, II, 998, 999, 1006, 1022

Wilkins, Samuel, II, 863

Wilkinson, Jemima, I, 615 n. 5; II, 736, 739–740

Wilkinson, John, I, 638

Willard, Jacob, I, 671, 779, 780

Willard, Samuel, I, 53, 87, 105–107

Willcox, Stephen, I, 171, 187

Willett, Thomas, I, 132–134, 142

Williams, Benjamin, I, 638

Williams, Israel, I, 517, 522, 527–528, 533, 535, 536, 539, 542, 546

Williams, Nathan, II, 805, 1098, 1114, 1157, 1171, 1175–1180, 1184

Williams, Roger, I, 6–8, 9, 14, 22, 26, 38 n. 33, 45 n. 59, 50, 61 n. 30, 63, 68, 79, 92, 109, 134, 150 n. 6, 251, 299, 309, 389, 400, 405, 542, 613, 618; II, 729, 737, 763, 1048, 1229; becomes a Baptist, I, 10; opposes baptism, I,10 n. 5; opposes hireling ministry, I, 56; debate with John Cotton, I, 92–102

Williams, Stephen, II, 715, 949

Williams College, II, 890, 1123–1125, 1131

Williamson, Timothy, II, 728

Willington, Conn., II, 949–950

Willoughby, Bliss, I, 395, 396; II, 793

Wilmarth, Elkanah, I, 638

Wilson, John (of Boston), I, 20, 103

Wilson, John (of N. H.), II, 840

Winchell, J. M., II, 1114

Winchester, Daniel, I, 472

Winchester, Elhanan, I, 436–437; II, 703–704, 717–722, 868, 930

Winchester, N. H., II, 858

Windham, Consociation, I, 368; II, 917

Windham Herald, II, 941

Windham, Conn., II, 1045

Windsor, Conn., II, 950; II, 1061–1062

Windsor, Mass., I, 626

Wingate, Paine, II, 862–863, 868–870, 871

Winslow, Job, I, 206–207

Winslow, Nathaniel, I, 205

Winsor, Joseph, II, 704

Winsor, Samuel Sr., I, 309–311

Winsor, Samuel Jr., I, 497–498

Winthrop, John Sr., I, 7, 10, 11 n. 7, 16, 23, 102, 117

Winthrop, John Jr., I, 51, 61, 77

Winthrop, Stephen, I, 102

Wise, John, I, 179, 400

Witchcraft, I, 335, II, 772

Witter, William, I, 18–19, 22, 50, 67

Woburn, Mass., I, 67, 73, 74, 84–89; II, 746–747

Wolcott, Oliver, II, 1023, 1025, 1033, 1043

Wolcott, William, I, 14

Wood, Amos, II, 851, 852, 853, 860

Wood, Jonathan, I, 431–433, 478, 480

Wood, Timothy, II, 954

Woods, Henry, I, 599

Woods, Leonard, II, 1114, 1027

Woodstock Association, II, 701, 826

Woodstock, Vt., II, 793–794, 801–803, 809, 815, 825

Woodward, Aaron, II, 825

Woodward, Nehemiah, II, 825

Worcester Baptist Association, II, 1142

Worcester, Noah, II, 699–700

Worcester, Samuel, I, 691; II, 1115

Worthington, Elias, II, 953–956

Worthington, John, I, 518–520

Wrentham, Mass., I, 463

Wright, Eliphalet, I, 399, 413

Yale College, I, 114, 215, 265, 282, 285, 286, 355; and Separates, I, 362; and Separate Baptists, I, 491, 492, 499; II, 918, 924, 974, 1027, 1029, 1030, 1034

Yankees and Yorkers, II, 830

Yarmouth, Mass., I, 119 n. 14, 372

York, Maine, I, 547

Young, Dan, I, 896–911

Young, Nathan, I, 479